ESSENTIALS
OF
MANAGEMENT
SCIENCE

Applications to Decision Making

ESSENTIALS OF MANAGEMENT SCIENCE

Applications to Decision Making

David R. Anderson
University of Cincinnati
Cincinnati, Ohio

Dennis J. Sweeney
University of Cincinnati
Cincinnati, Ohio

Thomas A. Williams
Rochester Institute of Technology
Rochester, New York

WEST PUBLISHING CO.
St. Paul New York
Los Angeles San Francisco

To: Krista and Mark
Mark, Linda, Brad, Tim, and Scott
Cathy and David

COPYRIGHT © 1978 By
WEST PUBLISHING CO.
50 West Kellogg Boulevard
P.O. Box 3526
St. Paul, Minnesota 55165
Printed in the United States of America

Library of Congress Cataloging in Publication Data
Anderson, David Ray, 1941–
    Essentials of management science.
    Includes index.
    1. Decision-making—Mathematical models.
2. Statistical decision.   3. Operations research.
I. Sweeney, Dennis J., joint author. II. Williams,
Thomas Arthur, 1944–   joint author.   III. Title.
HD30.23.A47   658.4′033   77-14598
ISBN 0-8299-0147-7
    3rd Reprint—1980

CONTENTS

CONTENTS

CONTENTS

CONTENTS

CHAPTER 13. THE TRANSPORTATION PROBLEM   361

CHAPTER 14. PROJECT SCHEDULING: PERT/CPM   398

CONTENTS

CONTENTS

PREFACE

The purpose of this book is to provide students, primarily in the fields of administration and economics, with a sound conceptual understanding of the role that management science plays in the decision–making process. The text is concerned primarily with that part of management science which we refer to as quantitative approaches to decision making. Over the past few years, many quantitative aids have been developed for making better decisions. This text describes what these quantitative aids are, how they work, and how they can be applied by the decision maker.

We have written this book with the needs of the nonmathematician in mind; it is applications oriented. In each chapter, a problem situation is described in conjunction with the quantitative procedure being introduced. The development of the quantitative technique or model includes applying it to the problem situation in order to generate a solution or recommended decision. We believe that this approach helps to motivate the student by demonstrating not only how the procedure works, but also how it can be applied and how it contributes to the decision–making process.

The only mathematical prerequisite for this text is a course in college algebra. Although the text has been written at a low level of mathematical sophistication, we have not "ducked" difficult topics by trying to dismiss their complexity with one or two sentence explanations. The underlying concern in covering every topic has been, "Will the student understand this technique and see its application to decision making." As a consequence, the readability of the text for students with limited mathematical backgrounds and no previous exposure to management science is a significant feature of the book.

The problems at the end of each chapter are an important part of the book. In addition to reinforcing the materials in the chapters, the problems are suggestive of the types of situations in which the methods can be applied. A good number of the examples are actually scaled down versions of problems that have been encountered in practice.

Throughout the text we have utilized notation that is generally accepted for the topic being covered. In this regard students that pursue study beyond the level of this text will find the difficulties of reading more advanced material minimized. To assist in further study, we have included a bibliography at the end of the text.

The text has been designed such that the instructor has substantial flexibility in terms of selecting topics to meet specific course needs. While many variations are possible, the following one–quarter and one–semester courses are illustrative of the options available.

Possible Course Outlines

One–Quarter	*One–Semester*
Introduction (Chapter 1)	Introduction (Chapter 1)
Probability Concepts (Chapters 2 & 3)	Probability Concepts (Chapters 2 & 3)
Decision Theory (Chapter 4)	Decision Theory (Chapters 4 & 5)
Linear Programming and Selected Applications (Chapters 8 and 11)	Linear Programming and Selected Applications (Chapters 8 & 11)
PERT (Section 14.1)	Assignment Problem (Chapter 12)
Inventory Models (Sections 15.1 and 15.2)	Transportation Problem (Chapter 13)
Computer Simulation (Sections 16.1 thru 16.4)	PERT/CPM (Sections 14.1 and 14.2)
	Inventory Models (Sections 15.1 and 15.2)
	Computer Simulation (Sections 16.1 thru 16.4)
	Waiting Line Models (Sections 17.1 thru 17.7)

For students who have previously studied probability and its use in the decision–making process, the course content could be modified such that Chapters 2 and 3 are either covered rather quickly for review purposes or omitted altogether. In such cases the instructor could elect to spend additional time on the above topics or include one or two additional topics such as decision theory (Chapter 6), utility (Chapter 7), linear programming (Chapters 9 and 10), Markov processes (Chapter 18) and/or management information systems (Chapter 19).

Accompanying the text is a complete package of support materials, including a statement of learning objectives for each chapter, solutions for all problems, transparency masters, and a student study guide with self-correcting exercises. The study guide was coauthored by John Lawrence and Barry Pasternack (California State University at Fullerton). In addition, adopters will be provided with a bank of questions and problems specifically designed for examination purposes. The test bank was prepared by Randall Byers (University of Idaho). We believe that the applications orientation of the text combined with this package of support materials provides an ideal basis for introducing students to the essentials of management science.

We would like to express our appreciation to Donald Adolphson (University of Washington), Edward Baker (University of Maryland), Stephen Becktold (Florida State University), Stanley Brooking (University of Southern Mississippi), Randall Byers (University of Idaho), Ron Ebert (University of Missouri), John Flueck (Temple University), Roger Glaser (Florida

International University), Jack Goodwin (Texas Tech University), Rebecca Klemm (Temple University), John Lawrence (California State University at Fullerton), Cynthia Ma (Ball State University), Richard K. Martin (University of Cincinnati), Patrick McKeown (University of Georgia), Barnett Parker (Oakland University), Wayland Smith (Western Michigan University), Bill Truscott (McMaster University), William Verdini (Arizona State University), Robert Winkler (Indiana University), and Ed Winkofsky (Virginia Polytechnic Institute) for their helpful comments and suggestions during the development of this manuscript. In addition, we are especially indebted to Linda Leininger and Phyllis Trosper for the many hours they devoted to typing and retyping the drafts of this book.

1
Introduction

Management Science is a broad discipline which includes all rational approaches to managerial decision making that are based upon an application of scientific methodology. The management science function considers organizational objectives and resources and, by using a scientific problem-solving approach, attempts to establish long- and/or short-range policies and decisions that are in the best interest of an organization. A management science problem may be as specific as improving the efficiency of a production line or as broad as establishing a long-range corporate strategy that involves a combination of financial, marketing, and manufacturing considerations.

Under the broad heading of management science, the disciplines of operations research, decision sciences, information sciences, behavioral sciences, and some aspects of systems analysis are often included. While a precise definition of each is not necessary for our purposes, it is important to realize that studies, projects, or analyses employing methodology from one or more of the above scientific disciplines could correctly be called a management science activity.

This book is concerned primarily with the portion of management science that deals with quantitative approaches to decision making. Over the past few years, many new and important quantitative techniques have been developed as aids in the decision-making process. However, the emphasis of this book is not on the techniques per se; rather it is on showing how they can contribute to a better decision-making process. Our approach is to describe decision-making situations in which quantitative techniques have been successfully applied and then show how the appropriate quantitative analysis can be utilized by the manager to make better decisions.

While a variety of names exist for the body of knowledge and methodology involving quantitative approaches to decision making, one of the most widely known and accepted names is *operations research* (OR). Actually operations research may be more broadly defined to include a multidisciplinary scientific approach to decision making. Under this definition, many use the terms "operations research" and "management science" almost interchangeably. In practice, operations research studies are frequently conducted by an operations research team which might consist of a quantitative specialist, an engineer, an accountant, a behavioral scientist, and an expert from the particular problem area being studied (such as, for example, marketing, finance, or manufacturing). While the analysis of a problem situation almost always includes some qualitative considerations, a significant portion of most operations research studies is based upon quantitative decision-making techniques. Thus in this text, when we use the term ''operations research,'' we are specifically referring to the quantitative analysis and quantitative procedures that assist the decision-making process.

1.1 DOMINANCE OF THE PROBLEM

A central theme in the operations research or quantitative approach to decision making is problem orientation. Nearly all operations research projects begin with recognition by management of a problem situation which does not have an obvious solution. Operations researchers or quantitative analysts may then be asked to assist in identifying the ''best'' decision or solution for the problem. Reasons why a quantitative approach might be used in the decision-making process include the following.

1. The problem is so complex that it is not possible for the manager to develop a good solution without the aid of quantitative specialists.
2. The problem is very important (for example, a great deal of money is involved), and the manager wants a thorough analysis before attempting a decision.
3. The problem is a new one, and the manager has no past experience upon which to draw.
4. The problem is a repetitive one, and the manager saves time by relying on a quantitative procedure to make the routine decision recommendation.

A survey[1] of corporate-level operations research activities identified some typical problem areas that have been the subject of operations research studies. These problem areas include

1. Distribution systems design (such as transportation networks, plant and warehouse location, etc.)
2. Inventory ordering and stocking decisions
3. Resource allocation for corporate activities
4. Capital investment analysis
5. Portfolio selection
6. Information systems design
7. Product mix and production decisions
8. New product analysis.

[1] Turban, E., ''A Sample Survey of Operations-Research Activities at the Corporate Level,'' *Operations Research,* vol. 20, pp. 708–721, 1972.

This is by no means an exhaustive list of the types of problems for which managers have found quantitative methodology to be beneficial, but it is indicative of the areas in which operations research or quantitative analysis procedures have been successfully applied. In many cases, substantial savings have been achieved as a result of employing quantitative approaches.

1.2 QUANTITATIVE ANALYSIS AND THE DECISION-MAKING PROCESS

The role of quantitative analysis in managerial decision making is best understood by considering the flowchart in Figure 1.1. We note that the process is initiated by the appearance of a problem. The manager is then charged with the responsibility of making a decision or selecting a course of action that will lead to the solution of the problem. In the decision-making process the manager will probably make an analysis of the problem which includes a statement of the specific objective, an identification of all constraints, an evaluation of alternative decisions, and a selection of the apparent "best" decision. This analysis process may take two basic forms: qualitative and quantitative. The qualitative analysis approach is based upon the manager's judgment and experience with similar problems. This type of analysis includes the manager's intuitive "feel" for the problem and is more an art than a science. If the manager has had experience with similar problems in the past, or if the problem is relatively simple, he may place heavy emphasis on this type of analysis and make the final decision accordingly. However, if the manager has had little experience with similar problems in the past, or if the

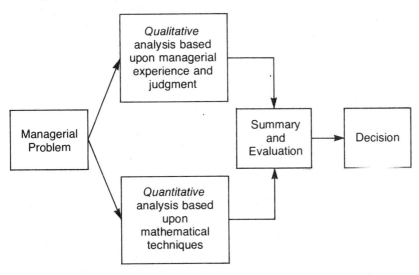

FIGURE 1.1 The Decision-Making Process

3

decision problem is sufficiently important and complex, then a quantitative analysis of the problem can be a very important consideration in the manager's final decision. In the quantitative approach to the problem, an analyst will concentrate on the quantitative facts or data associated with the problem and develop mathematical expressions that describe the objectives, constraints, and relationships that exist in the problem. Then, by using one or more quantitative techniques, the analyst will provide a recommendation for the manager based upon the quantitative aspects of the problem.

Both the qualitative and quantitative analysis of a problem provide important information for the manager or decision maker. In many cases a manager may draw on both sources and, through a comparison and evaluation of the information, make a final decision.

While skills in the qualitative approach are inherent in the manager and usually increase with his experience, the skills of the quantitative approach can only be learned by studying the assumptions and methods of quantitative analysis in detail. A manager can maximize his decision-making effectiveness by learning more about quantitative methodology and by better understanding its contribution to the decision-making process. The manager who is knowledgeable in quantitative decision-making procedures is in a much better position to compare and evaluate the qualitative and quantitative

TABLE 1.1. *Quantitative Techniques Used in Operations Research Projects*

Techniques	Frequency of Use (percent)
Statistical analysis*	29
Simulation	25
Linear programming	19
Inventory theory	6
PERT/CPM	6
Dynamic programming	4
Nonlinear programming	3
Queueing	1
Heuristic programming	1
Miscellaneous	6
Total	100

*Includes probability theory, regression analysis, exponential smoothing, statistical sampling, and tests of hypotheses.

4

sources of decision recommendations and ultimately combine the two sources in order to make the best possible decision.

The section of Figure 1.1 labeled "Quantitative analysis based upon mathematical techniques" encompasses most of the subject matter of this text. We will consider a managerial problem, introduce the appropriate quantitative methodology, and then develop and evaluate the recommended decision.

There are several important quantitative tools, or techniques, that have been found useful in this stage of the decision-making process. One of your objectives in studying this book should be to develop an understanding of what these techniques are, how they are used, and, most important, how they can aid the manager in making better decisions. According to the Turban study, the tools most frequently used are those presented in Table 1.1. This text includes an introductory coverage of most of these techniques. Since most students take a separate course in statistics, we have restricted our coverage in the statistical analysis area to probability and decision theory.

Let us now look more closely at the steps involved in carrying out the quantitative analysis of a managerial problem.

1.3 THE QUANTITATIVE ANALYSIS PROCESS

We begin our study of quantitative approaches to decision making by considering a five-step procedure: (1) problem definition, (2) model development, (3) data preparation, (4) model solution, and (5) report generation. We will refer to this procedure as the operations research or quantitative analysis process.

Problem Definition

As stated in Section 1.1, a central theme in the operations research approach to decision making is problem orientation. A clear and concise definition of the specific problem of interest is an essential first step of any operations research or quantitative analysis study. Obviously, if we are to proceed with scientific analyses and solution recommendation procedures, we must have a thorough definition of the problem we are attempting to solve.

The importance of the problem definition step should not be underestimated. Usually the problem starts with a rather broad or general description that takes time, imagination, and effort to transform into a well-defined problem. For example, a broadly described "excessive inventory" problem must be clearly defined in terms of a specific objective and constraints before we can proceed to the next step in the quantitative analysis process.

Model Development

Models are representations of real objects or situations. These representations, or models, can be presented in various forms. For example, a scale model of an airplane is a representation of a real airplane. Similarly, a child's toy truck is a model of a real truck. The model airplane and toy truck are examples of models that are physical replicas of real objects. In modeling terminology, physical replicas are referred to as *iconic* models.

A second classification of models refers to those that are physical in form but do not have the same physical appearance as the object being modeled. Such models are referred to as *analog* models. The speedometer of an automobile is an analog model in that the position of the needle on the dial represents the speed of the automobile. A thermometer is an analog model representing temperature.

A third classification of models—the primary types of models we will be studying—refers to models that represent the real situation by a system of symbols and mathematical relationships or expressions. Such models are referred to as *mathematical* models and are a critical part of any quantitative approach to decision making. For example, we know that the total profit from the sale of a product can be determined by multiplying the per unit profit by the quantity sold. If we let x represent the number of units sold and P the total profit, then, with a profit of \$10 per unit, we have the following mathematical model, or mathematical representation, of the total profit earned by selling x units of the product:

$$P = 10x. \tag{1.1}$$

The purpose or value of a model is that it enables us to draw conclusions about a real situation by studying and analyzing the model. For example, an airplane designer might test an iconic model of a new airplane design in a wind tunnel in order to learn about the potential flying characteristics of the full-size airplane. Similarly, we may use a mathematical model to draw conclusions about how much profit will be earned if a specified quantity of a particular product were sold. Using the mathematical model of equation (1.1), we would expect to obtain a \$30 profit from selling three units of the product. In both the airplane model and profit model examples, we are able to test and experiment with the model in order to learn about the real situation.

In general, experimenting with models requires less time and is less expensive than experimenting with the real object or situation. Certainly, a model airplane is quicker and less expensive to build and study than the full-size airplane. Similarly the mathematical model allows us to quickly identify profit expectations prior to actually producing and selling x units of the product. Thus, models also have the advantage of reducing the risk associated with the real situation. In particular, bad designs or bad decisions that

6

cause the model airplane to crash or the mathematical model to project a $10,000 loss can be avoided in the real situation.

The accuracy of the conclusions and decisions based on a model are dependent, however, upon how well the model represents the real situation. The more closely the model of the airplane represents the real airplane, the more accurate the conclusions and predictions about the flight characteristics will be. Similarly, the closer our mathematical model represents the company's true profit–volume relationship, the more accurate our profit projections will be.

Since this text deals with mathematical models, let us look more closely at the mathematical modeling process. When we initially consider a managerial problem, we will usually find that the problem definition phase of the analysis leads us to a specific objective, such as maximizing profits or minimizing costs, and possibly a set of restrictions or constraints, such as production capacities. The success of our mathematical model and quantitative approach to decision making will depend upon how accurate we are in expressing the objective and constraints in terms of mathematical equations or relationships.

The mathematical expression that describes the problem's objective is referred to as the *objective function*. For example, the profit equation $P = 10x$ might represent an objective function when we are attempting to maximize profit. A production capacity constraint would be necessary if we find that it takes 5 man-hours to produce each unit of the product and that there are only 40 man-hours of production time available per week. Using x to indicate the number of units to produce each week, we can represent the production time constraint by

$$5x \leq 40. \tag{1.2}$$

The value of $5x$ is the total production time required to produce the x units; the symbol $\leq$ indicates that the production time required must be less than or equal to the 40 hours available.

The question or decision problem is, how many units of the product should be scheduled each week in order to maximize profit. A complete mathematical model for this simple production problem is

> maximize $\quad P = 10x \qquad$ objective function
>
> subject to (s.t.)
>
> $$\left. \begin{array}{r} 5x \leq 40 \\ x \geq 0 \end{array} \right\} \quad \text{constraints.}$$

The $x \geq 0$ constraint requires the production quantity x to be greater than or equal to zero, which simply recognizes the fact that it is not possible to manufacture a negative number of units. The optimal solution to this model

7

can be easily calculated and is given by $x = 8$. The associated profit is \$80. This model is an example of a linear programming model. In subsequent chapters we will discuss more complicated mathematical models and learn how to solve them in situations where the answers are not nearly so obvious.

In the above mathematical model the profit per unit (\$10), the production time per unit (5 man-hours), and the production capacity (40 man-hours) are environmental factors that are not under the control of the manager or decision maker. Such environmental factors, which can affect both the objective function and the constraints, are referred to as the *uncontrollable inputs* to the model. The inputs which are controlled or determined by the decision maker are referred to as the *controllable inputs* to the model. In the above example the production quantity x is the controllable input to the model. The controllable inputs are the decision alternatives specified by the manager and thus are also referred to as the *decision variables* of the model.

Once all controllable and uncontrollable inputs are specified, the objective function and constraints can be evaluated and the output of the model determined. In this sense, the output of the model is simply the projection of what would happen if the particular environmental factors and decisions occurred in the real situation. A flowchart of how controllable and uncontrollable inputs are transformed by the mathematical model into output is shown in Figure 1.2. A similar flowchart for the production model is shown in Figure 1.3.

As stated earlier, the uncontrollable inputs are those which the decision maker cannot influence. The specific controllable and uncontrollable inputs of a model depend upon the particular problem or decision-making situation. In our production problem the number of man-hours available, 40, was an uncontrollable input. However, if it were possible to hire more employees, the number of man-hours available would become a controllable input and, therefore, a decision variable in our model.

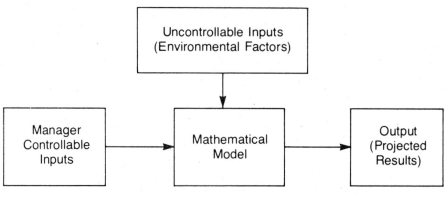

FIGURE 1.2 Flowchart of the Process of Transforming Model Inputs into Output

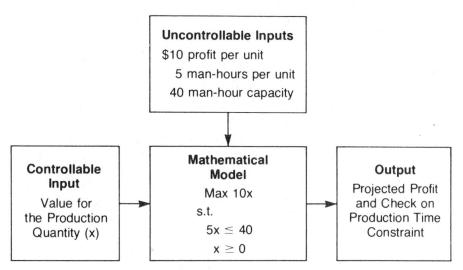

FIGURE 1.3   Flow Chart for the Production Model

Uncontrollable inputs can either be known exactly or be uncertain and subject to variation. If all uncontrollable inputs to a model are known and cannot vary, we have a *deterministic* model. Corporate income tax rates are not under the influence of the manager and thus constitute an uncontrollable input in many decision models. Since these rates are known and fixed (at least in the short run), a mathematical model with corporate income tax rates as the only uncontrollable input would be a deterministic model. The distinguishing feature of a deterministic model is that the uncontrollable input values are known in advance. Thus we can determine the output and project the results associated with a particular decision alternative.

If any of the uncontrollable inputs are uncertain and subject to variation, we have a *stochastic* model. An uncontrollable input to many production planning models is demand for the product. Since future demand may be any of a range of values, a mathematical model which treats the uncontrollable input, demand, with uncertainty could be called a stochastic model. In our profit maximizing model, the number of man-hours required per unit, the total man-hours available, and the unit profit were all uncontrollable inputs. Since the uncontrollable inputs were all known to take on fixed values, we had a deterministic model. If, however, the number of man-hours required per unit of production could vary from 3 to 6 hours depending upon the quality of the raw material, we would have had a stochastic model. The distinguishing feature of a stochastic model is that we cannot determine in advance the value of the output because the specific value of the uncontrollable input is unknown. In this respect, stochastic models are often more difficult to analyze.

9

Data Preparation

The third step in the quantitative analysis of a managerial problem is the preparation of the data required by the model. Data in this sense refer to the values of the uncontrollable inputs to the model. All uncontrollable inputs or data must be specified before we can analyze the model and select a recommended decision or solution for the problem.

In our production model the values of the uncontrollable inputs or data were $10 per unit for profit, 5 man-hours per unit for production time, and 40 man-hours for production capacity. In our development of the model these data values were known and thus were incorporated into the model as it was being developed. If the model is relatively small and the uncontrollable input values or data required are few, the quantitative analyst will probably combine model development and data preparation into one step. That is, in these situations the data values are inserted as the equations of the mathematical model are developed.

However, in most modeling situations one will find that the data, or uncontrollable input values, are not readily available. In these situations the quantitative analyst may know that the model will need profit per unit, production time, and production capacity data, but the values are not known until the accounting, production, and engineering departments can be consulted. Rather than attempting to collect the required data as the model is being developed, the analyst will usually adopt a general notation for the model development step and then perform a separate data preparation step to obtain the uncontrollable input values required by the model.

Using the general notation of

p = profit per unit
t = production time in man-hours per unit
c = production capacity in man-hours

the model development step of our production model would have resulted in the following general model:

$$\max \quad px$$
$$\text{s.t.}$$
$$tx \leq c$$
$$x \geq 0.$$

Then a separate data preparation step to find the values for p, t, and c can be used to complete the model.

Many inexperienced quantitative analysts or operations researchers assume that once the problem has been defined and a general model developed, the problem is essentially solved. These people tend to believe that data preparation is a trivial step in the process and can be simply handled by clerical staff. Actually, especially when we are dealing with a large-scale model with numerous data input values, this assumption could not be further from the truth. For example, a moderate-sized linear programming model with 50 decision variables and 25 constraints will have over 1300 data elements that must be identified in the data preparation step. The time required to prepare these data and the possibility of data collection errors will make the data preparation step a critical part of the quantitative analysis process.

Model Solution

Once the model development and data preparation steps have been completed, we can proceed to the model solution step. In this phase, the analyst will attempt to identify the values of the decision variables that provide the "best" output for the model. The specific decision variable value or values providing the "best" output will be referred to as the *optimal* solution for the model. These will be the recommended decisions based on the quantitative analysis process. For our production problem the model solution step involves finding the value of the production quantity decision variable x that maximizes profit while not exceeding the production capacity constraint.

One procedure we might follow in the model solution step involves a trial-and-error approach in which we use the model to test and evaluate alternative values for the decision variables. In our example, this would mean testing and evaluating the model under various production quantities or values of x. Referring to Figure 1.3, we see that we could input trial values for x and check the corresponding output for projected profit and satisfaction of the production time constraint. If a particular decision alternative does not satisfy one or more of the model constraints, the decision alternative is rejected as being *infeasible,* regardless of the objective function value. If all constraints are satisfied, the decision alternative is *feasible* and is a candidate for the "best" solution or recommended decision. Through this trial-and-error process of evaluating selected decision alternatives, a decision maker can identify a good, and possibly the best, feasible solution to the problem. This solution is the recommended decision for the problem under study.

Table 1.2 shows the results of a trial-and-error approach to solving the production model of Figure 1.3. The recommended decision is a production quantity of 8, since the feasible solution with the highest projected profit occurs at $x = 8$.

While the trial-and-error solution process is often acceptable and can provide valuable information for the manager, it has the drawbacks of not necessarily providing the one best solution and of being inefficient in that numerous calculations will be necessary if many decision alternatives are tried. For example, the relatively simple problem of assigning 10 employees to 10 tasks has over 3 million possible solutions. Thus, quantitative analysts have developed special solution procedures for many models that are much

11

TABLE 1.2   *Trial-and-Error Solution for the Production*
             Model of Figure 1.3.

Decision Alternative (Production Quantity) x	Projected Profit	Total Man-Hours of Production	Feasible Solution (Capacity = 40)
0	0	0	Yes
2	20	10	Yes
4	40	20	Yes
6	60	30	Yes
8	80	40	Yes
10	100	50	No
12	120	60	No

more efficient than the trial-and-error approach. Throughout this text you will be introduced to solution procedures that are applicable to the specific mathematical models that will be formulated. While some relatively small models or problems can be solved by hand calculations, many of the solution procedures will require the use of a computer.

In addition, it is important to realize that the model development and model solution steps are not completely separable. While we may want to develop an accurate model or representation of the actual problem situation, we also want to be able to identify a solution to the problem. If we approach the model development step by attempting to find the most accurate and realistic mathematical model, we may find the model so large and complex that we are unable to obtain a solution. In this case a simpler and perhaps more easily understood model with a readily available solution procedure is preferred, even if the recommended solution is only a rough approximation of the best decision. As you learn more about the quantitative solution procedures available, you will have a better idea of the types of mathematical models that can be developed and solved.

Report Generation

The final step in the quantitative analysis process is the preparation of managerial reports based upon the model's solution. Referring to Figure 1.1, we see that the solution based upon the quantitative analysis of a problem is one of the inputs that is considered by the manager when making a final decision. Thus it is essential that the results of the model and quantitative analysis

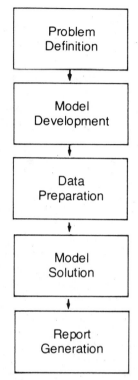

FIGURE 1.4   Steps of the Quantitative Analysis Process

appear in a managerial report which can be easily understood by the decision maker. The report will include the recommended decision and other pertinent information about the model results that may be helpful to the decision maker.

Figure 1.4 summarizes the five-step quantitative analysis process.

1.4 SUMMARY

This is a book about how quantitative approaches to decision problems may be used to help managers make better decisions. The focus of the text is on the decision-making process and on the role of quantitative analysis in that process. We have discussed the problem orientation of this process and, in general, have shown how mathematical models can be used in this type of analysis.

The difference between the model and the situation or managerial problem it represents is an important point. Mathematical models are abstractions of real-world situations and, as such, cannot capture all the aspects of the real situation. However, if a model can capture the major relevant aspects of the problem and provide a solution recommendation, it can be a valuable aid to decision making.

One of the characteristics of operations research or quantitative analysis that will become increasingly apparent as we proceed through the text is the search for the best solution to problems. In carrying out the quantitative analysis of problems, we shall be attempting to develop procedures for finding the optimal solutions to managerial decision problems. The block labeled "model solution" in Figure 1.4 shows where these procedures are applied in the quantitative analysis process.

1.5 GLOSSARY

1. *Model*—Representation of a real object or situation.
2. *Iconic model*—Physical replica or representation of a real object.
3. *Analog model*—While physical in form, a model that does not have a physical appearance similar to the real object or situation it represents.
4. *Mathematical model*—Mathematical symbols and expressions used to represent a real situation.
5. *Objective function*—A mathematical expression used to identify the objective of a problem situation.
6. *Constraints*—Restrictions or limitations imposed on the problem situation.
7. *Controllable input*—The decision alternatives or inputs that can be specified by the decision maker.
8. *Uncontrollable input*—The environmental factors or inputs that cannot be specified by the decision maker.
9. *Deterministic model*—A model where all uncontrollable inputs are known and cannot vary.
10. *Stochastic model*—A model where at least one uncontrollable input is uncertain and subject to variation.
11. *Feasible solution*—A decision alternative or solution that satisfies all constraints.
12. *Infeasible solution*—A decision alternative or solution that violates one or more constraints.
13. *Optimal solution*—A feasible solution that provides the best possible value of the objective function.

1.6 PROBLEMS

1. Define the terms "management science" and "operations research."
2. Discuss the different roles played by the qualitative and quantitative approaches to managerial decision making. Why is it important for a

manager or decision maker to have a good understanding of both these approaches to decision making?

3. A firm has just completed a new plant which will produce over 500 different products using over 50 different production lines and machines. The product scheduling decisions are critical in that sales will be lost if customer demands are not met on time. If no one in the firm has had experience with this production operation and if new production schedules must be generated each week, why should the firm consider a quantitative approach to the production scheduling problem?

4. List and discuss the five steps of the quantitative approach to decision making.

5. List and give an example of the three types of models discussed in this chapter.

6. What are the advantages of analyzing and experimenting with a model of a real object or situation?

7. Recall the production model from Figure 1.3:

max $10x$

s.t.

$$5x \leq 40$$
$$x \geq 0.$$

Suppose the firm in this example considers a second product which has a unit profit of $5 and requires 2 man-hours for each unit produced. Use y as the number of units of product 2 produced.

   a. Show the mathematical model when both products are considered simultaneously.

   b. Identify the controllable and uncontrollable inputs for this model.

   c. Draw the flowchart of the input–output process for this model (see Figure 1.3).

   d. What are the optimal solution values of x and y?

8. Is the model developed in Problem 7 a deterministic or a stochastic model? Explain.

9. Suppose we modify the model in Figure 1.3 to obtain the following mathematical model:

max $10x$

s.t.

$$ax \leq 40$$
$$x \geq 0$$

where a is the number of man-hours required for each unit produced. (With $a = 5$, we saw that the optimal solution was $x = 8$.) If we have a stochastic model with $a = 3$, $a = 4$, $a = 5$, or $a = 6$ as the possible values for the number of man-hours required per unit, what is the optimal value for x? What problems does this stochastic model cause?

15

10. Suppose a firm is reviewing its purchasing operation in an attempt to reduce the ordering and shipping costs associated with purchases from its supplier. Let

D = annual demand for a product
Q = quantity ordered each time an order is placed with the supplier
C_0 = fixed cost of placing an order (time, paper, telephone, and transportation expenses).

    a. Develop the mathematical model for the number of orders placed per year.
    b. Develop the mathematical model for the total annual ordering cost.
    c. If $D = 2000$, $Q = 100$, and $C_0 = \$50$, what is total annual ordering cost?
    d. If management specifies the annual cost for ordering the product is to be $500, what is your recommended order quantity?

11. Suppose you are going on a weekend trip to a city that is d miles away. Develop a model that determines your round trip gasoline costs. What assumptions or approximations do you have to make in order to treat this model as a deterministic model? Are these assumptions or approximations acceptable to you as a decision maker?

12. Suppose that a manager has a choice between the following two mathematical models of a given situation: (a) a relative simple model that is a reasonable approximation of the real situation, and (b) a thorough and complex model that is the most accurate mathematical representation of the real situation possible. Why might the model described in (a) be preferred by the manager?

2
Introduction to Probability

Throughout your career, whether it be in business, industry, government, etc., you will undoubtedly be faced with decision-making situations which involve an uncertain future. Perhaps you will encounter some of the following situations involving uncertainty.

1. What is the "chance" that sales will decrease if the price of the product is increased?
2. What is the "likelihood" that the new assembly method will increase productivity?
3. How "likely" is it that the project will be completed on time?

The material that you will find useful in effectively dealing with such uncertainties is contained under the heading of probability. In everyday terminology, *probability* can be thought of as a numerical measure of the "chance" or "likelihood" that a particular event will occur. For example, if we consider the event "rain tomorrow," we understand that when the television weather report indicates "a near-zero probability of rain," there is almost no chance of rain. However, if a .90 probability of rain is reported, we know that it is very likely or almost certain that rain will occur. A .50 probability indicates that rain is just as likely to occur as not to occur.

As the previous discussion suggests, probabilities are assigned on a scale from 0 to 1, where a probability of 0 indicates the event cannot occur and a probability of 1 indicates the event is certain to occur. Probabilities between 0 and 1 represent varying degrees of likelihood that an event will occur. Figure 2.1 depicts this view of probability.

The reason that probability is important in decision making is that it provides a mechanism for measuring and analyzing the uncertainties associated with future events. For example, the manager or decision maker who feels there is a "good chance" that sales will decrease if prices are increased may use probability to measure or express his belief. Perhaps in this case the "good chance" translates to a .85 probability. Whenever probability values are used to measure future uncertainties, methods of probability theory can be used to provide additional information which may ultimately lead to improved decision recommendations.

In this chapter, we introduce the fundamental concepts of probability and begin to illustrate their use as decision-making tools. In subsequent chapters,

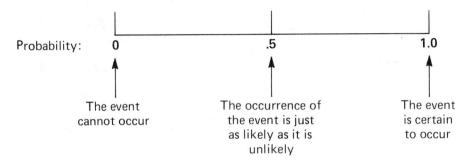

FIGURE 2.1 *Probability as a Numerical Measure of the Likelihood of Occurrence*

we extend these basic notions of probability and demonstrate additional ways that probability can be used to assist in the decision-making process.

2.1 EXPERIMENTS AND THE SAMPLE SPACE

Using the terminology of probability, we define an *experiment* to be any process which generates well-defined outcomes. By this we mean that in any single repetition of the experiment, *one and only one* of the possible experimental outcomes can occur. Several examples of experiments and their associated outcomes are as follows.

Experiment	Experimental Outcomes
Tossing a coin	Head, tail
Selecting a part for inspection	Defective, nondefective
Contacting a potential customer	Purchase, no purchase
Rolling a die	One, two, three, four, five, six
Playing a football game	Win, lose, tie

The first step in analyzing a particular experiment is to carefully define the outcomes of the experiment. When we have defined *all* possible experimental outcomes, we have identified the *sample space* for the experiment. That is, the sample space is defined as the set of all possible experimental outcomes. Any one particular experimental outcome is referred to as a *sample point*.

Let us consider the experiment of rolling a die, where the experimental outcomes are defined in terms of the number appearing on the face of the die. In this experiment, the numerical values 1, 2, 3, 4, 5, and 6 represent all the possible experimental outcomes or sample points for the experiment. If we let S denote the sample space, we can describe the sample space and sample points for the die-rolling experiment with the following set notation.

18

$$S = \{1, 2, 3, 4, 5, 6\}$$

As another example, suppose we consider an experiment involving the tossing of two coins. Assume that we are interested in defining the experimental outcomes in terms of the pattern of heads and tails appearing on the two coins. How many experimental outcomes or sample points are possible for this experiment?

Before you attempt to answer this question, let us introduce a rule which is often helpful in terms of determining the number of sample points in an experiment.

A Counting Rule

If an experiment can be described as a sequence of k steps in which there are n_1 possible results on the first step, n_2 possible results on the second step, and so on, then the total number of distinct sequences is given by

$$(n_1)(n_2) \ldots (n_k).$$

Thus, if we look at the experiment of tossing two coins as a sequence of first tossing one coin ($n_1 = 2$) and then tossing the other coin ($n_2 = 2$), we can see from the counting rule that there must be $(2)(2) = 4$ distinct sample points or experimental outcomes. These sample points are as follows.

Sample Point or Experimental Outcome	First Coin	Second Coin
E_1	Head	Head
E_2	Head	Tail
E_3	Tail	Head
E_4	Tail	Tail

We have used the symbol E with a subscript to denote the experimental outcomes or sample points for the experiment. Thus, using E_1, E_2, E_3, and E_4 as defined above, we can describe the sample space (S) for the two coin tossing experiment as follows:

$$S = \{E_1, E_2, E_3, E_4\}$$

Figure 2.2 provides a *tree diagram* which also shows the four sample points for this experiment.

While many of the basic concepts of probability, including experiments, sample points, and sample spaces, are rather easily introduced and demonstrated for experiments involving the rolling of a die or the tossing of coins,

19

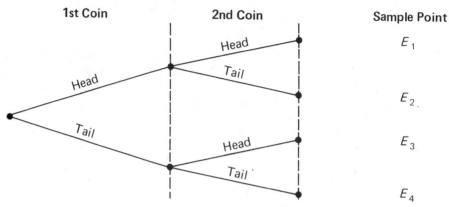

FIGURE 2.2   Tree Diagram for the Experiment of Tossing Two Coins

the concepts are of little practical value unless they can be applied to actual problem situations. Thus, we now describe how the concepts presented thus far can be used to help analyze a problem currently facing the Kentucky Power and Light Company. Specifically, we want to demonstrate how the company's problem situation can be viewed as an experiment. We will then attempt to define the appropriate sample points and sample space for the experiment.

The Kentucky Power and Light Problem

The Kentucky Power and Light Company (KP&L) is currently starting work on a project designed to increase the power capacity of its plants in northern Kentucky. The project is divided into two major stages: stage 1 (design) and stage 2 (construction). While each stage will be scheduled and controlled as thoroughly as possible, ultimately each stage of the project will be completed either earlier than scheduled, later than scheduled, or on time. The times required to complete the stages are summarized below.

	Stage 1	Stage 2
Early Completion	2 months	6 months
On-Time Completion	3 months	7 months
Late Completion	4 months	8 months

KP&L is primarily concerned with the delay problems that occur whenever a stage of the project is completed late. That is, if stage 1 requires 4 months to complete or if stage 2 requires 8 months to complete, KP&L will experience a "stage-delay" problem. Such problems are of major concern to

TABLE 2.1 **Listing of Experimental Outcomes or Sample Points for the KP&L Problem**

Experimental Outcome	Stage 1 (Design)	Stage 2 (Construction)	Sample Point Notation
1	Early	Early	E_1
2	Early	On time	E_2
3	Early	Late	E_3
4	On time	Early	E_4
5	On time	On time	E_5
6	On time	Late	E_6
7	Late	Early	E_7
8	Late	On time	E_8
9	Late	Late	E_9

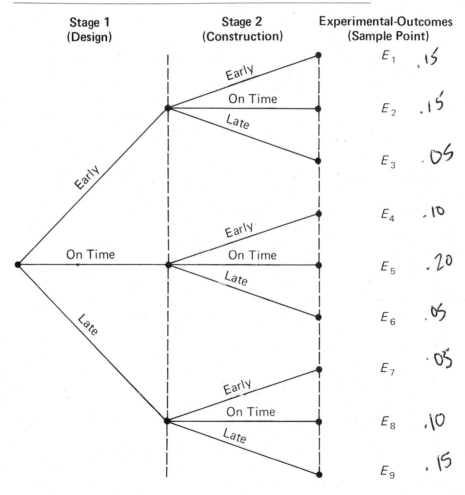

FIGURE 2.3 **Tree Diagram for the KP&L Project**

21

KP&L because they cause cost overruns and require additional managerial effort to reschedule related phases of the project. Thus, KP&L's management would like a thorough analysis of the project, including probability assessments for encountering stage-delay problems.

In probability terminology the KP&L project can be viewed as an experiment. At the completion of the "experiment" or project, the firm will observe an experimental outcome describing what happened at each stage of the project. For example, one experimental outcome is stage 1 completed early and stage 2 completed late. Another experimental outcome is stage 1 completed late and stage 2 completed on time. Since each stage can be completed in three different ways (early, late, or on time) and since the project involves a sequence of two stages, the counting rule tells us there are a total of (3)(3) = 9 experimental outcomes or sample points for the project. Table 2.1 lists these nine experimental outcomes, and Figure 2.3 shows a tree diagram indicating how these outcomes or sample points occur. Using the E notation defined in Table 2.1, the sample space for the KP&L project experiment can be described with the following set notation.

$$S = \{E_1, E_2, E_3, E_4, E_5, E_6, E_7, E_8, E_9\}.$$

2.2 EVENTS

Continuing with the KP&L problem, recall that KP&L's management is specifically concerned about stage-delay problems. Thus, KP&L is particularly interested in the following two events:

A = the event that stage 1 is completed late,
B = the event that stage 2 is completed late.

Referring to Table 2.1, we see that sample points E_7, E_8, and E_9 correspond to event A, while sample points E_3, E_6, and E_9 correspond to event B. Thus, in set notation the events are written

$$A = \{E_7, E_8, E_9\}$$

and

$$B = \{E_3, E_6, E_9\}.$$

Note that events A and B are defined by a collection of sample points. In a formal sense, this is precisely what we mean by an event. Until now, we have used the term "event" much as it would be used in everyday language; however, from this point on, we will use the formal definition of an *event* as a collection of sample points.

Union of Events

Given two or more events, we may want to consider forming more complex events by combining two or more of the original events. For example, considering the two events A and B, we might want to form the *union* of A and B, which is the event containing *all sample points belonging to A or B or both*. This union is denoted by $A \cup B$.

In the KP&L problem, where event A is stage 1 completed late and event B is stage 2 completed late, KP&L's management might be concerned about the event of either *A or B or both* occurring. That is, KP&L's management may be concerned about cost overruns and rescheduling problems if stage 1 or stage 2 or both stages are completed late. With

$$A = \{E_7, E_8, E_9\},$$

and

$$B = \{E_3, E_6, E_9\},$$

we have
$$A \cup B = \{E_3, E_6, E_7, E_8, E_9\}.$$

Note that the sample points in $A \cup B$ are the "stage-delay" sample points for KP&L, since all have either stage 1 or stage 2 or both being completed late.

A graphical device that is often useful in depicting operations involving events is a *Venn diagram*. In a Venn diagram the sample space is usually represented as a rectangle, and the events of interest are represented as circles or subsets of the rectangle. The shaded region of Figure 2.4 illustrates the use of a Venn diagram to depict the union of events A and B.

Intersection of Events

Another way of combining events is referred to as the intersection. For example, if we have two events A and B, we could form the *intersection* of A

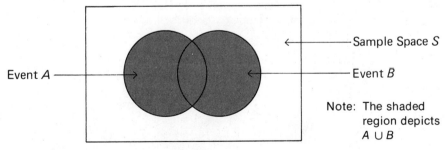

Note: The shaded region depicts $A \cup B$

FIGURE 2.4 *The Union of Events A and B*

Sample Space S
Event A
Event B
Note: The shaded region depicts $A \cap B$

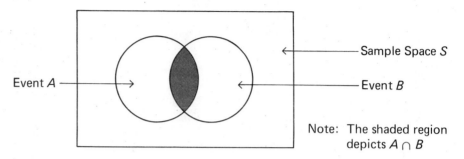

FIGURE 2.5 The Intersection of Events A and B.

and B by defining the event containing all sample points belonging to *both A and B.* This intersection is denoted $A \cap B$.

In the KP&L problem, the intersection of A and B refers to sample points where both stage 1 and stage 2 are completed late. Referring to the definitions of A and B, we see that only one sample point, E_9, is in both A and B. Thus, we have

$$A \cap B = \{E_9\}.$$

Note that E_9 is the only sample point having both stages completed late. The Venn diagram illustrating the intersection of two events is shown in Figure 2.5.

Complement of an Event

Given an event A, the *complement* of A is defined to be the event consisting of all sample points which are *not* in A. The complement of A is denoted by the symbol $\bar{A}$.

In the KP&L problem, where

$$A = \{E_7, E_8, E_9\},$$

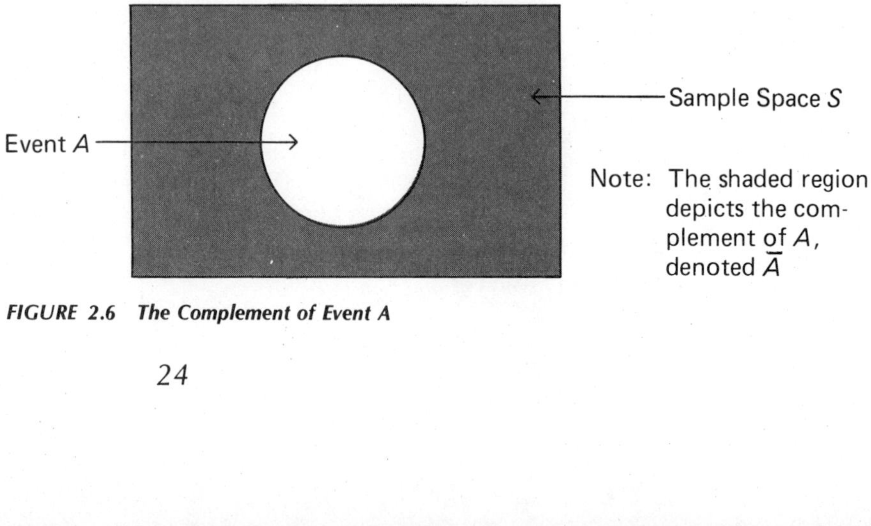

Sample Space S
Event A
Note: The shaded region depicts the complement of A, denoted $\bar{A}$

FIGURE 2.6 The Complement of Event A

we would define the complement of A as follows:

$$\overline{A} = \{E_1, E_2, E_3, E_4, E_5, E_6\}.$$

In this case, $\overline{A}$ can be interpreted as the event of state 1 *not* being completed late. Thus the sample points of $\overline{A}$ are the ones where stage 1 is completed either early or on time. The Venn diagram of the complement is shown in Figure 2.6.

Mutually Exclusive Events

Two or more events are said to be *mutually exclusive* if the events do not have any sample points in common. That is, events A and B are mutually exclusive if the occurrence of one event precludes the occurrence of the other event. Thus a requirement for A and B to be mutually exclusive is that their intersection must not contain any sample points; that is, $A \cap B$ must be empty. Figure 2.7 shows the Venn diagram for two mutually exclusive events.

In the KP&L problem, are the events $A = \{E_7, E_8, E_9\}$ and $B = \{E_3, E_6, E_9\}$ mutually exclusive? Since the intersection $A \cap B = \{E_9\}$ has a sample point, we would have to conclude events A and B are *not* mutually exclusive. The experimental outcome E_9 would cause both events A and B to occur.

However, suppose we let

C = the event that stage 1 is completed early;

thus

$$C = \{E_1, E_2, E_3\}.$$

Now are events A and C mutually exclusive? Yes, since they do not have any sample points in their intersection. Obviously, stage 1 cannot be completed late and early at the same time.

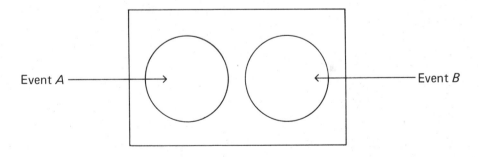

Event A ⟶   ⟵ Event B

FIGURE 2.7   Mutually Exclusive Events

25

Mutually Exclusive and Collectively Exhaustive Events

Consider the following three events:

C = The event stage 1 is completed early
 = $\{E_1, E_2, E_3\}$,
G = the event stage 1 is completed on time
 = $\{E_4, E_5, E_6\}$,
A = the event stage 1 is completed late
 = $\{E_7, E_8, E_9\}$.

Since these three events do not have any sample points in common, they are mutually exclusive. Moreover, the union of the three events is

$$C \cup G \cup A = \{E_1, E_2, E_3, E_4, E_5, E_6, E_7, E_8, E_9\}.$$

But this is the entire sample space S. Since these three mutually exclusive events collectively make up or exhaust the sample space, we refer to these three events as being mutually exclusive and collectively exhaustive. Note that the fact that these three events are mutually exclusive and collectively exhaustive implies that KP&L will observe one and only one of the above three events.

2.3 ASSIGNING PROBABILITIES

At the beginning of this chapter, we stated that probability was a numerical measure of the likelihood that an event will occur. In order to determine the probability for any particular event, we can begin with an assignment of a probability for each of the experimental outcomes or sample points. Then, using various laws of probability, we can calculate the probability of other events. In assigning probabilities to the experimental outcomes, there are a number of acceptable approaches; however, regardless of the approach taken, the following *two basic requirements* must be satisfied.

1. The probability values assigned to each sample point must be between 0 and 1. That is, if we let E_i indicate the sample point and $P(E_i)$ indicate the probability of the sample point, we must have

    $$0 \leq P(E_i) \leq 1, \text{ for all } i. \tag{2.1}$$

2. The sum of *all* the sample point probabilities must be 1. For example, if a sample space has k sample points, we must have

$$P(E_1) + P(E_2) + \cdots + P(E_k) = \sum_{i=1}^{k} P(E_i) = 1. \tag{2.2}$$

26

Thus, any method of assigning probability values to the experimental outcomes which satisfies these two requirements is acceptable. In practice, the following three methods are usually used:

1. Classical method
2. Relative frequency method
3. Subjective method.

Classical Method

To illustrate the classical method of assigning probabilities, let us consider the experiment of flipping a coin. On any one flip, we can observe one of two experimental outcomes: a head or a tail. Intuitively, it would seem reasonable to assume that the two possible outcomes are equally likely. Therefore, since one of the two equally likely outcomes is a head, we should logically conclude that the probability of observing a head is 1/2, or .50. Similarly, the probability of observing a tail is also .50. When the equally likely outcome assumption is used as a basis for assigning probabilities, the approach is referred to as the *classical method*.

Relative Frequency Method

Now suppose a firm is considering marketing a new product and is interested in the probability that a customer makes a purchase. When we contact a potential customer, there are two possible outcomes: the customer purchases the product or the customer does not purchase the product. However, in this case, we are *not* willing to make the assumption that the experimental outcomes are equally likely; thus the classical method of assigning probabilities is inappropriate. Further, suppose that in a test market evaluation of the product, 400 potential customers were contacted; 100 actually purchased the product, while 300 did not. Since we have, in effect, repeated the experiment of contacting one customer 400 times and have found that the product was purchased 100 times, we might decide to assign a probability of $100/400 = .25$ to the experimental outcome of purchasing the product. Similarly, $300/400 = .75$ could be assigned to the experimental outcome of not purchasing the product. This approach to assigning probabilities is referred to as the *relative frequency* method.

Subjective Method

While both the classical and relative frequency methods are objective ways of assigning probabilities, they cannot be applied to all situations where

27

probability assessments are desired. In situations where the experimental outcomes are not equally likely and where experimental or historical relative frequency data are unavailable, another method of assigning probabilities is needed. This third method is referred to as the *subjective method*.

Consider the next basketball or football game your school team will play. What is the probability that your team will win? The experimental outcomes of a win, a loss, and in the case of football, a tie, are not necessarily equally likely. Also, unless the teams involved have played each other several times previously this year, there is no relative frequency data available relevant to this upcoming game. Thus, if you want an estimate of the probability of winning, you must use your subjective opinion of its value. In this case, you are the expert; you know your team, its record, its current injuries, and so forth. Is the probability of winning near 1? If your team is nationally ranked and playing a home game against a team with a 1-win and 6-loss record, perhaps you would be willing to assign a .90 probability to winning. On the other hand, if your team is playing the nation's number 1 team and you have just learned your team's star player is out of the lineup because of injuries, you might want to lower your subjective probability of winning to .30 or perhaps even lower. In using the subjective method to assign probabilities to the experimental outcomes, you may use any data you have available: your experience, your intuition, etc. However, after considering all available information, you must specify a probability value that expresses *your degree of belief* that the team will win its next game.

In many business and economic decision problems, subjective probability estimates are an important source of assigned probabilities. In cases where the equally likely experimental outcome assumption is unacceptable and where experimental data is unavailable, the subjective method must be used to assign probabilities. However, even in those situations where either the classical or relative frequency approach can be applied, it is often still desirable to incorporate subjective input to account for intangible considerations. In such cases, the best probability estimates are obtained by combining both objective and subjective procedures. We will now investigate how the methods of assigning probabilities to the experimental outcomes can be applied in the KP&L problem.

Probabilities for The KP&L Problem

Given the above methods, let us consider assigning probabilities for the KP&L project. In KP&L's situation, it would seem unreasonable to assume that the nine sample points are equally likely; hence the classical method is not applicable. In addition, we might be inclined to reject the relative frequency approach on grounds that this is the first time this particular project has been attempted. However, if a number of "similar" projects have been conducted in the past, KP&L might consider using historical data to compute the relative frequencies of the possible outcomes. If historical data were not available, KP&L would have no choice but to ask the knowledgeable individuals within the firm to provide their best subjective probability estimates. For the KP&L problem, let us assume that only very limited historical data from "similar" projects were available; thus the subjective method was used to obtain the final probability estimates as shown in Table 2.2. Note that these are a valid set of probability assignments, since both equations (2.1) and (2.2) are satisfied.

TABLE 2.2 *Probability Assignments for the KP&L Problem*

Stage 1 (Design)	Stage 2 (Construction)	Sample Point E_i	Probabilities $P(E_i)$
Early	Early	E_1	.15
Early	On time	E_2	.15
Early	Late	E_3	.05
On time	Early	E_4	.10
On time	On time	E_5	.20
On time	Late	E_6	.05
Late	Early	E_7	.05
Late	On time	E_8	.10
Late	Late	E_9	.15
		Total	1.00

Computing the Probability of Events

Given the probabilities of the sample points as shown in Table 2.2, we can compute the probability of any event KP&L management might want to consider from the following rule.

The probability of any event is equal to the sum of the probabilities of the sample points in the event.

Using this rule, we can compute the probability of stage 1 being completed late (event A) and stage 2 being completed late (event B). Since we showed in Section 2.2 that $A = \{E_7, E_8, E_9\}$, the probability of A is given by

$$P(A) = P(E_7) + P(E_8) + P(E_9)$$
$$= .05 + .10 + .15 = .30.$$

Similarly, since $B = \{E_3, E_6, E_9\}$, we have

$$P(B) = P(E_3) + P(E_6) + P(E_9)$$
$$= .05 + .05 + .15 = .25.$$

29

Also, since $A \cap B = \{E_9\}$, then

$$P(A \cap B) = P(E_9) = .15.$$

While we could continue to use this rule to compute the probability for any event of interest, we will now consider alternate approaches that simplify the probability calculations.

2.4 LAWS OF PROBABILITY

The Addition Law

The *addition law* can be used to compute the probability of the union of two events. Under this law, the probability of a union $(A \cup B)$ is given by

$$P(A \cup B) = P(A) + P(B) - P(A \cap B). \tag{2.3}$$

In the KP&L problem, let us define

H = the event that at least one stage of the project is completed late.

Recall that either stage being delayed is the union of A and B. Thus $H = A \cup B$. With $P(A) = .30, P(B) = .25$, and $P(A \cap B) = .15$, we can use equation (2.3) to find that

$$P(H) = P(A \cup B) = .30 + .25 - .15 = .40.$$

Thus, there is a .40 probability that at least one stage of the project will be delayed and possibly cause cost and/or rescheduling problems.

In Section 2.2 we found that

$$A \cup B = \{E_3, E_6, E_7, E_8, E_9\}.$$

Therefore,

$$P(H) = P(A \cup B) = P(E_3) + P(E_6) + P(E_7) + P(E_8) + P(E_9)$$
$$= .05 + .05 + .05 + .10 + .15 = .40.$$

Note, however, for this problem, as well as for more complex problems, the use of the addition law is an easier way to compute the probability of the union.

To obtain an intuitive understanding of the addition law, note that the first two terms in the addition law, $P(A) + P(B)$, account for all the sample points in $A \cup B$. However, since the sample points in the intersection $A \cap B$ are in both A and B, when we compute $P(A) + P(B)$, we are, in effect, double counting the sample points in $A \cap B$. We correct for this double counting by subtracting $P(A \cap B)$.

For the special case of *mutually exclusive events*, $A \cap B$ has no sample points. Therefore, $P(A \cap B) = 0$, and the addition law can be expressed as

$$P(A \cup B) = P(A) + P(B).$$

Using the Complement

Since the complement of an event A, written $\bar{A}$, contains all the sample points not in A, and since the sum of the probabilities of all sample points must be 1, we know that

$$P(A) + P(\bar{A}) = 1.$$

Therefore, another important relationship of probability is

$$P(A) = 1 - P(\bar{A}). \tag{2.4}$$

This relationship can be used to compute $P(A)$ whenever the probability of the complement of A is known or readily available. For example, suppose KP&L is interested in the probability of event J, where

J = the event that both stages of the project are completed without delay.

This event represents the case in which both stages are completed on time or early.

While we could go back and identify the sample points in event J, we might note that we have previously defined H to be the event that at least one stage of the project is completed late. Therefore, H is the complement of J; that is, $H = \bar{J}$. Since we have found $P(H) = .40$, using equation (2.4) we have

$$P(J) = 1 - P(\bar{J}) = 1 - .40 = .60.$$

Thus, there is a .60 probability of completing the project without stage-delay problems.

Law of Conditional Probability

A very important area of probability is concerned with determining the probability of one event given that another event is known to have occurred. For example, in the KP&L problem, suppose that part way through the project, we find that stage 1 is completed late; that is, we know event A has occurred. As we start stage 2, we might ask for a revised or updated probability of stage 2 being completed late (event B). The fact that stage 1 is late is unfortunate; however, now that we know this event has occurred, how should we adjust our probability estimate for stage 2, if at all. That is, we would like to know the probability of event B *given* that event A has occurred. In probability notation, this is written $P(B|A)$, where the " $|$ " is used to denote we are interested in event B "given" that event A has already occurred.

In general, with two events A and B, the laws of conditional probability for B given A and A given B are as follows

$$P(B|A) = \frac{P(A \cap B)}{P(A)} \qquad (2.5)$$

$$P(A|B) = \frac{P(A \cap B)}{P(B)} \qquad (2.6)$$

Recall that our previous probability calculations showed that $P(A) = .30$, $P(B) = .25$, and $P(A \cap B) = .15$. We can now use equation (2.5) to find the probability that stage 2 is completed late (event B) given that stage 1 is completed late (event A).

$$P(B|A) = \frac{.15}{.30} = .50$$

Note that originally we found $P(B) = .25$; however, given that event A has occurred, we would now revise the probability of B to .50. This shows the rather strong effect that progress at stage 1 has on stage 2. If stage 1 experiences problems, it is a signal that there is an increased probability of encountering difficulty or delay problems at stage 2.

To obtain an intuitive understanding of the use of equation (2.5) as applied to the KP&L problem, consider the Venn diagram shown in Figure 2.8. The shaded region of Figure 2.8 depicts the event A, whereas the cross-hatched region denotes the event $(A \cap B)$. We know that once A has occurred, the only way we can also observe event B is for event $(A \cap B)$ to occur. Thus, of the probability of A equal to .30, we know that .15 can be attributed to the event that we also observe B; that is, $P(A \cap B) = .15$. Hence, the probability of observing event B given that event A has occurred is equal to .15/.30 = .50. What we are really saying is that given event A has occurred, there is a "50% chance" that we will also observe event B, because the probability of the event $(A \cap B)$ accounts for 50% of the probability of A.

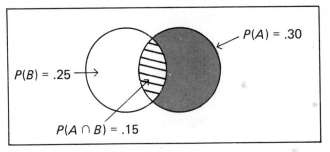

FIGURE 2.8 Venn Diagram for Illustrating Conditional Probability.

The Multiplication Law

The addition law of probability is used to compute the probability of a union of two events. We now show how the *multiplication law* can be used to find the probability of an intersection of two events. The multiplication law is easily derived from the law of conditional probability. Using equations (2.5) and (2.6) and solving for $P(A \cap B)$, we can write the multiplication law as follows:

$$P(A \cap B) = P(A)P(B \mid A) \tag{2.7}$$

or

$$P(A \cap B) = P(B)P(A \mid B). \tag{2.8}$$

The multiplication law is useful in situations where probabilities such as $P(A), P(B), P(B \mid A)$, and/or $P(A \mid B)$ are known, but $P(A \cap B)$ is not. In the KP&L problem, the multiplication law could have been used to estimate the probability of both stages being completed late if subjective probability estimates had been assigned to $P(A)$ and $P(B \mid A)$ directly. For example, suppose KP&L had directly estimated the probability of stage 1 being completed late, $P(A) = .30$, and the probability of stage 2 being completed late given stage 1 was completed late, $P(B \mid A) = .50$. We could then have used equation (2.7) to compute the probability of both stages being completed late.

$$P(A \cap B) = P(A)P(B \mid A)$$
$$= (.30)(.50) = .15.$$

Independent Events

In the KP&L problem, we saw that $P(B) = .25$, while $P(B \mid A) = .50$. This clearly shows that completing stage 1 late, event A, has an effect or influence on the probability of completing stage 2 late, event B. In this case, and in similar situations where $P(B \mid A) \neq P(B)$, we would say events A and B are *dependent* events; that is, the probability of event B is altered if event A occurs. On the other hand, if the occurrence of event A did not cause us to change the probability of event B, we would say the events are independent. This leads us to the following general definition of the independence of two events, A and B.

Two events, A and B are *independent* if

$$P(B \mid A) = P(B)$$

or

$$P(A \mid B) = P(A).$$

Otherwise, the events are *dependent*.

33

Using the definition of independence, we can substitute $P(B)$ for $P(B \mid A)$ and $P(A)$ for $P(A \mid B)$ in equations (2.7) and (2.8). Thus, for the *special case of independent events*, the multiplication law becomes

$$P(A \cap B) = P(A)P(B). \tag{2.9}$$

To see how the concept of independent events can be used in calculating probabilities, let us suppose KP&L has a second major project under way at another location approximately 250 miles from the first project. This second project is being handled by a completely different engineering and construction group. Thus, KP&L's management is convinced that the two projects are completely unrelated or, in probability terms, independent.

Recall that for our original KP&L project, we found the probability of a delay on at least one stage of the project to be .40. Let us denote this probability for the original project by $P(D_1) = .40$. Suppose a separate probability analysis of the second project shows the probability of a delay on at least one stage of this project to be .25; that is $P(D_2) = .25$. Making use of the fact that the two projects are unrelated, we may conclude that events D_1 and D_2 are independent. Then, using equation (2.9), we can compute the probability that both projects will experience delay problems. Thus,

$$P(D_1 \cap D_2) = P(D_1) \, P(D_2) = (.40)(.25) = .10.$$

Using this value in the addition law now provides the probability that project 1 and/or project 2 will experience delay problems. Hence,

$$P(D_1 \cup D_2) = P(D_1) + P(D_2) - P(D_1 \cap D_2)$$
$$= .40 + .25 - .10 = .55.$$

What do these two new probability values tell KP&L's management? The .10 value should be reasonably good news in that it shows a low probability of experiencing cost overruns and rescheduling problems on both projects. However, the $P(D_1 \cup D_2) = .55$ may cause some concern, since it shows a better than 50-50 chance that the firm will experience delay problems on at least one project.

2.5 HOW PROBABILITY HELPS IN THE DECISION-MAKING PROCESS

Let us pause for a moment and review how some of the fundamental concepts of probability have helped the KP&L management better understand the uncertainties associated with the projects. The probabilities we have computed thus far are summarized in Table 2.3.

If you were the manager of the KP&L projects, perhaps this probability information would be of some interest to you. For example, the .40 probability of late completion on at least one stage of the original project might

TABLE 2.3   *Probabilities Associated with the KP&L Project*

Event	Probability
Stage 1 completed late	.30
Stage 2 completed late	.25
Both stages completed late	.15
At least one stage completed late	.40
Project completed without delays	.60
Stage 2 completed late given stage 1 completed late	.50
Two major projects	
Both experience delays	.10
At least one experiences delay	.55

seem undesirably high. Knowing this information, you might consider action that could be taken to reduce this probability. Note also the critical impact that stage 1 has on stage 2. The initial probability of stage 2 being completed late is .25; however, if stage 1 is completed late, the probability of completing stage 2 late is increased to .50. This suggests immediate emphasis should be placed on ensuring that stage 1 is not delayed. Also, note the calculations point out that there is a .55 probability that at least one of the two major projects will experience some sort of delay problem.

Although the probability calculations do not directly recommend decisions for the KP&L manager, they do provide valuable insights into the problem in terms of helping the manager better understand the uncertainties associated with the project. Perhaps the probability information will be used as the basis for a revised scheduling or project control procedure. If some action is taken that causes a change in the probabilities of the outcomes, the new probability values can be computed, and a similar probability analysis can be made to see how the action taken affects the probabilities for events such as those shown in Table 2.3.

Like all quantitative techniques, the value of the output information is highly dependent upon the quality of the input data. In the KP&L problem, assuming that the sample space has been correctly defined and that the subjective probability estimates are realistic, the probability information generated can be quite valuable. In later chapters, we will show how such probability information can be combined with monetary considerations to provide economically sound decision recommendations.

2.6   BAYES' THEOREM

We pointed out in the discussion of conditional probability that being able to revise or update probabilities based on new information is an important phase of probability analysis. Often, we start out with initial or *prior* prob-

35

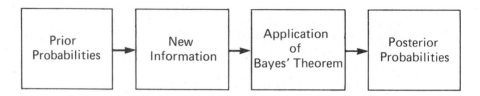

FIGURE 2.9   *Probability Revision Using Bayes' Theorem*

ability estimates for specific events of interest. Then, from sources such as a sample, a special report, a product test, and the like, we obtain some additional information about the events. Given this new information, we want to revise and update the prior probability values. The new or revised probabilities for the events are referred to as *posterior* probabilities. *Bayes' theorem* provides a means of computing these revised probabilities. The steps of this probability revision process are shown in Figure 2.9.

As an illustration of Bayes' theorem, let us consider the screening process used for new loan applications at the C&H Savings and Loan Association. Since loans granted by the firm are eventually repaid or defaulted, the purpose of the screening process is to classify each loan applicant as a good risk or bad risk based on an estimate of the probability that the loan will be repaid. The first step in the process involves a meeting between the loan applicant and the company's loan officer. Based on a personal assessment of the applicant's character, the loan officer provides an initial subjective estimate of the probability that the loan will be repaid. Later, when the written application form is received, information such as the applicant's age, education, years of employment, credit record, and so forth will be used to revise the loan officer's probability estimate.

For example, suppose for a particular loan applicant, the company's loan officer provides an initial probability estimate for repaying the loan of .50, which implies the probability of a default is also .50. Letting

A_1 = the event the loan is repaid
A_2 = the event the loan is defaulted,

we see the loan officer has specified the prior probabilities of $P(A_1) = .50$ and $P(A_2) = .50$.

We note that the events of interest in this example are mutually exclusive and collectively exhaustive. Thus, $P(A_1 \cap A_2) = 0$, and the sum of the prior probabilities $P(A_1) + P(A_2)$ equals 1. In all applications of Bayes' theorem, the events of interest will be mutually exclusive and collectively exhaustive.

Returning to our example, suppose the written application identifies the applicant as a college graduate. Furthermore suppose company records show that of all recently repaid loans, 40% were loans to college graduates. Moreover, of all recently defaulted loans, 10% were loans to college graduates. If we let

36

B = the event the loan applicant is a college graduate,

the above information provides a basis for estimating $P(B|A_1)$ = .40 and $P(B|A_2)$ = .10.

We would now like to know how information that the applicant is a college graduate should be used to modify the loan officer's prior probabilities. That is, what are the posterior probabilities, $P(A_1|B)$ and $P(A_2|B)$? These posterior probabilities may help determine whether the applicant is a good or bad risk.

In order to see how Bayes' theorem is applied and at the same time understand why the formula for Bayes' theorem works, let us look closely at the calculation of the posterior probability $P(A_1|B)$. That is, what is the probability that the applicant repays the loan given he is a college graduate?

Since the probability we are seeking, $P(A_1|B)$, is a conditional probability, we can start with the conditional probability law expressed in equation (2.6). That is,

$$P(A_1|B) = \frac{P(A_1 \cap B)}{P(B)} .$$

Next, using the multiplication law of equation (2.8), we can substitute $P(A_1)P(B|A_1)$ for $P(A_1 \cap B)$, which gives

$$P(A_1|B) = \frac{P(A_1)P(B|A_1)}{P(B)} \tag{2.10}$$

The above equation is one form of writing Bayes' theorem.

For the C&H Savings and Loan Association problem, $P(A_1)$ = .50 and $P(B|A_1)$ = .40 are known; however, $P(B)$, the probability that the applicant is a college graduate, must be determined before we can compute the desired posterior probability. Figure 2.10 should be helpful in determining how to compute $P(B)$.

In Figure 2.10 the tree diagram shows that there are two outcomes that result in the applicant being a college graduate: the applicant will repay the loan and is a college graduate ($A_1 \cap B$) and the applicant will not repay the loan and is a college graduate ($A_2 \cap B$). Since these two events are mutually exclusive, the probability of event B is given by

$$P(B) = P(A_1 \cap B) + P(A_2 \cap B).$$

Returning to the multiplication law, and as shown in Figure 2.10, we know that

$$P(A_1 \cap B) = P(A_1) \, P(B|A_1)$$

and

$$P(A_2 \cap B) = P(A_2) \, P(B|A_2).$$

37

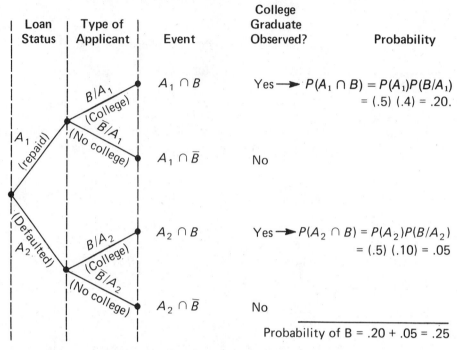

Loan Status	Type of Applicant	Event	College Graduate Observed?	Probability

FIGURE 2.10 Tree Diagram Representation of Bayes' Theorem Calculations

Therefore,

$$P(B) = P(A_1) P(B|A_1) + P(A_2) P(B|A_2). \tag{2.11}$$

Using the probability values for the C&H problem, we find

$$P(B) = (.5)(.40) + (.5)(.10) = .25.$$

This probability calculation tells us that if we had not seen the application form, we should have assigned a .25 probability to the event that the new applicant was a college graduate.

We now return to Bayes' theorem, equation (2.10), and find the desired posterior probability as follows.

$$P(A_1|B) = \frac{(.50)(.40)}{.25} = .80.$$

Thus we know that based on the information that the applicant is a college graduate, the probability the applicant will repay the loan has been revised from .50 to .80. The new information places the applicant in a much better risk category.

Note that by substituting equation (2.11) for $P(B)$ into equation (2.10), we obtain the following expression for $P(A_1|B)$.

$$P(A_1|B) = \frac{P(A_1)P(B|A_1)}{P(A_1)P(B|A_1) + P(A_2)P(B|A_2)} \qquad (2.12)$$

This is another way of writing Bayes' theorem when there are only two events A_1 and A_2. Generalizing equation (2.12) to the case where there are n mutually exclusive and collectively exhaustive events $A_1, A_2, \ldots, A_n$, Bayes' theorem for computing the posterior probability of any event A_i is given by

$$P(A_i|B) = \frac{P(A_i)P(B|A_i)}{P(A_1)P(B|A_1) + P(A_2)P(B|A_2) + \cdots + P(A_n)P(B|A_n)} \qquad (2.13)$$

where $P(A_i)$ = prior probability of event A_i,

$\quad P(B|A_i)$ = conditional probability of event B given A_i,

$\quad P(A_i|B)$ = posterior probability of A_i given B.

In the C&H problem, we have found that the probability of repayment, given the applicant is a college graduate, is .80. This implies that the probability of defaulting, given the applicant is a college graduate, must be $1 - .80 = .20$. Using equation (2.13) directly would have also provided this probability.

$$P(A_2|B) = \frac{P(A_2)P(B|A_2)}{P(A_1)P(B|A_1) + P(A_2)P(B|A_2)}$$

$$= \frac{(.5)(.10)}{(.5)(.40) + (.5)(.10)} = \frac{.05}{.25} = .20$$

The general formula for Bayes' theorem, equation (2.13), is somewhat complicated; therefore, a tabular approach to computing the revised or posterior probabilities is often preferred.

The Tabular Approach

The following step-by-step procedure shows how the tabular approach is applied.

Step 1. Prepare a table with the following three columns:

> Column 1—the list of mutually exclusive and collectively exhaustive events for which probabilities are desired,
> Column 2—prior probabilities,
> Column 3—conditional probability of the new information *given* each event.

This step for the C&H example is as follows:

Events A_i	Prior Probabilities $P(A_i)$	Conditional Probabilities $P(B\|A_i)$
A_1	.50	.40
A_2	.50	.10

Step 2. Compute the probabilities of each $(A_i \cap B)$ by the multiplication law

$$P(A_i \cap B) = P(A_i)P(B\mid A_i).$$

These probabilities are referred to as the *joint probabilities* for each event A_i and the new information B. Summarize these calculations in a column as follows:

Joint Probabilities $P(A_i \cap B)$
$(.50)(.40) = .20$
$(.50)(.10) = .05$

Step 3. Sum the joint probability column to find the probability of the new information, $P(B)$. That is,

$$P(B) = P(A_1 \cap B) + P(A_2 \cap B) = .20 + .05 = .25.$$

Step 4. Compute the posterior probabilities using the basic relationship of conditional probability

$$P(A_i\mid B) = \frac{P(A_i \cap B)}{P(B)}.$$

These calculations are as follows:

Posterior Probabilities $P(A_i\|B)$
$.20/.25 = .80$
$.05/.25 = \underline{.20}$
1.00

A summary of the calculations involved in the tabular approach is presented in Table 2.4.

TABLE 2.4 *A Summary of Bayes' Theorem Calculations for the C&H Savings and Loan Association*

Events A_i	Prior Probabilities $P(A_i)$	Conditional Probabilities $P(B\|A_i)$	Joint Probabilities $P(A_i \cap B)$	Posterior Probabilities $P(A_i\|B)$
A_1	.50	.40	.20	.20/.25 = .80
A_2	.50	.10	.05	.05/.25 = .20
	1.00		$P(B) = .25$	1.00

We note that the tabular approach results in exactly the same posterior probabilities as obtained by applying equation (2.13); however, the tabular approach does make it somewhat easier to carry out the calculations involved.

2.7 SUMMARY

In this chapter, we have introduced basic probability concepts and illustrated how probability analysis can be used to provide helpful decision-making information. We described how probability can generally be interpreted as a numerical measure of the likelihood that an event will occur. In addition, we saw that the probability of an event could be computed either by summing the probabilities of the experimental outcomes (sample points) of the event or by using the relationships established by laws of probability. For cases where additional information is available, we showed how Bayes' theorem could be used to obtain revised or posterior probabilities.

2.8 GLOSSARY

1. *Probability*—A numerical measure of the likelihood that an event will occur.
2. *Experiment*—Any process that generates well-defined outcomes.
3. *Sample points*—The individual outcomes of an experiment.
4. *Sample space*—The set of all possible sample points.
5. *Tree diagram*—A graphical device helpful in defining sample points of an experiment that consists of a sequence of trials.
6. *Event*—A collection of sample points or experimental outcomes.
7. *Union of events A and B (A ∪ B)*—The event containing all sample points that are in *A* or in *B* or in both.
8. *Venn diagram*—A graphical device for depicting the sample space and operations involving events.

9. *Intersection of A and B (A ∩ B)*—The event containing all sample points that are in both *A* and *B*.
10. *Complement of event A($\overline{A}$)*—The event containing all sample points that are not in *A*.
11. *Mutually exclusive events*—Events that have no sample points in common; that is, *A* ∩ *B* is empty.
12. *Collectively exhaustive events*—A group of events that contain all the sample points in the sample space.
13. *Basic requirements of probability*—Two principles or requirements that restrict the manner in which probability assignments can be made.
14. *Classical method*—A method of assigning probabilities that assumes the experimental outcomes are equally likely.
15. *Relative frequency method*—A method of assigning probabilities based upon experimentation or historical data.
16. *Subjective method*—A method of assigning probabilities based upon judgment.
17. *Addition law*—A probability law used to compute the probability of a union, $P(A \cup B) = P(A) + P(B) - P(A \cap B)$.
18. *The law of conditional probability*—A probability law concerned with determining the probability of an event given that another event has occurred.
19. *Multiplication law*—A probability law used to compute the probability of an intersection, $P(A \cap B) = P(A) P(B|A)$.
20. *Independent events*—Two events, *A* and *B*, where $P(A|B) = P(A)$ or $P(B|A) = P(B)$; that is, the events have no influence on each other.
21. *Prior probabilities*—Initial estimates of the probabilities of events.
22. *Posterior probabilities*—Revised probabilities of events based on additional information.
23. *Bayes' theorem*—A method used to compute posterior probabilities.

2.9 PROBLEMS

1. Many states design their automobile license plates such that space is available for up to six letters or numbers.
    a. If a state decides to use only numerical values for the license plates, how many different license plate numbers are possible? Assume 000000 is an acceptable license plate number, although it will only be used for display purposes at the license bureau. (Hint: Use the counting rule).
    b. If the state decides to use two letters followed by four numerical values, how many different license plate numbers are possible? Assume the letters I and O will *not* be used because of their similarity to numerical values 1 and 0.

   c.   Would larger states such as New York and California tend to use more or less letters in license plates than the smaller states? Explain.

2. A financial manager has just made two new investments, one in the oil industry and one in municipal bonds. After a 1-year period, each of the investments will be classified as either successful or unsuccessful. Consider the two investments as an experiment.

   a.   How many sample points exist for this experiment?

   b.   Show a tree diagram and list the sample points.

   c.   Let O = the event that the oil investment is successful, M = the event that the municipal bond investment is successful.
List the sample points in O and in M.

   d.   List the sample points in the union of the events $(O \cup M)$.

   e.   List the sample points in the intersection of the events $(O \cap M)$.

   f.   Are events O and M mutually exclusive? Explain.

3. An individual has purchased common stock in firms A and B. On a given day the price of each stock may rise, remain unchanged, or drop. Consider the experiment of what happens to the prices of the two stocks during a 1-day period.

   a.   How many sample points exist for this experiment?

   b.   Show a tree diagram and list the sample points.

   c.   Let A = the event that stock A shows a price increase, B = the event that stock B shows a price increase.
List the sample points in A and in B.

   d.   List the sample points in the union of the events $(A \cup B)$.

   e.   List the sample points in the intersection of the events $(A \cap B)$.

   f.   Are events A and B mutually exclusive? Explain.

   g.   List the sample points in the complement of A.

4. Consider an experiment where eight experimental outcomes exist. Using the E notation, we denote the experimental outcomes as $E_1, E_2, \ldots, E_8$. Suppose the following events are identified:

$A = \{E_1, E_2, E_3\}$
$B = \{E_2, E_4\}$
$C = \{E_1, E_7, E_8\}$
$D = \{E_5, E_6, E_7, E_8\}$.

Determine the sample points making up the following events:

   a. $A \cup B$ g. D

   b. $C \cup D$ h. $A \cup \overline{D}$

   c. $A \cap B$ i. $A \cap \overline{D}$

   d. $C \cap D$ j. Are A and B mutually exclusive?

   e. $B \cap C$ k. Are B and C mutually exclusive?

   f. $\overline{A}$ l. Are A, B, and D collectively exhaustive?

                 m. Define an event G such that G, B, and D are mutually exclusive and collectively exhaustive.

43

5. Consider the experiment of rolling a pair of dice. Suppose we are interested in the sum of the face values showing on the dice.
   a. How many sample points are possible? (Hint: Use the counting rule.)
   b. List the sample points.
   c. What is the probability of obtaining a 7?
   d. What is the probability of obtaining a value of 9 or greater?
   e. Since there are six possible *even* values (2, 4, 6, 8, 10, and 12) and only five possible *odd* values (3, 5, 7, 9, and 11), the dice should show even values more often than odd values. Do you agree with this statement? Explain.
   f. What method did you use to assign the probabilities above?

6. A marketing manager is attempting to assign probability values to the possible profits and losses resulting from a new product. Relying on subjective probabilities, his probability estimates are as follows:
   P(Profit over \$10,000) = .25
   P (Profit from \$0 to \$10,000) = .50
   P(Loss) = .15.
   Before he uses these estimates to perform further probability calculations, what advice would you offer?

7. Referring to Problem 4 and assuming the classical method is an appropriate way of establishing probabilities, find the following probabilities:
   a. $P(A), P(B), P(C)$, and $P(D)$
   b. $P(A \cap B)$
   c. $P(A \cup B)$
   d. $P(A \mid B)$
   e. $P(B \mid A)$
   f. $P(B \cap C)$
   g. $P(B \mid C)$
   h. Are B and C independent events?

8. In a particular resort area on the west coast of Florida the probability of the sun shining on a given day is .80. The probability of rain is .10. In addition, the probability that the resort experiences both sunshine and rain during the same day is .05. If the experiment involves the weather possibilities during a 1-day period,
   a. Are sun and rain mutually exclusive events? Explain
   b. Are sun and rain independent events?
   c. If we know that it rained on a given day, what is the probability that the resort also had sunshine during the day?

9. In a research study investigating the relationship between smoking and heart disease, a sample of 1000 men over 50 years of age provided the following data.
   180 had heart disease.
   300 were classified as smokers.
   100 had heart disease and were classified as smokers.

80 had heart disease and were classified as nonsmokers.

a.   Given that a man over 50 years of age is a smoker, use the above data to estimate the probability that he has heart disease.

b.   Given that a man over 50 years of age is a nonsmoker, what is the probability that he has heart disease?

c.   Does the research show that heart disease and smoking are independent events? Use probability values to justify your answer.

d.   What conclusion would you draw about the effect of smoking on heart disease?

10.   For the Kentucky Power and Light Company problem presented in this chapter, we found the probability of both stages being completed *without* delays to be .60. We also found that the probability of stage 1 being completed late was .30, while the probability of stage 2 being completed late was .25.

a.   What is the probability that stage 1 is completed without delay problems (that is, either early or on time)?

b.   What is the probability that stage 2 is completed without delay problems?

c.   What is the probability that stage 2 is completed without delay problems given that stage 1 is completed without delay problems?

d.   Do the above results support the manager's belief that good results at stage 1 will improve chances of good results at stage 2? Explain.

11.   A market survey of 800 people found that 400 people could recall a television commercial advertising a particular new product, while 400 could not recall the commercial. Of the 800 people, 240 had actually purchased the product. In addition, a total of 160 people had both seen the commercial *and* purchased the product.

Let T = event of seeing the television commercial, B = event of buying or purchasing the product.

a.   Find $P(T)$, $P(B)$, and $P(T \cap B)$.

b.   Are T and B mutually exclusive events? Use probability values to explain.

c.   If a person could recall seeing the television commercial, what is the probability that he purchased the product?

d.   Are T and B independent events? Use probability values to explain.

12.   Cooper Realty is a small real estate company located in Albany, New York, specializing primarily in residential listings. The firm has recently become interested in the probability of one of its listings being sold within a certain number of days. An analysis of company sales of 800 homes for the previous 2 years produced the data shown below.

a.   If A is defined as the event that a home is listed for over 90 days before being sold, estimate the probability of A.

b.   If B is defined as the event that the initial asking price is under $25,000, estimate the probability of B.

c.   What is the probability of $A \cap B$?

| | | Days Listed Until Sold | | | |
		Under 30	30–90	Over 90	Totals
Initial asking price	Under $25,000	50	40	10	100
	$25,000–$50,000	20	150	80	250
	$50,000–$75,000	20	280	100	400
	Over $75,000	10	30	10	50
	Totals	100	500	200	800

Total Homes Sold

d. Assuming that a contract has just been signed to list a home that has an initial asking price of less than $25,000, what is the probability that it will take Cooper Realty more than 90 days to sell the home?

e. Are the events A and B independent?

13. A purchasing agent has placed two rush orders for a particular raw material from two different suppliers, A and B. If neither order arrives in 2 weeks the production process must be shutdown until at least one of the orders arrives. The probability that supplier A can deliver the material in 2 weeks is .40, while the probability that supplier B can deliver the material in 2 weeks is .50.

   a. What is the probability that both suppliers deliver the material in 2 weeks? Since two separate suppliers are involved, we are willing to assume independence.

   b. What is the probability that at least one supplier delivers the material in 2 weeks?

   c. What is the probability that the production process is shut down in 2 weeks because of a shortage in raw material (that is, both orders are late)?

14. In the evaluation of a sales training program, a firm found that of 50 salesmen making a bonus last year, 20 had attended a special sales training program. If the firm has 200 salesmen, and we let B = the event a salesman makes a bonus, S = the event a salesman attends the sales training program,

   a. Find $P(B)$, $P(S|B)$ and $P(S \cap B)$.

   b. Assume that 40% of the salesmen have attended the training program. What is the probability that a salesman makes a bonus, given that the salesman attended the sales training program, $P(B|S)$?

   c. If the firm evaluates the training program in terms of the effect it has on the probability of a salesman making a bonus, what is your evaluation of the training program? Comment on whether B and S are dependent or independent events.

15. A company has studied the number of lost-time accidents occurring at its Brownsville, Texas, plant. Historical records show 6% of the employees had lost-time accidents last year. Management believes a special safety program will reduce the accidents to 5% during the current year. In addition, it is estimated that 15% of those having lost-time accidents last year will have a lost-time accident during the current year.
    a. What percent of the employees will have lost-time accidents in both years?
    b. What percent of the employees will have at least one lost-time accident over the 2-year period?

16. In a study of television viewing habits among married couples, a researcher found that for a popular Saturday night program, 25% of the husbands viewed the program regularly, while 30% of the wives viewed the program regularly. The study found that for couples in which the husband watches the program regularly, 80% of the wives also watch regularly.
    a. What is the probability both the husband and wife watch the program regularly?
    b. What is the probability that at least one—husband or wife—watches the program regularly?
    c. What percentage of married couples do not have at least one regular viewer of the program?

17. Suppose the loan officer in the C&H Savings and Loan Association problem interviews a new loan applicant and estimates the prior probability of the applicant repaying the loan to be .70.
    a. If subsequent examination of the written application shows that the loan applicant is a college graduate, what is the revised probability that he will repay the loan? Recall,
    P(College grad | Repaid loan) = .40,
    P(College grad | Defaulted loan) = .10.
    b. If the loan applicant is *not* a college graduate, what is the probability that he will repay the loan?

18. A salesman for Business Communication Systems, Inc. sells automatic envelope-addressing equipment to businesses. The probability of making a sale to a new customer is .10. During the initial contact with a customer, sometimes the salesman will be asked to call back later. Of the 30 most recent sales, 12 were made to customers who initially told the salesman to call back later. Of 100 customers who did not make a purchase, 17 had initially asked the salesman to call back later. If a customer asks the salesman to call back later, should the salesman do so? What is the probability of making a sale to a customer who has asked the salesman to call back later?

19. Migliori Industries, Inc. manufactures a gas-saving device for use on

gas forced-air residential furnaces. The company is presently trying to determine the probability that sales of this product will exceed 25,000 units during next year's winter sales period. The company believes that sales of the product depend, to a large extent, on the winter conditions. Management's best estimate is that the probability that sales will exceed 25,000 units if the winter is severe is .8, and that this probability drops to .5 if the winter conditions are moderate. If the weather forecast is .7 for a severe winter and .3 for moderate conditions, what is Migliori's probability that sales will exceed 25,000 units?

20. The Dallas IRS auditing staff is concerned with identifying potential fraudulent tax returns. Based upon past experience, they believe that the probability of finding a fraudulent return, given that the return contains deductions for contributions exceeding the IRS standard, is 0.20. Given that the deductions for contributions are less than the IRS standard, the probability of a fraudulent return decreases to .02. If 8% of all returns exceed the IRS standard for deductions as a result of contributions, what is the best estimate of the percentage of fraudulent returns?

21. An oil company has purchased an option on land in Alaska. Preliminary geological studies have assigned the following prior probabilities:
P(High-quality oil) = .50,
P (Medium-quality oil) = .20,
P(No oil) = .30.
  a. What is the probability of finding oil?
  b. After 200 feet of drilling on the first well, a soil test is taken. The probabilities of finding this particular type of soil were as follows:
  P(Soil | High-quality oil) = .20,
  P(Soil | Medium-quality oil) = .80,
  P(Soil | No oil) = .20.
  How should the firm interpret the soil test? What are the revised probabilities and what is the new probability of finding oil?

22. In the setup of a manufacturing process, a machine is either correctly or incorrectly adjusted. The probability of a correct adjustment is .90. When correctly adjusted, the machine operates with a 5% defective rate; however, if incorrectly adjusted, a 75% defective rate occurs.
  a. After the machine starts a production run, what is the probability that a defect is observed when one part is tested?
  b. Suppose the one part selected by an inspector is found to be defective? What is the probability that the machine is incorrectly adjusted? What action would you recommend?
  c. Before following your recommendation in (b) above, a second part is tested and found to be good. Using your revised probabilities from (b) as the most recent prior probabilities, compute the revised

48

probability of an incorrect adjustment, given that the second part is good. What action would you recommend now?

23. The Wayne Manufacturing Company purchases a certain part from three suppliers A, B, and C. A supplies 60% of the parts; B, 30%; and C, 10%. The quality of parts is known to vary between suppliers, with A, B, and C parts having a .25%, 1%, and 2% defective rate, respectively. The parts are used in one of the company's major products.

   a. What is the probability that the company's major product is assembled with a defective part?

   b. When a defective part is found, which supplier is the likely source?

3
Probability Distributions

In this chapter, we continue the study of probability as a decision-making tool by introducing the concept of a random variable and its probability distribution. This concept is extremely helpful in providing probability information pertaining to a wide variety of problems and/or decision-making situations. Specifically, we use a random variable to describe numerically the experimental outcomes. Then, we show how knowledge about the probability distribution of the random variable can be used to provide useful information for decision making.

3.1 RANDOM VARIABLES

Recall that in Chapter 2 we defined an experiment as any process which generates well-defined outcomes. We now want to concentrate on the process of assigning *numerical values* to the experimental outcomes. This is where the use of a random variable comes into play. For any particular experiment, a random variable can be defined such that each possible experimental outcome generates one numerical value for the random variable. For example, if we consider the experiment of selling automobiles for one day at a particular dealership, we could elect to describe the experimental outcomes in terms of the *number* of cars sold. In this case, if

x = number of cars sold,

x is referred to as a random variable. The particular numerical value that the random variable takes on depends upon the outcome of the experiment. That is, we will not know the specific value of the random variable until we have observed the experimental outcome. For example, if on a given day, three cars were sold, the random variable would take on the value "3." If on another day (a repeat of the experiment), four cars were sold, the random variable would take on the value "4." Thus we see that the purpose of a random variable is to provide a numerical description of the outcome of an experiment.

A random variable is like any other *variable* in the sense that it may take on a number of different values. However, when the numerical values of a variable depend directly upon the chance outcomes of an experiment, we call the variable a random variable. Formally, we define a random variable as follows.

A *random variable* is a numerical description of the outcome of an experiment.

Some additional examples of experiments and associated random variables are given below.

Experiment	Random Variable (x)	Possible values for the Random Variable
Make 100 sales calls	x = Total number of sales	0,1,2, . . . ,100
Inspect a shipment of 70 radios	x = Number of defective radios	0,1,2, . . . , 70
Work 1 year on a project to build a new library	x = Percent of project completed after 6 months	$0 \leq x \leq 100$

Although many experiments such as those listed above have experimental outcomes which lend themselves quite naturally to numerical values, others do not. Note, for example, the process of tossing a coin one time. The experimental outcome will either be a head or a tail, neither of which has a natural numerical value. However, if we want to express the outcomes in terms of a random variable, we obviously need a rule that can be used to assign a numerical value to each of the experimental outcomes. For example, we could let y denote a random variable, where

$y = 1$ if the experimental outcome is a head
$y = 0$ if the experimental outcome is a tail.

While the numerical values for the random variable y are arbitrary, they are acceptable in terms of the definition of a random variable. Namely, y is a random variable because it describes the experimental outcomes numerically.

A random variable may be classified as either discrete or continuous, depending upon the specific numerical values it can have. A random variable that may only take on a finite or countable number of different values is referred to as a *discrete* random variable. For example, the number of units sold, the number of defects observed, or the number of customers that enter a bank during one day of operation are examples of discrete random variables. On the other hand, random variables such as weight, time, or temperature which may take on an infinite number of values over a range or interval are referred to as *continuous* random variables.

51

3.2 A DISCRETE RANDOM VARIABLE—AN EXAMPLE

In order to demonstrate the use of a discrete random variable, let us consider the sales of automobiles at DiCarlo Motors, Inc. in Saratoga, New York. In particular the owner of DiCarlo Motors is interested in the daily sales volume for automobiles. In this situation, we could let x be a random variable denoting the number of cars sold on a given day. Since sales records show that five is the maximum number of cars that DiCarlo has ever sold during one day and since DiCarlo believes that the previous history of sales adequately represents what will occur in the future, we would expect the random variable x to take on one of the numerical values 0, 1, 2, 3, 4, or 5. Since the possible values of the random variable are finite, we would classify x as a discrete random variable.

The Probability Distribution of a Discrete Random Variable

Once we have defined an appropriate discrete random variable for a particular situation, we can determine the probability associated with each value of the random variable. In the DiCarlo Motors problem, we are interested in determining the probabilities of x being 0, 1, 2, 3, 4, or 5. In other words, we would like to know the probabilities associated with each possible daily sales volume for automobiles.

Suppose that in checking DiCarlo's sales records, we find that over the past year the firm has been open for business on exactly 300 days. The sales volumes generated and the frequency of their occurrence are summarized below.

Sales Volume	Number of Days
No Sales	54
Exactly 1 car	117
Exactly 2 cars	72
Exactly 3 cars	42
Exactly 4 cars	12
Exactly 5 cars	3
Total	300

In other problems, the classical or subjective method might be used to assign probabilities to the values of the random variable, but in this case, we assume that the owner of DiCarlo Motors believes that the relative frequency method will provide a reasonable means of assessing the probabilities. Since no sales means $x = 0$, we would assign $54/300 = .18$ as the proba-

TABLE 3.1   The Probability Distribution for the Number of
            Cars Sold per Day

x	$P(x)$
0	.18
1	.39
2	.24
3	.14
4	.04
5	.01

bility that the random variable x takes on the value 0. Using the notation $P(x)$ to represent the probability that x takes on a specific value, we see for $x = 0$, $P(0) = .18$. For $x = 1$, we have $P(1) = 117/300 = .39$. Similarly, computing the relative frequencies for the other possible values of x, we can develop a table of x and $P(x)$ values as shown in Table 3.1. This table, which shows all

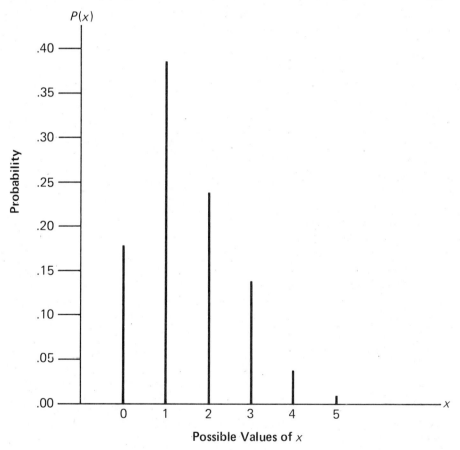

FIGURE 3.1   Graphical Representation of the Probability
             Distribution for Number of Cars Sold per Day

53

possible values of x and the associated probabilities $P(x)$, is the *probability distribution* for the random variable.

We can also depict the probability distribution of x graphically. In Figure 3.1 the values of the random variable x are represented on the horizontal axis and the probabilities, $P(x)$, on the vertical axis. This graph shows the probability distribution for the random variable.

In the development of the probability distribution for any discrete random variable, the following two conditions must always be satisfied.

1. $P(x) \geq 0$
2. $\Sigma P(x) = 1$

Condition 1 is the requirement that the probabilities associated with each value of x must be greater than or equal to zero, while condition 2 points out that the sum of the probabilities for all values of the random variable must be equal to one. Referring to Table 3.1 or Figure 3.1, we see that the probabilities are all greater than or equal to zero. In addition, we note that

$$\Sigma P(x) = P(0) + P(1) + P(2) + P(3) + P(4) + P(5)$$
$$= .18 + .39 + .24 + .14 + .04 + .01 = 1.00.$$

Therefore, since the above conditions are satisfied, the distribution depicted for DiCarlo Motors is a legitimate probability distribution.

Once a random variable and its probability distribution have been developed to describe numerically the experimental outcomes, a number of further computations that are useful in analysis and decision making can be performed. However, before discussing these further computations, let us note that the information already developed (that is, the probability distribution) can be helpful to DiCarlo in the analysis of his operations. The information in Table 3.1 provides DiCarlo with information about the possible levels of daily sales (the values the random variable can take on) together with the probability that each of these levels will occur. For example, the following observations can be made.

There is a .18 probability that no cars will be sold in a day.

There is a .82 probability of at least one sale in a day.

The most probable sales volume is 1 with $P(1) = .39$.

There is a .05 probability of an outstanding sales day with four or five cars sold.

Expected Value

Once we have constructed the probability distribution for a random variable, we may want to compute the *expected value* or *mean* of the random variable. The expected value of a random variable is the weighted average of all possible values of the random variable, where the weights are the probabilities associated with the values. The mathematical formula for computing the expected value of a discrete random variable x is

$$\mu = \Sigma x P(x). \tag{3.1}$$

The Greek symbol μ (mu) is referred to as the expected value or mean of x. Equation (3.1) tells us that in order to compute the expected value of a random variable, we must multiply each value of the random variable by its corresponding probability and then add the resulting terms. The calculation of the expected value of the random variable, number of daily sales, for DiCarlo Motors is shown below.

x	$P(x)$	$xP(x)$
0	.18	$0(.18) = .00$
1	.39	$1(.39) = .39$
2	.24	$2(.24) = .48$
3	.14	$3(.14) = .42$
4	.04	$4(.04) = .16$
5	.01	$5(.01) = .05$
		$\mu = \Sigma x P(x) = 1.50$

We see that 1.50 is the mean or expected number of cars sold per day.

The expected value of a random variable can be thought of as an "average" value. That is, for experiments that can be repeated numerous times, the expected value can be interpreted as the "long-run" average value for the random variable. However, the expected value is not necessarily the number we think the random variable will be the next time the experiment is conducted. In fact, it is impossible for DiCarlo to sell exactly 1.5 cars on any one day. But, if we envision selling cars at DiCarlo Motors for many days into the future, the expected value of 1.5 cars provides a good estimate of the average daily sales volume.

The expected value can be important to the manager from both a planning and a decision-making point of view. For example, suppose DiCarlo Motors will be open 60 days during the next 3 months. How many cars can the owner expect to sell during this period of time? Although we cannot specify the exact sales for any one day, the expected value of 1.50 cars provides an expected sales estimate of $60(1.50) - 90$ cars for the next 3-month period. In terms of setting sales quotas and/or planning orders, the expected value may be helpful decision-making information.

It is important to note that probability problems often involve nonrepeatable experiments. That is, unlike the DiCarlo Motors' daily sales problem, many experiments are "one time only" occurrences. Thus, we could not interpret the expected value of a random variable as the "long-run" average if the experiment could not be repeated a large number of times. In these situations, the expected value of a random variable as computed with equation (3.1) should be interpreted simply as the weighted average for the random variable. Of course, if the decision maker is willing to think in terms of the experiment being "hypothetically" repeated a large number of times, the "long-run average" interpretation can be made.

Variance

While the expected value gives us an idea of the average or central value for the random variable, often we would also like a measure of the dispersion or variability of the values of a random variable. For example, if the values of the random variable ranged from quite large to quite small, we would want a "large" value for our measure of variability. On the other hand, if the values of the random variable showed only modest variation, we would want a relatively "small" value for our measure of variability. In dealing with random variables, the *variance* is used to measure or summarize the variability in the values of the random variable. The mathematical formula for the variance of a discrete random variable is given by

$$\sigma^2 = \Sigma(x - \mu)^2 P(x). \tag{3.2}$$

The Greek symbol σ^2, stated "sigma squared." is the common notation for the variance of a random variable.

As you can see, an essential part of the variance formula is a *deviation,* $(x - \mu)$, which measures how far a particular value of the random variable is from the expected value or mean, μ. In computing the variance of a random variable, the deviations are squared and then weighted by the corresponding probability $P(x)$. The sum of these weighted squared deviations for all values of the random variable is referred to as the variance. A large value of σ^2 indicates that the random variable exhibits substantial variability, while a small value of σ^2 indicates low variability. The calculation of the variance for the number of daily sales in the DiCarlo Motors problem is given as follows.

x	$(x - \mu)$	$(x - \mu)^2$	$P(x)$	$(x - \mu)^2 P(x)$
0	$(0 - 1.50) = -1.50$	2.25	.18	$2.25(.18) = .4050$
1	$(1 - 1.50) = - .50$	.25	.39	$.25(.39) = .0975$
2	$(2 - 1.50) = .50$	.25	.24	$.25(.24) = .0600$
3	$(3 - 1.50) = 1.50$	2.25	.14	$2.25(.14) = .3150$
4	$(4 - 1.50) = 2.50$	6.25	.04	$6.25(.04) = .2500$
5	$(5 - 1.50) = 3.50$	12.25	.01	$12.25(.01) = .1225$
				$\sigma^2 = \Sigma(x - \mu)^2 P(x) = 1.2500$

The variance for the number of cars sold per day is 1.25.

56

Another measure of the variability of a random variable is the *standard deviation, σ,* which is simply defined as the positive square root of the variance. For DiCarlo Motors, the standard deviation of the number of cars sold per day is

$$\sigma = \sqrt{1.25} = 1.118.$$

For purposes of managerial interpretation, the standard deviation is usually preferred over the variance, since it is measured in the same units as the random variable ($\sigma = 1.118$ cars sold per day). The variance (σ^2) is measured in squared units and is thus more difficult for a manager to interpret.

Our use and interpretation of the variance and standard deviation are currently limited to comparisons of the variability of random variables. For example, if the daily sales at another DiCarlo dealership in Albany, New York, reported $\sigma^2 = 2.56$ and $\sigma = 1.6$, we could conclude that the number of cars sold per day is more stable (that is, exhibits less variability) at the DiCarlo Motor's Sarotoga dealership. Later in this chapter when we discuss the normal probability distribution, we will see that knowledge of the variance and standard deviation is necessary for a number of probability calculations.

3.3   THE BINOMIAL DISTRIBUTION

In this section we consider a class of experiments that possesses the following characteristics.

1. The experiment can be described in terms of a sequence of n identical trials.
2. Two outcomes are possible on each trial. We refer to one outcome as *success* and the other as *failure*.
3. The probabilities of the two outcomes do not change from one trial to the next.
4. The trials are independent.

For example, consider the situation of an insurance agent who contacts 10 different families. The outcome associated with visiting each family can be referred to as a success if the family purchases an insurance policy and a failure if not. If we assume the probability of selling a policy is the same for each family, and if the decision to purchase or not purchase insurance by one family does not affect the decision for any other family, then we have an example of an experimental situation that exhibits the above four characteristics.

Experiments which satisfy conditions 2, 3, and 4 are said to be generated by a *Bernoulli process*. If, in addition, condition 1 is satisfied (there are n trials), the experiment is called a binomial experiment. An important discrete

57

random variable associated with the binomial experiment is the number of successful outcomes in the n trials. If we let x denote the value of this random variable, then x can have a value of 0, 1, 2, 3, . . . , n, depending upon the number of successes observed in the n trials. The probability distribution associated with this random variable is called the *binomial probability distribution.*

In the DiCarlo Motors situation, the probability distribution was specified by providing a table or graph of the values of the random variable together with the probability associated with each value. In cases where the binomial distribution is applicable, a mathematical formula can be used to easily compute the probability associated with any value of the random variable. We now show how such a formula can be derived in the context of an example problem.

The Nastke Clothing Store Problem

As an illustration of the binomial probability distribution, let us consider the possible purchases made by customers who enter the Nastke clothing store. To keep the problem relatively small, let us restrict attention to the next three customers who enter the store. If, based on past experience, the store manager estimates the probability that any one customer will make a purchase to be .30, what is the probability that exactly two of the next three customers make a purchase? What is the probability that none of the three make a purchase? While other questions may also be asked, we first want to demonstrate that three customers entering the clothing store can be viewed as a binomial experiment. Checking the four requirements for a binomial experiment, we see the following.

1. The experiment can be described as a sequence of three identical trials—one trial for each of the three customers who will enter the store.
2. Two outcomes—the customer makes a purchase (success) or the customer does not make a purchase (failure)—are possible for each trial or customer.
3. The probability of the purchase (.30) and no purchase (.70) outcomes are assumed to be the same for all customers.
4. The purchase decision of each customer is independent of the decisions of the other customers.

Thus, if we define the random variable x as the number of customers making a purchase (that is, the number of successes in the three trials), we see that the requirements of the binomial probability distribution have been satisfied.

In Figure 3.2, we show a tree diagram of the Nastke problem with three customers entering the store. A success (S) indicates a purchase, and a failure (F) indicates no purchase. Note that the random variable of interest

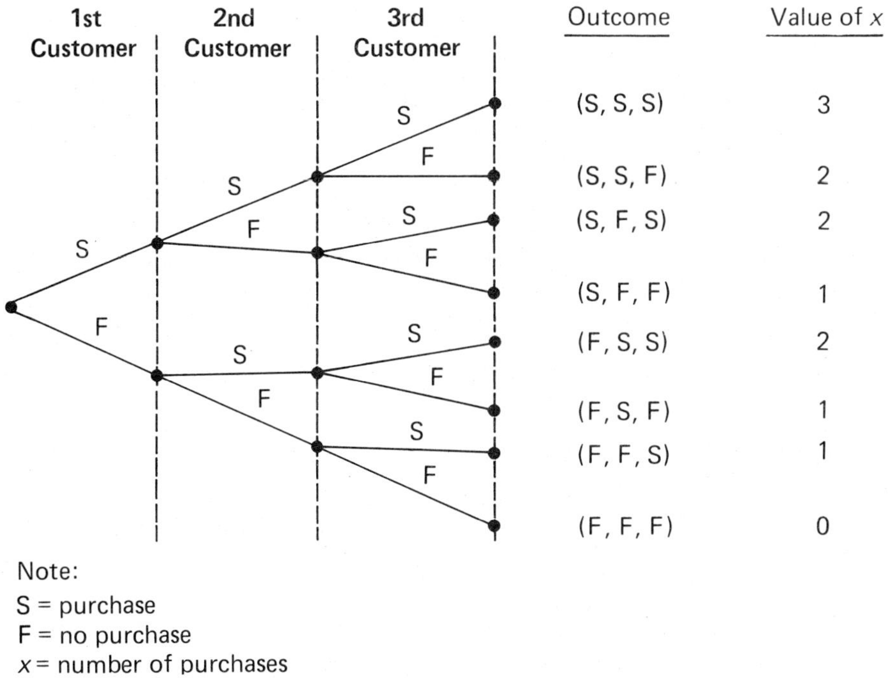

1st Customer	2nd Customer	3rd Customer	Outcome	Value of x

Outcome	Value of x
(S, S, S)	3
(S, S, F)	2
(S, F, S)	2
(S, F, F)	1
(F, S, S)	2
(F, S, F)	1
(F, F, S)	1
(F, F, F)	0

Note:
S = purchase
F = no purchase
x = number of purchases

FIGURE 3.2 Tree Diagram for the Nastke Clothing Store Problem

(number of purchases) is discrete and denotes the number of successes or purchases for the three customers.

Let us now attempt to determine the probability that exactly two of the three customers will make a purchase. We denote this probability as $P(2)$. Looking at Figure 3.2, we see that there are only three possible outcomes in which exactly two successes occur: (1) (S,S,F); (2) (S,F,S); (3) (F,S,S). Since these three outcomes represent three mutually exclusive events, we can compute $P(2)$ by adding the probability of these three experimental outcomes. Let us start with the outcome (S,S,F). To observe this outcome the first customer must make a purchase, the second customer must make a purchase, and the third customer must leave without making a purchase. Since these events are independent, the probability of their joint occurrence must equal the product of their respective probabilities. Hence, the probability of observing this outcome must equal $(.3)(.3)(.7) = (.30)^2(.70) = .063$.

Similar computations for the other two outcomes yielding exactly two successes give the following results.

Outcome	Probability
(S,F,S)	$(.30)(.70)(.30) = (.30)^2(.70) = .063$
(F,S,S)	$(.70)(.30)(.30) = (.30)^2(.70) = .063.$

59

Again, since the three experimental outcomes corresponding to two successes are mutually exclusive, we can apply the addition law (Chapter 2) to obtain

$$P(2) = .063 + .063 + .063$$
$$= .189.$$

We can now generalize the above development to the case of a binomial experiment involving n trials with p equal to the probability of success on any one trial, while $(1 - p)$ is the probability of failure on one trial. Given a binomial experiment involving n trials, the probability of obtaining any one outcome of exactly x successes is given by the formula

$$p^x(1 - p)^{n-x}. \tag{3.3}$$

The exponent on p represents the number of successes and the exponent on $(1 - p)$ represents the number of failures in the sequence of n trials. For the Nastke problem with $n = 3$ and $p = .30$, the probability of one outcome with exactly $x = 2$ successes is given by formula (3.3) as

$$(.30)^2(.70)^1 = .063.$$

Since, in general, there may be more than one experimental outcome corresponding to x successes, we must multiply the value of formula (3.3) by the number of experimental outcomes yielding exactly x successes in n trials. This number can be computed from the following formula[1]

$$\frac{n!}{x!(n - x)!} \tag{3.4}$$

where

$$n! = n(n - 1)(n - 2) \ . \ . \ . \ (2)(1) \tag{3.5}$$

Thus for the Nastke problem with $n = 3$ and $x = 2$, formula (3.4) would have told us there were

$$\frac{3!}{2!1!} = \frac{(3)(2)(1)}{(2)(1)(1)} = \frac{6}{2} = 3$$

experimental outcomes providing exactly two successes. Multiplying formula (3.3) by formula (3.4) would have told us that the probability of exactly two purchases is $3(.063) = .189$.

Combining (3.3) and (3.4) into one equation provides the mathematical formula for the binomial probability distribution.

---

[1] This is the formula commonly used to determine the number of combinations of n objects selected x at a time. For the binomial experiment, this combinatorial formula provides the number of experimental outcomes having x successes in n trials.

$$P(x) = \frac{n!}{x!(n-x)!} p^x (1-p)^{n-x} \qquad (3.6)$$

Equation (3.6) shows that if an experiment possesses the binomial properties, by specifying the number of trials (n) and the probability of success on each trial (p), we can compute the probability for any particular number of successes (x). Table 3.2 depicts the probability distribution of x for the Nastke clothing store problem. Note that for all four values of the random variable, 0, 1, 2, and 3, equation (3.6) was used to compute the corresponding probability. A graph of the probability distribution is provided in Figure 3.3.

If we consider any variation of the Nastke experiment, such as 10 customers rather than 3 entering the store, the binomial probability function given by equation (3.6) is still applicable. For example, the probability of making exactly four sales to 10 potential customers entering the store is

$$P(4) = \frac{10!}{4!6!}(.30)^4(.70)^6 = .2001.$$

This is a binomial experiment with $n = 10$, $x = 4$, and $p = .30$.

Based on equation (3.6), tables have been developed which provide the probability of x successes in n trials for a binomial experiment. These tables are generally easier and quicker to use than equation (3.6), especially when the number of trials involved is large. Such a table of binomial probability values is provided in Appendix A. In order to use this table, it is necessary to specify the values of n, p, and x for the binomial experiment of interest. To see how this table is used, refer to it to verify the probability of four successes in 10 trials for the Nastke clothing store problem. Note that the value of $P(4) = .2001$ can be read directly from Appendix A, making it unnecessary to perform the calculations required by equation (3.6).

TABLE 3.2   Probability
Distribution for
the Number of
Customers Making
a Purchase

x	$P(x)$	
0	$\frac{3!}{0!3!}(.30)^0(.70)^3 =$	.343
1	$\frac{3!}{1!2!}(.30)^1(.70)^2 =$	.441
2	$\frac{3!}{2!1!}(.30)^2(.70)^1 =$	.189
3	$\frac{3!}{3!0!}(.30)^3(.70)^0 =$	.027
		1.000

(Note: $0! = 1$)

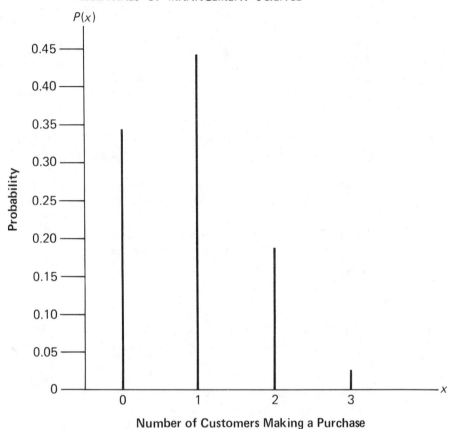

FIGURE 3.3 *Graphical Representation of the Probability Distribution of x for the Nastke Clothing Store Problem*

The Expected Value and Variance for the Binomial Probability Distribution

Given the data in Table 3.2, we can use equation (3.1) to compute the expected value or expected number of customers making a purchase.

$$\mu = \Sigma x P(x) = 0(.343) + 1(.441) + 2(.189) + 3(.027) = .9$$

Note that we could have obtained this same expected value simply by multiplying n times p. That is, $np = 3(.30) = .90$. For the special case of a binomial probability distribution, the expected value of the random variable is given by

$$\mu = np. \tag{3.7}$$

Suppose that during the next month, Nastke's clothing store expects 1000 customers to enter the store. What is the expected number of customers who will make a purchase? The answer is $\mu = np = (1000)(.3) = 300$. Thus, in order to increase the expected number of sales, Nastke's must either induce more customers to enter the store and/or somehow increase the probability that any individual customer will make a purchase after entering. Again, we see that knowledge of the expected value of a random variable can be important in determining what action, if any, should be taken.

For the special case of a binomial distribution, the variance of the random variable can be computed as follows:

$$\sigma^2 = np(1 - p) \tag{3.8}$$

For the Nastke clothing store problem with three customers, we see the variance and standard deviation for the number of customers making a purchase are as follows:

$$\sigma^2 = np(1 - p) = 3(.3)(.7) = .63$$

and

$$\sigma = \sqrt{.63} = .79.$$

Problem 11 at the end of the chapter will ask you to use the probability distribution of Table 3.2 and the variance expression of equation (3.2) to illustrate that for the Nastke clothing store binomial probability distribution, the variance is equal to $np(1 - p)$.

3.4 CONTINUOUS RANDOM VARIABLE—AN EXAMPLE

So far we have only considered random variables that can take on a finite or countable number of values; that is, discrete random variables. In this section we introduce random variables which can take on an infinite number of values in any range or interval. Such random variables are said to be continuous. Examples of continuous random variables are as follows.

1. The *number of ounces* of soup in a can labeled 8 ounces.
2. The *total flight time* of an airplane traveling from Chicago to New York.
3. The *lifetime* of the picture tube in a new color television set.
4. The *drilling depth* required to reach oil in an off-shore drilling operation.

The above random variables are considered continuous because if we identify any two possible values for the random variable, it will always be possible that a value between the first two values could occur. For example, suppose that in checking the filling weights for the cans of soup, we find one can having 8.2 ounces and another 8.3 ounces. Other cans could weigh 8.25 ounces, 8.225 ounces, and so forth. In fact, the actual weight can be any numerical value between 0 ounces for an empty can to, say, 10.00 ounces for a can filled to capacity. Since there are an infinite number of values in this interval, we can no longer list each value of the random variable and then identify its associated probability. In fact, for continuous random variables we will need to introduce a new method for computing the probabilities associated with the values of the random variable.

Let us consider the random variable x which indicates the total flight time of an airplane traveling from Chicago to New York. Since we cannot count and list each of the possible values for the flight time, x is a continuous rather than a discrete random variable. Let us assume that the absolute minimum time for the flight is 2 hours, while the absolute maximum time is 2 hours and 20 minutes. Thus, in terms of minutes, the total flight time can be any value in the interval from 120 minutes to 140 minutes. For example, the total flight time might be 124 minutes, 125.48 minutes, etc. In addition, let us assume that sufficient actual flight data are available to conclude that the probability of a flight time between 120 and 121 minutes is the same as the probability of a flight time within any other 1-minute interval up to and including 140 minutes. With every 1-minute interval being equally likely, the random variable x is said to have a *uniform probability distribution.* The function, referred to as the *probability density function,* which describes the uniform probability distribution for the flight time random variable is[2]

$$f(x) = \begin{cases} 1/20 & \text{for } 120 \le x \le 140 \\ \\ 0 & \text{elsewhere.} \end{cases} \tag{3.9}$$

A graph of this probability density function is shown in Figure 3.4.

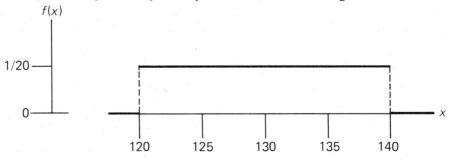

FIGURE 3.4   *Uniform Probability Density Function for Flight Time*

[2] In general, the uniform probability density function for a random variable x is

$$f(x) = \begin{cases} \dfrac{1}{b - a} & \text{for } a \le x \le b \\ \\ 0 & \text{elsewhere.} \end{cases}$$

Note that in the total flight time example, $a = 120$ and $b = 140$.

64

In the graph of the probability density function, $f(x)$ represents the height of the function at any particular value of x. Because we have a *uniform* probability density function, the height is the same for each value of x between 120 and 140.

Perhaps the biggest difference in dealing with discrete and continuous random variables has to do with how we express probability for the various possible values of the random variable. For each value of a discrete random variable, we determined the probability of x having *exactly* that value. That is, we found $P(x)$. However, since a continuous random variable has an infinite number of possible values, we can no longer attempt to identify the probability for each specific value of x. In fact the probability that a continuous random variable takes on any particular value is zero. Rather, we must consider probability only in terms of the likelihood that a random variable has a value within a *specified interval*. For example, in our flight time problem, an acceptable probability question is, what is the probability the flight time is between 120 and 130 minutes? That is, $P(120 \leq x \leq 130) = ?$.

Area as a Measure of Probability

Since the flight time must be between 120 and 140 minutes and since the probability was described as being uniform over this interval, perhaps you feel confident in saying $P(120 \leq x \leq 130)$ is .50. Indeed, this is correct.

Now let us make an observation about the graph shown in Figure 3.4. Specifically, what is the *area under the curve* in the interval from 120 to 130. Note that the region is rectangular in shape and that the area of a rectangle is simply the width times the height. With the width of the interval equal to $130 - 120 = 10$ and the height of the graph $f(x) = 1/20$, we have area = width times height = $10(1/20) = 10/20 = .50$. This is shown in Figure 3.5.

What observation can you make about area and probability? For our example, they are identical! Indeed, this is true for all continuous random

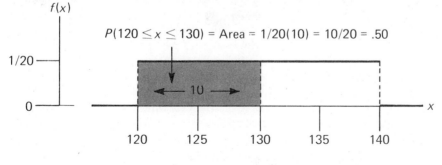

Flight Time in Minutes

FIGURE 3.5 Area Provides Probability of Flight Time

variables. Namely, once a probability density function $f(x)$ has been identified for a continuous random variable, then the probability that x takes on a value between some lower value a and some higher value b can be found by computing the *area* under the graph of $f(x)$ over the interval a to b.

Once we have the appropriate probability distribution and accept the interpretation of area as probability, we can answer any number of probability questions. For example, what is the probability of a flight time between 128 and 136 minutes? The width of the interval is $136 - 128 = 8$. With the uniform height of 1/20, we see $P(128 \leq x \leq 136) = 8(1/20) = 8/20 = .40$.

Note that $P(120 \leq x \leq 140) = 20(1/20) = 1$. That is the total area under the curve is equal to 1. This property holds for all continuous probability distributions and is the analog of the condition that the sum of the probabilities has to equal 1 for a discrete probability distribution. For a continuous probability distribution, we must also require that $f(x) \geq 0$ for all values of x. This is the analog of the requirement that $P(x) \geq 0$ for discrete probability distributions.

In conclusion, then, in regard to continuous random variables, two major differences stand out as compared to our treatment of discrete random variables.

1. We no longer talk about the probability of the random variable taking on a particular value but instead talk about the probability of the random variable assuming a value within some given interval.
2. The probability of the random variable taking on a value within some given interval from a to b is defined to be the area under the graph of the probability density function between a and b. As a result, the probability a continuous random variable will take on any particular value is zero.

3.5 THE NORMAL DISTRIBUTION

Perhaps the most important distribution used to describe a continuous random variable is the *normal probability distribution*. The normal probability distribution is applicable in a great many practical problem situations. Its probability density function has the form of the bell-shaped curve shown in Figure 3.6.

We saw in the previous section that when we deal with a continuous random variable, the graph of the probability distribution is determined by a probability density function $f(x)$. While the $f(x)$ function was rather simple for the uniform probability distribution, it is rather complex for the normal distribution. The normal probability density function is given by

$$f(x) = \frac{1}{\sqrt{2\pi}\sigma} e^{-\frac{(x-\mu)^2}{2\sigma^2}} \quad \text{for all values of } x \tag{3.10}$$

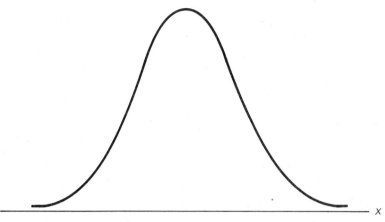

FIGURE 3.6   Bell-Shaped Curve of the Normal
            Probability Distribution

where

μ = mean or expected value of the random variable x

σ^2 = variance of the random variable x

σ = standard deviation of the random variable x

π = 3.14159

e = 2.71828.

Recall now that the $f(x)$ value corresponds to the height of the curve at a particular value of x. Thus, once the mean (μ) and either the standard deviation (σ) or the variance (σ^2) are specified, we can use equation (3.10) to draw the graph or curve for the specific normal distribution. For example, let us consider a normal distribution with a mean of 50 and a standard deviation of 10. Substituting $\mu = 50$ and $\sigma = 10$ into equation (3.10) provides the following probability density function.

$$f(x) = \frac{1}{\sqrt{2\pi}\,(10)}\, e^{-\frac{(x-50)^2}{2(100)}} \tag{3.11}$$

Figure 3.7 depicts the graph of this probability distribution.

Figure 3.8 shows two other normal distributions: one with $\mu = 50$ and $\sigma = 15$ and the other with $\mu = 50$ and $\sigma = 7.5$. Note in particular the effect the standard deviation, σ, has on the general shape of the normal curve. Specifically, a larger standard deviation tends to flatten and broaden the distribution curve. This, of course, is what we should expect, since larger values of σ indicate a larger variability in the values of the random variable.

In order to present the procedure used to compute probabilities associated

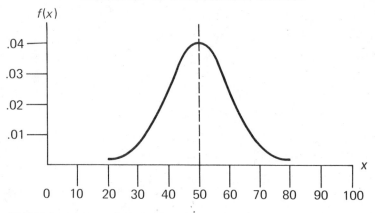

FIGURE 3.7 *A Normal Distribution with $\mu = 50$ and $\sigma = 10$*

with a random variable having a normal distribution, we must first introduce the *standard normal distribution*.

The Standard Normal Distribution

A random variable which has a normal distribution with a mean of 0 and a standard deviation of 1 is said to have a standard normal distribution. We will use the letter z to designate this particular random variable. Thus, for a standard normal random variable z, we can let $\mu = 0$ and $\sigma = 1$ in equation (3.10) in order to determine the probability density function for the standard normal distribution. Hence, we see that

$$f(z) = \frac{1}{\sqrt{2\pi}} e^{-z^2/2}. \tag{3.12}$$

The graph of the standard normal distribution is shown in Figure 3.9. Note

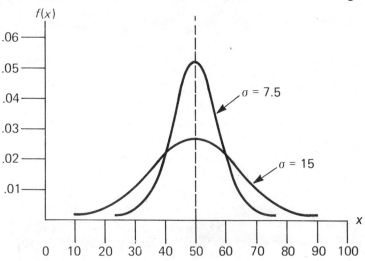

FIGURE 3.8 *Other Normal Distributions with $\mu = 50$*

68

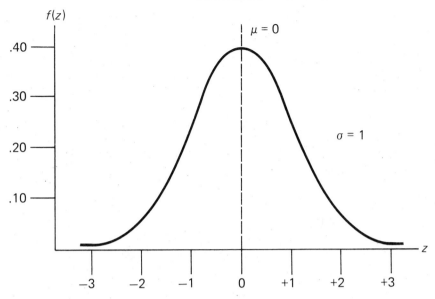

FIGURE 3.9   The Standard Normal Distribution

that while it has the same general appearance as other normal distributions, it has the special properties of $\mu = 0$ and $\sigma = 1$.

Now let us recall the procedure for finding probabilities associated with a continuous random variable. That is, if we want to know the probability of the random variable having a value in a specified interval from a to b, we have to find the area under the curve in the interval from a to b. Finding the area or probability for a uniform distribution was relatively easy, since all we had to do was multiply the width of the interval by the height of the curve. However, at first glance, finding the area under the normal distribution curve appears to be much more difficult, since the height of the curve varies. The mathematical technique for obtaining this area is beyond the scope of this text, but fortunately tables are available which provide areas or probability values for the standard normal distribution. Table 3.3 is such a table of areas. This table also appears as Appendix B at the end of the book.

Let us see how Table 3.3 is used to find areas or probabilities. First note that values of z appear in the left-hand column, with the second decimal value of z appearing in the top row. For example, for a z value of 1.00, we find the 1.0 in the left-hand column and 0.00 in the top row. Then, by looking in the body of the table, we find a value of 0.3413 corresponding to the 1.00 value for z. The value 0.3413 is interpreted as the area under the curve between the mean $z = 0.00$ and $z = 1.00$. This is shown in Figure 3.10. Thus the values in Table 3.3 provide *the area under the curve between the mean ($z = 0.00$) and any specified value of z.* For another example, use the table to show that the area or probability of a z value in the interval $z = 0.00$ to $z = 1.25$ is 0.3944.

69

TABLE 3.3   *Areas or Probabilities for the Standard Normal Distribution*

z	0.00	0.01	0.02	0.03	0.04	0.05	0.06	0.07	0.08	0.09
0.0	0.0000	0.0040	0.0080	0.0120	0.0160	0.0199	0.0239	0.0279	0.0319	0.0359
0.1	0.0398	0.0438	0.0478	0.0517	0.0557	0.0596	0.0636	0.0675	0.0714	0.0753
0.2	0.0793	0.0832	0.0871	0.0910	0.0948	0.0987	0.1026	0.1064	0.1103	0.1141
0.3	0.1179	0.1217	0.1255	0.1293	0.1331	0.1368	0.1406	0.1443	0.1480	0.1517
0.4	0.1554	0.1591	0.1628	0.1664	0.1700	0.1736	0.1772	0.1808	0.1844	0.1879
0.5	0.1915	0.1950	0.1985	0.2019	0.2054	0.2088	0.2123	0.2157	0.2190	0.2224
0.6	0.2257	0.2291	0.2324	0.2357	0.2389	0.2422	0.2454	0.2486	0.2518	0.2549
0.7	0.2580	0.2612	0.2642	0.2673	0.2704	0.2734	0.2764	0.2794	0.2823	0.2852
0.8	0.2881	0.2910	0.2939	0.2967	0.2995	0.3023	0.3051	0.3078	0.3106	0.3133
0.9	0.3159	0.3186	0.3212	0.3238	0.3264	0.3289	0.3315	0.3340	0.3365	0.3389
1.0	0.3413	0.3438	0.3461	0.3485	0.3508	0.3531	0.3554	0.3577	0.3599	0.3621
1.1	0.3643	0.3665	0.3686	0.3708	0.3729	0.3749	0.3770	0.3790	0.3810	0.3830
1.2	0.3849	0.3869	0.3888	0.3907	0.3925	0.3944	0.3962	0.3980	0.3997	0.4015
1.3	0.4032	0.4049	0.4066	0.4082	0.4099	0.4115	0.4131	0.4147	0.4162	0.4177
1.4	0.4192	0.4207	0.4222	0.4236	0.4251	0.4265	0.4279	0.4292	0.4306	0.4319
1.5	0.4332	0.4345	0.4357	0.4370	0.4382	0.4394	0.4406	0.4418	0.4429	0.4441
1.6	0.4452	0.4463	0.4474	0.4484	0.4495	0.4505	0.4515	0.4525	0.4535	0.4545
1.7	0.4554	0.4564	0.4573	0.4582	0.4591	0.4599	0.4608	0.4616	0.4625	0.4633
1.8	0.4641	0.4649	0.4656	0.4664	0.4671	0.4678	0.4686	0.4693	0.4699	0.4706
1.9	0.4713	0.4719	0.4726	0.4732	0.4738	0.4744	0.4750	0.4756	0.4761	0.4767
2.0	0.4772	0.4778	0.4783	0.4788	0.4793	0.4798	0.4803	0.4808	0.4812	0.4817
2.1	0.4821	0.4826	0.4830	0.4834	0.4838	0.4842	0.4846	0.4850	0.4854	0.4857
2.2	0.4861	0.4864	0.4868	0.4871	0.4875	0.4878	0.4881	0.4884	0.4887	0.4890
2.3	0.4893	0.4896	0.4898	0.4901	0.4904	0.4906	0.4909	0.4911	0.4913	0.4916
2.4	0.4918	0.4920	0.4922	0.4925	0.4927	0.4929	0.4931	0.4932	0.4934	0.4936
2.5	0.4938	0.4940	0.4941	0.4943	0.4945	0.4946	0.4948	0.4949	0.4951	0.4952
2.6	0.4953	0.4955	0.4956	0.4957	0.4959	0.4960	0.4961	0.4962	0.4963	0.4964
2.7	0.4965	0.4966	0.4967	0.4968	0.4969	0.4970	0.4971	0.4972	0.4973	0.4974
2.8	0.4974	0.4975	0.4976	0.4977	0.4977	0.4978	0.4979	0.4979	0.4980	0.4981
2.9	0.4981	0.4982	0.4982	0.4983	0.4884	0.4984	0.4985	0.4985	0.4986	0.4986
3.0	0.4986	0.4987	0.4987	0.4988	0.4988	0.4989	0.4989	0.4989	0.4990	0.4990

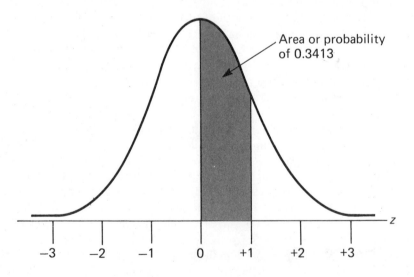

Area or probability of 0.3413

FIGURE 3.10   *Probability of z Between 0.00 and +1.00*

70

Now what is the probability of obtaining a z value between $z = -1.00$ and $z = 1.00$? We already have used Table 3.3 to find that the probability of a z value between $z = 0.00$ and $z = 1.00$ is 0.3413. Note now that the normal distribution is symmetric in the sense that the shape of the curve to the left of the mean is the mirror image of the shape of the curve to the right of the mean. The probability of a z value between $z = 0.00$ and $z = -1.00$ is the same as between $z = 0.00$ and $z = 1.00$, that is, 0.3413. Thus the probability of a z value between $z = -1.00$ and $z = 1.00$ must be 0.3413 + 0.3413 = 0.6826. This is shown graphically in Figure 3.11.

Similarly, we can find that the probability of a z value between -2.00 and $+2.00$ is 0.4772 + 0.4772 = 0.9544, while the probability of a z value between -3.00 and $+3.00$ is 0.4986 + 0.4986 = 0.9972. Since we know the total probability or total area under the curve for any continuous random variable must be 1.0000, the probability of 0.9972 tells us that virtually all values of z must fall between -3.00 and $+3.00$. Note that the figures depicting the standard normal distribution show this graphically.

As two final examples of computing areas for the standard normal distribution, let us find (1) the probability that z is *greater than* 2.00 and (2) the probability that z is between 1.00 and 2.00. For $P(z > 2.00)$, we see from Table 3.3 that the area between $z = 0.00$ and $z = 2.00$ is 0.4772. With 0.5000 as the total area above the mean, the area above $z = 2.00$ must be 0.5000 − 0.4772 = 0.0228. This is shown graphically below.

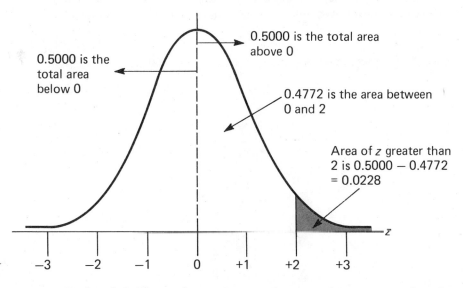

For $P(1.00 \leq z \leq 2.00)$, we know the area between the mean $z = 0$ and $z = 2.00$ is 0.4772, while the area between the mean $z = 0$ and $z = 1.00$ is 0.3413. Thus the area between $z = 1.00$ and $z = 2.00$ must be 0.4772 − 0.3413 = 0.1359. This result is shown graphically as follows.

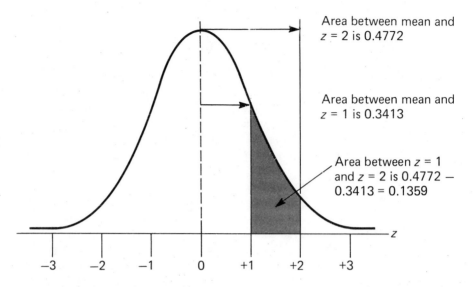

Area between mean and $z = 2$ is 0.4772

Area between mean and $z = 1$ is 0.3413

Area between $z = 1$ and $z = 2$ is 0.4772 − 0.3413 = 0.1359

Computing Probabilities for Any Normal Distribution by Converting to the Standard Normal Distribution

The reason we have been discussing the standard normal distribution so extensively is that probabilities for any normal distribution can be easily computed by first converting to the standard normal distribution. Thus, when we have a normal distribution with any mean, μ, and any standard deviation, σ, we can answer probability questions about this distribution by converting to the standard normal distribution and then using Table 3.3 and the appropriate z values to find the area or probability values. The formula used to convert a normal random variable x with mean μ and standard deviation σ to

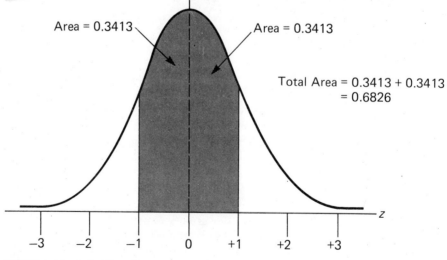

Area = 0.3413

Area = 0.3413

Total Area = 0.3413 + 0.3413 = 0.6826

FIGURE 3.11   Probability of z Between −1.00 and +1.00

72

the standard normal distribution is given by

$$z = \frac{x - \mu}{\sigma}. \tag{3.13}$$

Note that a value of x equal to its mean, μ, results in $z = (\mu - \mu)/\sigma = 0$. Thus, we see x at its mean, μ, corresponds to z at its mean, 0. Now suppose x is one standard deviation above its mean; that is, $x = \mu + \sigma$. Applying equation (3.13), the corresponding z values is $z = (\mu + \sigma - \mu)/\sigma = \sigma/\sigma = +1$. Thus, we see x at one standard deviation above the mean is equivalent to $z = 1$. In other words, we can interpret the z value as *the number of standard deviations an x value is from its mean μ.*

To see how this conversion enables us to compute probabilities for any normal distribution, let us consider an example. Suppose we have a normal distribution with $\mu = 10$ and $\sigma = 2$. What is the probability that the random variable x is between 10 and 14? Using equation (3.13) we see

$$\text{at } x = 10, z = \frac{10 - 10}{2} = 0$$

and

$$\text{at } x = 14, z = \frac{14 - 10}{2} = 2.$$

Thus the answer to our question is given by the probability that z is between 0 and 2. In other words, the probability we are seeking is the probability that the random variable x is between its mean and two standard deviations above the mean. Using $z = 2.00$, Table 3.3 shows us that the probability is 0.4772. Hence, the probability x is between 10 and 14 is 0.4772.

The Grear Tire Company

For an application of the normal probability distribution, let us suppose that the Grear Tire Company has just developed a new steel-belted radial tire that will be sold through a national chain of discount stores. Since the tire is a new product, Grear's management believes the mileage guarantee offered with the tire will be an important factor in the acceptance of the product. Before finalizing the tire mileage guarantee policy, Grear's management would like some probability information concerning the number of miles the tires will last.

Based on actual road tests with the tires, Grear's engineering group has estimated the mean tire mileage at $\mu = 36,500$ miles and the standard deviation at $\sigma = 5,000$ miles. In addition, the data collected indicates that a normal distribution is a reasonable assumption.

Using the normal distribution, what percentage of the tires can be expected to last more than 40,000 miles? In other words, what is the probability that the tire mileage will exceed 40,000? This question can be interpreted as trying to find the area of the shaded region on the following graph.

73

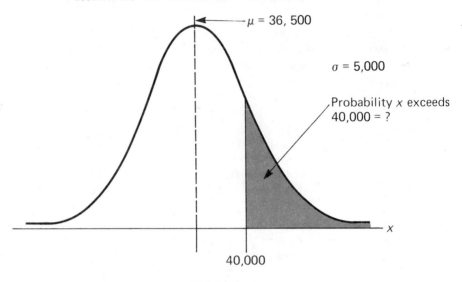

Tire Mileage

At $x = 40,000$, we have

$$z = \frac{x - \mu}{\sigma} = \frac{40,000 - 36,500}{5,000} = \frac{3,500}{5,000} = .70.$$

Using Table 3.3, we see that the area between the mean and $z = .70$ is 0.2580. Thus, $0.5000 - 0.2580 = 0.2420$ is the probability x will exceed 40,000. We can conclude that about 24.2% of the tires will exceed 40,000 in mileage.

Let us now assume Grear is considering a guarantee that will provide a discount on a new set of tires if the original tires do not exceed the mileage stated in the guarantee. What should the guarantee mileage be if Grear would like no more than 10% of the tires to be eligible for the discount guarantee? This question is interpreted graphically below.

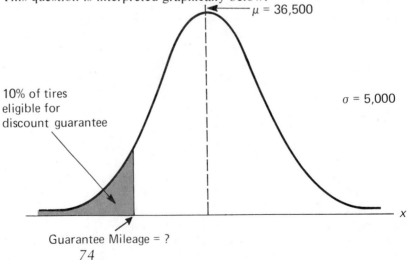

In the above graph, 40% of the area must be between the mean and the unknown guarantee mileage. Looking up 0.4000 in the body of Table 3.3, we see that this area occurs at approximately 1.28 standard deviations below the mean. To find the mileage corresponding to 1.28 standard deviations below the mean, we compute

$$x = \mu - 1.28\sigma$$
$$= 36,500 - 1.28\,(5,000) = 30,100.$$

Thus, a guarantee of 30,100 miles will meet the requirement that approximately 10% of the tires will be eligible for the guarantee. Perhaps, with this information, the firm will set its final tire mileage guarantee policy at 30,000 miles.

Again we see the important role that probability distributions play in providing decision-making information. Namely, once a probability distribution is established for a particular problem situation, it can be used rather quickly and easily to provide probability data about the problem. While the data does not make a decision recommendation directly, it does provide information that helps the decision maker better understand the problem. Ultimately, this information may assist the decision maker in reaching a good decision.

3.6 SUMMARY

In this chapter the concept of a random variable and its probability distribution was introduced. We saw that random variables were used to provide numerical descriptions of experimental outcomes. Such a numerical description is necessary if further computations, such as calculating expected values and variances, are to be performed. We have seen that discrete probability distributions can be represented either by tables or graphs that show the values of the random variable together with the associated probabilities or by a formula which can be used to compute probabilities given values for the random variable. The DiCarlo Motor's situation illustrated the tabular presentation, and the binomial distribution provided an illustration of a discrete probability distribution for which a formula was available to compute probabilities. The binomial distribution is important in applications of probability analysis, and special tables have been developed to make it easier to identify the appropriate probabilities. Such a table is provided in Appendix A.

With continuous random variables, it was necessary to associate probability with the area under the curve defined by the probability density function. The probability that a continuous random variable x takes on a value in the interval $a \leq x \leq b$ is given by the area under the curve between *a* and *b*. The uniform probability distribution was used to demonstrate the computation of areas or probabilities for continuous random variables. The remaining section of the chapter was devoted to the normal probability distribution. In particular, we demonstrated how the standard normal distribution could be used to provide probability information about any particular normally distributed random variable.

3.7 GLOSSARY

1. *Random variable*—A numerical description of the experimental outcomes.
2. *Discrete random variable*—A random variable that can only take on a finite or countable number of values.
3. *Continuous random variable*—A random variable that can take on an infinite number of values in an interval or range.
4. *Discrete probability distribution*—The values of the random variable and the associated probabilities. It can be provided in the form of a table, graph, or equation.
5. *Expected value*—The weighted average of the values of the random variable in which the probabilities are the weights. If an experiment could be repeated a large number of times, the expected value could be interpreted as the long-run average.
6. *Variance*—A measure of the dispersion or variability in the random variable.
7. *Standard deviation*—The positive square root of the variance.
8. *Binomial distribution*—The probability distribution for a discrete random variable denoting the number of successes in *n* trials.
9. *Probability density function*—The function that describes the distribution of a continuous random variable.
10. *Normal distribution*—A continuous probability distribution that is bell-shaped and determined by the parameters μ (mean) and σ (standard deviation).
11. *Standard normal distribution*—A normal distribution with a mean of 0 and a standard deviation of 1.

3.8 PROBLEMS

1. The probability distribution for the random variable, "number of telephone calls occurring at a business office in a 10-minute time period," is as follows:

Number of Calls	Probability
0	.05
1	.12
2	.19
3	.30
4	.22
5	.10
6	.02

    a.   Is this an acceptable probability distribution? Why?

    b.   What is the expected number of calls?

    c.   What is the variance and standard deviation?

2.   Which of the following are and which are not probability distributions? Explain.

x_1	$P(x_1)$	x_2	$P(x_2)$	x_3	$P(x_3)$
0	.20	0	.25	−1	.20
1	.30	2	.05	0	.50
2	.25	4	.10	1	−.10
3	.35	6	.60	2	.40

3.   The number of weekly lost-time injuries at a particular plant has the following probability distribution.

Number of Injuries	Probabilities
0	.05
1	.20
2	.40
3	.20
4	.15

    a.   Compute the expected value.

    b.   Compute the variance.

4.   Assume that the plant in Problem 3 initiated a safety training program and that the number of lost-time injuries during the 20 weeks following the training program was as follows:

Number of Injuries	Number of Weeks
0	2
1	8
2	6
3	3
4	1

a. Show the probability distribution for the above data.
b. Compute the expected value and variance and use both to evaluate the effectiveness of the safety training program.

5. A retailer has shelf space for two units of a highly perishable item which must be disposed of at the end of the day if it is not sold. Each unit costs $2.50 and sells for $5.00. Demand probabilities are as follows: P(demand = 0) = .40, P(demand = 1) = .20, and P(demand = 2) = .40.

Let y be a random variable indicating daily profit resulting if a retailer stocks two units each day.

Let x be a random variable indicating daily profit if a retailer stocks one unit each day.

a. Show the probability distributions for y and x.
b. Using the expected values of y and x, determine whether the retailer would be better off stocking one or two units per day.

6. A firm estimates the probability of employee disciplinary problems on a particular day to be .10.

a. What is the probability that the company experiences a week (5 working days) without a disciplinary problem?
b. What is the probability of exactly 2 days with disciplinary problems in a 2-week period (10 working days)?
c. What is the probability of at least 2 days with disciplinary problems in a 4-week period?

7. Suppose a salesman makes a sale on 20% of his calls.

a. If the salesman makes three calls per day, what is the probability that he makes more than three sales in a 5-day week?
b. If the salesman works 50 weeks per year and makes a commission of $100 per sale, how many sales can he be expected to make annually and what is his expected annual income?

8. The salesman in Problem 7 is being asked by his sales manager to make one extra call per day. If the salesman increases his calls from three to four per day, what is his probability of making more than three sales per week and how much of an increase can he expect in his annual income?

9. In an audit of a company's billings, an auditor randomly selects five bills. If 3% of all bills contain an error, what is the probability that the auditor will find

a. exactly one bill in error?
b. at least one bill in error?

10. A salesman contacts eight potential customers per day. From past experience, it is known that the probability of a potential customer making a purchase is .10.

a. What is the probability the salesman makes *exactly* two sales in a day?
b. What is the probability the salesman makes *at least* two sales in a day?

   c. What percentage of the days will the salesman not make a sale?

   d. What is the expected number of sales per day? Over a 5-day week, how many sales are expected?

11. For the special case of a binomial random variable, we showed that the variance measure could be computed from the formula $\sigma^2 = np(1 - p)$. For the Nastke clothing store problem data in Table 3.2, we found $\sigma^2 = np(1 - p) = .63$. Use the general definition of variance for a discrete random variable [equation (3.2)] and the data in Table 3.2 to verify that the variance is, in fact, .63.

12. A manufacturing process produces parts that are classified as either defective or acceptable. If the probability that the process produces a defective part is 0.10, how many defective parts would you expect to find in a lot of 500 parts? What is the variance of the number of defective parts in the lot?

13. In an office building, the waiting time for an elevator is found to be uniformly distributed between 0 minutes and 5 minutes.

   a. What is the probability density function $f(x)$ for this uniform distribution?

   b. What is the probability of waiting longer than 3.5 minutes?

   c. What is the probability the elevator arrives in the first 45 seconds?

   d. What is the probability of a waiting time between 1 and 3 minutes?

   e. What is the expected waiting time?

14. The demand for a new product is assumed to be normally distributed with $\mu = 200$ and $\sigma = 40$. Letting x be the units demanded, find the following:

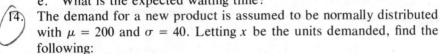

   a. $P(180 \leq x \leq 220)$

   b. $P(x \geq 250)$

   c. $P(x \leq 100)$

   d. $P(225 \leq x \leq 250)$

15. A soup company markets eight varieties of homemade soup throughout the eastern states. The standard size soup can holds a maximum of 11 ounces, while the label on each can advertises contents of $10\frac{3}{4}$ ounces. The extra $\frac{1}{4}$ ounce is to allow for the possibility of the automatic filling machine placing more soup than the company actually wants in a can. Past experience shows that the number of ounces placed in a can is approximately normally distributed with a mean of 10.75 and a standard deviation of 0.1 ounces. What is the probability that the machine will attempt to place more than 11 ounces in a can, causing an overflow to occur?

16. The sales of High-Brite Toothpaste are believed to be approximately normally distributed with a mean of 10,000 tubes per week and a standard deviation of 1500 tubes per week.

   a. What is the probability that more than 12,000 tubes will be sold in any given week?

b.   In order to have a .95 probability that the company will have sufficient stock to cover the weekly demand, how many tubes should be
produced?

17.   Ward Doering Auto Sales is considering offering a special service contract that will cover the total cost of any service work required on
leased vehicles. Based upon past experience, Ward estimates that
yearly service costs are approximately normally distributed with a
mean of $150 and a standard deviation of $25.

a.   If Ward offers the service contract to customers for a yearly charge
of $200, what is the probability that any one customer's service
costs will exceed the contract price of $200?

b.   What is Ward's expected profit per service contract?

18.   The attendance at home football games is normally distributed with a
mean of 45,000 and a standard deviation of 3000.

a.   What percentage of the time should attendance be between 44,000
and 48,000?

b.   What is the probability of exceeding 50,000?

c.   80% of the time the attendance should be at least how many?

19.   Assume that the test scores from a college admissions test are normally
distributed with a mean of 450 and a standard deviation of 100.

a.   What percentage of the people taking the test score between 400
and 500?

b.   Suppose someone receives a score of 630. What percentage of the
people taking the test score better? What percentage score worse?

c.   If a particular university will not admit anyone scoring below 480,
what percentage of the persons taking the test would be acceptable
to the university?

20.   The lifetime of a color television picture tube is normally distributed
with a mean of 7.8 years and a standard deviation of 2 years.

a.   What is the probability that a picture tube will last more than 10
years?

b.   If the firm guarantees the picture tube for 2 years, what percentage
of the television sets sold will have to be replaced because of
picture tube failure?

c.   If the firm is willing to replace the picture tubes in a maximum of
1% of the television sets sold, what guarantee period can be offered
for the television picture tubes?

21.   A machine fills containers with a particular product. The standard deviation of filling weights is known from past data to be .6 ounces. If only
2% of the containers have less than 18 ounces, what is the mean filling
weight for the container? Assume the filling weights are normally
distributed.

4

Introduction to Decision Theory

In Chapters 2 and 3 we discussed the role that probability plays in measuring the uncertainty associated with a given problem situation. We now show how probability information can be combined with payoff measures such as profits, costs, and the like to identify economically sound decision recommendations. The procedures appropriate for such an analysis usually come under the heading of decision theory or decision analysis. When a decision maker is faced with several decision alternatives and an uncertain pattern of future events, decision theory can lead to good decisions.

We begin our study of decision theory in this chapter by considering problem situations in which there are a reasonably small number of decision alternatives and possible future events. The concept of a payoff table is introduced to provide a structure for this type of decision situation and to illustrate the fundamentals involved in the decision theory approach to any situation. In Chapters 5, 6, and 7, we extend the decision theory approach to more complex decision-making situations.

4.1 STRUCTURING THE DECISION SITUATION: PAYOFF TABLES

In order to illustrate the decision theory approach let us consider the case of Political Systems, Inc. (PSI), a newly formed computer service firm specializing in information services such as surveys, data analysis, and so on, for individuals running for political office. PSI is in the final stages of selecting a computer system for its midwest branch located in Chicago. While the firm has decided on a computer manufacturer, it is currently attempting to determine the size of the computer system that would be the most economical to lease. We will use decision theory to help PSI make its computer-leasing decision.

The first step in the decision theory approach for a given problem situation is to identify the alternatives that may be considered by the decision maker. For PSI, the final decision will be to lease one of three computer systems which differ in size or capacity. The three decision alternatives, denoted by d_1, d_2, and d_3, are as follows:

d_1 = lease the large computer system

d_2 = lease the medium-sized computer system

d_3 = lease the small computer system.

Obviously, the determination of the best decision will depend upon what PSI management foresees as the possible market acceptance of their service and consequently the possible demand or load on the PSI computer system. Often the future events associated with a problem situation are uncertain. That is, while a decision maker may have an idea of the variety of possible future events, he will be unsure as to which particular event will occur. Thus, the second step in a decision theory approach is for the analyst to identify the future events that he believes might occur. These future events, which are not under the control of the decision maker, are referred to as the *states of nature* for the problem. It is assumed that the list of possible states of nature includes everything that can happen and that the individual states of nature do not overlap; that is, the states of nature are defined so that one and only one of the listed states of nature will occur. Thus the states of nature are mutually exclusive and collectively exhaustive events.

When asked about the states of nature for the PSI decision problem, the firm's management viewed the possible acceptance of their service as an either-or situation. That is, PSI management believed that the firm's overall level of acceptance in the marketplace would be one of two possibilities: high acceptance or low acceptance. Thus the PSI states of nature, denoted by s_1 and s_2, are as follows:

s_1 = high customer acceptance of PSI services

s_2 = low customer acceptance of PSI services.

Given the three decision alternatives and the two states of nature, which computer system should PSI lease? In order to answer this question, we will need information on the profit associated with each combination of a decision alternative and a state of nature. For example, what profit would PSI experience if the firm decided to lease the large computer system d_1 and market acceptance was high s_1? What profit would PSI experience if the firm decided to lease the large computer system d_1 and market acceptance was low s_2? And so on.

In decision theory terminology, we refer to the outcome resulting from making a certain decision and the occurrence of a particular state of nature as the *payoff*. Using the best information available, management of PSI has estimated the payoffs or profits for the PSI computer leasing problem. These estimates are presented in Table 4.1. A table of this form is referred to as a *payoff table*. In general, entries in a payoff table can be stated in terms of profits, costs, or any other measure of output that may be appropriate for the particular situation being analyzed. The notation we will use for the entries in

TABLE 4.1   Payoff Table for the PSI Computer
            Leasing Problem

			States of Nature	
			High Acceptance s_1	Low Acceptance s_2
Decision Alternatives	Lease a large system	d_1	$200,000	$-20,000
	Lease a medium sized system	d_2	$150,000	$ 20,000
	Lease a small system	d_3	$100,000	$ 60,000

Profit or
payoff

the payoff table is $V(d_i, s_j)$, which denotes the payoff associated with decision alternative d_i and state of nature s_j. Using this notation we see that $V(d_3, s_1) = \$100,000$.

The identification of the decision alternatives, the states of nature, and the determination of the payoff associated with each decision alternative and state of nature combination are the first three steps in the decision theory approach. The question we now turn to is, How can the decision maker best utilize the information presented in the payoff table to arrive at a decision? As we shall see, there are several criteria that may be used.

4.2 TYPES OF DECISION-MAKING SITUATIONS

Before discussing specific decision-making criteria, let us consider the types of decision-making situations that we may encounter. The classification scheme for decision-making situations is based on the knowledge the decision maker has about the states of nature. In this regard, there are two types of decision-making situations.

1. Decision making under certainty—the process of choosing a decision alternative when the state of nature is known.
2. Decision making under uncertainty—the process of choosing a decision alternative when the state of nature is not known.

In the case of decision making under certainty, there will be only one column in the payoff table, and the optimal decision is the one corresponding to the largest payoff in the column. For example, if PSI knew for certain that market acceptance of its service was going to be high, column s_2 could be removed from the payoff table, and the optimal solution would be the large system d_1, since d_1 provides the largest profit ($200,000) in the s_1 column.

83

Most situations in which the decision theory approach is applied, however, involve decision making under uncertainty. In these cases the selection of the best alternative is more difficult. First the decision maker must select a criterion. Then he must determine which decision alternative is best under the chosen criterion.

4.3 CRITERIA FOR DECISION MAKING UNDER UNCERTAINTY WITHOUT USING PROBABILITIES

In some situations of decision making under uncertainty, the decision maker may have very little confidence in his ability to assess the probabilities of the various states of nature. In such cases, the decision maker might prefer to choose a decision criterion that does not require any knowledge of the probabilities of the states of nature. Three of the most popular criteria available for these cases are maximin (or minimax), maximax (or minimin), and minimax regret.

Because different criteria will sometimes lead to different decision recommendations, it is important for the decision maker to know the criteria available and then select the specific criterion which, according to his judgment, is the most appropriate. We now discuss the above three criteria for decision making under uncertainty by showing how each could be used to solve the PSI computer leasing problem.

Maximin

The *maximin* decision criterion is a pessimistic or conservative approach to arriving at a decision. In this approach the decision maker attempts to *maxi*mize his *min*imum possible profits; hence the term maximin. Using the information contained in the payoff table, the decision maker would first list the minimum payoff that is possible for each decision alternative. He would then select the decision from the new list that results in maximum payoff. Table 4.2 illustrates this process for the PSI problem.

Since $60,000, corresponding to the decision to lease a small system yields the maximum of the minimum payoffs, the decision to lease a small system is recommended as the maximin decision. This decision criterion is considered conservative because it concentrates on the worst possible payoffs and then recommends the decision alternative that avoids the possibility of extremely "bad" payoffs. In using the maximin criterion, PSI is guaranteed a profit of at least $60,000. While PSI may still make more, it *cannot* make less than the maximin criterion value of $60,000.

For problems in which costs are to be minimized, the conservative maxi-

TABLE 4.2 PSI Minimum Payoff for Each Decision Alternative

Decision Alternatives		Minimum Payoff	
Large system	d_1	$-20,000	
Medium system	d_2	$20,000	Maximum of the minimum payoff values
Small system	d_3	$60,000	

min approach is reversed in that the decision maker first lists the maximum cost for each decision alternative. The recommended decision then corresponds to the *mini*mum to the *max*imum costs. Thus, this criterion, used for minimization problems, is referred to as *minimax*.

Maximax

While maximin offers a pessimistic decision criterion, maximax provides an optimistic criterion. Using this criterion for maximization problems, the decision maker selects the decision that *maxi*mizes his *max*imum payoff hence the name *maximax*. In applying this criterion, the decision maker first determines the maximum payoff possible for each decision alternative. The decision maker then identifies the decision that provides the overall maximum payoff. Table 4.3 shows the result of applying this criterion for the PSI problem.

Since $200,000, corresponding to the decision to lease a large system, yields the maximum of the maximum payoffs, the decision to lease a large system is the recommended maximax decision. This decision criterion reflects an optimistic point of view because it simply recommends the decision alternative that provides the possibility of obtaining the best of all payoffs, $200,000. While the use of this criterion provides the opportunity for a large payoff, it also exposes the company to the possibility of a $20,000 loss.

TABLE 4.3 PSI Maximum Payoff for Each Decision Alternative

Decision Alternative		Maximum Payoff	
Large system	d_1	$200,000	Maximum of the maximum payoff values
Medium system	d_2	$150,000	
Small system	d_3	$100,000	

For minimization problems, the maximax criterion reverses to the *mini*mum of the *mini*mum cost values, or the *minimin* criterion.

Minimax Regret

Suppose we make the decision to lease the small system d_3 and afterwards learn that market acceptance of the PSI service is high s_1. Table 4.1 shows the resulting profit to be $100,000. However, now that we know state of nature s_1 has occurred, we see that the large system decision d_1 yielding a profit of $200,000 would have been the optimal decision. This difference between the optimal payoff ($200,000) and the payoff experienced ($100,000) is referred to as the *opportunity loss* or *regret* associated with our d_3 decision when state s_1 occurs ($200,000 − $100,000 = $100,000). If we had made decision d_2 and state of nature s_1 had occurred, the opportunity loss or regret for this decision and state of nature would have been $200,000 − $150,000 = $50,000.

The general expression for opportunity loss or regret is given by:

$$R(d_i, s_j) = V^*(s_j) - V(d_i, s_j) \qquad (4.1)$$

where

$R(d_i, s_j)$ = regret associated with decision alternative d_i and state of nature s_j.

$V^*(s_j)$ = *best* payoff value under state of nature s_j.[1]

For our d_3 decision and state of nature s_1, $V^*(s_1) = \$200,000$ and $V(d_3, s_1) = \$100,000$. Thus

$$R(d_3, s_1) = \$200,000 - \$100,000 = \$100,000.$$

Using equation (4.1), we can compute the regret associated with all combinations of decision alternatives d_i and states of nature s_j. We simply replace each entry in the payoff table with the value found by subtracting it from the largest entry in its column. Table 4.4 shows the regret, or opportunity loss, table for the PSI problem.

The next step in applying the minimax regret criterion requires the decision analyst to identify the maximum regret for each decision alternative.

---

[1] In cost minimization problems $V^*(s_j)$ will be the smallest entry in column j. Thus, for minimization problems, formula (4.1) must be changed to $R(d_i, s_j) = V(d_i, s_j) - V^*(s_j)$.

TABLE 4.4 *Regret or Opportunity Loss Table for the PSI Problem*

			States of Nature	
			High Acceptance s_1	Low Acceptance s_2
	Large system	d_1	0	$80,000
Decision Alternatives	Medium system	d_2	$50,000	$40,000
	Small system	d_3	$100,000	0

Regret or opportunity loss

These data are shown in Table 4.5. The final decision is made by selecting the alternative corresponding to the *mini*mum of the *max*imum regret values; hence the name *minimax regret*. For the PSI problem, the decision to lease a medium-sized computer system, with a corresponding regret of $50,000, is the recommended minimax regret decision.

Note that the three decision criteria discussed in this section have each led to different recommendations. This is not in itself bad. It simply reflects the difference in decision-making philosophies that underly the various criteria. Ultimately, the decision maker will have to choose the most appropriate criterion and then make the final decision accordingly. The major criticism of the criteria discussed in this section is that they do not consider any information about the probabilities of the various states of nature. In the next section we discuss criteria that utilize probability information in selecting a decision alternative.

TABLE 4.5 *PSI Maximum Regret or Opportunity Loss for Each Decision Alternative*

Decision Alternatives		Maximum Regret or Opportunity Loss	
Large system	d_1	$ 80,000	Minimum of the maximum regret
Medium system	d_2	$ 50,000	
Small system	d_3	$100,000	

4.4 CRITERIA FOR DECISION MAKING UNDER UNCERTAINTY USING PROBABILITIES

In many situations, good probability estimates can be developed for the states of nature. Two decision criteria which make use of these probability estimates in the selection of a decision alternative are expected monetary value and expected opportunity loss. Let us now see how these criteria can be applied when making decisions under uncertainty.

Expected Monetary Value

The *expected monetary value* criterion requires the analyst to compute the expected value for each decision alternative and then select the alternative yielding the best expected value. Let

$P(s_j)$ = probability of occurrence for state of nature s_j
N = number of possible states of nature.

Since one and only one of the N states of nature can occur, we recall that the associated probabilities must satisfy the following two conditions:

$$P(s_j) \geq 0 \qquad \text{for all states of nature } j \tag{4.2}$$

and

$$\sum_{j=1}^{N} P(s_j) = P(s_1) + P(s_2) + \cdots + P(s_N) = 1. \tag{4.3}$$

The expected monetary value of a decision alternative d_i is given by

$$\mathrm{EMV}(d_i) = \sum_{j=1}^{N} P(s_j)V(d_i, s_j). \tag{4.4}$$

In words, the expected monetary value of a decision alternative is the sum of weighted payoffs for the alternative. The weight for a payoff is the probability of the associated state of nature and therefore the probability that the payoff occurs. Let us now return to the PSI problem to see how the expected monetary value criterion can be applied.

Suppose PSI management believes that the high acceptance state of nature, while very desirable, has only a 0.3 probability of occurrence, while the low acceptance state of nature has a 0.7 probability. Thus $P(s_1) = 0.3$ and $P(s_2) = 0.7$. Using the payoff values $V(d_i, s_j)$ shown in Table 4.1 and equation (4.4), expected monetary values for the three decision alternatives can be calculated:

EMV(d_1) = 0.3(200,000) + 0.7(−20,000) = $46,000

EMV(d_2) = 0.3(150,000) + 0.7(20,000) = $59,000

EMV(d_3) = 0.3(100,000) + 0.7(60,000) = $72,000.

Applying the expected monetary value criterion to this profit maximization problem, the small system decision d_3 with an expected monetary value of $72,000 is the recommended decision.

Note, however, that if the probabilities of the states of nature change, a different decision alternative might be selected. For example, if $P(s_1) = 0.6$ and $P(s_2) = 0.4$, we find the following expected monetary values.

EMV(d_1) = 0.6($200,000) + 0.4(−$20,000) = $112,000

EMV(d_2) = 0.6($150,000) + 0.4($20,000) = $98,000

EMV(d_3) = 0.6($100,000) + 0.4($60,000) = $84,000

Thus, we now see that decision alternative d_1 with an expected monetary value of $112,000 is the recommended decision with these probabilities.

Expected Opportunity Loss

In the previous section we defined the concept of an opportunity loss or regret associated with each decision alternative and state of nature combination. For PSI we developed the opportunity loss table shown in Table 4.4. The *expected opportunity loss* criterion uses the probabilities of the states of nature as weights for the opportunity loss values and computes the expected value of the opportunity loss (EOL) as follows:

$$EOL(d_i) = \sum_{j=1}^{N} P(s_j)R(d_i, s_j) \qquad (4.5)$$

where $R(d_i, s_j)$ denotes the regret or opportunity loss for decision alternative d_i and state of nature s_j [see equation (4.1)].

Again using $P(s_1) = 0.3$ and $P(s_2) = 0.7$ for PSI and the opportunity loss data of Table 4.4, the expected opportunity losses for the three decision alternatives become

EOL(d_1) = 0.3(0)   + 0.7(80,000) = $56,000

EOL(d_2) = 0.3(50,000) + 0.7(40,000) = $43,000

EOL(d_3) = 0.3(100,000) + 0.7(0)   = $30,000.

Since we would want to minimize the expected opportunity loss, the small system decision d_3 with the smallest loss of $30,000 is recommended.

While expected opportunity loss offers an alternate criterion and approach to decision making under uncertainty, the optimal decision using the expected opportunity loss criterion will *always* be the same as the optimal decision using the expected monetary value criterion. Since the recommended decisions are identical, only one criterion need be applied in a given decision-making situation. In practice the expected monetary value has been the most widely used and accepted criterion for decision making under uncertainty. However, the expected opportunity loss provides the same result, and as we will see in section 4.6, the (EOL) associated with the best decision provides an indication of the value of collecting additional information about the probabilities for the states of nature.

4.5 DECISION TREES

While decision problems involving a modest number of decision alternatives and a modest number of states of nature can be analyzed by using payoff tables, they can also be analyzed by using a graphical representation of the decision-making process called a *decision tree*.

Figure 4.1 shows a decision tree for the PSI computer leasing problem. Note that the tree shows the natural or logical progression that will occur in the decision-making process. First the firm must make its decision $(d_1, d_2,$ or

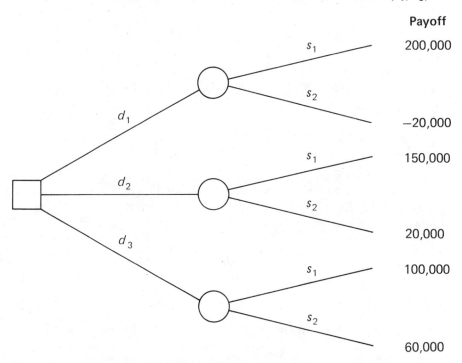

FIGURE 4.1 *Decision Tree for the PSI Problem.*

d_3) and then, once in operation, the state of nature (s_1 or s_2) will occur. The number at each endpoint of the tree represents the payoff associated with a particular chain of events. For example, the topmost payoff of 200,000 arises whenever management makes the decision to purchase a large system (d_1) and market acceptance turns out to be high (s_1). The next lower terminal point of $-20,000$ is reached when management has made the decision to lease the large system (d_1) and the true state of nature turns out to be a low degree of market acceptance (s_2). Thus, we see that each possible sequence of events for the PSI problem is represented in the decision tree.

Using the general terminology associated with decision trees, we will refer to the intersection or junction points of the tree as *nodes* and the arcs or connectors between the nodes as *branches*. Figure 4.2 shows the PSI decision tree with the nodes numbered 1 to 4 and the branches labeled as decision or state-of-nature branches. When the branches *leaving* a given node are decision branches, we refer to the node as a decision node. Decision nodes are denoted by squares. Similarly, when the branches leaving a given node are state-of-nature branches, we refer to the node as a state-of-nature node.

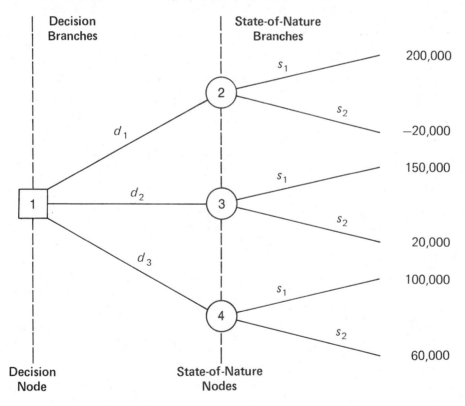

FIGURE 4.2 PSI Decision Tree with Node and Branch Labels

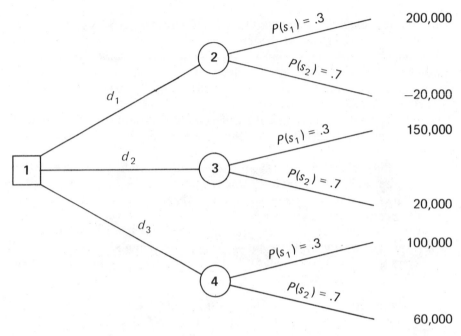

FIGURE 4.3 PSI Decision Tree with State-of-Nature Branch Probabilities

State-of-nature nodes are denoted by circles. Using this node-labeling procedure, node 1 is a decision node, whereas nodes 2, 3, and 4 are state-of-nature nodes.

At decision nodes the decision maker *selects* the particular decision brancn $(d_1, d_2, $ or $d_3)$ that will be taken. Selecting the best branch is equivalent to making the best decision. However the state-of-nature branches are not controlled by the decision maker; thus the specific branch followed from a state of nature node depends upon the probabilities associated with the branches. Using $P(s_1) = .3$ and $P(s_2) = .7$, we show the PSI decision tree with state-of-nature branch probabilities in Figure 4.3.

We will now use the branch probabilities and the expected monetary value criterion to arrive at the optimal decision for PSI. Working *backward* through the decision tree, we first compute the expected monetary value at each state-of-nature node. That is, at each state-of-nature node, we weight the possible payoffs by their chance of occurrence. The expected monetary values for nodes 2, 3, and 4 are computed as follows:

EMV(node 2) = 0.3(200,000) + 0.7(−20,000) = \$46,000

EMV(node 3) = 0.3(150,000) + 0.7(20,000) = \$59,000

EMV(node 4) = 0.3(100,000) + 0.7(60,000) = \$72,000.

We now continue backward through the tree to the decision node. Since the expected monetary values for nodes 2, 3, and 4 are known, the decision maker can view decision node 1 as follows.

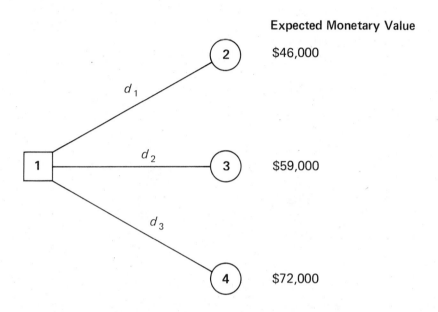

Expected Monetary Value

$46,000

$59,000

$72,000

Since the decision maker controls the branch leaving a decision node and since we are trying to maximize expected profits, the best decision branch at node 1 is d_3. Thus the decision tree analysis had led us to recommend d_3 with an expected monetary value of $72,000. Note that this is the same recommendation that was obtained using the expected monetary value criterion in conjunction with the payoff table.

We have seen how decision trees can be used to analyze a decision under risk. While other decision problems may be substantially more complex than the PSI problem, if there are a reasonable number of decision alternatives and states of nature, the decision tree approach outlined here can be used. First the analyst must draw a decision tree consisting of decision and state-of-nature nodes and branches that describe the sequential nature of the problem. Assuming that the expected monetary value criterion is to be used, the next step is to determine the probabilities for each of the state-of-nature branches and compute the expected monetary value at each state-of-nature node. The decision branch leading to the state of nature node with the highest expected monetary value is then selected. The decision alternative associated with this branch is the best decision using the expected monetary value criterion.

93

4.6 EXPECTED VALUE OF PERFECT INFORMATION

At the end of Section 4.4, we stated that the expected opportunity loss criterion was useful in determining the value of collecting additional information about the probabilities of the states of nature. Suppose now that PSI had the opportunity to conduct a market research study to thoroughly evaluate consumer need for its service. Such a study could help by improving the current probability assessments for the states of nature. On the other hand, if the cost of obtaining such information exceeded its value, PSI should not seek it.

To help determine the maximum possible value of additional information for PSI, we have reproduced PSI's opportunity loss table below (Table 4.6). Recall that the optimal decision using either the expected monetary value or expected opportunity loss criterion was to lease the small system, d_3. Let us now concentrate on the losses associated with this decision.

We see that if state of nature s_1 occurs, d_3 will not have been the best decision, and PSI will have an opportunity loss of $100,000 because d_1 was not selected. That is, given perfect information that s_1 was going to occur, PSI could increase its profit $100,000 by selecting d_1 instead of d_3. On the other hand, if state of nature s_2 occurs, d_3 will have been the best decision, and the opportunity loss will be $0. Thus, perfect information that s_2 was going to occur would be of no value to the company, since PSI would have made the optimal decision without it.

What is the expected value of this perfect information? Using $P(s_1) = .3$ and $P(s_2) = .7$ and the opportunity loss values, we see that 30% of the time PSI could save $100,000, while 70% of the time the savings would be $0. Thus, the *expected value of perfect information* (EVPI) for PSI's problem is given by

$$EVPI = (0.3)(\$100,000) + (0.7)(\$0) = \$30,000.$$

Note that EVPI is the same as the *expected opportunity loss of the optimal decision* (see Section 4.4). If we have used expected opportunity loss as a decision criterion or if in our analysis we have computed the expected oppor-

TABLE 4.6 Opportunity Loss Table for the PSI Problem

| | | States of Nature | |
		High Acceptance s_1	Low Acceptance s_2
Decision Alternatives	Large system d_1	0	$80,000
	Medium system d_2	$ 50,000	$40,000
	Small system d_3	$100,000	0

tunity loss of the optimal decision, we, in effect, have computed the expected value of perfect information.

Generally speaking, we would not expect a market research study to provide "perfect" information, but the information provided might be worth a good portion of the $30,000. In any case, PSI's management knows it should never pay more than $30,000 for any information, no matter how good. Provided the market survey cost is reasonably small, say $5000 to $10,000, it appears economically desirable for PSI to consider the market research study.

Before ending this chapter, we note the general expression for computing the expected value of perfect information (EVPI) from a payoff table.

Let d^* = optimal decision for the problem prior to obtaining information,

$\quad P(s_j)$ = probability of state of nature j,

$\quad\quad N$ = number of states of nature, and

$R(d^*, s_j)$ = opportunity loss or regret value for decision d^* and state of nature s_j.

Then we have the following expression for EVPI.

$$\text{EVPI} = \sum_{j=1}^{N} P(s_j)R(d^*, s_j)$$

4.7 SUMMARY

In this chapter we have introduced the decision theory approach to decision making. We have discussed in detail the procedures designed to solve problems with discrete states of nature and decision alternatives. The goal of the decision theory approach is to identify the best decision alternative given an uncertain pattern of future events (that is, states of nature).

After defining decision making under certainty and uncertainty, we discussed the decision criteria of maximin, maximax, and minimax regret for solving problems of decision making under uncertainty without using probabilities. The criteria of expected monetary value and expected opportunity loss were then introduced for solving problems of decision making under uncertainty when it was desired to make use of the probability information available. Decision trees provided a graphical representation of the sequential nature of the decision process and an alternative to the payoff table for determining the expected monetary value of a decision alternative.

Finally, we discussed the value of obtaining additional information to revise the probabilities of the states of nature. The expected value of perfect information was found to place an upper limit on the value of such information.

4.8 GLOSSARY

1. *States of nature*—The uncontrollable future events that can affect the outcome of a decision.
2. *Payoff*—The outcome measure such as profit, cost, and so forth. Each combination of a decision alternative and a state of nature has a specific payoff.
3. *Payoff table*—A tabular representation of the payoffs for a decision problem.
4. *Decision making under certainty*—The process of choosing a decision alternative when the state of nature is known.
5. *Decision making under uncertainty*—The process of choosing a decision alternative when the state of nature is not known.
6. *Maximin*—A maximization decision criterion for decisions under uncertainty that seeks to maximize the minimum payoff.
7. *Minimax*—A minimization decision criterion for decisions under uncertainty that seeks to minimize the maximum cost.
8. *Maximax*—A maximization decision criterion for decisions under uncertainty that seeks to maximize the maximum payoff.
9. *Minimin*—A minimization decision criterion for decisions under uncertainty that seeks to minimize the minimum payoff.
10. *Opportunity loss or regret*—The amount of loss (lower profit or higher cost) resulting from not making the best decision for each state of nature.
11. *Minimax regret*—A maximization or minimization decision criterion for decisions under uncertainty that seeks to minimize the maximum regret.
12. *Expected monetary value*—A decision criterion for decisions under uncertainty. The expected monetary value weights the payoff for each decision by its probability of occurrence.
13. *Expected opportunity loss*—The expected value criterion applied to opportunity loss or regret values. Also, a decision criterion for decisions under uncertainty.
14. *Decision tree*—A graphical representation of the decision-making situation from decision to state of nature to payoff.
15. *Nodes*—The intersection or junction points of the decision tree.
16. *Branches*—Lines or arcs connecting nodes of the decision tree.
17. *Expected value of perfect information (EVPI)*—The expected value of information that would tell the decision maker exactly which state of nature was going to occur (that is, perfect information). EVPI is equal to the expected opportunity loss of the best decision alternative when no additional information is available.

4.9 PROBLEMS

1. Suppose that a decision maker faced with four decision alternatives and four states of nature develops the following profit payoff table.

	States of Nature			
Decisions	s_1	s_2	s_3	s_4
d_1	14	9	10	5
d_2	11	10	8	7
d_3	9	10	10	11
d_4	8	10	11	13

If the decision maker knows nothing about the chances or probability of occurrence of the four states of nature (that is, decision making under uncertainty), what is the recommended decision under each of the following criteria.
a. Maximin
b. Maximax
c. Minimax regret
Which decision criterion do you prefer? Explain. Is it important for the decision maker to establish the most appropriate decision criterion before analyzing the problem? Explain.

2. Assume the payoff table in Problem 1 provides *cost* rather than profit payoffs. What is the recommended decision under each of the following criteria?
a. Minimax
b. Minimin
c. Minimax regret

3. Suppose that the decision maker in Problem 1 obtains some information that enables the following probability estimates.
$P(s_1) = 0.5$
$P(s_2) = 0.2$
$P(s_3) = 0.2$
$P(s_4) = 0.1$
a. Use the expected monetary value criterion to determine the optimal decision.
b. Now assume that the entries in the payoff table are costs and use the expected monetary value criterion to determine the minimum cost solution.

c. Show that the expected opportunity loss criterion leads to the same decisions recommended by the expected monetary value criterion in parts (a) and (b).

4. Hale's TV Productions is considering producing a pilot for a comedy series for a major TV network. While the network may reject the pilot and the series, it may also purchase the program for one or two years. While Hale may decide to produce the pilot Hale has an offer of $100,000 to transfer the rights for the series to a competitor. Hale's profits are summarized in the following payoff table.

		Reject	1 Year	2 Years	
			States of Nature		
Produce pilot	d_1	−100	50	150	Profit in
Sell to competitor	d_2	100	100	100	$\$\times 10^3$

If the probability estimates for the states of nature are P (Reject) = 0.2, P(1 Year) = 0.3, P(2 Year) = 0.5, what should the company do? What is the maximum Hale should be willing to pay for inside information on what the network will do?

5. McHuffter Condominiums, Inc., of Pensacola, Florida, has recently purchased land near the Gulf and is attempting to determine the size of the condominium development it should build. Three sizes of developments are being considered: small (d_1), medium (d_2), and large (d_3). At the same time an uncertain economy makes it difficult to ascertain the demand for the new condominiums. McHuffter's management realizes that a large development followed by a low demand could be very costly to the company. However, if McHuffter makes a conservative small development decision and then finds a high demand, the firm's profits will be lower than they might have been. With the three levels of demand—low, medium, and high—McHuffter's management has prepared the following payoff table.

		Low	Medium	High
			Demand	
	Small	400	400	400
Decision	Medium	100	600	600
	Large	−300	300	900

Profit in $\$\times 10^3$

a. If nothing is known about the demand probabilities, show the decision recommendations under the maximin, maximax, and minimax regret criteria.

b. If P (Low) $= 0.20$, P (Medium) $= 0.35$, and P (High) $= 0.45$, what is the decision recommended under the expected monetary value criterion?

c. What is the expected value of perfect information?

6. Construct a decision tree for the McHuffter Condominiums problem (Problem 5). What is the expected value at each state of nature node? What is the optimal decision?

7. Martin's Service Station is considering investing in a heavy-duty snow plow this fall. Martin has analyzed the situation carefully and feels this would be a very profitable investment if the snowfall is heavy. A small profit could still be made if the snowfall is moderate, but Martin would lose money if snowfall is light. Specifically, Martin forecasts a profit of $7000 if snowfall is heavy, $2000 if it is moderate, and a $9000 loss if it is light. Based on the weather bureau's long-range forecast, Martin estimates P (heavy snowfall) $= .4$, P (moderate snowfall) $= .3$, and P (light snowfall) $= .3$.

a. Prepare a decision tree for Martin's problem.

b. Using the expected monetary value criterion, would you recommend that Martin invest in the snowplow?

8. Refer again to the investment problem faced by Martin's Service Station (Problem 7). Martin can purchase a blade to attach to his service truck that can also be used to plow driveways and parking lots. Since this truck must also be available to service cars, Martin will not be able to generate as much revenue plowing snow if he elects this alternative. But he will keep his loss smaller if there is light snowfall. Under this alternative Martin forecasts a profit of $3500 if snowfall is heavy, $1000 if it is moderate and a $1500 loss if snowfall is light.

a. Prepare a new decision tree showing all three alternatives.

b. Using the expected monetary value criterion, what is the optimal decision?

c. Develop a table showing the opportunity loss for each decision/state-of-nature combination. Which decision minimizes expected opportunity loss?

d. What is the expected value of perfect information.

9. The Gorman Manufacturing Company must decide whether it should purchase a component part from a supplier or manufacture the component at its Milan, Michigan, plant. If demand is high, it would be to Gorman's advantage to manufacture the component. However, if demand is low, Gorman's unit manufacturing cost will be high as a result of underutilization of equipment. The projected profit in thousands of dollars for Gorman's manufacture or buy decision is shown below.

	Demand		
	Low	Medium	High
Manufacture Component	−20	40	100
Purchase Component	10	45	70

The states of nature have the following probabilities: P(Low demand) = .35, P(Medium demand) = .35, and P(High demand) = .30.
  a. Use a decision tree to recommend a decision.
  b. Use EVPI to determine whether Gorman should attempt to obtain a better estimate of demand.

10. In order to save on gasoline expenses, Ron and Jerry agreed to form a car pool for traveling to and from work. After limiting the travel routes to two alternatives, Ron and Jerry could not agree on the best way to travel to work. Jerry preferred the expressway since it was usually the fastest; however, Ron pointed out that traffic jams on the expressway sometimes led to long delays. Ron preferred the somewhat longer, but more consistent, Queen City Avenue. While Jerry still preferred the expressway, he agreed with Ron that they should take Queen City Avenue if the expressway had a traffic jam. Unfortunately, they did not know the state of the expressway ahead of time. The following payoff table provides the one-way time estimates for traveling to or from work.

	States of Nature	
	Expressway Open s_1	Expressway Jammed s_2
Expressway d_1'	25	45
Queen City Avenue d_2	30	30

Travel time in minutes

After driving to work on the expressway for 1 month (20 days), they found the expressway jammed three times. Assuming these days were representative of future days, should they continue to use the expressway for traveling to work? Explain. Would it make sense not to adopt the expected value criterion for this particular problem? Explain.

11. In Problem 10, suppose that Ron and Jerry wished to determine the best way to return home in the evenings. In 20 days of traveling home on the expressway, they found the expressway jammed six times.

Using the travel time table shown in Problem 10, what route would you recommend they take on their way home in the evening? If they had perfect information about the traffic condition of the expressway, what would be their savings in terms of expected travel time?

12. A firm produces a perishable food product at a cost of $10 per case. The product sells for $15 per case. For planning purposes the company is considering possible demands of 100, 200, or 300 cases. If the demand is less than production, the excess production is lost. If demand is more than production, the firm, in an attempt to maintain a good service image, will satisfy the excess demand with a special production run at a cost of $18 per case. The product, however, always sells at the $15 per case price.

    a. Set up the payoff table for this problem.
    b. If $P(100) = 0.2, P(200) = 0.2$, and $P(300) = 0.6$, use the expected opportunity loss criterion to determine the solution.
    c. What is the EVPI?

13. The Kremer Chemical Company has a contract with one of its customers to supply a unique liquid chemical product that will be used by the customer in the manufacturing of a lubricant for airplane engines. Because of the chemical process used by the Kremer Company, batch sizes for the liquid chemical product must be 1000 pounds. The customer has agreed to adjust his manufacturing to the full batch quantities and will order either one, two, or three batches every 6 months. Since an aging process of 2 months exists for the product, Kremer will have to make its production (how-much-to-order) decision before its customer places an order. Thus Kremer can list the product demand alternatives of 1000, 2000, or 3000 pounds, but the exact demand is unknown.

    Kremer's manufacturing costs are $15 per pound, and the product sells at the fixed contract price of $20 per pound. If the customer orders more than Kremer has produced, Kremer has agreed to absorb the added cost of filling the order by purchasing a higher quality substitute product from another chemical firm. The substitute product, including transportation expenses, will cost Kremer $24 per pound. Since the product cannot be stored more than 4 months without spoilage, Kremer cannot inventory excess production until the customer's next 6-month order. Therefore if the customer's current order is less than Kremer has produced, the excess production will be reprocessed and is valued at $5 per pound.

    The inventory decision in this problem is how much should Kremer produce given the above costs and the possible demands of 1000, 2000, or 3000 pounds? Based on historical data and an analysis of the customer's future demands Kremer has assessed the following probability distribution for demand.

Demand	Probability
1000	0.3
2000	0.5
3000	0.2
	1.0

a. Develop a payoff table for the Kremer problem.

b. How many batches should Kremer produce every 6 months?

c. How much of a discount should Kremer be willing to allow the customer for specifying in advance exactly how many batches will be purchased?

14. A quality control procedure involves 100% inspection of parts received from a supplier. Historical records show the following defective rates have been observed.

Defective %	Probability
0%	.15
1%	.25
2%	.40
3%	.20

The cost for the quality control 100% inspection is $250 for each shipment of 500 parts. If the shipment is not 100% inspected, defective parts will cause rework problems later in the production process. The rework cost is $25 for each defective part.

a. Complete the following payoff table where the entries represent the total cost of inspection and reworking.

	Percent Defective			
	0%	1%	2%	3%
100% inspection	$250	$250	$250	$250
No inspection				

b. The plant manager is considering eliminating the inspection process in order to save the $250 inspection cost per shipment. Do you support this action? Use EMV to justify your answer.

c. Show the decision tree for this problem.

15. Milford Trucking located in Chicago has requests to haul two shipments, one to St. Louis and one to Detroit. Because of a scheduling

102

problem, Milford will only be able to select one of these assignments. The St. Louis customer has guaranteed a return shipment, but the Detroit customer has not. Thus if Milford accepts the Detroit shipment and cannot find a Detroit-to-Chicago return shipment, the truck will return to Chicago empty. The payoff table showing profit is as follows.

	Return Shipment from Detroit s_1	No Return Shipment from Detroit s_2
St. Louis d_1	2000	2000
Detroit d_2	2500	1000

a. If the probability of a Detroit return shipment is 0.4, what should Milford do?

b. What is the expected value of information that would tell Milford whether or not Detroit had a return shipment?

5
Decision Theory: Revision of Probabilities

In situations involving decision making under uncertainty, we have seen how probability information about the states of nature affects the expected value calculations and thus possibly the decision recommendation. Decision makers frequently have preliminary or prior probability estimates for the states of nature which are initially the best probability values available. However, in order to make the best possible decision, the decision maker may want to seek additional information about the states of nature. This new information can be used to revise or update the prior probabilities so that the final decision is based upon more accurate probability estimates for the states of nature. We shall see that Bayes' theorem (see Chapter 2) plays a central role in determining how new information can be combined with the prior probabilities to compute revised probabilities for the states of nature.

The seeking of additional information is most often accomplished through experiments designed to provide the most current data available about the states of nature. Raw material sampling, product testing, and test market research are examples of experiments that may enable a revision or updating of the state-of-nature probabilities.

In this chapter we reconsider the PSI computer leasing problem of Chapter 4 and show how new information can be used to revise the state-of-nature probabilities. We then show how these revised probabilities can be used to develop an optimal decision strategy for PSI.

5.1 CALCULATING REVISED PROBABILITIES

Let us reconsider the PSI problem introduced in Chapter 4. The PSI payoff and opportunity loss tables are reproduced in Tables 5.1 and 5.2, respectively.

Recall that management had assigned a probability of 0.3 to the state of nature s_1 and a probability of 0.7 to the state of nature s_2. At this point, we will refer to these initial probability estimates, $P(s_1)$ and $P(s_2)$, as the *prior* probabilities for the states of nature. Using these prior probabilities, we found that the decision to lease the small system d_3 was optimal, yielding an

TABLE 5.1 Payoff Table for the PSI Computer Leasing Problem

| | | | State of Nature | |
			High Acceptance s_1	Low Acceptance s_2
Decision Alternatives	Lease a large system	d_1	$200,000	$-20,000
	Lease a medium sized system	d_2	$150,000	$20,000
	Lease a small system	d_3	$100,000	$60,000

Profit or payoff

expected monetary value of $72,000. Applying the criterion of minimizing expected opportunity loss we obtained the same decision recommendation and also learned that the expected opportunity loss (EOL) of the optimal decision d_3 was $30,000. In addition, we showed that since the expected value of perfect information was equal to the EOL of the optimal decision, the expected value of new information about the states of nature could potentially be worth as much as $30,000.

Suppose that PSI decides to consider hiring a market research firm to study the potential acceptance of the PSI service. The market research study will provide new information which can be combined with the prior probabilities through a Bayesian procedure to obtain updated or revised probability estimates for the states of nature. These revised probabilities are called *posterior* probabilities (see Chapter 2). The complete process of revising probabilities is depicted in Figure 5.1.

TABLE 5.2 Opportunity Loss Table for the PSI Computer Leasing Problem

| | | | State of Nature | |
			High Acceptance s_1	Low Acceptance s_2
Decision Alternatives	Large system	d_1	0	$80,000
	Medium system	d_2	$50,000	$40,000
	Small system	d_3	$100,000	0

Regret or opportunity loss

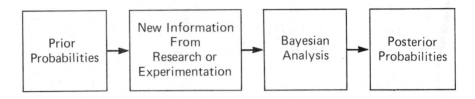

FIGURE 5.1 Probability Revision Based on New Information

We usually refer to the new information obtained through research or experimentation as an *indicator*. Since in many cases the experiment conducted to obtain the additional information will consist of taking a statistical sample, the new information is also often referred to as *sample information*.

Using the indicator terminology, we can denote the outcomes of the PSI marketing research study as follows.

I_1 = favorable market research report; that is, in the market research study, the individuals contacted generally express considerable interest in PSI's services.

I_2 = unfavorable market research report; that is, in the market research study the individuals contacted generally express little interest in PSI's services.

Given one of these possible indicators, our objective is to provide improved estimates of the probabilities of the various states of nature based upon the findings of the market research study. The end result of the Bayesian revision process depicted in Figure 5.1 is a set of posterior probabilities of the form $P(s_j \mid I_k)$, where $P(s_j \mid I_k)$ represents the conditional probability that state of nature s_j will occur given that the outcome of the market research study was indicator I_k.

To make effective use of this indicator information we must know something about the probability relationships between the indicators and the states of nature. For example, in the PSI problem, given that the state of nature ultimately turns out to be high customer acceptance, what is the probability that the market research study will result in a favorable report? In this case we are asking about the conditional probability of indicator I_1, given state of nature s_1, written $P(I_1 \mid s_1)$. In order to carry out the analysis, we will need conditional probability relationships for all indicators given all states of nature; that is, $P(I_1 \mid s_1), P(I_1 \mid s_2), P(I_2 \mid s_1),$ and $P(I_2 \mid s_2)$. Historical relative frequency data and/or subjective probability estimates are usually the primary source for these conditional probability values.

In the PSI case the past record of the marketing research company on similar studies has led to the following estimates of the relevant conditional probabilities.

States of Nature	Market Research Report	
	Favorable I_1	Unfavorable I_2
High acceptance s_1	$P(I_1 \mid s_1) = 0.8$	$P(I_2 \mid s_1) = 0.2$
Low acceptance s_2	$P(I_1 \mid s_2) = 0.1$	$P(I_2 \mid s_2) = 0.9$

Note that these probability estimates indicate that a great degree of confidence can be placed in the market research report. When the true state of nature is s_1, the market research report will be favorable 80% of the time and unfavorable only 20% of the time. When the true state is s_2, the report will make the correct indication 90% of the time. Now let us see how this additional information can be incorporated into the decision-making process.

We are now ready to compute the revised, or posterior probabilities for the states of nature. Let us assume that a favorable market research report (I_1) has been received and see how the posterior probabilities $P(s_1 \mid I_1)$ and $P(s_2 \mid I_1)$ can be computed. The tabular format for applying Bayes' theorem (see Chapter 2) is shown in Table 5.3.

TABLE 5.3 Probability Revision Given A Favorable
          Market Research Report (I_1)

State of Nature	Prior Probabilities $P(s_j)$	Conditional Probabilities $P(I_1 \mid s_j)$	Joint Probabilities $P(I_1 \cap s_j)$	Posterior Probabilities $P(s_j \mid I_1)$	
s_1	0.3	0.8	0.24	$.24/.31 =$	$.7742$
s_2	0.7	0.1	0.07	$.07/.31 =$	$.2258$
	1.0		$P(I_1) = 0.31$		1.0000

In the calculations depicted in Table 5.3 we see that by multiplying the prior probabilities, $P(s_j)$, by the conditional probability, $P(I_1 \mid s_j)$, we obtain the joint probabilities, $P(I_1 \cap s_j)$. That is

$$P(I_1 \cap s_j) = P(s_j) P(I_1 \mid s_j).$$

This result follows from the multiplication law of probability developed in Chapter 2. In addition, we see that by summing the joint probabilities, we obtain $P(I_1) = 0.31$; note that this is the probability of getting a favorable market research report. Then the posterior probabilities are computed from the conditional probability relationship

$$P(s_j \mid I_1) = \frac{P(I_1 \cap s_j)}{P(I_1)}.$$

107

Thus,

$$P(s_1 \mid I_1) = \frac{0.24}{0.31} = .7742$$

and

$$P(s_2 \mid I_1) = \frac{0.07}{0.31} = .2258.$$

Recall that this is the general procedure we introduced in Chapter 2 for computing revised probabilities.

The posterior probabilities $P(s_1 \mid I_1)$ and $P(s_2 \mid I_1)$ now provide the probability estimates for each state of nature if the market research study is favorable. For example, $P(s_1 \mid I_1) = 0.7742$ indicates that there is a 0.7742 probability that the market acceptance will be high (s_1), provided the market research report is favorable. However, we realize that the final market acceptance of the PSI service may still be low, even though the market research report is favorable. This probability is given by $P(s_2 \mid I_1) = 1 - P(s_1 \mid I_1) = 0.2258$. Note, however, that the state-of-nature probabilities given I_1 (that is, the posterior probabilities) have been substantially revised from the prior values of $P(s_1) = 0.3$ and $P(s_2) = 0.7$.

The revised probabilities corresponding to an unfavorable market research indicator (I_2) are shown in Table 5.4.

TABLE 5.4 *Probability Revision Given an Unfavorable Market Research Report (I_2)*

State of Nature	Prior Probabilities $P(s_j)$	Conditional Probabilities $P(I_2 \mid s_j)$	Joint Probabilities $P(I_2 \cap s_j)$	Posterior Probabilities $P(s_j \mid I_2)$
s_1	0.3	0.2	0.06	.0870
s_2	0.7	0.9	0.63	.9130
	1.0		$P(I_2) = 0.69$	1.0000

The calculations in Tables 5.3 and 5.4 provided the probabilities of the indicators, $P(I_1)$ and $P(I_2)$, as well as all the desired posterior or revised probabilities. Given this new probability information, we are now ready to see how an optimal decision strategy can be developed for PSI, provided the market research study is conducted.

5.2 DEVELOPING A DECISION STRATEGY

A decision strategy or a decision rule is a policy that is to be followed by the decision maker. In the PSI case, a decision strategy would consist of a rule to follow based on the outcome of the market research study. The rule or

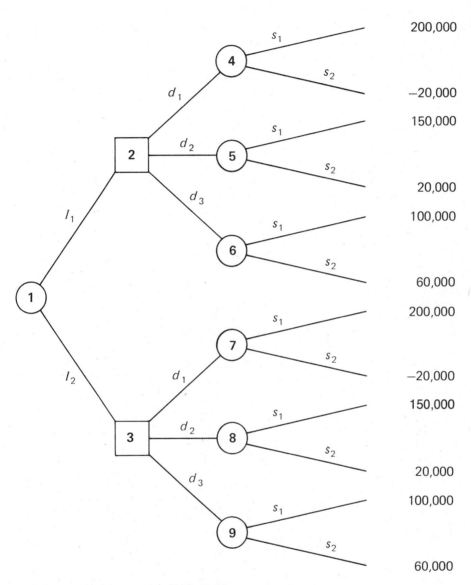

FIGURE 5.2 *Decision Tree for the PSI Problem*

decision strategy would recommend a particular decision based upon whether the market research report was favorable or unfavorable. We will employ a decision tree analysis to find the optimal decision strategy for PSI.

Figure 5.2 shows the decision tree for the PSI computer leasing problem, provided a market research study is conducted. Note that as you move from left to right, the tree shows the natural or logical order that will occur in the decision-making process. First, the firm will obtain the market research

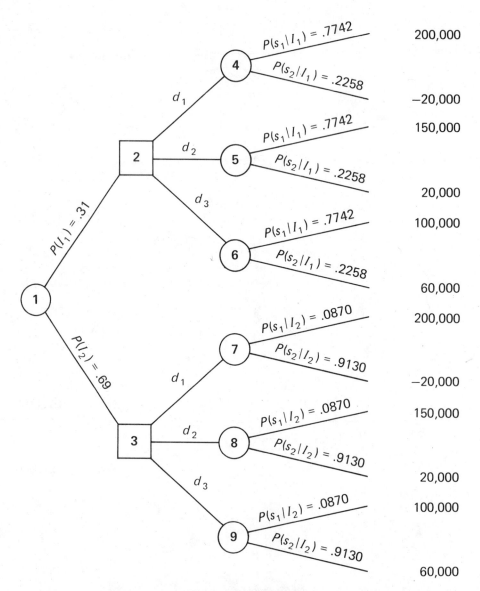

FIGURE 5.3   PSI Decision Tree with Indicator and State-of-Nature Branch Probabilities

report indicator (I_1 or I_2); then a decision (d_1, d_2, or d_3) will be made; and finally the state of nature (s_1 or s_2) will occur. The decision and the state of nature combine to provide the final profit or payoff.

Note that, using decision tree terminology, we have now introduced an *indicator node*, node 1, and *indicator branches* I_1 and I_2. Since the branches emanating from indicator nodes are not under the control of the decision maker but are determined by chance, these nodes are depicted by a circle just like the state-of-nature nodes. We see that nodes 2 and 3 are decision nodes, while nodes 4, 5, 6, 7, 8, and 9 are state-of-nature nodes. For decision nodes the decision maker must select the specific branch, d_1, d_2, or d_3, that will be taken. Selecting the best decision branch is equivalent to making the best decision. However, since the indicator and state-of-nature branches are not controlled by the decision maker, the specific branch leaving an indicator or a state-of-nature node will depend upon the probability associated with the branch. Looking back to our revised probability calculations in the previous section (Tables 5.3 and 5.4), we see that the probabilities associated with the indicator and state-of-nature branches have been identified. The decision tree for the PSI problem, including indicator and state-of-nature probabilities is shown in Figure 5.3.

We can now use the branch probabilities and the expected monetary value criterion to arrive at the optimal decision for PSI. Working backward through the decision tree, we first compute the expected monetary value at each state-of-nature node. That is, at each state-of-nature node the possible payoffs are weighted by their chance of occurrence. Thus the expected monetary values for nodes 4 through 9 are computed as follows:

$$\text{EMV(node 4)} = (.7742)(200,000) + (.2258)(-20,000) = 150,324$$
$$\text{EMV(node 5)} = (.7742)(150,000) + (.2258)(\ 20,000) = 120,646$$
$$\text{EMV(node 6)} = (.7742)(100,000) + (.2258)(\ 60,000) = \ 90,968$$
$$\text{EMV(node 7)} = (.0870)(200,000) + (.9130)(-20,000) = \ -860$$
$$\text{EMV(node 8)} = (.0870)(150,000) + (.9130)(\ 20,000) = \ 31,310$$
$$\text{EMV(node 9)} = (.0870)(100,000) + (.9130)(\ 60,000) = \ 63,480.$$

We now continue backward through the decision tree to the decision nodes. Because the expected values for nodes 4, 5, and 6 are known, the decision maker can view decision node 2 as follows.

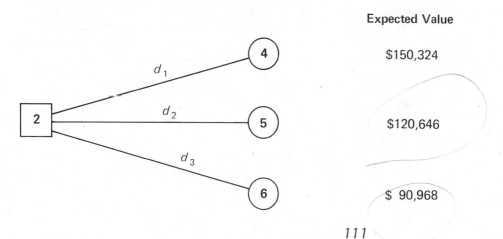

Expected Value

$150,324

$120,646

$ 90,968

Since the decision maker controls the branch leaving a decision node and since we are trying to maximize expected profits, the optimal decision at node 2 is d_1. Thus, since d_1 leads to an expected value of $150,324, we say EMV(node 2) = $150,324 if the optimal decision of d_1 is made.

A similar analysis of decision node 3 shows that the optimal decision branch at this node is d_3. Thus, EMV(node 3) becomes $63,480, provided the optimal decision of d_3 is made.

As a final step, we can continue working backward to the indicator node and establish its expected value. The branches at node 1 are as follows:

	Decision	Expected Value

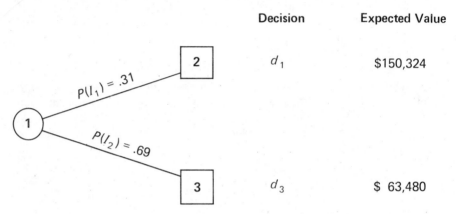

	Decision	Expected Value
2	d_1	$150,324
3	d_3	$ 63,480

Since node 1 has probability branches, we cannot select the best branch. Rather, we must compute the expected value over all possible branches. Thus we have

$$\text{EMV(node 1)} = (0.31)(\$150,324) + (0.69)(\$63,480) = \$90,402.$$

The value of $90,402 is viewed as the expected value of the optimal decision strategy when the market research study is used.

Note that the final decision has not yet been determined. We will need to know the results of the market research study before deciding to lease a large system (d_1) or a small system (d_3). The results of the decision theory analysis at this point, however, have provided us with the following optimal *decision strategy* if the market research study is conducted.

Thus we have seen how the decision tree approach can be used to develop optimal decision strategies for decisions under uncertainty when exper-

Decision Strategy	
If	Then
Report favorable (I_1)	Lease large system (d_1)
Report unfavorable (I_2)	Lease small system (d_3)

iments are used to provide additional information. While other decision strategy problems may not be as simple as the PSI problem, the approach we have outlined is still applicable. First, draw a decision tree consisting of indicator, decision, and state-of-nature nodes and branches such that the tree describes the specific decision-making process. Posterior probability calculations must be made in order to establish indicator and state-of-nature branch probabilities. Then, by working backward through the tree, computing expected values at state-of-nature and indicator nodes and selecting the best decision branch at decision nodes, the analyst can determine an optimal decision strategy and the associated expected value for the problem.

5.3 EXPECTED VALUE OF SAMPLE INFORMATION

In the PSI problem, management now has a decision strategy of leasing the large computer system if the market research report is favorable and leasing the small computer system if the market research report is unfavorable. Since the additional information provided by the market research firm will result in an added cost for PSI in terms of the fee paid to the research firm, PSI management may question the value of this market research information.

The value of information is often measured by calculating what is referred to as the *expected value of sample information* (EVSI). For maximization problems[1]

$$\text{EVSI} = \begin{bmatrix} \text{expected value of the} \\ \text{optimal decision } with \\ \text{sample information} \end{bmatrix} - \begin{bmatrix} \text{expected value of the} \\ \text{optimal decision } without \\ \text{sample information} \end{bmatrix} \quad (5.1)$$

For PSI the market research information is considered the "sample" information. The decision tree calculations indicated that the expected value of the optimal decision with the market research information was $90,402 while the expected value of the optimal decision without the market research information was $72,000. Using equation (5.1), the expected value of the market research report is

$$\text{EVSI} = \$90,402 - \$72,000 = \$18,402.$$

[1] In minimization problems, the expected value with sample information will be less than or equal to the expected value without sample information. Thus in minimization problems

$$\text{EVSI} = \begin{bmatrix} \text{expected value of the} \\ \text{optimal decision without} \\ \text{sample information} \end{bmatrix} - \begin{bmatrix} \text{expected value of the} \\ \text{optimal decision with} \\ \text{sample information} \end{bmatrix}$$

Thus PSI should be willing to pay up to $18,402 for the market research information.

Efficiency of Sample Information

In Section 4.6 we saw the expected value of perfect information (EVPI) for the PSI problem was $30,000. Although we never expected the market research report to obtain perfect information, we can use an *efficiency* measure to express the value of the report. With perfect information having an efficiency rating of 100%, the efficiency rating (E) for sample information is computed as follows:

$$E = \frac{\text{EVSI}}{\text{EVPI}} \times 100.$$

For our PSI example,

$$E = \frac{18,402}{30,000} \times 100 = 61\%.$$

In other words, the information from the market research firm is 61% as "efficient" as perfect information.

Low efficiency ratings for information might lead the decision maker to look for other types of information. On the other hand, high efficiency ratings indicate that the information is almost as good as perfect information and additional sources of information are probably not worthwhile.

5.4 SUMMARY

In this chapter we have shown how new information can be used to revise the probabilities for the states-of-nature and thus increase the expected payoff of the decision recommendation. In the case where a decision maker elects to seek additional information, it is appropriate to develop a decision strategy which will provide a recommended decision based on the outcome of the information collection. The expected value of perfect information is an upper limit on the value of additional information to the decision maker. However, since additional information is generally not perfect information, the expected value of sample information is used to measure the value of the new information. The efficiency of the new information is given by the ratio of EVSI to EVPI.

5.5 GLOSSARY

1. *Indicator*—Information about the states of nature obtained by experimentation. An indicator may be the result of a sample.

2. *Prior probabilities*—The probabilities of the states of nature prior to obtaining experimental information.
3. *Posterior (revised) probabilities*—The probabilities of the states of nature after adjusting the prior probabilities based upon given indicator information.
4. *Bayesian revision*—The process of adjusting the prior probabilities to create the posterior probabilities based upon information obtained by experimentation.
5. *Expected value of sample information (EVSI)*—The difference between the expected value of an optimal strategy based on new information and the "best" expected value without any new information. It is a measure of the economic value of new information.
6. *Efficiency*—The ratio of EVSI to EVPI; perfect information is 100% efficient.

5.6 PROBLEMS

1. Suppose you are given a decision situation with three possible states of nature: s_1, s_2, and s_3. The prior probabilities are $P(s_1) = 0.2$, $P(s_2) = 0.5$, and $P(s_3) = 0.3$. Indicator information I is obtained, and it is known that $P(I \mid s_1) = 0.1$, $P(I \mid s_2) = 0.05$, and $P(I \mid s_3) = 0.2$. Compute the revised or posterior probabilities: $P(s_1 \mid I), P(s_2 \mid I)$, and $P(s_3 \mid I)$.

2. The payoff table for a decision problem with two states of nature and three decision alternatives is presented below.

	s_1	s_2
d_1	15	10
d_2	10	12
d_3	8	20

The prior probabilities for s_1 and s_2 are $P(s_1) = 0.8$ and $P(s_2) = 0.2$.
   a. Using only the prior probabilities and the expected monetary value criterion, find the optimal decision.
   b. Find the EVPI.
   c. Suppose some indicator information, I, is obtained with $P(I \mid s_1) = 0.2$ and $P(I \mid s_2) = 0.75$. Find the posterior probabilities $P(s_1 \mid I)$ and $P(s_2 \mid I)$. Recommend a decision alternative based on these probabilities.

3. Consider the following decision tree representation of a decision theory problem with two indicators, two decision alternatives, and two states of nature.

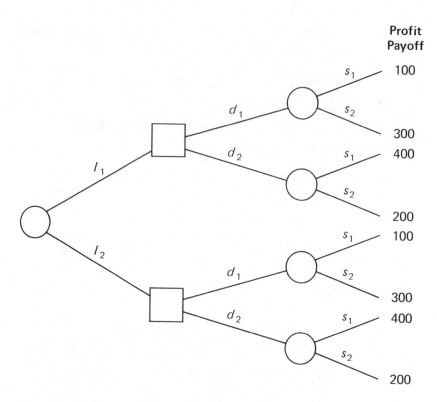

Profit
Payoff

s_1 100

d_1

s_2 300

d_2 s_1 400

s_2

200

s_1 100

d_1 s_2

300

d_2 s_1 400

s_2

200

Assume the following probability information is given.

$P(s_1) = 0.4$ $P(I_1 \mid s_1) = 0.8$ $P(I_2 \mid s_1) = 0.2$
$P(s_2) = 0.6$ $P(I_1 \mid s_2) = 0.4$ $P(I_2 \mid s_2) = 0.6$

a. What are the values for $P(I_1)$ and $P(I_2)$?
b. What are the values of $P(s_1 \mid I_1)$, $P(s_2 \mid I_1)$, $P(s_1 \mid I_2)$, and $P(s_2 \mid I_2)$?
c. Use the decision tree approach and determine the optimal decision strategy. What is the expected value of your solution?

4. The payoff table for Problem 3 is as follows.

	s_1	s_2
d_1	100	300
d_2	400	200

a. What is your decision without the indicator information?
b. What is the expected value of the indicator or sample information EVSI?
c. What is the expected value of perfect information EVPI?
d. What is the efficiency of the indicator information?

5. The payoff table for Hale's TV Productions (Problem 4.4) is as follows.

		States of Nature		
		s_1	s_2	s_3
Produce pilot	d_1	−100	50	150
Sell to competitor	d_2	100	100	100
Probability of states of nature		0.2	0.3	0.5

Thousands of dollars

For a consulting fee of $2500 an agency will review the plans for the comedy series and indicate the overall chances of a favorable network reaction to the series. If the special agency review results in a favorable (I_1) or an unfavorable (I_2) evaluation, what should Hale's decision strategy be? Assume Hale believes the following conditional probabilities are realistic appraisals of the agency's evaluation accuracy.

$$P(I_1 \mid s_1) = 0.3 \quad P(I_2 \mid s_1) = 0.7$$
$$P(I_1 \mid s_2) = 0.6 \quad P(I_2 \mid s_2) = 0.4$$
$$P(I_1 \mid s_3) = 0.9 \quad P(I_2 \mid s_3) = 0.1$$

a. Show the decision tree for this problem.
b. What is the recommended decision strategy and the expected value, assuming the agency information is obtained?
c. What is the EVSI? Is the $2500 consulting fee worth the information? What is the maximum Hale should be willing to pay for the consulting information?

6. McHuffter Condominiums (Problem 4.5) is conducting a survey which will help evaluate the demand for the new condominium development. McHuffter's payoff table (profit) is as follows.

		States of Nature		
		Low	Medium	High
		s_1	s_2	s_3
Small	d_1	400	400	400
Decision Medium	d_2	100	600	600
Large	d_3	−300	300	900
Probability of states of nature		0.20	0.35	0.45

The survey will result in three indicators of demand [weak (I_1), average (I_2), or strong (I_3)], where the conditional probabilities are as follows.

	$P(I_k \mid s_k)$		
	I_1	I_2	I_3
s_1	0.6	0.3	0.1
s_2	0.4	0.4	0.2
s_3	0.1	0.4	0.5

a. What is McHuffter's optimal strategy?
b. What is the value of the survey information?
c. What are the EVPI and the efficiency of the survey information?

7. The payoff table for Martin's Service Station (Problems 4.7 and 4.8) is as follows:

		Snowfall		
		s_1 Heavy	s_2 Moderate	s_3 Light
Purchase snowplow	d_1	7000	2000	−9000
Do not invest	d_2	0	0	0
Purchase blade	d_3	3500	1000	−1500
Probabilities of states of nature		.4	.3	.3

Suppose Martin decides to wait to check the September temperature pattern before making a final decision. Estimates of the probabilities associated with an unseasonably cold September (I) are as follows: $P(I \mid s_1) = .30$, $P(I \mid s_2) = .20$, and $P(I \mid s_3) = .05$. If Martin observes an unseasonably cold September, what is the recommended decision? If Martin does not observe an unseasonably cold September, what is the recommended decision?

8. A food processor considers daily production runs of 100, 200, or 300 units. Possible demands for the product are 100, 200 or 300 cases. The payoff table is as follows:

			Demand		
			s_1 100	s_2 200	s_3 300
Production	d_1	100	500	200	−100
	d_2	200	−400	800	700
	d_3	300	−1000	−200	1600

a. If $P(s_1) = .20$, $P(s_2) = .20$, and $P(s_3) = .60$, what is your recommended production quantity?

b. On some days, the firm receives phone calls for advance orders and on some days, it does not. Let I_1 = advance orders are received and I_2 = no advance orders are received. If $P(I_2 \mid s_1) = .80$, $P(I_2 \mid s_2) = .40$, and $P(I_2 \mid s_3) = .10$, what is your recommended production quantity for days the company does not receive any advance orders?

9. The Gorman Manufacturing Company (Problem 4.9) has the following payoff table for a make-or-buy decision:

		Demand		
		s_1 Low	s_2 Medium	s_3 High
Manufacture component	d_1	-20	40	100
Purchase component	d_2	10	45	70
Probabilities		.35	.35	.30

A test market study of the potential demand for the product is expected to report either a favorable (I_1) or unfavorable (I_2) condition. The relevant conditional probabilities are as follows.

$$P(I_1 \mid s_1) = .10 \qquad P(I_2 \mid s_1) = .90$$
$$P(I_1 \mid s_2) = .40 \qquad P(I_2 \mid s_2) = .60$$
$$P(I_1 \mid s_3) = .60 \qquad P(I_2 \mid s_3) = .40$$

a. What is the probability the market research report will be favorable?

b. What is Gorman's optimal decision strategy?

c. What is the expected value of the market research information?

d. What is the efficiency of the information?

10. The traveling time to work for Ron and Jerry (Problem 4.10) has the following time payoff table:

		States of Nature Expressway	
		Open s_1	Jammed s_2
Expressway	d_1	25	45
Queen City Avenue	d_2	30	30
Probability of states of nature		0.85	0.15

After a period of time Ron and Jerry noted that the weather seemed to affect the traffic conditions on the expressway. They identified three weather conditions (indicators) with the following conditional probabilities.

I_1 = clear
I_2 = overcast
I_3 = rain

$P(I_1 \mid s_1) = 0.8 \qquad P(I_2 \mid s_1) = 0.2 \qquad P(I_3 \mid s_1) = 0.0$
$P(I_1 \mid s_2) = 0.1 \qquad P(I_2 \mid s_2) = 0.3 \qquad P(I_3 \mid s_2) = 0.6$

a. Show the decision tree for the problem of traveling to work.
b. What is the optimal decision strategy and the expected travel time?
c. What is the efficiency of the weather information?

11. The research and development (R&D) manager for Beck Company is trying to decide whether or not to fund a project to develop a new lubricant. It is assumed the project will be a major technical success, a minor technical success, or a failure. The company has estimated that the value of a major technical success is $150,000, since the lubricant can be used in a number of products the company is making. If the project is a minor technical success, its value is $10,000, since Beck feels the knowledge gained will benefit some other ongoing projects. If the project is a failure, it will cost the company $100,000.

Based on the opinion of the scientists involved and the manager's own subjective assessment, the assigned prior probabilities are as follows:

P(major success) = 0.15
P(minor success) = 0.45
P(failure) = 0.40

a. Using the expected monetary value criterion, should the project be funded?
b. Suppose that a group of expert scientists from a research institute could be hired as consultants to study the project and make a recommendation. If this study were to cost $30,000, should the Beck Company consider hiring the consultants?

12. Consider again the problem faced by the R&D manager of Beck Company (Problem 11). Suppose an experiment can be conducted to explore the technical feasibility of the project. There are three possible outcomes for the experiment.

I_1 = prototype lubricant works well at all temperatures,
I_2 = prototype lubricant works well only at temperatures above $10°$,
I_3 = prototype lubricant does not work well at any temperature.

Suppose that we can determine the following conditional probabilities.

$$P(I_1 \mid \text{major success}) = .70$$
$$P(I_1 \mid \text{minor success}) = .10$$
$$P(I_1 \mid \text{failure}) = .10$$

$$P(I_2 \mid \text{major success}) = .25$$
$$P(I_2 \mid \text{minor success}) = .70$$
$$P(I_2 \mid \text{failure}) = .30$$

$$P(I_3 \mid \text{major success}) = .05$$
$$P(I_3 \mid \text{minor success}) = .20$$
$$P(I_3 \mid \text{failure}) = .60$$

a. Assuming the experiment is conducted and the prototype lubricant works well at all temperatures, should the project be funded?

b. Assuming the experiment is conducted and the prototype lubricant works well only at temperatures above 10°, should the project be funded?

c. Develop a decision strategy that Beck's R&D manager can use to recommend a funding decision based on the outcome of the experiment.

d. Find the EVSI for the experiment. How efficient is the information in the experiment?

13. The payoff table for the Kremer Chemical Company (Problem 4.13) is as follows:

			Demand		
			s_1 1000	s_2 2000	s_3 3000
Production	1000	d_1	5000	1000	−3000
Quantity	2000	d_2	−5000	10000	6000
	3000	d_3	−15000	0	15000
Probabilities			.30	.50	.20

Kremer has identified a pattern in the demand for the product based on customer's previous order quantity. Let

I_1 = customers last order was 1000 pounds,
I_2 = customers last order was 2000 pounds,
I_3 = customers last order was 3000 pounds.

The conditional probabilities are as follows:

$P(I_1 \mid s_1) = .10$	$P(I_2 \mid s_1) = .30$	$P(I_3 \mid s_1) = .60$
$P(I_1 \mid s_2) = .30$	$P(I_2 \mid s_2) = .30$	$P(I_3 \mid s_2) = .40$
$P(I_1 \mid s_3) = .80$	$P(I_2 \mid s_3) = .20$	$P(I_3 \mid s_3) = .00.$

121

a. Develop an optimal decision strategy for Kremer.

b. What is the EVSI?

c. What is the efficiency of the information for the most recent order?

14. Milford Trucking Company (Problem 4.15) has the following payoff table.

		Return Shipment From Detroit s_1	No Return Shipment From Detroit s_2
St. Louis	d_1	2000	2000
Detroit	d_2	2500	1000
Probabilities		.40	.60

a. Milford can phone a Detroit truck dispatch center and determine if the general Detroit shipping activity is busy (I_1) or slow (I_2). If the report is busy, the chances of obtaining a return shipment will increase. Suppose the following conditional probabilities are given.

$$P(I_1 \mid s_1) = 0.6 \qquad P(I_2 \mid s_1) = 0.4$$
$$P(I_1 \mid s_2) = 0.3 \qquad P(I_2 \mid s_2) = 0.7$$

Should Milford obtain the phone information?

b. If the Detroit report is busy (I_1), what is the probability Milford obtains a return shipment if it makes the trip to Detroit?

c. What is the efficiency of the phone information?

15. The quality control inspection process (Problem 4.14) has the following payoff table:

		Percent Defective			
		s_1 0%	s_2 1%	s_3 2%	s_4 3%
100% Inspection	d_1	250	250	250	250
No inspection	d_2	0	125	250	375
Probabilities		.15	.25	.40	.20

Suppose a sample of five parts is selected from the shipment and one defect is found.

a. Let I = one defect in a sample of five. Use the binomial probability distribution (Section 3.3) to compute $P(I \mid s_1), P(I \mid s_2), P(I \mid s_3)$, and $P(I \mid s_4)$, where the state of nature identifies the value for p.

b. If I occurs, what are the revised probabilities for the states of nature?

c. Should the entire shipment be 100% inspected whenever one defect is found in a sample of five?

d. What is the cost savings associated with the sample information?

6

Decision Theory with the Normal Distribution

The PSI computer leasing problem analyzed in Chapters 4 and 5 had a relatively small number of states of nature and decision alternatives. Thus, a payoff table and/or a decision tree provided an effective means of describing and analyzing the problem. In many decision situations, however, it is necessary to consider numerous or even an infinite number of states of nature and/or decision alternatives. Obviously the payoff table or decision tree approach to structuring these problems would not be possible. The purpose of this chapter is to demonstrate how the decision theory approach can be extended to solve these new types of problems.

We begin by considering a problem situation involving two decision alternatives and numerous states of nature. Here the normal probability distribution is used to describe the possible states of nature. Later in the chapter we examine a problem situation in which both the number of decision alternatives and the number of states of nature are numerous. In this general problem situation, we continue to use the normal probability distribution to describe the possible states of nature and employ a technique called incremental analysis to select an optimal solution. While it is possible to use other continuous probability distributions for the states of nature, we emphasize the normal distribution primarily because of its wide applicability in many practical decision situations. We leave the treatment of other continuous probability distributions to more advanced texts on decision theory.

6.1 A NEW PRODUCT DECISION

The D. J. Smith Manufacturing Company must make a decision concerning the market introduction of a new product. The new product development group has recently completed work on a product which the firm will consider introducing into the market next fall. A prototype, which has been tested in the laboratory and by a consumer panel, has been found to perform satisfactorily. Thus the Smith Company is now faced with choosing one of the following decision alternatives:

d_1 = Add the new product to the product line and begin full-scale production at the earliest possible date.

124

d_2 = Withhold approval of the new product and do not attempt to introduce it into the market at this time.

We see that Smith's decision problem involves two decision alternatives: introduce or do not introduce the new product. Typically, the resolution of problems such as this involves a marketing and production feasibility study which provides the decision maker with data pertaining to the cost, potential demand, and profit associated with the new product. The decision to introduce the product will involve equipment purchases, production line setup, training of sales personnel, and promotion. The only way these costs can be recovered is if there are sufficient sales of the product.

Suppose the relevant financial data for the new product are as follows.

Fixed Costs:

Equipment purchases	$ 50,000
Production setup	25,000
Sales force training and promotion	45,000
Total	$120,000

Variable Cost per Unit Produced:

Material	$ 4
Labor	3
Miscellaneous (transportation, commissions, etc.)	3
Total	$10 per unit

Selling Price: $16 per unit

The *fixed costs* are the one-time costs the company will incur if the decision is made to introduce the new product. Consequently, if Smith decides to introduce the product and then experiences a zero sales volume, the firm will still incur the $120,000 fixed cost. On the other hand, the *variable cost* per unit is the cost that is directly proportional to volume. For example, if Smith's volume is 5 units, then the variable cost will be 5 × $10 = $50; for 500 units, the variable cost will be 500 × $10 = $5,000; and so on.

Additional information needed for a decision analysis of Smith's problem is a forecast of the demand for the new product. The demand level together with the fixed and variable costs determine the profit for the new product. For example sales of 30,000 units would result in a $60,000 profit. The calculations are presented below.

Total Revenue (30,000 × $16)		$480,000
Expenses		
Fixed cost	$120,000	
Variable cost (30,000 × $10)	300,000	
Total expense		420,000
Profit		$ 60,000

Note that the amount of demand for the new product represents the state of nature in this problem. In addition, since product demand could technically be any number greater than or equal to zero, we see that the payoff table approach of listing all the possible states of nature (demands) is not feasible. However, it is possible to develop a mathematical expression for profit given each of the decision alternatives. Let

x = demand for the new product in units

TR = total revenue generated from sales of the product

TC = total cost of x units of the product

P = profit.

The total revenue expression is given by

$TR = 16x$

where \$16 is the unit selling price of the product. The total cost expression (fixed cost plus variable cost) is given by

$TC = 120,000 + 10x.$

Thus the expression for profit is obtained by subtracting total cost from total revenue.

$$P = TR - TC = 16x - (120,000 + 10x)$$
$$= 6x - 120,000. \qquad (6.1)$$

Of course, the decision not to introduce the product will result in $P = 0$ regardless of what demand might have been. Some additional economic analysis must be made before we can arrive at a recommended decision for the Smith Company problem.

6.2 BREAK-EVEN ANALYSIS

In decisions such as the one faced by Smith, the decision maker is often interested in knowing the volume or demand that will be necessary for the firm to "break even" on the decision to introduce the product. That is, the decision maker wants to know what the demand will have to be in order for revenue from the sale of the product to exactly equal the total cost associated with the product. This demand volume is referred to as the *break-even point*. A demand exceeding the break-even point results in a profit for the firm, while a demand below the break-even point results in a loss.

Let us calculate the break-even point for d_1, the decision to introduce the new product. Let x_b equal the level of sales that will allow the firm to break even. At the break-even point, x_b, we must have total revenue equal to total cost resulting in a zero profit. Hence, the break-even point wil! be the level of demand that results in a zero profit. Thus, using equation (6.1), we have

$$P = 6x_b - 120,000 = 0$$
$$6x_b = 120,000$$
$$x_b = 20,000.$$

Figure 6.1 shows graphically the calculation of the break-even point.

The decision maker now knows that a demand of more than 20,000 units will be required in order to realize a profit if d_1 is selected; if demand is less, a loss will be incurred. In order to proceed further with our decision analysis, we must know the probability of the various levels of demand.

6.3 ESTIMATING THE PROBABILITY DISTRIBUTION OF DEMAND

We have already established that the actual demand for the new product could be any number greater than or equal to zero. In practical applications,

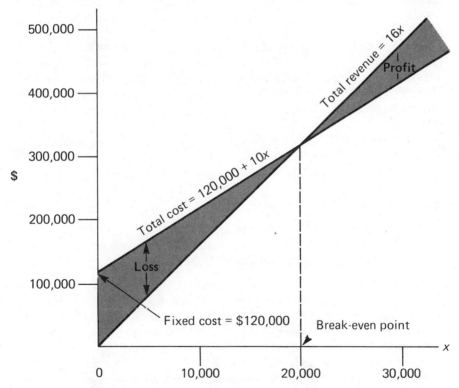

FIGURE 6.1 Break-even Analysis for the Smith Company Problem

it is common to use a normal distribution as the forecast of sales for a new product in this type of situation. If the decision maker feels that the probability distribution for demand is symmetric and takes the form of a bell-shaped curve, then a normal distribution can be used with some confidence to describe demand for the new product. A typical normal curve for demand is shown below.

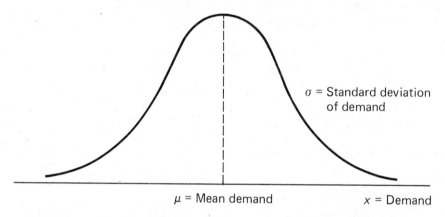

σ = Standard deviation of demand

μ = Mean demand x = Demand

Recall from Chapter 3 that the highest point on the curve corresponds to the mean (μ) or expected value of demand, and the standard deviation (σ) measures the variability of the demand about the mean. Thus, in order to completely describe the normal curve used to approximate demand, we must determine the mean demand level (μ) and the standard deviation (σ) of demand.

Assuming that Smith is satisfied that a normal curve can provide a good representation of the probability distribution of demand, let us see how values for μ and σ might be found. Suppose Smith's marketing manager has expressed his opinions about demand for the new product in the following two statements.

1. The most likely value of demand is 21,000 units.
2. There is a 10% chance of selling over 25,000 units and, at the same time, a 10% chance of selling less than 17,000 units.

For any continuous probability distribution, the most likely value corresponds to the highest point on the curve which, for the normal distribution, corresponds to the mean. Thus, using the information in (1) above, we can select the most likely value of demand (21,000 units) as the mean of the distribution (that is, μ = 21,000). Figure 6.2 shows a normal distribution for demand based on the above information.

We note that the information contained in the marketing manager's second statement is supportive of our choice of a normal distribution to approximate demand. The manager has indicated that the area under the curve between

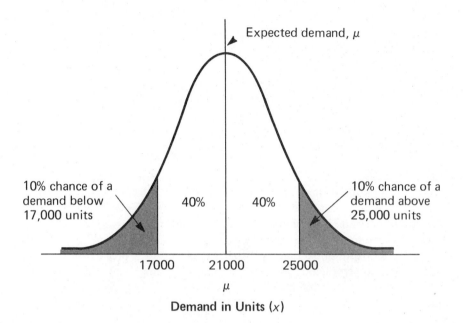

FIGURE 6.2 The Normal Distribution of Demand for Smith's New Product

the mean and 4000 units above the mean (.40) is exactly equal to the area under the curve between the mean and 4000 units below the mean. This suggests a belief on his part that the demand distribution is symmetric. The information relating probability statements to the demands of 25,000 and 17,000 units can now be used to estimate the standard deviation for the demand distribution.

Recall from Chapter 3 that in order to find areas under the curve for a normal distribution we must first convert to a standard normal random variable, z. In our particular application where x represents the demand in units, z would represent the number of standard deviations x lies above or below the mean μ. The formula for computing the number of standard deviations that x lies away from the mean μ is

$$z = \frac{x - \mu}{\sigma} \ .$$

Using the standard normal distribution in Appendix B, we see that the area under the curve between the mean and $z = 1.28$ standard deviations above the mean is .40. Since the normal distribution is symmetric, the area under the curve between the mean and 1.28 standard deviations below the mean is also .40. We can use this information to compute an estimate of the standard deviation of demand for Smith.

Using $x = 25,000$, $\mu = 21,000$, and $z = 1.28$ in the above formula for a standard normal random variable, we obtain

$$1.28 = \frac{25,000 - 21,000}{\sigma},$$

or $1.28\sigma = 25,000 - 21,000 = 4000$,

and $\sigma = \dfrac{4000}{1.28} = 3125$ units.

Thus, given the information provided by the marketing manager, we have been able to estimate that demand is normally distributed with a mean of 21,000 units and a standard deviation of 3125 units. We now have all the information needed to recommend a decision alternative to Smith.

Prior to attempting to select the best decision, let us use the derived probability distribution to calculate the probability of a profit or loss if the new product is introduced. We first compute the number of standard deviations from the mean to the break-even point, $x_b = 20,000$. With $\mu = 21,000$ and $\sigma = 3125$ we obtain

$$z = \frac{x_b - \mu}{\sigma} = \frac{20,000 - 21,000}{3125} = -.32.$$

Using Appendix B, we find $z = -.32$ corresponds to an area of .1255. Thus the probability of a profit and a loss is computed as follows:

$$P(\text{Profit}) = P(x > x_b) = .1255 + .5000 = .6255$$

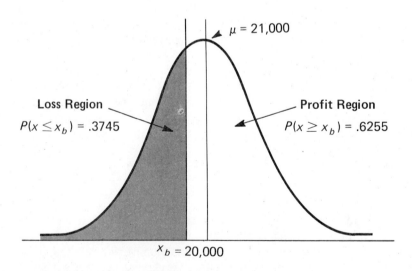

FIGURE 6.3 *Break-even Point and Probabilities of Profit and Loss for Smith Company Problem*

and

$$P(\text{Loss}) = 1 - P(\text{Profit}) = 1 - .6255 = .3745.$$

These probabilities are shown in Figure 6.3.

6.4 SELECTING A DECISION: THE MEAN AS A CERTAINTY EQUIVALENT

In Chapter 4, we showed how to use the expected monetary value criterion in decision situations where probability estimates were available for the states of nature. We now apply this criterion to Smith's problem. Recall that Smith has two decision alternatives: introduce the new product, d_1, or do not introduce it, d_2. It should be clear that d_2 results in an expected monetary value of \$0; that is, the profit will be \$0 regardless of the level of demand that might have occurred. Thus, we only need concern ourselves with calculating the expected monetary value of decision alternative d_1. If it is greater than zero, we will recommend d_1; if it is less than zero, we will recommend d_2.

Recall that the profit expression for the new product is given by

$$\text{Profit} = P = 6x - 120,000.$$

We can see that in this case, profit is a linear function of the number of units demanded. That is, the graph of profit versus number of units demanded is a straight line. It turns out that whenever we have a *linear profit function,* the expected monetary value for the associated decision alternative is easy to compute. For example, to compute the expected monetary value for decision alternative d_1, we simply substitute the mean (μ) for demand (x) in our profit expression; the resulting profit is the expected monetary value of decision alternative d_1. Thus, for Smith's problem, the expected monetary value of d_1 is

$$\begin{aligned}
\text{EMV}(d_1) &= \$6(21,000) - 120,000 \\
&= 6000.
\end{aligned}$$

In cases such as this (linear profit function), the decision maker can act as though he "knew for certain" that the actual value of demand would be equal to the mean level of demand μ. Thus, we refer to the mean of the probability distribution of demand as a *certainty equivalent* for the actual demand.

Returning to the Smith problem, we are now ready to make a decision recommendation. Since $\text{EMV}(d_1) = \$6000$ is greater than $\text{EMV}(d_2) = 0$, the EMV criterion indicates that Smith should introduce the new product. However, since $\text{EMV}(d_1) = \$6000$ is not that much greater than $\text{EMV}(d_2) = 0$, and since there is a significant probability of incurring a loss (.3745), Smith might prefer to do some further study before making a final decision on the product. For example, as we saw in the previous chapter, the expected value of perfect information (EVPI) indicates how much the expected payoff or expected profit could be increased if the decision maker had "perfect" information about the states of nature. Thus, before finalizing decision d_1 as recommended above, Smith might want to compute the EVPI associated with the decision. If the EVPI is large, Smith might want to consider obtaining additional information about the demand for the new product before proceeding with the implementation of decision d_1.

6.5 EVPI WITH THE NORMAL DISTRIBUTION

Looking closely at the calculations of the preceding section, we see that the profit function and the mean demand, μ, were the only two inputs needed to determine the decision that maximized expected monetary value. This was because the mean can be used as a certainty equivalent for actual demand whenever we have a linear profit function. Thus, you may wonder why we went to the effort of computing the standard deviation, σ, of demand when it was not used in selecting a decision alternative. The answer is that this measure of the variability of demand is needed to determine the risk associated with a particular decision. Specifically, we will see that the standard deviation must be known in order to compute the expected value of perfect information.

Recall that in Chapter 4 we introduced the concept of expected opportunity loss as a decision criterion that could be used as an alternative to the expected monetary value criterion. In addition, we noted that the expected opportunity loss (EOL) of the optimal decision was important because it could be interpreted as the expected value of perfect information. That is, the expected opportunity loss of the optimal decision told us how much we could expect to increase our profit if we had perfect information about the states of nature.

Let us return to the Smith Company problem and compute the EVPI or EOL associated with d_1, the decision to begin marketing the new product. This calculation involves first identifying the opportunity loss resulting from each possible demand and then weighting the loss by the probability of its occurrence. Note that if demand (x) exceeds the break-even point $x_b = 20,000$ units, the decision to market the product is the *best* decision. For this case, the opportunity loss is zero regardless of the amount by which demand exceeds the break-even point. Therefore

if $x \geq x_b$, then opportunity loss (OL) = \$0.

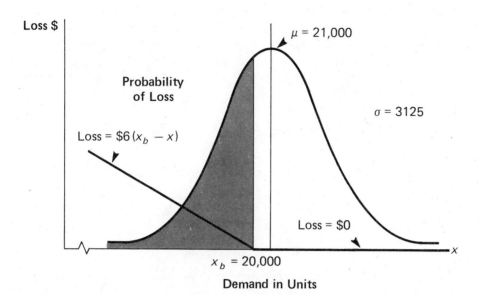

FIGURE 6.4 *Opportunity Loss Function for d_1 and Demand Distribution for Smith Company*

However if demand turns out to be less than the 20,000 unit break-even point, the decision not to introduce the product (yielding a payoff of $0) would have been the best decision. In this case the opportunity loss associated with the decision to market the product is just the actual loss that would occur if demand is less than the break-even point. For example, when $x = 19,999$ (one unit below the break-even point), we can use the product's profit expression, equation (6.1), to see that the loss would be $6. For $x = 19,998$ (two units below the break-even point), the loss would be $12, and so on. For the Smith Company, the opportunity loss expression when demand is less than the break-even point is as follows:

$$OL = 6(x_b - x).$$

Since the opportunity loss is a linear function of the demand x, we say we have a *linear loss function.*[1] A graph of the loss function associated with the decision to introduce the new product, d_1, is shown in Figure 6.4. To the right of the break-even point, $x_b = 20,000$, we see the loss function is zero. But to the left of the break-even point, it increases at the rate of $6 per unit decrease of demand.

[1] If our calculations had found the break-even point to be above the mean demand, decision d_2 would have been the optimal decision. In this case the linear loss function would have been as follows:

$$OL = \begin{cases} 6(x - x_b) & \text{for } x \geq x_b \\ 0 & \text{for } x \leq x_b. \end{cases}$$

133

Given the opportunity loss function and the probability distribution for demand, we can now calculate the expected opportunity loss of the optimal decision or, equivalently, the expected value of perfect information EVPI. We will describe the general procedure for a decision situation having the following characteristics:

1. two decision alternatives,
2. a normal distribution describes the states of nature, and
3. a linear loss function.

When a problem situation exists with the above characteristics, such as in the Smith Company's problem, the following expression[2] can be used to compute the expected value of perfect information.

$$\text{EVPI} = \text{EOL} = k\sigma L_N(z_b) \tag{6.2}$$

where

$$k = \text{per unit loss in the linear loss function}$$
$$\sigma = \text{standard deviation of the normal distribution}$$
$$z_b = \left| \frac{x_b - \mu}{\sigma} \right| = \text{absolute value of the number of standard deviations from the mean to the break-even point}$$
$$L_N(z_b) = \text{value of the } \textit{unit normal loss integral} \text{ (see Appendix C).}$$

For the data in the Smith Company problem, we have

$$k = 6$$
$$\sigma = 3125$$
$$z_b = \left| \frac{x_b - \mu}{\sigma} \right| = \left| \frac{20,000 - 21,000}{3125} \right| = .32.$$

Referring to Appendix C, we find

$$L_N(.32) = .2592.$$

Therefore,

$$\text{EVPI} = \text{EOL}(d_1) = 6(3125)(.2592) = \$4,860.$$

If the Smith Company feels that the EOL of $4860 represents a serious economic risk, it should consider generating additional information which could be used to revise or refine the forecast of the demand. In any case, we know that the EVPI or EOL value indicates that the company should never pay more than $4860 for additional information about potential demand no matter how good the information promises to be. If Smith's management

---

[2] The mathematics required to derive the EVPI expression under the assumption of a normal distribution is beyond the scope of this text. Thus, we merely present the EVPI or EOL formula and concentrate on the calculation and interpretation of its value.

believes that the $4860 EOL is not unreasonably high, they might decide to accept this risk and not seek additional information. In this case, our decision theory analysis recommends that the new product should be introduced into the market with an expected monetary value or expected payoff of $6000.

6.6 DECISION THEORY WITH NUMEROUS DECISION ALTERNATIVES

In the previous sections of this chapter, we have seen how the decision theory approach could be extended to problem situations involving two decision alternatives and a very large or perhaps infinite number of states of nature. In this section, we further extend our analysis to consider problem situations in which both the number of decision alternatives and the number states of nature are very large or infinite. The solution technique we utilize to solve such problems is called incremental analysis. Let us begin by considering how incremental analysis can be used to solve a single-period inventory problem.

A *single-period* inventory model refers to an inventory situation in which *one* order is placed for the product, and at the end of the period the product has either soldout or there is a surplus of unsold items which will be sold for a salvage value. The single-period model occurs in situations involving seasonal or perishable items that cannot be carried in inventory and sold in future periods. Seasonal clothing (such as bathing suits, winter coats, and so on) are typically handled in a single-period manner. In these situations a buyer places one preseason order for each item and then experiences a stockout or holds a clearance sale on the surplus stock at the end of the season. No items are carried in inventory and sold the following year. Newspapers are another example of a product that is ordered one time and is either sold or not sold during the single period. While newspapers are ordered daily, they cannot be carried in inventory and sold in later periods. Thus, newspaper orders may be treated as a sequence of single-period models; that is, each day or period is separate and a single-period inventory decision must be made each period (day). For this reason the single-period inventory problem is sometimes referred to as the *newsboy problem*. Since we only order once for the period, the only inventory decision we must make is how much of the product to order at the start of the period.

Obviously, if the demand were known for our single-period inventory situation, the solution would be easy; we would simply order the amount we knew we were going to sell. However, in most single-period models, the exact demand will not be known. In fact, forecasts may show that demand can have a wide variety of values. In these cases, it is usually reasonable to approximate the demand with a continuous probability distribution such as the normal.

The decision alternatives for the single-period inventory model are the order quantities the decision maker wants to consider. Since under ideal conditions, the decision maker would order an amount exactly equal to the demand, it seems reasonable to consider one possible order quantity or decision alternative for each possible demand level. Thus, in situations where a large or perhaps infinite number of demands (states of nature) are encountered, the decision theory approach must be able to consider an equally large number of decision alternatives. With so many possible decision alternatives, it will be impossible to calculate the expected monetary value for each alternative and then select the one with the largest EMV. Incremental or marginal analysis offers an efficient means of selecting a decision alternative in this situation.

Incremental Analysis

Incremental analysis is a procedure which allows us to calculate the decision alternative yielding the largest EMV without having to compute the EMV for each alternative. Let us see how this approach can be used to solve the single-period inventory problem faced by the Johnson Shoe Company.

Suppose that the Johnson Shoe Company is considering ordering a new white fashion shoe for men that has just been shown at a buyers' meeting in New York City. The shoe will be part of the company's spring-summer promotion and will be sold through nine retail stores in the Chicago area. The shoes will cost $20 per pair and retail for $30 per pair. If all the shoes are not sold by July 15, the company will have a July–August clearance sale and will be able to sell all surplus shoes at $15 per pair. How many pairs of size 10D shoes would you order for this single-period inventory problem?

The obvious question at this time is, what are the possible levels of demand that we might experience for this shoe and what are the probabilities associated with these levels? Suppose that management has followed the procedure discussed in Section 6.3 and concluded that a normal distribution with mean $\mu = 1000$ and standard deviation $\sigma = 100$ provides a good approximation to the probability distribution of demand for the size 10D shoes (see Figure 6.5).

Incremental analysis attacks the "how-much-to-order" decision by determining the cost or loss associated with both stocking and not stocking *one additional unit*. Suppose we decide to order the average or expected number of shoes demanded. Figure 6.5 shows that this expected demand would be 1000 pairs of size 10D white shoes. Next, suppose a manager asks us to consider incrementing the order size by 1 to an order quantity of 1001 pairs of shoes. Is it economically desirable to make this one unit increment in the order size? We can make this decision by analyzing the incremental effect of the one additional unit in terms of the cost or loss that might result. Suppose

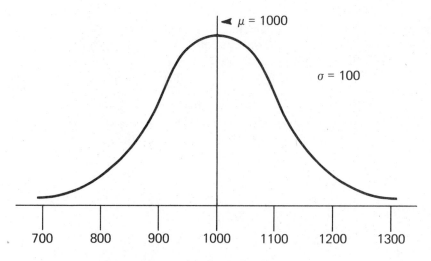

FIGURE 6.5 *Normal Distribution of Demand for the Johnson Shoe Company Size 10D White Shoes*

we decide to stock the one additional unit and then find it is not needed; what is our loss? Your answer should be $5, the $20 cost per unit minus $15 salvage value per unit. The $5 cost is the opportunity loss associated with stocking an extra unit when the best decision would have been not to order an additional unit. Now suppose we decide not to stock the one additional unit. A loss associated with this decision will occur if we find later that the unit could have been sold. In this case we have lost the opportunity to make a sale and its associated profit. Thus we have an opportunity loss of $10, the profit we could have made on the sale of this unit. An unsatisfied demand could also result in a loss of goodwill, which would be reflected as an increase in the opportunity loss.

The general expressions for the two types of losses are as follows:

$$L_S = c - s \tag{6.3}$$
$$L_{NS} = (p - c) + g \tag{6.4}$$

where

L_S = loss of *stocking* one unit and finding it *could not* be sold
L_{NS} = loss of *not stocking* one unit and finding it *could* have been sold
p = selling price per unit
s = salvage value per unit
c = cost per unit
g = goodwill or other added cost per unit due to shortage.

Assume the Johnson Shoe Company did not specify a goodwill cost, and thus the opportunity loss of not stocking an additional unit when it is needed is $10.

137

When working with uncertain demands, we know we have to consider the probability of obtaining specific demands and thus the probability of obtaining the losses associated with these demands. For example, when considering order sizes of 1000 or 1001 units, the loss of $5 associated with stocking the extra unit can only occur when the demand is less than or equal to 1000 and the extra unit is not sold. Similarly the $10 loss associated with not stocking the extra unit can only occur when the demand exceeds 1000 and the unstocked unit could have been sold. These conditions are summarized below.[3]

Order Quantity	Possible Loss	Probability Loss Occurs
Incremental unit stocked (Q=1001)	$L_S = \$5$	P (demand $\leq$ 1000)
Incremental unit not stocked (Q=1000)	$L_{NS} = \$10$	P (demand $>$ 1000)

By looking at the demand probability distribution in Figure 6.5, we see that P(demand $\leq$ 1000) = 0.50, and therefore P(demand $>$ 1000) = 1 − P(demand $\leq$ 1000) = 0.50. By multiplying the possible losses by the probability of obtaining the loss, we have the expected opportunity loss of the two decisions: to stock or not stock an additional unit.

$$\text{EOL}(Q = 1001) = L_S \cdot P(\text{demand} \leq 1000) = \$5(0.5) = \$2.50$$
$$\text{EOL}(Q = 1000) = L_{NS} \cdot P(\text{demand} > 1000) = \$10(0.5) = \$5.00.$$

Now what is our decision, do we order $Q = 1001$ or $Q = 1000$? Since the expected loss is greater for $Q = 1000$, we want to avoid this loss, and thus we should stock the additional unit, making $Q = 1001$. The manager might ask us to again consider incrementing our order by one additional unit to $Q = 1002$.

While we could follow the process of a unit-by-unit analysis, it would be very time-consuming and cumbersome. We would have to evaluate $Q = 1001$ versus $Q = 1002$, $Q = 1002$ versus $Q = 1003$, and so on, until we found the expected loss of an incremental unit equal to the expected loss without the incremental unit; that is, the optimal order quantity Q^* occurs when the incremental analysis shows

$$\text{EOL}(Q^* + 1) = \text{EOL}(Q^*) \tag{6.5}$$

[3] Since we have a continuous probability distribution for demand, a slightly more accurate approximation to the probabilities involved could be obtained by calculating P(demand $\leq$ 1000.5) and P(demand $>$ 1000.5). However, the additional accuracy is not significant and has no effect on the development which follows.

138

and there is no economic advantage to increasing the order quantity by the incremental unit.

Using D to indicate demand, equation (6.5) can be written as

$$L_S P(D \leq Q^*) = L_{NS} P(D > Q^*).$$

Since we know

$$P(D > Q^*) = 1 - P(D \leq Q^*)$$

we have

$$L_S P(D \leq Q^*) = L_{NS}[1 - P(D \leq Q^*)].$$

Solving for $P(D \leq Q^*)$, we have

$$P(D \leq Q^*) = \frac{L_{NS}}{L_S + L_{NS}}. \qquad (6.6)$$

Since we have already calculated the opportunity losses to be

$$L_{NS} = \$10 \quad \text{and} \quad L_S = \$5,$$

equation (6.6) for the Johnson Shoe Company becomes

$$P(D \leq Q^*) = \frac{10}{5 + 10} = .6667.$$

Thus we can find the optimal order quantity Q^* by returning to the assumed probability distribution shown in Figure 6.5 and finding a Q^* that will provide $P(D \leq Q^*) = .6667$. In order to do this, we must refer to Appendix B.

From Appendix B we see that .6667 of the area under the curve for a normal distribution lies at $z = +0.43$ standard deviations about the mean. Since the average demand is given by $\mu = 1000$ and the standard deviation is $\sigma = 100$,

$$Q^* = \mu + z\sigma$$
$$= 1000 + 0.43(100) = 1043.$$

Thus with this assumed normal probability distribution of demand the Johnson Shoe Company should order 1043 pairs of the 10D white shoes. Figure 6.6 shows the result of our calculations.

The results of our analysis of the Johnson Shoe Company problem can be generalized to develop an optimal decision rule for any single-period inventory problem. Equation (6.6) can be used to find the optimal order quantity any time the probability distribution for demand is normal or for any other continuous probability distribution. In the case of a discrete probability distribution of demand, it is usually not possible to select an order quantity such that equation (6.6) will be satisfied as an equality. Instead we first restrict consideration to those order sizes corresponding to possible demand

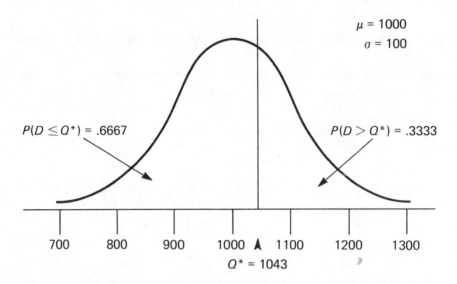

FIGURE 6.6 Optimal Order Quantity for the Johnson Shoe
Company Size 10D White Shoes

levels. Then it turns out that the optimal order quantity is given by the smallest value of Q^* that will satisfy equation (6.7) below.

$$P(D \leq Q^*) \geq \frac{L_{NS}}{L_S + L_{NS}} \tag{6.7}$$

Problem 15 at the end of the chapter provides practice in making this calculation for a discrete demand distribution.

6.7 SUMMARY

In this chapter we have extended the decision theory approach to problems involving a very large or infinite number of decision alternatives and possible states of nature. We were unable to use the payoff table or decision tree approach to solve these problems because of the large number of decision alternatives and states of nature. We found, however, that alternative methods of solving the problem were available.

In the cases where profit is a linear function, we are able to use the mean of the probability distribution for the states of nature as a certainty equivalent. Thus, in order to calculate the decision yielding the highest expected monetary value, it was only necessary to calculate the break-even point and compare it with the mean of the probability distribution. However we found that in order to determine the risk involved with a recommended decision, it was necessary to know the complete probability distribution. We needed to know the standard deviation, as well as the mean, for the normal distribution in order to calculate the expected opportunity loss or EVPI.

140

Incremental analysis was employed to determine an optimal decision rule for a single-period inventory problem which involved numerous decision alternatives as well as numerous states of nature. The best order quantity was found as that point where the opportunity loss of stocking an additional unit was equal to the opportunity loss from not stocking the unit.

6.8 GLOSSARY

1. *Fixed cost*—One-time costs that are not related to volume.
2. *Variable costs*—Costs that depend directly on volume with higher volumes providing proportionally higher costs.
3. *Break-even point*—A volume level where total revenue exactly equals total cost. Volumes above the break-even point result in profits, while volumes below the break-even point result in losses.
4. *Linear profit function*—An equation relating profit and volume such that profit is a linear function of volume.
5. *Certainty equivalent*—A value that can be used in place of knowledge of the entire probability distribution in many decision-making applications. For example, with a linear profit function the mean of the probability distribution for demand can be used as a certainty equivalent in computing expected profit.
6. *Linear loss function*—An equation relating loss and volume such that loss is a linear function of volume.
7. *Unit normal loss integral*—Tabular values (Appendix C) used to compute the expected opportunity loss of an optimal solution for two-action, normal distribution decision theory problems having a linear loss function.
8. *Single-period inventory models*—Inventory models in which it is assumed that only one order is placed for the product, and at the end of the sales period, the item has either sold out or the surplus of unsold items is sold for a salvage value.
9. *Newsboy problem*—A special case of the single-period inventory problem where it is desired to determine the number of daily newspapers for a newsboy to order.
10. *Incremental or marginal analysis*—The solution technique whereby the analyst considers the marginal profit or cost associated with incrementing the order quantity by one unit.

6.9 PROBLEMS

1. Based on the EVPI calculated in Section 6.5, suppose that the D. J. Smith Company decided to hire a market research firm to make an independent study of the demand for the new product. As a result of the additional information provided by a market research survey, Smith

revised the demand forecast for its new product such that it was best described by a normal distribution with $\mu = 18,500$ and $\sigma = 800$. What is now the recommended decision for Smith's new product? Calculate the new EVPI and comment on the need for a further revised forecast of demand.

2. The Korach Office Furniture Company is considering manufacturing a luxurious office swivel chair which would be sold primarily for executive conference rooms. The planned selling price is $480 per chair. The fixed cost for developing and manufacturing the chair is $200,000, while the variable cost would be $280 per chair.

    a. What is the break-even volume? Show the break-even analysis graphically.

    b. Assuming that demand for the chair is normally distributed with $\mu = 925$ and $\sigma = 125$, should Korach manufacture the chair?

    c. What is the EVPI? Would you suggest collecting information that might improve the accuracy of the demand forecast? Explain.

    d. Based on the above data, what is the minimum selling price per chair Korach could charge and still break even at a 925-unit demand?

3. Suppose for an extra $25,000 investment in fixed cost (that is, a total fixed cost of $225,000), the Korach Company in Problem 2 believes the variable cost per chair can be reduced to $230. Assuming the normal distribution with $\mu = 925$ and $\sigma = 125$ is still the best forecast of demand available, what is your recommended decision? What is the expected profit? What is the EVPI?

4. A book publisher expects a new college textbook to have sales of 40,000 units. However, because of uncertainties in the sales volume, the publisher has agreed that a normal distribution with $\mu = 40,000$ and $\sigma = 10,000$ is a reasonable approximation of the demand. The selling price is $18 per book, the variable cost is $14 per book, and the fixed publishing costs for the text are $90,000.

    a. What is the break-even point and the recommended decision?

    b. What is the expected profit?

    c. What is the EVPI?

    d. What is the probability that this text will show a profit?

    e. Is your decision in part (a) a safe or risky decision? Explain.

5. Suppose the most likely demand for a product is 3500 units with a .50 probability that the demand will be between 3000 and 4000 units.

    a. Assuming a normal distribution of demand, what is the appropriate standard deviation?

    b. For a break-even point of 3800 units, what is the probability the product will yield a profit?

6. The marketing manager of the Utter CB Radio Company estimates the demand for the company's new 40-channel radio will be around 12,000

units during the first year it is on the market. He also believes there is a 20% chance that over 15,000 units will be sold.

    a. Assuming that a normal distribution is used to describe the demand for the radio, what is the appropriate standard deviation (σ)?

    b. What is the probability the firm sells over 10,000 units during the first year?

    c. Is it very likely that demand could reach 20,000 units? What is this probability?

7. The Carolina Bicycle Company has designed a new 20 inch bicycle which it is considering manufacturing. The fixed cost is estimated to be $175,000 with a variable cost of $50 per bicycle. The bicycle will sell for $89.

    a. Show graphically the break-even analysis for this problem.

    b. If the expected demand is 4000 units, what should the firm do and what is its expected profit?

    c. Why would it be desirable to attempt to define a complete probability distribution for demand? That is, what additional decision-making information could be obtained if a normal distribution of the demand could be defined?

8. Harding, Inc. has just accepted a $150,000 government contract to manufacture an air pollution measuring device which will be used by the Environmental Protection Agency. The device is a one-of-a-kind model and will be tested in the Pittsburgh area. If results of the test are favorable, additional units will be manufactured. If Harding's fixed costs for the contract are $30,000 and additional costs are expected at the rate of $20,000 per month, how long can Harding take to complete the contract work and still break even? Suppose the contract completion time is assumed to follow a normal distribution with $\mu = 5$ months and $\sigma = 1$ month. What is the expected profit for Harding? What is the probability the contract will result in a loss? Do you agree with the original decision to accept the contract? What is the EVPI?

9. A perishable dairy product is ordered daily at a particular supermarket. The product, which costs $1.19 per unit, sells for $1.65 per unit. If units are unsold at the end of the day, the supplier takes them back at a rebate of $1 per unit. Assume that daily demand is approximately normal distribution with $\mu = 150$ and $\sigma = 30$.

    a. What is your recommended daily order quantity for the supermarket?

    b. What is the probability that the supermarket sells all the units it orders?

    c. In problems such as these, why would the supplier offer a rebate as high as $1? For example, why not offer a nominal rebate of, say, 25¢ per unit? What happens to the supermarket order quantity as the rebate is reduced?

10. A retail outlet sells a seasonal product for $10 per unit. The cost of the product is $8 per unit. All units not sold during the regular season are sold for half the retail price in an end-of-season clearance sale. Assume that demand for the product is normal with $\mu = 500$ and $\sigma = 100$.
    a. What is the recommended order quantity?
    b. What is the probability that at least some customers will ask to purchase the product after the outlet is sold out? That is, what is the probability of a stock out using your order quantity in part (a)?
    c. Suppose the owner's policy is that in order to keep customers happy and returning to the store later, stockouts' should be avoided if at all possible. What is your recommended order quantity if you get the owner to agree to a .15 probability of stockout?
    d. Using your answer to part (c), what is the goodwill cost you are assigning to a stockout? That is, how many dollars per unit is the owner implying he would pay to avoid a stockout?

11. The J&B Card Shop sells calendars with different colonial pictures shown for each month. The once-a-year order for each year's calendar is placed in September. From past experience the demand for the calendars can be approximated by a normal distribution with $\mu = 500$ and $\sigma = 120$. The calendars cost $1.50 each, and J&B sells them for $3 each.
    a. If J&B throws out all unsold calendars at the end of the year (that is, salvage value is zero), how many calendars should be ordered?
    b. If J&B reduces the calendar price to $1 in July of each year and can sell all surplus calendars at this price, how many calendars should be ordered?

12. A popular newsstand in a large metropolitan area is attempting to determine how many copies of the Sunday paper it should purchase each week. Demand for the newspaper on Sundays can be approximated by a normal distribution with $\mu = 450$ and $\sigma = 100$. The newspaper costs the newsstand 35¢ a copy and sells for 50¢ a copy. The newsstand does not receive any value from surplus papers and thus absorbs a 100% loss on all unsold papers.
    a. How many copies of the Sunday paper should be purchased each week?
    b. What is the probability the newsstand has a stockout?
    c. The manager of the newsstand is concerned about the newsstand's image if the probability of stockout is high. The customers often purchase other items after coming to the newsstand for the Sunday paper. Frequent stockouts would cause customers to go to another newsstand. The manager agrees that a 50¢ loss of goodwill cost should be assigned to any stockout. What is the new recommended order quantity and the new probability of a stockout?

13. The Gilbert Air-Conditioning Company is considering the purchase of a

144

special shipment of portable air conditioners manufactured in Japan. Each unit will cost Gilbert $80, and it will be sold for $125. Gilbert does not want to carry surplus air conditioners over until the following year. Thus all supplies will be sold to a wholesaler who has agreed to take all surplus units for $50 per unit. The probability distribution for air conditioner demand is as follows:

Interval	Estimated Probability
0 but less than 10	.30
10 but less than 20	.35
20 but less than 30	.20
30 but less than 40	.10
40 to 50	.05

Use incremental analysis to find the recommended order quantity for Gilbert.

14. Referring to Problem 13, suppose the air conditioner demand had been approximated by a normal distribution with $\mu = 20$ and $\sigma = 8$.
   a. What is the recommended order quantity under this assumed demand distribution?
   b. What is the probability Gilbert will sell all units it orders?

15. The McCormick Hardware Store places one order for riding lawn mowers each February. The lawn mowers being purchased this year cost $300 and sell for $425. In the past, McCormick has always been able to sell all surplus lawn mowers during the September "end-of-summer" sale. The clearance sale price for these lawn mowers will be $250. If the following probability distribution for demand is assumed, how many lawn mowers should McCormick order?

Demand for Lawn Mowers	Probability
0	.10
1	.15
2	.30
3	.20
4	.15
5	.10

7
Utility and Decision Making

In Chapters 4, 5, and 6 we have expressed the payoffs associated with the combination of a decision alternative and a state of nature solely in terms of monetary values. When probability information was available about the states of nature, we recommended using expected monetary value or, equivalently, expected opportunity loss as a decision criterion. Indeed, in many business decision-making situations, expected monetary value is an excellent criterion. However, there are situations in which the expected monetary value criterion does not lead to the "best" decision alternative.

By "best" decision alternative, we mean the one that is preferred by the decision maker, taking into account not only the expected monetary value but also many other factors, such as the ability to make a very large profit or the possibility of incurring a large loss. Examples of situations in which expected monetary value does not lead to the selection of the most preferred alternative are numerous. One such example is the decision by most people to carry insurance. Clearly the decision to carry insurance on a house does not provide a higher expected monetary value than not carrying such insurance. Otherwise, insurance companies could not pay expenses and make a profit. Similarly, many people buy tickets to state lotteries knowing that the expected monetary value of such a decision is negative.

Should we conclude that persons or businesses that participate in lotteries or buy insurance do so because they are unable to determine which decision alternative leads to the highest expected monetary value? On the contrary, we take the view that in these cases, monetary value is not the proper measure of the true worth of the outcome to the decision maker.

We will see that in those cases where expected monetary value does not lead to the most preferred decision alternative, expressing the value (or worth) of an outcome in terms of its *utility* will permit the use of *expected utility* as a preferred decision criterion.

7.1 THE MEANING OF UTILITY

Utility is a measure of the total worth of a particular outcome which reflects the decision maker's attitude toward a collection of factors such as profit, loss, and risk. Researchers have found that as long as the monetary values of

146

payoffs stay within a range that is considered reasonable to the decision maker, expected monetary value is a good decision criterion. However, when the payoffs or losses become extreme, most decision makers are not satisfied with the expected monetary value criterion.

As an example of a case where utility theory can help in selecting the best decision alternative, let us consider the problem faced by Swofford, Inc., a relatively small real estate investment firm located in Atlanta, Georgia. Swofford currently has two investment opportunities which require approximately the same cash outlay. The cash requirements necessary prohibit Swofford from making more than one investment at this time. Consequently, there are three possible decision alternatives that may be considered.

The three decision alternatives, denoted by d_1, d_2, and d_3, are as follows:

d_1 = make investment A,

d_2 = make investment B,

d_3 = do not invest.

The monetary payoffs associated with the investment opportunities depend largely upon what happens to the real estate market during the next 6 months. Either real estate prices will go up, prices will remain stable, or prices will go down. Thus, the Swofford states of nature, denoted by s_1, s_2, and s_3, are as follows:

s_1 = real estate prices go up,

s_2 = real estate prices remain stable,

s_3 = real estate prices go down.

Using the best information available, Swofford has estimated the profits or payoffs associated with each decision alternative and state-of-nature combination. The resulting payoff table is shown in Table 7.1.

TABLE 7.1 Payoff Table for Swofford, Inc.

| | | States of Nature | | |
		Prices up s_1	Prices stable s_2	Prices down s_3
Decision	Investment A d_1	$30,000	$20,000	-$50,000
Alternatives	Investment B d_2	$50,000	-$20,000	-$30,000
	Do not invest d_3	0	0	0

Swofford's best estimate of the probability that prices will go up is 0.30; the best estimate of the probability that prices will remain stable is 0.50; and the best projection of the probability that real estate prices will go down is

147

0.20. Thus, the expected monetary values for the three decision alternatives are

$$EMV(d_1) = 0.3(30,000) + 0.5(\quad 20,000) + 0.2(-50,000) = \quad 9000$$
$$EMV(d_2) = 0.3(50,000) + 0.5(-20,000) + 0.2(-30,000) = -1000$$
$$EMV(d_3) = 0.3(\quad 0 \quad) + 0.5(\quad 0 \quad) + 0.2(\quad 0 \quad) = \quad 0$$

Using the expected monetary value criterion, the optimal decision is to select investment A with an expected monetary value of $9000. Is this really the best decision alternative? Let us consider some other very relevant company factors that relate to Swofford's capability for absorbing a loss as great as $50,000 if investment A is made and prices actually go down.

It turns out that Swofford's current financial position is very weak. This was partly reflected in Swofford's ability to undertake at most one investment at the current time. More importantly, however, the firm's president feels that if the next investment results in substantial losses, Swofford's future will be in jeopardy. Although the expected monetary value criterion leads to a recommendation for d_1, do you think this is the decision the firm's president would prefer?

He might. But we suspect that unless the firm's president is a real gambler he would select d_2 or d_3 in order to avoid the possibility of incurring a $50,000 loss. In fact, it is reasonable to believe that if a loss as great as even $30,000 could possibly drive Swofford's out of business, the president would select d_3, feeling that both investment A and investment B are too great a risk for a firm in Swofford's current financial position.

The way we can resolve the dilemma created by applying the EMV criterion is to first determine the utility to Swofford's of the various monetary outcomes. Recall that the utility of any monetary outcome is the total worth of that outcome taking into account the risks and payoffs involved. If the utilities for the various outcomes are correctly assessed, then the decision alternative with the highest expected utility is the most preferred or best alternative. In the next section, we will see how to determine the utility of the monetary outcomes in such a fashion that the alternative with the highest expected utility is most preferred.

7.2 DEVELOPING UTILITIES FOR MONETARY PAYOFFS

The procedure we shall use to establish utility values for the payoffs in Swofford's problem situation requires that we first assign a utility value to the best and worst possible payoffs in the decision situation. Any values will work as long as the utility assigned to the best payoff is greater than the utility assigned to the worst payoff. In this case, $50,000 is the best payoff and −$50,000 is the worst. Suppose then that we arbitrarily make the following assignments to these two payoffs.

Utility of −$50,000 = $U(-50,000)$ = 0
Utility of $50,000 = $U(\ \ 50,000)$ = 10.

Now, let us see how we can determine the utility associated with every other payoff.

Consider the process of establishing the utility of a payoff of $30,000. First, we ask Swofford's president to state a preference between a guaranteed $30,000 payoff and the opportunity to engage in the following lottery or bet.

Lottery: Swofford's obtains a payoff of $50,000
           with probability p and a payoff of −$50,000
           with probability $(1 - p)$.

Obviously, if p is "very close" to 1, Swofford's president would prefer the lottery to the certain payoff of $30,000, since the firm would virtually guarantee itself a payoff of $50,000. On the other hand, if p is "very close" to 0, Swofford's president would clearly prefer the guarantee of $30,000. In any event, as p changes continuously from 0 to 1, the preference for the guaranteed payoff of $30,000 will change at some point into a preference for the lottery. At this value of p, Swofford's president would have no greater preference for the guaranteed payoff of $30,000 than for the lottery. For example, let us assume that when $p = 0.95$, Swofford's president is indifferent between the certain payoff of $30,000 and the lottery. Given this value of p, we can compute the utility of a $30,000 payoff as follows:

$$
\begin{aligned}
U(30,000) &= p\ U(50,000) + (1 - p)\ U(-50,000) \\
&= 0.95(10) + (0.05)(0) \\
&= 9.5
\end{aligned}
$$

Obviously, if we had started with a different assignment of utilities for a payoff of $50,000 and −$50,000, we would have ended up with a different utility for $30,000. For example, if we had started with an assignment of 100 for $50,000 and 10 for −$50,000, the utility of a $30,000 payoff would be

$$
\begin{aligned}
U(30,000) &= 0.95(100) + 0.05(10) \\
&= 95 + 0.5 \\
&= 95.5.
\end{aligned}
$$

Hence, we must conclude that the utility assigned to each payoff is not unique but merely depends upon the initial choice of utilities for the best and worst payoffs. We will discuss this further at the end of this section. For now, however, we will continue to use a value of 10 for the utility of $50,000 and 0 for the utility of −$50,000.

Before computing the utility for the other payoffs, let us consider the significance of Swofford's president assigning a utility of 9.5 to a payoff of $30,000. Clearly, when $p = 0.95$, the expected monetary value of the lottery is

$$\begin{aligned} \text{EMV(lottery)} &= 0.95(\$50,000) + 0.05(-\$50,000) \\ &= \$47,500 - \$2500 \\ &= \$45,000 \end{aligned}$$

We see that although the expected monetary value of the lottery when $p = 0.95$ is $45,000, Swofford's president would just as soon take a guaranteed payoff of $30,000. Thus, Swofford's president is taking a conservative or risk-avoiding viewpoint. The president would rather have $30,000 for certain than risk anything greater than a 5% chance of incurring a loss of $50,000. One can view the difference between the EMV of $45,000 and the $30,000 amount for certain as the "risk premium" Swofford's would be willing to pay to avoid the 5% chance of losing $50,000. Thus, in this case, expected monetary value is not a true measure of the president's actual preference.

To compute the utility associated with a payoff of $-\$20,000$, we must ask Swofford's president to state a preference between a guaranteed $-\$20,000$ payoff and the opportunity to engage in the following lottery.

Lottery: Swofford's obtains a payoff of $50,000 with probability p and a payoff of $-\$50,000$ with probability $(1 - p)$.

Note that this is exactly the same lottery we used to establish the utility of a payoff of $30,000. In fact, this will be the lottery used to establish the utility for any monetary value in the Swofford payoff table. Using this lottery, then, we must ask Swofford's president to state the value of p that would make him indifferent between a guaranteed payoff of $-\$20,000$ and the lottery. For example, we might begin by asking the president to choose between a certain loss of $20,000 and the lottery with a payoff of $50,000 with probability $p = 0.90$ and a payoff of $-\$50,000$ with probability $(1 - p) = 0.10$. What answer do you think we would get? Surely, with this high probability of obtaining a payoff of $50,000, the president would elect the lottery. Next, we might ask if $p = 0.85$ would result in indifference between the loss of $20,000 for certain and the lottery. Again, the president might tell us that the lottery would be preferred. Suppose we continue in this fashion until we get to $p = .55$, where we find that with this value of p, the president is indifferent between the payoff of $-\$20,000$ and the lottery. That is, for any value of p less than 0.55, the president would rather take a loss of $20,000 for certain than risk the potential loss of $50,000 with the lottery, and for any value of p above 0.55, the president would elect the lottery. Thus the utility assigned to a payoff of $-\$20,000$ is

$$U(-\$20,000) = p\ U(50,000) + (1 - p)U(-\$50,000)$$
$$= 0.55(10) + 0.45(0)$$
$$= 5.5.$$

Again, let us examine the significance of this assignment as compared to the expected monetary value criterion. When $p = 0.55$, the expected monetary value of the lottery is

$$EMV(\text{lottery}) = 0.55(\$50,000) + 0.45(-\$50,000)$$
$$= \$27,500 - \$22,500$$
$$= \$5000.$$

Thus, Swofford's president would just as soon absorb a loss of $20,000 for certain as take the lottery, even though the expected monetary value of the lottery is $5,000. Once again, we see the conservative or risk-avoiding point of view of Swofford's president.

In the above two examples where we computed the utility for a specific monetary payoff M, we first found the probability p where the decision maker was indifferent between a guaranteed payoff of M and a lottery with a payoff of $50,000 with probability p and $-\$50,000$ with probability $(1 - p)$. The utility of M was then computed as

$$U(M) = pU(\$50,000) + (1 - p)U(-\$50,000)$$
$$= p(10) + (1 - p)0$$
$$= 10p.$$

Using the above procedure, utility values for the rest of the payoffs in Swofford's problem were developed. The results are presented in Table 7.2.

TABLE 7.2 Utility of Monetary Payoffs for the
Swofford, Inc. Problem

Monetary Value	Indifference Value of P	Utility Value
$50,000	Does not apply	10.0
30,000	0.95	9.5
20,000	0.90	9.0
0	0.75	7.5
− 20,000	0.55	5.5
− 30,000	0.40	4.0
− 50,000	Does not apply	0

Now that we have determined the utility value of each of the possible monetary values, we can write our original payoff table in terms of utility values. Table 7.3 shows the utility for the various outcomes in the Swofford problem. The notation we will use for the entries in the utility table is $u(d_i, s_j)$, which denotes the utility associated with decision alternative d_i and state of nature s_j. Using this notation, we see that $u(d_2, s_3) = 4.0$.

TABLE 7.3 *Utility Table for Swofford, Inc.*

		Prices up s_1	Prices stable s_2	Prices down s_3
	Investment A d_1	9.5	9.0	0
Decision				
	Investment B d_2	10.0	5.5	4.0
Alternatives				
	Do not invest d_3	7.5	7.5	7.5

The Expected Utility Criterion

We can now apply the *expected utility* criterion (EU) to select an optimal decision alternative for Swofford, Inc. The expected utility criterion requires the analyst to compute the expected utility for each decision alternative and then select the alternative yielding the best expected utility. If there are N possible states of nature, the expected utility of a decision alternative d_i is given by

$$EU(d_i) = \sum_{j=1}^{N} P(s_j)u(d_i, s_j)$$

The expected utility for each of the decision alternatives in the Swofford problem is computed below.

$$EU(d_1) = 0.3(9.5) + 0.5(9.0) + 0.2(0) = 7.35$$
$$EU(d_2) = 0.3(10) + 0.5(5.5) + 0.2(4.0) = 6.55$$
$$EU(d_3) = 0.3(7.5) + 0.5(7.5) + 0.2(7.5) = 7.5$$

We see that the optimal decision using the expected utility criterion is d_3, do not invest. The ranking of alternatives according to the president's utility assignments is given below.

Ranking of Decision Alternatives	Expected Utility	Expected Monetary Value
Do not invest	7.50	0
Investment A	7.35	9000
Investment B	6.55	−1000

Note that while investment A had the highest expected monetary value of $9000, our analysis indicates that Swofford should decline this investment. The rationale behind not selecting investment A is that the .20 probability of a $50,000 loss was considered to involve a very serious risk by Swofford's president. The seriousness of this risk and its associated impact on the company was not adequately reflected when the expected monetary value criterion was employed. It was necessary to assess the utility for each payoff in order to adequately take this risk into account.

In the Swofford problem, we have been using a utility of 10 for the largest possible payoff and 0 for the smallest. Since the choice of values could have been anything, we might have chosen 1 for the utility of the largest payoff and 0 for the utility of the smallest. Had we made this choice, the utility for any monetary value M would have been the value of p at which the decision maker was indifferent between a payoff of M for certain and a lottery in which the best payoff is obtained with probability p and the worst payoff is obtained with probability $(1 - p)$. Thus the utility for any monetary value would have been equal to the probability of earning the highest payoff. Often, this choice is made because of the ease in computation. We chose not to do so to emphasize the distinction between the utility values and the indifference probabilities for the lottery.

7.3 SUMMARY OF STEPS FOR DETERMINING THE UTILITY FOR MONEY

Before considering other aspects of utility, let us summarize the steps involved in determining the utility for money and using it within the decision theory framework. The steps outlined below state in general terms the procedure used to solve the Swofford, Inc. investment problem. The steps are as follows:

1. Develop a payoff table using monetary values.
2. Identify the best and worst payoff values in the table and assign each a utility value with U(best payoff) $> U$(worst payoff).
3. For every other monetary value M in the original payoff table, perform Steps a through c below in order to determine its utility value.
   a. Define the following lottery: The best payoff is obtained with probability p and the worst payoff is obtained with probability $(1 - p)$.
   b. Determine the value of p such that the decision maker is indifferent between a payoff of M for certain and the lottery defined in (a).
   c. Calculate the utility of M as follows: $U(M) = pU$(best payoff) $+ (1 - p)U$(worst payoff).
4. Convert the payoff table from monetary values to the calculated utility values.

5. Apply the expected utility criterion to the utility table and select the decision alternative with the best expected utility.

7.4 RISK AVOIDERS VERSUS RISK TAKERS

The financial position of Swofford, Inc. was such that the firm's president evaluated investment opportunities from a conservative or risk-avoiding point of view. However, if the firm had a surplus of cash and a very stable future, we might have found Swofford's president looking for investment alternatives which, while perhaps risky, contained a potential for substantial profit. If the president had behaved in this manner, he would be classified as a risk taker. In this section, we analyze the decision problem faced by Swofford from the point of view of a decision maker who would be classified as a risk taker. We then compare the conservative or risk-avoiding point of view of Swofford's president to the behavior of a decision maker who is a risk taker.

Given the decision problem faced by Swofford, Inc. and using the general procedure for developing utilities as discussed in Section 7.3, a risk taker might express the utility of the various payoffs as shown in Table 7.4. As before, we have taken $U(50,000) = 10.0$ and $U(-50,000) = 0$. Note carefully the difference in behavior between that reflected in Table 7.4 and Table 7.2. That is, in determining the value of p at which the decision maker is indifferent between a payoff of M for certain and a lottery in which $50,000 is obtained with probability p and $-$50,000 with probability $(1 - p)$, the risk taker is willing to accept a greater risk of incurring a loss of $50,000 in order to gain the opportunity to realize a profit of $50,000.

To help develop the utility table for the risk taker, we have reproduced the Swofford, Inc. payoff table in Table 7.5.

Using these payoffs and the risk taker's utility values given in Table 7.4, we can now write the risk taker's utility table as shown in Table 7.6.

TABLE 7.4 Revised Utility Values for the
Swofford, Inc. Problem Assuming
a Risk Taker

Monetary Value	Indifference Value of p	Utility Value
$50,000	Does not apply	10.0
30,000	.50	5.0
20,000	.40	4.0
0	.25	2.5
−20,000	.15	1.5
−30,000	.10	1.0
−50,000	Does not apply	0

TABLE 7.5   Payoff Table for the Swofford, Inc. Problem

		States of Nature		
		s_1	s_2	s_3
Decision Alternatives	Investment A	$30,000	$20,000	-$50,000
	Investment B	$50,000	-$20,000	-$30,000
	Do not invest	0	0	0

TABLE 7.6   Utility Table of a Risk Taker for the Swofford, Inc. Problem

		States of Nature		
		s_1	s_2	s_3
Decision Alternatives	Investment A	5.0	4.0	0.0
	Investment B	10.0	1.5	1.0
	Do not invest	2.5	2.5	2.5

The expected utility calculations now show

$$EU(d_1) = 0.3(5) + 0.5(4.0) + 0.2(0.0) = 3.50$$
$$EU(d_2) = 0.3(10) + 0.5(1.5) + 0.2(1.0) = 3.95$$
$$EU(d_3) = 0.3(2.5) + 0.5(2.5) + 0.2(2.5) = 2.5$$

What is the recommended decision? Perhaps somewhat to your surprise, the analysis recommends investment B, with the highest expected utility of 3.95. Recalling this investment had a -$1000 expected monetary value, why is it now the recommended decision? Remember that the decision maker in this revised problem is a risk taker with high utilities associated with large profits. Thus, although the expected profit of investment B is negative, utility analysis has shown that this decision maker is enough of a risk taker to prefer investment B and its potential for the $50,000 profit.

Using the above utility values and the expected utility criterion, the order of preference and the associated expected monetary values are as follows:

Ranking of Decision Alternatives	Expected Utility	Expected Monetary Value
Investment B	3.95	-$1000
Investment A	3.50	$9000
Do not invest	2.50	0

When we compare the above utility analysis for a risk taker with the more conservative, risk-avoider preferences of the president of Swofford, Inc., we see, even with the same decision problem, how different attitudes toward risk can lead to different recommended decisions. The utility values established by Swofford's president indicated that the firm should not invest at this time, while the utilities established by the risk taker showed a preference for investment B. Note that both of these decisions differ from the best expected monetary value decision, which was investment A.

We can obtain another perspective of the difference in behavior between a risk avoider and a risk taker by developing a graph that depicts the relationship between monetary value and utility. The horizontal axis of the graph will be used to represent monetary values, and the vertical axis will represent the utility associated with each monetary value. Now, consider the data in Table 7.2, with a utility value corresponding to each monetary value for the original Swofford, Inc. problem. These values can be plotted on a graph such as in Figure 7.1, and a curve can be drawn through the observed points. The resulting curve is the utility function for money for Swofford's president. Recall that these points reflected the conservative or risk-avoiding nature of Swofford's president. Hence, we refer to the curve in Figure 7.1 as a utility

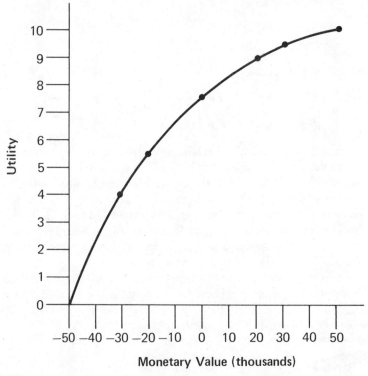

FIGURE 7.1   Utility Function for Money for the Risk Avoider

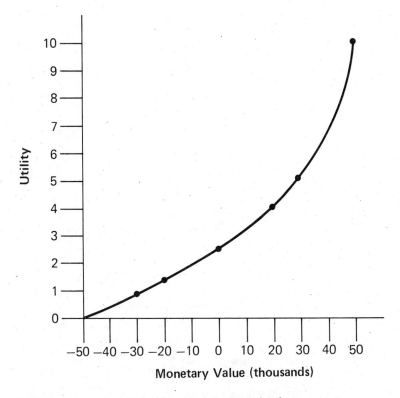

FIGURE 7.2   Utility Function for Money for the Risk Taker

function for a risk avoider. Using the data in Table 7.4, developed for a risk taker, we can plot these points on a graph such as in Figure 7.2. The resulting curve depicts the utility function for a risk taker.

By looking at the utility functions of Figures 7.1 and 7.2, we can begin to generalize about the utility functions for risk avoiders and risk takers. Although the exact shape of the utility function will vary from one decision maker to another, we can see the general shape of these two classifications of utility functions. The utility function for the risk-avoider class shows a diminishing marginal return for money. For example, the increase in utility going from a monetary value of −$30,000 to $0 is 7.5 − 4.0 = 3.5, whereas the increase in utility in going from $0 to $30,000 is only 9.5 − 7.5 = 2.0. On the other hand the utility function for a risk taker shows an increasing marginal return for money. For example, in Figure 7.2, we see that the increase in utility in going from −$30,000 to $0 is 2.5 − 1.0 = 1.5, whereas the increase in utility in going from $0 to $30,000 is 5.0 − 2.5 = 2.5. Note also that in either case, the utility function is always increasing. That is, more money leads to more utility. This is a property possessed by all utility functions.

We concluded above that the utility function for a risk avoider shows a

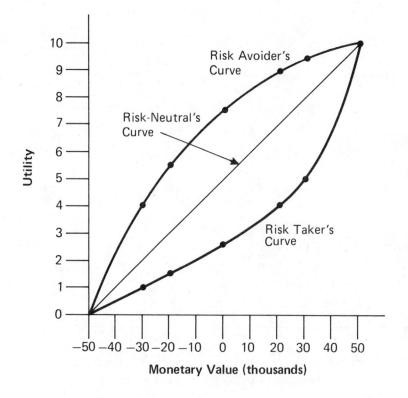

FIGURE 7.3   Utility Functions for Risk Avoider, Risk Taker,
and Risk-Neutral

diminishing marginal return for money and that the utility function for a risk taker shows an increasing marginal return. When the marginal return for money is neither decreasing nor increasing but remains constant, the corresponding utility function describes the behavior of a decision maker who is neutral to risk. The following characteristics are associated with a risk-neutral decision maker.

1. The utility function can be drawn as a straight line connecting the "best" and the "worst" points.
2. The expected utility criterion and the expected monetary value criterion result in the same action.

Figure 7.3 depicts the utility function of a risk-neutral decision maker using the Swofford, Inc. problem data. For comparison purposes, we also show the utility functions for the cases where the decision maker is either a risk taker or a risk avoider.

158

7.5 EXPECTED MONETARY VALUE VERSUS EXPECTED UTILITY AS A DECISION-MAKING CRITERION

In many decision-making problems, expected monetary value and expected utility will lead to identical recommendations. In fact, this will always be true if the decision maker is neutral to risk. In general, if the decision maker is "almost" risk-neutral over the range of payoffs (from lowest to highest) for a particular decision problem, the expected monetary value criterion is a good one. The trick is in recognizing the range of monetary values over which a decision maker's utility function is risk-neutral.

It is generally agreed that when the payoffs for a particular decision-making problem fall into a reasonable range—the best is not too good and the worst is not too bad—decision makers tend to express preferences in agreement with the expected monetary value criterion. Thus, as a general guideline, we suggest asking the decision maker to consider the best and worst possible payoffs for a problem and assess their reasonableness. If the decision maker believes they are in the "reasonable" range, the expected monetary value criterion can be used. However, if the payoffs appear unreasonably large or unreasonably small (for example, a huge loss) and if the decision maker feels monetary values do not adequately reflect his true preferences for the payoffs, a utility analysis of the problem should be considered.

Unfortunately, the determination of the appropriate utilities is not a trivial task. As we have seen, measuring utility requires a degree of subjectivity on the part of the decision maker, and different decision makers will have different utility functions. This aspect of utility often causes decision makers to feel uncomfortable about using the utility criterion in decision making. However, if we encounter a decision situation in which we are convinced monetary value is not necessarily the primary measure of performance and if we agree that a quantitative analysis of the decision problem is desirable, then some form of utility analysis must be performed.

7.6 SUMMARY

In this chapter we have suggested that expected utility should be used as a criterion in many decision situations in which the expected monetary value criterion would lead to unacceptable decisions. Unlike monetary value, utility is a measure of the total worth of an outcome resulting from the choice of a decision alternative and the occurrence of a state of nature. As such, utility takes into account the decision maker's attitude toward the profit, loss, and the risk associated with an outcome. In our examples we have seen how the use of utility analysis can lead to decision recommendations that differ from those that would be selected under the expected monetary value criterion.

While admittedly a decision maker's utility can be difficult to measure, we have offered a step-by-step procedure that can be used to determine a decision maker's utility for money. Using the decision maker's evaluation of a lottery involving only the best and worst payoffs, the procedure provides a method whereby each entry in the payoff table can be converted to a utility value. Then the expected utility criterion can be used to select the best decision alternative.

Even with utility as a measure of worth, we saw how the analysis for a conservative or risk-avoiding decision maker could lead to different decision recommendations than for a risk taker. In cases where the decision maker is risk-neutral, however, we saw that the recommendations using the expected utility criterion are identical to the recommendations using the expected monetary value criterion.

7.7 GLOSSARY

1. *Utility*—A measure of the total worth of an outcome reflecting a decision maker's attitude toward considerations such as profit, loss, and intangibles such as risk.
2. *Lottery*—A hypothetical investment alternative with a probability p of obtaining the best possible payoff and a probability of $(1 - p)$ of obtaining the worst possible payoff in a payoff table.
3. *Utility function for money*—A curve that depicts the relationship between monetary value and utility.
4. *Risk avoider*—A decision maker who tends to avoid decisions which have the risk of a low or extremely bad payoff.
5. *Risk taker*—A decision maker who tends to prefer decisions which, although risky, have a possibility for a high or extremely good payoff.
6. *Risk-neutral Decision Maker*—A decision maker who is neutral to risk. For this decision maker the expected monetary value criterion yields results identical to those obtained with the expected utility criterion.
7. *Expected utility criterion*—A decision criterion which requires the analyst to compute the expected utility for each decision alternative and then select the alternative yielding the best expected utility.

7.8 PROBLEMS

1. A firm has three investment alternatives. The payoff table and associated probabilities are as follows:

		Economic Conditions			
		Up	Stable	Down	
	d_1	100	25	0	
Investment	d_2	75	50	25	← Thousands of dollars
	d_3	50	50	50	
Probabilities		.40	.30	.30	

a. Using the EMV criterion, which decision is preferred?

b. For the lottery having a payoff of $100,000 with probability p and $0 with probability $(1 - p)$, two decision makers expressed the following indifference probabilities.

Profit	Indifference Probability (p)	
	Decision Maker A	Decision Maker B
75,000	.80	.60
50,000	.60	.30
25,000	.30	.15

   Find the most preferred decision for each decision maker using the expected utility criterion.

c. Why don't A and B select the same decision alternative?

2. Alexander Industries is considering purchasing an insurance policy for its new office building in St. Louis, Missouri. The policy has an annual cost of $10,000. If minor fire damage occurs to the office building, a cost of $100,000 is anticipated, while a major or total destruction carries a cost of $200,000. The payoff table, including the state of nature probabilities, is as follows:

			Damage			
			s_1 None	s_2 Minor	s_3 Major	
	Purchase insurance	d_1	10,000	10,000	10,000	
Decision Alternatives	Do not purchase insurance	d_2	0	100,000	200,000	←Cost
	Probability of occurrence over a 1-year period		96	.03	.01	

a. Using the expected monetary value criterion, what decision do you recommend?

b. What lottery would you use to assess utilities? (Note that since the data are costs, the best payoff is $0.)

c. Assume we found the following indifference probabilities for the Lottery defined in part (b).

Cost	Indifference Probability
10,000	$p = .99$
100,000	$p = .60$

What decision would you recommend?

d. Do you favor using the expected monetary value or expected utility criterion for this decision problem? Why?

3. In a certain state lottery, a lottery ticket costs $2. In terms of the decision to purchase or not to purchase a lottery ticket, suppose the following payoff table applies.

			Outcomes	
			s_1 Win	s_2 Loss
Decision Alternatives	Purchase lottery ticket	d_1	300,000	-2
	Do not purchase lottery ticket	d_2	0	0

a. If a realistic estimate of the chances of winning are 1 in 250,000 use the expected monetary value criterion to recommend a decision.

b. If a particular decision maker assigns an indifference probability of .000001 to the $0 payoff, would this individual purchase a lottery ticket? Use the expected utility criterion to justify your answer.

4. There are two different routes for traveling between two cities. Route A normally takes 60 minutes, while route B normally takes 45 minutes. If traffic problems are encountered on route A, the travel time increases to 70 minutes, while traffic problems on route B increase travel time to 90 minutes. The probability of the delays are .20 for route A and .30 for route B.

a. Using the expected value criterion, what is the recommended route?

b. If utilities are to be assigned to the travel times, what is the appropriate lottery? Note that the smaller times should reflect higher utilities.

c. Using the lottery of part (b), assume that the decision maker expresses indifference probabilities of

$p = .80$ for 60 minutes
$p = .60$ for 70 minutes.

What route should this decision maker select? Is the decision maker a risk taker or a risk avoider?

5. Three decision makers have assessed utilities for the following decision problem.

		States of Nature		
		s_1	s_2	s_3
Decision	d_1	20	50	−20
Alternatives	d_2	80	100	−100

← Payoff in dollars

The indifference probabilities are as follows:

Payoffs	Indifference Probabilities (p)		
	Decision Maker A	Decision Maker B	Decision Maker C
100	1.00	1.00	1.00
80	.95	.70	.90
50	.90	.60	.75
20	.70	.45	.60
−20	.50	.25	.40
−100	.00	.00	.00

a. Plot the utility function for money for the three decision makers.
b. Classify each decision maker as a risk avoider, a risk taker, or risk-neutral.
c. For the payoff of 20, what is the premium the risk avoider will pay to avoid risk? What is the premium the risk taker will pay to have the opportunity of the high payoff?

6. In Problem 5, if $P(s_1) = .25$, $P(s_2) = .50$, and $P(s_3) = .25$, find a recommended decision for each of the three decision makers. Note that for the same decision problem, different utilities can lead to different decisions.

7. Suppose that the point spread for a particular sporting event is 10 points and that with this spread you are convinced you would have a .60 probability of winning a bet on your team. However, the local bookie will only accept a $1000 bet. Assuming such bets are legal, would you bet on your team? (Disregard any commission charged by the bookie.)

163

Remember *you* must pay losses out of your own pocket. Your payoff table is as follows:

			States of Nature	
			s_1 You Win	s_2 You Lose
Decision	Bet	d_1	1000	−1000
Alternatives	Don't bet	d_2	0	0

a. What decision does EMV recommend?
b. What is *your* indifference probability for the $0 payoff? (While this is not easy, be as realistic as possible. Remember, this is required if we are to do an analysis that reflects your attitude toward risk.)
c. What decision would you make based on the expected utility criterion? In this case, are you a risk taker or risk avoider?
d. Would other individuals assess the same utility values you do? Explain.
e. If your decision in part (c) was to place the bet, repeat the analysis assuming a minimum bet of $10,000.

8. A Las Vegas roulette wheel has 38 different numerical values. If an individual bets on one number and wins, the payoff is 35 to 1.
   a. Show a payoff table for a $10 bet on one number using decision alternatives of bet and do not bet.
   b. What is the EMV decision?
   c. Do the Las Vegas casinos want risk-taking or risk-avoiding customers? Explain.
   d. What range of utility values would a decision maker have to assign to the $0 payoff in order to have expected utility justify his decision to place the $10 bet?

9. A new product has the following profit projections and associated probabilities.
   a. Use the EMV criterion to make the decision of whether or not to market the new product.
   b. Because of the high dollar values involved, especially the possibil-

Profit	Probability
$150,000	.10
$100,000	.25
$ 50,000	.20
0	.15
−$ 50,000	.20
−$100,000	.10

ity of a $100,000 loss, the marketing vice president has expressed some concern about the use of the EMV criterion. As a consequence, if a utility analysis is performed, what is the appropriate lottery?

c. Assume that the following indifference probabilities are assigned:

Profit	Indifference Probability (p)
100,000	.95
50,000	.70
0	.50
−50,000	.25

Do the utilities reflect the behavior of a risk taker or a risk avoider?

d. Use the expected utility criterion to make a recommended decision.

e. Should the decision maker feel comfortable with the final decision recommended by the analysis?

10. A television network has been receiving low ratings for its programs. Currently, management is considering two alternatives for the Monday night 8:00 P.M.–9:00 P.M. time slot: a western program with a well-known star or a musical-variety program with a relatively unknown husband and wife team. The percent of viewing audience estimates depend on the degree of program acceptance. The relevant data are below.

Program Acceptance	Percent of Viewing Audience	
	Western	Musical-Variety
High	30%	40%
Moderate	25%	20%
Poor	20%	15%

The probabilities associated with program acceptance levels are as follows:

Program Acceptance	Probability	
	Western	Musical-Variety
High	.30	.30
Moderate	.60	.40
Poor	.10	.30

a. Using the expected value criterion, which program should the network choose?
b. Assuming a utility analysis is desired, what is the appropriate lottery?
c. Using the appropriate lottery in part (b), assume the network's program manager has assigned the following indifference probabilities:

Percent of Audience	Indifference Probability (p)
30%	.40
25%	.30
20%	.10

Using utility measures, which program would you recommend? Is the manager in this problem a risk taker or a risk avoider?

8

Linear Programming: The Graphical Method

Linear programming is a mathematical technique that has been developed to help managers make decisions. Let us begin our discussion by presenting some typical problems in which linear programming can be used.

1. A manufacturer wants to develop a production schedule and an inventory policy that will satisfy sales demand in future periods. Ideally the schedule and policy will enable the company to satisfy demand and at the same time *minimize* the total production and inventory costs.
2. A financial analyst must select an investment portfolio from a variety of stock and bond investment alternatives. The analyst would like to establish the portfolio that *maximizes* the return on investment.
3. A marketing manager wants to determine how he should allocate a fixed advertising budget among alternative advertising media such as radio, television, newspaper, and magazine. The manager would like to determine the media schedule that *maximizes* the advertising effectiveness.
4. A company has warehouses in a number of locations throughout the United States that are intended to serve its many markets. Given a set of customer demands for its products, the company would like to determine which warehouse should ship how much product to which customers so that the total transportation costs are *minimized*.

Although these are but a few of the possible applications where linear programming has been used successfully, the examples do point out the broad nature of the types of problems that can be tackled using linear programming. Even though the applications are diverse, a close scrutiny of the examples points out one basic property that all these problems have in common. That is, in each example problem we were concerned with *maximizing* or *minimizing* some quantity. In example 1 we wanted to minimize costs; in example 2 we wanted to maximize return on investment; in example 3 we wanted to maximize total advertising effectiveness; and in example 4 we wanted to minimize total transportation costs. In linear programming terminology the maximization or minimization of a quantity is referred to as the *objective* of the problem. Thus the objective of all linear programs is to maximize or minimize some quantity.

A second property common to all linear programming problems is that there are restrictions or *constraints* that limit the degree to which we can pursue our objective. In example 1 the manufacturer is restricted in terms of how far he can reduce costs by the constraints that guarantee that product demand be satisfied and by the constraints that indicate that production capacities are limited. The financial analyst's portfolio problem is constrained by the total amount of investment funds available and the maximum amounts that can be invested in each stock or bond. The marketing manager's media selection decision is constrained by a fixed advertising budget and the availability of the various media. In the transportation problem the minimum cost shipping schedule is constrained by the supply of product available at each warehouse. Thus constraints are another general feature of every linear programming problem.

Although we have yet to define linear programming in a formal manner, we have nonetheless been able to talk about some typical problems where linear programming has been applied, and as a result we have been able to recognize two properties that are common to all linear programs: the objective and the constraints. In the following discussion we will illustrate how linear programming can be used to solve problems of the above nature. In the process, we will also arrive at a formal definition of linear programming.

8.1 A SIMPLE MAXIMIZATION PROBLEM

Let us consider the problem currently being analyzed by the management of Par, Inc., a small manufacturer of golf equipment and supplies. Par has been convinced by its distributor that there is an existing market for both a medium- and a high-priced golf bag. In fact, the distributor is so confident of the market that if Par can make the bags at a competitive price, the distributor has agreed to purchase everything Par can manufacture over the next 3 months.

After a thorough investigation of the steps involved in manufacturing a golf bag, Par has determined that each golf bag produced will require the following operations:

1. Cutting and dyeing of material
2. Sewing
3. Finishing (such as inserting umbrella holder, club separators, etc.)
4. Inspection and packaging.

The head of manufacturing has analyzed each of the operations and has concluded that if the company produces a medium priced standard model, each bag produced will require $\frac{7}{10}$ hour in the cutting and dyeing department,

TABLE 8.1 Production Operations and Production Requirements per Bag

| | Production Time (hours) | | | |
Product	Cutting and Dyeing	Sewing	Finishing	Inspection and Packaging
Standard bag	$\frac{7}{10}$	$\frac{1}{2}$	1	$\frac{1}{10}$
Deluxe bag	1	$\frac{5}{6}$	$\frac{2}{3}$	$\frac{1}{4}$

$\frac{1}{2}$ hour in the sewing department, 1 hour in the finishing department, and $\frac{1}{10}$ hour in the inspection and packaging department. Similarly, the more expensive deluxe model will require 1 hour of cutting and dyeing time, $\frac{5}{6}$ hour of sewing time, $\frac{2}{3}$ hour of finishing time, and $\frac{1}{4}$ hour of inspection and packaging time. This production information is summarized in Table 8.1.

The accounting department has analyzed these production figures, assigned all relevant variable costs, and has arrived at prices for both bags that will result in a profit of $10 for every standard bag and $9 for every deluxe bag produced.

In addition, the head of manufacturing has studied his work load for the next 3 months and estimates that he should have available a maximum of 630 hours of cutting and dyeing time, 600 hours of sewing time, 708 hours of finishing time, and 135 hours of inspection and packaging time. Par's problem then is to determine how many standard and how many deluxe bags should be produced in order to *maximize* profit. If you were in charge of production scheduling for Par, Inc., what decision would you make, given the above information? That is, how many standard and how many deluxe bags would you produce in the next 3 months? Write your decision in the spaces below. Later you can check and see how good your decision was.

| Number of Standard Bags | Number of Deluxe Bags | Total Profit |

8.2 THE OBJECTIVE FUNCTION

As we pointed out earlier, every linear programming problem has a specific objective. For the Par, Inc., problem, the objective is to maximize profit.

We can write this objective in a more specific form with the introduction of some simple notation. Let

x_1 = the number of standard bags Par, Inc., produces

x_2 = the number of deluxe bags Par, Inc., produces.

Then Par's profit will be made up of two parts, (1) the profit made by producing x_1 standard bags and (2) the profit made by producing x_2 deluxe bags. Since Par makes $10 for every standard bag produced, the company will make 10x_1$ if x_1 standard bags are produced. Also, since Par makes $9 for every deluxe bag produced, the company will make 9x_2$ if x_2 deluxe bags are produced. If we denote the total profit with the symbol z, then in terms of our notation

$$\text{total profit} = z = \$10x_1 + \$9x_2.$$

From now on we will just assume that the profit is measured in dollars, and will write our expression for total profit without the dollar signs. That is,

$$\text{total profit} = z = 10x_1 + 9x_2. \tag{8.1}$$

The solution to Par's problem, then, is to make the *decision* that will maximize total profit. That is, Par, Inc., must determine the values of the variables x_1 and x_2 that will yield the highest possible value of z. In linear programming terminology we refer to x_1 and x_2 as the *decision variables*. Since the objective—maximize total profit—is a *function* of these decision variables, we refer to $10x_1 + 9x_2$ as the *objective function*. Thus in linear programming terminology we say that Par's goal or objective is to maximize the value of its objective function. Using max as an abbreviation for maximize, we can now write our objective as follows:

$$\max z = \max 10x_1 + 9x_2. \tag{8.2}$$

Suppose Par decided to make 400 standard bags and 200 deluxe bags. What would the profit be for this particular production combination? In terms of our decision variables x_1 and x_2, this production combination would mean that

$$x_1 = 400 \quad \text{and} \quad x_2 = 200.$$

The corresponding profit would be

$$
\begin{aligned}
z &= 10(400) + 9(200) \\
&= 4000 + 1800 \\
&= 5800.
\end{aligned}
$$

What if Par decided upon a different production combination such as producing 800 standard bags and no deluxe bags? In this case Par's profit would be

$$z = 10(800) + 9(0)$$
$$= 8000.$$

Certainly the latter production combination is better for Par, Inc., in terms of the stated objective of maximizing profit. However, it may not be possible for Par, Inc., to manufacture 800 standard bags and no deluxe bags. Let us look at the number of hours that will be required for each of the four operations if we consider this particular production combination. Using the data in Table 8.1 you can see that this particular product combination would require 560 hours of cutting and dyeing time, 400 hours of sewing time, 800 hours of finishing time, and 80 hours of inspection and packaging time. Can Par, Inc., produce 800 standard bags? The answer is ''no'' because one department—the finishing department—does not have a sufficient number of hours available. Thus, because of the constraints on the number of hours available, Par, Inc., is not able to consider 800 standard bags and no deluxe bags as an acceptable production alternative. In fact, Par, Inc., can consider only the production alternatives that have total hour requirements less than or equal to the maximum hours available for each of the four operations.

In the Par, Inc., problem any particular production combination of standard and deluxe bags is referred to as a *solution* to the problem. However, only those solutions which satisfy *all* the constraints of the problem are referred to as *feasible solutions*. The particular feasible production combination or feasible solution that results in the largest profit will be referred to as the *optimal* production combination or, equivalently, the *optimal solution* to the problem. At this point, however, we have no idea what the optimal solution will be because we have not developed a procedure for identifying feasible solutions. The procedure for determining the feasible solutions requires us to first identify all the constraints of the problem.

8.3 THE CONSTRAINTS

We know that every bag has to go through four manufacturing operations. Since there is a limited amount of production time available for each of these operations, we can expect four restrictions or constraints that will limit the total number of golf bags Par can produce. Hence the next step in our linear programming approach to this problem will be to specify clearly all the constraints associated with the problem.

Cutting and Dyeing Capacity Constraint

From our production information (see Table 8.1) we know that every standard bag Par manufactures will use $\frac{7}{10}$ hour of cutting and dyeing time. Hence the total number of hours of cutting and dyeing time used in the manufacture of x_1 standard bags will be $\frac{7}{10}x_1$. On the other hand, every deluxe bag Par produces will use 1 hour of cutting and dyeing time, so x_2 deluxe bags will use $1x_2$ hours of cutting and dyeing time. Thus the total cutting and dyeing time required for the production of x_1 standard bags and x_2 deluxe bags is given by

$$\text{total cutting and dyeing time required} = \tfrac{7}{10}x_1 + 1x_2.$$

Since the head of manufacturing has stated that Par has at most 630 hours of cutting and dyeing time available, it follows that the product combination we select must satisfy the requirement

$$\tfrac{7}{10}x_1 + 1x_2 \leq 630. \tag{8.3}$$

Sewing Capacity Constraint

We know that every standard bag manufactured will require $\frac{1}{2}$ hour of sewing time and every deluxe bag manufactured will require $\frac{5}{6}$ hour of sewing time. Since there are 600 hours of sewing time available, it follows that

$$\tfrac{1}{2}x_1 + \tfrac{5}{6}x_2 \leq 600. \tag{8.4}$$

Finishing Capacity Constraint

Every standard bag produced will require 1 hour of finishing time, and every deluxe bag produced will require $\frac{2}{3}$ hour of finishing time. Since there are 708 hours of finishing time available, we may represent this constraint mathematically as

$$1x_1 + \tfrac{2}{3}x_2 \leq 708. \tag{8.5}$$

Inspection and Packaging Constraint

For the inspection and packaging operation we have 135 hours of time available. Since every standard bag requires $\frac{1}{10}$ hour and every deluxe bag requires $\frac{1}{4}$ hour, we must require that

$$\tfrac{1}{10}x_1 + \tfrac{1}{4}x_2 \leq 135. \tag{8.6}$$

We now have specified the mathematical relationships for the constraints associated with our four production operations. Are there any other constraints we may have forgotten? Can Par, Inc., produce a negative number of standard or deluxe bags? Clearly, the answer is "no!" Thus in order to

172

prevent our decision variables x_1 and x_2 from having negative values, we must add two additional constraints

$$x_1 \geq 0 \quad \text{and} \quad x_2 \geq 0. \tag{8.7}$$

These constraints ensure that the solution to our problem will contain non-negative values and are thus referred to as the *nonnegativity constraints*. These nonnegativity constraints, which require *all* decision variables to be greater than or equal to zero, are a general feature of all linear programming problems and will be written in the following abbreviated form:

$$x_1, x_2 \geq 0.$$

8.4 THE MATHEMATICAL STATEMENT OF THE PAR, INC., PROBLEM

The mathematical statement or mathematical formulation of our Par, Inc., problem is now complete. We have succeeded in translating the objective and constraints of the "real-world" problem into a set of mathematical relationships which we refer to as a *mathematical model*. We can now write the complete mathematical model for the Par, Inc., problem as follows:

$$\max \quad 10x_1 + 9x_2$$

subject to (s.t.)

$\frac{7}{10}x_1 + 1x_2 \leq 630$	cutting and dyeing
$\frac{1}{2}x_1 + \frac{5}{6}x_2 \leq 600$	sewing
$1x_1 + \frac{2}{3}x_2 \leq 708$	finishing
$\frac{1}{10}x_1 + \frac{1}{4}x_2 \leq 135$	inspection and packaging
$x_1, x_2 \geq 0.$	

Our job now is to find that product mix (that is, the combination of x_1 and x_2) which satisfies all the constraints and, at the same time, yields a value for the objective function that is greater than or equal to the value given by any other feasible solution. Once we have done this, we will have found the optimal solution to our problem.

The above mathematical model of the Par, Inc., problem is what is known as a *linear program*. You can see that the problem has the objective and constraints that we said earlier were common properties of all linear programs. But what is the special feature of this mathematical model that makes us want to call it a *linear* program? The special feature of this model that makes it a linear program is that the objective function is a linear function of the decision variables, and the constraint functions (the left-hand sides of the constraint inequalities) are also linear functions of the decision variables.

Mathematically speaking, we refer to functions where each of the variables appears in a separate term and is raised to the first power as *linear functions.* Our objective function $(10x_1 + 9x_2)$ is linear since each decision variable appears in a separate term and has an exponent of one. If the objective function had appeared as $(10x_1{}^2 + 9\sqrt{x_2})$ it would not have been a linear function, and we would not have had a linear program. The amount of production time required in the cutting and dyeing department $(\frac{7}{10}x_1 + 1x_2)$ is also a linear function of the decision variables for the same reasons. Similarly, the functions on the left-hand side of all the constraining inequalities (the constraint functions) are linear functions. Thus we see that our mathematical formulation of the Par, Inc., problem is indeed a linear program.

8.5 THE GRAPHICAL SOLUTION APPROACH

An easy way to solve a simple linear programming problem that contains only two decision variables is the graphical solution procedure. Although the graphical method is awkward in solving three-variable problems and cannot be used for larger problems, the insight gained from studying this method will be invaluable as an aid to understanding some of the more advanced concepts to be discussed later in the book. In addition, the graphical method provides an intuitive basis for more practical solution methods such as the Simplex method which we will discuss in Chapter 9.

Let us begin our graphical solution procedure by developing a graph that can be used to display the possible solutions (x_1 and x_2 values) for the Par, Inc., problem. On our graph (Figure 8.1) the values of x_1 will be shown on the horizontal axis, and the values of x_2 will be shown on the vertical axis. Any point on the graph can be identified by the x_1 and x_2 values which indicate the position of the point along the x_1 and x_2 axes, respectively. Since every point (x_1, x_2) corresponds to a possible solution, every point on our graph is called a *solution point*. The solution point where $x_1 = 0$ and $x_2 = 0$ is referred to as the origin of the graph.

Our next step will be to show graphically which of the possible combinations of x_1 and x_2, that is, solution points, correspond to feasible solutions to our linear program. Since in our linear programming problem both x_1 and x_2 must be nonnegative, we need only consider points where $x_1 \geq 0$ and $x_2 \geq 0$. This is indicated in Figure 8.2 by arrows pointing in the direction of production combinations that will satisfy the nonnegativity relationships in the problem. In all future graphs we will assume that the nonnegativity relationships hold, and hence we will only draw the portion of the graph corresponding to nonnegative x_1 and x_2 values.

Earlier we saw that the inequality representing the cutting and dyeing constraint was of the form

$$\tfrac{7}{10}x_1 + 1x_2 \leq 630.$$

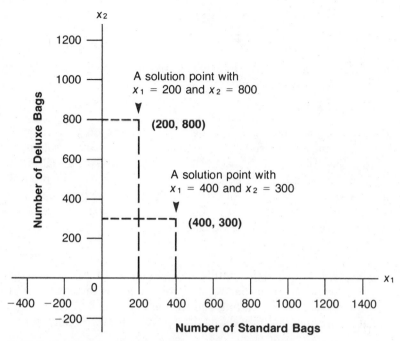

FIGURE 8.1   Graph of Solution Points for the Two-Variable Par, Inc., Problem

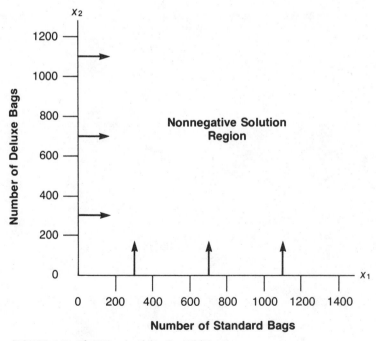

FIGURE 8.2   The Nonnegativity Constraints

To show all solution points that satisfy this relationship, we start by graphing the line corresponding to the equation

$$\tfrac{7}{10}x_1 + 1x_2 = 630.$$

The graph of this equation is found by identifying two points that lie on the line and then drawing a line through the points. Setting $x_1 = 0$ and solving for x_2 we see that the point $(x_1 = 0, x_2 = 630)$ satisfies the above equation. To find a second point satisfying this equation we set $x_2 = 0$ and solve for x_1. By doing this we get $\tfrac{7}{10}x_1 + 1(0) = 630$, or $x_1 = 900$. Thus a second point satisfying the equation is $(x_1 = 900, x_2 = 0)$. Given these two points we may now graph the line corresponding to the equation

$$\tfrac{7}{10}x_1 + 1x_2 = 630.$$

This line, which will be called the cutting and dyeing *constraint line,* is shown in Figure 8.3. For purposes of identification we label this line "C & D" to indicate that it represents the cutting and dyeing constraint.

Recall that the inequality representing the cutting and dyeing constraint is

$$\tfrac{7}{10}x_1 + 1x_2 \leq 630.$$

Can you identify all of the solution points that satisfy this constraint? Well, since we have the line where $\tfrac{7}{10}x_1 + 1x_2 = 630$, we know any point on this

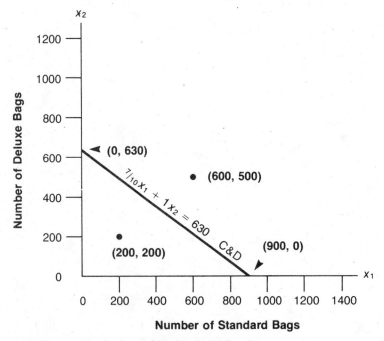

FIGURE 8.3 *The Cutting and Dyeing Constraint Line*

line must satisfy the constraint. But where are the solution points satisfying $\frac{7}{10}x_1 + 1x_2 < 630$? Let us consider two solution points ($x_1 = 200, x_2 = 200$) and ($x_1 = 600, x_2 = 500$). You can see from Figure 8.3 that the first solution point is below the constraint line and the second is above the constraint line. Which of these solutions will satisfy the cutting and dyeing constraint? For the point ($x_1 = 200, x_2 = 200$) we see that

$$\tfrac{7}{10}x_1 + 1x_2 = \tfrac{7}{10}(200) + 1(200) = 340.$$

Since the 340 hours is less than the 630 hours available, the $x_1 = 200$, $x_2 = 200$ production combination, or solution point, satisfies the constraint. For $x_1 = 600, x_2 = 500$ we have

$$\tfrac{7}{10}x_1 + 1x_2 = \tfrac{7}{10}(600) + 1(500) = 920.$$

Since the 920 hours is greater than the 630 hours available, the $x_1 = 600$, $x_2 = 500$ solution point does not satisfy the constraint and is thus an unacceptable production alternative.

Are you ready to answer the question of where are the solution points that satisfy the cutting and dyeing constraint? Your answer should be that any point *below* the cutting and dyeing constraint line satisfies the constraint. You may want to prove this to yourself by selecting additional solution points above and below the constraint line and checking to see if the solutions satisfy the constraints. You will see that for the $\leq$ constraints only solution points on or below the constraint line satisfy the constraint. In Figure 8.4 we indicate all such points by shading the region of the graph corresponding to the solution points that satisfy the cutting and dyeing constraint.

Next let us identify all solution points that satisfy the sewing constraint

$$\tfrac{1}{2}x_1 + \tfrac{5}{6}x_2 \leq 600.$$

We start by drawing the constraint line corresponding to the equation

$$\tfrac{1}{2}x_1 + \tfrac{5}{6}x_2 = 600.$$

As before, the graphing of a line is most easily done by finding two points on the line and then connecting them. Thus we first set x_1 equal to zero and solve for x_2, which yields the point ($x_1 = 0, x_2 = 720$). Next we set x_2 equal to zero and solve for x_1, which gives the second point ($x_1 = 1200, x_2 = 0$). In Figure 8.5 we have drawn the line corresponding to the sewing constraint. For identification purposes, we label this line "S." Using the same approach as for the cutting and dyeing constraint, we realize that only points on or below the line will satisfy the sewing time constraint. Thus in Figure 8.5 we have shaded the region corresponding to all feasible production combinations or feasible solution points for the sewing operation.

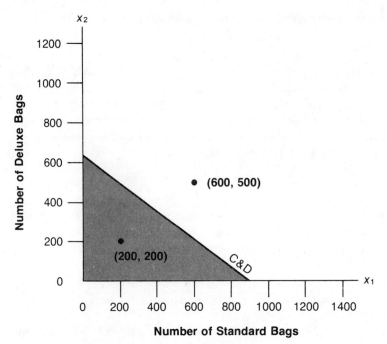

FIGURE 8.4 *Feasible Region for the Cutting and*
Dyeing Constraint

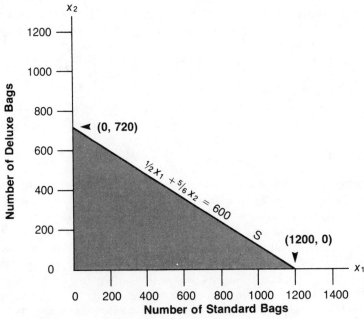

FIGURE 8.5 *Feasible Region for the Sewing Constraint*

178

In a similar manner, we can determine the set of all feasible production combinations for each of the remaining constraints. The results are shown in Figures 8.6 and 8.7. For practice, try to graph the feasible solution region for the finishing (F) constraint and the inspection and packaging (I & P) constraint and see if your results agree with those shown in Figures 8.6 and 8.7.

We now have four separate graphs showing the feasible solution points for each of the four constraints. In a linear programming problem we need to identify the solution points that satisfy *all* the constraints *simultaneously*. To find these solution points, we can draw our four constraints on one graph and observe the region containing the points that do in fact satisfy all the constraints.

The graphs in Figures 8.4 to 8.7 can be superimposed to obtain one graph with all four constraints. This combined-constraint graph is shown in Figure 8.8. The shaded region in this figure includes every solution point that satisfies all the constraints. Since solutions that satisfy all the constraints are termed *feasible solutions*, the shaded region is called the feasible solution region, or simply the *feasible region*. Any point on the boundary of the feasible region or within the feasible region is a *feasible solution point*. You may want to check points outside the feasible region to prove to yourself that these solution points violate one or more of the constraints and are thus infeasible or unacceptable.

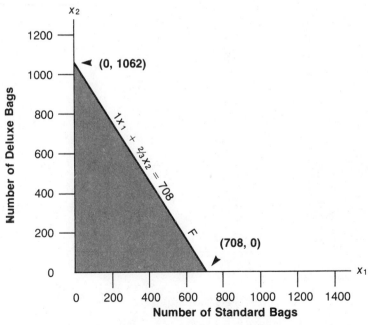

FIGURE 8.6   *Feasible Region for the Finishing Constraint*

179

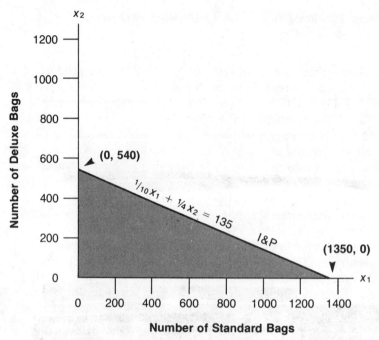

FIGURE 8.7 *Feasible Region for the Inspection and Packaging Constraint*

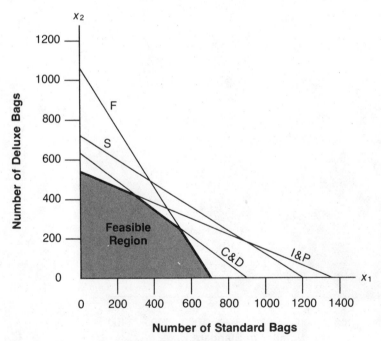

FIGURE 8.8 *Feasible Solution Region for the Par, Inc., Problem*

180

Now that we have identified the feasible region we are ready to proceed with the graphical solution method and find the optimal solution to the Par, Inc., problem. Recall that the optimal solution for any linear programming problem is the feasible solution that provides the best possible value of the objective function. We could arbitrarily select feasible solution points (x_1, x_2) and compute the associated profit $10x_1 + 9x_2$. However, the difficulty with this approach is that there are too many feasible solutions (actually an infinite number), and thus it would not be possible to evaluate all feasible solutions. Hence this trial-and-error procedure would not guarantee that the optimal solution could be obtained. Thus we would like a systematic way of identifying the feasible solution that does in fact maximize the profit for Par, Inc.

Let us start this final step of our graphical solution procedure by drawing the feasible region on a separate graph. This is shown in Figure 8.9.

Rather than selecting an arbitrary feasible solution and computing the associated profit, let us select an arbitrary profit and identify all of the feasible solution points (x_1, x_2) that yield the selected profit. For example, what

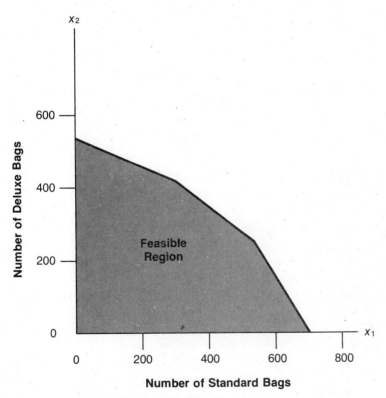

FIGURE 8.9 *Feasible Solution Region for the Par, Inc., Problem*

181

feasible solution points provide a profit of $1800? That is, we are asking what values of x_1 and x_2 in the feasible region will make the objective function

$$10x_1 + 9x_2 = 1800.$$

The above expression is simply the equation of a line. Thus all feasible solution points (x_1, x_2) yielding a profit of $1800 must be on the line. We learned earlier in this section how to graph a constraint line. The procedure for graphing our profit or objective function line is the same. Letting $x_1 = 0$, we see that x_2 must be 200 and thus the solution point ($x_1 = 0, x_2 = 200$) is on the line. Similarly, by letting $x_2 = 0$ we see that the solution point ($x_1 = 180$, $x_2 = 0$) is also on the line. Drawing the line through these two solution points will identify all the solution points that have a profit of $1800. A graph of this profit line is presented in Figure 8.10.

Since our objective is one of finding the feasible solution point that has the highest profit, let us proceed by selecting higher profit values and finding the feasible solution points that yield the stated profits. For example, what solution points provide a $3600 profit? What solution points provide a $5400

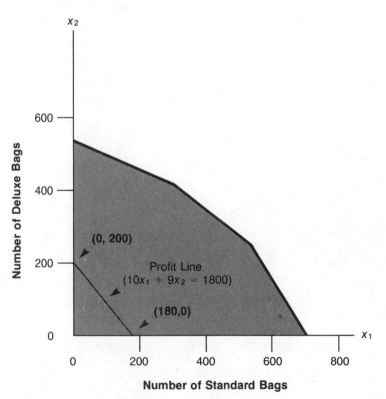

FIGURE 8.10 $1800 Profit Line for the Par, Inc., Problem

profit? To answer these questions we must find the x_1 and x_2 values that are on the following lines:

$$10x_1 + 9x_2 = 3600$$

and

$$10x_1 + 9x_2 = 5400.$$

Using our previous procedure for graphing profit and constraint lines, we have drawn the $3600 and $5400 profit lines on the graph in Figure 8.11. While not all solution points on the $5400 profit line are in the feasible region, at least some points on the line are, and thus we can obtain a feasible production combination that provides a $5400 profit.

Can we find a solution yielding even higher profits? Look at Figure 8.11 and see what general observations you can make about the profit lines. You should be able to identify the following properties: (1) the profit lines are *parallel* to each other, and (2) higher profit lines occur as we move farther from the origin.

These properties, which hold for all two-decision-variable linear pro-

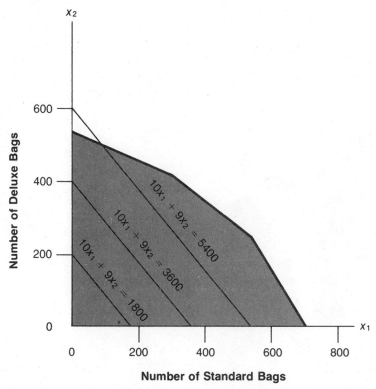

FIGURE 8.11   Selected Profit Lines for the Par, Inc., Problem

grams, can now be used to determine the optimal solution to our problem. We know that if we continue to move our profit line farther from the origin so that it remains parallel to the other profit lines, we can obtain solution points that yield higher and higher values for the objective function. However, at some point we will find that any further outward movement will place the profit line outside the feasible region. Since points outside the feasible region are unacceptable, the point in the feasible region which lies on the highest profit line is the optimal solution to our linear program.

You should now be able to identify the optimal solution point for the Par, Inc., problem. Use a ruler or a straight piece of paper and move the profit line as far from the origin as you can. What is the last point in the feasible region that you reach? This point, which is the optimal solution, is shown graphically in Figure 8.12

The optimal values of the decision variables x_1 and x_2 are the x_1 and x_2 values at the optimal solution point. Depending upon the accuracy of your graph, you may or may not be able to read the *exact* x_1 and x_2 values from the graph. The best we can do with respect to the optimal solution point in Figure 8.12 is to conclude that the optimal production combination consists

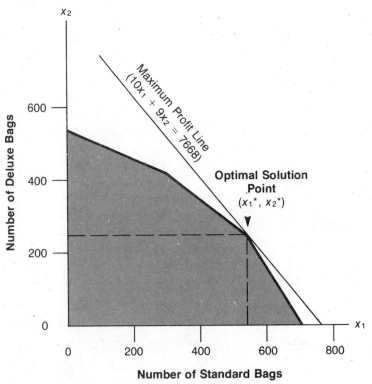

FIGURE 8.12   *Optimal Solution Point for the*
Par, Inc., Problem

184

of approximately 550 standard bags (x_1) and 250 deluxe bags (x_2). As you will see later, the actual x_1 and x_2 values at the optimal solution point are $x_1 = 540$ and $x_2 = 252$. In Section 8.7 we will show how to compute these exact optimal solution values.

The optimal solution of 540 standard bags and 252 deluxe bags yields a profit of $10(540) + 9(252) = \$7668$. How close did you come to the actual optimal solution with your decision from Section 8.1?

In addition to the optimal solution and the expected profit, the management of Par, Inc., will probably want information about the production time requirements for each production operation. We can determine this information by substituting the optimal x_1 and x_2 values into the constraints of our linear program. For the Par, Inc., problem the production time requirements using equations (8.3) through (8.6) are as follows:

$\frac{7}{10}(540) + 1(252) = 630$ hours of cutting and dyeing time

$\frac{1}{2}(540) + \frac{5}{6}(252) = 480$ hours of sewing time

$1(540) + \frac{2}{3}(252) = 708$ hours of finishing time

$\frac{1}{10}(540) + \frac{1}{4}(252) = 117$ hours of inspection and packaging time.

We can tell management that the production of 540 standard bags and 252 deluxe bags will require all available cutting and dyeing time (630 hours) and all available finishing time (708 hours), while 120 hours of sewing time $(600 - 480)$ and 18 hours of inspection and packaging time $(135 - 117)$ remain idle.

Could we have used our graphical analysis to provide some of this production information? The answer is "yes." By finding our optimal solution point on Figure 8.8 we can see that the cutting and dyeing and the finishing constraints restrict or bind our feasible region at this point. Thus this solution point requires the use of all available time for these two operations. On the other hand, since the sewing and the inspection and packaging constraints are not restricting the feasible region at the optimal solution point, we can expect some unused time for these two operations.

As a final comment on the graphical analysis of the Par, Inc., problem, we call your attention to the sewing capacity constraint as shown in Figure 8.8. Note in particular that this constraint did not affect the feasible region. That is, the feasible region would be the same whether the sewing capacity constraint was included or not. This tells us that there is enough sewing time available to accommodate any production level that can be achieved by the other three departments. Since the sewing constraint does not affect the feasible region and thus cannot affect the optimal solution, it is called a *redundant* constraint. Redundant constraints can be dropped from the problem without having any effect upon the optimal solution.[1]

[1] We point out here that in many linear programming problems, redundant constraints are not always discarded because often these constraints are not recognizable as redundant until after the problem has been solved.

185

Summary of the Graphical Solution Procedure for Maximization Problems

As you have seen, the graphical solution procedure is one method of solving two-variable linear programming problems such as the Par, Inc., problem. The steps of the graphical solution procedure for a maximization problem are outlined below.

1. Prepare a graph of the feasible solution points for each of the constraints.
2. Determine the feasible solution region by identifying the solution points that satisfy all the constraints simultaneously.
3. Draw a profit line showing all values of the x_1 and x_2 variables that yield a specified value of the objective function.
4. Move parallel profit lines toward higher profits (usually away from the origin) until further movement would take the profit line completely outside the feasible region.
5. The feasible solution point that is touched by the highest possible profit line is the optimal solution.
6. Determine, at least approximately, the optimal values of the decision variables by reading the x_1 and x_2 values at the optimal solution point directly from the graph.

8.6 EXTREME POINTS AND THE OPTIMAL SOLUTION

Let us suppose that the profit for the Par, Inc., standard bag is reduced from $10 to $5 per bag, while the profit for the deluxe bag and all the constraint conditions remain unchanged. Our complete linear programming model of this new problem is identical to the mathematical model in Section 8.4, except for the following revised objective function:

$$\max z = \max 5x_1 + 9x_2.$$

How does this change in the objective function affect the optimal solution to our Par, Inc., problem? In Figure 8.13 we show the graphical solution of the Par, Inc., problem with the revised objective function. Note that since our constraints have not changed, the feasible solution region has also not changed. However, our profit lines have been altered to reflect the new objective function.

By moving the profit line in a parallel manner away from the origin, we found the optimal solution point shown in Figure 8.13. The exact values of the decision variables at this point are $x_1 = 300$ and $x_2 = 420$. Thus the reduced profit for the standard bags has caused us to change our optimal solution. In fact, as you may have suspected, we are cutting back the pro-

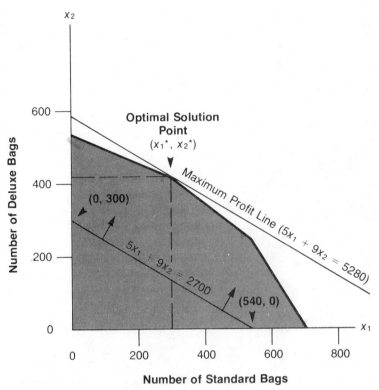

FIGURE 8.13   Optimal Solution Point for the Par, Inc., Problem with an Objective Function of $5x_1 + 9x_2$

duction of the lower profit standard bags and increasing the production of the higher profit deluxe bags.

What have you noticed about the location of the optimal solutions in the two linear programming problems that we have solved thus far? Look closely at the graphical solutions in Figures 8.12 and 8.13. An important observation that you should be able to make is that the optimal solutions occur at one of the vertices or "corners" of the feasible region. In linear programming terminology these vertices are referred to as the *extreme points* of the feasible region. Thus the Par, Inc., problem has five vertices or five extreme points for its feasible region (see Figure 8.14). We can now state our observation about the location of optimal solutions as follows:

The optimal solution to a linear programming problem occurs at an extreme point of the feasible solution region for the problem.

This is a very important property of all linear programming problems because it says that if you are looking for the optimal solution to a linear programming problem, you do not have to evaluate all feasible solution points. In fact, you *only* have to consider the feasible solutions that occur at

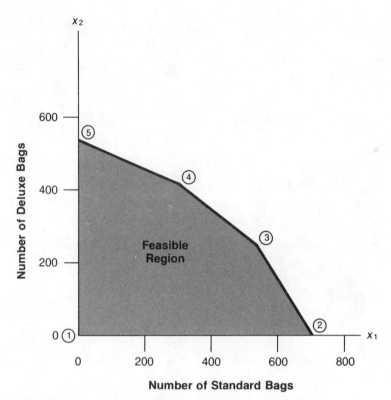

FIGURE 8.14   The Five Extreme Points of the Feasible Region for the Par, Inc., Problem

the extreme points of the feasible region. Thus for the Par, Inc., problem, instead of computing and comparing the profit for all feasible solutions, we know that we can find the optimal solution for the problem by evaluating the five extreme-point solutions and selecting the one that provides the highest profit. Actually the graphical solution procedure is nothing more than a convenient way of identifying the optimal extreme points for two-variable problems.

To help convince yourself that the optimal solution to a linear program always occurs at an extreme point, select several different objective functions for the Par, Inc., problem and graphically find the optimal solution for each case. You will see that as you move the profit lines away from the origin, the last feasible solution point—the optimal solution point—is always one of the extreme points.

What happens if the highest profit line coincides with one of the constraint lines on the boundary of the feasible region? This case is shown for a $4x_1 + 10x_2$ objective function in Figure 8.15. Does an optimal solution still occur at an extreme point? The answer is "yes." In fact, for this case the

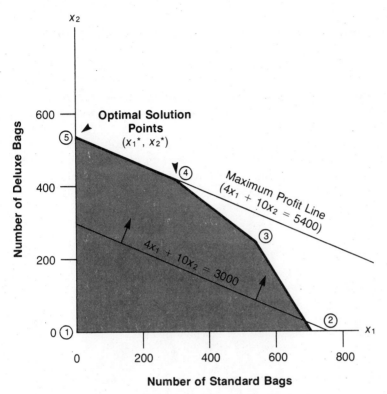

FIGURE 8.15 *Optimal Solution Points for the Par, Inc., Problem with an Objective Function of $4x_1 + 10x_2$*

optimal solution occurs at extreme point ④, extreme point ⑤, and any solution point on the line joining these two points. This is the special case of alternate optimal solutions which will be discussed in detail in Chapter 10. Here we are merely concerned with noting that if alternate optimal solutions exist, one optimal solution to the linear programming problem can still always be found by evaluating the extreme point solutions.

8.7 SIMULTANEOUS LINEAR EQUATIONS

The graphical solution method is a convenient way to find optimal extreme point solutions for two-variable linear programming problems. For problems having more than two decision variables, however, this method is unacceptable. In Chapter 9 we will introduce a general algebraic solution procedure, the Simplex method, which can be used to find optimal extreme point solutions for linear programming problems having as many as several thousand decision variables. The mathematical steps of the Simplex method are based in part upon concepts from the area of simultaneous linear equations. Thus in order to prepare you for using the Simplex method and understanding how the method identifies optimal extreme point solutions, we must briefly study simultaneous linear equations. We shall find that knowledge about simultaneous linear equations is also helpful in identifying the exact x_1 and x_2 values at the optimal extreme point in a graphical solution of a two-variable problem.

If we have a system of two or more linear equations involving the variables $x_1, x_2, x_3, \ldots$, then we say we have a system of simultaneous linear equations. For example, the following is a system of two simultaneous linear equations involving two variables:

$$2x_1 + 1x_2 = 16 \tag{8.8}$$
$$-1x_1 + \tfrac{1}{2}x_2 = 2. \tag{8.9}$$

A solution to a system of simultaneous linear equations is any combination of values for the variables $x_1, x_2, x_3, \ldots$, that satisfies all the equations at the same time. The solution to the above system of simultaneous equations is $x_1 = 3, x_2 = 10$, as you can easily verify by substituting these values into equations (8.8) and (8.9). These solution values were found by the use of elementary row operations which we will now discuss.

Elementary Row Operations

A solution to a set of simultaneous linear equations can be found by applying a sequence of the following two *elementary row operations:*

1. Multiplying a row or equation by a nonzero number, and
2. Adding one row or equation multiplied by a nonzero number to another row or equation.

These elementary row (equation) operations will change the coefficients of the variables in the linear equations. However, it is important to realize that although the coefficients of the variables may change, *the elementary row operations do not change the solution $(x_1, x_2, x_3, \ldots,)$ to the set of linear equations.* That is, while the linear equations may appear in a different form after applying the elementary row operations, the same values of the variables $(x_1, x_2, x_3, \ldots,)$ solve them. We will show how these elementary row operations can be used to obtain the solution to a set of linear equations after we have given examples of how the elementary row operations can change the coefficients of the variables in an equation.

Let us return to the two-variable simultaneous *linear equations* (8.8) and (8.9). Operation 1 states that we can multiply any row or equation by a nonzero value and the solution will not be changed. To illustrate this operation, we multiply equation (8.8) by 3 and equation (8.9) by -2. The resulting set of linear equations is

$$6x_1 + 3x_2 = 48 \qquad\qquad (8.10)$$
$$2x_1 - 1x_2 = -4. \qquad\qquad (8.11)$$

While the coefficients of the variables and the right-hand sides of the equations have changed, the solution to the equations has not. That is, $x_1 = 3$ and $x_2 = 10$ satisfy equations (8.10) and (8.11) as well as the original set of simultaneous linear equations (8.8) and (8.9).

To illustrate elementary row operation 2, let us multiply equation (8.9) by -4 and add the resulting equation to equation (8.8):

$$-4(-1x_1 + \tfrac{1}{2}x_2 = 2) \to 4x_1 - 2x_2 = -8$$

added to equation (8.8) $\qquad \underline{2x_1 + 1x_2 = 16}$

yields $\qquad\qquad\qquad\quad 6x_1 - 1x_2 = 8 \qquad\qquad (8.12)$

Leaving equation (8.9) unchanged, we have the following set of linear equations:

$$6x_1 - 1x_2 = 8 \qquad\qquad (8.12)$$
$$-1x_1 + \tfrac{1}{2}x_2 = 2. \qquad\qquad (8.9)$$

Again, you can see that $x_1 = 3$ and $x_2 = 10$ still solves the system of equations. The important feature of elementary row operations is that even though they change the coefficients of the linear equations, the solution to the resulting system is the same as the solution to the original system.

Solving a Set of Linear Equations by Elementary Row Operations

We now show how elementary row operations can be used to put the linear equations in a form that will allow us to easily determine the solution. Consider again the simultaneous linear equations

$$2x_1 + 1x_2 = 16 \qquad\qquad (8.8)$$
$$-1x_1 + \tfrac{1}{2}x_2 = 2. \qquad\qquad (8.9)$$

We know that the elementary row operations can be used to change the coefficients of the variables without changing the value of the solution. Therefore suppose we could convert the left-hand side of equation (8.8) into the form

$$1x_1 + 0x_2$$

and the left-hand side of equation (8.9) into the form

$$0x_1 + 1x_2$$

by performing row operations.

The solution to the set of linear equations could be easily determined because the right-hand side value of the first equation would be the value of x_1 and the right-hand side value of the second equation would be the value of x_2. Let us see what elementary row operations must be performed in order to put our linear equations in the above form.

Multiplying equation (8.8) by $\frac{1}{2}$ yields

$$1x_1 + \tfrac{1}{2}x_2 = 8. \tag{8.13}$$

Adding 1 times this equation to equation (8.9) we have

$$0x_1 + 1x_2 = 10. \tag{8.14}$$

This is the exact form we want for the second equation. To get our first equation in the desired form we can multiply equation (8.14) by $-\frac{1}{2}$ and add the resulting equation to equation (8.13). Thus we obtain

$$1x_1 + 0x_2 = 3. \tag{8.15}$$

Equations (8.14) and (8.15) are now in the form that easily provides the solution $x_1 = 3$ and $x_2 = 10$.

Thus elementary row operations can be used to change the coefficients of the variables so that the solution can be easily obtained. The exact sequence of elementary row operations is up to you. A variety of sequences can be used to obtain the solution for the equations.

Finding the Exact Location of Graphical Solution Extreme Points

Let us consider extreme point ③ of the Par, Inc., problem as shown in Figure 8.16. In our graphical solution procedure of Section 8.5 we identified extreme point ③ as the optimal solution to the original Par, Inc., problem. However, we had difficulty reading the exact values of x_1 and x_2 at extreme point ③ directly from the graph. Actually, the best we could do was to arrive at approximate values for the decision variables.

Referring to Figure 8.16, can you see a way to find the values of x_1 and x_2 at extreme point ③ without having to read the values directly from the graph? What constraint lines determine the exact location of extreme point ③? You should be able to see that the cutting and dyeing constraint line and the finishing constraint line combine to determine this extreme point. That is, extreme point ③ is on both the cutting and dyeing constraint line

$$\tfrac{7}{10}x_1 + 1x_2 = 630 \tag{8.16}$$

and the finishing constraint line

$$1x_1 + \tfrac{2}{3}x_2 = 708. \tag{8.17}$$

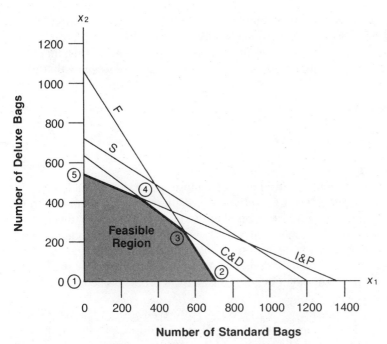

FIGURE 8.16   *Feasible solution region for the Par, Inc., problem*

Thus the values of the decision variables x_1 and x_2 at extreme point ③ must satisfy the simultaneous linear equations given by equation (8.16) and (8.17).

We can use our elementary row operations on equations (8.16) and (8.17) in order to find the solution. Multiplying equation (8.16) by $\frac{10}{7}$ yields

$$1x_1 + \tfrac{10}{7} x_2 = 900. \tag{8.18}$$

Multiplying equation (8.18) by -1 and adding the result to equation (8.17) gives

$$0x_1 - \tfrac{16}{21}x_2 = -192. \tag{8.19}$$

Multiplying equation (8.19) by $-\frac{21}{16}$ gives the following desired equation form:

$$0x_1 + 1x_2 = 252. \tag{8.20}$$

Multiplying equation (8.21) by $-\frac{10}{7}$ and adding the result to equation (8.18) provides the other desired equation form:

$$1x_1 + 0x_2 = 540. \tag{8.21}$$

You can now see that the x_1 and x_2 values at the extreme point by the cutting and dyeing constraint line and the finishing constraint line must be exactly $x_1 = 540$ and $x_2 = 252$.

We have now seen how the solution of simultaneous linear equations can enable us to find exact extreme point solutions when the values cannot be accurately determined from the graph. Problem 8 at the end of this chapter asks you to use the simultaneous linear equation procedure to show that the exact solution at extreme point ④ is $x_1 = 300$ and $x_2 = 420$.

8.8 A SIMPLE MINIMIZATION PROBLEM

While we have been studying a maximization problem, you will see that some linear programming problems are more naturally formulated as minimization problems. For example consider the case of a manufacturer who has contracted to sell a certain number of units of his product to various buyers. He is no longer concerned with how many units to produce. His problem is one of minimizing the total cost of production subject to the constraints that he must satisfy demand. As an illustration of how this type of minimization problem might occur, consider the problem encountered by Photo Chemicals, Inc.

Photo Chemicals produces two types of picture-developing fluids. Both products cost Photo Chemicals $1 per gallon to produce. Based upon an analysis of current inventory levels and outstanding orders for the next month, Photo Chemical's management has specified that at least 30 gallons of product 1 and at least 20 gallons of product 2 must be produced during the next 2 weeks. Management has also stated that an existing inventory of highly perishable raw material required in the production of both fluids must be used within the next 2 weeks. The current inventory of the perishable raw material is 80 pounds. While more of this raw material can be ordered if necessary, any that is not used within the next 2 weeks will spoil; hence the management requirement that at least 80 pounds must be used in the next 2 weeks. Furthermore it is known that product 1 requires 1 pound of this perishable raw material per gallon produced, and product 2 requires 2 pounds of the raw material per gallon.

In summary, management is looking for a minimum cost production plan that uses at least the 80 pounds of perishable raw material currently in inventory, and provides at least 30 gallons of product 1 and 20 gallons of product 2. What is this minimum cost solution?

To answer this question, let us attempt to write the problem in the form of a linear program. Following a procedure similar to the one used for the Par, Inc. problem, we will first define the decision variables and the objective function for the problem. Let

x_1 = the number of gallons of product 1 produced
x_2 = the number of gallons of product 2 produced

Since the production costs for Photo Chemicals, Inc., are $1 for each gallon of product 1 and each gallon of product 2 produced, the objective function representing total cost is

$$1x_1 + 1x_2. \tag{8.22}$$

Using the z notation for the value of the objective function, the minimum cost objective can be written as

$$\min z = \min 1x_1 + 1x_2. \tag{8.23}$$

Next let us consider the constraints placed on the Photo Chemical, Inc., problem. For the perishable raw material constraint, we know that product 1 uses 1 pound of raw material and product 2 uses 2 pounds of raw material. Thus the total number of pounds of raw material required to produce x_1 units of product 1 and x_2 units of product 2 is

$$1x_1 + 2x_2. \tag{8.24}$$

Since we are constrained to use *at least* 80 pounds of the perishable raw material, the complete raw material constraint becomes

$$1x_1 + 2x_2 \geq 80. \tag{8.25}$$

Introducing the constraints of at least 30 gallons of product 1 ($x_1 \geq 30$), at least 20 gallons of product 2 ($x_2 \geq 20$), and the nonnegativity constraints (x_1, $x_2 \geq 0$), we have the following linear programming formulation of our problem:

$$
\begin{aligned}
\min \quad & 1x_1 + 1x_2 \\
\text{s.t.} \quad & \\
& 1x_1 + 2x_2 \geq 80 \quad \text{raw material} \\
& 1x_1 \geq 30 \quad \text{product 1} \\
& \phantom{1x_1 +{}} 1x_2 \geq 20 \quad \text{product 2} \\
& x_1, x_2 \geq 0.
\end{aligned}
$$

Since the Photo Chemicals, Inc. problem has only two decision variables, we can use the graphical solution procedure to find the optimal production quantities or optimal decisions. The graphical method for this problem, just as in the Par, Inc. problem, requires us first to graph all constraint lines and then to find the feasible solution points for the constraints. Note that in the Photo Chemicals, Inc. problem the greater-than-or-equal-to constraints will cause the feasible solution points to be above the constraint lines. The constraint lines and the feasible region are shown in Figure 8.17.

In order to determine the minimum value of our cost ($1x_1 + 1x_2$), we begin by drawing the cost line corresponding to a particular value of cost, $z = 1x_1 + 1x_2$. For example, we might start by drawing the line $1x_1 + 1x_2 = 80$. In Figure 8.18 we show the equation of this line. Clearly,

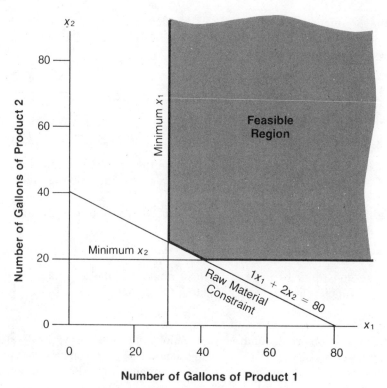

FIGURE 8.17 Set of feasible solutions for the Photo Chemicals, Inc., problem.

there are many points in the feasible region yielding this cost value (for example, $x_1 = x_2 = 40$).

To find the values of x_1 and x_2 which yield the minimum cost solution we move our cost line in a lower left direction until, if we moved it any further, it would be entirely outside the feasible region. We see that the line $1x_1 + 1x_2 = 55$ intersects the feasible region at the point ($x_1 = 30, x_2 = 25$). Thus the optimal solution to our problem is $x_1 = 30, x_2 = 25$, with a corresponding objective function value of 55. Also in Figure 8.18 we see that the raw material constraint and the minimum x_1 constraint are binding and that, just as in the Par, Inc., maximization problem, the optimal solution occurs at an extreme point of the feasible region.

Note that in the Par, Inc., maximization problem all the constraints were of the $\leq$ type and in the Photo Chemicals, Inc., minimization problem all the constraints were of the $\geq$ type. Although this pattern of constraints may occur in other linear programming problems, we caution you *not* to expect maximization problems to have only $\leq$ constraints and minimization problems to have only $\geq$ constraints. In fact, linear programming problems that

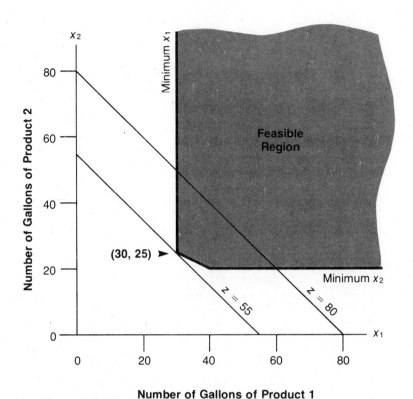

FIGURE 8.18 Graphical solution for the Photo Chemicals, Inc., problem.

are either maximization or minimization may have some $\leq$ constraints, some $\geq$ constraints, and some equality ($=$) constraints. The equality constraints mean that the optimal solution must satisfy the constraint conditions exactly as defined by the constraint lines.

An example of a linear program with each of the three constraint types is as follows:

min $\quad 2x_1 + 2x_2$

s.t.

$$1x_1 + 3x_2 \leq 12$$
$$3x_1 + 1x_2 \geq 13$$
$$1x_1 - 1x_2 = 3$$
$$x_1, x_2 \geq 0.$$

Problem 20 at the end of the chapter will ask you to solve the above linear program using the graphical solution procedure.

Summary of the Graphical Solution Procedure for Minimization Problems

The steps of the graphical solution procedure for a minimization problem are outlined below:

1. Prepare a graph of the feasible solution points for each of the constraints.
2. Determine the feasible solution region by identifying the solution points that satisfy all the constraints simultaneously.
3. Draw a cost line showing all values of the x_1 and x_2 variables that yield a specified value of the objective function.
4. Move parallel cost lines toward lower costs (usually toward the origin) until further movement would take the cost line completely outside the feasible region.
5. The feasible extreme point that is touched by the lowest possible cost line is the optimal solution.
6. Determine, at least approximately, the optimal values of the decision variables by reading the x_1 and x_2 values at the optimal solution point directly from the graph.

8.9 STANDARD FORM

We stated in Section 8.7 that the algebraic solution to linear programming problems will involve solving simultaneous linear equations. In fact, we will have one linear equation for each constraint in the linear programming problem. Since linear programming problems almost always contain some constraints with inequality relationships, that is $\leq$ and $\geq$ relationships, we will need a standard procedure for converting each inequality constraint to a linear equation or equality (=) form. When all the constraints of a linear programming problem have been written as equality relationships, we say the problem has been written in its *Standard* form. You will see later that we will convert every linear programming problem to its Standard form before beginning the Simplex solution method.

Let us return to the original Par, Inc., problem and see how we can write this problem in its Standard form. The linear programming model of the Par, Inc., problem is

$$\max \quad 10x_1 + 9x_2$$

s.t.

$$\tfrac{7}{10}x_1 + 1x_2 \leq 630$$
$$\tfrac{1}{2}x_1 + \tfrac{5}{6}x_2 \leq 600$$
$$1x_1 + \tfrac{2}{3}x_2 \leq 708$$
$$\tfrac{1}{10}x_1 + \tfrac{1}{4}x_2 \leq 135$$
$$x_1, x_2 \geq 0.$$

In order to transform the above formulation into its Standard form, we must write the constraints corresponding to the four production operations as equalities. Let us begin with the first constraint

$$\tfrac{7}{10}x_1 + 1x_2 \leq 630.$$

To make this constraint an equality, we must add something to the left-hand side to make up for the difference between 630 and ($\tfrac{7}{10}x_1 + 1x_2$). Since the left-hand side of the constraint varies depending on the values of x_1 and x_2, the amount we add to the left-hand side must be a variable. We refer to a variable that is added to the left-hand side of any less-than-or-equal-to constraint to create an equality as a *slack variable*. Thus by adding a slack variable (s_1) to the left-hand side, the first constraint can be written as the following equation:

$$\tfrac{7}{10}x_1 + 1x_2 + 1s_1 = 630.$$

If a particular production combination specifies $x_1 = 100$ and $x_2 = 100$, then

$$\tfrac{7}{10}(100) + 1(100) + 1s_1 = 630$$

or

$$s_1 = 460.$$

If $x_1 = 500$ and $x_2 = 200$, then

$$\tfrac{7}{10}(500) + 1(200) + 1s_1 = 630$$

or

$$s_1 = 80.$$

The physical interpretation of the value of slack variable s_1 is that s_1 indicates the remaining cutting and dyeing production time available after producing x_1 units of the standard bag and x_2 units of the deluxe bag.

Using s_2 as the slack variable for the sewing constraint, s_3 for the finishing constraint, and s_4 for the inspection and packaging constraint, the remaining three constraints can be written as the following three linear equations:

$$\tfrac{1}{2}x_1 + \tfrac{5}{6}x_2 + 1s_2 \qquad\qquad = 600$$
$$1x_1 + \tfrac{2}{3}x_2 \qquad + 1s_3 \qquad = 708$$
$$\tfrac{1}{10}x_1 + \tfrac{1}{4}x_2 \qquad\qquad + 1s_4 = 135.$$

In each case the value of the slack variable indicates the excess production time for the corresponding operation after x_1 standard bags and x_2 deluxe bags have been produced.

Since we have added four new variables to the problem, we have to be sure to include these variables in the objective function. Since the excess time available for any operation makes no contribution to profit, the profit coefficient associated with each slack variable will be zero. Thus the Par, Inc. linear programming problem can now be written in Standard form:

$$\max \quad 10x_1 + 9x_2 + 0s_1 + 0s_2 + 0s_3 + 0s_4$$

s.t.

$$\frac{7}{10}x_1 + 1x_2 + 1s_1 \qquad\qquad\qquad = 630$$
$$\tfrac{1}{2}x_1 + \tfrac{5}{6}x_2 \qquad + 1s_2 \qquad\qquad = 600$$
$$1x_1 + \tfrac{2}{3}x_2 \qquad\qquad + 1s_3 \qquad = 708$$
$$\tfrac{1}{10}x_1 + \tfrac{1}{4}x_2 \qquad\qquad\qquad + 1s_4 = 135$$
$$x_1, x_2, s_1, s_2, s_3, s_4 \geq 0.$$

We have used the s notation for the slack variables to make it easy to recall that these added variables are slack variables and not the original decision variables (x_1 and x_2). While the four slack variables could have been called x_3, x_4, x_5, and x_6, we believe the s notation is more descriptive.

Also note that we have expanded the nonnegativity constraints to include the four new slack variables. To see why the slack variables must be constrained to nonnegative values, recall that our original cutting and dyeing constraint was

$$\frac{7}{10}x_1 + 1x_2 \leq 630. \tag{8.26}$$

Written in its equality form we had

$$\frac{7}{10}x_1 + 1x_2 + 1s_1 = 630. \tag{8.27}$$

What would it mean if s_1 were negative? A negative s_1 would mean that in order to satisfy equation (8.27) the quantity $\frac{7}{10}x_1 + 1x_2$ would have to be greater than 630. Since this would violate the original cutting and dyeing constraint, equation (8.26), negative s_1 values are unacceptable. In addition, negative slack variables would indicate a negative excess capacity which has no physical interpretation. Thus the nonnegativity constraints apply to all slack variables as well as to the original decision variables.

In the Photo Chemicals, Inc., problem we encountered greater-than-or-equal-to constraints. In order to see how these constraints are converted to the equality relationships required by the Standard form, let us return to the Photo Chemicals problem.

$$\min \quad 1x_1 + 1x_2$$

s.t.

$$1x_1 + 2x_2 \geq 80$$
$$1x_1 \qquad \geq 30$$
$$1x_2 \geq 20$$
$$x_1, x_2 \geq 0.$$

Using the raw material constraint as an example, we have

$$1x_1 + 2x_2 \geq 80.$$

Since the left-hand side of the constraint varies depending upon the values of x_1 and x_2, and since the left-hand side must be greater than or equal to 80, we must subtract an amount from the left-hand side in order to achieve the equality form. We refer to a variable that is subtracted from the left-hand side of any greater-than-or-equal-to constraint as a *surplus variable*. Thus by subtracting a surplus variable (s_1) from the left-hand side of the first constraint, it can be written as the following equation:

$$1x_1 + 2x_2 - 1s_1 = 80.$$

If our production combination specifies $x_1 = 50$ and $x_2 = 25$, then

$$1(50) + 2(25) - 1s_1 = 80$$

or

$$s_1 = 20.$$

The physical interpretation of the value of the surplus variable s_1 is that it indicates the extra pounds of raw material used to produce x_1 units of product 1 and x_2 units of product 2, over and above the minimum usage level of 80 pounds.

Note that it is our practice to use the s notation for surplus as well as for slack variables. We can always interpret an s variable by referring to the original linear programming formulation to see if the associated constraint is a less-than-or-equal-to (slack variable) or a greater-than-or-equal-to (surplus variable) constraint.

Using s_2 as a surplus variable for the product 1 minimum quantity constraint and s_3 for the product 2 minimum quantity constraint, zero cost coefficients for all surplus variables in the objective function, and adding nonnegativity constraints for the surplus variables, the Photo Chemicals, Inc., problem can now be written in the following Standard form:

$$\min \quad 1x_1 + 1x_2 + 0s_1 + 0s_2 + 0s_3$$

s.t.

$$
\begin{aligned}
1x_1 + 2x_2 - 1s_1 & && = 80 \\
1x_1 && - 1s_2 && = 30 \\
1x_2 && - 1s_3 & = 20 \\
x_1, x_2, s_1, s_2, s_3 & \geq 0.
\end{aligned}
$$

Since we have seen in Section 8.8 that linear programming problems may have a mixture of $\leq$, $\geq$, or $=$ constraint forms, it is possible to have Standard forms that contain both slack and surplus variables. For example, the linear programming problem presented in Section 8.8 containing all three constraint forms has the following Standard form:

$$\min \quad 2x_1 + 2x_2 + 0s_1 + 0s_2$$

s.t.

$$
\begin{aligned}
1x_1 + 3x_2 + 1s_1 \qquad &= 12 \\
3x_1 + 1x_2 \qquad - 1s_2 &= 13 \\
1x_1 - 1x_2 \qquad &= \ \ 3 \\
x_1, x_2, s_1, s_2 &\geq 0.
\end{aligned}
$$

Note that s_1 is a slack variable, while s_2 is a surplus variable. Also, since the third constraint was already an equality, we did not have to utilize a slack or a surplus variable for this constraint.

As a final point, it is important to realize that the Standard form of a linear programming problem is equivalent to the original formulation of the problem. That is, the optimal solution to any linear programming problem is the same as the optimal solution to the Standard form of the problem. Thus the Standard form has not changed our basic problem; it has only changed how we write the constraints for the problem. Writing a linear programming problem in its Standard form is a necessary step to obtain the set of linear equations required by the Simplex solution procedure.

8.10 SUMMARY

We have seen how two problems, the Par, Inc., and the Photo Chemicals, Inc., problems, could be formulated as linear programs and solved by a graphical procedure. In studying the graphical solution procedure we noted that an optimal solution to every linear programming problem occurs at one of the extreme points of the feasible region.

In the process of formulating a mathematical model of these problems we developed the following general definition of a linear program.

A linear program is a mathematical model which has the following properties:

1. A linear objective function which is to be maximized or minimized
2. A set of linear constraints
3. Variables which are all restricted to nonnegative values.

Although the algebraic solution to linear programs using the Simplex method will not be presented until the next chapter, it was pointed out that solving simultaneous linear equations will be an important part of this solution procedure. We saw how elementary row operations could be used to find solutions to such systems of linear equations and how this method could be used to find exact solutions to a linear programming problem after a graphical solution procedure had been used to identify the binding constraints.

We have seen how slack variables can be used to write less-than-or-equal-to constraints in equality form and how surplus variables can be used to write greater-than-or-equal-to constraints in equality form. The value of a slack variable can usually be interpreted as the amount of unused resource, while the value of a surplus variable indicates the amount required over and above some stated minimum. We saw in Section 8.9 that when all constraints have been written as equalities, the linear program has been written in its Standard form.

8.11 GLOSSARY

1. *Objective function—All* linear programs have a linear objective function that is either to be maximized or minimized. In most linear programming problems the objective function will be used to measure the profit or cost of a particular solution.
2. *Constraint*—An equation or inequality which rules out certain combinations of variables as feasible solutions.
3. *Constraint function*—The left-hand side of a constraint relationship (that is the portion of the constraint containing the variables).
4. *Solution*—Any set of values for the variables.
5. *Optimal solution*—A feasible solution that maximizes or minimizes the value of the objective function.
6. *Nonnegativity constraints*—A set of constraints that requires all variables to be nonnegative.
7. *Mathematical model*—A representation of a problem where the objective and all constraint conditions are described by mathematical expressions.
8. *Linear program*—A mathematical model with a linear objective function, a set of linear constraints, and nonnegative variables.
9. *Linear equations or functions*—Mathematical expressions in which the variables appear in separate terms and are raised to the first power.
10. *Feasible solution*—A solution which satisfies all the constraints.
11. *Feasible region*—The set of all possible feasible solutions.
12. *Redundant constraint*—A constraint which does not affect the feasible region. If a constraint is redundant it could be removed from the problem without affecting the feasible region.
13. *Extreme point*—Graphically speaking, extreme points are the feasible solution points occurring at the vertices or "corners" of the feasible region. With two variables, extreme points are determined by the intersection of the constraint lines. An important property of extreme points is that the optimal solution to a linear program always occurs at an extreme point.

14. *Simultaneous linear equations*—A system of linear equations which has a solution if a set of values for the variables satisfies all equations.
15. *Elementary row operations*—A procedure for finding solutions to a system of simultaneous linear equations.
16. *Standard form*—A linear program in which all of the constraints are written as equalities. The optimal solution of the Standard form of a linear program is the same as the optimal solution of the original formulation of the linear program.
17. *Slack variable*—A variable added to the left-hand side of a less-than-or-equal-to constraint to convert the constraint into an equality. The value of this variable can usually be interpreted as the amount of unused resource.
18. *Surplus variable*—A variable subtracted from the left-hand side of a greater-than-or-equal-to constraint to convert the constraint into an equality. The value of this variable can usually be interpreted as the amount over and above the required minimum level.

8.12 PROBLEMS

1. Consider the following linear programming problem:

   $$\max \quad 1x_1 + 1x_2$$

   s.t.
   $$1x_1 + 2x_2 \leq 6$$
   $$6x_1 + 4x_2 \leq 24$$
   $$x_1, x_2 \geq 0.$$

   a. Find the optimal solution using the graphical procedure.
   b. If the objective function were changed to $1x_1 + 3x_2$, what would be the optimal solution?
   c. How many extreme points are there on your graph? What are the x_1 and x_2 values at each extreme point?

2. Consider the following linear programming problem:

   $$\max \quad 2x_1 + 3x_2$$

   s.t.
   $$3x_1 + 3x_2 \leq 12$$
   $$\tfrac{2}{3}x_1 + 1x_2 \leq 4$$
   $$1x_1 + 2x_2 \leq 6$$
   $$x_1, x_2 \geq 0.$$

   a. Find the optimal solution using the graphical procedure.
   b. Does this problem have a redundant constraint? If so, what is it?

204

Does the solution change if the redundant constraint is removed from the problem?

3. Suppose that the management of Par, Inc., encounters each of the following situations:

   a. The accounting department revises its profit estimate on the deluxe bags to $18 per bag.

   b. A new low-cost material is available for the standard bag, and the profit per standard bag can be increased to $20 per bag. (Assume the profit of the deluxe bag is the original $9 value.)

   c. New sewing equipment is available and would increase the sewing operation capacity to 750 hours. (Assume $10x_1 + 9x_2$ is the appropriate objective function.)

   If each of the above conditions is encountered separately, what do you recommend under each case? That is, what is the optimal solution and profit for each situation?

4. Which of the following mathematical relationships could be found in a linear programming model and which could not? For the relationships that are unacceptable for linear programs, state your reasons.

   a. $6x_1 - 2x_2 + \frac{1}{2}x_3 \leq 100$
   b. $-1x_1 + 2x_2{}^2 + 1x_3 = 50$
   c. $2x_1 \qquad + 5x_3 \leq 10$
   d. $1x_1 + 2x_2 + 1x_1x_2 = 25$
   e. $3\sqrt{x_1} + 2x_2 + 1x_3 \leq 5$
   f. $1x_1 + 1x_2 + 1x_3 \leq 20.$

5. Grippo Golf Glove Company makes two different brands of golf gloves. One is a full-fingered glove and the other is a half-fingered model. Grippo currently has orders for more gloves than it can produce in time for the upcoming golf season. The scarce resource in the manufacture of these gloves is labor time.

   Grippo has available 400 hours in the cutting and sewing department, 250 hours in the finishing department, and 150 hours in the packaging and shipping department.

   The department time requirements and the profit per box (1 gross) are given below.

| | Production Time (hours) | | | |
	Cutting and Sewing	Finishing	Packaging and Shipping	Profit
Full finger	3	$1\frac{1}{2}$	1	$30
Half finger	$1\frac{1}{2}$	2	1	$25

Find the optimal product mix for Grippo, assuming the company wants to maximize profit.

What is the maximum amount of profit Grippo can earn?

6. The URNUTZ Company manufactures and sells two products. The company makes a profit of $7 for each unit of product 1 and a profit of $6 for each unit of product 2 sold. The man-hour requirements for the products in each of the three production departments are summarized below:

	Product 1	Product 2
Department 1	$\frac{1}{3}$	$\frac{1}{2}$
Department 2	$\frac{1}{4}$	$\frac{1}{6}$
Department 3	$\frac{1}{2}$	$\frac{3}{8}$

The supervisors of these departments have estimated that the following number of man-hours will be available during the next month: 200 manhours in department 1, 150 man-hours in department 2, and 500 man-hours in department 3.

Assuming that URNUTZ is interested in maximizing profits,

a. Show the linear programming model of this problem.

b. Find the optimal solution using the graphical procedure.

7. The Sweet Tooth Candy Company has a limited supply of two chocolate ingredients that are used in the production of candy bar products. There are 8000 ounces available of XJ100 and 7000 ounces of XJ200. Both ingredients are made especially for Sweet Tooth by the Marcus T. Cavity Chocolate Compound Company. Sweet Tooth uses the two ingredients to produce either Crunch-A-Munch Bars or Golden-Goodie Bars. Each Crunch-A-Munch Bar uses $\frac{1}{4}$ ounce of XJ100 and $\frac{1}{2}$ ounce of XJ200. Each Golden-Goodie Bar requires $\frac{1}{2}$ ounce of XJ100 and $\frac{1}{4}$ ounce of XJ200. In addition, the marketing department of Sweet Tooth estimates they will be able to sell at most 10,000 Crunch-A-Munch Bars. If Sweet Tooth makes a profit of $0.05 on each Crunch-A-Munch and $0.02 on each Golden Goodie, what product mix should the company employ? Solve this problem using the graphical procedure.

8. What constraint lines combine to form extreme point ④ of the Par, Inc., problem (see Figure 8.16)? Use the solution of simultaneous linear equations to show that the exact values of x_1 and x_2 at this extreme point are $x_1 = 300$ and $x_2 = 420$.

9. An oil refinery in Tulsa, Oklahoma, sells 60% of its oil production to a distributor in Chicago and 40% to a distributor in Atlanta. Another refinery in New Orleans, Louisiana, sells 30% of its oil production to

206

the same Chicago distributor and 70% to the same Atlanta distributor. If we know the Chicago distributor received 120,000 gallons of oil from the two plants and the Atlanta distributor received 180,000 gallons from the two plants during the last month, how many gallons of oil were produced at each of the two plants? (Hint: Let x_1 = gallons at the Tulsa plant and x_2 = gallons at the New Orleans plant. Then define a linear equation for each distributor and solve the two simultaneous linear equations.)

10. Use elementary row operations to find the solution to the following set of linear equations:

$$1x_1 - 2x_2 + 3x_3 = 9$$
$$2x_1 - 1x_2 + 1x_3 = 4$$
$$1x_1 + 2x_2 - 1x_3 = 1.$$

11. Consider the following linear program:

$$\min \quad 1.5x_1 + 2x_2$$

s.t.

$$2x_1 + 2x_2 \geq 8$$
$$2x_1 + 6x_2 \geq 12$$
$$x_1, x_2 \geq 0.$$

Identify the feasible region and solve by the graphical procedure.

12. For the above problem, use the graphical procedure to find the optimal solution when the objective function is

$$\min \quad 1.5x_1 + 1x_2.$$

13. Doc's Dog Kennel's Inc., provides overnight lodging for a variety of pets. A particular feature at Doc's is the quality of care the pets receive, including excellent food. The kennel's dog food is made by mixing two brand-name dog food products to obtain what Doc's calls the "well-balanced dog diet." The data for the two dog foods are below.

Dog Food	Cost per Ounce	Protein (percent)	Fat (percent)
Bark Bits	$0.03	30	10
Canine Chow	$0.025	20	20

If Doc wants to be sure that his dogs receive at least 5 ounces of protein and 2 ounces of fat per day, what is the minimum cost mix of the two dog food products?

14. Jack Kammer has been trying to figure out the correct amount of fertilizer that should be applied to his lawn. After getting his soil

207

analyzed at the local agricultural agency, he has been advised to put at least 60 pounds of nitrogen, 24 pounds of phosphorous compounds, and 40 pounds of potassium compounds on the lawn this season. One third of the mixture is to be applied in May, one third in July, and one third in late September. After checking the local discount stores, Jack finds that one store is currently having a sale on packaged fertilizer. One type on sale is the 20-5-20 mixture consisting of 20% nitrogen, 5% phosphorous compounds, and 20% potassium compounds, and selling at $4 for a 20-pound bag. The other type on sale is a 10-10-5 mixture selling for $5 for a 40 pound bag. Jack would like to know how many bags of each type he should purchase so he can combine the ingredients to form a mixture that will meet the minimum agricultural agency requirements. Like all homeowners plagued with large lawns, Jack would like to spend as little as possible to keep his lawn healthy. What should Jack do?

15. Write the following linear program in Standard form:

$$\max \quad 5x_1 + 2x_2 + 8x_3$$

s.t.

$$1x_1 - 2x_2 + \tfrac{1}{2}x_3 \leq 420$$
$$2x_1 + 3x_2 - 1x_3 \leq 610$$
$$6x_1 - 1x_2 + 3x_3 \leq 125$$
$$x_1, x_2, x_3 \geq 0.$$

16. Given the following linear program:

$$\max \quad 3x_1 + 4x_2$$

s.t.

$$-1x_1 + 2x_2 \leq 8$$
$$1x_1 + 2x_2 \leq 12$$
$$2x_1 + 1x_2 \leq 16$$
$$x_1, x_2 \geq 0.$$

a. Write this problem in its Standard form.
b. Solve the above problem using the graphical procedure.
c. What are the values of the three slack variables at the optimal solution?

17. For the following linear program:

$$\max \quad 10x_1 + 2.5x_2$$

s.t.

$$5x_1 + 1x_2 \leq 15$$
$$6x_1 + 4x_2 \leq 24$$
$$1x_1 + 1x_2 \leq 5$$
$$x_1, x_2 \geq 0.$$

   a. Write this problem in its Standard form.
   b. Solve the above problem using the graphical procedure.
   c. What are the values of the three slack variables at the optimal solution?

18. For the following linear program:

$$\min \quad 3x_1 + 2x_2$$

s.t.

$$1x_1 + 1x_2 \geq 10$$
$$2x_1 + 1x_2 \geq 12$$
$$1x_2 \leq 4$$
$$x_1, x_2 \geq 0.$$

   a. Write this problem in its Standard form.
   b. Solve the above problem using the graphical procedure.
   c. What are the values of the slack and surplus variables?

19. Consider the following linear program:

$$\max \quad 1x_1 + 2x_2$$

s.t.

$$1x_1 \qquad \leq 5$$
$$1x_2 \leq 4$$
$$2x_1 + 2x_2 = 12$$
$$x_1, x_2 \geq 0.$$

   a. Graphically show the feasible region.
   b. What are the extreme points of the feasible region?
   c. Find the optimal solution by the graphical procedure.

20. Consider the following linear program:

$$\min \quad 2x_1 + 2x_2$$

s.t.

$$1x_1 + 3x_2 \leq 12$$
$$3x_1 + 1x_2 \geq 13$$
$$1x_1 - 1x_2 = 3$$
$$x_1, x_2 \geq 0.$$

   a. Graphically show the feasible region.
   b. What are the extreme points of the feasible region?
   c. Find the optimal solution by the graphical procedure.

21. The Death-to-Weeds Company is a major manufacturer of weed killers for home use. It currently has available 175 pounds of K-20 and 900 pounds of K-25 weed killing concentrates used in the manufacture of a number of Death-to-Weeds products. The company will use these concentrates in the production of Dandelion-Do-In and Quack-Killer, two of the most profitable company products. Each unit of Dandelion-Do-In

uses $\frac{1}{4}$ pound of K-20 and 1 pound of K-25. Each unit of Quack-Killer requires $\frac{1}{6}$ pound of K-20 and $1\frac{1}{2}$ pounds of K-25. The company has enough packaging material to produce as much Dandelion-Do-In as desired but is limited to a maximum of 400 units of Quack-Killer. If the profit contribution for both products is $6 per unit produced, how many units of each product should the company manufacture? Solve this problem using the graphical procedure.

22. Speen Food Supplies, Inc., is a manufacturer of frozen pizzas. Art Speen, president of Speen Food Supplies, personally supervises the production of both types of frozen pizzas produced by the company: Speen's regular and Speen's super-deluxe. Art makes a profit of $0.50 for each regular produced and $0.75 for each super-deluxe. He currently has 150 pounds of dough mix available and 800 ounces of topping mix. Each regular pizza uses 1 pound of dough mix and 4 ounces of topping, whereas each super-deluxe uses 1 pound of dough mix and 8 ounces of topping mix. Based upon past demand, Art knows that he can sell at most 75 super-deluxe pizzas and 125 regular pizzas. How many regular and super-deluxe pizzas should Art make in order to maximize profits?
   a. Solve this problem graphically.
   b. Show the problem in its Standard form.
   c. What are the values and interpretations of all slack variables? Which constraints are binding the optimal solution?

23. Wilkinson Motors, Inc., sells standard automobiles and station wagons. The firm makes $200 profit for each automobile it sells and $250 profit for each station wagon it sells. The company is planning next month's order which the manufacturer says cannot exceed 300 automobiles and 150 station wagons. Dealer preparation time requires 2 hours for each automobile and 3 hours for each station wagon. Next month the company has 900 hours of shop time available for new car preparation. How many automobiles and station wagons should be ordered so that profit is maximized?
   a. Show the linear programming model of the above problem.
   b. Show the Standard form and identify the slack variables.
   c. Identify the extreme points of the feasible region.
   d. Solve graphically.

24. Ryland Farms in northwestern Indiana grows soybeans and corn on its 500 acres of land. An acre of soybeans brings a $50 profit and an acre of corn brings a $100 profit. Because of government regulations, no more than 200 acres can be planted in soybeans. During the planting season 1200 man-hours of planting time will be available. Each acre of soybeans requires 2 man-hours, while each acre of corn requires 6 man-hours. How many acres of soybeans and how many acres of corn should be planted in order to maximize profits?

   a.   Show the linear programming model of the above problem.

   b.   Show the Standard form and identify all slack variables.

   c.   Solve graphically.

   d.   Identify all the extreme points of the feasible region.

   e.   If the farm could get either more man-hours of labor or additional land, which should it attempt to obtain? Why?

25. The marketing department of KT Company is interested in finding out how to get the most audience exposure from its current advertising budget. The company would like to determine how much of its advertising budget should be spent on each of three media: radio, television, and newspaper.

    Each dollar spent on radio advertising is worth six exposure points to the company. Similarly, KT believes it will get five and eight exposure points, respectively, for every dollar spent on television and newspaper advertising.

    KT's total advertising budget consists of $10,000. However, because of an agreement with a local television station, KT may not spend more than half as much on radio advertising as it does on television. In addition, the combined expenditure on television and newspaper advertising may not exceed 80% of the total advertising expenditure.

    Assuming that KT is interested in maximizing its exposure points, formulate this problem as a linear program. (Hint: Let x_1 = dollars spent on radio, x_2 = dollars spent on television, and x_3 = dollars spent on newspaper.) Set up the Standard form for this problem and interpret all slack variables. (You do not have to solve this problem.)

9
Linear Programming: The Simplex Method

We have learned how to find the optimal solution for two-variable linear programming problems using the graphical procedure. However, most real-world problems contain more than two decision variables and thus are too large for this solution technique. An algebraic solution procedure, the Simplex method, will have to be used to solve these larger linear programming problems. Computer programs of the Simplex method have been used to solve linear programming problems having as many as several thousand variables and constraints.

In this chapter we first present the Simplex method in a step-by-step fashion using the Par, Inc., maximization problem of Chapter 8. We will then use the Photo Chemicals, Inc., example of Chapter 8 to show how the Simplex method can be used to solve minimization problems. After the method has been developed for these particular problems, we set forth the general Simplex procedure which can be used to solve any linear program.

9.1 AN ALGEBRAIC OVERVIEW OF THE SIMPLEX METHOD

Let us return to the Par, Inc., problem which is written below in its Standard form:

$$\max \quad 10x_1 + 9x_2 + 0s_1 + 0s_2 + 0s_3 + 0s_4 \tag{9.1}$$

s.t.

$$\tfrac{7}{10}x_1 + 1x_2 + 1s_1 \qquad\qquad\qquad\qquad = 630 \tag{9.2}$$
$$\tfrac{1}{2}x_1 + \tfrac{5}{6}x_2 \qquad + 1s_2 \qquad\qquad\quad = 600 \tag{9.3}$$
$$1x_1 + \tfrac{2}{3}x_2 \qquad\qquad + 1s_3 \qquad\quad = 708 \tag{9.4}$$
$$\tfrac{1}{10}x_1 + \tfrac{1}{4}x_2 \qquad\qquad\qquad + 1s_4 = 135 \tag{9.5}$$
$$x_1, x_2, s_1, s_2, s_3, s_4 \geq 0. \tag{9.6}$$

What is involved in finding the optimal solution to this problem algebraically? First note that equations (9.2) to (9.5), the constraint equations, form a system of four simultaneous linear equations in six variables. In order to satisfy the constraints of the Par, Inc., problem, the optimal solution must be a solution to this set of linear equations. Whenever a set of simultaneous equations has more variables than constraints, we can expect an infinite number of solutions. Thus any algebraic procedure for solving linear programs must be capable of finding solutions to systems of simultaneous equations involving more variables than equations.

Second, note that not every solution to equations (9.2) to (9.5) is a feasible solution to the linear program. That is, we cannot expect every solution to equations (9.2) to (9.5) to also satisfy the nonnegativity conditions ($x_1, x_2, s_1,$ $s_2, s_3, s_4 \geq 0$). Thus, we see that an algebraic procedure for solving linear programming problems should be capable of eliminating from consideration those solutions to equations (9.2) to (9.5) which do not also satisfy the nonnegativity requirement.

Finally, an algebraic procedure for solving linear programs must be capable of picking one of these feasible solutions as the one which maximizes the objective function. The *Simplex method* is an algebraic procedure with all three of the capabilities outlined above.

Since our system of equations (9.2) to (9.5) has more variables (six) than equations (four), the Simplex method finds solutions for these equations by assigning zero values for any two of the variables and then solving for the values of the remaining four variables. To illustrate this procedure, suppose we set $x_2 = 0$ and $s_1 = 0$. Our system of equations then becomes

$$\frac{7}{10}x_1 \qquad\qquad\qquad = 630 \qquad\qquad (9.7)$$
$$\tfrac{1}{2}x_1 + 1s_2 \qquad\qquad = 600 \qquad\qquad (9.8)$$
$$1x_1 \qquad + 1s_3 \qquad = 708 \qquad\qquad (9.9)$$
$$\frac{1}{10}x_1 \qquad\qquad + 1s_4 = 135 \qquad\qquad (9.10)$$

By setting $x_2 = 0$ and $s_1 = 0$ we have in effect reduced our system of linear equations to four variables and four equations. Using the elementary row operations introduced in Chapter 8, we can solve for the values of the remaining four variables.

Multiplying the first row by $\frac{10}{7}$ we have

$$1x_1 = 900.$$

Using additional row operations to obtain a zero coefficient for x_1 in all other equations, our system of linear equations reduces to

$$1x_1 \qquad\qquad = \quad 900$$
$$1s_2 \qquad\qquad = \quad 150$$
$$1s_3 \qquad = -192$$
$$1s_4 = \quad 45.$$

We now have one solution to our original set of four equations and six variables. This solution is

$$\begin{bmatrix} x_1 \\ x_2 \\ s_1 \\ s_2 \\ s_3 \\ s_4 \end{bmatrix} = \begin{bmatrix} 900 \\ 0 \\ 0 \\ 150 \\ -192 \\ 45 \end{bmatrix}$$

Using the above procedure, we have found what is known as a *basic solution* to our linear programming problem. In general, if we have a Standard form linear programming problem consisting of n variables and m equations, where n is greater than m, a basic solution can be obtained by setting $n - m$ of the variables equal to zero and solving the m constraint equations

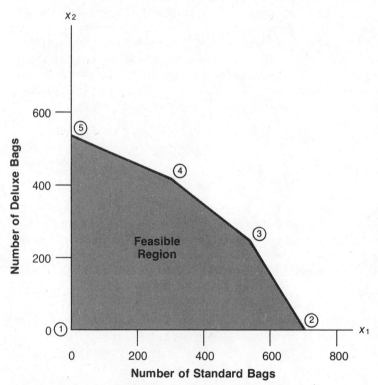

FIGURE 9.1   *The five extreme points of the feasible region for the Par, Inc., problem.*

214

for the remaining m variables.[1] In terms of our Par, Inc., problem, a basic solution can be obtained by setting *any* two variables equal to zero and then solving the system of four equations for the remaining four variables. We shall refer to the $n - m$ variables set equal to zero as the *nonbasic* variables and the remaining m variables (usually nonzero) as the *basic* variables. Thus in the above example, x_2 and s_1 are the nonbasic variables and x_1, s_2, s_3 and s_4 are the basic variables.

Certainly the above basic solution is not feasible since the nonnegativity conditions are not satisfied (that is, s_3 is less than zero). Thus we see that a basic solution does *not* have to be a feasible solution. However, when a basic solution is also feasible, we refer to it as a *basic feasible solution*. For example, if we set $x_1 = 0$ and $x_2 = 0$, we can solve for s_1, s_2, s_3, and s_4. Doing this, our system of equations becomes

$$
\begin{aligned}
s_1 \quad &= 630 \\
s_2 \quad &= 600 \\
s_3 \quad &= 708 \\
s_4 &= 135.
\end{aligned}
$$

Thus, the solution corresponding to $x_1 = 0$ and $x_2 = 0$ is

$$
\begin{bmatrix} x_1 \\ x_2 \\ s_1 \\ s_2 \\ s_3 \\ s_4 \end{bmatrix} = \begin{bmatrix} 0 \\ 0 \\ 630 \\ 600 \\ 708 \\ 135 \end{bmatrix}
$$

Clearly, this solution represents a basic one to our problem since it was obtained by setting two of the variables equal to zero and solving for the other four. Moreover, it is a basic feasible solution since each of the variables is greater than or equal to zero. Referring to Figure 9.1, we see that this basic feasible solution corresponds to extreme point ① of the feasible region ($x_1 = 0$ and $x_2 = 0$). Thus in this case, a basic feasible solution corresponds to an extreme point. This is not just a coincidence, but an important property of all basic feasible solutions. That is, basic feasible solutions always occur at the extreme points of the feasible region. *In other words, a basic feasible solution and an extreme point solution are one and the same.*

A basic feasible solution to the system of m constraint equations and n

---

[1] There are cases where a unique solution cannot be found for the resulting system of m equations in m variables. However, these cases are exceptions to the rule and will never be encountered when using the Simplex method.

variables is required as a starting point for the Simplex method. Such a solution can be easily found by setting all the decision variables equal to zero. This corresponds to selecting the origin (extreme point ① in the Par, Inc., problem) as the initial basic feasible solution for the Simplex procedure. From this starting point, the Simplex method successively generates basic feasible solutions to our system of equations, making sure that the objective function increases for each new solution. Since, as we saw in Chapter 8, an optimal solution to a linear programming problem always occurs at an extreme point, and since a basic feasible solution and an extreme point solution are synonymous, the Simplex method must eventually locate an optimal solution to the problem. Thus the Simplex method can be described as an iterative procedure for moving from one basic feasible solution (extreme point) to another until the optimal solution is reached. The way in which this iterative procedure is carried out, is the subject of the remainder of this chapter.

9.2 TABLEAU FORM

As we discussed in Section 9.1, the Simplex method always begins with a basic feasible solution and then moves from one basic feasible solution to another until the optimal basic feasible solution (extreme point) is reached. Thus prior to beginning the Simplex method, we must find an initial basic feasible solution for our system of constraint equations. Recall that for our Par, Inc., problem, the Standard form was

$$\max \quad 10x_1 + 9x_2 + 0s_1 + 0s_2 + 0s_3 + 0s_4$$

s.t.

$$\frac{7}{10}x_1 + 1x_2 + 1s_1 \qquad\qquad\qquad = 630$$
$$\frac{1}{2}x_1 + \frac{5}{6}x_2 \qquad + 1s_2 \qquad\qquad = 600$$
$$1x_1 + \frac{2}{3}x_2 \qquad\qquad + 1s_3 \qquad = 708$$
$$\frac{1}{10}x_1 + \frac{1}{4}x_2 \qquad\qquad\qquad + 1s_4 = 135$$
$$x_1, x_2, s_1, s_2, s_3, s_4 \geq 0.$$

As we saw in Section 9.1, it is very easy to find an initial basic feasible solution for this problem. We simply set $x_1 = 0$ and $x_2 = 0$ and solve for s_1, s_2, s_3, and s_4. Thus we obtain the solution $x_1 = 0, x_2 = 0, s_1 = 630, s_2 = 600$, $s_3 = 708$, and $s_4 = 135$. The reason that this basic feasible solution was so easy to find is that as soon as x_1 and x_2 had been set equal to zero, the values for the remaining variables could simply be read from the right-hand side of the constraint equations. If we study this particular system of equations closely, we can identify two properties that make it possible to easily find a basic feasible solution.

The first property enables us to find a basic solution. Loosely stated, this property says that m of the variables ($m = 4$ in this case) must each have both a coefficient of one in exactly one equation and appear with a zero coefficient in all other equations. Then if these m variables are made basic by setting the other $(n - m)$ variables equal to zero, the values of the basic variables can be read from the right-hand side of the constraint equations. In the example the variables s_1, s_2, s_3, and s_4 satisfy this first property. The second property enables us to easily find a basic feasible solution for a linear program. This property requires that the values on the right-hand side of the constraint equations be nonnegative. In our example we see that this property is also satisfied.

If we can write our linear programming problem in a form which satisfies the first property, then the values of the basic variables are given by the right-hand sides of the constraining equations. If, in addition, the second property is satisfied, the values of the variables will be nonnegative and the basic solution will also be feasible.

If a linear programming problem satisfies both of the above properties, it is said to be in *Tableau form*. We note that the Standard form representation of the Par, Inc., problem is already in Tableau form. In fact, the Standard form and the Tableau form representations of linear programs that have all less-than-or-equal-to constraints, and nonnegative right-hand side values are the same. However, as we shall see later in this chapter, there are many linear programming problems for which Standard form and Tableau form are not the same.

Let us pause for a moment and reflect on the reason for introducing the notion of Tableau form. Since the Simplex method always begins with a basic feasible solution and since the Tableau form provides an easy way of obtaining an initial basic feasible solution, putting a linear programming problem into Tableau form is an important step in preparing the problem for solution by the Simplex method. Thus the following three steps are necessary in order to prepare a linear programming problem for solution using the Simplex method:

Step 1: Formulate the problem.
Step 2: Set up the Standard form representation of the problem.
Step 3: Set up the Tableau form representation of the problem.

9.3 SETTING UP THE INITIAL SIMPLEX TABLEAU

After a linear programming problem has been converted to Tableau form, we have available an initial basic feasible solution which can be used to begin the Simplex method. The next step is to set up the initial *Simplex tableau*.

The Simplex tableau provides a convenient means for keeping track of and performing the calculations necessary during the Simplex solution procedure.

Part of the initial Simplex tableau is simply a table containing all the information shown in the Tableau form representation of a linear program. If we adopt the general notation

c_j = objective function coefficient for variable j

b_i = right-hand side value for constraint i

a_{ij} = coefficient associated with variable j in constraint i

we can show this portion of the Simplex tableau as follows:

c_1	c_2	$\cdots$	c_n	
a_{11}	a_{12}	$\cdots$	a_{1n}	b_1
a_{21}	a_{22}	$\cdots$	a_{2n}	b_2
$\cdot$	$\cdot$	$\cdots$	$\cdot$	$\cdot$
$\cdot$	$\cdot$	$\cdots$	$\cdot$	$\cdot$
$\cdot$	$\cdot$	$\cdots$	$\cdot$	$\cdot$
a_{m1}	a_{m2}	$\cdots$	a_{mn}	b_m

In the above partial tableau, the horizontal and vertical lines are used to separate the different parts of the Tableau form representation of a linear program. The upper horizontal line separates the coefficients of the variables in the objective function from the coefficients of the variables in the constraint equations. The vertical line can be interpreted as an equality line; the values to the left of this line are the coefficients of the variables in the constraint equations, and those to the right of the line are the right-hand side values of the constraint equations.

Later we may want to refer to all the objective function coefficients, all the right-hand side values, or all the coefficients in the constraints. To do this we will find the following general notation helpful:

c row $\quad$ = row of objective function coefficients

b column = column of right-hand side values of the constraint equations

A matrix $\,$ = m rows and n columns of coefficients of the variables in the constraint equations.

Using this notation, we can show the above portion of the Simplex tableau as follows:

c row	
A matrix	b column

Before we can apply the Simplex method, two more rows and two more columns will have to be added to our tableau. However, before defining these new rows and columns, let us set up the partial Simplex tableau for our Par, Inc., example problem. The Tableau form (the same as Standard form in this case) for the Par, Inc., problem is

$$\max \quad 10x_1 + 9x_2 + 0s_1 + 0s_2 + 0s_3 + 0s_4$$

s.t.

$$\frac{7}{10}x_1 + 1x_2 + 1s_1 \qquad\qquad\qquad = 630$$
$$\frac{1}{2}x_1 + \frac{5}{6}x_2 \qquad + 1s_2 \qquad\qquad = 600$$
$$1x_1 + \frac{2}{3}x_2 \qquad\qquad + 1s_3 \qquad = 708$$
$$\frac{1}{10}x_1 + \frac{1}{4}x_2 \qquad\qquad\qquad + 1s_4 = 135$$
$$x_1, x_2, s_1, s_2, s_3, s_4 \geq 0.$$

A partial Simplex tableau can then be written as

	Coefficients of the Objective Function						Constants on the Right-hand Side of the Constraints
	10	9	0	0	0	0	
	7/10	1	1	0	0	0	630
Constraint	1/2	5/6	0	1	0	0	600
coefficients	1	2/3	0	0	1	0	708
	1/10	1/4	0	0	0	1	135

Notice that the row above the first horizontal line contains the coefficients of the objective function for our Par, Inc., problem in Tableau form. The elements appearing between the horizontal lines and to the left of the vertical line are simply the coefficients of the constraint equations, whereas the elements to the right of the vertical line are the right-hand side values of the constraint equations. It may be easier to recall that each of the rows contains the coefficients of one constraint equation, if we note that each of the columns is associated with one of the variables. For example, x_1 corresponds to the first column, x_2 the second, s_1 the third, and so on. To help us keep this in mind, we will write the variable associated with each column directly above the column. Doing this, we get

x_1	x_2	s_1	s_2	s_3	s_4	
10	9	0	0	0	0	
7/10	1	1	0	0	0	630
1/2	5/6	0	1	0	0	600
1	2/3	0	0	1	0	708
1/10	1/4	0	0	0	1	135

219

We stated earlier that the Simplex method must be started with a basic feasible solution. Certainly, one basic feasible solution for the Par, Inc., problem is the one we found in Section 9.2 from the Tableau form of our problem. This solution corresponds to a product combination of zero standard bags and zero deluxe bags and is represented by the solution

$$\begin{bmatrix} x_1 \\ x_2 \\ s_1 \\ s_2 \\ s_3 \\ s_4 \end{bmatrix} = \begin{bmatrix} 0 \\ 0 \\ 630 \\ 600 \\ 708 \\ 135 \end{bmatrix}$$

Note that the initial Simplex tableau contains the Tableau form of the problem, and thus it is easy to find the above basic feasible solution from the initial Simplex tableau. As you can see, a column in the Simplex tableau which has a 1 in the only nonzero position is associated with each basic variable. Such columns are known as *unit columns* or *unit vectors*. Also a row of the tableau is associated with each basic variable. This row can be identified by the fact that it contains the 1 in the unit column. The value of each basic variable is then given by b_i in the row associated with the basic variable. For example, s_3 has a 1 in row 3; therefore the value of this basic variable is given by $s_3 = b_3 = 708$. This procedure is shown in Table 9.1.

At this point we have seen how to go about finding an initial basic feasible solution and setting up a partial Simplex tableau. We know that the Simplex method proceeds from one basic feasible solution to another until the optimal basic feasible solution is reached. In the next section we discuss how the Simplex method moves from our initial basic feasible solution to a better one.

TABLE 9.1   Illustration of Procedure for Finding Values of
Basic Variables from the Simplex Tableau

x_1	x_2	s_1	s_2	s_3	s_4	
10	9	0	0	0	0	
7/10	1	1	0	0	0	630
1/2	5/6	·0	1	0	0	600
1	2/3	0	0	1	0	708
1/10	1/4	0	0	0	1	135

Row associated with s_3 ——→ 1 ... 708 ←—— value of s_3

220

9.4 IMPROVING THE SOLUTION

To improve the solution we will have to generate a new basic feasible solution (extreme point) that yields a larger profit. To do this we will have to change the set of basic variables, that is, we will have to select one of the current nonbasic variables to bring into solution and one of the current basic variables to leave the solution in such a fashion that the new basic feasible solution yields a larger value for the objective function. The Simplex method provides us with an easy way to carry out this change in the basic feasible solution.

For convenience we will add two new columns to the present form of the Simplex tableau in order to keep track of the basic variables and the profit associated with these variables. One column will be labeled *Basis* and the other c_j. Under the column labeled *Basis* we shall list the names of the current basic variables, and under the column labeled c_j we shall list the profit corresponding to each of these basic variables. For the Par, Inc., problem this results in the following initial Simplex tableau:

Basis	c_j	x_1	x_2	s_1	s_2	s_3	s_4	
		10	9	0	0	0	0	
s_1	0	7/10	1	1	0	0	0	630
s_2	0	1/2	5/6	0	1	0	0	600
s_3	0	1	2/3	0	0	1	0	708
s_4	0	1/10	1/4	0	0	0	1	135

We note in the *Basis* column that s_1 is listed first since its value is given by b_1; s_2 second since its value is given by b_2, and so on.

Can we improve upon our present basic feasible solution? To find out if this is possible, we introduce two new rows into our tableau. The first row, labeled z_j, will represent the *decrease* in the value of the objective function that will result if one unit of the variable corresponding to the jth column of the A matrix is brought into solution. For example, z_1 will represent the decrease in profit that will result if one unit of x_1 is brought into solution.

Let us see why a decrease in profit might result if we bring x_1 into solution. If one unit of x_1 is produced, we will have to change the value of some of the current basic variables in order to satisfy our constraint equations. In the first constraint equation we have

$$\tfrac{7}{10}x_1 + 1x_2 + 1s_1 = 630.$$

If we are considering making x_1 some positive value, we will have to reduce x_2 and/or s_1 in order to satisfy this constraint. Since x_2 is already zero (x_2 is a nonbasic variable), it cannot be reduced any further. Thus the value of s_1 will be reduced if x_1 is made positive. This reduction in the value of a basic variable may result in a reduction in the value of the objective function. The amount of the reduction depends of course upon the coefficient of s_1 in the objective function. In this case, since s_1 is a slack variable, its coefficient is zero; thus reducing s_1 will not decrease the value of the objective function.

On the other hand, every unit of x_1 introduced will improve the value of the objective function by the amount c_1, which in our Par, Inc., problem is the \$10 profit associated with each standard bag produced. Since the value of the objective function will decrease by z_1 for each unit of x_1 produced, the net change in the value of the objective function that results due to one unit of x_1 being introduced is given by $c_1 - z_1$. The next row we introduce into our tableau, which we refer to as the *net evaluation row,* will contain the value of $c_j - z_j$ for every variable (column) in the tableau. In terms of position in the tableau, the z_j and $c_j - z_j$ rows will be placed directly under the A matrix in the existing tableau. Now let us return to the original question of which variable we should make basic by calculating the entries in the net evaluation row for the Par, Inc., problem.

If we were to bring one unit of x_1 into the solution, we see from analyzing the constraint equations that we would have to give up $\frac{7}{10}$ hour of cutting and dyeing time, $\frac{1}{2}$ hour of sewing time, 1 hour of finishing time, and $\frac{1}{10}$ hour of inspection and packaging time. Thus we note that the coefficients in the x_1 column indicate how many units of each basic variable will be driven out of solution when one unit of x_1 is brought in. In general, all the column coefficients can be interpreted this way. Thus, if we were to bring one unit of x_2 into solution, we would have to give up 1 unit of s_1, $\frac{5}{6}$ unit of s_2, $\frac{2}{3}$ unit of s_3, and $\frac{1}{4}$ unit of s_4.

To calculate how much the objective function will decrease when one unit of a nonbasic variable is brought into solution, we must know the value of the objective function coefficients for the basic variables. These values are given in the c_j column of our tableau. Hence *the values in the z_j row can be calculated by multiplying the elements in the c_j column by the corresponding elements in the columns of the A matrix and summing them.* Thus we get

$$z_1 = 0(\tfrac{7}{10}) + 0(\tfrac{1}{2}) + 0(1) + 0(\tfrac{1}{10}) = 0$$
$$z_2 = 0(1) + 0(\tfrac{5}{6}) + 0(\tfrac{2}{3}) + 0(\tfrac{1}{4}) = 0$$
$$z_3 = 0(1) + 0(0) + 0(0) + 0(0) = 0$$
$$z_4 = 0(0) + 0(1) + 0(0) + 0(0) = 0$$
$$z_5 = 0(0) + 0(0) + 0(1) + 0(0) = 0$$
$$z_6 = 0(0) + 0(0) + 0(0) + 0(1) = 0.$$

We see that since the initial basic feasible solution consists entirely of slack variables, and since the c_j values for these variables are all zero, reducing the value of these slack variables when a nonbasic variable is introduced into solution causes no decrease in profit.

222

Since the objective function coefficient for x_1 is 10, the value of $c_1 - z_1$ is $10 - 0 = 10$, which indicates that the net result of bringing a unit of x_1 into the *current solution* will be an increase in profit of $10. Hence in the net evaluation row corresponding to x_1 we enter the value of 10.

In the same manner we can calculate the corresponding z_j and $c_j - z_j$ values for the remaining variables. The result is the following complete initial Simplex tableau.

		x_1	x_2	s_1	s_2	s_3	s_4	
Basis	c_j	10	9	0	0	0	0	
s_1	0	7/10	1	1	0	0	0	630
s_2	0	1/2	5/6	0	1	0	0	600
s_3	0	1	2/3	0	0	1	0	708
s_4	0	1/10	1/4	0	0	0	1	135
	z_j	0	0	0	0	0	0	0
	$c_j - z_j$	10	9	0	0	0	0	

PROFIT

In this tableau we also see a 0 in the z_j row in the last column. This zero represents the profit associated with the current basic solution. This value was obtained by multiplying the values of the basic variables, which are given in the last column, times their corresponding contribution to profit as given in the c_j column.

By looking at the net evaluation row, we see that every standard bag Par produces will increase the value of the objective function by $10, and every deluxe bag will increase the value of the objective function by $9. Given only this information it would make sense to produce as many standard bags as possible. We know that every standard bag produced uses $\frac{7}{10}$ hour of cutting and dyeing time. Therefore, if we produce x_1 standard bags, we will use $\frac{7}{10}x_1$ hours of cutting and dyeing time. Since we only have 630 hours of cutting and dyeing time available, the maximum possible value of x_1, considering the cutting and dyeing constraint, can be calculated by solving the equation

$$\tfrac{7}{10}x_1 = 630.$$

Thus there is only enough time available in the cutting and dyeing department to manufacture a maximum of 900 standard bags.

In a similar manner, every standard bag produced uses $\frac{1}{2}$ hour of the available 600 hours of sewing time; therefore, the maximum number of standard bags we can produce and still satisfy the sewing constraint is given by

$$\tfrac{1}{2}x_1 = 600.$$

This indicates that x_1 could be at most 1200. But we know that it is impossible to produce 1200 standard bags since we do not have enough cutting and dyeing time available. In fact, we saw that we only have enough capacity in the cutting and dyeing department to make 900 standard bags. Considering these constraints simultaneously, the cutting and dyeing time is more restrictive. From the finishing constraint, we see that x_1 standard bags would use $1x_1$ of the available 708 hours of finishing time. Solving the equation

$$1x_1 = 708$$

shows that in terms of the three constraints considered so far, we can produce at most 708 standard bags.

In the inspection and packaging department every standard bag produced uses $\frac{1}{10}$ hour of inspection and packaging time. Since there is only 135 hours available we can solve

$$\tfrac{1}{10}x_1 = 135$$

to find the largest number of standard bags that can be processed by the inspection and packaging department is 1350. Thus when we consider all the constraints together, we see that the most restrictive constraint in terms of the maximum number of standard bags we can produce is the finishing constraint. That is, making 708 standard bags will use all the finishing capacity available. Hence if x_1 is introduced into solution at its maximum value, we will produce 708 standard bags ($x_1 = 708$), and there will be no slack time in the finishing department ($s_3 = 0$).

In making our decision to produce as many standard bags as possible, we have changed the set of variables in our basic feasible solution. The previous nonbasic variable x_1 is now a basic variable with $x_1 = 708$, while the previous basic variable s_3 is now a nonbasic variable with $s_3 = 0$. This interchange of roles between two variables is the essence of the Simplex method. That is, the way the Simplex method moves from one basic feasible solution to another is by selecting a nonbasic variable to replace one of the current basic variables. This process of moving from one basic feasible solution to another is called an *iteration*.

Before presenting general rules for carrying out the steps of the Simplex method, let us consider the following constraint equation which might appear in the Tableau form of a linear program:

$$-\tfrac{2}{3}x_1 + 0x_2 + 1s_2 = 500.$$

Suppose that s_2 is a basic variable and x_1 and x_2 are nonbasic variables. Since the coefficient of x_1 is negative ($-\tfrac{2}{3}$), every unit of x_1 introduced into solution would require the basic variable s_2 to increase by $\tfrac{2}{3}$ of a unit in order to maintain the constraint equation. Thus no matter how large we make x_1, the basic variable s_2 will also become larger and hence will never be driven out of the basic solution (that is, forced to zero). Similarly, since the coefficient of x_2 is zero, making x_2 basic would not affect the value of s_2. No matter how large we make x_2, the basic variable s_2 would remain unchanged and could never be driven out of solution. Thus if the coefficient of a nonbasic variable

224

is less than or equal to zero in some constraint, then that constraint can never limit the number of units of the nonbasic variable that can be brought into solution. Hence the basic variable associated with that constraint can never be driven out of solution. Therefore, in determining which variable should leave the current basis we only need to consider rows of our tableau in which the coefficient of the incoming nonbasic variable is *strictly positive*. With this additional consideration in mind, we now present the general Simplex rules for selecting a nonbasic variable to enter the basis and a current basic variable to leave the basis.

Criterion for Entering a New Variable Into the Basis

Look at the net evaluation row and select as the variable to enter the basis that variable which will cause the largest per unit increase in the objective function. Let us say that this variable corresponds to column j in the A portion of the tableau.

Criterion for Removing a Variable from the Current Basis

For each row i compute the ratio b_i/a_{ij} for every a_{ij} greater than zero. This ratio tells us the maximum amount of the variable x_j that can be brought into solution and still satisfy the constraint equation represented by that row. The minimum of these ratios tells us which constraint will be most restrictive if x_j is introduced into the solution. Hence we get the following rule for selecting the variable to remove from the current basis. For all the ratios b_i/a_{ij} where $a_{ij} > 0$ select the basic variable corresponding to the minimum value of these ratios as the variable to leave the basis.

Let us illustrate the above procedure by applying it to our Par. Inc., example problem. For illustration purposes we have added an extra column showing the b_i/a_{ij} ratios for the initial Simplex tableau associated with our Par, Inc., problem.

Basis	c_j	x_1 10	x_2 9	s_1 0	s_2 0	s_3 0	s_4 0		$\dfrac{b_i}{a_{i1}}$
s_1	0	7/10	1	1	0	0	0	630	$\dfrac{630}{7/10} = 900$
s_2	0	1/2	5/6	0	1	0	0	600	$\dfrac{600}{1/2} = 1200$
s_3	0	①	2/3	0	0	1	0	708	$\dfrac{708}{1} = 708$
s_4	0	1/10	1/4	0	0	0	1	135	$\dfrac{135}{1/10} = 1350$
	z_j	0	0	0	0	0	0	0	
	$c_j - z_j$	10	9	0	0	0	0		

We see that $c_1 - z_1 = 10$ is the largest positive value in the $c_j - z_j$ row. Hence x_1 is selected to become the new basic variable. Checking the ratios b_i/a_{i1} for $a_{i1} > 0$, we see that $b_3/a_{31} = 708$ is the minimum of these ratios. Thus the current basic variable associated with row 3 (s_3) is the variable selected to leave the basis. In our tableau we have circled a_{31}, $\textcircled{1}$, to indicate that the variable corresponding to the first column is to enter the basis and to indicate that the basic variable corresponding to the third row is to leave the basis. Adopting the usual linear programming terminology, we refer to this circled element as the *pivot element*.

We now see that to improve the current solution of $x_1 = 0$, $x_2 = 0$, $s_1 = 630$, $s_2 = 600$, $s_3 = 708$, and $s_4 = 135$, we should increase x_1 to 708. This would call for the production of 708 standard bags at a corresponding profit of $\$10 \times 708$ units $= \$7080$. In doing so, we will use all the available finishing capacity, and thus s_3 will be reduced to zero. Hence, x_1 will become the new basic variable replacing s_3 in the old basis.

9.5 CALCULATING THE NEXT TABLEAU

We saw in the previous section that our initial basic feasible solution could be improved by introducing x_1 into the basis to replace s_3. Before we can determine if this new basic feasible solution can be improved upon, it will be necessary to develop the corresponding Simplex tableau.

Recall that our initial Simplex tableau is simply a table containing the coefficients of the Tableau form for our linear programming problem. Because of the special properties of the Tableau form representation, our initial Simplex tableau contained a unit column corresponding to each of the basic variables. Thus the value of the basic variable with a 1 in row i could be found by simply reading the ith element of the last column in the Simplex tableau, b_i.

Now we will formulate a new tableau in which all the columns associated with the new basic variables are unit columns and such that the value of the basic variable in row i is given by b_i. Thus we would like to make the column in our new tableau corresponding to x_1 look just like the column corresponding to s_3 in our original tableau. Hence our goal is to get the column in our A matrix corresponding to x_1 to appear as

0

0

1

0.

The way in which we transform the Simplex tableau so that it still represents an equivalent system of constraint equations with the above properties

226

is to employ the elementary row operations discussed in Chapter 8. You will recall that there were two row operations that we could perform on a system of equations and still retain an equivalent system. (1) we could multiply any row by a nonzero number, and (2) we could multiply any row by a nonzero number and add it to another now. By performing these row operations, we will be able to change the column for the variable entering the basis to a unit column and, at the same time, change the last column of the tableau so that it contains the values of the new basic variables. We emphasize that performing these operations will in no way affect the solution to our problem, since the feasible solutions to the constraint equations are not changed by these elementary row operations.

Clearly, many of the numerical values in our new Simplex tableau are going to change as the result of performing these row operations. However, we know that after the row operations are performed, the new Simplex tableau will still represent an equivalent system of equations. Nonetheless, because the elements in the new Simplex tableau will usually change as the result of the required row operations, our present method of referring to elements in the Simplex tableau may lead to confusion. Let us see why this is so.

Up to now we have made no distinction between the A matrix and b column for the Tableau form and the corresponding portions of the Simplex tableau. Indeed, we showed that the initial Simplex tableau was formed by properly placing the a_{ij}, c_j, and b_i elements as given in the Tableau form into the Simplex tableau. From now on we will refer to the portion of the Simplex tableau that initially contained the a_{ij} values with the symbol $\overline{A}$, and the portion of the tableau that initially contained the b_i values with the symbol $\overline{b}$. In terms of the Simplex tableau, elements in $\overline{A}$ will be denoted by $\overline{a}_{ij}$ and elements in $\overline{b}$ will be denoted by $\overline{b}_i$. We recognize that using this notation we will have $\overline{A} = A$ and $\overline{b} = b$ in our initial Simplex tableau. However, in subsequent Simplex tableaus this relationship will usually not hold. This notation will avoid any possible confusion when we wish to distinguish between the original constraint coefficient values a_{ij} and right-hand side values b_i of the Tableau form, and the Simplex tableau elements $\overline{a}_{ij}$ and $\overline{b}_i$.

Now let us illustrate the procedure for calculating the next tableau by returning to the Par, Inc., problem. Recall that our goal is to get the column in the $\overline{A}$ portion of the tableau corresponding to x_1 to appear as

$$\begin{bmatrix} \overline{a}_{11} \\ \overline{a}_{21} \\ \overline{a}_{31} \\ \overline{a}_{41} \end{bmatrix} = \begin{bmatrix} 0 \\ 0 \\ 1 \\ 0 \end{bmatrix}$$

Since we already have $\overline{a}_{31} = 1$ in the initial Simplex tableau, no row operations need to be performed on the third row of our tableau.

227

In order to set $a_{11} = 0$, we multiply our *pivot row* (the row corresponding to the finishing constraint) by $-\frac{7}{10}$ to obtain the equivalent equation

$$-\tfrac{7}{10}(1x_1 + \tfrac{2}{3}x_2 + 0s_1 + 0s_2 + 1s_3 + 0s_4) = -\tfrac{7}{10}(708)$$

or

$$-\tfrac{7}{10}x_1 - \tfrac{14}{30}x_2 - 0s_1 - 0s_2 - \tfrac{7}{10}s_3 - 0s_4 = -495.6. \tag{9.11}$$

Now let us consider the cutting and dyeing constraint equation which is

$$\tfrac{7}{10}x_1 + 1x_2 + 1s_1 + 0s_2 + 0s_3 + 0s_4 = 630. \tag{9.12}$$

Let us add equation (9.11) to the cutting and dyeing constraint equation (9.12). Dropping the terms with zero coefficients and performing this addition, we get

$$(\tfrac{7}{10}x_1 + 1x_2 + 1s_1) + (-\tfrac{7}{10}x_1 - \tfrac{14}{30}x_2 - \tfrac{7}{10}s_3) = 630 - 495.6$$

or

$$0x_1 + \tfrac{16}{30}x_2 + 1s_1 - \tfrac{7}{10}s_3 = 134.4. \tag{9.13}$$

Since this is just a simple row operation, we will have an equivalent system of equations if equation (9.12) is replaced by equation (9.13). Making this substitution in our original Simplex tableau, we see that we have obtained a zero in the first position in the x_1 column (that is, $\bar{a}_{11} = 0$).

Basis	c_j	x_1	x_2	s_1	s_2	s_3	s_4	
		10	9	0	0	0	0	
		0	16/30	1	0	−7/10	0	134.4
		1/2	5/6	0	1	0	0	600
		1	2/3	0	0	1	0	708
		1/10	1/4	0	0	0	1	135
	z_j							
	$c_j - z_j$							

We still need to set the elements in the second row and the fourth row of the x_1 column equal to zero. Can you find a way to do this? Recall that we accomplished this result for row 1 by multiplying the pivot row by a nonzero constant $(-\frac{7}{10})$ and then adding the result to the first row. Note that our constant in this case was just the negative of the coefficient in the first row and x_1 column. Thus to get the element in the second constraint corresponding to the x_1 column equal to zero, we multiply the pivot row by $-\frac{1}{2}$ and then add this result to the second constraint. This gives us the result

$$(\tfrac{1}{2}x_1 + \tfrac{5}{6}x_2 + 1s_2) + (-\tfrac{1}{2}x_1 - \tfrac{1}{3}x_2 - \tfrac{1}{2}s_3) = 600 - 354$$

which is equivalent to

$$0x_1 + \tfrac{1}{2}x_2 + 0s_1 + 1s_2 - \tfrac{1}{2}s_3 + 0s_4 = 246.$$

This becomes the new representation of the second constraint equation in our Simplex tableau.

To obtain a zero in the a_{41} position, we just multiply our pivot row by $-\tfrac{1}{10}$ and then add the result to the last row. The resulting constraint equation is

$$0x_1 + \tfrac{22}{120}x_2 + 0s_1 + 0s_2 - \tfrac{1}{10}s_3 + 1s_4 = 64.2.$$

Placing these last two equations into our new tableau gives us the following Simplex tableau:

Basis	c_j	x_1 10	x_2 9	s_1 0	s_2 0	s_3 0	s_4 0	
s_1	0	0	16/30	1	0	−7/10	0	134.4
s_2	0	0	1/2	0	1	−1/2	0	246
x_1	10	1	2/3	0	0	1	0	708
s_4	0	0	22/120	0	0	−1/10	1	64.2
	z_j							7080
	$c_j - z_j$							

Since s_1, s_2, x_1, and s_4 are the basic variables in this tableau, x_2 and s_3 are set equal to 0, and we can read the solution for s_1, s_2, x_1 and s_4 directly from the tableau:

$$s_1 = 134.4$$
$$s_2 = 246$$
$$x_1 = 708$$
$$s_4 = 64.2$$

The profit corresponding to this solution is \$7080. Note that this value for profit was obtained by multiplying the solution values for our basic variables in the $\bar{b}$ column times their corresponding objective function coefficients as given in the c_j column, that is $7080 = 0(134.4) + 0(246) + 10(708) + 0(64.2)$. We still have not calculated any entries in the z_j and $c_j - z_j$ rows. Before doing so, let us reflect for a moment on the present solution.

Interpreting the Results of an Iteration

Starting with one Simplex tableau, changing the basic variables, and finding a new Simplex tableau is referred to as an iteration of the Simplex method. In our example the initial basic feasible solution was

$$
\begin{bmatrix} x_1 \\ x_2 \\ s_1 \\ s_2 \\ s_3 \\ s_4 \end{bmatrix} = \begin{bmatrix} 0 \\ 0 \\ 630 \\ 600 \\ 708 \\ 135 \end{bmatrix}
$$

with a corresponding profit of $0. One iteration of the Simplex method moved us to another basic feasible solution where the value of the objective function was $7080. This new basic feasible solution was

$$
\begin{bmatrix} x_1 \\ x_2 \\ s_1 \\ s_2 \\ s_3 \\ s_4 \end{bmatrix} = \begin{bmatrix} 708 \\ 0 \\ 134.4 \\ 246 \\ 0 \\ 64.2 \end{bmatrix}
$$

Graphically this iteration moved us from one extreme point to another extreme point along the edge of our feasible region. In Figure 9.2 we see that our initial basic feasible solution corresponded to extreme point ①. The first iteration moved us in the direction of the greatest per unit increase in profit, that is, along the x_1 axis. We moved away from extreme point in the x_1 direction until we could move no further without violating one of the constraints. The tableau we calculated after one iteration represents the basic feasible solution corresponding to extreme point ②.

We know that the slack variables represent the unused capacity associated with each constraint. Noting the value of s_1 in our Simplex tableau, we see that the unused cutting and dyeing capacity is 134.4 hours. Does this seem reasonable? Since our solution indicated that we should make 708 standard bags, and since each standard bag requires $\frac{7}{10}$ hour of cutting and dyeing time, the total number of hours used in producing the 708 standard bags is $\frac{7}{10}$ (708) = 495.6. Since we started with 630 hours, we now have 134.4 hours of unused time available. Similarly, since every standard bag produced requires $\frac{1}{2}$ hour of sewing time, the total amount of sewing time used in producing 708 standard bags is 354 hours. We started with 600 hours of sewing time; therefore 246 hours remain. Every standard bag requires 1 hour of finishing time. Thus since 708 hours of finishing time are available, we will use all the finishing time by producing 708 standard bags. This is the reason you see that the finishing constraint is binding at extreme point ②. Producing 708 stan-

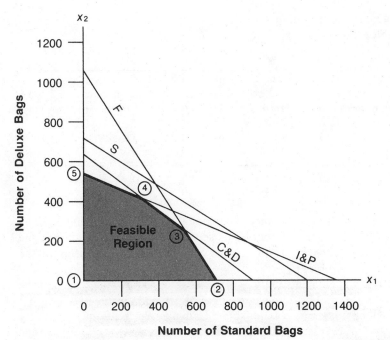

*FIGURE 9.2   Feasible solution region for the Par, Inc.,
             problem.*

dard bags will use $\frac{1}{10}(708) = 70.8$ hours of inspection and packaging time, leaving a slack of 64.2 hours in this department.

Moving toward a Better Solution

We are ready to start things all over again. The next question we must ask ourselves is, can we find a new basic feasible solution (extreme point) that will increase the value of the objective function any further? To answer this, we need to calculate our z_j and $c_j - z_j$ rows for the current Simplex tableau.

Recall that the elements in the z_j row can be calculated by multiplying the elements in the c_j column of the Simplex tableau by the corresponding elements in the columns of the $\overline{A}$ matrix and summing. Thus we get

$$
\begin{aligned}
z_1 &= 0(0) &&+ 0(0) &&+ 10(1) + 0(0) &&= 10 \\
z_2 &= 0(\tfrac{16}{30}) &&+ 0(\tfrac{1}{2}) &&+ 10(\tfrac{2}{3}) + 0(\tfrac{22}{120}) &&= \tfrac{20}{3} \\
z_3 &= 0(1) &&+ 0(0) &&+ 10(0) + 0(0) &&= 0 \\
z_4 &= 0(0) &&+ 0(1) &&+ 10(0) + 0(0) &&= 0 \\
z_5 &= 0(-\tfrac{7}{10}) &&+ 0(-\tfrac{1}{2}) &&+ 10(1) + 0(-\tfrac{1}{10}) &&= 10 \\
z_6 &= 0(0) &&+ 0(0) &&+ 10(0) + 0(1) &&= 0.
\end{aligned}
$$

231

Subtracting z_j from c_j to obtain the net evaluation row, we get the complete Simplex tableau:

		x_1	x_2	s_1	s_2	s_3	s_4	
Basis	c_j	10	9	0	0	0	0	
s_1	0	0	16/30	1	0	−7/10	0	134.4
s_2	0	0	1/2	0	1	−1/2	0	246
x_1	10	1	2/3	0	0	1	0	708
s_4	0	0	22/120	0	0	−1/10	1	64.2
	z_j	10	20/3	0	0	10	0	7080
	$c_j - z_j$	0	7/3	0	0	−10	0	

Before considering the question of changing the basis and moving on to an even better basic feasible solution, let us see if we can interpret some of the numerical values appearing in the above Simplex tableau in terms of the original Par, Inc., problem.

We know that the elements in the x_2 column indicate how much each of the four basic variables will have to change in order to produce one unit of x_2 and still satisfy all the constraint relationships. Using the *Basis* column to identify the basic variable corresponding to each element in the x_2 column, we can see that introducing one unit of x_2 will force us to decrease s_1 by $\frac{16}{30}$ of a unit, s_2 by $\frac{1}{2}$ of a unit, x_1 by $\frac{2}{3}$ of a unit, and s_4 by $\frac{22}{120}$ of a unit.

Why does producing one deluxe bag require us to decrease the production of standard bags by $\frac{2}{3}$ of a unit? Notice that when we decided to produce 708 standard bags we used all the finishing time available. Since every unit of x_2 we produce requires $\frac{2}{3}$ hour of finishing time ($\bar{a}_{32} = \frac{2}{3}$), and every unit of x_1 requires 1 full hour, we see that in order to produce a unit of x_2 we will have to cut back $\frac{2}{3}$ of a unit of x_1 in order to free up enough finishing time. Thus $\bar{a}_{32} = \frac{2}{3}$ does indeed indicate correctly how many units of the basic variable x_1 must be given up if one unit of x_2 is introduced.

In our original tableau (*look back and check this*) we saw that each deluxe bag required 1 hour of cutting and dyeing time. Why then is $\bar{a}_{12} = \frac{16}{30}$? Once again, each deluxe bag we produce will kick out $\frac{2}{3}$ of a standard bag from the solution, and hence free up $\frac{2}{3}$ of the cutting and dyeing time required for one standard bag. Since each standard bag requires $\frac{7}{10}$ hour, we see that $\frac{2}{3}(\frac{7}{10}) = \frac{14}{30}$ hour would be made available because $\frac{2}{3}$ of a standard bag leaves the solution. Since each deluxe bag requires 1 hour of cutting and dyeing time, the net effect of producing one deluxe bag is to really only use up an additional $(1 - \frac{14}{30}) = \frac{16}{30}$ hour of cutting and dyeing time. The remaining coefficients in the x_2 column can be interpreted in the same manner.

To see why $c_2 - z_2 = \frac{7}{3}$ we note that since the basic variables s_1, s_2, and s_4 are slack variables and have zero objective function coefficients, their reduction when one unit of x_2 is brought into solution does not decrease total profit. However, since the profit associated with each unit of x_1 is $10, the $\frac{2}{3}$

232

reduction will cost us $\$\frac{20}{3}$. On the other hand, every unit of x_2 we bring into solution increases profit by \$9, or $\$\frac{27}{3}$. Thus the net increase in the value of the objective function resulting from a one unit increase in x_2 will be given by $\$\frac{27}{3} - \frac{20}{3} = \$\frac{7}{3}$.

Note that for all the basic variables s_1, s_2, x_1, and s_4 the value of $c_j - z_j$ is equal to zero. Since each of these variables is associated with a unit column in our Simplex tableau, we can interpret this as meaning that bringing one unit of a basic variable into solution would force us to remove one unit of the same basic variable. The result obviously is no net change in the value of the objective function. From a physical point of view the argument is even simpler. Consider, for example, x_1. Since we are producing all the standard bags we can, no additional profit can be realized from their further production. Thus the net improvement in the objective function must be zero.

In summary we note that at each iteration of the Simplex method

1. The value of the current basic feasible solution can be found in the $\bar{b}$ column of the Simplex tableau;
2. The value of $c_j - z_j$ for each of the basic variables is equal to zero;
3. The coefficients in a particular column of the $\bar{A}$ portion of the Simplex tableau indicate how much the current basic solution will change if one unit of the variable associated with that column is introduced.

Let us now analyze the net evaluation row to see if we can introduce a new variable into the basis and continue to improve the objective function. Using our rule for determining which variable should enter the basis next, we select x_2, since it has the highest positive coefficient in the net evaluation row.

In order to determine which variable will be removed from the basis when x_2 enters, we must compute for each row i the ratio $\bar{b}_i/\bar{a}_{i2}$ (remember though that we only compute this ratio if $\bar{a}_{i2}$ is greater than zero) and then select the variable corresponding to the minimum ratio as the variable to leave the basis. As before, we will show these ratios in an extra column of the Simplex tableau. Thus our extended tableau becomes

Basis	c_j	x_1 10	x_2 9	s_1 0	s_2 0	s_3 0	s_4 0		$\bar{b}_i$ $\bar{a}_{i2}$
s_1	0	0	16/30	1	0	−7/10	0	134.4	$\frac{134.4}{16/30} = 252$
s_2	0	0	1/2	0	1	−1/2	0	246	$\frac{246}{1/2} = 492$
x_1	10	1	2/3	0	0	1	0	708	$\frac{708}{2/3} = 1062$
s_4	0	0	22/120	0	0	−1/10	1	64.2	$\frac{64.2}{22/120} = 350.18$
	z_j	10	20/3	0	0	10	0	7080	
	$c_j - z_j$	0	7/3	0	0	−10	0		

233

Since 252 is the minimum ratio, s_1 will be the variable that will leave the basis. Our pivot element will be $\bar{a}_{12} = \frac{16}{30}$, which is circled in the above tableau. The variable x_2 must now be made a basic variable. This means that we must perform the row operations necessary to convert the x_2 column into a unit column; that is, we will have to transform the second column in our tableau to the form

$$\begin{bmatrix} 1 \\ 0 \\ 0 \\ 0 \end{bmatrix}$$

We can do this by performing the following steps:

Step 1: Multiply every element in row 1 by 30/16. Note that this will get us a 1 in position $\bar{a}_{12}$.

Step 2: Multiply the new row 1 by $(-1/2)$ and add the result to row 2. This will set $\bar{a}_{22} = 0$.

Step 3: Multiply the new row 1 by $(-2/3)$ and add the result to row 3. This will set $\bar{a}_{32} = 0$.

Step 4: Multiply the new row 1 by $(-22/120)$ and add the result to row 4. This will give us a zero in position $\bar{a}_{42}$.

The above elementary row operations again change the appearance of our Simplex tableau, but do not alter the solutions to the system of equations contained in the tableau. The only difference is that now we have x_2, s_2, x_1, and s_4 as the basic variables, and s_1 and s_3 as the nonbasic variables. The new tableau resulting from these row operations is presented below:

Basis	c_j	x_1 10	x_2 9	s_1 0	s_2 0	s_3 0	s_4 0	
x_2	9	0	1	30/16	0	$-210/160$	0	252
s_2	0	0	0	$-15/16$	1	25/160	0	120
x_1	10	1	0	$-20/16$	0	300/160	0	540
s_4	0	0	0	$-11/32$	0	45/320	1	18
	z_j							7668
	$c_j - z_j$							

Note that the profit corresponding to this basic feasible solution is $252(9) + 120(0) + 540(10) + 18(0)$, or 7668, and that the basic variables are $x_2 = 252, s_2 = 120, x_1 = 540$, and $s_4 = 18$.

This basic feasible solution corresponds to extreme point ③ in Figure

9.2. As you may recall from the graphical solution in Chapter 8, this is the optimal solution to the Par, Inc., problem. However, the Simplex method has not yet identified this solution as optimal. Thus we must continue to investigate whether or not it makes sense to bring any other variable into the basis and move to another basic feasible solution. As we saw before, this involves calculating the z_j and $c_j - z_j$ rows and then selecting the variable to enter the basis that corresponds to the highest positive value in the net evaluation row.

After performing the z_j and $c_j - z_j$ calculations for our current solution, we obtain the following complete Simplex tableau:

Basis	c_j	x_1 10	x_2 9	s_1 0	s_2 0	s_3 0	s_4 0	
x_2	9	0	1	30/16	0	−210/160	0	252
s_2	0	0	0	−15/16	1	25/160	0	120
x_1	10	1	0	−20/16	0	300/160	0	540
s_4	0	0	0	−11/32	0	45/320	1	18
z_j		10	9	70/16	0	111/16	0	7668
$c_j - z_j$		0	0	−70/16	0	−111/16	0	

Looking at the net evaluation row we see that every element is zero or negative. Since $c_j - z_j$ is less than or equal to zero for both of our nonbasic variables s_1 and s_3, if we attempt to bring a nonbasic variable into the basis at this point, it will result in lowering the current value of the objective function. Hence the above tableau represents the optimal solution to our linear programming problem.

Stopping Criterion

The optimal solution to a linear programming problem has been reached when there are no positive values in the net evaluation row of the Simplex tableau. If all entries in the net evaluation row are zero or negative, we stop the calculations and our optimal solution is given by the current Simplex tableau.

Interpretation of Optimal Solution

We see that in the final solution to our Par, Inc., problem the basic variables are x_2, s_2, x_1, and s_4. The complete optimal solution to the Par, Inc., problem is thus

$$\begin{bmatrix} x_1 \\ x_2 \\ s_1 \\ s_2 \\ s_3 \\ s_4 \end{bmatrix} = \begin{bmatrix} 540 \\ 252 \\ 0 \\ 120 \\ 0 \\ 18 \end{bmatrix}$$

That is, our optimal solution is $x_1 = 540$, $x_2 = 252$, $s_1 = 0$, $s_2 = 120$, $s_3 = 0$, and $s_4 = 18$ with a corresponding value of the objective function of \$7668. Thus if the management of Par, Inc., wants to maximize profit, they should produce 540 standard bags and 252 deluxe bags. In addition, management should note that there will be 120 hours of idle time in the sewing department and 18 hours of idle time in the inspection and packaging department. If it is possible to make alternate use of these additional resources, management should plan to do so.

You can also see that with $s_1 = 0$ and $s_3 = 0$ there is no slack time available in the cutting and dyeing and the finishing departments. The constraints for these operations are both binding in our optimal solution (see Figure 9.2). If it is possible to obtain additional man-hours for these two departments, management should consider doing so.

9.6 TABLEAU FORM—THE GENERAL CASE

In Section 9.2 we pointed out how setting up the Tableau form of a linear programming problem is a necessary step in preparation for the Simplex solution procedure. You may recall that the Tableau form had two important properties: (1) the b column values (right-hand side values) were nonnegative, and (2) with m constraints, m columns of the A matrix were unit columns with the 1's of the unit columns all in different rows.

The purpose of the Tableau form is to make it easy to identify an initial basic feasible (extreme point) solution in order to start the Simplex procedure.

When we formulated the Par, Inc., problem we found that the right-hand side values were all nonnegative [property (1) satisfied], and that the Standard form of the four less-than-or-equal-to constraints provided four unit columns for the slack variables associated with the constraints [property (2) satisfied]. Thus we were lucky in this particular case in that the Standard form of the Par, Inc., problem was also the Tableau form. However, when we encounter negative right-hand side values, greater-than-or-equal-to constraints, and/or equality constraints we will have to take additional steps in order to convert a linear program into its Tableau form. The necessary steps are outlined in this section.

Negative Right-Hand Sides

What if one or more of the values on the right-hand side of our constraints are *negative?* For example, suppose that management of Par, Inc., had specified that the number of standard bags produced had to be less than or equal to the number of deluxe bags after 25 deluxe bags had been saved for display purposes. We could formulate this constraint as

$$1x_1 \leq 1x_2 - 25. \tag{9.14}$$

Subtracting x_2 from both sides of the inequality allows us to place all the variables on the left-hand side of the constraint and the constant on the right-hand side. Thus we have

$$1x_1 - 1x_2 \leq -25. \tag{9.15}$$

Our standard procedure of adding a slack variable ($x_1 - x_2 + s_1 = -25$) to obtain the Tableau form is unacceptable since our constraint would not satisfy the Tableau form requirement of nonnegative right-hand sides. Thus we must look for ways to remove the negative right-hand side values before we can set up our Tableau form representation of the problem. This is relatively easy to do. There are three separate cases to consider. We must consider whether the constraint in question is an equality, greater-than-or-equal-to, or less-than-or-equal-to constraint.

Case 1: Equality Constraint

For example,

$$6x_1 + 3x_2 - 4x_3 = -20.$$

We need only multiply both sides of the equation by -1 in order to obtain

$$-6x_1 - 3x_2 + 4x_3 = 20$$

which has an acceptable right-hand side value for the Tableau form.

Case 2: Greater-than-or-Equal-to Constraint

For example,

$$6x_1 + 3x_2 - 4x_3 \geq -20.$$

What would happen if we multiplied both sides by -1? The rule is that if you multiply both sides of an inequality by a negative number, the sign of the inequality changes direction. For example, the inequality $1 \geq -2$ is certainly true. However, if we multiply both sides by -1 we must change the direction of the inequality in order to have the correct relationship $-1 \leq 2$. Similarly, multiplying the above constraint by -1 and changing the direction of the inequality yields

$$-6x_1 - 3x_2 + 4x_3 \leq 20.$$

This constraint can now be treated the same as any ordinary less-than-or-equal-to constraint by adding a slack variable to the left-hand side.

Case 3: Less-than-or-Equal-to Constraint

For example,

$$6x_1 + 3x_2 - 4x_3 \leq -20.$$

We multiply both sides by -1 and change the direction of the inequality to get

$$-6x_1 - 3x_2 + 4x_3 \geq 20.$$

Using this method, the Par, Inc., constraint (9.15) could be rewritten as

$$-1x_1 + 1x_2 \geq 25. \tag{9.16}$$

Now we have the usual situation for a greater-than-or-equal-to constraint. That is, all we need to do now to obtain the Standard form is to subtract a surplus variable from the left-hand side.

Summarizing, we see that any time the original formulation of a linear program contains a negative right-hand side we should perform the preliminary operations outlined above before adding slack and surplus variables.

Greater-than-or-Equal-to Constraints

Suppose that in the Par, Inc., problem management wanted to ensure that at least 100 bags of each model were produced. We could incorporate these new restrictions by adding a constraint that ensures that x_1 will be greater than or equal to 100 bags, and adding another constraint that ensures that x_2 will be greater than or equal to 100 bags; that is, we can add the constraints

$$1x_1 \geq 100 \tag{9.17}$$
$$1x_2 \geq 100. \tag{9.18}$$

With these two additions our modified problem can now be written as

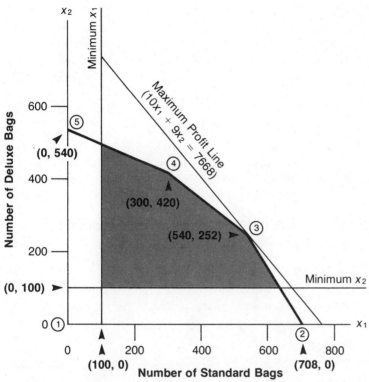

FIGURE 9.3 *Graphical solution to the modified Par, Inc., problem.*

$$\max z = 10x_1 + 9x_2$$

$$\text{s.t.} \quad \tfrac{7}{10}x_1 + 1x_2 \le 630$$

$$\tfrac{1}{2}x_1 + \tfrac{5}{6}x_2 \le 600$$

$$1x_1 + \tfrac{2}{3}x_2 \le 708$$

$$\tfrac{1}{10}x_1 + \tfrac{1}{4}x_2 \le 135$$

$$1x_1 \qquad \ge 100$$

$$1x_2 \ge 100$$

$$x_1, x_2 \ge 0.$$

The graphical solution to this problem is shown in Figure 9.3 and is the same as the solution to the original Par, Inc., problem. However, if we are going to use the Simplex method for solving this problem, we need to know how to put the greater-than-or-equal-to constraints into the Tableau form.

We can first use slack and surplus variable to write this Par, Inc., program in the following Standard form:

239

$$\text{max} \quad 10x_1 + 9x_2 + 0s_1 + 0s_2 + 0s_3 + 0s_4 + 0s_5 + 0s_6$$

$$
\begin{array}{llll}
\text{s.t.} & \tfrac{7}{10}x_1 + 1x_2 + 1s_1 & = 630 & (9.19) \\
& \tfrac{1}{2}x_1 + \tfrac{5}{6}x_2 \qquad + 1s_2 & = 600 & (9.20) \\
& 1x_1 + \tfrac{2}{3}x_2 \qquad\qquad + 1s_3 & = 708 & (9.21) \\
& \tfrac{1}{10}x_1 + \tfrac{1}{4}x_2 \qquad\qquad\qquad + 1s_4 & = 135 & (9.22) \\
& 1x_1 \qquad\qquad\qquad\qquad\qquad\qquad - 1s_5 & = 100 & (9.23) \\
& \qquad 1x_2 \qquad\qquad\qquad\qquad\qquad\qquad - 1s_6 & = 100 & (9.24)
\end{array}
$$

$$x_1, x_2, s_1, s_2, s_3, s_4, s_5, s_6 \geq 0.$$

Now let us reconsider the way we generated an initial basic feasible solution to get the Simplex method started. We set $x_1 = 0, x_2 = 0$, and selected the slack variables as our initial basic variables. Extending this notion to our current problem would suggest setting $x_1 = 0, x_2 = 0$, and selecting as initial basic variables the slack and surplus variables. However, looking at the graphical representation of this problem (Figure 9.2) we see that the solution corresponding to the origin is no longer feasible. The inclusion of the two greater-than-or-equal-to constraints $x_1 \geq 100$ and $x_2 \geq 100$ has made the basic solution with $x_1 = x_2 = 0$ infeasible.

To see this another way look at equations (9.23) and (9.24) in the Standard form representation of the problem. When x_1 and x_2 are set equal to zero, equations (9.23) and (9.24) reduce to

$$-1s_5 = 100$$

and

$$-1s_6 = 100.$$

Thus setting x_1 and x_2 equal to zero gives us the basic solution

$$
\begin{bmatrix} s_1 \\ s_2 \\ s_3 \\ s_4 \\ s_5 \\ s_6 \end{bmatrix}
=
\begin{bmatrix} 630 \\ 600 \\ 708 \\ 135 \\ -100 \\ -100 \end{bmatrix}
$$

Clearly this is not a basic feasible solution since s_5 and s_6 violate the nonnegativity requirements. Thus our former method of creating an initial basic feasible solution by setting each of the decision variables to zero will not work. The difficulty here is that the Standard form and the Tableau form are only equivalent for problems with less-than-or-equal-to constraints.

In order to set up the Tableau form for this problem, we shall resort to a mathematical "trick" that will enable us to find an initial basic feasible solution in terms of the slack variables s_1, s_2, s_3, and s_4, and two new variables we shall denote as a_1 and a_2. These two new variables constitute the mathematical "trick." Variables a_1 and a_2 really have nothing to do with the Par, Inc., problem, but merely serve to enable us to set up the Tableau form and thus obtain an initial basic feasible solution. Since these new variables have been artificially created by us in order to get things going, we will refer to such variables as *artificial variables*. We caution the student to avoid confusing the notation for artificial variables with that used for elements of the A matrix. Elements of the A matrix always have two subscripts, whereas artificial variables only have one.

With the addition of two artificial variables, we can convert our Standard form representation of the modified Par, Inc., problem into the Tableau form. We add an artificial variable, a_1 to equation (9.23) and an artificial variable, a_2, to equation (9.24) to obtain the following representation of the system of equations in Tableau form:

$$
\begin{aligned}
\tfrac{7}{10}x_1 + 1x_2 + 1s_1 &&&&&&&&= 630 \\
\tfrac{1}{2}x_1 + \tfrac{5}{6}x_2 &&+ 1s_2 &&&&&&= 600 \\
1x_1 + \tfrac{2}{3}x_2 &&&&+ 1s_3 &&&&= 708 \\
\tfrac{1}{10}x_1 + \tfrac{1}{4}x_2 &&&&&&+ 1s_4 &&= 135 \\
1x_1 &&&&&&&&- 1s_5 \quad + 1a_1 &= 100 \\
1x_2 &&&&&&&&- 1s_6 \quad + 1a_2 &= 100
\end{aligned}
$$

$$x_1, x_2, s_1, s_2, s_3, s_4, s_5, s_6, a_1, a_2 \geq 0.$$

Since the variables s_1, s_2, s_3, s_4, a_1, and a_2 each appear only once with a coefficient of 1, and since the right-hand sides are nonnegative, both requirements of the Tableau form have been satisfied.

We can now obtain an initial basic feasible solution to the system of equations in the Tableau form by setting $x_1 = x_2 = s_5 = s_6 = 0$. This complete solution is

$$
\begin{bmatrix} x_1 \\ x_2 \\ s_1 \\ s_2 \\ s_3 \\ s_4 \\ s_5 \\ s_6 \\ a_1 \\ a_2 \end{bmatrix}
=
\begin{bmatrix} 0 \\ 0 \\ 630 \\ 600 \\ 708 \\ 135 \\ 0 \\ 0 \\ 100 \\ 100 \end{bmatrix}
$$

241

Is this solution feasible in terms of our real-world problem? No. It does not satisfy the requirements that we produce at least 100 each of standard and deluxe bags. Thus we must make an important distinction between a basic feasible solution for the Tableau form of our problem and a basic feasible solution for the real-world problem. A basic feasible solution for the Tableau form of a linear programming problem is not always a basic feasible solution to the real-world problem. This is because of the appearance of the artificial variables in the Tableau form of the problem. However, since the Standard form representation of the problem does not include any of these artificial variables, a basic feasible solution for the Standard form representation will be feasible for the real-world problem. We see, then, that the Standard form representation is equivalent to the original problem whereas, whenever we have to add artificial variables, the Tableau form representation is not.

As we saw earlier in this chapter, the reason for creating the Tableau form was to obtain an initial basic feasible solution to get the Simplex method started. Thus we see that whenever it is necessary to introduce artificial variables, the initial Simplex solution will not in general be feasible for the real-world problem. This situation is not as difficult as it might seem, however, since the only time we *must* have a feasible solution is at the *last* iteration of the Simplex method (that is, the optimal solution must be feasible). Thus if we could devise some means to guarantee that the artificial variables would be driven out of the basis before the optimal solution was reached, there would be no difficulty.

The way in which we guarantee that these artificial variables will be driven out before the optimal solution is reached is to assign a very large cost to each of these variables in the objective function. For example, in the problem we are currently considering, we assign a very large negative number as the profit coefficient of each artificial variable in the objective function of the Tableau form. Hence if these variables are in solution, they will necessarily be substantially reducing profits. As a result, these variables will be eliminated from the basis as soon as possible, and this is precisely what we want to happen.

As an alternative to picking a large negative number like $-100,000$ for the profit coefficient, we will denote the profit coefficient of each artificial variable by $-M$. Here it is assumed that $-M$ represents some very large negative number. This notation will make it easier for us to keep track of the elements of the Simplex tableau which depend on the profit coefficients of the artificial variables. Using $-M$ as the profit coefficient for the artificial variables, we can now write the objective function for the Tableau form of our problem:

$$\max z = 10x_1 + 9x_2 + 0s_1 + 0s_2 + 0s_3 + 0s_4 + 0s_5 + 0s_6 - Ma_1 - Ma_2.$$

Thus in terms of our new artificial variables a_1 and a_2, we can now write the following initial Simplex tableau:

Basis	c_j	x_1 10	x_2 9	s_1 0	s_2 0	s_3 0	s_4 0	s_5 0	s_6 0	a_1 $-M$	a_2 $-M$	
s_1	0	7/10	1	1	0	0	0	0	0	0	0	630
s_2	0	1/2	5/6	0	1	0	0	0	0	0	0	600
s_3	0	1	2/3	0	0	1	0	0	0	0	0	708
s_4	0	1/10	1/4	0	0	0	1	0	0	0	0	135
a_1	$-M$	①	0	0	0	0	0	-1	0	1	0	100
a_2	$-M$	0	1	0	0	0	0	0	-1	0	1	100
	z_j	$-M$	$-M$	0	0	0	0	M	M	$-M$	$-M$	$-200M$
	$c_j - z_j$	$10 + M$	$9 + M$	0	0	0	0	$-M$	$-M$	0	0	

The above tableau corresponds to the solution $s_1 = 630$, $s_2 = 600$, $s_3 = 708$, $s_4 = 135$, $a_1 = 100$, $a_2 = 100$, and $x_1 = x_2 = s_5 = s_6 = 0$. In terms of our tableau, this is a basic feasible solution since all the variables are greater-than-or-equal-to zero and $n - m$ of the variables are equal to zero. However, in terms of our modified Par, Inc., problem, $x_1 = x_2 = 0$ is clearly not feasible. This difficulty is caused by the fact that the artificial variables are in our current basic solution at positive values. Let us complete the Simplex solution to this problem and see if the artificial variables are driven out of solution as we hope they will be.

We see that at the first iteration, x_1 will be brought into the basis and a_1 will be driven out. The Simplex tableau after this iteration is presented below.

Result of iteration 1:

Basis	c_j	x_1 10	x_2 9	s_1 0	s_2 0	s_3 0	s_4 0	s_5 0	s_6 0	a_1 $-M$	a_2 $-M$	
s_1	0	0	1	1	0	0	0	7/10	0	$-7/10$	0	560
s_2	0	0	5/6	0	1	0	0	1/2	0	$-1/2$	0	550
s_3	0	0	2/3	0	0	1	0	1	0	-1	0	608
s_4	0	0	1/4	0	0	0	1	1/10	0	$-1/10$	0	125
x_1	10	1	0	0	0	0	0	-1	0	1	0	100
a_2	$-M$	0	①	0	0	0	0	0	-1	0	1	100
	z_j	10	$-M$	0	0	0	0	-10	M	10	$-M$	$1000 - 100M$
	$c_j - z_j$	0	$9 + M$	0	0	0	0	10	$-M$	$-M - 10$	0	

The current solution is still not feasible since artificial variable a_2 is in the basis at a positive value. It does not satisfy the $x_2 \geq 100$ requirement. Graphically we see in Figure 9.4 that this iteration has moved us from the origin (labeled Ⓐ) to point Ⓑ which is still not in the feasible region.

243

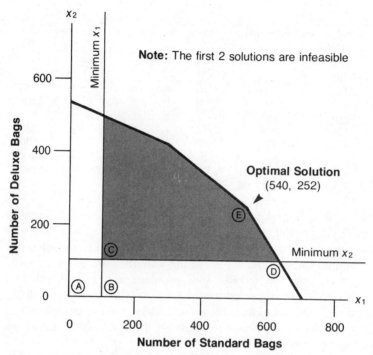

FIGURE 9.4 *Sequence of simplex solutions to modified Par, Inc., problem.*

At the next iteration x_2 will be brought into solution and a_2 will be driven out. The Simplex tableau after this iteration is presented below:

Result of iteration 2:

Basis	c_j	x_1 10	x_2 9	s_1 0	s_2 0	s_3 0	s_4 0	s_5 0	s_6 0	a_1 $-M$	a_2 $-M$	
s_1	0	0	0	1	0	0	0	7/10	1	−7/10	−1	460
s_2	0	0	0	0	1	0	0	1/2	5/6	−1/2	−5/6	$466\frac{2}{3}$
s_3	0	0	0	0	0	1	0	①	2/3	−1	−2/3	$541\frac{1}{3}$
s_4	0	0	0	0	0	0	1	1/10	1/4	−1/10	−1/4	100
x_1	10	1	0	0	0	0	0	−1	0	1	0	100
x_2	9	0	1	0	0	0	0	0	−1	0	1	100
	z_j	10	9	0	0	0	0	−10	−9	10	9	1900
	$c_j - z_j$	0	0	0	0	0	0	10	9	−10	−9	

The current solution is now feasible since all the artificial variables have been driven out of solution. Thus we now have the situation where the basic feasible solution contained in the Simplex tableau is also a basic feasible

244

solution to the real-world problem. As you can see from Figure 9.4 the current solution corresponds to point Ⓒ on the corner of the feasible region.

The next two iterations of the Simplex method move us from point Ⓒ to Ⓓ and from Ⓓ to Ⓔ on our graph. The resulting Simplex tableaus are given below:

Result of iteration 3:

Basis	c_j	x_1 10	x_2 9	s_1 0	s_2 0	s_3 0	s_4 0	s_5 0	s_6 0	a_1 −M	a_2 −M	
s_1	0	0	0	1	0	−7/10	0	0	(16/30)	0	−16/30	2432/30
s_2	0	0	0	0	1	−1/2	0	0	3/6	0	−3/6	588/3
s_5	0	0	0	0	0	1	0	1	2/3	−1	−2/3	1624/3
s_4	0	0	0	0	0	−1/10	1	0	11/60	0	−11/60	1376/30
x_1	10	1	0	0	0	1	0	0	2/3	0	−2/3	1924/3
x_2	9	0	1	0	0	0	0	0	−1	0	1	100
z_j		10	9	0	0	10	0	0	−7/3	0	7/3	$7313\frac{1}{3}$
$c_j - z_j$		0	0	0	0	−10	0	0	7/3	−M	−M − 7/3	

Result of iteration 4:

Basis	c_j	x_1 10	x_2 9	s_1 0	s_2 0	s_3 0	s_4 0	s_5 0	s_6 0	a_1 −M	a_2 −M	
s_6	0	0	0	30/16	0	−210/160	0	0	1	0	−1	152
s_2	0	0	0	−15/16	1	25/160	0	0	0	0	0	120
s_5	0	0	0	−20/16	0	300/160	0	1	0	−1	0	440
s_4	0	0	0	−11/32	0	45/320	1	0	0	0	0	18
x_1	10	1	0	−20/16	0	300/160	0	0	0	0	0	540
x_2	9	0	1	30/16	0	−210/160	0	0	0	0	0	252
z_j		10	9	70/16	0	111/16	0	0	0	0	0	7668
$c_j - z_j$		0	0	−70/16	0	−111/16	0	0	0	−M	−M	

Just as with the graphical approach, we see that the addition of the two greater-than-or-equal-to constraints has not changed our optimal solution. However, it has taken us more iterations to get to this point. This is because it took us two iterations to eliminate the artificial variables and hence obtain a basic feasible solution for the real-world problem.

Fortunately once we obtain the initial Simplex tableau using artificial variables, we need not concern ourselves with worrying about whether the basic solution at a particular iteration is feasible for the real-world problem. We need only follow all the rules for the Simplex method. If we reach the stopping criterion (that is, all $c_j - z_j \leq 0$) and all the artificial variables have been eliminated from the solution, then we have found the optimal solution to our linear program. On the other hand, if we reach the stopping criterion and one or more of the artificial variables remains in solution at a positive value, then there is no feasible solution to the real-world problem. This special case will be discussed in more detail in the next chapter.

Equality Constraints

When an equality constraint occurs in a linear programming problem, we need only add an artificial variable to get an initial basic feasible solution for our Simplex tableau. For example, if we had the equality constraint

$$6x_1 + 4x_2 - 5x_3 = 30$$

we would simply add an artificial variable, say a_1, to enable us to create an initial basic feasible solution in our tableau. The above equation would then become

$$6x_1 + 4x_2 - 5x_3 + 1a_1 = 30.$$

Once we have created the Tableau form by adding artificial variables to all the equality constraints, the Simplex method proceeds in exactly the same manner as for the greater-than-or-equal-to constraint situation.

Summary of the Steps to Create the Tableau Form

1. If the original formulation of the linear program contains one or more negative right-hand side values, multiply the corresponding constraint(s) by -1 and change the direction of the inequalities. This will provide an equivalent linear program with nonnegative right-hand side values. We can then follow steps 2 to 4 below to obtain the Tableau form and an initial basic feasible solution.
2. For $\leq$ constraints, simply add a slack variable to each less-than-or-equal-to constraint to obtain an equality. The coefficient of the slack variable in the objective function is assigned a value of zero. This gives us the Tableau form, and the slack variable becomes one of the variables in our initial basic feasible solution.
3. For equality constraints, add an artificial variable to each equality constraint to obtain the Tableau form. The coefficient of this artificial variable in the objective function is assigned a value of $-M$. This artificial variable becomes part of our initial basic feasible solution.
4. For $\geq$ constraints, subtract a surplus variable to obtain an equality. Then add an artificial variable to get the Tableau form of the problem. This artificial variable becomes part of the initial basic feasible solution. The coefficient of the artificial variable in the objective function is $-M$.

To get some practice applying the above principles, let us now convert the following numerical example into the Tableau form and set up the initial Simplex tableau.

$$\max \quad 6x_1 + 3x_2 + 4x_3 + 1x_4$$

s.t.

$$
\begin{aligned}
-2x_1 - \tfrac{1}{2}x_2 + 1x_3 - 6x_4 &= -60 \\
1x_1 \qquad\qquad 1x_3 + \tfrac{2}{3}x_4 &\leq 20 \\
-1x_2 - 5x_3 \qquad &\leq -50 \\
x_1, x_2, x_3, x_4 &\geq 0.
\end{aligned}
$$

In order to handle the negative right-hand side values in constraints 1 and 3, we multiply both constraints by -1 and reverse the direction of the inequality to obtain the following linear program:

$$\max \quad 6x_1 + 3x_2 + 4x_3 + 1x_4$$

s.t.

$$
\begin{aligned}
2x_1 + \tfrac{1}{2}x_2 - 1x_3 + 6x_4 &= 60 \\
1x_1 \qquad + 1x_3 + \tfrac{2}{3}x_4 &\leq 20 \\
1x_2 + 5x_3 \qquad &\geq 50 \\
x_1, \quad x_2, x_3, x_4 &\geq 0.
\end{aligned}
$$

By using slack and surplus variables where appropriate, we obtain the following Standard form representation:

$$\max \quad 6x_1 + 3x_2 + 4x_3 + 1x_4 + 0s_1 + 0s_2$$

s.t.

$$
\begin{aligned}
2x_1 + \tfrac{1}{2}x_2 - 1x_3 + 6x_4 &= 60 & (9.25)\\
1x_1 + 0x_2 + 1x_3 + \tfrac{2}{3}x_4 + 1s_1 &= 20 & (9.26)\\
0x_1 + 1x_2 + 5x_3 + 0x_4 - 1s_2 &= 50 & (9.27)\\
x_1, x_2, x_3, x_4, s_1, s_2 &\geq 0.
\end{aligned}
$$

In order to obtain the Tableau form, we must add an artificial variable to equations (9.25) and (9.27). Adding artificial variable a_1 to equation (9.25) and artificial variable a_2 to equation (9.27), we get

$$\max \quad 6x_1 + 3x_2 + 4x_3 + 1x_4 + 0s_1 + 0s_2 - Ma_1 - Ma_2$$

s.t.

$$
\begin{aligned}
2x_1 + \tfrac{1}{2}x_2 - 1x_3 + 6x_4 \qquad\qquad + 1a_1 \qquad &= 60 \\
1x_1 + 0x_2 + 1x_3 + \tfrac{2}{3}x_4 + 1s_1 \qquad &= 20 \\
0x_1 + 1x_2 + 5x_3 + 0x_4 - 1s_2 + 1a_2 &= 50 \\
x_1, x_2, x_3, x_4, s_1, s_2, a_1, a_2 &\geq 0.
\end{aligned}
$$

The initial Simplex tableau corresponding to this Tableau form is

247

Basis	c_j	x_1 6	x_2 3	x_3 4	x_4 1	s_1 0	s_2 0	a_1 $-M$	a_2 $-M$	
a_1	$-M$	2	1/2	-1	6	0	0	1	0	60
s_1	0	1	0	1	2/3	1	0	0	0	20
a_2	$-M$	0	1	5	0	0	-1	0	1	50
	z_j	$-2M$	$-1\frac{1}{2}M$	$-4M$	$-6M$	0	M	$-M$	$-M$	$-110M$
	$c_j - z_j$	$2M + 6$	$1\frac{1}{2}M + 3$	$4M + 4$	$6M + 1$	0	$-M$	0	0	

9.7 SOLVING THE MINIMIZATION PROBLEM USING THE SIMPLEX METHOD

There are two ways in which we can solve a minimization problem using the Simplex method. The first requires that we change the rule used to introduce a variable into solution. Recall that in the maximization case, we selected the variable with the largest positive $c_j - z_j$ as the variable to introduce next into the basis. This was because the value of $c_j - z_j$ told us the amount the objective function would increase if one unit of the variable in column j was brought into the basis. To solve the minimization problem we can simply reverse this rule. That is, we can select the variable with the most negative $c_j - z_j$ as the one to introduce next. Of course, this means our stopping rule will also have to be changed. In the minimization case we stop when every value in the net evaluation row is nonnegative. When this condition occurs, we have an optimal solution to the minimization problem.

Let us look at the second way in which we can solve a minimization problem using the Simplex method. This second approach is the one we shall use in the remainder of the book whenever we are required to solve a minimization problem. The approach relies on a well-known mathematical "trick" often employed in optimization problems. It turns out that if one wishes to solve the problem, minimize z subject to a set of constraints (linear or otherwise),[2] an equivalent problem is, maximize $-z$ subject to the same constraints. These problems are equivalent in the sense that the same solution which minimizes z also maximizes $-z$. The only difference is that the value of the solution to one is the negative of the solution to the other. That is,

$$\min z = -\max (-z).$$

[2] z is being used to indicate the value of the objective function.

Consider the data in Table 9.2, which shows the values of the objective function z and $-z$ for selected feasible solutions to the Photo Chemicals, Inc., problem introduced in Section 8.8. As you can see, the values of x_1 and x_2 that minimize z are also the values of x_1 and x_2 that maximize $-z$. Moreover, we see that the value of the solution that minimizes $z = 1x_1 + 1x_2$, that is, $z = 55$, is the negative of the value of the solution that maximizes $-z = -1x_1 - 1x_2$. Thus we see that if we want to solve min $(1x_1 + 1x_2)$, we need only solve the problem max $(-1x_1 - 1x_2)$ and multiply the value of the solution by -1. This relationship will always hold true and will be the method we shall use to solve minimization problems.

TABLE 9.2 *Comparison of Feasible Solutions to Show that the min z Solution is the max (−z) Solution*

Selected Feasible Solutions		$z = 1x_1 + 1x_2$	$-z = -1x_1 - 1x_2$
$x_1 = 40$	$x_2 = 40$	80	-80
$x_1 = 40$	$x_2 = 30$	70	-70
$x_1 = 40$	$x_2 = 20$	60	-60
$x_1 = 30$	$x_2 = 40$	70	-70
$x_1 = 30$	$x_2 = 30$	60	-60
$x_1 = 30$	$x_2 = 25$	55 [min value of z]	-55 [max value of (−z)]

Employing the max $(-z)$ approach to solving the minimization problem means that we can follow exactly the same Simplex solution procedure that was outlined for the maximization problem earlier. The only change necessary is that we multiply the objective function by -1 before setting up the Standard form representation. Let us see how this procedure works for the Photo Chemicals problems we solved graphically in Section 3.8.

We previously saw that the Photo Chemicals problems could be formulated as

$$\text{min} \quad 1x_1 + 1x_2$$

s.t.

$$1x_1 \qquad \geq 30$$
$$1x_2 \geq 20$$
$$1x_1 + 2x_2 \geq 80$$
$$x_1, x_2 \geq 0.$$

To solve the problem using our maximization Simplex procedure, we first multiply the objective function by -1 in order to convert the minimization problem into the following equivalent maximization problem:

$$\max \quad -1x_1 - 1x_2$$

s.t.

$$
\begin{aligned}
1x_1 \quad &\geq 30 \\
1x_2 &\geq 20 \\
1x_1 + 2x_2 &\geq 80 \\
x_1, x_2 &\geq 0.
\end{aligned}
$$

After subtracting surplus variables, we obtain the following Standard form representation for our problem:

$$\max \quad -1x_1 + 1x_2 + 0s_1 + 0s_2 + 0s_3$$

s.t.

$$
\begin{aligned}
1x_1 + 0x_2 - 1s_1 \qquad\qquad &= 30 \\
0x_1 + 1x_2 \qquad - 1s_2 \qquad &= 20 \\
1x_1 + 2x_2 \qquad\qquad - 1s_3 &= 80 \\
x_1, x_2, s_1, s_2, s_3 &\geq 0.
\end{aligned}
$$

Since our problem is one involving $\geq$ constraints, we must add artificial variables to obtain the Tableau form. After adding artificial variables to each of our constraints, we get the following Tableau form for our Photo Chemicals problem:

$$\max \quad -1x_1 - 1x_2 + 0s_1 + 0s_2 + 0s_3 - Ma_1 - Ma_2 - Ma_3$$

s.t.

$$
\begin{aligned}
1x_1 + 0x_2 - 1s_1 \qquad\qquad + 1a_1 \qquad\qquad &= 30 \\
0x_1 + 1x_2 \qquad - 1s_2 \qquad + 1a_2 \qquad &= 20 \\
1x_1 + 2x_2 \qquad\qquad - 1s_3 \qquad\qquad + 1a_3 &= 80 \\
x_1, x_2, s_1, s_2, s_3, a_1, a_2, a_3 &\geq 0.
\end{aligned}
$$

The initial Simplex tableau becomes

Basis	c_j	x_1 -1	x_2 -1	s_1 0	s_2 0	s_3 0	a_1 $-M$	a_2 $-M$	a_3 $-M$	
a_1	$-M$	1	0	-1	0	0	1	0	0	30
a_2	$-M$	0	(1)	0	-1	0	0	1	0	20
a_3	$-M$	1	2	0	0	-1	0	0	1	80
	z_j	$-2M$	$-3M$	M	M	M	$-M$	$-M$	$-M$	$-130M$
	$c_j - z_j$	$-1 + 2M$	$-1 + 3M$	$-M$	$-M$	$-M$	0	0	0	

Three iterations of the Simplex method are required to reach an optimal solution to this problem. The results of each iteration are summarized below.

Result of iteration 1:

250

Basis	c_j	x_1	x_2	s_1	s_2	s_3	a_1	a_2	a_3	
		-1	-1	0	0	0	$-M$	$-M$	$-M$	
a_1	$-M$	①	0	-1	0	0	1	0	0	30
x_2	-1	0	1	0	-1	0	0	1	0	20
a_3	$-M$	1	0	0	2	-1	0	-2	1	40
z_j		$-2M$	-1	M	$-2M+1$	M	$-M$	$-1+2M$	$-M$	$-70M-20$
$c_j - z_j$		$-1+2M$	0	$-M$	$-1+2M$	$-M$	0	$-3M+1$	0	

Result of iteration 2:

Basis	c_j	x_1	x_2	s_1	s_2	s_3	a_1	a_2	a_3	
		-1	-1	0	0	0	$-M$	$-M$	$-M$	
x_1	-1	1	0	-1	0	0	1	0	0	30
x_2	-1	0	1	0	-1	0	0	1	0	20
a_3	$-M$	0	0	1	②	-1	-1	-2	1	10
z_j		-1	-1	$-M+1$	$-2M+1$	M	$-1+M$	$-1+2M$	$-M$	$-10M-50$
$c_j - z_j$		0	0	$-1+M$	$-1+2M$	$-M$	$-2M+1$	$-3M+1$	0	

Result of iteration 3:

Basis	c_j	x_1	x_2	s_1	s_2	s_3	a_1	a_2	a_3	
		-1	-1	0	0	0	$-M$	$-M$	$-M$	
x_1	-1	1	0	-1	0	0	1	0	0	30
x_2	-1	0	1	$1/2$	0	$-1/2$	$-1/2$	0	$1/2$	25
s_2	0	0	0	$1/2$	1	$-1/2$	$-1/2$	-1	$1/2$	5
z_j		-1	-1	$1/2$	0	$1/2$	$1/2$	0	$-1/2$	-55
$c_j - z_j$		0	0	$-1/2$	0	$-1/2$	$-M-1/2$	$-M$	$-M+1/2$	

It turns out that the third iteration provides us with the optimal solution (all $c_j - z_j$ values are ≤ 0). Looking back to the solution obtained using the graphical procedure, we see that this is indeed the same solution.

Now referring to Figure 8.17, look at the path we followed in going from the origin to the optimal solution. We started at the origin ($x_1 = 0, x_2 = 0$) with our initial Simplex tableau. Our first iteration took us from the origin to the point ($x_1 = 0, x_2 = 20$). Note that at this point we were still in the infeasible region. The second iteration took us to the point ($x_1 = 30, x_2 = 20$) as x_1 was introduced into solution. However, we still did not have a feasible solution to our real-world problem. Finally, the last iteration took us to

251

$(x_1 = 30, x_2 = 25)$. This is a feasible solution, as we can easily verify from the graph. Indeed, it is also the optimal solution to our problem. Note that the optimal solution from our tableau shows that we produce 30 units of product 1 and 25 units of product 2 and that with $s_2 = 5$, we will have a surplus of 5 units of product 2 over what was required.

Now we are able to solve minimization problems as well as maximization problems. Actually we had this ability all along. We just did not recognize until now that any minimization problem could be converted to an equivalent maximization problem by simply multiplying the objective function by -1. In the next chapter we concentrate on discussing some important special cases that may occur when trying to solve any linear programming problem. We only consider the case for maximization problems, recognizing that all minimization problems may be placed into this form.

9.8   SUMMARY

In Chapter 8 we saw how small linear programs could be solved using a graphical approach. In this chapter the Simplex method was developed as a procedure for solving larger linear programs. Actually the Simplex method is also an easy way to solve small linear programs by hand calculations. However, as problems get larger, even the Simplex method becomes too cumbersome for efficient hand computation. As a result, we must utilize a computer if we want a solution to larger linear programs in any reasonable length of time.

We described how developing the Tableau form of a linear program was a necessary step in the Simplex solution procedure. In addition, we have shown in this chapter how to convert greater-than-or-equal-to constraints, equality constraints, and constraints with negative right-hand side values into the form required for writing a linear program in the Tableau form. Doing this required noting that when both sides of an inequality are multiplied by -1, the direction of the inequality changes, and that for linear programs with greater-than-or-equal-to constraints and/or equality constraints it is necessary to introduce artificial variables in order to go from Standard to Tableau form. We assigned an objective function coefficient of $-M$, where M is a very large number, to these variables. Thus if there was a feasible solution to the real-world linear program, these artificial variables would be driven out of solution before the Simplex method reached its stopping criterion.

We then presented two techniques for solving minimization problems. The first involved changing the Simplex rules for introducing a variable into solution and changing the stopping criterion. The second approach enabled us to solve any minimization problem using the same rules as for a maximization problem. That is, we showed that minimizing z was equivalent to

252

maximizing $-z$. The only difference was that the value of the solution to max $(-z)$ was the negative of the value of the solution to min z Thus to solve a minimization problem using our maximization Simplex rules, we multiply each decision variable coefficient in the objective function by -1 and then apply the maximization procedure. When we get the optimal solution to this problem, we multiply the value of the optimal solution by -1 to get the value of the optimal solution for our original minimization problem.

As a review of the material in this chapter we present here a detailed step-by-step procedure for solving linear programs using the Simplex method.

Step 1: Formulate a linear programming model of the real-world problem. This is done to obtain a mathematical representation of the problem.

Step 2: Define an equivalent linear program by:
    a. multiplying negative right-hand side constraints by -1 and changing the direction of the inequalities;
    b. if it is a min z problem, change to max $(-z)$.
    This is an equivalent mathematical representation which is ready for the maximization Simplex method.

Step 3: Set up the Standard form representation of the linear program. This is done to make every constraint an equality and is the first step in preparing the problem for solution using the Simplex method.

Step 4: Set up the Tableau form representation of the linear program. This is necessary in order to obtain an initial basic feasible solution. All linear programs must be put in this form before the initial Simplex tableau can be set up.

Step 5: Set up the Simplex tableau. This is used to keep track of the calculations made as we carry out the Simplex method. The solution corresponding to the initial Simplex tableau is always the origin. That is, in the initial solution all the decision variables are equal to zero.

Step 6: Choose the variable with the largest $c_j - z_j$ to introduce into solution. The value of $c_j - z_j$ tells us the amount by which the value of the objective function will increase for every unit of x_j introduced into the solution.

Step 7: Choose as the pivot row that row with the smallest ratio by b_i/a_{ij}, $a_{ij} > 0$. This determines which variable will leave the basis when x_j enters. It also tells us how many units of x_j can be introduced into solution before the basic variable in the ith row equals zero.

Step 8: Perform the necessary row operations to convert column j to a unit column.
    a. Multiply the pivot row by the constant necessary to make the pivot element a 1.
    b. Obtain zeros in all the other rows by multiplying the new pivot

row by an appropriate constant and adding it to the appropriate row.

Once these row operations have been performed, we can read the values of our basic variables from the $\bar{b}$ column of our tableau.

Step 9: Test for optimality. If $c_j - z_j \leq 0$ for all columns, we have the optimal solution. If not, return to Step 6.

If $c_j - z_j \leq 0$ for all variables, there is no variable that we can introduce which will cause the objective function to increase, and hence we have the optimal solution.

Some additional notation was introduced in this chapter. We use $\bar{A}$ and $\bar{a}_{ij}$ to denote the positions in the Simplex tableau corresponding to the A matrix in the Tableau form representation of our linear program. Similarly, we used $\bar{b}$ and $\bar{b}_i$ to denote the positions in the Simplex tableau corresponding to the b column in our Tableau form representation.

9.9 GLOSSARY

1. *Simplex method*—An algebraic procedure for solving linear programs. It moves from one basic feasible solution (extreme point) to another, making sure that the objective function increases at each iteration until the optimal solution is reached.

2. *Basic solution*—For a general linear program with n variables and m constraints a basic solution may be found by setting $(n - m)$ of the variables equal to zero and solving the constraint equations for the values of the other m variables. If a unique solution exists, it is a basic solution.

3. *Basic feasible solution*—A basic solution which is also in the feasible region (that is, it satisfies the nonnegativity requirement). A basic feasible solution corresponds to an extreme point.

4. *Tableau form*—The form in which a linear program must be written prior to setting up the initial Simplex tableau. When a linear program is written in this form, its A matrix contains m unit columns corresponding to basic variables, and the values of these basic variables are given by the b column. A further requirement is that the entries in the b column be greater than or equal to zero. This requirement provides us with a basic feasible solution.

5. *Simplex tableau*—A table used to keep track of the calculations made when the Simplex solution method is employed.

6. *Unit vector or unit column*—A vector or column of a matrix, which has a zero in every position except one. In the nonzero position there is a 1.

7. *Net evaluation row*—The $c_j - z_j$ row. The jth element in this row indicates the amount the value of the objective function will increase if one unit of x_j is introduced into the solution.

254

8. *Current solution*—When carrying out the Simplex method, the current solution refers to the current basic feasible solution (extreme point).
9. *Basis*—The set of variables which are not restricted to equal zero in the current basic solution. The variables which make up the basis are termed basic variables, and the remaining variables are called nonbasic variables.
10. *Iteration*—An iteration of the Simplex method consists of the sequence of steps performed in moving from one basic feasible solution to another.
11. *Pivot column*—The column corresponding to the nonbasic variable that is about to be introduced into the basic feasible solution.
12. *Pivot row*—The row in the Simplex tableau corresponding to the basic variable that will leave the solution as the algorithm iterates from one basic feasible solution to another.
13. *Pivot element*—The element of the Simplex tableau that is in both the pivot row and pivot column.
14. *Artificial variable*—A variable that has no physical meaning in terms of the original linear programming problem, but serves merely to enable a basic feasible solution to be created for starting the Simplex method. Artificial variables are assigned an objective function coefficient of $-M$, where M is a very large number.

9.10 PROBLEMS

1. The following partial initial Simplex tableau is given:

Basis	c_j	x_1	x_2	x_3	s_1	s_2	s_3	
		5	20	25	0	0	0	
	2	1	0	1	0	0		40
	0	2	1	0	1	0		30
	3	0	$-1/2$	0	0	1		15
z_j								
$c_j - z_j$								

a. Complete the initial tableau.
b. Write the problem in its Tableau form.
c. What is the initial basis? Does this correspond to the origin? Explain.
d. What is the value of the objective function at this initial solution?
e. For the next iteration, what variable should enter the basis and what variable should leave the basis?

f. How many units of the entering variable will be in the next solution? Before making this first iteration, what should be the value of the objective function after the first iteration?

g. Find the optimal solution using the Simplex method.

2. Solve the following linear program using the graphical approach. Next set the linear program up in Tableau form and use the Simplex method to solve. Show on your graph the sequence of extreme points generated by the Simplex method.

$$\max \quad 1x_1 + 1x_2$$

s.t.

$$\tfrac{1}{2}x_1 + 1x_2 \leq 3$$
$$2x_1 + 1x_2 \leq 5$$
$$x_1, x_2 \geq 0.$$

3. Explain in your own words why the Tableau form and the Standard form are the same for problems with less-than-or-equal-to constraints and nonnegative b_i.

4. Solve the Ryland Farm problem (Problem 8.24) using the Simplex method. Compare each iteration to the graphical solution procedure.

5. Solve the Wilkinson Motor, Inc., problem (Problem 8.23) using the Simplex method. Compare each iteration to the graphical solution procedure.

6. Solve the following linear program:

$$\max \quad 3x_1 + 5x_2 + 1x_3 + 2x_4$$

s.t.

$$\tfrac{1}{2}x_1 + \tfrac{7}{10}x_2 + \tfrac{1}{10}x_3 + \tfrac{4}{10}x_4 \leq 800$$
$$1x_1 + 1x_2 + \tfrac{8}{10}x_3 + \tfrac{1}{2}x_4 \leq 650$$
$$\tfrac{6}{10}x_1 + \tfrac{5}{10}x_2 + \tfrac{5}{10}x_3 + \tfrac{6}{10}x_4 \leq 480$$
$$x_1, x_2, x_3, x_4 \geq 0.$$

What are the values of your basic variables at each iteration?

7. Solve the following linear program:

$$\max \quad 5x_1 + 2x_2 + 8x_3$$

s.t.

$$1x_1 - 2x_2 + \tfrac{1}{2}x_3 \leq 420$$
$$2x_1 + 3x_2 - 1x_3 \leq 610$$
$$6x_1 - 1x_2 + 3x_3 \leq 125$$
$$x_1, x_2, x_3 \geq 0.$$

8. Solve the following linear program using both the graphical and the Simplex methods:

$$\max \quad 1x_1 + 1x_2$$

s.t.

$$1x_1 + 2x_2 \leq 6$$
$$6x_1 + 4x_2 \leq 24$$
$$x_1, x_2 \geq 0.$$

Show graphically how the Simplex method moves from one extreme point to another. Find the coordinates of all the extreme points of this problem.

9. How many basic solutions are there to a linear program which has eight variables and five constraints when written in Standard form?

10. Explain in your own words why when we are trying to determine which basic variable to eliminate at a particular iteration, we only consider the $\bar{a}_{ij}$ which are strictly greater than zero.

11. Find all of the basic solutions for the linear program in Problem 8. (Hint: There are six.) Which of these are extreme points?

12. Suppose that instead of picking the variable with the largest positive value in the net evaluation row to introduce at each iteration, we introduce any variable with a positive value of $c_j - z_j$ without regard to whether or not it is the largest value. Do you think we would still reach the optimal solution? Why or why not?

13. Suppose that we did not remove the basic variable with the smallest ratio of $\bar{b}_i/\bar{a}_{ij}$ at a particular iteration. What effect would this have on the Simplex tableau for our next solution?

14. Suppose a company manufactures three products from two raw materials where

	Product 1	Product 2	Product 3
Raw material A	3.5 lb	3 lb	1.5 lb
Raw material B	2.5 lb	2 lb	1 lb

If the company has available 50 pounds of material A and 100 pounds of material B and if the profits for the three products are $10, $10, and $7.50, how much of each product should be produced in order to maximize profits?

15. Liva's Lumber, Inc., manufactures three types of plywood. The data below summarize the production hours per unit in each of three production operations and other data for the problem:

Plywood	Operations (hours) I	II	II	Profit per Unit
Grade A	2	2	4	$40
Grade B	5	5	2	$30
Grade X	10	3	2	$20
Maximum time available	900	400	600	

How many units of each grade of lumber should be produced?

16. Ye Olde Cording Winery in Peoria, Illinois, makes three kinds of authentic German wine: Heidelberg Sweet, Heidelberg Regular, and Deutschland Extra Dry. The raw materials, labor, and profit for a gallon of each of these wines are summarized below:

Wine	Grapes Grade A (bushels)	Grapes Grade B (bushels)	Sugar (pounds)	Labor (man-hours)	Profit per Gallon
Heidelberg Sweet	1	1	2	2	$0.10
Heidelberg Regular	2	0	1	3	$0.12
Deutschland Extra Dry	0	2	0	1	$0.20

If the Winery has 150 bushels of grade A grapes, 150 bushels of grade B grapes, 80 pounds of sugar, and 225 man-hours available during the next week, what product mix of wines will maximize the company's profit?

a. Solve by the Simplex method.

b. Interpret all slack variables.

c. An increase in which resources could improve the company's profit?

17. Set up the Tableau form for the following linear program. (Do not attempt to solve.)

$$\min \quad 3x_1 + 2x_2 + 4x_3 - 1x_4$$

s.t.

$$1x_1 + 1x_2 \quad\quad\quad\quad\ \leq 40$$
$$2x_1 - 3x_2 + 3x_3 - 4x_4 \geq 10$$
$$1x_1 \quad\quad + 2x_3 + 1x_4 = 20$$
$$x_1, x_2, x_3, x_4 \geq 0.$$

18. Set up the Tableau form for the following linear program. (Do not attempt to solve.)

258

$$\text{min} \quad 2x_1 + 5x_2 + 3x_3$$

s.t.

$$
\begin{aligned}
4x_1 + 2x_2 - 1x_3 &= 15 \\
3x_1 \qquad\quad + 2x_3 &\geq 10 \\
+ 1x_2 - 1x_3 &\leq -5 \\
-2x_1 + 2x_2 \qquad\quad &= -8 \\
x_1, x_2, x_3 &\geq 0.
\end{aligned}
$$

19. Solve the following linear program:

$$\text{min} \quad 3x_1 + 4x_2 + 8x_3$$

s.t.

$$
\begin{aligned}
2x_1 + 1x_2 \qquad\quad &\geq 6 \\
2x_2 + 4x_3 &\geq 8 \\
x_1, x_2, x_3 &\geq 0.
\end{aligned}
$$

20. Solve the following linear program:

$$\text{min} \quad 4x_1 + 2x_2 + 3x_3$$

s.t.

$$
\begin{aligned}
1x_1 + 3x_2 \qquad\quad &\geq 15 \\
1x_1 \qquad\quad + 2x_3 &\geq 10 \\
2x_1 + 1x_2 \qquad\quad &\geq 20 \\
x_1, x_2, x_3 &\geq 0.
\end{aligned}
$$

21. Ajax Fuels, Inc., is developing a new additive for airplane fuels. The additive is a mixture of three liquid ingredients A, B, and C. For proper performance, the total amount of additive must be at least 10 ounces for each gallon of fuel. However, because of safety reasons the amount of additive should not exceed 15 ounces in each gallon of fuel. The mix of ingredients in the additive is also critical. At least $\frac{1}{4}$ of an ounce of ingredient A must be used for every ounce of ingredient B and at least 1 ounce of ingredient C must be used for every ounce of ingredient A. If the costs of ingredients A, B, and C are \$0.10, \$0.03, and \$0.09 per ounce, respectively, find the minimum-cost mixture of A, B, and C for the additive and the amount of additive that should be used for every gallon of airplane fuel.

22. Supersport Footballs, Inc., has just received an order for 1000 of their All-Pro model footballs. Because Supersport is the sole manufacturer of NFL footballs, the current production run must result in at least 1000 All-Pro models. Supersport also manufactures a College model and a High-School model. All three footballs require operations in the follow-ing departments: cutting and dyeing, sewing, and inspection and pack-

aging. The production times and maximum production availabilities are shown below:

Model	Production Time (minutes) Cutting and Dyeing	Sewing	Inspection and Packaging
All-Pro	12	15	3
College	10	15	4
High-School	8	12	2
Time available	300 hours	200 hours	100 hours

a. If Supersport realizes a profit of $3 for each All-Pro model, $5 for each College model, and $4 for each High-School model, how many footballs of each type should be produced?

b. If Supersport can increase sewing time to 300 hours and inspection and packaging time to 150 hours by using overtime, what is your recommendation?

23. Captain John's Yachts, Inc., located in Fort Lauderdale, Florida, rents three types of ocean-going boats: sailboats, cabin cruisers, and Captain John's favorite, the luxury yachts. Captain John advertises his boats with his famous "you rent—we pilot" slogan, which means that the company supplies the captain and crew for each rented boat. Each rented boat, of course, has one captain, but the crew sizes (that is, deck hands, galley, and so on) differ. The crew requirements, in addition to a captain, and 1 for sailboats, 2 for cabin cruisers, and 3 for yachts. Currently Captain John has rental requests for all of his boats: 4 sailboats, 8 cabin cruisers, and 3 luxury yachts. However, he only has 10 employees who qualify as captains and an additional 18 employees who qualify for the crew positions. If Captain John's daily profit is $50 for sailboats, $70 for cruisers, and $100 for luxury yachts, how many boats of each type should he rent?

24. The Our-Bags-Don't-Break (OBDB) plastic bag company manufactures three plastic refuse bags for home use: a 20-gallon garbage bag, a 30-gallon garbage bag, and a 33-gallon leaf and grass bag. Using purchased plastic material, three operations are required to produce each end product: cutting, sealing, and packaging. The production time required to process each type of bag in every operation, as well as the maximum daily production time available for each operation, are shown below. Note that the production time figures in this table are per box of each type of bag.

Type of Bag	Production Time (seconds)		
	Cutting	Sealing	Packaging
20 gallons	2	2	3
30 gallons	3	2	4
33 gallons	3	3	5
Time available	2 hours	3 hours	4 hours

If OBDB makes a profit of $0.10 for each box of 20-gallon bags produced, $0.15 for each box of 30-gallon bags, and $0.20 for each box of 33-gallon bags, what is the optimal product mix?

25. Kirkman Brothers ice cream parlors sell three different flavors of Dairy Sweet ice milk: chocolate, vanilla, and banana. Because of extremely hot weather and a high demand for its products, Kirkman has run short of its supply of ingredients: milk, sugar and cream. Hence Kirkman will not be able to fill all the orders received from its retail outlets, the ice cream parlors. As a result of these circumstances, Kirkman has decided to make the best amounts of the three flavors given the constraints on supply of the basic ingredients. The company will then ration the ice milk to the retail outlets.

Kirkman has collected the following data on profitability of the various flavors, availability of supplies, and amounts required by each flavor.

Flavor	Profit per Gallon	Usage per Gallon		
		Milk (gallons)	Sugar (pounds)	Cream (gallons)
Chocolate	$1.00	0.45	0.50	0.10
Vanilla	$0.90	0.50	0.40	0.15
Banana	$0.95	0.40	0.40	0.20
Maximum available		200	150	60

Determine the optimal product mix for Kirkman Brothers. What additional resources could be used?

26. Uforia Corporation sells two different brands of women's perfume: Incentive and Temptation No. 1. Uforia sells exclusively through department stores and employs a three-man sales staff to call on its customers.

The amount of sales time necessary for each of the salesmen to sell one case of each product varies with the experience and ability of the salesmen. Data on the average times for each of Uforia's salesmen are presented below.

Salesman	Average Sales Time per Case (minutes)	
	Incentive	Temptation No. 1
John	10	15
Alex	15	10
Red	12	6

Each of the salesmen spends approximately 80 hours per month in the actual selling of these two products. Each case of Incentive and Temptation No. 1 sells at a profit of $30 and $25, respectively.

Uforia has a twofold problem. First it would like to know how many cases of each perfume to produce over the next month in order to maximize profit. Second the corporation would like to know how much of each salesman's time should be allocated to each of the products.

Use linear programming to solve the above problems for Uforia. (Hint: Let x_1 = number of cases of Incentive sold by John, x_2 = number of cases of Temptation No. 1 sold by John, x_3 = number of cases of Incentive sold by Alex, and so on.)

27. The We-Survey-Anything market research company has just been hired by Ace Industries to investigate consumer reaction to Ace's newly introduced product. The contract calls for a door-to-door survey with the following stipulations:
   a. At least 200 households with no children be contacted, either during the day or evening.
   b. At least 400 households with children be contacted, either during the day or evening.
   c. The total number of households contacted during the evening be at least as great as the number contacted during the day.
   d. A sample of at least 1000 families be contacted during the study.
   Based upon previous interviews, management has developed the following interview costs:

Household	Interview Cost	
	Day	Evening
Children	$10	$12
No children	$ 8	$10

What household-time-of-day plan should the company use in order to minimize interview costs while satisfying contract requirements?

28. The Our-Paint-Dries-Quickest (OPDQ) paint company produces two interior enamels: Quick-Dry and Super-Speedie. Both enamels are

manufactured from premix silicate base and linseed oil solutions, which OPDQ purchases from a number of different suppliers. Currently only two types of premix solutions are available. Type A contains 60% silicates and 40% linseed oil, whereas type B contains 30% silicates and 70% linseed oil. Type A costs $0.50 per gallon and type B costs $0.75 per gallon. If each gallon of Quick-Dry requires at least 25% silicates and 50% linseed oil, and each gallon of Super-Speedie requires at least 20% silicates but at most 50% linseed oil, how many gallons of each premix should OPDQ purchase in order to produce exactly 100 gallons of Quick-Dry and 100 gallons of Super-Speedie?

29. Suppose the management at Par, Inc., learned that the accounting department made a mistake and that the profit on the deluxe bag was really $18 per bag. Shown below is a partial Simplex tableau corresponding to the optimal basic feasible solution with $c_1 = 10$ and $c_2 = 9$. The only difference is that we have changed c_2 to 18.

a. Calculate the remainder of the Simplex tableau and show that the Simplex method indicates that the current solution is not optimal.

b. Find the optimal solution with $c_2 = 18$. What new variable enters the basis? What variable leaves?

c. Refer to the original graphical solution in Figure 8.17. What extreme point is now optimal? What constraints are now binding?

Basis	c_j	x_1 10	x_2 18	s_1 0	s_2 0	s_3 0	s_4 0	
x_2	18	0	1	30/16	0	−21/16	0	252
s_2	0	0	0	−15/16	1	25/160	0	120
x_1	10	1	0	−20/16	0	300/160	0	540
s_4	0	0	0	−11/32	0	45/320	1	18
z_j								
$c_j - z_j$								

30. Catalina Yachts, Inc., is a builder of cruising sailboats. They manufacture three models of sailboats: the C-32, the C-40, and the C-48. The company, because of its excellent reputation, is in the enviable position of being able to sell all the boats it manufactures. Catalina is currently in the process of taking orders for the coming year. The company has asked you to determine for them how many orders for each model it should accept in order to maximize profits.

The manufacture of each model requires differing amounts of time spent on each of three operations: molding, carpentry, and finishing. The number of days required to perform each of these activities on the three models is given below.

Model	Production Time (man-days)		
	Molding	Carpentry	Finishing
C-32	3	5	4
C-40	5	12	5
C-48	10	18	8

Based on past experience, management expects the profit per boat to be $5000 on the C-32, $10,000 on the C-40, and $20,000 on the C-48.

Catalina currently has 40 people employed in manufacturing these sailboats: 10 in molding, 20 in carpentry, 10 in finishing, and on the average each employee works 240 days per year. The only other constraint is a management-imposed restriction on the number of C-48 models that can be sold. Because Catalina does not want the C-48 to become commonplace, it will not take orders for over 20 of this model.

31. The World-Wide Grocery Store Company, in preparation for the up-coming holiday season, has just purchased the following quantities of nuts.

Type of Nut	Amount (pounds)
Almonds	6000
Brazil	7500
Filberts	7500
Pecans	4000
Walnuts	7500

They would like to package these nuts in 1-pound bags and are presently considering producing a regular mix (consisting of 10% pecans, 15% almonds, 25% filberts, 25% brazil, 25% walnuts), a deluxe mix (20% of each type of nut), and individual bags of each type of nut. The profit figures for each bag they produce are as follows:

Type of Bag	Profit per Bag
Regular mix	$0.20
Deluxe mix	$0.25
Almonds	$0.05
Brazil	$0.10
Filberts	$0.10
Pecans	$0.05
Walnuts	$0.15

Your job is to formulate a linear program that World-Wide could use in order to determine how many bags of each type they should produce to maximize profits. Solve the linear program you formulate in order to obtain the optimal solution.

32. The employee credit union for Ivory Tower University is planning its usage of funds for the coming year. The credit union makes four different kinds of loans to members, each of which has a different rate of return. Also, in order to stabilize income, the company is permitted to invest up to 30% of its money in "risk-free" securities. The various revenue-producing investments together with their annual return are as follows:

Type of Investment	Annual Rate of Return (percent)
Automobile loans (secured)	8
Signature loans	12
Furniture loans (secured)	10
Other secured loans	11
Securities (risk-free)	9

Credit union policy and state law impose the following restrictions on the composition of the above company assets: Securities may not exceed 30% of the total amount of funds available for investment and signature loans may not exceed 10% of total loans. Furniture loans plus "other secured loans" may not exceed 50% of total secured loans (the total of all three types). Signature loans plus "other secured loans" may not exceed the amount invested in risk-free securities.

The credit union would like to determine how much of its funds should be allocated to each of the investments in order to maximize profits. The firm expects to have $3 million to invest in the coming year. Formulate this problem as a linear program.

33. In Section 9.6 we defined a modified Par, Inc., problem where the minimum production levels for each golf bag were given by

$$x_1 \geq 100$$
$$x_2 \geq 100.$$

While it was perfectly acceptable to use these constraints in the Simplex procedure, consider the following variation. Since we know x_1 and x_2 will both be at least 100, let us define new decision variables x_1' and x_2' where

x_1' = production of standard bags above the 100-unit minimum
x_2' = production of deluxe bags above the 100-unit minimum.

265

Thus if we know the values of x_1' and x_2', we can find our total production x_1 and x_2 by

$$x_1 = 100 + x_1'$$
$$x_2 = 100 + x_2'.$$

Return to the Par, Inc., problem in Section 9.1 and substitute the expression $x_1 = 100 + x_1'$ and $x_2 = 100 + x_2'$ into the linear program. State the linear program in terms of the x_1' and x_2' decision variables.

What is the primary advantage of this procedure? Solve the linear program for the optimal value of the x_1' and x_2' variables. Do we obtain the same optimal production plan?

10
Linear Programming: Other Topics

In the previous two chapters we discussed what linear programming problems are and how they can be solved using the graphical solution method (Chapter 8) or the Simplex solution procedure (Chapter 9). In this chapter we introduce some special cases and difficulties that can arise when we attempt to solve linear programming problems. We demonstrate how these special cases affect both the graphical and Simplex solution methods. In addition, we discuss the important topic of sensitivity analysis.

10.1 INFEASIBILITY

Infeasibility comes about when there is no solution to the linear programming problem which satisfies all the constraints, including the nonnegativity conditions, $x_1, x_2, \ldots, x_n \geq 0$. Graphically, infeasibility means that a feasible region does not exist; that is, there are no points which satisfy all the constraining equations and the nonnegativity conditions simultaneously. To illustrate this situation, let us look again at the problem faced by Par, Inc.

Suppose that management had specified that at least 500 of the standard bags and 360 of the deluxe bags must be manufactured. The graph of our solution region may now be constructed to reflect these requirements (see Figure 10.1).

The shaded area in the lower left-hand portion of the graph depicts those points satisfying the departmental constraints on the availability of time. The shaded area in the upper right-hand portion depicts those points satisfying the minimum production requirements of 500 standard and 360 deluxe bags. But there are no points satisfying both sets of constraints. Thus we see that if management imposes these minimum production requirements, there will be no feasible solution to the linear programming model.

How should we interpret this infeasibility in terms of our current problem? First we should tell management that, given the resources available (that is, cutting and dyeing time, sewing time, finishing time, and inspection and packaging time) it is not possible to make 500 standard bags and 360 deluxe bags. Moreover, we can tell management exactly how much of each resource

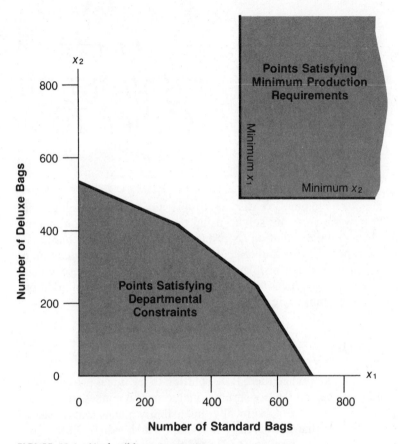

FIGURE 10.1 *No feasible region for the Par, Inc. problem with production requirements of 500 standard and 360 deluxe bags.*

must be expended in order to make it possible to manufacture 360 deluxe and 500 standard bags. The following minimum amounts of resources must be available.

Thus we need 80 more hours of cutting and dyeing time, 32 more hours of finishing time, and 5 more hours of inspection and packaging time in order to meet management's requirement.

If after seeing our report, management still wants to manufacture 500 standard and 360 deluxe bags, it must somehow provide additional resources. Perhaps this will mean hiring another person to work in the cutting and dyeing department, transferring a person from elsewhere in the plant to work part-time in the finishing department, or having the sewing people help

Operation	Minimum Required Resources (hours)	Available Resources (hours)
Cutting and dyeing	$\frac{7}{10}(500)+1(360)=710$	630
Sewing	$\frac{1}{2}(500)+\frac{5}{6}(360)=550$	600
Finishing	$1(500)+\frac{2}{3}(360)=740$	708
Inspection and packaging	$\frac{1}{10}(500)+\frac{1}{4}(360)=140$	135

out periodically with the inspection and packaging. As you can see, there are many possibilities for corrective management action, once we discover there is no feasible solution. The important thing for us to realize is that linear programming analysis can help us determine whether or not management's plans are feasible. By analyzing the problem using linear programming, we are often able to point out infeasible conditions and initiate corrective action.

Now that we have explored the implications of infeasibility in the context of a graphical solution, let us see how infeasibility is identified in the Simplex tableau. We mentioned earlier, in conjunction with artificial variables, that infeasibility in terms of the Simplex tableau meant that our stopping criteria would indicate an optimal solution while one or more of the artificial variables still remained in solution at a positive value. As an illustration of this phenomenon, we present the Simplex solution to the current modification of the Par, Inc. problem for which we just saw graphically there is no feasible solution.

Initial tableau:

Basis	c_j	x_1	x_2	s_1	s_2	s_3	s_4	s_5	s_6	a_1	a_2	
		10	9	0	0	0	0	0	0	$-M$	$-M$	
s_1	0	7/10	1	1	0	0	0	0	0	0	0	630
s_2	0	1/2	5/6	0	1	0	0	0	0	0	0	600
s_3	0	1	2/3	0	0	1	0	0	0	0	0	708
s_4	0	1/10	1/4	0	0	0	1	0	0	0	0	135
a_1	$-M$	①	0	0	0	0	0	-1	0	1	0	500
a_2	$-M$	0	1	0	0	0	0	0	-1	0	1	360
	z_j	$-M$	$-M$	0	0	0	0	M	M	$-M$	$-M$	$-860M$
	c_j-z_j	$M+10$	$M+9$	0	0	0	0	$-M$	$-M$	0	0	

Two iterations of the Simplex method provide the following final tableau:

Basis	c_j	x_1 x_2	s_1	s_2 s_3 s_4	s_5	s_6	a_1	a_2	
		10 9	0	0 0 0	0	0	$-M$	$-M$	
x_2	9	0 1	1	0 0 0	7/10	0	$-7/10$	0	280
s_2	0	0 0	$-5/6$	1 0 0	$-1/12$	0	1/12	0	$116\frac{2}{3}$
s_3	0	0 0	$-2/3$	0 1 0	16/30	0	$-16/30$	0	$21\frac{1}{3}$
s_4	0	0 0	1/4	0 0 1	$-9/120$	0	9/120	0	15
x_1	10	1 0	0	0 0 0	-1	0	1	0	500
a_2	$-M$	0 0	-1	0 0 0	$-7/10$	-1	7/10	1	80
	z_j	10 9	$9+M$	0 0 0	$\dfrac{-37+7M}{10}$	M	$\dfrac{37-7M}{10}$	$-M$	$7520-80M$
	c_j-z_j	0 0	$-9-M$	0 0 0	$\dfrac{37-7M}{10}$	$-M$	$\dfrac{-37-8M}{10}$	-0	

Just as you might have expected, one of the artificial variables, a_2, is in the final solution. Notice that $c_j - z_j \le 0$ for all the variables; therefore, according to the rules we established earlier, this should be the optimal solution. But this solution is not feasible for our real-world problem, since it has $x_1 = 500$ and $x_2 = 280$. (Recall that we had to make at least 360 deluxe bags.) The fact that artificial variable a_2 is in solution at a value of 80 tells us that the final solution violates the sixth constraint ($x_2 \ge 360$) by 80 units.

In summary, a linear program is infeasible if there is no solution which satisfies all the constraints and nonnegativity conditions simultaneously. Graphically, we recognize this situation as the case where there is no feasible region. In terms of the Simplex solution procedure, we know that if one or more of the artificial variables remain in the final solution at a positive value, there is no feasible solution to the real-world problem. In closing we note that for linear programming problems with all $\le$ constraints and nonnegative right-hand sides there will always be a feasible solution. Since it is not necessary to introduce artificial variables to set up the initial Simplex tableau, there could not possibly be an artificial variable in the final solution.

10.2 UNBOUNDEDNESS

A solution to a linear programming problem is *unbounded* if the value of the solution may be made infinitely large without violating any of the constraints. This condition might be termed, "managerial utopia." If this condition were to occur in a profit maximization problem, it would be possible for the manager to achieve any level of profit he wanted.

In linear programming models of real-world problems the occurrence of an unbounded solution means that the problem has been improperly formulated. We know from our own experience and observations that it is not possible to increase profits indefinitely. Therefore we must conclude that if a profit maximization problem results in an unbounded solution, our mathematical model is not a sufficiently accurate representation of the real-world problem. Usually one or more constraints have been overlooked in setting up the model.

Graphically speaking, if a linear programming problem has an unbounded solution, the feasible region extends to infinity in some direction. As an illustration, consider the simple numerical example

$$\text{max} \quad 2x_1 + 1x_2$$

$$\text{s.t.}$$

$$1x_1 \quad \geq 2$$
$$1x_2 \leq 5$$
$$x_1, x_2 \geq 0.$$

In Figure 10.2 we have graphed the feasible region associated with this problem. Note that we can only indicate part of the feasible region, since the feasible region extends indefinitely in the direction of the x_1 axis. Looking at the profit lines in Figure 10.2, we see that the solution to this problem may be made as large as we desire. That is, no matter what solution we pick, there will always be some feasible solution with a larger value. Thus we say that the solution to this linear program is *unbounded*.

If we are using the Simplex method of solution and the linear program is unbounded, we will automatically discover this before reaching a final tableau. What will happen is that the rule for determining the variable to remove from the solution will not work. Recall that we calculated the ratio $\bar{b}_i/\bar{a}_{ij}$ for each of the elements of column j which were *positive*. Then we picked the smallest ratio to tell us which variable to remove from the current basic feasible solution.

As you will recall from Chapter 9, the coefficients in a particular column of $\bar{A}$ indicate how much each of the current basic variables will decrease if one unit of the variable associated with that particular column is brought into solution. For example, if $\bar{a}_{34} = 2$, then the value of the basic variable associated with the third row will decrease by two units if one unit of the variable associated with the fourth column is brought into solution. Suppose, then, that for a particular linear program we found that $c_3 - z_3 = 5 > 0$, and that all the $\bar{a}_{i3}$ in column 3 were ≤ 0. This would mean that each unit of x_3 brought into solution would increase the objective function by five units. Furthermore, since $\bar{a}_{i3} \leq 0$ for all i, this would mean that none of the current basic

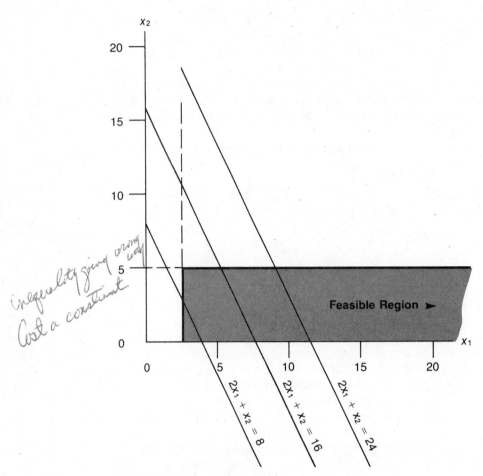

FIGURE 10.2 Example of an unbounded problem.

variables would be driven to zero, no matter how many units of x_3 we introduced. Thus we could introduce an infinite amount of x_3 into solution and still maintain feasibility. Since each unit of x_3 increases the objective function by five, you can see that we would have an unbounded solution in this case. Hence the way we recognize the unbounded situation is that all the $\bar{a}_{ij}$ are ≤ 0 in column j, and the Simplex method indicates the variable x_j is to be introduced into solution.

To show this explicitly, let us solve our unbounded example problem using the Simplex method. We first subtract a surplus variable, s_1, from the first constraint equation and add a slack variable, s_2, to the second constraint equation to obtain the Standard form. We then add an artificial variable, a_1, to the first constraint equation in order to obtain the Tableau form and set

272

up the initial Simplex tableau in terms of the basic variables a_1 and s_2. After bringing in x_1 at the first iteration, our Simplex tableau is as follows.

		x_1	x_2	s_1	a_1	s_2	
Basis	c_j	2	1	0	$-M$	0	
x_1	2	1	0	-1	1	0	2
s_2	0	0	1	0	0	1	5
	z_j	2	0	-2	2	0	4
	$c_j - z_j$	0	1	2	$-M-2$	0	

Since s_1 has the largest positive $c_j - z_j$, we know we can increase the value of the objective function most rapidly by bringing s_1 into the basis. But $\bar{a}_{13} = -1$ and $\bar{a}_{23} = 0$; hence we cannot form the ratio $\bar{b}_i/\bar{a}_{i3}$ for all positive $\bar{a}_{i3}$, since there are none. This is our indication that the solution to the linear program is unbounded. We can interpret this condition as follows.

Each unit of s_1 that we bring into the basis drives zero units of s_2 out of solution, and "gives" us an extra unit of x_1, since $\bar{a}_{13} = -1$. This is because s_1 is a surplus variable and can be interpreted as the amount of product 1 we produce over the minimum amount required; that is, $x_1 = 2$. Since our Simplex tableau has indicated that we can introduce as much of s_1 as we desire without violating any constraints, this tells us that we can make as much as we want above the minimum amount of x_1 required. Thus there will be no upper bound on the value of the objective function, since the objective function coefficient associated with x_1 is positive.

In summary, a maximization linear program is unbounded if it is possible to make the value of the optimal solution as large as desired without violating any of the constraints. We can recognize this condition graphically as the case where the feasible region extends to infinity in a direction of increase for the objective function. When employing the Simplex solution procedure, an unbounded linear program is easy to recognize. That is, if at some iteration the Simplex method tells us to introduce x_j into solution and all the $\bar{a}_{ij}$ are less than or equal to zero in the jth column, we recognize that we have a linear program having an unbounded solution.

We emphasize that the case of an unbounded solution will never occur in real-world cost minimization or profit maximization problems because it is not possible to reduce costs to minus infinity or to increase profits to plus infinity. Thus if we encounter this situation when solving a linear programming model in practice, we should go back and examine carefully our formulation of the problem to determine if we have made some error, or if the linear programming model is inappropriate.

10.3 ALTERNATE OPTIMAL SOLUTIONS

When we have a linear program which has two or more optimal solutions, we say the program has *alternate optima*. Graphically, this is the case when the objective function is parallel to one of the binding constraints. As an example, let us consider the original Par, Inc. problem with a slightly modified objective function:

max $7x_1 + 10x_2$ — *actually a constraint*

s.t.

$$\tfrac{7}{10}x_1 + 1x_2 \leq 630$$
$$\tfrac{1}{2}x_1 + \tfrac{5}{6}x_2 \leq 600$$
$$1x_1 + \tfrac{2}{3}x_2 \leq 708$$
$$\tfrac{1}{10}x_1 + \tfrac{1}{4}x_2 \leq 135$$
$$x_1, x_2 \geq 0.$$

The graphical solution is presented in Figure 10.3.

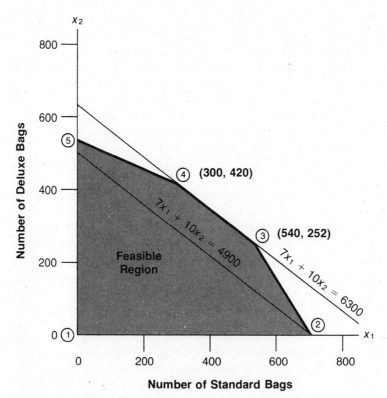

FIGURE 10.3 *Par, Inc. problem with a modified objective.*

The graph of the objective function for this problem is parallel to the cutting and dyeing constraint. As we move the profit line away from the origin in an effort to increase the value of the objective function, we see that the objective function is maximized when it coincides with the cutting and dyeing constraint. The optimal objective function value for this problem is 6300, and there are an infinite number of feasible points yielding this value. Any point on the line segment connecting the points (300, 420) and (540, 252) is optimal. In addition, we see that both of the end points are optimal:

$$7(300) + 10(420) = 2100 + 4200 = 6300$$
$$7(540) + 10(252) = 3780 + 2520 = 6300.$$

This condition of a linear program having alternate optima is an ideal situation for the practicing manager attempting to implement the linear programming solution. It means that several (actually an infinite number) combinations of the variables are optimal, and the manager can pick the one which is most expedient.

When using the Simplex method of solution, one will probably not recognize that a linear program has alternate optima until the final Simplex tableau. Then, if the program has alternate optima, $c_j - z_j$ will equal zero for one or more of the variables not in solution. For example, let us look at the final Simplex tableau for the problem portrayed graphically in Figure 10.3.

Basis	c_j	x_1 7	x_2 10	s_1 0	s_2 0	s_3 0	s_4 0	
x_1	7	1	0	10/3	0	0	−40/3	300
s_2	0	0	0	−10/18	1	0	−20/18	100
s_3	0	0	0	−22/9	0	1	64/9	128
x_2	10	0	1	−4/3	0	0	28/3	420
	z_j	7	10	10	0	0	0	6300
	$c_j - z_j$	0	0	−10	0	0	0	

All values in the net evaluation row are less than or equal to zero, indicating that we have reached the optimal solution. This solution yields $x_1 = 300$, $x_2 = 420$, $s_2 = 100$, and $s_3 = 128$. Notice, however, that the entry in the net evaluation row for s_4, $c_6 - z_6$, is equal to zero. This indicates that our linear program has alternate optima. Since $c_6 - z_6$ for s_4 is equal to zero, we could introduce s_4 into solution without changing the value of the optimal solution. The tableau, after introducing s_4, is presented below:

Basis	c_j	x_1 7	x_2 10	s_1 0	s_2 0	s_3 0	s_4 0	
x_1	7	1	0	−5/4	0	120/64	0	540
s_2	0	0	0	−30/32	1	10/64	0	120
s_4	0	0	0	−22/64	0	9/64	1	18
x_2	10	0	1	15/8	0	−84/64	0	252
	z_j	7	10	10	0	0	0	6300
	c_j-z_j	0	0	−10	0	0	0	

After introducing s_4 we have a different solution: $x_1 = 540$, $x_2 = 252$, $s_2 = 120$, and $s_4 = 18$. However, this solution is still optimal ($c_j - z_j \leq 0$ for all j). Another way to confirm that this solution is still optimal is to note that the value of the objective function has remained at 6300.

In summary, we can recognize that a linear program has alternate optima by observing graphically that the objective function is parallel to one of the binding constraints. When using the Simplex method, we can recognize alternate optima if $c_j - z_j$ equals zero for one of the variables not in solution.

10.4 DEGENERACY

A linear program is said to be *degenerate* if one or more of the variables in the basic solution has a value of zero. Degeneracy does not cause any particular difficulties for the graphical solution procedure; however, degeneracy can cause some difficulties when the Simplex method is used to solve a linear program.

To see how a degenerate linear program may come about, consider the following modification of the Par, Inc. problem:

max $10x_1 + 9x_2$

s.t. $\frac{7}{10}x_1 + 1x_2 \leq 630$

$\frac{1}{2}x_1 + \frac{5}{6}x_2 \leq 480$ Sewing capacity reduced to 480.

$1x_1 + \frac{2}{3}x_2 \leq 708$

$\frac{1}{10}x_1 + \frac{1}{4}x_2 \leq 135$

$x_1, x_2 \geq 0$.

Let us solve this new Par, Inc. problem using the Simplex method. The tableau after the first iteration is as follows.

276

Basis	c_j	x_1	x_2	s_1	s_2	s_3	s_4	
		10	9	0	0	0	0	
s_1	0	0	(16/30)	1	0	−7/10	0	134.4
s_2	0	0	1/2	0	1	−1/2	0	126
x_1	10	1	2/3	0	0	1	0	708
s_4	0	0	22/120	0	0	−1/10	1	64.2
z_j		10	20/3	0	0	10	0	7080
$c_j - z_j$		0	7/3	0	0	−10	0	

The entries in the net evaluation row indicate that we should introduce variable x_2 into solution. Calculating the appropriate ratios to determine the pivot element, we get

$$\frac{\bar{b}_1}{\bar{a}_{12}} = \frac{134.4}{\frac{16}{30}} = 252$$

$$\frac{\bar{b}_2}{\bar{a}_{22}} = \frac{126}{\frac{1}{2}} = 252$$

$$\frac{\bar{b}_3}{\bar{a}_{32}} = \frac{708}{\frac{2}{3}} = 1062$$

$$\frac{\bar{b}_4}{\bar{a}_{42}} = \frac{64.2}{\frac{22}{120}} = 350.2.$$

We see that there is a tie between the first and second *rows*. This is an indication that we will have a degenerate linear program at the next iteration. To see why, let us arbitrarily select one of the tied rows and perform the necessary row operations to remove the corresponding variable from the current basis. Let us select row 1 and thus remove variable s_1 from the current basis. The Simplex tableau after this iteration is as follows:

Basis	c_j	x_1	x_2	s_1	s_2	s_3	s_4	
		10	9	0	0	0	0	
x_2	9	0	1	30/16	0	−210/160	0	252
s_2	0	0	0	−15/16	1	25/160	0	0
x_1	10	1	0	−20/16	0	300/160	0	540
s_4	0	0	0	−11/32	0	45/320	1	18
z_j		10	9	70/16	0	111/16	0	7668
$c_j - z_j$		0	0	−70/16	0	−111/16	0	

Do you see anything unusual about this tableau? When we performed our iteration and introduced 252 units of x_2 into the basis, we not only drove s_1 out of solution setting s_1 equal to zero but we also drove s_2 to zero. Hence we have a solution where one of the basic variables is equal to zero. Whenever we have a tie in the minimum $\bar{b}_i/\bar{a}_{ij}$ ratios, there will always be a basic variable equal to zero in the next tableau. Since we are at the optimal solution in this case, we do not care that s_2 is in solution at a zero value. However, if this condition were to occur at some iteration prior to reaching the optimal solution, it is theoretically possible for the Simplex algorithm to cycle; that is, the algorithm could possibly alternate between the same set of nonoptimal points at each iteration and never reach the optimal solution. Cycling has not proved to be a significant difficulty in practice. Therefore we do not recommend introducing any special machinery into the Simplex algorithm to eliminate the possibility of degeneracy occurring. If while performing the iterations of the Simplex algorithm a tie occurs for the minimum $\bar{b}_i/\bar{a}_{ij}$ ratio, then we recommend simply selecting the upper row as the pivot row.

10.5 SENSITIVITY ANALYSIS

Sensitivity analysis is the study of how the optimal solution and the value of the optimal solution to a linear program change, given changes in the various coefficients of the problem. That is, we are interested in answering questions such as the following: (1) What effect will a change in the coefficients in the objective function (c_j) have? (2) What effect will a change in the right-hand side values (b_i) have? (3) What effect will a change in the coefficients in the constraining equations (a_{ij}) have? Since sensitivity analysis is concerned with how these changes affect the optimal solution, the analysis begins only after the optimal solution to the original linear programming problem has been obtained. Hence sensitivity analysis can be referred to as postoptimality analysis.

There are several reasons why sensitivity analysis is considered so important from a managerial point of view. First, consider the fact that businesses operate in a dynamic environment. Prices of raw materials change over time, companies purchase new machinery to replace old, stock prices fluctuate, employee turnovers occur, and so on. If a linear programming model has been used in a decision-making situation and later we find that changes in the situation cause changes in some of the coefficients associated with the initial linear programming formulation, we would like to determine how these changes affect the optimal solution to our original linear programming problem. Sensitivity analysis provides us with this information without requiring us to completely solve a new linear program. For example, if the profit for the Par, Inc., standard bags were reduced from $10 to $7 per bag, sensitivity analysis can tell the manager whether the production schedule of 540 standard bags and 252 deluxe bags is still the best decision or not. If it is, we will not have to solve a revised linear program with $7x_1 + 9x_2$ as the objective function.

Sensitivity analysis can also be used to determine how critical estimates of coefficients are in the solution to a linear programming problem. For example, suppose the management of Par, Inc., realizes the $10 profit coefficient for standard bags is a good but rough estimate of the profit the bags will actually provide. If sensitivity analysis shows that Par, Inc., should produce 540 standard bags and 252 deluxe bags as long as the actual profit for standard bags remains between $6 and $14, management can feel comfortable that the recommended production quantities are optimal. However, if the range for the profit of standard bags is $9.90 to $12, management may want to reevaluate the accuracy of the $10 profit estimate. Management would especially want to consider what revisions would have to be made in the optimal production quantities if the profit for standard bags dropped below the $9.90 limit.

As another phase of postoptimality analysis, management may want to investigate the possibility of adding resources to relax the binding constraints. In the Par, Inc., problem, management would possibly like to consider providing additional hours (such as overtime) for the cutting and dyeing and finishing operations. Sensitivity analysis can help answer the important questions of how much will each added hour be worth in terms of increasing profits, and what is the maximum number of hours that can be added before a different basic solution becomes optimal.

Thus you can see that through sensitivity analysis we will be able to provide additional valuable information for the decision maker. We begin our study of sensitivity analysis with the coefficients of the objective function.

10.6 SENSITIVITY ANALYSIS—THE COEFFICIENTS OF THE OBJECTIVE FUNCTION

In this phase of sensitivity analysis we will be interested in placing ranges on the values of the objective function coefficients such that as long as the actual value of the coefficient is within this range, the optimal solution will remain unchanged. As stated in the previous section, this information will tell us if we have to alter the optimal solution when a coefficient actually changes and will provide us with an indication of how critical the estimates of the coefficients are in arriving at the optimal solution.

In the following sensitivity analysis procedures we assume that only one coefficient changes at a time and that all other objective function coefficients remain at the values defined in the initial linear programming model. To illustrate the analysis for the coefficients of the objective function, let us again consider the final Simplex tableau for the Par, Inc., problem.

Basis	c_j	x_1 10	x_2 9	s_1 0	s_2 0	s_3 0	s_4 0	
x_2	9	0	1	30/16	0	−210/160	0	252
s_2	0	0	0	−15/16	1	25/160	0	120
x_1	10	1	0	−20/16	0	300/160	0	540
s_4	0	0	0	−11/32	0	45/320	1	18
	z_j	10	9	70/16	0	111/16	0	7668
	c_j-z_j	0	0	−70/16	0	−111/16	0	

Coefficients of the Nonbasic Variables

The sensitivity analysis procedure for coefficients of the objective function depends upon whether we are considering the coefficient of a basic or non-basic variable. For now, let us consider only the case of nonbasic variables.

Since the nonbasic variables are not in the solution, we are interested in the question of how much the objective function coefficient would have to change before it would be profitable to bring the associated variable into solution. Recall that it is only profitable to bring a variable into solution if its $c_j - z_j$ entry in the net evaluation row is greater than or equal to zero.

Let us denote a change in the objective function coefficient of variable x_j by Δc_j. Thus

$$\Delta c_j = c_j' - c_j \tag{10.1}$$

where

c_j = the value of the coefficient of x_j in the original linear program
c_j' = the new value of the coefficient of x_j.

Using this notation, we can write the new objective function coefficient as

$$c_j' = c_j + \Delta c_j. \tag{10.2}$$

It will be desirable to bring the nonbasic variable x_j into solution if the new objective function coefficient is such that $c_j' - z_j > 0$ (that is, if it will increase the value of the objective function). On the other hand, we will not want to bring the variable x_j into solution and thus will not change our current optimal solution as long as $c_j' - z_j \leq 0$. Our goal in this phase of sensitivity analysis is to determine the range of values that c_j' can take on without affecting the optimal solution.

Recall that z_j is computed by multiplying the coefficients of the *basic variables* (c_j column of the Simplex tableau) by the corresponding elements in the jth column of the $\bar{A}$ portion of the tableau. Thus a change in the objective function coefficient for a nonbasic variable cannot affect the value of the z_j. Therefore the values of c_j' that do not require us to change the optimal solution are given by

$$c_j' - z_j \leq 0.$$

Since z_j will be known in the final Simplex tableau, any new coefficient c_j' for a nonbasic variable such that

$$c_j' \leq z_j$$

will not cause a change in the current optimal solution.

Note that there is no lower limit on the new coefficient c_j'. This is certainly as expected, since we have a maximization objective function and thus lower and lower c_j' values will make the nonbasic variables even less desirable.

Thus for nonbasic variables we can now establish a range of c_j' values which will not affect the current optimal solution. We call this range the *range of insignificance* for the nonbasic variables. It is given by

$$-\infty < c_j' \leq z_j.$$

As long as the objective function coefficients for nonbasic variables remain within their respective ranges of insignificance, the nonbasic variables will remain at a zero value in the optimal solution. Thus the current optimal solution and the value of the objective function at the optimal solution will not change.

Coefficients of the Basic Variables

Let us start by asking how much the objective function coefficient of a basic variable would have to change before it would be profitable to change the current optimal solution. Again, realize that we will only change the current optimal solution if one or more of the net evaluation row values $c_j - z_j$ becomes greater than zero.

Let us consider a change in the objective function coefficient for the basic variable x_1 in the Par, Inc., problem. Let the new coefficient value be c_1'. Using equation (10.2), we can write $c_1' = c_1 + \Delta c_1$ where c_1 is the original coefficient 10 and Δc_1 is the change in the coefficient. Thus

$$c_1' = 10 + \Delta c_1. \tag{10.3}$$

Let us now see what happens to the final Simplex tableau of the Par, Inc., problem where the objective function coefficient for x_1 becomes $10 + \Delta c_1$. This tableau is given below.

Basis	c_j	x_1 $10+\Delta c_1$	x_2 9	s_1 0	s_2 0	s_3 0	s_4 0	
x_2	9	0	1	$\frac{30}{16}$	0	$-\frac{210}{160}$	0	252
s_2	0	0	0	$-\frac{15}{16}$	1	$\frac{25}{160}$	0	120
x_1	$10+\Delta c_1$	1	0	$-\frac{20}{16}$	0	$\frac{300}{160}$	0	540
s_4	0	0	0	$-\frac{11}{32}$	0	$\frac{45}{320}$	1	18
z_j		$10+\Delta c_1$	9	$\frac{70}{16}-\frac{20}{16}\Delta c_1$	0	$\frac{111}{16}+\frac{30}{16}\Delta c_1$	0	$7668+540\Delta c_1$
c_j-z_j		0	0	$-\frac{70}{16}+\frac{20}{16}\Delta c_1$	0	$-\frac{111}{16}-\frac{30}{16}\Delta c_1$	0	

How does the change of Δc_1 affect our final tableau? First, note that since x_1 is a basic variable, the new objective function coefficient $c_1' = 10 + \Delta c_1$ appears in the c_j column of the Simplex tableau. This means that the $10 + \Delta c_1$ value will affect the z_j values for several of the variables. By looking at the z_j row you can see that the new coefficient affects the z_j values of the basic variable x_1, both nonbasic variables (s_1 and s_3), and the objective function.

Recall that a decision to change the current optimal solution must be based on values in the net evaluation row. What variables have experienced a change in $(c_j - z_j)$ values because of the change Δc_1? As you can see, the change in the objective function coefficient for basic variable x_1 has caused changes in the $c_j - z_j$ values for both of the nonbasic variables. The $c_j - z_j$ values for all the basic variables remained unchanged; $c_j - z_j = 0$.

We have just identified the primary difference between the objective function sensitivity analysis procedures for basic and nonbasic variables. That is, a change in the objective function coefficient for a nonbasic variable only affects the $c_j - z_j$ value for that variable. However, a change in the objective function coefficient for a basic variable can affect the $c_j - z_j$ values for all nonbasic variables.

Returning to the Par, Inc., problem with the coefficient for x_1 changed to $10 + \Delta c_1$, we know that our current solution will remain optimal as long as all $c_j - z_j \leq 0$. Since the basic variables all still have $c_j - z_j = 0$, we will have to determine what range of values for Δc_1 will keep the $c_j - z_j$ values for all nonbasic variables less than or equal to zero.

For nonbasic variable s_1 we must have

$$-\tfrac{70}{16} + \tfrac{20}{16}\Delta c_1 \leq 0. \tag{10.4}$$

Solving for Δc_1, we see that it will not be profitable to introduce s_1 as long as

$$\tfrac{20}{16}\Delta c_1 \leq \tfrac{70}{16}$$
$$\Delta c_1 \leq \tfrac{16}{20}(\tfrac{70}{16}) = \tfrac{7}{2}$$
$$\Delta c_1 \leq 3.5.$$

For nonbasic variable s_3 we must have

$$-\tfrac{111}{16} - \tfrac{30}{16}\Delta c_1 \leq 0.$$

Solving for Δc_1, we see that it will not be profitable to introduce s_3 as long as

$$-\tfrac{30}{16}\Delta c_1 \leq \tfrac{111}{16}$$
$$\tfrac{30}{16}\Delta c_1 \geq -\tfrac{111}{16}$$
$$\Delta c_1 \geq \tfrac{16}{30}(-\tfrac{111}{10}) = -\tfrac{111}{30}$$
$$\Delta c_1 \geq -3.7.$$

Thus in order to keep the net evaluation row values of the nonbasic variables less than or equal to zero and to keep the current solution optimal, changes in c_1 cannot exceed a 3.5 increase ($\Delta c_1 \leq 3.5$) or a 3.7 decrease ($\Delta c_1 \geq -3.7$). Hence our current solution will remain optimal as long as

$$-3.7 \leq \Delta c_1 \leq 3.5. \tag{10.6}$$

From equation (10.3) we know that $\Delta c_1 = c_1' - 10$, where c_1' is the new value of the coefficient for x_1 in the objective function. Thus we can use equation (10.6) to define a range for the coefficient values of x_1 that will not cause a change in the optimal solution. This is done as follows:

$$-3.7 \leq (c_1' - 10) \leq 3.5.$$

Therefore,

$$6.3 \leq c_1' \leq 13.5.$$

The above result indicates to the decision maker that as long as the profit for one standard bag is between \$6.30 and \$13.50, the current production quantities of 540 standard bags and 252 deluxe bags will be optimal. We refer to the above range of values for the objective function coefficient of x_1 as the *range of optimality for* c_1.

To see how the management of Par, Inc., can make use of the above sensitivity analysis information, suppose that because of an increase in raw material prices, the profit of the standard bag is reduced to \$7 per unit. The range of optimality for c_1 indicates that the current solution $x_1 = 540$, $x_2 = 252$, $s_1 = 0$, $s_2 = 120$, $s_3 = 0$, and $s_4 = 18$ will still be optimal. To see the effect of this change, let us calculate the final Simplex tableau for the Par, Inc., problem after c_1 has been reduced to \$7:

Basis	c_j	x_1 7	x_2 9	s_1 0	s_2 0	s_3 0	s_4 0	
x_2	9	0	1	30/16	0	−210/160	0	252
s_2	0	0	0	−15/16	1	25/160	0	120
x_1	7	1	0	−20/16	0	300/160	0	540
s_4	0	0	0	−11/32	0	45/320	1	18
z_j		7	9	130/16	0	21/16	0	6048
$c_j - z_j$		0	0	−130/16	0	−21/16	0	

Since all the $c_j - z_j$ values are less than or equal to zero, the solution is optimal. As you can see, this solution is the same as our previous optimal solution. Note, however, that because of the decrease in profit for the standard bags, the total profit has been reduced to $7668 + 540\Delta c_1 = 7668 + 540(-3) = \$6048$.

What would happen if the profit per standard bag were reduced to $5? Again, we refer to the range of optimality for c_1. Since $c_1 = 5$ is outside the range, we know that a change this large will cause a new solution to be optimal. Consider the following Simplex tableau containing the same basic feasible solution but with the value of $c_1 = 5$.

Basis	c_j	x_1 5	x_2 9	s_1 0	s_2 0	s_3 0	s_4 0	
x_2	9	0	1	30/16	0	−210/160	0	252
s_2	0	0	0	−15/16	1	25/160	0	120
x_1	5	1	0	−20/16	0	300/160	0	540
s_4	0	0	0	−11/32	0	45/320	1	18
z_j		5	9	170/16	0	−39/16	0	4968
$c_j - z_j$		0	0	−170/16	0	39/16	0	

As expected, the solution $x_1 = 540$, $x_2 = 252$, $s_1 = 0$, $s_2 = 120$, $s_3 = 0$, and $s_4 = 18$ is no longer optimal. The coefficient for s_3 in the net evaluation row is now greater than zero. This implies that at least one more iteration must be performed to reach the optimal solution. Check for yourself to see that the new optimal solution will require production of 300 standard bags and 420 deluxe bags.

284

Thus we see how the range of optimality can be used to quickly determine whether or not a change in the objective function coefficient of a basic variable will cause a change in the optimal solution. Note that by using the range of optimality to determine whether or not the change in a profit coefficient for a basic variable is large enough to cause a change in the optimal solution, we can avoid the time-consuming process of reformulating and resolving the entire linear programming problem.

Returning to the final Simplex tableau for the original Par, Inc., problem, we can consider the effect of a change in the objective function coefficient for the basic variable x_2 by letting the new coefficient value be c_2'. Using equation (10.2) we have $c_2' = c_2 + \Delta c_2 = 9 + \Delta c_2$. Using $9 + \Delta c_2$ as the objective function coefficient in the final Simplex tableau and following the same sensitivity analysis procedure as for basic variable x_1, we can show the range of optimality for c_2 is

$$6.67 \leq c_2' \leq 14.29.$$

Thus, using sensitivity analysis, we see that as long as the profit for deluxe bags is between \$6.67 and \$14.29 per unit, the production quantities of 540 standard bags and 252 deluxe bags will remain optimal.

As a summary, we present the following managerial interpretation of sensitivity analysis for the objective function coefficients. Think of the basic variables as corresponding to our current product line and the nonbasic variables as representing other products we might produce. Within bounds, changes in the profit associated with one of the products in our current product line would not cause us to change our product mix or the amounts produced, but the changes would have an effect on our total profit. Of course, if the profit associated with one of our products changed drastically, we would change our product line (that is, move to a different basic solution). For products we are not currently producing (nonbasic variables) it is obvious that a decrease in per unit profit would not make us want to produce them. However, if the per unit profit for one of these products became large enough, we would want to consider adding it to our product line.

10.7 SENSITIVITY ANALYSIS—THE RIGHT-HAND SIDES

A very important phase of sensitivity analysis, both from a theoretical and practical point of view, is the study of the effect of changes of the right-hand sides on the optimal solution and the value of the optimal solution. By changes of the right-hand sides we mean simply changing the values of one of the elements in the b column of a linear program.

Quite often in linear programming problems we can interpret the b_i as the resources available. For example, in the Par, Inc., problem the right-hand side values represented the number of man-hours available in each of four departments. Thus valuable management information could be provided if we knew how much it would be worth to the company if one or more of these production time resources were increased. Sensitivity analysis of the right-hand sides can help provide this information.

Shadow Prices

The final Simplex tableau for the original Par, Inc., problem is shown below. Let us concentrate on the net evaluation row or $c_j - z_j$ values.

Basis	c_j	x_1	x_2	s_1	s_2	s_3	s_4	
		10	9	0	0	0	0	
x_2	9	0	1	30/16	0	−210/160	0	252
s_2	0	0	0	−15/16	1	25/160	0	120
x_1	10	1	0	−20/16	0	300/160	0	540
s_4	0	0	0	−11/32	0	45/320	1	18
z_j		10	9	70/16	0	111/16	0	7668
c_j-z_j		0	0	−70/16	0	−111/16	0	

What information is contained in the net evaluation row? As we developed the Simplex method, we learned that the $c_j - z_j$ values tell us how much the objective function changes as one unit of a variable is introduced into the solution. Thus when all $c_j - z_j \leq 0$, we know we cannot increase the value of the objective function and thus the optimal solution has been reached.

We want to see now how the $c_j - z_j$ values can also be used to determine how much additional resources are worth. For the Par, Inc., problem we have the following $c_j - z_j$ values for the slack variables.

Resource Constraint	Associated Slack Variable	Value of c_j-z_j at Optimum
Cutting and dyeing	s_1	−70/16
Sewing	s_2	0
Finishing	s_3	−111/16
Inspection and packaging	s_4	0

An important property of the net evaluation row is that the *negative* of the $c_j - z_j$ values for a slack variable associated with a constraint tells us how much the objective function will increase if one additional unit of the resource corresponding to the constraint is made available. Using this important property we could conclude that additional resources for Par, Inc., have the following values.

Resource	Value of an Additional Hour
Cutting and dyeing	70/16=$4.375
Sewing	0
Finishing	111/16=$6.9375
Inspection and packaging	0

The above values can be interpreted as the maximum value or price we would be willing to pay to obtain one additional unit of the resource. Because of this interpretation, the value of one additional unit of a resource is often called the *shadow price* of the resource.

Let us look more closely at these resource shadow prices to see if we can intuitively see why the negative of the $c_j - z_j$ values do in fact indicate the value of an additional unit of resource.

How much would you be willing to pay for additional resources in the sewing and inspection and packaging departments? Since slack time exists in these departments ($s_2 = 120$ and $s_4 = 18$), we already have excess capacity. Thus an additional unit of resources in either of these departments would simply increase the slack time. Clearly this is of no value to the company. In general, if a slack variable is a basic variable, in the optimal solution the shadow price of the corresponding resource is zero.

The slack variables associated with the cutting and dyeing and finishing departments are nonbasic variables in the optimal solution and are thus zero ($s_1 = s_3 = 0$). This indicates that all resources in these departments have been used. Thus the resource constraints corresponding to these two departments are the binding constraints. If Par, Inc., had additional resources available, it would obviously make sense to add production time in the cutting and dyeing and finishing departments.

To see why we place a 70/16 value on an additional unit of cutting and dyeing time, consider the following question: What happens if we bring one unit of s_1 into solution? We know that $c_j - z_j = -70/16$ tells us that profit will decrease by 70/16 for each unit of s_1 brought into solution. Having $s_1 = 1$ means we would only be using 629 hours in the cutting and dyeing department (that is, one hour of the 630 is slack time). Thus we see that decreasing our resource usage by one unit to 629 hours changes profit by $-70/16$. Hence

287

we conclude that the value of an additional unit of this resource is equal to 70/16. As a result, if we increase our resource usage by one unit to 631 hours, we should expect profit to increase by 70/16. Thus 70/16, or $4.375, is the value of an additional unit of cutting and dyeing time.

Shown below is the final Simplex tableau you would obtain if Par, Inc., had 631 hours of cutting and dyeing time available. As you can see, the profit has increased by $7672\frac{6}{16} - 7668 = \$4.375$ which is the shadow price of this resource.

Basis	c_j	x_1 10	x_2 9	s_1 0	s_2 0	s_3 0	s_4 0	
x_2	9	0	1	30/16	0	−210/160	0	$253\frac{14}{16}$
s_2	0	0	0	−15/16	1	25/160	0	$119\frac{1}{16}$
x_1	10	1	0	−20/16	0	300/160	0	$538\frac{12}{16}$
s_4	0	0	0	−11/32	0	45/320	1	$17\frac{21}{32}$
z_j		10	9	70/16	0	111/16	0	$7672\frac{6}{16}$
c_j-z_j		0	0	−70/16	0	−111/16	0	

Once we have used the shadow price concept to determine that one additional hour of cutting and dyeing time is worth $4.375, we might wonder how many additional hours of this resource it would be profitable to obtain. While we expect one additional unit to increase profit $4.375, two additional units 2($4.375) = $8.750, and three additional units 3($4.375) = $13.125, we cannot expect this increase in profit to continue without limit. In fact, as we increase the available cutting and dyeing time, at some point we will find that we are unable to use further amounts of this resource. At this point, additional units of the resource will be valued at $0. Thus the shadow price can only be interpreted as the marginal value of an additional unit of a resource. One can determine how many units of a resource can be obtained before the shadow price for the resource decreases. But the computations are rather detailed and beyond the scope of this text.[1]

10.8 SENSITIVITY ANALYSIS—THE COEFFICIENTS OF THE CONSTRAINTS

A change in one of the coefficients of the constraints can have a significant effect on the optimal solution to a linear programming problem. A complete

For a discussion of this see Anderson, Sweeney, and Williams, *Linear Programming for Decision Making,* West Publishing Company, 1974.

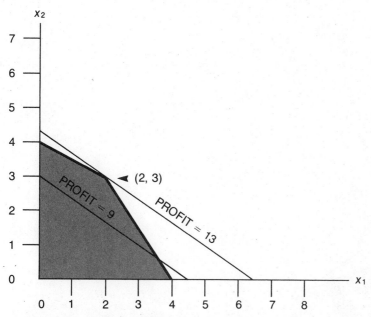

FIGURE 10.4 *Graphical solution of the example problem.*

discussion of the ramifications of making changes in the coefficients is beyond the scope of this text. However, we can make a few remarks based on an analysis of the graphical solution of the example problem shown below:

max $\quad 2x_1 + 3x_2$

s.t.

$$1x_1 + 2x_2 \leq 8$$
$$3x_1 + 2x_2 \leq 12$$
$$x_1, x_2 \geq 0.$$

The graphical solution to this problem is shown in Figure 10.4.

Suppose we make a change in the first constraint such that the coefficient associated with x_2 is 3. The problem now becomes

max $\quad 2x_1 + 3x_2$

s.t.

$$1x_1 + 3x_2 \leq 8$$
$$3x_1 + 2x_2 \leq 12$$
$$x_1, x_2 \geq 0.$$

The graphical solution to this problem is shown in Figure 10.5.

The optimal solution of $x_1 = 2$, $x_2 = 3$, and $z = 13$ for the original example has been revised to $x_1 = \frac{20}{7}$, $x_2 = \frac{12}{7}$, and $z = \frac{76}{7}$ as a result of this change. Thus the effect was to reduce the amount of x_2 in the optimal solution and to

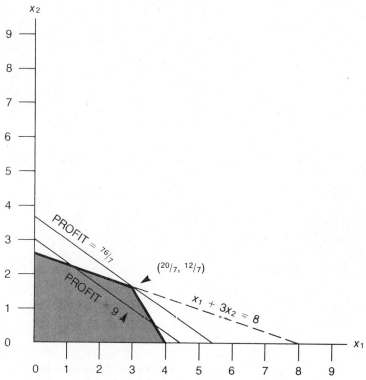

FIGURE 10.5 *Graphical solution of the example problem after changing a_{12} from 2 to 3.*

increase the amount of x_1. Graphically, we see that the slope and the x_2 intercept of the first constraint have changed. As a consequence, this has altered the feasible region and has caused a decrease in the value of the optimal solution.

The way to analyze qualitatively the effects of a change in a_{ij} for basic variable x_j is to think about the effect this change has on the constraining equation. Let us assume for the moment that all our constraints are of the less-than-or-equal-to type. Then if a_{ij} is increased and constraint i is binding, the value of the objective function will decrease, and the amount of x_j in the optimal solution will also decrease (assuming $x_j > 0$, that is, no degeneracy). If a_{ij} is decreased and constraint i is binding, then the value of the optimal solution will increase, and the amount of x_j will increase in the optimal solution. The converse of the above is true if our constraints are of the greater-than-or-equal-to type. For the case of equality constraints, additional analysis is necessary to determine the effect on the optimal solution. If one of the a_{ij} should change for a nonbinding constraint, this will have no effect on the optimal solution unless the change is large enough to make a new basis

290

optimal. In addition, if one of the a_{ij} change for a nonbasic variable, the change will have no effect on the optimal solution unless the change is large enough to cause the $c_j - z_j$ for that variable to become greater than or equal to zero.

A range can be computed for any a_{ij} such that values within the range do not require a new basis for the optimal solution. However, the calculations are much more complicated than they were for the coefficients of the objective function. Thus a detailed quantitative analysis of changes in the constraint coefficients is not elaborated upon here.

10.9 SUMMARY

This chapter has presented illustrations and discussions of the implications of infeasibility, unboundedness, alternate optima, and degeneracy. Toward this end we provided graphical illustrations and showed how to recognize and interpret all these solution possibilities when using the Simplex method.

We showed, through sensitivity analysis, how we could provide the decision maker with valuable information as to how the optimal solution and value of that solution could be expected to change, given a change in one of the coefficients of the problem. With respect to the objective function coefficients we calculated a range of optimality over which the basic variables could range with no resultant change in the optimal solution. Similarly, a range of insignificance was calculated for the objective function coefficients of the nonbasic variables. For the right-hand side values we described how shadow prices could be obtained from the final Simplex tableau and pointed out that these provided the marginal value of the corresponding resource. With respect to the A matrix our remarks were qualitative, since calculating the quantitative effect of a change in the a_{ij} is outside the scope of this text.

The calculations and the resulting conclusions we obtained from sensitivity analysis were based on the assumption that *only one* coefficient was being changed at a time and that all other coefficients remained fixed. It is possible through sensitivity analysis to study the effects of multiple changes in the problem coefficients, but the calculations are more complicated.

10.10 GLOSSARY

1. *Infeasibility*—Infeasibility occurs when there is no solution to the linear programming problem which satisfies all the constraints. If the final Simplex tableau consists of one or more artificial variables in solution at a positive value, we recognize that the optimal solution to the linear programming model is infeasible for our real-world problem.

2. *Unboundedness*—A solution to a linear programming problem is said to be unbounded if the value of the solution may be made infinitely large without violating any of the constraints. If at some iteration the Simplex method tells us to introduce x_j into solution and all the $\bar{a}_{ij}$ are less than or equal to zero in column j, then we have an unbounded solution.

3. *Alternate optima*—When a linear program has two or more optimal solutions, we say that the linear program has alternate optima. In the Simplex method we cannot usually recognize alternate optima until the final tableau. Then, if the program has alternate optima, $c_j - z_j$ will equal zero for one of the variables not in solution.

4. *Degeneracy*—A linear program is degenerate if one or more of the variables in the basic solution has a value of zero.

5. *Range of insignificance*—The range of values over which a c_j associated with a nonbasic variable may vary without causing any change in the optimal solution or the value of the objective function.

6. *Range of optimality*—The range of values over which a c_j associated with a basic variable may vary without causing any change in the optimal solution (that is, the values of all the variables will remain the same, but the value of the objective function will change).

7. *Shadow price*—The value of one additional unit of the resource associated with a linear programming constraint.

10.11 PROBLEMS

In Problems 1–9 we provide example linear programs that result in one or more of the following solution situations:

1. Optimal solution
2. Infeasible solution
3. Unbounded solution
4. Alternate optimal solution
5. Degenerate solution

For each linear program, determine the solution situations that exist and indicate how you identified each situation using the graphical and/or Simplex method. For the problems with alternate optimal solutions, calculate at least two optimal solutions. Solve Problems 1 to 5 using both the graphical and Simplex methods.

1. max $2x_1 + 4x_2$
s.t.
$$1x_1 + 1x_2 \le 5$$
$$-1x_1 + 1x_2 \ge 8$$
$$x_1, x_2 \ge 0.$$

2. max $1x_1 + 1x_2$
s.t.
$$4x_1 + 3x_2 \ge 12$$
$$2x_1 + 3x_2 \ge -6$$
$$1x_2 \ge 2$$
$$x_1, x_2 \ge 0.$$

3. min $3x_1 + 3x_2$

   s.t.

$$4x_1 + 1x_2 \geq 20$$
$$1x_1 \qquad\ \geq\ 2$$
$$2x_1 + 2x_2 \geq 16$$
$$x_1, x_2 \geq 0.$$

4. min $2x_1 + 1x_2$

   s.t.

$$1x_1 + 1x_2 = 600$$
$$1x_1 + 1x_2 \leq 700$$
$$1x_1 + \tfrac{3}{2}x_2 \leq 900$$
$$1x_1 \qquad\ \geq 200$$
$$x_1, x_2 \geq 0.$$

5. max $2x_1 + 4x_2$

   s.t.

$$1x_1 + \tfrac{1}{2}x_2 \leq 10$$
$$1x_1 + 1x_2 = 12$$
$$1x_1 + \tfrac{3}{2}x_2 \leq 18$$
$$x_1, x_2 \geq 0.$$

6. max $1x_1 + 2x_2 + 1x_3$

   s.t.

$$3x_1 + 4x_2 \qquad\quad \leq 12$$
$$2x_1 + 3x_2 - 1x_3 \geq\ 6$$
$$x_1, x_2, x_3 \geq 0.$$

7. max $2x_1 + 1x_2 + 1x_3$

   s.t.

$$2x_1 + 1x_2 + 1x_3 \geq\ 2$$
$$1x_1 + 2x_2 \qquad\ \leq 10$$
$$2x_1 + 4x_2 + 1x_3 \leq\ 8$$
$$x_1, x_2, x_3 \geq 0.$$

8. min $-4x_1 + 5x_2 + 5x_3$

   s.t.

$$-1x_2 + 1x_3 \geq\ 2$$
$$-1x_1 + 1x_2 + 1x_3 \geq\ 1$$
$$x_3 \leq -1$$
$$x_1, x_2, x_3 \geq 0.$$

9. min $1x_1 + 1x_2 + 1x_3$

   s.t.

$$1x_1 + 5x_2 + 2x_3 \geq 250$$
$$1x_2 + 2x_3 \geq\ 50$$
$$x_1, x_2, x_3 \geq 0.$$

10. In addition to their line of bicycles, Hot Wheels, Inc., manufactures three types of kiddie tricycles. They produce a model known as the Fat Wheel, a model called the Toad, and their ever popular model, the Ridge Runner. Hot Wheels manufactures these tricycle models on special order or whenever they have any slack time available during their bicycle production. Hot Wheels currently has some slack time available and would like to determine the optimal number of kiddie tricycles to produce in order to maximize the total number of tricycles produced, with the requirement that they produce at least twice as many Ridge Runners as they do of Fat Wheels plus Toads. (Historically, orders have normally been 2 : 1 in favor of the Ridge Runner model.) Each unit of the Fat Wheel and Toad requires 10 minutes of manufacturing time, whereas each unit of the Ridge Runner requires 4 minutes. In addition, Fat Wheels require 8 minutes of assembly time, Toads require 6 minutes, and Ridge Runners require 4 minutes. There are 40 hours of

manufacturing time and 20 hours of assembly time available. The warehouse has capacity to store a maximum of 150 tricycles. What should Hot Wheels do?

Consider the possibility of alternate optimal solutions. What flexibility does this provide for Hot Wheels?

11. The cook at Happy Harry's Lakeside Kiddie Resort has a problem. In addition to knowing how to cook just three different dishes, he has been told by Happy Harry to use as much as possible of the ingredients on hand in order to make up meals having the highest nutritional value possible (this is so that Harry can advertise that his resort is not only a fun place to get rid of the kids, but also a healthy place). The cook currently has 40 pounds of ingredient A available, 30 pounds of ingredient B, and 60 pounds of ingredient C. Each unit of recipe 1 calls for 1 pound of A, $\frac{1}{2}$ pound of B, and 1 pound of C. Each unit of recipe 2 requires 2 pounds of B and 1 pound of C. Each unit of recipe 3 requires 1 pound of both A and B, and 2 pounds of C. If one unit of recipe 1 contains 15 nutritional units, one unit of recipe 2 contains 30 nutritional units, and one unit of recipe 3 contains 25 nutritional units, how many units of each recipe should the cook make in order to maximize the nutritional value of the meals made. Set up this problem and solve using the Simplex method.

12. Consider the linear program:

$$\max \quad 15x_1 + 30x_2 + 20x_3$$

s.t.

$$1x_1 \qquad + 1x_3 \leq 4$$
$$\tfrac{1}{2}x_1 + 2x_2 + 1x_3 \leq 3$$
$$1x_1 + 1x_2 + 2x_3 \leq 6$$
$$x_1, x_2, x_3 \geq 0.$$

a. Find the optimal solution.
b. Calculate the range of optimality or range of insignificance (whichever is appropriate) for c_1.
c. What would be the effect of a five-unit increase in c_1 (from 15 to 20) on the optimal solution and the value of that solution?
d. Calculate the range of optimality or range of insignificance (whichever is appropriate) for c_3.
e. What would be the effect of a five-unit increase in c_3 (from 20 to 25) on the optimal solution and the value of that solution?

13. Consider again the linear programming problem presented in Problem 12.

a. How much will the value of the objective function change if b_1 is increased from 4 to 5?
b. How much will the value of the objective function change if b_2 is increased from 3 to 4?

c. How much will the value of the objective function change is b_3 is increased from 6 to 7?

14. Consider the following linear program:

$$\text{max} \quad 3x_1 + 1x_2 + 5x_3 + 3x_4$$

s.t.

$$3x_1 + 1x_2 + 2x_3 \qquad = 30$$
$$2x_1 + 1x_2 + 3x_3 + 1x_4 \geq 15$$
$$2x_2 \qquad + 3x_4 \leq 25$$
$$x_1, x_2, x_3, x_4 \geq 0.$$

a. Find the optimal solution.
b. Calculate the range of optimality or range of insignificance (whichever is appropriate) for c_3.
c. What would be the effect of a four-unit decrease in c_3 (from 5 to 1) on the optimal solution and the value of that solution?
d. Calculate the range of optimality or range of insignificance (whichever is appropriate) for c_2.
e. What would be the effect of a three-unit increase in c_2 (from 1 to 4) on the optimal solution and the value of that solution?

15. Consider the Par, Inc., problem which is formulated below:

$$\text{max} \quad 10x_1 + 9x_2$$

s.t.

$$\tfrac{7}{10}x_1 + 1x_2 \leq 630 \quad \text{cutting and dyeing}$$
$$\tfrac{1}{2}x_1 + \tfrac{5}{6}x_2 \leq 600 \quad \text{sewing}$$
$$1x_1 + \tfrac{2}{3}x_2 \leq 708 \quad \text{finishing}$$
$$\tfrac{1}{10}x_1 + \tfrac{1}{4}x_2 \leq 135 \quad \text{inspection and packaging}$$
$$x_1, x_2 \geq 0.$$

The final tableau is

Basis	c_j	x_1 10	x_2 9	s_1 0	s_2 0	s_3 0	s_4 0	
x_2	9	0	1	30/16	0	−210/160	0	252
s_2	0	0	0	−15/16	1	25/160	0	120
x_1	10	1	0	−20/16	0	300/160	0	540
s_4	0	0	0	−11/32	0	45/320	1	18
	z_j	10	9	70/16	0	111/16	0	7668
	c_j-z_j	0	0	−70/16	0	−111/16	0	

a. Calculate the range of optimality for the profit contribution c_2 of the deluxe bag.

295

b. If the profit per deluxe bag drops to $7 per unit, how will the optimal solution be affected?

c. What unit profit would the deluxe bag have to have before Par would consider changing its current production plan?

d. If the profit of the deluxe bags can be increased to $15 per unit, what is the optimal production plan? State what you think will happen before you compute the new optimal solution.

11
Linear Programming Applications

Our study thus far has been directed primarily toward obtaining an understanding of linear programming methodology. This background is essential for knowing when linear programming is an appropriate problem-solving tool and for interpreting the results of a linear programming solution to a problem. However, the benefits of this study will only be realized by learning how this methodology can be used to solve real-world decision-making problems. The purpose of this chapter is to show you how selected real-world decision-making problems can be formulated and solved using linear programming.

There are two ways in which one may develop skills in model building. (In this chapter, model building should be taken to mean formulating a linear program that is a "model" of the real-world decision-making problem for which a solution is desired.) The first way is by on-the-job experience. This is essentially a trial-and-error approach and obviously could not be attempted in a textbook. The second way in which one may develop these skills is by studying how others have developed successful models. In this chapter we attempt to develop your skills along these lines by presenting several reasonably detailed examples of successful linear programming applications. Relatively small problems will be used in the examples, but the principles being developed are applicable to much larger problems.

In practice, linear programming has proved to be one of the most successful quantitative aids for managerial decision making. Numerous applications have been reported in the chemical, airline, steel, paper, petroleum, and other industries. The specific problems studied have included production scheduling, capital budgeting, plant location, transportation, media selection, and many others.

As the variety of the applications mentioned would suggest, linear programming is a flexible problem-solving tool with applications in many disciplines. In this chapter we present introductory applications from the areas of finance, marketing, management, and accounting, as well as the standard linear programming applications in blending and diet problems. In addition, an application involving environmental protection is presented.

An understanding of the material presented in this chapter should give the reader an appreciation of the broad range of practical linear programming applications and provide a basis for the reader to further develop his modeling skills by creating similar and possibly new linear programming applications in his own field of interest.

11.1 FINANCIAL APPLICATIONS

Portfolio Selection

Portfolio selection problems are financial management situations in which a manager must select specific investments—for example, stocks, bonds— from a variety of investment alternatives. This type of problem is frequently encountered by managers of mutual funds, credit unions, insurance companies, and banks. The objective function for these problems is usually maximization of expected return or minimization of risk. The constraints usually take the form of restrictions on the type of permissible investments, state laws, company policy, maximum permissible risk, and so on.

Problems of this type have been formulated and solved using a variety of mathematical programming techniques. However, if in a particular portfolio selection problem it is possible to formulate a linear objective function and linear constraints, then linear programming can be used to solve the problem. In this section we show how a simplified portfolio selection problem can be formulated and solved as a linear program.[1]

Consider the case of Welte Mutual Funds, Inc., located in New York City. Welte has just obtained $100,000 by converting industrial bonds to cash and is now looking for other investment opportunities for these funds. Considering Welte's current investments, the firm's top financial analyst recommends that all new investments should be made in the oil industry, steel industry, or government bonds. Specifically, the analyst has identified five investment opportunities and projected their annual rates of return. The investments and rates of return are shown in Table 11.1.

Management of Welte has imposed the following investment guidelines.

1. Neither industry should receive more than 50% of the total new investment.
2. Government bonds should be at least 25% of the steel industry investments.
3. The investment in Pacific Oil, the high-return but high-risk investment, cannot be more than 60% of the total oil industry investment.

[1] For a discussion of some other approaches to portfolio selection, see Markowitz, H., *Portfolio Selection* (Cowles Foundation Monograph No. 16). New York: Wiley, 1959.

TABLE 11.1 *Investment Opportunities for Welte Mutual Funds*

Investment	Projected Rate of Return (percent)
Atlantic Oil	7.3
Pacific Oil	10.3
Midwest Steel	6.4
Huber Steel	7.5
Government bonds	4.5

What portfolio recommendations—investments and amounts—should be made for the available $100,000? Given the objective of maximizing projected return subject to the budgetary and managerially imposed constraints, we can answer this question by formulating a linear programming model of the problem. The solution to this linear programming model will then provide investment recommendations for the management of Welte Mutual Funds.

Let

x_1 = dollars invested in Atlantic Oil

x_2 = dollars invested in Pacific Oil

x_3 = dollars invested in Midwest Steel

x_4 = dollars invested in Huber Steel

x_5 = dollars invested in government bonds.

The complete linear programming model is as follows:

$$\max \quad 0.073x_1 + 0.103x_2 + 0.064x_3 + 0.075x_4 + 0.045x_5$$

s.t.

$$
\begin{aligned}
x_1 + x_2 + x_3 + x_4 + x_5 &= 100{,}000 \quad \text{available funds} \\
x_1 + x_2 &\le 50{,}000 \quad \text{oil industry maximum} \\
x_3 + x_4 &\le 50{,}000 \quad \text{steel industry maximum} \\
-\, 0.25x_3 - 0.25x_4 + x_5 &\ge 0 \quad \text{government bonds minimum} \\
-0.6x_1 + 0.4x_2 &\le 0 \quad \text{Pacific oil restriction} \\
x_1, x_2, x_3, x_4, x_5 &\ge 0.
\end{aligned}
$$

299

TABLE 11.2 Optimal Portfolio Selection for Welte Mutual Funds

Investment	Amount	Expected Annual Return
Atlantic Oil	$ 20,000	$1460
Pacific Oil	30,000	3090
Huber Steel	40,000	3000
Government bonds	10,000	450
	$100,000	$8000

Expected annual return of $8000=8%

The solution to this linear programming model is shown in Table 11.2.

We note that the optimal solution indicates that the portfolio should be diversified among all the investment opportunities except Midwest Steel. The projected expected annual return for this portfolio is 8%.

One shortcoming of the linear programming approach to the portfolio selection problem is that we may not be able to invest the exact amount specified in each of the securities. For example, if Atlantic Oil sold for $75 a share, we would have to purchase exactly $266\frac{2}{3}$ shares in order to spend exactly the recommended $20,000. The approach usually taken to avoid this difficulty is to purchase the largest possible whole number of shares with the amount of funds recommended (for example, 266 shares of Atlantic Oil). Hence we guarantee that our budget constraint will not be violated. This, of course, introduces the possibility that our solution will no longer be optimal, but the danger is slight if large numbers of securities are involved.

Financial Mix Strategy

Financial mix strategies involve the selection of means for financing company projects, inventories, production operations, and various other activities. In this section we illustrate how linear programming can be used to solve problems of this type by formulating and solving a problem involving the financing of production operations. In this particular application a financial decision must be made with regard to how much production is to be supported by internally generated funds and how much is to be supported by external funds.

The Jefferson Adding Machine Company will begin production of two new models of electronic adding machines during the next 3 months. Since this new line requires an expansion of the current production operation, the company will need operating funds to cover material, labor, and selling expenses during this initial production period. Revenue from this initial production run will not be available until after the end of the period. Thus the company must arrange financing for these operating expenses before production can begin.

Jefferson has $3000 in internal funds available to cover expenses of this operation. If additional funds are needed, they will have to be generated externally. A local bank has offered a line of short-term credit in an amount not to exceed $10,000. The interest rate over the life of the loan will be 12% per year on the average amount borrowed. One stipulation set by the bank requires that the remaining company cash allocated to this operation plus the accounts receivable for this product line must be at least twice as great as the outstanding loan plus interest at the end of the initial production period.

In addition to the financial restrictions placed on this operation, man-hour capacity is also a factor for Jefferson to consider. Specifically, only 2500 hours of assembly time and 150 hours of packaging and shipping time are available for the new product line during the initial 3-month production period. Relevant cost, price, and production time requirements for the two models are shown in Table 11.3.

Additional restrictions have been imposed by company management in order to guarantee that the market reaction to both products can be tested; that is, at least 50 units of model Y and at least 25 units of model Z must be produced in this first production period.

Since the cost of units produced on borrowed funds will in effect experience an interest charge, the profit margins for the units of models Y and Z produced on borrowed funds will be reduced. Hence we adopt the following notation for the decision variables in our problem:

x_1 = units of model Y produced with company funds

x_2 = units of model Y produced with borrowed funds

x_3 = units of model Z produced with company funds

x_4 = units of model Z produced with borrowed funds

TABLE 11.3   Cost, Price, and Manpower Data for the
            Jefferson Adding Machine Company

Model	Unit Cost (Materials and Other Variable Expenses)	Selling Price	Profit Margin	Man-Hours Required Assembly	Packaging and Shipping
Y	$ 50	$ 58	$ 8	12	1
Z	$100	$120	$20	25	2

How much will the profit margin be reduced for units produced on borrowed funds? To answer this question, one must know for how long the loan will be outstanding. We assume that all units of each model are sold as they are produced to independent distributors, and that the average rate of turnover of accounts receivable is 3 months. Since company management has specified that the loan is to be repaid by funds generated by the units produced on borrowed funds, the funds borrowed to produce one unit of model Y or Z will be repaid approximately 3 months later. Hence the profit margin for each unit of model Y produced on borrowed funds is reduced from \$8.00 to \$8.00 − (\$50 × 0.12 × $\frac{1}{4}$ yr.) = \$6.50, and the profit margin for each unit of model Z produced on borrowed funds is reduced from \$20.00 to \$20.00 − (\$100 × 0.12 × $\frac{1}{4}$ yr.) = \$17.00. With this information we can now formulate the objective function for Jefferson's financial mix problem:

$$\max \quad 8x_1 + 6.5x_2 + 20x_3 + 17x_4.$$

We can also specify the following constraints for the model:

$$
\begin{array}{lll}
12x_1 + 12x_2 + 25x_3 + 25x_4 \leq 2500 & \text{assembly} \\
x_1 + x_2 + 2x_3 + 2x_4 \leq 150 & \text{packaging and shipping} \\
50x_1 + 100x_3 \leq 3000 & \text{internal funds} \\
50x_2 + 100x_4 \leq 10{,}000 & \text{external funds} \\
x_1 + x_2 \geq 50 & \text{model Y requirement} \\
x_3 + x_4 \geq 25 & \text{model Z requirement}
\end{array}
$$

In addition, the following constraint must be included to satisfy the bank loan requirement:

cash + accounts receivable $\geq$ 2 (loan + interest).

This restriction must be satisfied at the end of the period. Recalling that accounts receivable are outstanding for an average of 3 months, the following relationships can be used to derive a mathematical expression for the above inequality at the end of the period.

$$
\begin{aligned}
\text{cash} &= 3000 - 50x_1 - 100x_3 \\
\text{accounts receivable} &= 58x_1 + 58x_2 + 120x_3 + 120x_4 \\
\text{loan} &= 50x_2 + 100x_4 \\
\text{interest} &= (0.12 \times \tfrac{1}{4} \text{ yr.})(50x_2 + 100x_4) = 1.5x_2 + 3x_4.
\end{aligned}
$$

Therefore the constraint resulting from the bank restriction can be written as:

$$3000 - 50x_1 - 100x_3 + 58x_1 + 58x_2 + 120x_3 + 120x_4 \geq 2(51.5x_2 + 103x_4)$$

or

$$-8x_1 + 45x_2 - 20x_3 + 86x_4 \leq 3000.$$

TABLE 11.4 Optimal Financial Mix for the Production of
Jefferson Adding Machines

	Units	Expected Profit
Model Y		
borrowed funds (x_2)	50	$ 325
Model Z		
company funds (x_3)	30	$ 600
borrowed funds (x_4)	15.7	$ 267
Total		$1192

The complete linear programming model for our problem can now be stated:

$$\max \quad 8x_1 + 6.5x_2 + 20x_3 + 17x_4$$

s.t.

$$12x_1 + 12x_2 + 25x_3 + 25x_4 \le 2500$$
$$x_1 + x_2 + 2x_3 + 2x_4 \le 150$$
$$50x_1 + 100x_3 \le 3000$$
$$50x_2 + 100x_4 \le 10{,}000$$
$$x_1 + x_2 \ge 50$$
$$x_3 + x_4 \ge 25$$
$$-8x_1 + 45x_2 - 20x_3 + 86x_4 \le 3000$$
$$x_1, x_2, x_3, x_4 \ge 0.$$

The solution to this four-variable seven-constraint financial mix problem is shown in Table 11.4. The optimal financial mix requires the company to use all its internal funds ($3000), but only slightly over $4000 of the available $10,000 line of credit.

11.2 MARKETING APPLICATIONS

Media Selection

Media selection applications of linear programming are aimed at helping marketing managers allocate a fixed advertising budget across various media. Potential advertising media include newspapers, magazines, radio commercials, television commercials, direct mailings, and others. In most of these applications the objective is taken to be the maximization of audience exposure. Restrictions on the allowable allocation usually arise through considerations such as company policy, contract requirements, and availability of media. In the application which follows we illustrate how a simple media selection problem might be formulated and solved using a linear programming model.

Consider the case of the Relax-and-Enjoy Lake Development Corporation. Relax-and-Enjoy is developing a lakeside community at a privately owned lake and is in the business of selling property for vacation and/or retreat cottages. The primary market for these lakeside lots includes all middle and upper income families within approximately 100 miles of the development. Relax-and-Enjoy has employed the advertising firm of Boone, Phillips, and Jackson to design the promotional campaign for the project.

After considering possible advertising media and the market to be covered, Boone has made the preliminary recommendation to restrict the first month's advertising to five sources. At the end of this month, Boone will then reevaluate its strategy based upon the month's results. Boone has collected data on the number of potential purchase families reached, the cost per advertisement, the maximum number of times each medium is available, and the expected exposure for each of the five media. The expected exposure is measured in terms of an exposure unit, a management judgment measure of the relative value of one advertisement in each of the media. These measures, based on Boone's experience in the advertising business, take into account such factors as audience profile (age, income, and education of the audience reached), image presented, and quality of the advertisement. The information collected to date is presented in Table 11.5.

Relax-and-Enjoy has provided Boone with an advertising budget of $30,000 for the first month's campaign. In addition, Relax-and-Enjoy has imposed the following restrictions on how Boone may allocate these funds. At least 10 television commercials must be used and at least 50,000 potential purchasers must be reached during the month. In addition no more than $18,000 may be spent on television advertisements. What advertising media selection plan should the advertising firm recommend?

The first step in formulating a linear programming model of this problem is the definition of the decision variables. We let

x_1 = number of times daytime TV is used

x_2 = number of times evening TV is used

x_3 = number of times daily newspaper is used

x_4 = number of times Sunday newspaper is used

x_5 = number of times radio is used.

With the overall goal of maximizing the expected exposure, the objective function becomes

$$\max \quad 65x_1 + 90x_2 + 40x_3 + 60x_4 + 20x_5.$$

TABLE 11.5   Advertising Media Alternatives for the Relax-
and-Enjoy Lake Development Corporation

Advertising Media	Number of Potential Purchase Families Reached	Cost per Advertise-ment	Maximum* Times Available Per Month	Expected Exposure Units
1. Daytime TV (1 min) Station WKLA	1000	$1500	15	65
2. Evening TV (30 sec) Station WKLA	2000	$3000	10	90
3. Daily news-paper (full page) The Morning Journal	1500	$400	25	40
4. Sunday newspaper magazine ($\frac{1}{2}$ page color) The Sunday Press	2500	$1000	4	60
5. Radio, 8:00 A.M. or 5:00 P.M. news (30 sec) Station KNOP	300	$100	30	20

* The maximum number of times the medium is available is either the maximum number of times the advertising medium occurs (that is, 4 Sundays for medium 4) or the maximum number of times Boone will allow the medium to be used.

The constraints for our model can now be formulated from the information given:

$$
\begin{array}{rcl}
x_1 & \leq & 15 \\
x_2 & \leq & 10 \\
x_3 & \leq & 25 \\
x_4 & \leq & 4 \\
x_5 & \leq & 30
\end{array}
\left. \right\} \begin{array}{l} \text{availability} \\ \text{of media} \end{array}
$$

$$1500x_1 + 3000x_2 + 400x_3 + 1000x_4 + 100x_5 \leq 30{,}000 \quad \text{budget}$$

$$
\left.
\begin{array}{rcl}
x_1 + x_2 & \geq & 10 \\
1500x_1 + 3000x_2 & \leq & 18{,}000
\end{array}
\right\} \begin{array}{l} \text{television} \\ \text{restrictions} \end{array}
$$

$$1000x_1 + 2000x_2 + 1500x_3 + 2500x_4 + 300x_5 \geq 50{,}000 \quad \begin{array}{l} \text{audience} \\ \text{coverage} \end{array}$$

$$x_1, x_2, x_3, x_4, x_5 \geq 0.$$

TABLE 11.6 Advertising Plan for Relax-and-Enjoy Lake
Development Corporation

Media	Frequency	Budget
Daytime TV	10	$15,000
Daily newspaper	25	10,000
Sunday newspaper	2	2,000
Radio	30	3,000
		$30,000

Total audience contacted=61,500

Expected exposure=2370

The solution to this five-variable nine-constraint linear programming model is presented in Table 11.6.

We point out that the above media selection model, probably more than most other linear programming models, requires crucial subjective evaluations as input. The most critical of these inputs is the expected exposure rating measure. While marketing managers may have substantial data concerning expected advertising exposure, the final coefficient that includes image and quality considerations is primarily based on managerial judgment. However, judgment input is a very acceptable way of obtaining necessary data for a linear programming model.

Another shortcoming of this model is that, even if the expected exposure measure were not subject to error, there is no guarantee that maximization of total expected exposure will lead to a maximization of profit. However, this is not a shortcoming of linear programming; rather, it is a shortcoming of the use of exposure as a criterion. Certainly if we were able to measure directly the effect of an advertisement on profit we would use total profit as our objective to be maximized.

In addition, you should be aware that the media selection model as formulated in this section does not include considerations such as the following:

1. Reduced exposure value for repeat media usage
2. Cost discounts for repeat media usage
3. Audience overlap by different media
4. Timing recommendation for the advertisement.

A more complex formulation—more variables and constraints—can often be used to overcome some of these limitations, but it will not always be possible to overcome all of them with a linear programming model. However, even in these cases, a linear programming model can often be used to arrive at a rough approximation to the best decision. Management evaluation

306

combined with the linear programming solution should then make possible the selection of an overall effective advertising strategy.

Marketing Strategy

One particular marketing strategy decision involves the optimal allocation of sales force and advertising effort. As we discussed in the previous section on media selection problems, one would like to make this decision in such a fashion as to maximize profit or sales. Unfortunately, one seldom has enough information to specify the relationship between the allocation of sales force and advertising effort and the ultimate criterion of profit or sales. We illustrate in this section a case where the company has been able to specify this relationship. Thus the marketing strategy decision can be made with the objective of maximizing profit.

Electronic Communications, Inc., manufactures portable radio systems that can be used for two-way communications. The company's new product, which has a range of up to 25 miles, is particularly suitable for use in a variety of applications such as mobile unit-home office systems, marina sales and service systems, and others. In these applications the two-way communication system enables an office to easily contact field salesmen, repairmen, and so on. The primary distribution channel for the product will be through industrial communications equipment distributors. However, the firm is also considering distribution through a national chain of discount stores and a marine equipment distributor. These latter two distribution channels have the advantage of allowing the product to reach individuals interested in radio-oriented hobbies and individuals desiring boat communication systems.

Because of differing distribution and promotional costs, the profitability of the product varies with the distribution alternative selected. In addition, the company's estimate of the advertising cost and salesman time per unit sold will vary with the different distribution channels. Since the company only produces these units on order, the number of units produced and number of units sold are the same.

Table 11.7 summarizes the data prepared by Electronic Communications

TABLE 11.7 Profit, Cost, and Time Data for Electronic Communications, Inc.

Distributor	Profit per Unit Sold	Estimated Average Advertising Cost per Unit Sold	Estimated Sales-Force Effort per Unit Sold (hours)
Industrial	$90	$10	2.5
Discount stores	70	18	3.0
Marine	84	8	3.0

with respect to profit, expected advertising effort per unit sold, and estimated sales force effort per unit sold. The advertising and sales force estimates are based upon past experience with similar radio equipment.

Company management has specified that at least 100 units must be distributed through the discount stores during the next 3 months. The firm has set the advertising budget at $5000 and stated that a maximum of 1200 man-hours of sales force time will be available during the current planning period. In addition, production capacity is 600 units.

The company is now faced with the task of establishing a profitable marketing strategy. Specifically, decisions need to be made on the following:

1. How many units should be produced and how should they be allocated to the three market segments?
2. How much advertising should be devoted to the three market segments?
3. How should the sales force effort be allocated among the three market segments?

Proceeding to a linear programming formulation of this problem, we define the following variables:

x_1 = units produced for the industrial market

x_2 = units produced for the discount store market

x_3 = units produced for the marine market.

In terms of this notation, the objective function and constraints can be written as follows:

$$\max \quad 90x_1 + 70x_2 + 84x_3$$

s.t.

$$
\begin{array}{llll}
10x_1 + 18x_2 + 8x_3 \le 5000 & \text{advertising budget} \\
2.5x_1 + 3x_2 + 3x_3 \le 1200 & \text{sales-force availability} \\
x_1 + x_2 + x_3 \le 600 & \text{production capacity} \\
x_2 \ge 100 & \text{minimum discount store volume} \\
x_1, x_2, x_3 \ge 0.
\end{array}
$$

The solution to this linear programming model is given in Table 11.8.

Sensitivity analysis techniques may provide the marketing manager with some additional valuable information. Specifically, the shadow prices for the advertising budget, sales force, and production capacity resources are 6, 12, and 0, respectively. Recall from Chapter 10 that a shadow price of zero for a slack variable indicated that an increase in the value of the right-hand side for the corresponding constraint would have no effect on profit. Therefore we can conclude in this case that the production capacity (constraint 3) is not restricting our profit. In fact, the slack variable associated with this constraint shows the excess production capacity to be 160 hours. That is, the

TABLE 11.8 *Profit Maximizing Marketing Strategy for Electronic Communications, Inc.*

Market Segment	Volume	Advertising Allocation	Sales Force Allocation (hours)	Production Time (hours)
Industrial	240	$2400	600	240
Discount store	100	1800	300	100
Marine	100	800	300	100
Total	440	$5000	1200	440

Profit projection = $37,000

current solution uses only 440 of the available 600 hours of production time.

The nonzero shadow prices mean that the corresponding constraints are binding. Therefore we know that we are using the maximum available advertising and sales force resources. The results in Table 11.8 confirm this analysis. The values of these shadow prices give the marginal value of additional advertising budget and sales force effort. Specifically, an additional advertising dollar has a potential of increasing the profit by $6, while an additional man-hour of sales force effort has a potential value of $12. Thus the manager should consider the possibility of obtaining these additional resources as long as the cost of the addition is less than the potential benefits. Recall, however, in Chapter 10 we saw that we cannot expect additional resources to increase profit without limit. In this case we might consider increasing the advertising budget and using part-time sales assistance. However, as we continue to increase these resources, sales will increase and production capacity will become binding, causing any additional advertising and sales efforts to be of no value.

11.3 MANAGEMENT APPLICATIONS

Production Scheduling

One of the richest areas of linear programming applications is production scheduling. The solution to a production scheduling problem enables the manager to establish an efficient low cost production schedule for one or more products over several time periods, such as, weeks, months, and so on. Essentially, a production scheduling problem can be viewed as a product mix problem for each of several periods in the future. The manager must determine the production levels that will allow the company to meet product demand requirements, given limitations on production capacity, manpower capacity, and storage space. At the same time it is desired to minimize the total cost of carrying out this task.

One major reason for the widespread application of linear programming to production scheduling problems is that these problems are of a recurring nature. A production schedule must be established for the current month, again for the next month, the month after that, and so on. When the production manager looks at the problem each month, he will find that while demands for his products have changed, production times, production capacities, storage space limitations, and so on, are roughly the same. Thus he is basically resolving the same problem he handled in previous months. Hence a general linear programming model of the production scheduling procedure may be frequently applied. Once the model has been formulated, the manager can simply supply the data—demands, capacities, and so on—for the given production period, and the linear programming model can then be used to develop the production schedule. Thus one linear programming formulation may have many repeat applications.

Let us consider the case of the Bollinger Electronics Company which produces two different electronic components for a major airplane engine manufacturer. The airplane engine manufacturer notifies the Bollinger sales office each quarter as to what the monthly requirements for components will be during each of the next 3 months. The monthly demands for the components may vary considerably depending upon the type of engines the airplane engine manufacturer is producing. The order shown in Table 11.9 has just been received for the next 3-month period.

After the order is processed, a demand statement is sent to the production control department. The production control department must then develop a 3-month production plan for the components. Knowing the preference of the production department manager for constant demand levels (such as balanced workload, constant machine and manpower utilization), the production scheduler might consider the alternative of producing at a constant rate for all 3 months. This would set monthly production quotas at 3000 units per month for component 322A and 1500 units per month for component 802B. Why not adopt this schedule?

While this schedule would obviously be quite appealing to the production department, it may be undesirable from a total cost point of view. In particular this schedule ignores inventory costs. Consider the projected inventory

TABLE 11.9 Three-Month Demand Schedule for Bollinger Electronics Company

	Month		
	April	May	June
Component 322A	1000	3000	5000
Component 802B	1000	500	3000

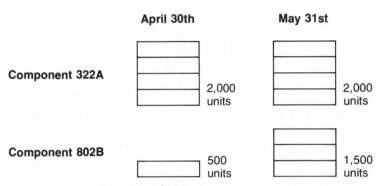

FIGURE 11.1 *Projected inventory levels under a constant rate production schedule.*

levels that would result from this schedule calling for constant production (Figure 11.1).

Thus we see that this production schedule would lead to high inventory levels. When we consider the cost of tied up idle capital and storage space, a schedule that provides lower inventory levels might be economically more desirable.

At the other extreme of the constant rate production schedule is the produce-to-meet-demand approach. While this schedule eliminates the inventory holding cost problem, the wide monthly production level fluctuation may cause some serious production problems and costs. For example, production capacity would have to be available to meet the total 8000-unit peak demand in June. Unless other components could be scheduled on the same production equipment in April and May, there would be significant unused capacity and thus low machine utilization in those months. In addition, the large production variations will require substantial manpower adjustments; employee turnover or training problems may be encountered. Thus it appears that the best production schedule will be one that compromises between the constant rate-high inventory and the variable rate-low utilization extremes.

The production scheduler will therefore want to identify and consider the following costs:

1. Production costs
2. Storage costs
3. Change in production level costs.

In the remainder of this section we show how a linear programming model of the production process for Bollinger Electronics can be formulated to account for these costs in such a fashion that the total system cost is minimized.

In order to develop our model we introduce a double subscript notation for

311

the decision variables in the problem. We let the first subscript indicate the product number and the second subscript the month. Thus in general we let x_{im} denote the production volume in units for product i in month m. Here $i = 1, 2$ and $m = 1, 2, 3$; $i = 1$ refers to component 322A, $i = 2$ refers to component 802B. The purpose of the double subscript is to provide a more descriptive notation. We could simply use x_6 to represent the number of units of product 2 produced in month 3, but we believe (as do many others) that x_{23} is more descriptive in that we know directly the product and month the variable represents.

If component 322A costs \$20 per unit produced and component 802B costs \$10 per unit produced, the production cost part of the objective function becomes

$$\text{production cost} = 20x_{11} + 20x_{12} + 20x_{13} + 10x_{21} + 10x_{22} + 10x_{23}.$$

You should note that in this particular problem the production cost per unit is the same each month, and thus we need not include production costs in our objective function; that is, no matter what production schedule is selected, the total production costs will remain the same. In cases where the cost per unit is expected to change each month, these variable production costs per unit per month must be included in the objective function. For the Bollinger Electronics problem we have elected to include them. This means that the value of the linear programming objective function will include all the costs associated with the problem.

To incorporate the inventory costs into our model, we introduce the following double subscripted decision variable that will indicate the number of units of inventory for each product for each month. We let s_{im} be the inventory level for product i at the end of month m.

Bollinger has determined that, on a monthly basis, inventory holding costs are 1.5% of the value of the product; that is, \$0.30 per unit for component 322A and \$0.15 per unit for component 802B. A common assumption made in linear programming approaches to the production scheduling problem is now invoked. We assume, monthly ending inventories are an acceptable approximation to the average inventory levels throughout the month. Given this assumption, the inventory holding cost portion of the objective function can be written as follows:

$$\text{inventory holding cost} = 0.30s_{11} + 0.30s_{12} + 0.30s_{13}$$
$$+ 0.15s_{21} + 0.15s_{22} + 0.15s_{23}.$$

In order to incorporate the costs due to fluctuations in production levels, we need to define the following additional decision variables:

I_m = increase in the production man-hours during month m.

D_m = decrease in the production man-hours during month m.

After estimating the effect of employee layoffs, turnovers, reassignment training costs, and other costs associated with fluctuating manpower requirements, Bollinger estimated that the cost associated with an increase in manpower was $10 per man-hour, while the cost associated with a decrease was only $2.50 per man-hour. Thus the third portion of our objective function can now be written:

production fluctuation costs $= 10I_1 + 10I_2 + 10I_3 + 2.5D_1 + 2.5D_2 + 2.5D_3.$

You should note that Bollinger has elected to measure the cost associated with production fluctuations as a function of the change in man-hours required. In other production scheduling problems such costs might be measured in terms of machine hours or in terms of total units produced.

Combining all three costs, our complete objective function becomes

$$\begin{aligned} \text{objective function} = {}& 20x_{11} + 20x_{12} + 20x_{13} + 10x_{21} + 10x_{22} + 10x_{23} \\ & + 0.30s_{11} + 0.30s_{12} + 0.30s_{13} + 0.15s_{21} + 0.15s_{22} \\ & + 0.15s_{23} + 10I_1 + 10I_2 + 10I_3 + 2.5D_1 + 2.5D_2 + 2.5D_3. \end{aligned}$$

Now let us consider the constraints. First we must guarantee that our schedule meets customer demand. Since the units shipped can come from the current month's production or from inventory carried over from previous periods, we have the following basic requirements:

$$\begin{pmatrix} \text{ending} \\ \text{inventory} \\ \text{from previous} \\ \text{month} \end{pmatrix} + \begin{pmatrix} \text{current} \\ \text{production} \end{pmatrix} \geq \begin{pmatrix} \text{this month's} \\ \text{demand} \end{pmatrix}$$

In fact, the difference in the left-hand side and the right-hand side will be the amount of ending inventory at the end of this month. Thus the demand requirement takes the form

$$\begin{pmatrix} \text{ending} \\ \text{inventory} \\ \text{from previous} \\ \text{month} \end{pmatrix} + \begin{pmatrix} \text{current} \\ \text{production} \end{pmatrix} - \begin{pmatrix} \text{ending} \\ \text{inventory} \\ \text{for this} \\ \text{month} \end{pmatrix} = \begin{pmatrix} \text{this} \\ \text{month's} \\ \text{demand} \end{pmatrix}$$

Suppose that the inventories at the beginning of our 3-month scheduling period were 500 units for component 322A and 200 units for component 802B. Recalling that the demand for both products in the first month (April) was 1000 units, the constraints for meeting demand in the first month become

$$500 + x_{11} - s_{11} = 1000$$
$$200 + x_{21} - s_{21} = 1000.$$

Moving the constants to the right-hand side, we have

TABLE 11.10 Machine, Manpower, and Storage Capacities
for Bollinger Electronics

	Machine Capacity (hours)	Manpower Capacity (hours)	Storage Capacity (square feet)
April	400	300	10,000
May	500	300	10,000
June	600	300	10,000

$$x_{11} - s_{11} = 500$$
$$x_{21} - s_{21} = 800.$$

Similarly, we need demand constraints for both products in the second and third months. These can be written as follows:

Month 2:
$$s_{11} + x_{12} - s_{12} = 3000$$
$$s_{21} + x_{22} - s_{22} = 500.$$
Month 3:
$$s_{12} + x_{13} - s_{13} = 5000$$
$$s_{22} + x_{23} - s_{23} = 3000.$$

If the company specifies a minimum inventory level at the end of the 3-month period of at least 400 units of component 322A and at least 200 units of component 802B, we can add the constraints

$$s_{13} \geq 400$$
$$s_{23} \geq 200.$$

Let us suppose that we have the following additional information available on machine manpower, and storage capacity given in Table 11.10. Machine, manpower, and storage space requirements are given in Table 11.11. To reflect these limitations, the following constraints are necessary:

TABLE 11.11 Machine, Manpower, and Storage Requirements for Components 322A and 802B.

	Requirements		
	Machine (hours/unit)	Manpower (hours/unit)	Storage (sq. ft./unit)
Component 322A	0.10	0.05	2
Component 802B	0.08	0.07	3

Machine capacity:

$$0.10x_{11} + 0.08x_{21} \leq 400 \quad \text{month } 1$$
$$0.10x_{12} + 0.08x_{22} \leq 500 \quad \text{month } 2$$
$$0.10x_{13} + 0.08x_{23} \leq 600 \quad \text{month } 3$$

Manpower capacity:

$$0.05x_{11} + 0.07x_{21} \leq 300 \quad \text{month } 1$$
$$0.05x_{12} + 0.07x_{22} \leq 300 \quad \text{month } 2$$
$$0.05x_{13} + 0.07x_{23} \leq 300 \quad \text{month } 3$$

Storage capacity:

$$2s_{11} + 3s_{21} \leq 10,000 \quad \text{month } 1$$
$$2s_{12} + 3s_{22} \leq 10,000 \quad \text{month } 2$$
$$2s_{13} + 3s_{23} \leq 10,000 \quad \text{month } 3.$$

One final set of constraints must be added. These are necessary in order to guarantee that I_m and D_m will reflect the increase or decrease in the number of man-hours used for production in month m. Suppose that the number of man-hours used for production of the two components in March, the month before the start of our planning period, had been 225. We can find the amount of the change in the manpower level for April from the relationship

$$\text{April usage} \quad - \text{March usage} = \text{change}$$
$$(0.05x_{11} + 0.07x_{21}) - \quad 225 \quad = \text{change}.$$

Note that the change can be positive or negative. A positive change reflects an increase in the man-hour level, and a negative change reflects a decrease. Using this relationship, we can now specify the following constraint for the change in the number of man-hours used in April:

$$(0.05x_{11} + 0.07x_{21}) - 225 = I_1 - D_1.$$

Of course we cannot have an increase and decrease in the same period, so either I_1 or D_1 will be zero. If April requires 245 man-hours, $I_1 = 20$ and $D_1 = 0$. If April requires only 175 man-hours, $I_1 = 0$ and $-D_1 = -50$; therefore $D_1 = 50$. This technique of denoting the change in man-hour requirements as the difference of two variables (I_m and D_m) means that, even though these variables will both be forced to assume nonnegative values by our linear programming model, we can represent both positive and negative fluctuations. Using the same approach in the following months (always subtracting the previous month's man-power levels from the current month's), we have the following constraints for the second and third months:

$$(0.05x_{12} + 0.07x_{22}) - (0.05x_{11} + 0.07x_{21}) = I_2 - D_2$$
$$(0.05x_{13} + 0.07x_{23}) - (0.05x_{12} + 0.07x_{22}) = I_3 - D_3.$$

Placing the variables on the left-hand side and the constants on the right-hand side, the complete set of manpower smoothing constraints can be written as

$$
\begin{aligned}
0.05x_{11} + 0.07x_{21} & & -I_1 + D_1 = 225 \\
-0.05x_{11} - 0.07x_{21} + 0.05x_{12} + 0.07x_{22} & & -I_2 + D_2 = 0 \\
-0.05x_{12} - 0.07x_{22} + 0.05x_{13} & & \\
+ 0.07x_{23} - I_3 + D_3 & = & 0.
\end{aligned}
$$

Our initially rather small two-product 3-month scheduling problem has now developed into an 18-variable 20-constraint linear programming problem. Notice that in our problem we were only concerned with one type of machine process, one type of manpower, and one type of storage area. In actual production scheduling problems you may encounter several machine types, several labor grades, and/or several storage areas. Thus you are probably beginning to realize how large-scale linear programs of production systems come about.

When we encounter a large-scale system, we look for ways to reduce the number of variables and the number of constraints so that our linear programming problem will be at least a little easier to solve. For the Bollinger Electronics Company production scheduling problem presented in this section, we can reduce the number of variables by noting the following:

$$
\begin{pmatrix} \text{ending} \\ \text{inventory} \\ \text{for a given} \\ \text{month} \end{pmatrix} = \begin{pmatrix} \text{inventory} \\ \text{at begin-} \\ \text{ning of the} \\ \text{planning} \\ \text{period} \end{pmatrix} + \begin{pmatrix} \text{all produc-} \\ \text{tion up to} \\ \text{and including} \\ \text{the current} \\ \text{month} \end{pmatrix} - \begin{pmatrix} \text{all ship-} \\ \text{ments or} \\ \text{demands up} \\ \text{to and in-} \\ \text{cluding the} \\ \text{current} \\ \text{month} \end{pmatrix}.
$$

Thus for component 322A we have

$$
\begin{aligned}
s_{11} &= 500 + x_{11} & - 1000 & & = x_{11} & - 500 \\
s_{12} &= 500 + x_{11} + x_{12} & - 1000 - 3000 & & = x_{11} + x_{12} & - 3500 \\
s_{13} &= 500 + x_{11} + x_{12} + x_{13} - 1000 - 3000 - 5000 & & = x_{11} + x_{12} + x_{13} - 8500.
\end{aligned}
$$

Similarly, for component 802B we have

$$
\begin{aligned}
s_{21} &= x_{21} & - 800 \\
s_{22} &= x_{21} + x_{22} & - 1300 \\
s_{23} &= x_{21} + x_{22} + x_{23} & - 4300.
\end{aligned}
$$

We can now return to the objective function and nonnegativity constraints of our linear programming formulation, and for every inventory variable s_{im} we can substitute the appropriate expression from above. What have we accomplished? We can now write the objective function and constraints with only the $x_{im}, I_m,$ and D_m variables, and our problem is reduced to a 12-variable

20-constraint problem. We have reduced the number of variables by 33%. In large-scale systems a reduction in variables of this magnitude can be quite significant.

The complete solution to the Bollinger Electronics Company production scheduling problem is shown in Table 11.12.

At first glance the variation in the production schedule may look rather strange. But let us examine the logic of the recommended solution. Recall that the inventory cost for component 802B is one half the inventory cost for component 322A. Therefore, as might be expected, component 802B tends to be carried in inventory, while the more expensive component 322A tends to be produced when demanded.

Why do we recommend producing over 2800 units of 802B in April when at least some of the units cannot be shipped until June? The answer to this is also logical. Recall that a manpower level of 225 man-hours was used in March. The low demand in April tends to dictate a manpower cutback; however, as you can see from the May and June demands, the firm would then have to rehire or add manpower in later months. The model is in effect smoothing the manpower requirements. Rather than recommending expensive manpower fluctuations, the linear programming model indicates it is cheaper to maintain a relatively high April production, even though it means a higher inventory cost for component 802B. Keeping the April labor force at 225 man-hours means that the only labor force change will be a 42.5 man-hour increase in May. This level will be maintained during the month of June.

We have seen in this illustration that a linear programming application of a relatively small two-product system (12 variables and 20 constraints) has

TABLE 11.12 Optimal Production, Manpower, and Inventory Policy for Bollinger Electronics Company

Schedule	April	May	June
Production			
Component 322A	500	3050	5350
Component 802B	2858	1642	—
Man-hours	225	267.5	267.5
Inventory			
Component 322A	—	50	400
Component 802B	2058	3200	200

Total cost (including production, inventory, and manpower smoothing costs)=$224,378

provided some valuable information in terms of identifying a minimum-cost production schedule. In larger systems, where the number of variables and constraints are too numerous to humanly track, linear programming models often provide significant cost savings for the firm.

Manpower Planning

Manpower planning or scheduling problems frequently occur when managers must make decisions involving departmental staffing requirements for a given period of time. This is particularly true when manpower assignments have some flexibility and at least some manpower can be assigned to more than one department or work center. This is often the case when employees have been cross-trained on two or more jobs. In the following example we present a product mix problem similar to the Par, Inc. problem and show how linear programming can be used to determine not only an optimal product mix but also an optimal manpower allocation for the various departments.

McCarthy's Everyday Glass Company is planning to produce two styles of drinking glasses during the next month. The glasses are processed in four separate departments. Excess equipment capacity is available and will not be a constraining factor. However, the company's manpower resources are limited and will probably constrain the production volume for the two products. The man-hour requirements per case produced (one dozen glasses) are shown in Table 11.13.

The company makes a profit of $1 per case of product 1 and $0.90 per case of product 2. If the number of man-hours available in each department is fixed, we can formulate McCarthy's problem as a standard product mix linear program. We use the usual notation:

x_1 = cases of product 1 manufactured

x_2 = cases of product 2 manufactured

b_i = man-hours available in department i, $i = 1, 2, 3, 4$.

TABLE 11.13 Man-Hours of Labor per Case of Product

Department	Product 1	Product 2
1	0.070	0.100
2	0.050	0.084
3	0.100	0.067
4	0.010	0.025

The linear program can be written as

max $1.00x_1 + 0.90x_2$

s.t.
$$0.070x_1 + 0.100x_2 \leq b_1$$
$$0.050x_1 + 0.084x_2 \leq b_2$$
$$0.100x_1 + 0.067x_2 \leq b_3$$
$$0.010x_1 + 0.025x_2 \leq b_4$$
$$x_1, x_2 \geq 0.$$

To solve the normal product mix problem we would ask the production manager to specify the man-hours available in each department b_1, b_2, b_3, and b_4); then we could solve for the profit maximizing product mix. However, in this case we assume that the manager has some flexibility in allocating manpower resources, and we would like to make a recommendation for this allocation as well as determining the optimal product mix.

Suppose that after consideration of the training and experience qualifications of the workers, we find this additional information:

Possible Labor Assignments	Man-Hours Available
Department 1 only	430
Department 2 only	400
Department 3 only	500
Department 4 only	135
Departments 1 or 2	570
Departments 3 or 4	300
Total	2335

Of the 2335 man-hours available for the month's production, we see that 870 man-hours can be allocated with some management discretion. The constraints for the man-hours available per department are as follows:

$$b_1 \leq 430 + 570 = 1000$$
$$b_2 \leq 400 + 570 = 970$$
$$b_3 \leq 500 + 300 = 800$$
$$b_4 \leq 135 + 300 = 435.$$

Since the 570 man-hours that have a flexible assignment between departments 1 and 2 cannot be assigned to both departments, we need the following additional constraint:

319

$$b_1 + b_2 \leq 430 + 400 + 570 = 1400.$$

Similarly, for the 300 man-hours that can be allocated between departments 3 and 4, we need the constraint:

$$b_3 + b_4 \leq 500 + 135 + 300 = 935.$$

In this formulation we are now treating the manpower assignments to departments as variables. The objective function coefficients for these variables will be zero since the b_i variables do not directly affect profit. Thus placing all variables on the left-hand side of the constraints, we have the following complete formulation:

$$\max \quad 1.00x_1 + 0.90x_2 + 0b_1 + 0b_2 + 0b_3 + 0b_4$$

s.t.

$$
\begin{array}{rcl}
0.070x_1 + 0.100x_2 - b_1 & \leq & 0 \\
0.050x_1 + 0.084x_2 \quad\quad - b_2 & \leq & 0 \\
0.100x_1 + 0.067x_2 \quad\quad\quad\quad - b_3 & \leq & 0 \\
0.010x_1 + 0.025x_2 \quad\quad\quad\quad\quad\quad - b_4 & \leq & 0 \\
b_1 & \leq & 1000 \\
b_2 & \leq & 970 \\
b_3 & \leq & 800 \\
b_4 & \leq & 435 \\
b_1 + b_2 & \leq & 1400 \\
b_3 + b_4 & \leq & 935
\end{array}
$$

$$x_1, x_2, b_1, b_2, b_3, b_4 \geq 0.$$

This linear programming model will actually solve two problems. (1) It will find the optimal product mix for the planning period, and (2) it will allocate manpower to the departments in such a fashion that profits will be maximized. The solution to this 6-variable 10-constraint model is shown in Table 11.14.

TABLE 11.14   *Optimal Production and Manpower Plans for McCarthy's Everyday Glass Company*

Production plan:	
Product 1 (x_1)=4700 cases	
Product 2 (x_2)=4543 cases	
Manpower plan:	
Department 1	783 hours
Department 2	617 hours
Department 3	774 hours
Department 4	161 hours
Total	2335 hours
Profit=$8789	

Note that the optimal manpower plan utilizes all 2335 man-hours of labor by making the most profitable manpower allocations. In this particular solution there is no idle time in any of the departments. While this will not always be the case in problems of this type, if the manager does have the freedom to assign certain employees to different departments, the effect will probably be a reduction in the overall idle time. The linear programming model automatically assigns such employees to the departments in the most profitable manner. If the manager had used his judgment to allocate the man-hours to the departments, and we had then solved the product mix problem with fixed b_i, we would in all probability have found slack in some departments while other departments represented bottlenecks because of insufficient resources.

Variations in the basic formulation of this section might be used in situations such as allocating raw material resources to products, allocating machine time to products, and allocating sales force time to product lines or sales territories.

11.4 ACCOUNTING APPLICATIONS

Audit Staff Assignments

A problem common to large and small CPA firms alike is the effective utilization of manpower resources. For many firms it is difficult to keep all employees engaged in productive (billable) assignments at certain times of the year. At other times, and this is more often the case, there is more work to be done than there are people to do it.

Especially at the busy or peak periods it is essential that the firm develop an efficient auditor-client schedule for its staff. In the following example we consider an audit staff assignment problem involving the assignment of senior accountants to manage audits so that all audits are completed with a minimum expenditure of man-hours.

The certified public accounting firm of Scott and Warner has three new clients who have just requested an audit by the firm. While the current auditing staff is overloaded, Scott and Warner would like to accommodate these new clients. After reviewing current audit progress reports, the manager in charge has identified four senior accountants who could possibly be assigned to supervise the audits for the new clients. However, all four senior accountants are busy and therefore each could handle at the most one of the new clients. Overall, manpower utilization is critical and the firm wants to be sure that the new client assignments are made in the most efficient manner (that is, minimum total man-hour requirement).

The differences in experience and ability among the senior accountants will cause the estimated audit completion times to differ from the various auditor-client assignments. After considering all possible assignments, the manager has made estimates of the audit completion times for each possible assign-

TABLE 11.15 *Estimated Audit Completion Time (in hours)*
for the Scott and Warner Accounting Firm

Senior Accountant	Client		
	Cincinnati Drug	Pruitt Trucking	Strom Foods
Warren	150	210	270
Kirkman	170	230	220
Howard	180	230	225
Phipps	160	240	230

ment. These data are summarized in Table 11.15. It is estimated, for example, that Kirkman would require 170 man-hours to complete the Cincinnati Drug audit while Warren would take 150 man-hours for this audit.

Let us attempt to formulate this auditor assignment problem as a linear programming problem. Once again we use double subscript notation for the decision variables.

$$x_{ij} = \begin{cases} 1 & \text{if senior accountant } i \text{ is assigned to client } j, \\ & i = 1, 2, 3, 4; j = 1, 2, 3 \\ 0 & \text{otherwise.} \end{cases}$$

Wait a minute, you say. How can these variables be appropriate linear programming decision variables when they can only take on the values of zero or one? Technically you are correct; they cannot be. Actually, the problem we are solving is a zero–one integer programming problem. However, this problem has a very nice feature that makes it possible for us to treat it as a linear programming problem; that is, the values of all the basic variables will be either zero or one at the extreme points of the feasible region, and since the optimal solution to a linear program lies at an extreme point, we will satisfy the requirement that $x_{ij} = 0$ or 1.

Using the above decision variables, the objective function calling for a minimization of total man-hours can be written as

$$\begin{aligned} \min \quad & +150x_{11} + 210x_{12} + 270x_{13} \\ & +170x_{21} + 230x_{22} + 220x_{23} \\ & +180x_{31} + 230x_{32} + 225x_{33} \\ & +160x_{41} + 240x_{42} + 230x_{43}. \end{aligned}$$

Constraints affecting this problem are that all three clients must be assigned exactly one senior accountant. These conditions are satisfied by the following constraints:

$$x_{11} + x_{21} + x_{31} + x_{41} = 1$$
$$x_{12} + x_{22} + x_{32} + x_{42} = 1$$
$$x_{13} + x_{23} + x_{33} + x_{43} = 1.$$

The fact that the firm will not allow any of the four senior accountants to take more than one additional assignment leads to the following set of constraints:

$$x_{11} + x_{12} + x_{13} \leq 1 \quad \text{Warren}$$
$$x_{21} + x_{22} + x_{23} \leq 1 \quad \text{Kirkman}$$
$$x_{31} + x_{32} + x_{33} \leq 1 \quad \text{Howard}$$
$$x_{41} + x_{42} + x_{43} \leq 1 \quad \text{Phipps.}$$

In addition, the nonnegativity constraints for all variables are included as usual.

The solution to this 12-variable 7-constraint linear programming model ($x_{12} = 1$, $x_{23} = 1$, $x_{41} = 1$) provides the auditor assignment plan that will minimize the total number of man-hours expended. This solution is shown in Table 11.16.

You will see in Chapter 12 that the problem we have just solved is a special linear program known as the assignment problem. In Chapter 12 you will also see a special solution procedure that has been developed for this class of problems.

For the audit staff assignment problem Summers[2] offers a more extensive linear programming formulation and analysis than we have presented in this section. Summers shows how additional constraints such as

1. maximum hours of auditor availability
2. maximum hours of auditor utilization
3. allowances for auditor vacation

TABLE 11.16   Minimum Man-Hours of Audit Staff Assignment for Scott and Warner

Client	Senior Accountant	Estimated Man-Hours
Cincinnati Drug	Phipps	160
Pruitt Trucking	Warren	210
Strom Foods	Kirkman	220
	Total	590
	Unassigned: Howard	

[2] Summers, E. L., "The Audit Staff Assignment Problem: A Linear Programming Analysis," *Accounting Review*, July, 1972.

4. assignments to professional development
5. assignments to specific audit activities

can be included in a linear programming formulation of the audit staff assignment problem. In addition, he discusses other alternatives for the objective function such as billable time and intangible benefits.

The Accounting Point of View

In attempting to classify linear programming applications for business and industry, we have found that in terms of problem content most applications are probably more readily identified as finance, marketing, or management oriented problems. However, if you consider the data requirements of these applications (costs, profit margins, and so on) you should begin to realize the importance of the accounting function in formulating linear programming models. Can you imagine trying to determine an optimal product mix without the accountant's analysis of material costs, labor costs, factory overhead, selling, and administrative expenses and the resulting product profitability?

Even if the applications of linear programming are not solely accounting problems, the accountant must still be aware of the business applications of the technique. Any time any department or division of a firm undertakes a cost control or a profit maximization project, the firm's accountants will become involved in the problem. The accountants must therefore be thoroughly familiar with the assumptions underlying linear programming approaches to these problems. With this background the accountant can provide valuable assistance in the formulation and evaluation of linear programming models. Thus we feel that almost all linear programming problems are accounting-related applications; that is, much of the data necessary for linear programming applications are provided by the accountant. Since the success of the application is critically dependent on the reliability of the data used, the accountant's role in linear programming applications can be quite significant.

11.5 INGREDIENT MIX APPLICATIONS

The Blending Problem

Blending problems arise whenever a manager must decide how to blend two or more resources in order to produce one or more products. In these situations the resources contain one or more essential ingredients that must be blended in such a manner that the final products will contain specific percentages of the essential ingredients. In most of these applications, then, management must decide how much of each resource to purchase in order to satisfy product specifications and product demands at minimum cost.

These types of problems occur frequently in the petroleum industry (such as blending crude oil to produce different octane gasolines), chemical industry (such as blending chemicals to produce fertilizers, weed killers, and so on), and food industry (such as blending input ingredients to produce soft drinks, soups, and so on). Because of their widespread application, our objective in this section is to illustrate how linear programming can be applied to solve these types of problems.

Consider the case of Beauty Suds, Inc., manufacturers of Wonderful Hair Shampoo. Beauty Suds is considering the production of a new product, Wonderful Plus Hair Shampoo. The new product is a blend of the company's standard shampoo base product, a new dandruff preventive, a perfume, and deionized water. The company has specified the following final product characteristics per gallon manufactured.

	Minimum	Maximum
Suds forming ingredient, grams	100	150
Dandruff ingredient, grams	50	50
Perfume ingredient, grams	20	30
Shampoo viscosity, centipoise	400	600

The cost and general characteristics of the four raw materials are as follows.

	Shampoo Base	Dandruff Preventive	Perfume	Deionized Water
Suds ingredient, g/gal	150	0	0	0
Dandruff ingredient, g/gal	10	500	0	0
Perfume ingredient, g/gal	15	0	200	0
Viscosity, centipoise	700	600	400	5
Cost per gallon	$3.00	$15.00	$60.00	$0.25

Assuming that all quantities of ingredients blend linearly by volume, the management of Beauty Suds would like to know how much of each raw material should be in each gallon of the new shampoo product in order to meet product requirements at minimum cost.

325

In order to formulate a linear programming model for the Beauty Suds blending problem, we begin by defining appropriate decision variables. Let

x_1 = gallons of standard shampoo base per gallon of shampoo

x_2 = gallons of dandruff preventive per gallon of shampoo

x_3 = gallons of perfume per gallon of shampoo

x_4 = gallons of deionized water per gallon of shampoo.

The objective function for our problem can then be written as follows:

$$\min 3x_1 + 15x_2 + 60x_3 + 0.25x_4.$$

To meet the requirements for the minimum and maximum amounts of suds-forming ingredient, dandruff ingredient, perfume ingredient, and shampoo viscosity, we formulate the following set of constraints:

$$
\begin{array}{lll}
150x_1 & \leq 150 & \\
150x_1 & \geq 100 & \text{suds} \\
10x_1 + 500x_2 & = 50 & \text{dandruff} \\
15x_1 \quad\quad + 200x_3 & \leq 30 & \\
15x_1 \quad\quad + 200x_3 & \geq 20 & \text{perfume} \\
700x_1 + 600x_2 + 400x_3 + 5x_4 \geq 400 & & \\
700x_1 + 600x_2 + 400x_3 + 5x_4 \leq 600 & & \text{viscosity.}
\end{array}
$$

In addition, to guarantee that the amount of raw material blended will produce exactly one gallon of Wonderful Plus Hair Shampoo, we require that

$$x_1 + x_2 + x_3 + x_4 = 1.$$

At the optimal solution then, if management requires 1000 gallons of the new product, they need only multiply the values of the decision variables by 1000. (Equivalently, we could have replaced the right-hand side of this constraint by 1000 and realized exactly the same solution.)

After adding the usual nonnegativity requirements, the complete linear programming model was solved using the Simplex method. The optimal solution is shown in Table 11.17.

We see that the optimal solution to the problem not only tells management how to blend the available resources to meet product specifications but also provides management with the cost of doing so. This additional information is often the most critical piece of information from management's point of view. For example, suppose a priori that management felt that it could not market the product unless the cost of raw materials for the new product was less than $7 per gallon. Given this a priori assessment, should management produce the new product? Clearly the answer is "yes," since the linear

TABLE 11.17   Optimal Solution for the Beauty Suds, Inc. Blending Problem

Material	Quantity (gallons)
Shampoo base	0.759
Dandruff preventive	0.085
Perfume	0.043
Water	0.113
Cost per gallon=$6.16	

programming solution to the problem shows management that the raw materials cost to produce the new product is $6.16 per gallon.

In the Beauty Suds blending problem we formulated as a linear programming model, we saw a problem situation wherein four different resources were blended to produce one product. In many blending problems, however, a number of different products must be produced. A descriptive approach to defining appropriate decision variables for these more general blending problems is to use double subscripted decision variables. The first subscript can be used to denote the resource and the second subscript to denote the product. Thus we let x_{ij} be the amount (such as, gallons) of resource i used to produce product j. Problem 4 at the end of this chapter describes a gasoline blending situation in which decision variables of the above type can be applied.

The Diet Problem

The diet problem is presented in this chapter in order to introduce the reader to this well-known application of linear programming. Typically the diet problem, or in agricultural applications the feed-mix problem, involves specifying a food or feed ingredient combination that will satisfy some minimal nutritional requirements at a minimum total cost. As a result, some authors view the diet problem as a special case of the general blending problem.

Let us consider the feed-mix form of the diet problem encountered by Bluegrass Farms, Inc., in Lexington, Kentucky. This company is experimenting with a special diet for its racehorses. The feed components available for the diet are a standard horse feed product, a vitamin enriched oat product, and a new vitamin and mineral feed additive. Table 11.18 shows the nutritional values and costs for the three components.

TABLE 11.18   Units of Feed Ingredient per Pound of Feed Component

Diet Requirement	Feed Component Enriched		
	Standard	Oats	Additive
Ingredient A	0.8	0.2	0
Ingredient B	1.0	1.5	3.0
Ingredient C	0.1	0.6	2.0
Cost per pound	$0.25	$0.50	$3.00

Suppose that the horse trainer sets the minimum daily diet requirement at three units of ingredient A, six units of ingredient B, and four units of ingredient C. Also suppose that for weight control, the trainer does not want the total daily feed to exceed 6 pounds. What is the optimal daily mix of the three components?

A linear programming model of this diet problem can be formulated as follows. Let

x_1 = pounds of the standard feed

x_2 = pounds of the enriched oats

x_3 = pounds of the additive.

With the overall goal of minimizing cost, the objective function becomes

min $0.25x_1 + 0.50x_2 + 3.00x_3$.

Using the information provided, the constraints for our problem are easily formulated as follows:

$$0.8x_1 + 0.2x_2 \qquad\qquad \geq 3 \qquad \text{ingredient A}$$
$$1.0x_1 + 1.5x_2 + 3.0x_3 \geq 6 \qquad \text{ingredient B}$$
$$0.1x_1 + 0.6x_2 + 2.0x_3 \geq 4 \qquad \text{ingredient C}$$
$$x_1 + \cdot \ \ x_2 + \quad x_3 \leq 6 \qquad \text{total weight}$$
$$x_1, x_2, x_3 \geq 0.$$

The minimum cost feed-mix solution for the above linear programming model is given in Table 11.19.

As we saw in the blending problem, the optimal solution for the Bluegrass Farms linear programming model tells management not only how to mix the three components to produce the desired product but also the cost of doing so. This latter piece of information is often the first thing management wants to know. For example, if Bluegrass Farms is presently purchasing a feed mix with similar characteristics for a daily cost of less than $5.97, it is doubtful whether they would consider producing this new special diet except on an experimental basis.

328

TABLE 11.19 Minimum Cost Diet for Bluegrass Farms, Inc., Horses

Standard feed, pounds	3.51
Enriched oats, pounds	0.95
Vitamin additive, pounds	1.54
Total, pounds	6.00
Daily cost=$5.97	

11.6 ENVIRONMENTAL PROTECTION APPLICATION

While linear programming has been applied primarily in business and industrial settings, the technique is of course not limited to these fields. Applications of linear programming to health care, environmental protection, and a variety of other problems society is currently faced with have been made. In this section we describe a problem that, although similar to some of the industrial problems we have studied in earlier sections, incorporates environmental considerations. Specifically, the linear programming model we present will assist a firm in making policy decisions of an antipollution nature.

Consider the problem faced by Skillings Industrial Chemicals, Inc., a refinery located in southwestern Ohio near the Ohio River. The company's major product is manufactured from a chemical process that requires two raw materials, A and B. The production of 1 pound of product requires 1 pound of material A and 2 pounds of material B. The output of this process also yields 1 pound of liquid waste materials and a solid waste by-product. The solid waste by-product is given to a local fertilizer plant as payment for picking up the by-product. Since the liquid waste material has virtually no market value, and since it is in liquid form, the refinery has been dumping it directly into the Ohio River. Skillings' manufacturing process is shown schematically in Figure 11.2.

Recent governmental pollution guidelines established by the Environmental Protection Agency will not permit this liquid waste disposal process to continue. Hence the refinery's research group has developed the following set of alternative uses for the waste material:

1. Produce a secondary product (K) by adding 1 pound of raw material A to every pound of liquid waste.
2. Produce another secondary product (M) by adding 1 pound of raw material B to every pound of liquid waste.
3. Specially treat the liquid waste so that it meets pollution standards before dumping it directly into the river.

329

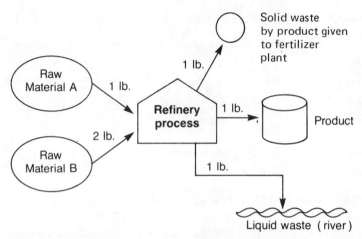

FIGURE 11.2   *Manufacturing Process at Skillings Industrial Chemicals, Inc.*

These three alternatives are depicted in Figure 11.3.

The company's management knows that the secondary products will be low in quality and will probably not be very profitable. Management also knows that the special treatment alternative will be a relatively expensive operation. The company's problem is to determine how to satisfy the pollution regulations and still maintain the highest possible profit. How should the waste material be handled? Should Skillings produce product K, product M, use the special treatment, or employ some combination of the three alternatives?

Since the waste disposal process will affect the production of the firm's primary product, the complete system—manufacturing process and waste disposal process—will have to be considered together in the analysis. Hope-

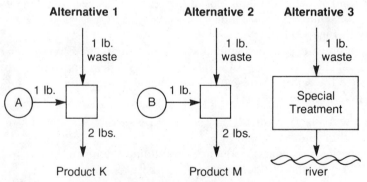

FIGURE 11.3   *Alternatives for Handling the Refinery Liquid Waste Material*

fully, Skillings will be able to satisfy the antipollution requirements and still make a satisfactory profit.

Considering the selling price, material costs, and manpower costs, the accounting department has prepared the following information with respect to product profit contribution.

Product	Profit Contribution per Pound
Primary	$2.10
Product K	−0.10
Product M	0.15

As you can see, the primary product is very profitable, while the secondary products are marginal. In fact, product K can only be produced at a loss. However, since product K provides a means for disposing of the waste material, it must still be considered as an alternative. Furthermore, suppose that the special treatment disposal cost is $0.25 per pound.

The ingredients required to make 1 pound of each product are summarized in Table 11.20.

Additional restrictions on our problem result from the fact that during any planning period the company will have limited amounts of raw materials available. During the production period of interest in our current problem, these maxima are 5000 pounds of material A and 7000 pounds of material B.

Let us see how we can formulate a linear programming model that will help management solve this problem. We let

x_1 = pounds of primary product

x_2 = pounds of secondary product K

x_3 = pounds of secondary product M

x_4 = pounds of liquid waste material processed by the special treatment.

Assuming that the liquid waste material is a zero-cost zero-profit by-product of the primary process, it will only incur additional cost if it has to be

TABLE 11.20 *Pounds of Ingredient Required per Pound of Product*

Ingredients	Primary Product	Product K	Product M
Raw material A	1	0.5	0.0
Raw material B	2	0.0	0.5
Waste	0	0.5	0.5

specially treated. Thus the objective function can be written as

$$\max \quad 2.10x_1 - 0.10x_2 + 0.15x_3 - 0.25x_4.$$

The raw material constraints are

$$
\begin{aligned}
1x_1 + 0.5x_2 \qquad\qquad &\leq 5000 \\
2x_1 \qquad\quad + 0.5x_3 &\leq 7000.
\end{aligned}
$$

We note that the production of both product K (x_2) and product M (x_3) depends upon the amount of liquid waste material available. Hence we must include a constraint on the amount of products x_2, x_3, and x_4 that can be produced. Since all the liquid waste material must be disposed of, we must require that

$$0.5x_2 + 0.5x_3 + 1x_4 = \text{total liquid waste material available.}$$

Since the amount of total liquid waste material generated is equal to the amount of primary product produced (see Figure 11.2), we can write the above requirement as

$$0.5x_2 + 0.5x_3 + 1x_4 = 1x_1$$

or

$$-1x_1 + 0.5x_2 + 0.5x_3 + 1x_4 = 0.$$

The solution to this four-variable three-constraint linear programming model provides the most profitable production and pollution control plan. The complete solution is shown in Table 11.21.

We see that the optimal solution to our linear programming model involves the production of product K and specially treated waste, both of which result in losses for the company. Does this seem reasonable in view of the fact that product M will enable Skillings to dispose of waste and still realize some contribution to profit? Let us see if we can answer this question by analyzing the optimal solution a bit more carefully.

TABLE 11.21   Optimal Production and Waste Management
             Plan for Skillings, Inc.

	Production (pounds)	Profit
Primary product	3500	$7350
Waste disposal		
Product K	3000	−$300
Specially treated waste	2000	−$500
	Total	$6550

In our model the primary product was so profitable when compared to the alternatives, we produced as much primary product as possible. Since B was the limiting raw material resource, all of B was used up in the production of the primary product. Thus since product M required raw material B, it was impossible to produce any amount of product M. Hence the waste material generated had to be disposed of using product K and the specially treated waste process.

11.7 SUMMARY

In this chapter we have tried to give the reader an appreciation and understanding of the broad range of situations in which linear programming may be a useful decision-making aid. Through illustrative situations we have formulated and solved problems from the areas of finance, marketing, management, and accounting. In addition we showed how linear programming could be applied to blending and diet problems. An application involving environmental protection showed the flexibility of linear programming in solving social problems.

All the illustrations presented in this chapter have been simplified versions of actual situations in which linear programming has been applied. In real-world applications the reader will find that the problem is not as concisely stated, that the data are not as readily available, and that the problem has a larger number of variables and constraints. However, a thorough study of the applications in this chapter is a good place for the reader who eventually hopes to apply linear programming to real-world problems to begin.

For the reader interested in learning about additional applications of linear programming, we suggest a text by Gass.[3] In this text the author presents a bibliography of over 100 business and industrial applications of the technique.

11.8 PROBLEMS

1. *Product mix.* A small job shop has purchased a new drill press which can be operated 40 hours per week. Two products are to be manufactured with this equipment. Product 1, which has a profit of 30 cents per unit, can be produced at the rate of 50 units per hour, and product 2, which has a profit of 50 cents per unit, can be produced at the rate of 40 units per hour. Based on current orders, 1000 units of product 1 and 500 units of product 2 must be manufactured each week.

[3] Gass, S. J., *An Illustrated Guide to Linear Programming.* New York: McGraw-Hill, 1970.

a. If the firm can sell all the units it produces, how many units of each product should be manufactured each week?

b. What is the profit contribution of an overtime hour for the drill press? Is there an upper limit on the amount of overtime you would want? Explain.

2. *Investment Planning.* The management of the Bordon Investment Company has three investment opportunities to consider over the next 18 months. The investments differ in terms of availability date, duration, rate of return, and maximum dollar amount. The data as summarized by one of the firm's financial analysts are as follows.

Investment	Available	Duration	Projected Annual Rate of Return	Maximum Amount
Mutual fund A	Now	No limit	0.09	No limit
Bond B	Now	12 months	0.12	$50,000
Stock C	6 months	No limit	0.14	$25,000

The firm can buy or sell the mutual fund or stock any time, but if the bond investment is made, the firm must keep it for the full year.

a. If the firm has $60,000 to invest over the next 18 months, develop the investment plan for each 6-month period that will maximize the return. Note that since investment decisions are made every 6 months, the rate of return over each 6-month period will be one half the annual rate. Assume that the total funds available to the firm at the start of period 2 are the original $60,000 plus any 6-month interest from the mutual fund and that the total funds available at the start of period 3 are the $60,000 plus interest from all previous investments.

b. If the company changed the upper limit on the stock to a maximum of $50,000, what would happen? Use the shadow price to help you answer this before you resolve the problem.

3. *Make or Buy.* The Carson Stapler Manufacturing Company forecasts a 5000 unit demand for its Sure-Hold model during the next quarter. This stapler is assembled from three major components: base, staple cartridge, and handle. Previously Carson has manufactured all three components. However, the 5000 forecasted units is a new high in sales volume, and it is doubtful that the firm will have production capacity to make all the components. The company is considering contracting a local firm to produce at least some of the components.

The production time requirements per unit are as follows:

Departments	Base (hours)	Cartridge (hours)	Handle (hours)	Total Department Time Available (hours)
A	0.03	0.02	0.05	400
B	0.04	0.02	0.04	400
C	0.02	0.03	0.01	400

After considering the firm's overhead, material, and labor costs, the accounting department has determined the unit manufacturing cost for each component. These data along with the purchase price quotations by the contracting firm are as follows.

Component	Manufacturing Cost	Purchase Cost
Base	$0.75	$0.95
Cartridge	$0.40	$0.55
Handle	$1.10	$1.40

a. Determine the make-or-buy decision for Carson that will meet the 5000-unit demand at a minimum total cost. How many units of each component should be made and how many purchased?
b. Which departments are limiting the manufacturing volume? If overtime could be considered at the additional cost of $3 per hour, which department(s) should be allocated the overtime? Explain.
c. Suppose that up to 80 hours of overtime can be scheduled in department A. What do you recommend?

4. *Blending Problem.* Seastrand Oil Company produces two grades of gasoline: regular and high octane. Both types of gasoline can be produced from two types of crude oil. Although both types of crude oil contain the two important compounds required to produce both gasolines, the percentage of important compounds in each type of crude oil differs, as well as the cost per gallon. The composition of each type of crude oil and the cost per gallon is shown below.

Type of Crude Oil	Cost	Compound c_1	Compound c_2
1	$0.10	20%	60%
2	$0.15	50%	30%

Daily demand for regular octane gasoline is 800,000 gallons, and daily demand for high octane is 500,000 gallons. Each gallon of regular must contain at least 40% of c_1, whereas each gallon of high octane can contain at most 50% of c_2. How many gallons of each type of crude oil should Seastrand Oil purchase in order to satisfy daily demand at minimum cost?

5. *Marketing Strategy*. In the marketing strategy problem encountered by Electronic Communications, Inc. (see Section 11.2), we found the advertising budget and sales force availability were the limiting constraints. Assume an additional $2000 is available for advertising and an additional 300 hours is available in sales force effort, how does the optimal solution change?

6. *Paper Trim Problem*. The Ferguson Paper Company produces rolls of paper for use in adding machines, desk calculators, and cash registers. The rolls, which are 200 feet long, are produced in widths of $1\frac{1}{2}$, $2\frac{1}{2}$, and $3\frac{1}{2}$ inches. The production process provides 200-foot rolls in 10-inch widths only. The firm must therefore cut the rolls to the desired final product sizes. The seven cutting alternatives and the amount of waste of each are as follows.

Cutting Alternative	Number of Rolls			Waste (inches)
	$1\frac{1}{2}$ in.	$2\frac{1}{2}$ in.	$3\frac{1}{2}$ in.	
1	6	0	0	1
2	0	4	0	0
3	2	0	2	0
4	0	1	2	$\frac{1}{2}$
5	1	3	0	1
6	1	2	1	0
7	4	0	1	$\frac{1}{2}$

The minimum production requirements for the three products are as follows.

Roll Width (inches)	Units
$1\frac{1}{2}$	1000
$2\frac{1}{2}$	2000
$3\frac{1}{2}$	4000

a. If the company wants to minimize the number of units of the 10-inch rolls that must be manufactured, how many units will be processed on each cutting alternative? How many rolls are required, and what is the total inches of waste?

b. If the company wants to minimize the waste generated, how many 10-inch units will be processed on each cutting alternative? How many rolls are required, and what is the total inches of waste?

c. What are the differences in approaches (a) and (b) to this trim problem? In this case, which objective do you prefer? Explain. What are the types of situations that would make the other objective the more desirable?

7. *Inspection.* The Get-Well Pill Company inspects capsule medicine products by passing the capsules over a special lighting table where inspectors visually check for cracked or partially filled capsules. Currently any of three inspectors can be assigned to the visual inspection task. The inspectors, however, differ in accuracy and speed abilities and are paid at slightly different wage rates. The differences are as follows.

Inspector	Speed (units per hour)	Accuracy (percent)	Hourly Wage
Davis	300	98	$2.95
Wilson	200	99	$2.60
Lawson	350	96	$2.75

Operating on a full 8-hour shift, the company needs at least 2000 capsules inspected with no more than 2% of these capsules having inspection errors. In addition, because of the fatigue factor of this inspection process, no one inspector can be assigned this task for more than four hours per day. How many hours should each inspector be assigned to the capsule inspection process during an 8-hour day? What volume will be inspected per day and what is the daily capsule inspection cost?

8. *Equipment Acquisition.* The Two-Rivers Oil Company near Pittsburgh transports gasoline to its distributors by trucks. The company has recently received a contract to begin supplying gasoline distributors in southern Ohio and has $300,000 available to spend on the necessary expansion of its fleet of gasoline tank trucks. Three types of gasoline tank trucks are available.

The company estimates that the monthly demand for the region will be a total of 550,000 gallons of gasoline. Because of the size and speed differences of the trucks, the different truck models will vary in terms of the number of deliveries or round trips possible per month. Trip capacities are estimated at 15 per month for the Super Tanker, 20 per

Truck Model	Capacity (gallons)	Purchase Cost	Monthly Operating Costs, Including Depreciation
Super Tanker	5000	$37,000	$550
Regular Line	2500	$25,000	$425
Econo-Tanker	1000	$16,000	$350

month for the Regular Line, and 25 per month for the Econo-Tanker. Based on maintenance and driver availability, the firm does not want to add more than 15 new vehicles to its fleet. In addition, the company would like to make sure it purchases at least three of the new Econo-Tankers to use on the short-run low-demand routes. As a final constraint, the company does not want more than half of the new models to be Super Tankers.

a. If the company wishes to satisfy the gasoline demand with a minimum monthly operating expense, how many models of each truck should be purchased?

b. If the company did not require at least three Econo-Tankers and allowed as many Super Tankers as needed, what would the company strategy be?

9. *Production Scheduling*. The Silver Star Bicycle Company will be manufacturing both men's and women's models for their Easy-Pedal 10-speed bicycles during the next 2 months, and the company would like a production schedule indicating how many bicycles of each model should be produced in each month. Current demand forecasts call for 150 men's and 125 women's models to be shipped during the first month and 200 men's and 150 women's models to be shipped during the second month. Additional data are shown below.

Model	Production Costs	Labor Required for Manufacturing (hours)	Labor Required for Assembly (hours)	Current Inventory
Men's	$40	10	3	20
Women's	$30	8	2	30

Last month the company used a total of 4000 man-hours of labor. The company's labor relations policy will not allow the combined total man-hours (manufacturing plus assembly) to increase or decrease by more than 500 man-hours from month to month. In addition, the company charges monthly inventory at the rate of 2% of the production cost based on the inventory levels at the end of the month. The company would like to have at least 25 units of each model in inventory at the end of the 2 months.

a. Establish a production schedule that minimizes production and inventory costs and satisfies the manpower smoothing, demand, and inventory requirements. What inventories will be maintained and what are the monthly man-hour requirements?

b. If the company changed the manpower level constraints so that monthly manpower increases and decreases could not exceed 250 man-hours, what would happen to the production schedule? How much will the cost increase? What would you recommend?

10. *Manpower Balancing.* The Patriotic Doll Company manufactures two kinds of dolls: the Betsy Ross and the George Washington. The assembly process for these dolls requires two people. The assembly times are as follows.

Doll	Assembler 1	Assembler 2
Betsy Ross	6 min.	2 min.
George Washington	3 min.	4 min.
Maximum hours available per day	8	8

The company policy is to balance work loads on all assembly jobs. In fact, management wants to schedule work so that no assembler will have more than 30 minutes more work per day than other assemblers. This means that in a regular 8-hour shift, all assemblers will be assigned at least $7\frac{1}{2}$ hours of work. If the firm makes a $2 profit for each George Washington doll and a $1 profit for each Betsy Ross doll, how many units of each doll should be produced per day? How much time will each assembler be assigned per day?

11. *Capital Budgeting.* The Ice-Cold Refrigerator Company can invest capital funds in a variety of company projects which have different capital requirements over the next 4 years. Faced with limited capital resources, the company must select the most profitable projects and budget for the necessary capital expenditures. The estimated project values, the capital requirements, and the available capital projections are as follows.

a. Which projects should the company select in order to maximize the present value of the invested funds? Show the capital budget for each year.

Hint: The decision must be made to accept or reject each project. This is similar to the auditor assignment problem (see Section

Project	Estimated Present Value	Capital Requirements			
		Year 1	Year 2	Year 3	Year 4
Plant expansion	$90,000	$15,000	$20,000	$20,000	$15,000
Warehouse expansion	$40,000	$10,000	$15,000	$20,000	$5,000
New machinery	$10,000	$10,000	0	0	$4,000
New product research	$37,000	$15,000	$10,000	$10,000	$10,000
Available capital funds		$30,000	$40,000	$30,000	$25,000

11.4) where we let $x = 1$ if the assignment was to be made and $x = 0$ if it was not to be made. Adopting a similar approach, we can let $x = 1$ if the project is accepted and $x = 0$ if it is rejected. Thus all variables must be constrained with $x \leq 1$. For this linear programming formulation of the capital budgeting problem the variables will be 0 (rejected), 1 (accepted), or a fraction between 0 and 1. Fractional values should be interpreted as insufficient funds for the complete project; therefore reject the project outright or proceed with the project in smaller increments, if possible. Actually, the method of integer programming could be used to require only 0 and 1 valued variables; however, a linear programming solution to the capital budgeting problem can still provide valuable information.

b. If the company could obtain an additional $10,000 in all 4 years, what would you recommend? What is the new solution?

12
The Assignmen Problem

The assignment problem is a special class of management science application that can occur in a variety of decision-making situations. Typical assignment problems involve assigning jobs to machines, assigning workers to tasks or projects, assigning salesmen to sales territories, assigning contracts to bidders, and so on. A distinguishing feature of the assignment problem is that *one* job, worker, etc., is assigned to *one and only one* machine, project, etc. Specifically, we are looking for the assignment decisions that will optimize a stated objective such as minimize costs, minimize time, or maximize profits.

12.1 ILLUSTRATIVE PROBLEM

As an illustration of the assignment problem, let us consider the case of Fowle Marketing Research, Inc., which has just received requests for market research studies from three new clients. The company is faced with the task of assigning project leaders to each of these three new research studies. Currently, three individuals are relatively free from other major commitments and are available for the project leader assignments. Fowle's management realizes, however, that the time required to complete each study will depend upon the experience and ability of the project leader assigned to the study. Since the three projects have been judged to have approximately the same priority, the company would like to assign project leaders such that the total expended effort (i.e. total man-days) required to complete all three projects is the minimum possible. If one project leader is to be assigned to one and only one client, what assignments should be made?

In order to answer this assignment question, Fowle's management must first consider all possible project leader-client assignments and then estimate the corresponding project completion times. Fowle's assignment alternatives and estimated project completion times in days are summarized in Table 12.1. For example, it is estimated that Terry would require 10 days to complete client A's project, while Carle would require approximately 9 days for the same project.

Since there are only three clients and three project leaders, we can enumerate all possible assignment alternatives and then pick the one yielding the minimum total completion time. First we could consider assigning Terry to

TABLE 12.1 Estimated Project Completion Times in Days for
the Fowle, Inc., Assignment Problem

Project Leader	Client A	B	C
Terry	10	15	9
Carle	9	18	5
McClymonds	6	14	3

either client A, B, or C, then assigning Carle to one of the remaining two clients, and finally assigning McClymonds to the remaining client. Thus in this case, there are only a total of $3 \times 2 \times 1 = 6$ possible assignment solutions. Table 12.2 shows all assignment solutions and their associated project completion times.

The optimal solution is clearly number 5, with Terry assigned to client B, Carle assigned to client C, and McClymonds assigned to client A. The total completion time for all three projects is 26 days.

The above enumeration approach, which worked quite well for solving this small problem, is a very inefficient way to solve larger assignment problems. For example, a problem requiring the assignment of four leaders to four clients would require us to consider $4 \times 3 \times 2 \times 1 = 24$ alternative assignment solutions. In general there are $n! = n \times (n - 1) \times (n - 2) \times \ldots \times 3 \times 2 \times 1$ possible solutions to an assignment problem which requires assigning n persons or objects to n tasks. For a relatively small problem with eight project leaders and eight tasks, there are $8! = 40{,}320$ possible solutions. Clearly it would be impractical to attempt solving such a problem by hand. Even for a large computer the enumeration approach is impractical, except for relatively small ($n \leq 15$) assignment problems.

TABLE 12.2 All Possible Assignment Solutions for the
Fowle, Inc., Assignment Problem

Project Leader	Assignment Solutions 1	2	3	4	5	6
Terry	A(10)	B(15)	C(9)	A(10)	B(15)	C(9)
Carle	B(18)	A(9)	A(9)	C(5)	C(5)	B(18)
McClymonds	C(3)	C(3)	B(14)	B(14)	A(6)	A(6)
Total completion time for all projects	31	27	32	29	26	33

Minimum-time solution

12.2 AN ASSIGNMENT PROBLEM SOLUTION ALGORITHM

The *Hungarian method* is an efficient solution procedure for assignment problems. We will develop this specialized algorithm by showing you how it may be used to solve the Fowle, Inc., problem. For convenience, we repeat below the estimated project completion times for the Fowle, Inc., assignment problem:

| | | Columns | | |
		A	B	C
Rows	Terry	10	15	9
	Carle	9	18	5
	McClymonds	6	14	3

Note that a table or matrix such as this will be associated with every assignment problem. In a general framework, the rows will consist of the objects we want to assign, and the columns will denote the tasks or items we want to assign the objects to. The entries inside our table or matrix will be the values associated with making a particular assignment. We saw that in the Fowle, Inc., problem these values represented estimated project completion times. In other situations the values may represent costs, profits, parts produced, and so on.

The solution procedure involves what is called *matrix reduction*. By subtracting and adding appropriate numbers in the matrix, the algorithm determines an optimal solution to the general assignment problem. Basically there are three major steps associated with the procedure. Let us consider Step 1, which shows the initial matrix reduction calculation.

Step 1: Reduce the matrix by subtracting the smallest element in each row from every element in that row and then subtracting the smallest element in each column from every element in that column.

Thus we first reduce the numbers in the matrix by subtracting the minimum value in each row from each element in the row. With the minimum values of 9 for row 1, 5 for row 2, and 3 for row 3, our reduced matrix becomes

The assignment problem represented by this reduced matrix is equivalent to our original assignment problem in the sense that the same solution will be

	A	B	C
Terry	1	6	0
Carle	4	13	0
McClymonds	3	11	0

optimal. The row 1 minimum element, 9, has been subtracted from every element in the first row. Since Terry must still be assigned to one of the clients, the only change is that in this revised problem his time for any assignment will be 9 days less. Similarly Carle and McClymonds are shown with completion times requiring 5 and 3 less days, respectively. Thus the only difference between this reduced assignment problem and the original one is that the value of every solution, including the optimal one, has been reduced by 9 + 5 + 3 = 17 days. Continuing Step 1 in the matrix reduction process, we subtract the minimum element in each column from every element in the column. This also leads to an equivalent assignment problem; that is, the same solution will still be optimal. The only difference is that the value of each solution in the new assignment problem is further reduced by the sum of the minimum values subtracted from the columns. With the minimum values of 1 for column 1, 6 for column 2, and 0 for column 3, our reduced matrix becomes

	A	B	C
Terry	0	0	0
Carle	3	7	0
McClymonds	2	5	0

Thus during this step we have subtracted 1 + 6 + 0 = 7 days from the table.

In Table 12.3 we show all six assignment solutions for this reduced assignment problem.

TABLE 12.3 All Possible Assignment Solutions for the Reduced Fowle, Inc., Assignment Problem

Project Leader	Assignment Solutions					
	1	2	3	4	5	6
Terry	A(0)	B(0)	C(0)	A(0)	B(0)	C(0)
Carle	B(7)	A(3)	A(3)	C(0)	C(0)	B(7)
McClymonds	C(0)	C(0)	B(5)	B(5)	A(2)	A(2)
Total reduced matrix time for all projects	7	3	8	5	2	9

↑
Minimum-time solution

Sum of row values subtracted 17
Sum of column values subtracted 7
Total 24

We note that the value of every solution has been reduced by the total amount of the subtractions, 24. Our goal now is to continue reducing the matrix until the value of one of the solutions is zero. Then, as long as there are no negative elements in the matrix, the zero solution will be the optimal solution. The way in which we perform this further reduction and recognize when we have reached an optimal solution is described in the following two steps.

Step 2: Find the *minimum* number of row and column straight lines necessary to cover all the zeros in the matrix. If the minimum number is the same as the number of rows (or equivalently, columns) in the matrix, an optimal assignment with value zero can be made. If the number of lines is less than the number of rows, go to Step 3.

Applying Step 2 we see, as shown below, that the minimum number of lines necessary to cover all the zeros is two. Thus we must continue to Step 3.

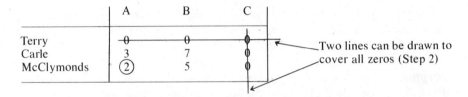

Step 3: Subtract the value of the smallest *unlined* element from every *unlined* element and add this value to every element at the *intersection* of two lines. All other elements remain unchanged. Return to Step 2 and continue until the condition of Step 2, the minimum number of lines necessary to cover all the zeros in the matrix is equal to the number of rows, is satisfied.

The minimum unlined element is 2. Note that in our previous matrix we circled this element for convenience in carrying out the computations of Step 3. Subtracting 2 from all unlined elements and adding 2 to the intersection element for Terry and client C, produces the new matrix shown below.

	A	B	C
Terry	0	0	2
Carle	1	5	0
McClymonds	0	3	0

We now return to Step 2, where we find that the minimum number of straight lines necessary to cover all the zeros is 3. The following matrix illustrates the Step 2 calculations:

345

	A	B	C
Terry	0	0	2
Carle	1	5	0
McClymonds	0	3	0

Three lines must be drawn to cover all zeros; therefore the optimal solution has been reached

According to Step 2, then, it must be possible to find an assignment with a value of zero. Such an assignment can be found and is indicated by the squares around the elements of the new reduced matrix shown below.

	A	B	C
Terry	0	[0]	2
Carle	1	5	[0]
McClymonds	[0]	3	0

If you make the mistake of drawing too many lines to cover the zeros in the reduced matrix and thus conclude an optimal solution has been reached when it has not, you will find you cannot identify a zero-value assignment. Thus if you think you have reached the optimal solution, but the zero-value assignments cannot be found, go back to the previous step and check to see if you have actually determined the *minimum* number of lines necessary to cover the zero elements.

Following Steps 2 and 3 always leads to an assignment problem that is equivalent to the original assignment problem. That is, the optimal assignment solutions are the same for the original and all reduced assignment problems considered. The matrix reduction method enables us to consider

TABLE 12.4 All Possible Assignment Solutions for the Completely Reduced Fowle, Inc., Assignment Problem

Project Leader	Alternative Solutions					
	1	2	3	4	5	6
Terry	A(0)	B(0)	C(2)	A(0)	B(0)	C(2)
Carle	B(5)	A(1)	A(1)	C(0)	C(0)	B(5)
McClymonds	C(0)	C(0)	B(3)	B(3)	A(0)	A(0)
Total reduced matrix time for all projects	5	1	6	3	0	7

Minimum-time solution

successively reduced problems until the minimum zero-value assignment is observed. Table 12.4 lists all alternative assignment solutions for the final reduced Fowle, Inc., assignment problem.

The value of the optimal assignment can be found by referring to the original assignment problem and summing the solution times associated with the optimal assignment; in this case Terry to B, Carle to C, and McClymonds to A. Following the procedure we obtain the solution time of $15 + 5 + 6 = 26$ days.

We have seen how the assignment problem solution algorithm can be applied to the Fowle Marketing Research assignment problem in order to find an optimal assignment solution. The solution procedure we have outlined involves finding minimization assignments when we have the same number of leaders as clients. However, through some simple modifications we will show you how to solve assignment problems when the number of people or objects (leaders) is not the same as the number of tasks (clients), and when the problem has a maximization objective.

Dummy Rows and Dummy Columns

The assignment solution algorithm we have just discussed requires an identical number of rows (people, objects, and so on) and columns (tasks, clients, and so on). Suppose that in the Fowle, Inc., example four project leaders had been available for assignment to the three new clients. Fowle still faces the same basic problem, namely, which project leaders should be assigned to which clients in order to minimize the total project completion times. The project completion time estimates with the new project leader alternative is shown in Table 12.5.

We have seen how to apply the assignment solution algorithm when the number of rows and columns are equal. Therefore we can apply the same procedure if we can add a new client, which would result in a 4×4 assignment problem. Since we do not have another client, we simply add a *dummy column* or a dummy client. Since this dummy client is nonexistent, the

TABLE 12.5 Estimated Project Completion Time, in Days, for the Fowle, Inc., Assignment Problem with Four Project Leaders

Project Leader	Client A	B	C
Terry	10	15	9
Carle	9	18	5
McClymonds	6	14	3
Higley	8	16	6

TABLE 12.6 Estimated Project Completion Time, in Days, for the Fowle, Inc., Assignment Problem

Project Leader	Client			
	A	B	C	D ◄──── Dummy client
Terry	10	15	9	0
Carle	9	18	5	0
McClymonds	6	14	3	0
Higley	8	16	6	0

project leader assigned to the dummy client in the optimal assignment solution will, in effect, be the unassigned project leader.

What project time estimates should be shown in this new dummy column? Actually any arbitrary value is acceptable as long as all project leaders are given the same completion time. However, since the dummy client assignment will not take place, a zero project completion time for all project leaders seems logical. Thus the 4 × 4 Fowle, Inc., assignment problem is shown in Table 12.6. Problem 3 at the end of the chapter asks you to use the Hungarian method to determine the optimal assignment solution to this problem.

Note that if we had considered the case of four new clients and only three project leaders, we would have had to add a *dummy row* or dummy project leader in order to apply the solution algorithm. The client receiving the dummy row assignment would not be assigned an immediate project leader and would have to wait until a new leader becomes available. Also note that in order to obtain an assignment problem form compatible with the solution algorithm, it may be necessary to add several dummy rows or dummy columns, but never both.

A Maximization Assignment Problem

Suppose that Salsbury Discounts, Inc., has just leased a new shopping center store and is attempting to determine where various departments should be located within the store. The store manager has four locations that have not yet been assigned a department and is considering five departments that might occupy the four locations. The departments under consideration are a shoe, a toy, an auto parts, a houseware, and a record department. The store manager would like to determine the optimal assignment of departments to locations in order to maximize profits. After a careful study of the layout of the remainder of the store, and based on his experience with similar stores, the store manager has made estimates of the expected annual profit for each department in each location. These are presented in Table 12.7.

TABLE 12.7   Estimated Annual Profit, in Thousands of
Dollars, for Each Department-Location
Combination

Department	Location 1	2	3	4
Shoe	10	6	12	8
Toy	15	18	5	11
Auto parts	17	10	13	16
Housewares	14	12	13	10
Records	14	16	6	12

We now have an assignment problem which requires a maximization objective. However, we have a problem involving more rows than columns. Thus we must first add a dummy column, corresponding to a dummy or fictitious location, in order to apply the Hungarian method solution procedure. Following the procedure discussed for adding dummy rows and dummy columns, the 5 × 5 Salsbury Discount, Inc., assignment problem is shown in Table 12.8.

We can obtain an equivalent minimization assignment problem by converting all the elements in the matrix to *opportunity losses*. This conversion is accomplished by subtracting every element in each column from the largest element in the column.

It turns out that finding the assignment that minimizes opportunity loss leads to the same solution that maximizes the value of the assignment in our original problem. Thus any maximization assignment problem can be converted to a minimization problem by converting the assignment matrix to one in which the elements represent opportunity losses. Hence we begin our solution to this maximization assignment problem by developing an assignment matrix in which each element represents the opportunity loss from not making the "best" assignment. This matrix is presented in Table 12.9.

TABLE 12.8   Estimated Annual Profit, in Thousands of
Dollars, for Each Department-Location
Combination, Including a Dummy Location

Department	Location 1	2	3	4	5 (Dummy location)
Shoe	10	6	12	8	0
Toy	15	18	5	11	0
Auto parts	17	10	13	16	
Housewares	14	12	13	10	
Record	14	16	6	12	0

TABLE 12.9   Opportunity Loss, in Thousands of Dollars,
for Each Department-Location Combination

Department	1	2	Location 3	4	5
Shoe	7	12	1	8	0
Toy	2	0	8	5	0
Auto parts	0	8	0	0	0
Housewares	3	6	0	6	0
Records	3	2	7	4	0

Dummy location (pointing to column 5)

The opportunity loss from putting the shoe department in location 1 is
$7000; that is, if we put the shoe department, instead of the best department
(auto parts), in that location, we forego the opportunity to make an
additional $7000 in profit. The opportunity loss associated with putting the
toy department in location 2 is zero since it yields the highest profit in that
location. What about the opportunity losses associated with the dummy
column? Well, the assignment of a department to this "dummy" location
means that the department will not be assigned a store location in the
optimal solution. Since all departments earn the same amount from this
dummy location, zero, the opportunity cost for each department is zero.

Following Steps 1, 2, and 3 of our assignment algorithm, we can proceed
to determine the optimal maximum profit assignment solution. Since each
row minimum and column minimum is already zero, the application of Step 1
does not change our matrix. Continuing to Step 2, we see that the minimum
number of lines required to cover all the zeros is 4. Thus we cannot find a
solution with a value of zero. The current matrix illustrating the results of
Step 2 is shown below. Note that the minimum unlined element is 1.

Department	1	2	Location 3	4	5
Shoe	7	12	①	8	0
Toy	2	0	8	5	0
Auto parts	0	8	0	0	0
Housewares	3	6	0	6	0
Records	3	2	7	4	0

Performing Step 3 leads to the following reduced assignment matrix:

Department	1	2	Location 3	4	5
Shoe	6	11	0	7	0
Toy	2	0	8	5	1
Auto parts	0	8	0	0	1
Housewares	3	6	0	6	1
Records	2	①	6	3	0

350

The minimum number of lines required to cover all the zeros is still 4. Repeating Step 3 with the minimum unlined element of 1 yields a new matrix:

Department	1	2	Location 3	4	5
Shoe	5	10	0	6	0
Toy	2	0	9	5	2
Auto parts	0	8	1	0	2
Housewares	2	5	0	5	1
Records	①	0	6	2	0

The minimum number of lines required to cover all the zeros is still 4. We again repeat Step 3 with 1 as the minimum element:

Department	1	2	Location 3	4	5
Shoe	4	10	0	5	[0]
Toy	1	[0]	9	4	2
Auto parts	0	9	2	[0]	3
Housewares	1	5	[0]	4	1
Records	[0]	0	6	1	0

The minimum number of lines needed is now five. Thus we can make an assignment with zero value. Hence we have found the optimal solution. The optimal solution, together with its resultant total profit, is presented in Table 12.10.

We note that since the optimal solution had the shoe department assigned to the dummy location, this department will not be included in the store layout.

TABLE 12.10   Maximum Profit Assignment for the Salsbury Discount Store

Department	Assigned Location	Estimated Profit
Toy	2	18
Auto parts	4	16
Housewares	3	13
Records	1	14
	Total	61

Unassigned: shoe department

Handling Unacceptable Assignments

Suppose that in the Salsbury Discounts, Inc., assignment problem, the store manager believed that the toy department should not be considered for location 2 and the auto parts department should not be considered for location 4. In essence, the store manager is saying that based on other considerations such as size of area, adjacent departments, and so on, the two assignments are unacceptable alternatives.

You may recall that in the discussion of artificial variables for linear programming (see Chapter 9) we attempted to guarantee that variables would not appear in the optimal solution by assigning them extremely high costs in a minimization problem and extremely low profits in a maximization problem. Using this same approach for the assignment problem, we define a value of $+M$ for unacceptable minimization assignments and a value of $-M$ for unacceptable maximization assignments, where M is an arbitrarily large value. In fact, M is assumed so large that M minus any value is still approximately M. Thus an M-valued cell in an assignment matrix maintains its M value throughout the matrix reduction calculations. Since an M-valued cell can never be zero, it can never be an assignment in the final solution.

The Salsbury Discount Store assignment problem with the two unacceptable assignments is shown in Table 12.11.

TABLE 12.11 Estimated Profit for the Department-Location Combinations

Department	Location 1	2	3	4	5
Shoe	10	6	12	8	0
Toy	15	$-M$	5	11	0
Auto parts	17	10	13	$-M$	0
Housewares	14	12	13	10	0
Records	14	16	6	12	0

When this assignment matrix is converted to the opportunity loss matrix, the $-M$ profit value will be changed to M. Problem 4 at the end of this chapter asks you to solve the above assignment problem.

Summary of the Assignment Problem Solution Algorithm

We will now restate and summarize the complete step-by-step solution algorithm for the assignment problem. For convenience in describing the calculations, we will restate the procedure in terms of two stages, (1) preparing the problem for solution by the Hungarian method, and (2) using the Hungarian method to solve the problem.

Preparing the Problem for Solution

Step 1: Set up a matrix with the m objects (rows) to be assigned to n tasks (columns).

Step 2: Enter the cost, profit, or other measure of performance in the matrix cell corresponding to each object-task combination. Use a $-M$ profit or a $+M$ cost if the specific object-task combination is unacceptable.

Step 3: If the number of rows is not equal to the number of columns, add dummy rows or dummy columns until the number of rows and number of columns are equal. Use 0 values for the new elements in the assignment matrix.

Step 4: If the problem involves maximization, convert the matrix to an opportunity loss matrix by subtracting each column entry from the maximum value in the column.

The Hungarian Solution Procedure

Step 1: Subtract the smallest element in each row from every element in that row, and then subtract the smallest element in each column from every element in that column.

Step 2: Find the minimum number of row and column straight lines necessary to cover all the zeros in the matrix. If the minimum number is the same as the number of rows, the optimal solution can be found by using the zero-value assignments. Otherwise go to Step 3.

Step 3: Locate the smallest unlined element. Subtract it from all unlined elements and add it to every element at the intersection of two lines. Repeat Steps 2 and 3 until the optimal solution is found.

12.3 A LINEAR PROGRAMMING FORMULATION OF THE ASSIGNMENT PROBLEM

In Section 11.4 we discussed how an audit staff assignment problem could be formulated and solved as a linear program. It was pointed out that the linear programming formulation of the problem, which involved decision variables that could only take on the values of 0 and 1, was really a zero-one integer programming problem. However, it was also mentioned that the values of all the basic variables will be equal to 0 or 1 at the extreme points of the feasible region for such problems. Therefore, since the optimal solution to a linear program lies at an extreme point, the optimal solution to a linear programming formulation of the assignment problem will have the basic variables all equal to 0 or 1. Thus solving the linear programming formulation provides the optimal solution to the assignment problem.

To expand on the linear programming approach in solving assignment problems, let us reconsider the Fowle Marketing Research problem with the four project leaders as shown in Table 12.5. Let us begin by defining the following decision variables:

$$x_{ij} = \begin{cases} 1 & \text{if project leader } i \text{ is assigned to client } j, \\ & i = 1, 2, 3, 4; j = 1, 2, 3 \\ 0 & \text{otherwise.} \end{cases}$$

Using the above decision variables, the objective function calling for the minimization of total days can be written as

$$\begin{aligned} \min \quad & 10x_{11} + 15x_{12} + 9x_{13} \\ + \ & 9x_{21} + 18x_{22} + 5x_{23} \\ + \ & 6x_{31} + 14x_{32} + 3x_{33} \\ + \ & 8x_{41} + 16x_{42} + 6x_{43}. \end{aligned}$$

The constraints affecting this problem are that all clients must receive exactly one project leader and that the project leaders cannot be assigned to more than one client. The first condition is satisfied by the following linear constraints:

$$\begin{aligned} x_{11} + x_{21} + x_{31} + x_{41} &= 1 \quad \text{client A} \\ x_{12} + x_{22} + x_{32} + x_{42} &= 1 \quad \text{client B} \\ x_{13} + x_{23} + x_{33} + x_{43} &= 1 \quad \text{client C.} \end{aligned}$$

The second condition is reflected in the following constraints:

$$\begin{aligned} x_{11} + x_{12} + x_{13} &\leq 1 \quad \text{Terry} \\ x_{21} + x_{22} + x_{23} &\leq 1 \quad \text{Carle} \\ x_{31} + x_{32} + x_{33} &\leq 1 \quad \text{McClymonds} \\ x_{41} + x_{42} + x_{43} &\leq 1 \quad \text{Higley.} \end{aligned}$$

In addition, the nonnegativity constraints for the variables are included as usual.

The solution to this 12-variable 7-constraint linear programming model provides a project leader assignment plan that will allow Fowle to complete the three projects with a minimum total number of days expended. Using the linear programming approach, we would obtain the same solution as obtained using the Hungarian method.

The general assignment problem is one that involves m objects and n tasks. If we let $x_{ij} = 1$ or 0 according to whether object i is assigned to task j or not, and if c_{ij} denotes the cost of assigning object i to task j, then we can write the general assignment model as follows:

$$\min \quad \sum_{i=1}^{m} \sum_{j=1}^{n} c_{ij} x_{ij}$$

s.t.

$$\sum_{j=1}^{n} x_{ij} \leq 1 \qquad i = 1, 2, \cdots, m$$

$$\sum_{i=1}^{m} x_{ij} = 1 \qquad j = 1, 2, \cdots, n$$

$$x_{ij} \geq 0 \qquad \text{for all } i \text{ and } j.$$

The above general model will not have a feasible solution if n exceeds m, that is, if the number of tasks exceeds the number of objects available for assignment. For example, if Fowle had five clients and only three project leaders available, that is, $n = 5$ and $m = 3$, our above model would not have a feasible solution. That is, the equality constraints specify that each client must be assigned a project leader, and it is impossible to assign three project leaders to five clients unless we allow project leaders to be assigned to more than one client. However, we know that our inequality constraints prohibit such assignments, and thus we must conclude that we cannot obtain a feasible solution. To get around this problem, we need only add two dummy project leaders to obtain a feasible linear programming solution. In the problem formulation, the cost for assigning the dummy leaders would be zero (that is, $c_{ij} = 0$ for all dummy project leaders). If this approach were employed, projects receiving a dummy project leader could not be started until a project leader became available sometime in the future.

We can handle the situation where some assignments are unacceptable by omitting the corresponding x_{ij} variables from the objective function and all the constraints. Thus these assignments will not be in the linear programming solution.

12.4 SUMMARY

In this chapter we have introduced you to the assignment problem. The Hungarian method for solving the assignment problem was presented and demonstrated. It was also shown that the assignment problem could be formulated and solved as a linear program.

12.5 *Glossary*

1. *Hungarian method*—An algorithm used to solve assignment problems.
2. *Matrix reduction*—The approach used by the Hungarian method which reduces the values of the assignments until a zero-value assignment can be made.

3. *Dummy row(s)*—Extra row(s) added to an assignment problem to provide the equal number of row(s) and columns required by the solution procedure.
4. *Dummy column(s)*—Extra column(s) added to an assignment problem to provide the equal number of rows and column(s) required by the solution procedure.
5. *Opportunity loss*—The difference between the "best" assignment in a column and another assignment in the column. The measure is used to solve maximization assignment problems.

12.6   PROBLEMS

1. Joe's Body Shop currently has three jobs unassigned. Jerry, Frank, and Paul are the employees available to work on these jobs. The following table shows the assignment alternatives and the estimated completion times in hours for each alternative:

Employees	Job A	B	C
Jerry	11	12	17
Frank	7	11	20
Paul	5	8	16

   a. Find the minimum time assignment by enumerating all possible assignment solutions.
   b. Use the Hungarian method to obtain the optimal solution to this problem.

2. In Problem 1 assume that an additional employee was available for possible assignment. The following table shows the assignment alternatives and the estimated completion times with the additional employee.

Employees	Job A	B	C
Jerry	11	12	17
Frank	7	11	20
Paul	5	8	16
Ralph	8	10	19

   a. What is the optimal assignment using the Hungarian method? Is there more than one optimal solution?

b. Did the addition of Ralph change the previous optimal assignment? What about the value of the assignment?

c. Which employee will remain unassigned in the optimal assignment?

3. Solve the Fowle Marketing Research, Inc., assignment problem when four project leaders are available for assignment to the three clients. The estimated project completion times in days are as follows:

	Client		
Project Leader	A	B	C
Terry	10	15	9
Carle	9	18	5
McClymonds	6	14	3
Higly	8	16	6

4. Solve the Salsbury Discount, Inc., department-location assignment problem for the estimated annual profit data provided in Table 12.11.

5. In a job shop operation, four jobs may be performed on any of four machines. The number of hours required for each job on each machine are summarized below. What is the minimum total time job-machine assignment?

	Machine			
Job	A	B	C	D
1	10	14	15	13
2	12	13	15	12
3	8	12	12	11
4	13	16	18	16

6. Four secretaries are available to type any of three reports. Given the typing times in hours shown below, what is the minimum total time secretary-report assignment?

	Report		
Secretary	A	B	C
Phyllis	12	12	20
Linda	10	12	24
Janet	15	15	24
Cathy	13	14	25

7. Mr. Jones has four sales territories to which he has to assign four salesmen. From past experience he is able to estimate the sales volume for each salesman in each sales territory. Find the salesman-territory assignments that maximize sales.

Salesman	Sales Territory			
	A	B	C	D
George	10	9	19	13
Rugo	15	13	20	11
Moose	12	12	15	9
Walker	18	10	14	15

8. Each Monday the drivers of the J. P. Trucking Company state their preferences for the various truck routes open during the following week. With one indicating a first choice and five indicating a last choice, what is the driver-route assignment that minimizes the sum of the choice values?

Driver	Route				
	A	B	C	D	E
1	3	2	1	4	5
2	4	1	2	3	5
3	5	1	2	4	3
4	4	1	2	5	3
5	5	1	2	3	4

9. A firm has four salesmen and four sales territories. Since the salesmen have different levels of experience and ability, they will differ in terms of the value of sales that can be generated in each territory. The firm's management has estimated the sales volume that can be expected from each salesman in each sales territory. These data are shown below. Note that the Jenkins-territory A and Brinkley-territory B assignments are unacceptable and carry a $-M$ sales volume. What are the salesman-territory assignments that maximize sales?

Salesman	Sales Territory			
	A	B	C	D
Jenkins	$-M$	60	50	50
Brinkley	60	$-M$	80	75
Goode	80	100	90	80
Nichols	65	80	75	70

10. Manager Sparky Gibson of the Hamilton White Sox baseball team is trying to establish his starting pitchers for the crucial three-game series with the Mt. Washington Tigers. Sparky has the following five pitchers available.

Minta—the ace of the staff who just pitched last night's extra inning game against the Northtown Giants

O'Donnel—The aging veteran who has three wins and six losses this season

Banks—the relief ace who has started only one game this season

Hudlow—the rookie who just arrived from the Delphi farm team

Nash—a 10-win, 4-loss right-hander who has been having arm problems.

Sparky knows that the Tigers are saving their ace pitcher for the third game of the series. After considering the Tigers' probable lineup and pitchers, Sparky has estimated the probability of winning each of the three games with each of the five starting pitcher alternatives.

The winning probabilities are as follows:

Starting Pitcher	Game		
	1	2	3
Minta	0.60	0.75	0.65
O'Donnel	0.40	0.45	0.45
Banks	0.50	0.45	0.35
Hudlow	0.30	0.50	0.20
Nash	0.40	0.45	0.30

a. Assuming each pitcher could only start one game in the series, what is the pitching rotation that will maximize the expected number of wins for the Sox?

b. If Nash reports that his arm is fine prior to the start of the first game and his probabilities of winning are revised to 0.60, 0.70, and 0.50 for the three games, how should Sparky alter the pitching rotation?

11. In Section 12.3 we stated that assignment problems can be formulated and solved by linear programming. In the linear programming formulation we let $x = 1$ if an assignment is made; $x = 0$ otherwise. Remember now that linear programming does not necessarily provide integer values for the variables. However, we will now illustrate that all the extreme points of the assignment formulation happen to be integer 0 or 1 solutions. Thus standard linear programming formulations of assignment problems will provide the necessary 0 or 1 solution values for the variables.

Consider the simple assignment problem, given the following cost data:

	Job	
Person	1	2
A	10	12
B	8	9

a. Formulate the problem as a linear program.
b. List all the basic feasible solutions for this problem.

13
The
Transportation
Problem

The problems and solution procedures presented in this chapter are concerned with the transportation or physical distribution of goods and services from several supply locations to several customer locations. Usually we have a fixed capacity or limited quantity of goods available at each supply location *(origin)* and a specified order quantity or demand at each customer location *(destination)*. With a variety of transportation or shipping routes and a variety of costs for these routes, we would like to determine how many units should be shipped from each origin to each destination so that all destination demands are satisfied and the total transportation costs are minimized.

While the model and solution procedures presented in this chapter have been used to solve problems having nothing to do with the transportation of goods or services, the majority of problems or applications, as the name implies, have been used in transportation decision situations. Thus let us begin by considering a problem involving the distribution or transportation of a product from three plants to four distribution centers.

13.1 THE FOSTER GENERATORS, INC, TRANSPORTATION PROBLEM

Foster Generators, Inc., is a firm that has production operations in Cleveland, Ohio; Bedford, Indiana; and York, Pennsylvania. Production capacities for these plants over the next 3-month planning period for one particular type of generator are as follows.

Plant	Three-Month Production Capacity (units)
Cleveland	5000
Bedford	6000
York	2500
Total	13,500

Suppose that the firm distributes its generators through four regional distribution centers located in Boston, Chicago, St. Louis, and Lexington, and that the 3-month forecasted demands for the distribution centers are as follows.

Distribution Center	Forecasted Three-Month Demand (units)
Boston	6000
Chicago	4000
St. Louis	2000
Lexington	1500
Total	13,500

Management would like to determine how much of its production should be shipped from each plant to each distribution center. Figure 13.1 shows graphically the distribution routes Foster can use.

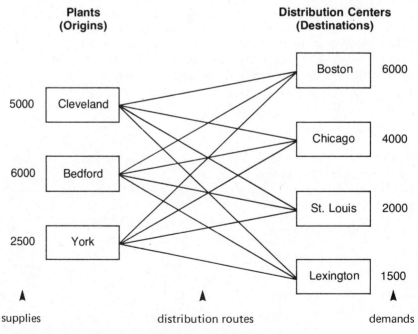

FIGURE 13.1 *Possible Distribution Routes for the Foster Generators Transportation Problem*

TABLE 13.1 Transportation Cost per Unit for the Foster
Generators Transportation Problem

		To Destination			
		Boston	Chicago	St. Louis	Lexington
From Origin	Cleveland	3	2	7	6
	Bedford	7	5	2	3
	York	2	5	4	5

With identical production costs at the three plants, the only relevant costs involved are transportation costs. Thus the problem becomes one of determining the distribution routes to be used and the quantity to be shipped via each route so that all distribution center demands can be met with a minimum total transportation cost. The cost for each unit shipped on each route is given in Table 13.1.

We will now discuss a procedure or algorithm that can be used to solve the Foster Generators transportation problem.

13.2 TRANSPORTATION PROBLEM
SOLUTION ALGORITHMS

The solution algorithms that we discuss for the transportation problem involve finding an initial feasible solution and then proceeding iteratively to make improvements in the solution until an optimal solution is reached. In order to conveniently summarize the data and to keep track of the algorithm calculations, a *transportation tableau* is usually employed. The transportation tableau for the Foster Generators problem is presented in Table 13.2.

Note that the twelve *cells* in the tableau correspond to the 12 shipping routes shown in Figure 13.1, that is, each cell corresponds to the route from one plant to one distribution center. The entries at the right-hand border of the tableau represent the supply available at each plant, and the entries at the bottom border represent the demand at each distribution center. The entries in the upper right-hand corner of each cell represent the per unit cost of shipping over that specific route.

Once the transportation tableau is complete, we can proceed with the calculations necessary to determine the minimum cost transportation decision. As stated, the first phase of the solution procedure involves finding an initial feasible solution. This can be accomplished by either using the northwest corner rule or Vogel's approximation method.

363

TABLE 13.2 Transportation Tableau for the Foster
Generators Transportation Problem

		To Destination				Origin Supply
		Boston	Chicago	St. Louis	Lexington	
	Cleveland	3	2	7	6	5000
From Origin	Bedford	7	5	2	3	6000
	York	2	5	4	5	2500
	Destination Demand	6000	4000	2000	1500	13,500

Cell corresponding to
shipments from Bedford
to Boston

Total supply
and total demand

The Northwest Corner Rule

The *northwest corner rule* for identifying an initial feasible solution requires
that we begin in the upper left-hand corner or cell of the tableau (the *northwest corner* on a map) and allocate units to routes in a "move-to-the-right-
and-down" fashion. For example, in the Foster Generators problem we
begin by allocating as many units as possible to the northwest corner; that is,
the Cleveland-Boston route. In this case we can only ship 5000 units over
this cell or route since the supply at Cleveland is only 5000. To identify a
shipment of 5000 units over the route, we write 5000 in the Cleveland-Boston
cell of our transportation tableau. Since this reduces our supply at Cleveland
from 5000 to 0, we cross out the 5000 supply value for Cleveland in the
tableau and replace it with the new revised value of 0. In addition, since 5000
units shipped along this route still leaves a demand of 1000 unsatisfied at
Boston, we cross out the 6000 Boston demand value and replace it with 1000.
Our transportation tableau now appears as shown on the top of page 365.

	Boston	Chicago	St. Louis	Lexington	Supply
Cleveland	3 — 5000	2	7	6	0 ~~5000~~
Bedford	7	5	2	3	6000
York	2	5	4	5	2500
Demand	~~6000~~ 1000	4000	2000	1500	

We continue the procedure by "moving down" the Boston column and shipping as many units as possible over the cell in row 2 and column 1: the Bedford-Boston route. Since the remaining Boston demand is only 1000 units, we will ship 1000 over the Bedford-Boston route and "move to the right" on the Bedford row, shipping as many as possible, 4000, over the Bedford-Chicago cell or route. The resulting tableau appears below.

	Boston	Chicago	St. Louis	Lexington	Supply
Cleveland	3 — 5000	2	7	6	0 ~~5000~~
Bedford	7 — 1000	5 — 4000	2	3	1000 ~~5000~~ ~~6000~~
York	2	5	4	5	2500
Demand	~~6000~~ ~~1000~~ 0	~~4000~~ 0	2000	1500	

Continuing in this "right-and-down" fashion, we obtain the following initial feasible transportation solution using the northwest corner rule.

	Boston	Chicago	St. Louis	Lexington	Supply
Cleveland	3 5000	2	7	6	0 ~~5000~~
Bedford	7 1000	5 4000	2 1000	3	0 ~~1000~~ ~~5000~~ ~~6000~~
York	2	5	4 1000	5 1500	0 ~~1500~~ ~~2500~~
Demand	~~6000~~ ~~1000~~ 0	~~4000~~ 0	~~2000~~ ~~1000~~ 0	~~1500~~ 0	

This solution is feasible since all the demand is satisfied and all the supply is used. However, we would be very fortunate indeed if this turned out to be the optimal solution. The total transportation cost that would result from this solution is calculated in Table 13.3.

The major advantage of using the northwest corner rule to find an initial feasible solution is that it is quick and easy to use. However, you might

TABLE 13.3 *Total Cost of Initial Feasible Solution Obtained Using the Northwest Corner Rule*

Route from	to	Units Shipped	Per Unit Cost	Total Cost
Cleveland	Boston	5000	$3	$15,000
Bedford	Boston	1000	$7	7000
Bedford	Chicago	4000	$5	20,000
Bedford	St. Louis	1000	$2	2000
York	St. Louis	1000	$4	4000
York	Lexington	1500	$5	7500
			Total	$55,500

366

suspect that the initial feasible solution obtained using this procedure will not be very good since the costs of shipping over each of the routes were totally ignored. This is the major shortcoming of the northwest corner rule. Vogel's approximation method overcomes this shortcoming by taking costs into account in the development of an initial feasible solution.

Vogel's Approximation Method

Vogel's approximation method (VAM) attempts to find a low-cost initial transportation solution by considering the costs associated with the transportation route alternatives. In order to apply VAM we first calculate for each row and column the penalty that will be incurred if, instead of shipping over the *best* route, we are forced to ship over the *second best* route. Let us apply VAM to develop an initial feasible solution for the Foster Generators problem. An initial set of row and column penalties for this problem has been calculated in the tableau below.

	Boston	Chicago	St. Louis	Lexington	Supply	Row Penalties
Cleveland	3	2	7	6	5000	1
Bedford	7	5	2	3	6000	1
York	2	5	4	5	2500	2
Demand	6000	4000	2000	1500		
Column Penalties	1	3	2	2		

For row 1 we see that the best or lowest cost route is the Cleveland-Chicago route at a cost of $2 per unit. If we are not allowed to ship any of the Cleveland production over this route and must ship over the second best route instead (the Cleveland-Boston route, at $3 per unit), the penalty we pay is $1 per unit. Similarly Bedford-St. Louis is the best route in row 2. If we are not allowed to ship over this best route, we will have to pay a penalty of $1 per unit. That is, the incremental cost is $1 per unit shipped over the second best route, Bedford-Lexington.

The penalties for each column are calculated similarly. For example, in column 3 the cheapest way to satisfy the St. Louis demand is to ship from Bedford. If we do not ship over this route, we must pay a penalty of $2 per unit corresponding to the incremental cost of shipping over the second best route, York-St. Louis. Thus the column penalty is 2.

Once *all* the row and column penalties have been calculated, we make an allocation to the cell for which the penalty would be greatest if we did not select this cell or route. That is, we locate the row or column with the largest penalty and then allocate the maximum number of units possible to the best cell in that row or column. In our problem, column 2 has the largest penalty, 3, and the Cleveland-Chicago route is the best in that column. Thus we allocate the maximum number of units possible, 4000, to this cell. Hence in our transportation tableau we write 4000 in the Cleveland-Chicago cell.

The allocation of 4000 units to the Cleveland-Chicago route satisfies all the Chicago demand, and hence we can line out column 2 and ignore it in the remainder of the calculations. In addition, we reduce the supply available at Cleveland by the amount shipped. Thus the revised supply at Cleveland is now $5000 - 4000 = 1000$ units. The resulting transportation tableau is shown below.

	Boston	Chicago	St. Louis	Lexington	Supply	Row Penalties
Cleveland	3	2 4000	7	6	1000 ~~5000~~	✗ 3
Bedford	7	5	2	3	6000	✗ 1
York	2	5	4	5	2500	✗ 2
Demand	6000	~~4000~~ 0	2000	1500		
Column Penalties	1	3	2	2		

Once column 2 has been lined out and the Cleveland supply and Chicago demand have been revised, we must recalculate our penalties in order to determine the next allocation. Our new tableau with the recalculated row penalties is presented below. Note that the *column* penalties remain unchanged since no rows were lined out in the previous step.

Row 1 now has the largest penalty, and thus we select the Cleveland-Boston route as the best cell or route. The maximum amount we can ship over this route is the remaining supply of 1000 units at Cleveland. Thus we allocate 1000 units to the cell in row 1 and column 1. Since all the Cleveland production has been shipped, we line out the Cleveland row and ignore it in the remainder of the calculations. The Boston demand can now be revised to $6000 - 1000 = 5000$ units. Our resulting transportation tableau is shown below.

	Boston	Chicago	St. Louis	Lexington	Supply	Row Penalties
Cleveland	3 — 1000	2 — 4000	7	6	0 ~~1000~~ ~~5000~~	~~1~~ ~~3~~
Bedford	7	5	2	3	6000	~~1~~ 1
York	2	5	4	5	2500	~~2~~ 2
Demand	~~6000~~ 5000	~~4000~~ 0	2000	1500		
Column Penalties	1	3	2	2		

Once row 1 has been lined out and the Cleveland supply and the Boston demand have been revised, we must recalculate new column penalties in order to determine the next allocation. Our new tableau with the recalculated column penalties is presented at the top of p. 370. Note that since column 1 turns out to have the maximum penalty, we have selected the York-Boston route as the best cell, and hence have allocated 2500 units over this route. Since this exhausts our supply at York, we have lined out the York row in this revised tableau.

	Boston	Chicago	St. Louis	Lexington	Supply	Row Penalties
Cleveland	3 / 1000	2 / 4000	7	6	0 / ~~1000~~ / ~~5000~~	~~X~~ 3
Bedford	7	5	2	3	6000	~~X~~ 1
York	2 / 2500	5	4	5	0 / ~~2500~~	~~2~~ 2
Demand	~~6000~~ ~~5000~~ 2500	~~4000~~ 0	2000	1500		
Column Penalties	~~1~~ 5	3	~~2~~ 2	~~2~~ 2		

	Boston	Chicago	St. Louis	Lexington	Supply	Row Penalties
Cleveland	3 / 1000	2 / 4000	7	6	0 / ~~1000~~ / ~~5000~~	~~X~~ 3
Bedford	7 / 2500	5	2 / 2000	3 / 1500	~~6000~~	~~X~~ 1
York	2 / 2500	5	4	5	0 / ~~2500~~	~~2~~ 2
Demand	~~6000~~ ~~5000~~ ~~2500~~	~~4000~~ 0	~~2000~~	~~1500~~		
Column Penalties	~~1~~ 5	3	~~2~~ 2	~~2~~ 2		

370

Since we have only one row left, it is not necessary to recalculate row or column penalties. All that we have to do to obtain an initial feasible solution is to allocate the 6000 units of supply at Bedford to the Boston, St. Louis, and Lexington destinations. Carrying out these remaining allocations results in the transportation tableau at the bottom of page 370.

This solution is feasible since all the demand is satisfied and all the supply is used. The total transportation cost resulting from this solution is calculated in Table 13.4.

TABLE 13.4   Total Cost of Initial Feasible Solution Obtained
Using Vogel's Approximation Method

Route from	to	Units Shipped	Per Unit Cost	Total Cost
Cleveland	Boston	1000	$3	$ 3000
Cleveland	Chicago	4000	$2	8000
Bedford	Boston	2500	$7	17,500
Bedford	St. Louis	2000	$2	4000
Bedford	Lexington	1500	$3	4500
York	Boston	2500	$2	5000
			Total	$42,000

Comparing Tables 13.3 and 13.4, we see that the initial feasible solution obtained using Vogel's approximation method results in a cost savings of $13,500. Considering only these cost savings, one is tempted to conclude that VAM is obviously the best way to find an initial feasible solution. However, neither method guarantees us the optimal solution and in rare cases the northwest corner rule actually provides a better initial feasible solution (see problem 13.3). Thus further calculations will be necessary regardless of whether the northwest corner rule or VAM is used to find an initial feasible solution. However, in most cases VAM will give a better initial feasible solution and also will tend to minimize the calculations necessary to reach the optimal solution. The major drawback of Vogel's approximation method is that it takes many more calculations to find an initial feasible solution than does the northwest corner rule. There are some studies that seem to indicate that the extra work necessary in using VAM to find an initial feasible solution is more than compensated for by the reduction in work necessary in the second phase of the solution procedure, where we must iterate from the initial feasible solution to the optimal solution.

Summary of Initial Feasible Solution Procedures

Before moving on to the second phase of the solution procedure and attempting to improve the initial feasible solution, let us restate the steps of the northwest corner rule and Vogel's approximation method for obtaining the initial transportation solution.

Northwest Corner Rule

Step 1: Starting with the upper left-hand cell (northwest corner) of the transportation tableau, assign as many units to this cell as possible. The amount assigned is the smaller of the row supply available or the column demand requirement.

Step 2: Reduce the row supply and the column demand by the amount assigned to the cell.

Step 3: If the row supply is now zero, move down the column to the next cell; if the column demand is now zero, move to the right on the row to the next cell; if both the row supply and the column demand are zero, move down one cell and to the right one cell to the next cell.

Step 4: For the next cell, as identified by Step 3, assign as many units as possible and return to Step 2 until an initial feasible solution is obtained.

Vogel's Approximation Method

Step 1: For each row and column of the transportation tableau, compute a penalty cost, which is the difference between the unit cost on the *second best* route in the row or column and the *best* route in the row or column.

Step 2: Identify the row or column with the highest penalty cost and assign as many units as possible to the *best* cell or route in the identified row or column.

Step 3: Reduce the row supply and the column demand by the amount assigned to the cell.

Step 4: If the row supply is now zero, eliminate the row; if the column demand is now zero, eliminate the column; if both the row supply and the column demand are zero, eliminate both the row and column.

Step 5: Compute the new row and column penalty costs for the transportation tableau after the Step 4 reduction and return to Step 2 until an initial feasible solution is obtained.

The Stepping-Stone Method

The *stepping-stone method* provides an iterative method for moving from the northwest corner or VAM initial feasible solution to an optimal solution. As we will discuss in detail later, this method can only be implemented if the initial feasible solution of an m-origin n-destination transportation problem uses $m + n - 1$ transportation routes. This condition requires the Foster Generators transportation problem to have $3 + 4 - 1 = 6$ transportation routes in the initial solution. For the Foster problem both the northwest corner rule solution (Table 13.3) and the VAM solution (Table 13.4) satisfy this condition; thus we may proceed with the stepping-stone method. Later we will show you what to do if the initial solution does not consist of $m + n - 1$ transportation routes.

Basically we will use the stepping-stone method to evaluate the economics of shipping via transportation routes that are not currently part of the transportation solution. If we can find cost-reducing routes, we will revise the current solution by making shipments via these new routes. By continuing to evaluate the costs associated with routes that are not in the current solution, we will know that we have reached the optimal solution when all routes not in the current solution would increase costs if they were brought into the solution.

To see how the stepping-stone method works, let us return to the VAM initial solution for the Foster Generators problem as presented below.

	Boston	Chicago	St. Louis	Lexington	Supply
Cleveland	3 1000	2 4000	7	6	5000
Bedford	7 2500	5	2 2000	3 1500	6000
York	2 2500	5	4	5	2500
Demand	6000	4000	2000	1500	

Suppose we were to allocate one unit to the route or cell in row 2 and column 2; that is, ship one unit on the currently unused route from Bedford to Chicago. In order to satisfy the Chicago demand exactly, we would have to reduce the number of units in the Cleveland-Chicago cell to 3999. But then we would have to increase the amount in the Cleveland-Boston cell to 1001 so that the total Cleveland supply of 5000 units can be shipped. Finally, we would reduce the Bedford-Boston cell by 1 in order to exactly satisfy the

373

Boston demand. The tableau below summarizes the series of adjustments we have described.

	Boston	Chicago	St. Louis	Lexington	Supply
Cleveland	3 1001 ~~1000~~	2 3999 ~~4000~~	7	6	5000
Bedford	7 2499 ~~2500~~	5 1	2 2000	3 1500	6000
York	2 2500	5	4	5	2500
Demand	6000	4000	2000	1500	

What is the added or reduced cost that will result from using the Bedford-Chicago route? Let us calculate the cost per unit change resulting from the one unit addition to the Bedford-Chicago route. The cost adjustments are as follows:

	Changes	Effect on Cost
Add 1 unit	Bedford–Chicago	+5
Reduce 1 unit	Cleveland–Chicago	−2
Add 1 unit	Cleveland–Boston	+3
Reduce 1 unit	Bedford–Boston	−7
	Total net effect	−1

Thus this analysis tells us that the transportation costs can be reduced by $1 for every unit shipped over the Bedford-Chicago route if corresponding changes are made in other routes as shown.

Before making additions to this new route, let us look at the general procedure for evaluating the costs associated with a new cell or route and then check all currently unused routes to find the best route to add to our current transportation solution.

The method we have just demonstrated for evaluating the Bedford-Chicago route is known as the stepping-stone method. Note that in considering the addition of this new route, we evaluated its effect on other routes

374

currently in the transportation solution, referred to as *occupied* cells. In total we considered changes in four cells, the new cell and three *current solution* or *occupied* cells. In effect, we can view these four cells as forming a path or *stepping-stone path* in the tableau, where the corners of the path are current solution cells. The idea is to view the tableau as a pond with the current solution cells as stones sticking up in the pond. To identify the stepping-stone path for a new cell, we want to move in horizontal and vertical directions using current solution cells as the stones at the corners of the path by which we can step from stone to stone and return to the new cell we initially started with. The dotted line in the following tableau represents the stepping-stone path for the Cleveland-St. Louis route or cell. In terms of a transportation tableau, the stepping-stone path represents the sequence of adjustments that are necessary to maintain a feasible solution, given that one unit is to be shipped through a new or currently unoccupied cell.

	Boston	Chicago	St. Louis	Lexington	Supply
Cleveland	3 1000	2 4000	7	6	5000
Bedford	7 2500	5	2 2000	3 1500	6000
York	2 2500	5	4	5	2500
Demand	6000	4000	2000	1500	

By using the stepping-stone path for a new cell, we can evaluate the costs associated with a one-unit addition to the new cell. For example, the Cleveland-St. Louis cell would result in the following changes:

	Changes	Effect on Cost
Add 1 unit	Cleveland–St. Louis	+7
Reduce 1 unit	Bedford–St. Louis	−2
Add 1 unit	Bedford–Boston	+7
Reduce 1 unit	Cleveland–Boston	−3
	Total net effect	+9

Thus we see that the Cleveland-St. Louis route is unattractive in that use of this route will result in a $9 per unit increase in the transportation cost.

Finding the stepping-stone path for each possible new cell will enable us to identify the cost effect for each new cell or route. Evaluating this cost effect for all possible new cells leads to the following transportation tableau. The per unit cost effect for each possible new cell is circled in the cell.

	Boston	Chicago	St. Louis	Lexington	Supply
Cleveland	3 1000	2 4000	7 (+9)	6 (+7)	5000
Bedford	7 2500	5 (−1)	2 2000	3 1500	6000
York	2 2500	5 (+4)	4 (+7)	5 (+7)	2500
Demand	6000	4000	2000	1500	

On the basis of the calculated per unit changes, we see that the best cell in terms of cost reduction is the Bedford-Chicago cell with a $1 decrease in cost for every unit shipped on this route. The question now is, how much should

	Boston	Chicago	St. Louis	Lexington	Supply
Cleveland	3 3500	2 1500	7	6	5000
Bedford	7	5 2500	2 2000	3 1500	6000
York	2 2500	5	4	5	2500
Demand	6000	4000	2000	1500	

we ship over this new route? Since the total cost decreases by $1 per unit shipped, we would like to ship the maximum possible number of units. We know from our previous stepping-stone calculation that each unit shipped over the Bedford-Chicago route results in an increase of one unit shipped from Cleveland to Boston and a decrease of one unit in both the amount shipped from Bedford to Boston (currently 2500) and the amount shipped from Cleveland to Chicago (currently 4000). Because of this, the maximum we can ship over the Bedford-Chicago route is 2500, which results in no units being shipped from Bedford to Boston. The tableau corresponding to this new solution is presented on the bottom of page 376.

Note that the only changes from the previous tableau are located on the stepping-stone path originating in the Bedford-Chicago cell. We can now use the stepping-stone method to recalculate the per unit changes resulting from attempting to add new cells or routes to our current solution. Doing so we get the tableau below. Note that the stepping-stone path used to evaluate the York-St. Louis cell is indicated by the dashed line in the tableau.

	Boston	Chicago	St. Louis	Lexington	Supply
Cleveland	3 3500	2 1500	7 ⑧	6 ⑥	5000
Bedford	7 ①	5 2500	2 2000	3 1500	6000
York	2 2500	5 ④	4 ⑥	5 ⑥	2500
Demand	6000	4000	2000	1500	

The per unit change for every possible new cell is now greater than or equal to zero. Thus since there is no new route which will decrease the total cost, we have reached the optimal solution. The optimal solution together with its total cost is summarized in Table 13.5.

The most difficult part of the solution procedure we have outlined is the identification of every stepping-stone path so that we can calculate the cost per unit change in the total cost. There is an easier way to make these cost per unit calculations; it is called the modified distribution (MODI) method. While we will not derive the method, we will demonstrate how it can be used to calculate the per unit changes for the new or unoccupied cells.

TABLE 13.5 *Optimal Solution to the Foster Generators Transportation Problem*

Route from	to	Units Shipped	Per Unit Cost	Total Cost
Cleveland	Boston	3500	$3	$10,500
Cleveland	Chicago	1500	$2	3000
Bedford	Chicago	2500	$5	12,500
Bedford	St. Louis	2000	$2	4000
Bedford	Lexington	1500	$3	4500
York	Boston	2500	$2	5000
				$39,500

Modified Distribution (MODI) Method

The MODI method requires that we define an index u_i for each row of the tableau and an index v_j for each column of the tableau. The values of these indices are found by requiring that the cost coefficient for each current solution or occupied cell equal $u_i + v_j$. If we define c_{ij} to be the per unit cost of shipping from plant i to distribution center j, then we require that $u_i + v_j = c_{ij}$ for each occupied cell in order to calculate the per unit changes in the final tableau of the Foster Generators problem.

Requiring that $u_i + v_j = c_{ij}$ for all the occupied cells in the final tableau of the Foster Generators problem leads to a system of six equations and seven variables.

Occupied Cell:
    Cleveland-Boston $u_1 + v_1 = 3$
    Cleveland-Chicago $u_1 + v_2 = 2$
    Bedford-Chicago $u_2 + v_2 = 5$
    Bedford-St. Louis $u_2 + v_3 = 2$
    Bedford-Lexington $u_2 + v_4 = 3$
    York-Boston $u_3 + v_1 = 2.$

Since there is one more variable than equation in the above system, we can freely pick a value for one of the variables and then solve for the others. Thus we shall always choose $u_1 = 0$ and then solve for the values of the other variables. Setting $u_1 = 0$, we get the following system of equations:

$$0 + v_1 = 3 \qquad u_2 + v_3 = 2$$
$$0 + v_2 = 2 \qquad u_2 + v_4 = 3$$
$$u_2 + v_2 = 5 \qquad u_3 + v_1 = 2.$$

Solving these equations leads to the following values for $u_1, u_2, u_3, v_1, v_2, v_3$, and v_4.

$$u_1 = 0 \qquad v_1 = 3$$
$$u_2 = 3 \qquad v_2 = 2$$
$$u_3 = -1 \qquad v_3 = -1$$
$$ \qquad v_4 = 0.$$

Now let us define $e_{ij} = c_{ij} - u_i - v_j$, where the value of e_{ij} represents the per unit change in total cost resulting from allocating one unit to the unoccupied cell in row i and column j. Rewriting the final tableau for the Foster Generators problem and replacing the previous marginal information with the values of u_i and v_j we obtain

u_i \ v_j	3	2	-1	0
0	3 3500	2 1500	7 ⑧	6 ⑥
3	7 ①	5 2500	2 2000	3 1500
-1	2 2500	5 ④	4 ⑥	5 ⑥

Note how much easier it is to compute the net changes using the MODI method. For example, $e_{13} = c_{13} - u_1 - v_3 = 7 - 0 - (-1) = 8$ represents the net change in the total cost that would result from allocating one unit to cell 1,3. We also observe that these e_{ij} calculated by the MODI method are exactly the same as the net changes calculated by the stepping-stone method. It is still necessary to search for a stepping-stone path to determine which route to close once the best route to open has been identified. However, it is not necessary to generate a stepping-stone path for any of the other unoccupied cells. Thus a considerable savings in the work required at each iteration can be obtained by employing the MODI method in the calculation of the e_{ij} for each unoccupied cell.

Summary of the Stepping-Stone and MODI Algorithms

The stepping-stone and modified distribution methods were presented as procedures for improving an initial feasible transportation solution until an optimal solution is reached. Below we restate the detailed steps of these algorithms.

Stepping-Stone Method: Given the transportation tableau with an initial solution and $m + n - 1$ occupied cells, the stepping-stone method is as follows.

Step 1: For each unoccupied cell, identify its stepping-stone path through the transportation tableau.

Step 2: Compute the per unit change (e_{ij}) from adding one unit to each unoccupied cell as follows:

    a. Label the starting or unoccupied cell under consideration as cell 1 and number sequentially 2, 3, 4, . . . the occupied cells on the corners of its stepping-stone path.

    b. The per unit change from adding one unit to the unoccupied cell is found by adding the unit shipping costs of all *odd*-numbered cells on the path and subtracting the unit shipping costs of all *even*-numbered cells on the path.

Step 3: In a minimization problem, if the per unit changes for all unoccupied cells are nonnegative, the solution is optimal. However, if negative per unit changes exist, identify the best cell (most negative per unit change) and continue.

Step 4: For the best cell, identify the sequentially numbered occupied cells on the corners of its stepping-stone path as under Step 2. Determine the even-numbered stepping-stone cell over which the smallest quantity is being shipped. Add this quantity to the new cell and all odd-numbered cells. Subtract this quantity from all even-numbered cells. Return to Step 1.

Modified Distribution (MODI) Method: Given the transportation tableau with an initial solution and $m + n - 1$ occupied cells, the MODI method is as follows.

Step 1: Letting $u_1 = 0$, use the occupied cells of the transportation tableau to compute row indices $u_2, u_3,$ . . . and column indices $v_1, v_2, v_3,$ . . . such that

$$u_i + v_j = c_{ij}$$

for all occupied cells.

380

Step 2: Compute the cost e_{ij} of adding one unit to each unoccupied cell by

$$e_{ij} = c_{ij} - u_i - v_j.$$

Step 3: Follow Step 3 of the stepping-stone method.
Step 4: Follow Step 4 of the stepping-stone method.

13.3 HANDLING SPECIAL SITUATIONS

We will now discuss how to handle the following special transportation problem situations:

1. Total supply not equal to total demand
2. Maximization objective
3. Unacceptable transportation routes
4. Transportation tableaus with less than $m + n - 1$ occupied cells.

One situation that often occurs is the case where the total supply is not equal to the total demand. This situation can be handled easily by our solution procedure if we first introduce a dummy plant or dummy distribution center; that is, if total supply is greater than total demand, we introduce a *dummy destination* (distribution center) with demand exactly equal to the excess of supply over demand. Similarly, if total demand is greater than total supply, we introduce a *dummy origin* (plant) with supply exactly equal to the excess of demand over supply. In either the excess demand or excess supply case, we assign cost coefficients of zero to every route into a dummy distribution center and every route out of a dummy plant. This is because when the solution is implemented, no shipments will actually be made from a dummy plant or to a dummy distribution center.

The transportation model can also be used to solve problems involving maximization of an objective. The only modification in our solution procedure necessary for problems of this type is in the selection of an unoccupied cell to which units will be allocated. Instead of picking the cell with the most negative e_{ij} value, we pick that cell for which e_{ij} is largest; that is, we pick the cell which will cause the largest per unit increase in the objective function.

In the assignment problem, we saw that unacceptable assignments carry an extremely large cost of M in order to keep them out of solution. Thus if we have a transportation route from an origin to a destination that for some reason cannot be used, we simply assign this route a value of M, and thus this route will not enter the solution. Unacceptable routes would be assigned a value of $-M$ in a maximization problem.

A final difficulty that can occur when applying our solution procedure is referred to as *degeneracy*. This happens when there are less than $m + n - 1$ occupied cells in an m-origin n-destination transportation tableau and causes problems in that there are not enough cells to identify all stepping-stone paths or all u_i and v_j in the MODI method. To handle this situation, we artificially create an occupied cell; that is, we place a 0, representing nothing being shipped, in one of the unoccupied cells and then treat it as if it were occupied. Note, however, that we must choose the unoccupied cell in which to place the 0 so that once it is placed, all stepping-stone paths and all the u_i and v_j can be determined.

Let us now illustrate with another example how the above difficulties can be resolved. Suppose we have three plants (origins) with production capacities as follows.

Plants	Production Capacity
P_1	50
P_2	40
P_3	30
Total	120

We also have demand for our product at three retail outlets. The demand forecasts for the current planning period are presented below.

Retail Outlets	Forecasted Demand
R_1	45
R_2	15
R_3	30
Total	90

The production cost at each plant is different, and the sales prices at the retail outlets vary. Taking prices, production costs, and shipping costs into consideration, the profits for producing one unit at plant i, shipping it to retail outlet j, and selling it at retail outlet j are presented in Table 13.6.

TABLE 13.6 *Profit per Unit for Producing at Plant i and Selling at Retail Outlet j*

	Retail Outlets		
	R_1	R_2	R_3
P_1	2	8	10
P_2	6	11	6
P_3	12	7	9

382

We note first that the total production capacity exceeds the total demand at the retail outlets. Thus we must introduce a dummy retail outlet with demand exactly equal to the excess of production capacity. We therefore add retail outlet R_4 with a demand of 30 units. The per unit profit for shipping from each plant to retail outlet R_4 is set to zero, since these units will not actually be shipped. An initial feasible solution for this problem obtained by the northwest corner rule is presented below:

	R_1	R_2	R_3	R_4	Supply
P_1	2 / 45	8 / 5	10	0	50
P_2	6	11 / 10	6 / 30	0	40
P_3	12	7	9	0 / 30	30
Demand	45	15	30	30	

With this solution as a starting point we can attempt to use the MODI method to calculate the row and column indices u_i and v_j. Unfortunately,

u_i \ v_j	2	8	3		Supply
0	2 / 45	8 / 5	10	0	50
3	6	11 / 10	6 / 30	0	40
	12	7	9	0 / 30	30
Demand	45	15	30	30	

383

whenever the number of occupied cells is less than the number of rows plus the number of columns minus 1, it will not be possible to calculate all the u_i and v_j; that is, degeneracy occurs. In this case, since the number of rows is 3 and the number of columns is 4, anytime the number of occupied cells is less than 6 we will have a degenerate solution. From the tableau at the bottom of page 383 we see that it is not possible to calculate u_3 or v_4 using the initial feasible solution.

We must artificially create a sixth occupied cell by placing 0 in any cell that will allow us to complete the calculation of the u_i and v_j. Thus we place a 0 in row 3 and column 3 and treat the corresponding cell as if it were occupied. Then we can complete our calculations of the u_i and v_j. The result of this calculation together with the e_{ij} for each unoccupied cell is presented below.

u_i \ v_j	2	8	3	−6	Supply
0	[2] 45	[8] 5	[10] ⑦	[0] ⑥	50
3	[6] ①	[11] 10	[6] 30	[0] ③	40
6	[12] ④	[7] ⑦ (−7)	[9] 0	[0] 30	30
Demand	45	15	30	30	

Since this is a maximization problem, we pick the cell with the largest e_{ij} to make an allocation, that is, the route from P_1 to R_3 with $e_{13} = 7$ should be selected. Applying the stepping-stone procedure, we see that the maximum amount we can ship over this route before the cell in row 1 and column 2 becomes unoccupied is 5. Making the appropriate adjustments and recalculating the e_{ij} we obtain a new tableau at the top of page 385.

The route from P_3 to R_1 with $e_{31} = 11$ now results in the largest increase. Our stepping-stone path (dashed line) indicates that 0 units is the maximum that can be shipped over this route if we are to maintain a feasible solution in our tableau, that is, if we attempted to ship any positive amount we would end up with the amount shipped from P_3 to R_3 being negative.

Making the appropriate adjustments for 0 units being shipped and recalculating the e_{ij}, we obtain a new tableau. Note that we no longer have an

u_i \ v_j	2	15	10	1	Supply
0	2 45	8 (−7)	10 5	0 (−1)	50
−4	6 (8)	11 15	6 25	0 (3)	40
−1	12 (11)	7 (−7)	9 0	0 30	30
Demand	45	15	30	30	

u_i \ v_j	2	15	10	−10	Supply
0	2 45	8 (−7)	10 5	0 (10)	50
−4	6 (8)	11 15	6 25	0 (14)	40
10	12 0	7 (−18)	9 (−11)	0 30	30
Demand	45	15	30	30	

entry in the P_3–R_3 cell since the 0 units previously there have been moved to the P_3–R_1 cell.

In iterating to this tableau we see that there is really no change in the shipping pattern. However, the maximum net change is now $e_{24} = 14$. Thus we make an allocation to the route P_2–R_4. Note from the stepping-stone path that we will ship 25 units. Also since cell P_3–R_1 is on the stepping-stone path, we will increase the number of units shipped from P_3 to R_1 from 0 to 25. Our new tableau is given at the top of page 386.

u_i \ v_j	2	1	10	−10	Supply
0	[2] 20	[8] ⑦	[10] 30	[0] ⑩	50
10	[6] ⑥̄(−6) 15	[11]	[6] (−14) 25	[0]	40
10	[12] 25	[7] (−4)	[9] (−11)	[0] 5	30
Demand	45	15	30	30	

We next allocate to the P_1–R_4 route since e_{14} is the largest e_{ij}. The maximum that can be shipped over this route is 5. The next tableau is shown below.

u_i \ v_j	2	11	10	0	Supply
0	[2] 15	[8] (−3)	[10] 30	[0] 5	50
0	[6] (4)	[11] 15	[6] (−4)	[0] 25	40
10	[12] 30	[7] (−14)	[9] (−11)	[0] (−10)	30
Demand	45	15	30	30	

We now ship 15 units over the route P_2–R_1. The result of this iteration is the following tableau.

u_i \ v_j	6	11	10	0
0	2 / (-4)	8 / (-3)	10 / 30	0 / 20
0	6 / 15	11 / 15	6 / (-4)	0 / 10
6	12 / 30	7 / (-10)	9 / (-7)	0 / (-6)

Since all the e_{ij} are now less than or equal to zero, we have reached the optimal solution to this maximization transportation problem.

When applying the above procedures to solve a transportation problem it may happen that there are alternate optimal solutions to the problem. We will discover this condition whenever the e_{ij} for an unoccupied cell is equal to zero in the final transportation tableau. This condition implies that we could allocate units to be unoccupied cell with a zero e_{ij} without causing a change in the value of the solution. Hence another optimal solution could be found by allocating units to that route.

Summary of Solution Procedure for Transportation Problems

Let us now summarize in a step-by-step fashion the solution procedure that we have developed for transportation problems.

Step 1: Find an initial feasible solution using either the northwest corner rule or Vogel's approximation method.

Step 2: Use the MODI method to determine the per unit change in the value of the current solution that would result from making an allocation to any unoccupied cell. If degeneracy occurs, it will be necessary to artificially create an occupied cell by shipping 0 units over a route in order to calculate all the u_i and v_j.

Step 3: Determine if making an allocation to any of the unoccupied cells will cause an improvement in the value of the current solution. If not, the optimum has been reached.

387

Step 4: Allocate as many units as possible to that unoccupied cell that will cause the greatest per unit improvement in the value of the solution. Use the stepping-stone method to determine which currently occupied cell becomes unoccupied. Return to Step 2.

13.4 A LINEAR PROGRAMMING FORMULATION OF THE TRANSPORTATION PROBLEM

Like the assignment problem, the transportation problem can be formulated and solved using linear programming. In order to show the linear programming formulation of the transportation problem, we must introduce some additional notation. Let

i = index for origins, $i = 1, 2, \ldots, m$

j = index for destinations, $j = 1, 2, \ldots, n$

x_{ij} = number of units shipped from origin i to destination j

c_{ij} = cost per unit of shipping from origin i to destination j

s_i = supply or capacity in units at origin i

d_j = demand in units at destination j

The general linear programming formulation of the m-origin n-destination transportation problem is

$$\min \ \sum_{i=1}^{m} \sum_{j=1}^{n} c_{ij}x_{ij}$$

s.t.

$$\sum_{j=1}^{n} x_{ij} \leq s_i \qquad i = 1, 2, \ldots, m \quad \text{(supply)}$$

$$\sum_{i=1}^{m} x_{ij} = d_j \qquad j = 1, 2, \ldots, n \quad \text{(demand)}$$

$$x_{ij} \geq 0 \qquad \text{for all } i \text{ and } j.$$

You might notice that the supply constraints are inequalities in this formulation. As long as total supply is at least as great as total demand, a feasible solution will result, and all demands will be met. It is not necessary to introduce a dummy destination in the case where total supply is greater than total demand. If we encounter a transportation problem where total supply ($\sum_{i=1}^{m} s_i$) is less than total demand ($\sum_{j=1}^{n} d_j$), there will be no feasible solution to the problem, that is, we know in advance that demands cannot be satisfied unless

$$\sum_{i=1}^{m} s_i \geq \sum_{j=1}^{n} d_j.$$

We can still generate a minimum transportation cost solution for the available supply and at the same time identify the destinations that will not receive the requested demand by creating a dummy origin or source with a supply exactly equal to the difference between the total demand and total supply. If we let s_{m+1} indicate the fictitious supply, then

$$s_{m+1} = \sum_{j=1}^{n} d_j - \sum_{i=1}^{m} s_i.$$

Essentially, we create a dummy origin with a capacity of s_{m+1}.

The result of introducing this dummy origin is to make total supply equal to total demand. Thus the modified linear programming model will have a feasible solution. Since no shipments will actually be made from the dummy origin, all objective function cost coefficients for this source can be set equal to zero. Thus

$$c_{m+1,1} = c_{m+1,2} = \ldots = c_{m+1,n} = 0.$$

In the linear programming formulation of the transportation problem, the case of unacceptable routes is easy to handle. We simply remove the x_{ij} corresponding to an unacceptable route from the problem formulation. Then it will not be possible for the optimal solution to include units shipped over the unacceptable route.

In the case where some routes have a limited shipping capacity, additional constraints can be added to the linear programming model. For example, suppose that the route from origin 2 to destination 3 had a maximum shipping capacity of 50 units. The following constraint can be added to guarantee that the route capacity will be met:

$$x_{23} \leq 50.$$

In general, if L_{ij} represents the route capacity from origin i to destination j, additional constraints of the form

$$x_{ij} \leq L_{ij}$$

will be needed.

13.5 SUMMARY

In this chapter we have introduced the transportation problem and have presented a number of approaches to solving decision-making problems that can be formulated in the framework of a general transportation situation. It should be apparent that the assignment problem discussed in Chapter 12 is really a special case of the transportation problem; that is, an assignment problem can be viewed as a transportation problem in which each origin has exactly one unit to ship and each destination has a demand for exactly one unit. Hence the solution methods developed for the transportation problem could also be used to solve the assignment problem. The chapter concluded with a discussion of how a transportation problem could be formulated as a linear program, and hence solved using the Simplex method described in Chapter 9.

13.6 GLOSSARY

1. *Origin*—A source or supply location in a transportation problem.
2. *Destination*—A customer or demand location in a transporation problem.
3. *Transportation tableau*—A table showing origins, destinations, routes, costs, supplies, and demands in a transportation problem. The tableau is used to facilitate the solution algorithm calculations.
4. *Cell*—A section of a transportation tableau corresponding to a route between a specific origin and a specific destination.
5. *Occupied cell*—A cell indicating that some quantity greater than zero is assigned to its corresponding route.
6. *Northwest corner rule*—An algorithm used to find an initial feasible solution to a transportation problem.
7. *Vogel's approximation method*—An algorithm used to find an initial feasible solution to a transportation problem.
8. *Stepping-stone method*—A transportation algorithm used to find the optimal solution to a transportation problem.
9. *Stepping-stone path*—A path in a transportation tableau beginning and ending with the same unoccupied cell and having occupied cells on the corners of the path.
10. *Modified distribution method (MODI)*—An algorithm used to find the optimal solution to a transportation problem.
11. *Degeneracy*—A situation that occurs when there are less than $m + n - 1$ occupied cells in a transportation tableau.
12. *Dummy origin*—An origin added to make total supply equal to total demand in a transportation problem. The supply at the dummy origin is equal to the excess of demand over the current supply.
13. *Dummy destination*—A destination added to make total supply equal total demand in a transportation problem. The demand at the dummy destination is equal to the excess of supply over the demand.

13.7 PROBLEMS

1. Consider the following initial transportation tableau.

		Destinations		
		Watkins Glenn	Penn Yan	Supply
Origins	Elmira	8 _300_	6 _300_	300
	Endicott	5 _200_	6	200
	Endwell	7 _350_	10 _300_	300
	Demand	500	300	

$u_1 + v_2 = 6 = v_2$

$u_2 + v_1 = 5 \quad 5$

$u_3 + v_1 = 7 \quad 7$

$u_2 + u_2 = 6 - 0$

a. Use the northwest corner rule to find an initial solution.
b. Use the stepping-stone method to find an optimal solution.

2. a. For Problem 1 use Vogel's approximation method to find an initial solution.
   b. Use the MODI method to evaluate all unassigned routes.

3. a. Construct an example of a transportation problem in which the northwest corner rule leads to a better initial feasible solution than Vogel's approximation method.
   b. For your example problem, find the initial feasible solution using both methods and show that the value of the solution obtained using the northwest corner rule is better.

4. Consider the following transportation problem.

		Destinations			
		Boston	Atlanta	Houston	Supply
	Detroit	5	2	3	100
Origins	St. Louis	8	4	3	300
	Denver	9	7	5	300
	Demand	300	200	200	

a. Use the northwest corner rule to find an initial solution.

b. Use the stepping-stone method to find an optimal solution.

c. How would the optimal solution change if we want to ship 100 units on the Detroit-Atlanta route?

5. a. Use Vogel's approximation method to find an initial solution to Problem 4.

b. Use the MODI method to find an optimal solution.

c. Compare the northwest corner rule and Vogel's approximation method in terms of their relative advantages.

6. Suppose that in Problem 4 a labor dispute temporarily eliminates the Denver-Boston and the St. Louis-Atlanta routes. How should the firm revise its shipping schedules in order to maintain a minimum total transportation cost solution? The transportation tableau with an M unit cost assigned to the unacceptable routes is as follows.

		Destinations			
		Boston	Atlanta	Houston	Supply
Origins	Detroit	5	2	3	100
	St. Louis	8	M	3	300
	Denver	M	7	5	300
	Demand	300	200	200	

What effect did the elimination of these two routes have on the firm's total transportation costs?

7. Consider the transportation tableau with the feasible solution shown below.

	D_1	D_2	D_3	Supply
O_1	6 100	7 50	9	150
O_2	4 100	4	3 150	250
O_3	6	5 100	4	100
Demand	200	150	150	

(handwritten annotations:)

$6 \quad 7 \quad 5$

$u_1 + v_3 = 9$

$u_2 + v_3 = 4$

$u_3 + v_1 = 6$

$u_3 + v_3 = 4$

$u_1 + v_1 = 6 = v_1 \; 6$

$u_1 + v_2 = 7 \quad v_2 = 7$

$u_2 + v_1 = 4 \quad u_2 = -2$

$u_2 + v_3 = 3 \quad v_3 = 5$

$u_3 + v_2 = 5 \quad u_3 = -2$

$u_3 + v_2$

Use the MODI method and the initial feasible solution given above to find the minimum cost solution to this problem.

8. Solve the following transportation problem.

	Destinations			
	D_1	D_2	D_3	Supply
O_1	1	3	4	200
O_2	2	6	8	500
O_3	2	5	7	300
Demand	200	100	400	

a. Identify any degenerate solutions that occur in your search for an optimal solution.

b. Since total supply (1000 units) exceeds total demand (700 units), which origins may consider alternate uses for their excess supply and still maintain a minimum total transportation cost solution?

9. Klein Chemicals, Inc., produces a special oil base material that is currently in short supply. Four of Klein's customers have already placed orders which in total exceed the combined capacity of Klein's two plants. Klein's management faces the problem of deciding how many units it should supply to each customer. Since the four customers are in different industries, the pricing structure enables different prices to be charged to different customers. However, slightly different production costs at the two plants and varying transportation costs between the plants and customers make a "sell to the highest bidder" strategy unacceptable. After considering price, production costs, and transportation costs, Klein has established the following profit per unit for each plant–customer alternative.

		Customers		
Plant	D_1	D_2	D_3	D_4
Kokomo	$20	$17	$16	$16
Clarksville	$19	$15	$14	$17

The plant capacities and customer orders are as follows:

Plant Capacity		Orders	
Kokomo	5000 units	D_1	2000 units
Clarksville	3000 units	D_2	5000 units
		D_3	3000 units
		D_4	2000 units

How many units should each plant produce for each customer in order to *maximize* profits? Which customer demands will not be met?

10. Sound Electronics, Inc., produces a battery-operated tape recorder at plants located in Martinsville, North Carolina; Plymouth, New York; and Franklin, Missouri. The unit transportation cost for shipments from the three plants to distribution centers in Chicago, Dallas, and New York are as follows.

	To		
From	Chicago	Dallas	New York
Martinsville	1.45	1.60	1.40
Plymouth	1.10	2.25	0.60
Franklin	1.20	1.20	1.80

After considering transportation costs, management has decided that under no circumstances will it use the Plymouth-Dallas route. The plant capacities and distributor orders for the next month are as follows.

Plant	Capacity (units)	Distributor	Orders (units)
Martinsville	400	Chicago	400
Plymouth	600	Dallas	400
Franklin	300	New York	400

Because of different wage scales at the three plants, the unit production cost varies from plant to plant. If the costs are $29.50/unit at Martinsville, $31.20/unit at Plymouth, and $30.35 at Franklin, find the production and distribution plan that minimizes production and transportation costs.

11. The Ace Manufacturing Company has orders for three similar products.

Product	Orders (units)
A	500
B	1200
C	2000

Three machines are available for the manufacturing operations. All three machines can produce all the products at the same production rate. However, because of varying defect percentages of each product on each machine, the unit costs of the products vary depending upon the machine used. Machine capacities for the next week and the unit costs are as follows.

Machine	Capacity (units)
I	1500
II	1500
III	1000

		Products		
		A	B	C
	I	0.50	0.60	0.55
Machine	II	0.70	0.60	0.65
	III	0.60	0.45	0.50

a. Use the transportation model to develop the minimum cost production schedule for the products and machines.

b. Do alternate optimal production schedules exist? If the production manager would like the minimum cost schedule to have the smallest possible number of changeovers of products on machines, which solution would you recommend?

12. Consider the following transportation problem:

Origins		Destinations A	B	C	Supply
	1	10	15	9	1
	2	9	18	5	1
	3	6	14	3	1
Demand		1	1	1	

a. Use the northwest corner rule to find an initial solution.
b. Use the MODI method to find an optimal solution.
c. Could this problem have been solved using the assignment algorithm of Chapter 12?

397

14

Project Scheduling: PERT/CPM

In many situations, managers assume the responsibility for planning, scheduling, and controlling projects that involve numerous separate jobs or tasks performed by a variety of departments, individuals, and so forth. Often these projects are so large and/or so complex that the manager cannot possibly keep all the information pertaining to the plan, schedule, and progress of the project in his head. In these situations the techniques of PERT (Program Evaluation and Review Technique) and CPM (Critical Path Method) have proved to be extremely valuable in assisting managers in carrying out their project management responsibilities.

PERT and CPM have been used to plan, schedule, and control a wide variety of projects such as

1. research and development of new products and processes
2. construction of plants, buildings, highways, and the like
3. maintenance of large and complex equipment
4. design and installation of new systems such as manufacturing, computers, accounting, and so forth.

In projects such as these, PERT and CPM are used to manage the *time* aspect of the project. That is, the purpose of PERT and CPM is to see that all components of the project are completed as scheduled in order to ensure that the entire project will be completed on time. In addition, a modification of the PERT and CPM techniques, referred to as PERT/Cost, can be used to plan, schedule, and control the *cost* associated with the project. Specifically, PERT/Cost provides the additional information necessary to see that all components of the project stay within their allotted costs and that the entire project is completed within its budget. Let us begin our discussion of the PERT, CPM, and PERT/Cost project management techniques by seeing how PERT can be used to assist a project manager.

14.1 PERT

PERT was developed in the late 1950s for planning, scheduling, and controlling the Polaris missile project. Since then, it has been used to assist managers in the planning, scheduling, and controlling of a wide variety of projects consisting of numerous specific jobs or *activities,* each of which must be completed in order to complete the entire project. A critical task for the project manager in such situations is to schedule and coordinate the activities so that the entire project is completed on time. A complicating factor in carrying out this task is the interdependence of the activities; for example, some activities depend upon the completion of other activities before they can even be started. When we realize that projects can have as many as several thousand specific activities, we see why project managers look for procedures that will help them answer questions such as the following:

1. What is the expected project completion date?
2. What is the scheduled start and completion date for each specific activity?
3. Which activities are "critical" and must be completed *exactly* as scheduled in order to keep the project on schedule?
4. How long can "noncritical" activities be delayed before they cause a delay in the total project?

As you will see, PERT can be used to answer the above questions.

An Example—The Daugherty Porta-Vac Project

The H. S. Daugherty Company has manufactured industrial vacuum cleaning systems for a number of years. Recently a member of the company's new product research team submitted a report suggesting the company consider manufacturing a cordless vacuum cleaner that could be powered by a rechargeable battery. The vacuum cleaner, referred to as a Porta-Vac, could be used for light industrial cleaning and could contribute to Daugherty's expansion into the household market. Hopefully the new product could be manufactured at a reasonable cost, and its portability and no-cord convenience would make it extremely attractive.

Daugherty's top management would like to initiate a project to study the feasibility of proceeding with the Porta-Vac idea. The result of the feasibility project will be a report recommending the action to be taken for the new product. In order to complete this project, we will need information from the firm's research and development, product testing, manufacturing, cost estimating, and market research groups. How long do you think this feasibility study project will take? When should we tell the product testing group to schedule their work? Obviously, you do not have enough information to answer these questions at this time. In the following discussion we will learn how PERT can be used to answer these questions and provide the complete schedule and control information for the project.

Developing the PERT Network

The first step in the PERT project scheduling process is to determine all specific activities that make up the project. The list of activities for this Porta-Vac feasibility project is shown in Table 14.1. The development of this list is a key step in the project. Since we will be planning the entire project and estimating the project completion date based on our list of activities, poor planning and omissions of activities will be disastrous and lead to completely inaccurate schedules. We will assume that careful planning of the Porta-Vac project has been completed and that Table 14.1 lists all project activities.

Note that Table 14.1 contains additional information in the column labeled "immediate predecessors." Recall that we mentioned earlier that the project activities have interdependencies; thus, in order to plan, schedule, and control the project, we will need information about the relationships among the activities. One way to obtain this information is to determine the *immediate predecessors* for each activity, where the immediate predecessors are all the activities that must immediately precede the given activity. For example, the market survey (activity H) shows activities B and E as immediate predecessors. This simply means that planning the market research (activity B) and preparing the marketing brochure (activity E) must be completed before the market survey can be started.

In Figure 14.1 we have drawn a picture that not only depicts the activities listed in Table 14.1 but also portrays the predecessor relationships among the

TABLE 14.1   Activity List for the Daugherty Porta-Vac Project

Activity	Description	Immediate Predecessors
A	R & D product design	—
B	Plan market research	—
C	Routing (manufacturing engineering)	A
D	Build prototype model	A
E	Prepare marketing brochure	A
F	Cost estimates (industrial engineering)	C
G	Preliminary product testing	D
H	Market survey	B, E
I	Pricing and forecast report	H
J	Final report	F, G, I

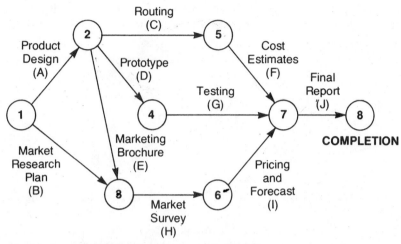

FIGURE 14.1 *PERT Network of the Porta-Vac Project*

activities. We refer to this graphical representation as the *PERT network* for the Porta-Vac project. As you can see, a PERT network consists of numbered circles which are interconnected by several arrows. In general network terminology, the circles are called *nodes* and the arrows connecting the nodes are called *branches* or *arcs*. In a PERT network the arrows that connect the circles correspond to the activities in the project, and the nodes indicate the start or finish of the activities. When *all* the activities leading into a node have been completed, the node is referred to as an *event*. Thus the circle containing the number 3, referred to in network terms as node 3, can be technically referred to as an event when activities B and E are completed. Thus, an event denotes a point in time which corresponds to the completion of a specific phase of the project.

While the case did not arise in the Porta-Vac PERT network, you may encounter other PERT networks in which two activities appear to have the same starting and ending nodes. Consider the following portion of a project activity table.

Activity	Immediate Predecessors
A	–
B	–
C	A
D	A, B

401

Note that activities C and D both have a predecessor in common. If we were to attempt to draw a PERT network corresponding to this situation, we might obtain the following network.

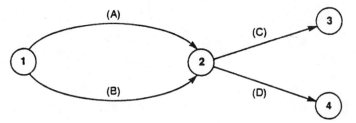

The problem here is that this network shows both A and B as immediate predecessors of activity C. This problem arises because activities A and B appear to have the same starting and ending nodes. A PERT network avoids this situation by inserting a *dummy activity* so that the network can be drawn as follows.

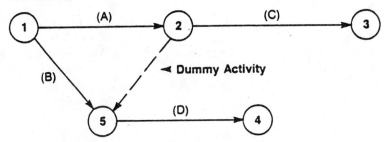

The dummy activity, illustrated by a dashed arrow, enables us to draw the PERT network with the proper precedence relations; by using a dummy activity, we can properly reflect that activity C cannot begin until A is completed and that activity D cannot begin until both A and B are completed. Such dummy activities will carry zero completion times in our analysis of the PERT network.

Activity Times

Once we have established a PERT network for our project, we will need information on the time required to complete each activity. This information will be used in the calculation of the duration of the entire project and the scheduling of the specific activities. Accurate activity time estimates are essential for successful project management. Errors in activity time estimates will cause errors in scheduling and project completion date projections.

For repeat projects such as construction and/or maintenance projects, managers may have the experience and historical data necessary to provide accurate activity time estimates. However, for new or unique projects, activity time estimation may be significantly more difficult. In fact, in many cases activity times are uncertain and perhaps best described by a range of possible values rather than one specific activity time estimate. In these instances the uncertain activity times are treated as random variables with associated probability distributions and the PERT procedure is used to provide probability statements about the project meeting specific completion dates.

In order to incorporate uncertain activity times into the PERT network model, we will need to obtain three time estimates for each activity. The three estimates are:

optimistic time a—the activity time if everything progresses in an *ideal* manner

most probable time m—the most likely activity time under normal conditions

pessimistic time b—the activity time if we encounter significant breakdowns and/or delays.

The three estimates enable the manager to make his best guess of the most likely activity time and then express his uncertainty by providing estimates ranging from the best (optimistic) possible time to the worst (pessimistic) possible time.

As an illustration of the PERT procedure with uncertain activity times, let us consider the optimistic, most probable, and pessimistic time estimates for the Porta-Vac activities as presented in Table 14.2.

TABLE 14.2 Optimistic, Most Probable, and Pessimistic Activity Time Estimates in Weeks for the Porta-Vac Project

Activity	Optimistic a	Most Probable m	Pessimistic b
A	4	5	12
B	1	1.5	5
C	2	3	4
D	3	4	11
E	2	3	4
F	1.5	2	2.5
G	1.5	3	4.5
H	2.5	3.5	7.5
I	1.5	2	2.5
J	1	2	3

Using the product design activity A as an example, we see that management estimates that this activity will require from 4 weeks (optimistic) to 12 weeks (pessimistic) to complete with the most likely time 5 weeks. If the activity could be repeated a large number of times, what would be the average time for the activity? The PERT procedure estimates this average or *expected time t* from the following formula:

$$t = \frac{a + 4m + b}{6} \tag{14.1}$$

For activity A we have an estimated average or expected completion time of

$$t = \frac{4 + 4(5) + 12}{6} = \frac{36}{6} = 6 \text{ weeks.}$$

Equation (14.1) is based on the PERT assumption that the uncertain activity times are best described by a *beta probability distribution;* that is, equation (14.1) provides the average time for the special case of a beta probability distribution as the best description of the variability in activity times. This distribution assumption, which was judged to be reasonable by the developers of PERT, provides the time distribution for activity A as shown in Figure 14.2.

For uncertain activity times we can use the common statistical measure of the *variance* to describe the dispersion or variation in the activity time values. In PERT we compute the variance of the activity times from the following formula.[1]

$$\text{variance of activity time} = \left(\frac{b - a}{6}\right)^2 \tag{14.2}$$

As you can see, the difference between the pessimistic *b* and optimistic *a* time estimates greatly affects the value of the variance. With large differences in these two values, management has a high degree of uncertainty in the activity time. Accordingly, the variance given by equation (14.2) will be large.

Referring to activity A we see that the measure of uncertainty, that is, the variance, of this activity, denoted as σ_A^2, is

$$\sigma_A^2 = \left(\frac{12 - 4}{6}\right)^2 = \left(\frac{8}{6}\right)^2 = 1.78.$$

The expected times and variances for the Porta-Vac activities, as computed using the data in Table 14.2 and equations (14.1) and (14.2) are given in Table 14.3.

[1] The variance equation is based on the notion that a standard deviation is approximately 1/6 of the difference between the extreme values of the distribution: $(b - a)/6$. The variance is simply the square of the standard deviation.

404

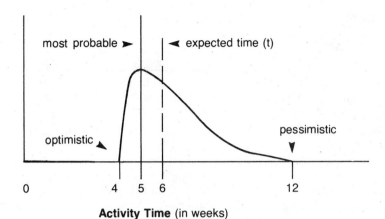

Activity Time (in weeks)

*FIGURE 14.2   Activity Time Distribution for the Product Design
Activity A of the Porta-Vac Project*

The Critical Path Calculation

Once we have the PERT network and the expected activity times, we are
ready to proceed with the calculations necessary to determine the expected
project completion date and a detailed activity schedule. In our initial calculations we will treat the expected activity time (Table 14.3) as the *fixed length*

*TABLE 14.3   Expected Times and Variances for the Porta-
Vac Activities*

Activity	Expected Time t (in weeks)	Variance
A	6	1.78
B	2	0.44
C	3	0.11
D	5	1.78
E	3	0.11
F	2	0.03
G	3	0.25
H	4	0.69
I	2	0.03
J	2	0.11
Total	32	

or *known duration* of each activity. Later we will analyze the effect of activity time variability.

While Table 14.3 indicates that the total expected time to complete all the work for the Porta-Vac project is 32 weeks, we can see from the network (Figure 14.1) that several of the activities can be conducted simultaneously (A and B, for example). Being able to work on two or more activities simultaneously will have the effect of making the total project completion time shorter than 32 weeks. However, the desired project completion time information is not directly available from the data in Table 14.3.

In order to arrive at a project duration estimate we will have to analyze the network and determine what is called its critical path. A *path* is a sequence of connected activities that lead from the starting node (1) to the completion node (8). The connected activities defined by nodes 1-2-5-7-8 form a path consisting of activities, A, C, F, and J. Nodes 1-2-4-7-8 define the path associated with activities A, D, G, and J. Since *all* paths must be traversed in order to complete the project, we need to analyze the amount of time the various paths require. In particular, we will be interested in the longest path through the network. Since all other paths are shorter in duration, the longest path demermines the expected total time or expected duration of the project. If activities on the longest path are delayed, the entire project will be delayed. Thus the longest path activities are the *critical activities* of the project and the longest path is called the *critical path* of the network. If managers wish to reduce the total project time, they will have to reduce the length of the critical path by shortening the duration of the critical activities. The following discussion presents a step-by-step procedure or algorithm for finding the critical path of a PERT network.

Starting at the network's origin (node 1) and using a starting time of 0, compute an *earliest start* and *earliest finish* time for each activity in the network. Write the earliest start time at the beginning of the activity and the earliest finish time at the end of the activity. Using activity A as an example, we have

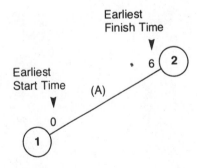

Let

ES = earliest start time
EF = earliest finish time
  t = expected activity completion time.

The following expression can be used to find the earliest finish time for a given activity:

$$EF = ES + t. \tag{14.3}$$

Given $ES = 0$ and $t = 6$ for activity A, the earliest finish time was found to be $EF = 0 + 6 = 6$.

Recall that a PERT event does not occur until all activities leading into the node have been completed. Activities leaving a node cannot be started until all preceding activities have been completed and the event has occurred. This logic leads to the following rule for determining earliest start times of activities.

Earliest Start Time Rule: The earliest start time for an activity leaving a particular node is equal to the *largest* value of the earliest finish times for all activities entering the node.

Applying this rule to the portion of the network involving nodes 1, 2, 3, and 6, we obtain the following:

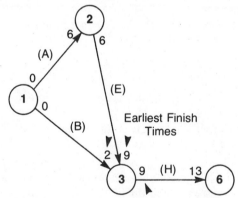

Note: Event 3 occurs at time 9

Earliest start time for activity H

Proceeding in a *forward pass* through the network, we can establish first an earliest start and then an earliest finish time for each activity. The Porta-Vac network with ES and EF values is shown in Figure 14.3.

Note that the earliest finish time for activity J, the last activity, is 17 weeks. Thus the earliest completion time for the entire project is 17 weeks.

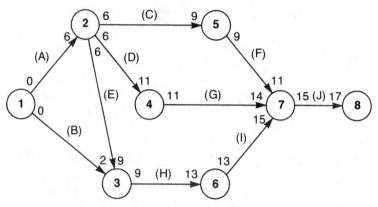

FIGURE 14.3 *Earliest Start and Earliest Finish Activity Times for the Porta-Vac Network*

We now continue our algorithm for finding the critical path by making a *backward pass* calculation. Starting at the completion point (node 8) and using a latest finish time of 17 for activity J, we trace back through the network computing a latest start and latest finish time for each activity.

Letting

LS = latest starting time
LF = latest finishing time,

the following expression can be used to find the latest start time for a given activity:

$$LS = LF - t. \tag{14.4}$$

Given an LF = 17 and $t = 2$ for activity J, the latest start time for this activity can be computed as LS = $17 - 2 = 15$.

The following rule is necessary in order to determine the latest finish time for any activity in the network.

Latest Finish Time Rule: The latest finish time for an activity entering a particular node is equal to the *smallest* value of the latest starting times for all activities leaving the node.

Logically the above rule states that the latest time an activity can be finished is equal to the earliest (smallest) value for the latest start time of following activities. The complete network with the LS and LF backward pass calculations is shown in Figure 14.4.

By comparing the earliest start time and the latest start time (or earliest finish and latest finish times) for each activity, we can find the amount of slack or free time associated with each of the activities. *Slack* is defined as

408

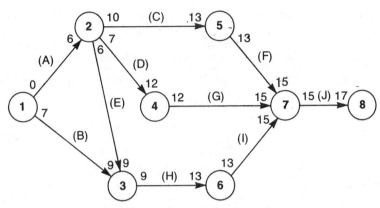

FIGURE 14.4 Latest Start and Latest Finish Activity Times
for the Porta-Vac Project

the length of time an activity can be delayed without affecting the completion date for the project. Using

$$slack = LS - ES = LF - EF \qquad (14.5)$$

we see that the slack associated with activity C is $LS - ES = 10 - 6 = 4$ weeks. This means that the routing activity can be delayed up to 4 weeks (start anywhere between weeks 6 and 10), and the project can still be completed in 17 weeks. This activity is not a critical activity and is not part of the critical path.

Using equation (14.5) we see that the slack associated with activity E is $6 - 6 = 0$. Thus the marketing brochure activity must be held to the 6-week start time schedule. This activity cannot be delayed without affecting the entire project. Thus activity E is a critical activity and is on the critical path. In general, the critical path activities are the activities with zero slack. An activity schedule shown in Table 14.4 is helpful in identifying the critical path. We see that the critical path for the Porta-Vac Project is made up of activities A, E, H, I, and J. In addition, Table 14.4 shows the slack or delay that can be tolerated for the noncritical activities before they will cause a project delay.

Variability in the Project Completion Date

While during the critical path calculations we treated the activity times as fixed at their expected values, we are now ready to consider the uncertainty in the activity times and determine the effect this uncertainty or variability has on the project completion date. Recall that the critical path determines the duration of the entire project. For the Porta-Vac project the critical path of A-E-H-I-J resulted in an expected project completion time of 17 weeks.

TABLE 14.4   Activity Schedule in Weeks for the Porta-Vac Project

Activity	Earliest Start	Latest Start	Earliest Finish	Latest Finish	Slack (LS−ES)	Critical Path
A	0	0	6	6	0	Yes
B	0	7	2	9	7	
C	6	10	9	13	4	
D	6	7	11	12	1	
E	6	6	9	9	0	Yes
F	9	13	11	15	4	
G	11	12	14	15	1	
H	9	9	13	13	0	Yes
I	13	13	15	15	0	Yes
J	15	15	17	17	0	Yes

Just as the critical path activities govern the expected project completion date, variation in critical path activities can cause significant variation in the completion date. Variation in noncritical path activities will ordinarily have no effect on the project completion date because of the slack time associated with these activities. However, if a noncritical activity were delayed long enough to expend all of its slack time, then that activity would become part of a new critical path, and further delays would extend the project completion date. Variability leading to a longer total time for the critical path activities will always extend the project completion date. On the other hand, variability in critical path activities resulting in a shorter critical path will enable an earlier than expected completion date, unless the activity times on the other paths become critical. The PERT procedure uses the variance in the critical path activities to determine the variance in the project completion date.

If we let T denote the project duration, then T, which is determined by the critical activities A-E-H-I-J in the Porta-Vac problem, has the expected value of

$$T = t_A + t_E + t_H + t_I + t_J$$
$$= 6 + 3 + 4 + 2 + 2 = 17 \text{ weeks.}$$

Similarly the variance in the project duration is given by the sum of the variance of the critical path activities. Thus the project time variance, σ^2, for the Porta-Vac project is given by

$$\sigma^2 = \sigma_A^2 + \sigma_E^2 + \sigma_H^2 + \sigma_I^2 + \sigma_J^2$$
$$= 1.78 + 0.11 + 0.69 + 0.03 + 0.11 = 2.72.$$

This formula is based on the assumption that all the activity times are independent. If two or more activities are dependent, the formula only provides an approximation to the variance of the project completion time. The closer the activities are to being independent, the better the approximation.

Since we know that the standard deviation is the square root of the variance, we can compute the standard deviation, σ, for the Porta-Vac project completion time as follows:

$$\sigma = \sqrt{\sigma^2} = \sqrt{2.72} = 1.65.$$

A final assumption of PERT, that the distribution of the project completion time T follows a normal or bell-shaped distribution,[2] allows us to draw the distribution shown in Figure 14.5.

With this distribution we can compute the probability of meeting a specified project completion date. For example, suppose that management has allotted 20 weeks for the Porta-Vac project. While we expect completion in 17 weeks, what is the probability that we will meet the 20-week deadline? Using the normal distribution from Figure 14.5, we are asking for the probability that $T \leq 20$. This is shown graphically in Figure 14.6.

By computing the z value of $(20-17)/1.65 = 1.82$ and using the tables for the normal distribution (see Appendix B), we see that the probability of meeting the deadline is $0.4656 + 0.5000 = 0.9656$. Thus, while activity time variability may cause the project to exceed the 17-week expected duration,

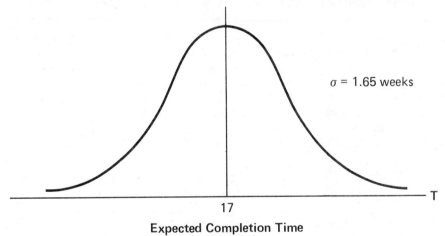

$\sigma = 1.65$ weeks

17

**Expected Completion Time
(17 weeks)**

*FIGURE 14.5 PERT Normal Distribution of the Project
Completion Time for the Porta-Vac Project*

---

[2] The use of the normal distribution is based on the central limit theorem, which indicates that the sum of independent activity times follows a normal distribution as the number of activities becomes large.

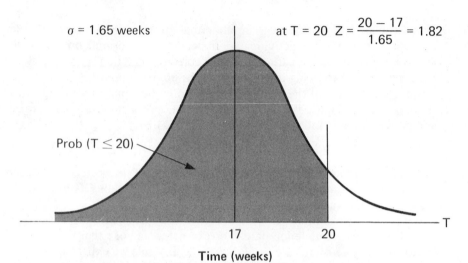

$\sigma = 1.65$ weeks   at T = 20 $Z = \dfrac{20 - 17}{1.65} = 1.82$

Prob (T ≤ 20)

17   20

Time (weeks)

FIGURE 14.6 *Probability of a Porta-Vac Project Completion*
Date Prior to the 20-Week Deadline

there is an excellent chance that the project will be completed before the 20-week deadline. Similar probability calculations can be made for other project deadline possibilities.

Summary of PERT Procedure

Before discussing the contributions of PERT, let us briefly review the process of analyzing a project using the PERT procedure. In analyzing *any* project using PERT, we perform the following steps.

Step 1: Develop a list of activities that make up the project, including immediate predecessors.

Step 2: Draw a PERT network corresponding to the activity list developed in Step 1.

Step 3: Estimate the expected activity time and the variance for each activity.

Step 4: Using the expected activity time estimates, determine the earliest start time and the earliest finish time for each activity; the earliest finish time for the complete project corresponds to the earliest finish time for the last activity.

Step 5: After determining the latest start time and the latest finish time for each activity, compute the slack associated with each activity; the critical path activities are the activities with zero slack.

Step 6: Use the variability in the critical path activity times to estimate the variability of the project completion date; then, using the normal distribution, compute the probability of meeting a specified completion date.

412

Contributions of PERT

At the beginning of this section we stated that project managers look for procedures that will help them answer many important questions regarding the planning and controlling of projects. Let us reconsider these questions in light of the information our PERT analysis has provided to assist management in planning controlling the Porta-Vac project.

1. What is the expected project completion date?
    Answer: PERT has shown management that the expected project duration is 17 weeks.
2. What is the scheduled start and completion date for each specific activity?
    Answer: PERT has provided management with a detailed activity schedule that shows the earliest start, latest start, earliest finish, and latest finish for each activity (Table 14.4).
3. Which activities are "critical" and must be completed *exactly* as scheduled in order to keep the project on schedule?
    Answer: PERT has provided management with the critical activities A-E-H-I-J.
4. How long can "noncritical" activities be delayed before they cause a delay in the total project?
    Answer: The detailed activity schedule (Table 14.4) shows management the slack time available for each activity.

In addition to the above information, management has also been provided with information about the probability of meeting a specific deadline.

In the management of any project, the above information is important and valuable. While larger projects may substantially increase the time required to draw the PERT network and to make the necessary calculations, the PERT procedure and contributions in the larger projects are identical to those observed in the Porta-Vac project. Furthermore, computer packages currently exist that carry out the steps of the PERT procedure, thus relieving the applications analyst from having to carry out the details of the technique using hand calculation procedures.

The PERT procedure discussed in this section has been based on using three estimates of completion times for an activity in order to arrive at an expected activity time. This procedure has enabled us to make the contributions listed above. In some cases a project manager may only wish to provide a single estimate of the expected activity times. In these situations, PERT is still applicable. However, we will be unable to prepare an analysis of the variability in activity times unless the manager can also provide direct estimates of the activity time variances.

413

14.2 CPM

CPM (Critical Path Method) is a network-based procedure developed to assist in planning, scheduling, and controlling multiactivity projects. While similar to PERT in many respects, CPM provides the important capability of allowing the project manager to allocate additional resources to critical activities so that the critical path and thus the project duration can be shortened. CPM, however, uses only a single estimate of activity times and thus does not consider the effects of uncertainty or variability in the activity times. Because of the single activity time estimates, CPM is perhaps most applicable to repeating or recurring projects where experience and historical data provide good estimates of actual activity times. Projects involving construction and maintenance programs have been typical areas for CPM project management applications.

In order to illustrate CPM, let us consider the simple CPM network shown in Figure 14.7.

Actually this network is identical to the PERT-type networks in that the arcs represent the activities or work to be performed, and the nodes represent the activity starting and finishing points. Assume that the network in Figure 14.7 refers to the five activities of a major overhaul and maintenance project for a two-machine manufacturing system. The activities and estimated completion times are presented in Table 14.5.

Critical path calculations for a CPM network are identical to the procedures we used to find the critical path of a PERT network. Making the forward pass and backward pass calculations, we can obtain the activity schedule shown in Table 14.6. As you can see, the zero slack times and thus the critical path are associated with activities A-B-E or nodes 1-2-4-5. The length of the critical path and thus the project is 12 days.

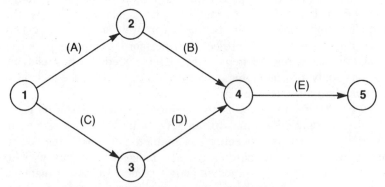

FIGURE 14.7 CPM Network of a Two-Machine Maintenance Project

TABLE 14.5 *Activity List for a Two-Machine Maintenance Project*

Activity	Description	Expected Time (in days)
A	Overhaul machine I	7
B	Adjust machine I	3
C	Overhaul machine II	6
D	Adjust machine II	3
E	Test system	2

Crash Capabilities of CPM

Now suppose that the current production levels make it imperative for the maintenance project to be completed within 2 weeks or 10 working days. By looking at the length of the critical path of the network (12 days), we realize that it is impossible to meet the project completion date unless we can shorten selected activity times. This shortening of activity times, which usually can be achieved by adding resources such as manpower or overtime, is referred to as *crashing* the activity times. However, since the added resources associated with crashing activity times usually result in added project costs, we will want to identify the least cost activities to crash and then crash only the amount necessary to meet the desired project completion date.

In order to determine just where and how much to crash activity times, we will need information on how much each activity can be crashed and how

TABLE 14.6 *Activity Schedule for the Maintenance Project*

Activity	Earliest Start	Latest Start	Earliest Finish	Latest Finish	Slack (LS−ES)	Critical Path
A	0	0	7	7	0	Yes
B	7	7	10	10	0	Yes
C	0	1	6	7	1	
D	6	7	9	10	1	
E	10	10	12	12	0	Yes

much the crashing process costs. Possibly the best way to accomplish this is to ask management for the following information on each activity:

1. Estimated activity cost under the normal or expected activity time.
2. Activity completion time under maximum crashing (that is, shortest possible activity time)
3. Estimated activity cost under maximum crashing.

Let

τ = normal activity time
τ' = crashed activity time (at maximum crashing)
C_n = normal activity cost
C_c = crashed activity cost (at maximum crashing).

We can compute the *maximum* possible activity time reduction M due to crashing as follows:

$$M = \tau - \tau'. \tag{14.6}$$

On a per unit time basis (for example, per day), the crashing cost K for each activity is given by

$$K = \frac{C_c - C_n}{M}. \tag{14.7}$$

For example, if activity A has a normal activity time of 7 days at a cost of $500 and a maximum crash activity time of 4 days at a cost of $800, we have $\tau = 7$, $\tau' = 4$, $C_n = 500$, and $C_c = 800$. Thus using equations (14.6) and (14.7) we see that activity A can be crashed a maximum of

$$M_A = 7 - 4 = 3 \text{ days}$$

at a crashing cost of

$$K_A = \frac{800 - 500}{3} = \frac{300}{3} = \$100 \text{ per day.}$$

CPM makes the assumption that any portion or fraction of the activity crash time can be achieved for a corresponding portion of the activity crashing cost. For example, if we decided to crash activity A by only $1\frac{1}{2}$ days, CPM assumes that this can be accomplished with an added cost of $1\frac{1}{2}(\$100) = \$150$, which results in a total activity cost of $\$500 + \$150 = \$650$. Figure 14.8 shows the graph of the time-cost reltionship for activity A.

The complete normal and crash activity data for our example project are given in Table 14.7.

Now the question is, which activities would you crash and how much should these activities be crashed in order to meet the 10-day project completion deadline with a minimum cost? Your first reaction to this question is possibly to consider crashing the critical path activities, A, B, or E. Since

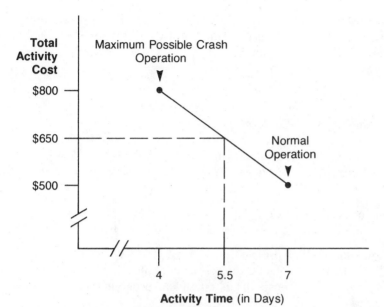

FIGURE 14.8   Time–Cost Relationship for Activity A

activity A has the lowest crashing costs of the three, crashing this activity by 2 days will reduce a A-B-E path to the desired 10 days. While this is correct, be careful, because as you crash the current critical path activities, other paths may become critical. Thus you will need to check the critical path in the revised network and perhaps either identify additional activities to crash or modify your initial crashing decision. Although you may be able to use this trial-and-error approach to making crashing decisions in a small net-

TABLE 14.7   Normal and Crash Activity Data for the Maintenance Project

Activity	Normal Time τ	Crash Time τ	Total Normal Cost C_n	Total Crash Cost C_c	Maximum Crash Days $(M=\tau-\tau')$	Crash Cost per Day $K = \dfrac{C_c-C_n}{M}$
A	7	4	$500	$800	3	$100
B	3	2	$200	$350	1	$150
C	6	4	$500	$900	2	$200
D	3	1	$200	$500	2	$150
E	2	1	$300	$550	1	$250
			$1700	$3100		

417

work, in larger CPM networks you will need a mathematical procedure in order to arrive at the optimal decision. The following discussion shows how linear programming can be used to solve the CPM network crashing problem.

A Linear Programming Model of CPM

While several solution procedures and variations exist for the CPM crashing procedure, the following linear programming model is one approach used to analyze CPM networks. First we define the decision variables. Let

x_i = time of occurrence of event i, i = 1, 2, 3, 4, 5
y_j = amount of crash time used for activity j, j = A, B, C, D, or E.

Since the total normal time project cost is fixed at \$1700 (see Table 14.7), we can minimize the total project cost (normal cost plus crash cost) simply by minimizing the crashing costs. Thus our linear programming objective function becomes

$$\min \sum_j K_j y_j \tag{14.8}$$

or

$$\min \quad 100y_A + 150y_B + 200y_C + 150y_D + 250y_E \tag{14.9}$$

where K_j is the crash cost for activity j, j = A, B, C, D, E on a per unit time basis.[3]

The constraints on the model involve describing the network, limiting the activity crash times, and meeting the project completion date. Of these, constraints used to describe the network are perhaps the most difficult. These constraints are based on the following conditions.

1. The time of occurrence of event i (x_i) must be greater than or equal to the activity completion time for all activities leading into the node or event.
2. An activity start time is equal to the occurrence time of its preceding node or event.
3. An activity time is equal to its normal time less the length of time it is crashed.

Using an event occurrence time of zero at node 1 ($x_1 = 0$), we can create the following set of network description constraints:

---

[3] Note that the x_j variables indicating event occurrences do not result in costs; thus, they have zero coefficients in the objective function.

Event 2:

$$x_2 \geq \tau_A - y_A + 0$$

Occurrence time for event 2 ... Actual time for activity A ... Start time for activity A ($x_1 = 0$)

$$x_2 \geq 7 - y_A$$

or

$$x_2 + y_A \geq 7. \tag{14.10}$$

Event 3:

$$x_3 > \tau_c - y_c + 0$$
$$x_3 + y_c \geq 6. \tag{14.11}$$

Since two activities enter event or node 4, we have the following two constraints:

Event 4:

$$x_4 \geq \tau_B - y_B + x_2$$
$$x_4 \geq \tau_D - y_D + x_3 \tag{14.12}$$

or

$$-x_2 + x_4 + y_B \geq 3$$
$$-x_3 + x_4 + y_D \geq 3. \tag{14.13}$$

Event 5:

$$x_5 \geq \tau_E - y_E + x_4$$

or

$$-x_4 + x_5 + y_E \geq 2. \tag{14.14}$$

The five constraints (8.10)–(8.14) are necessary to describe our CPM network.

The maximum allowable crash time constraints are

$$y_A \leq 3 \tag{14.15}$$
$$y_B \leq 1 \tag{14.16}$$
$$y_c \leq 2 \tag{14.17}$$
$$y_D \leq 2 \tag{14.18}$$
$$y_E \leq 1 \tag{14.19}$$

and the project completion date provides another constraint:

$$x_5 \leq 10. \tag{14.20}$$

Adding the nonnegativity restrictions and solving the above 9-variable

11-constraint [(14.10)–(14.20)] linear programming model provides the following solution:

$$x_2 = 5 \qquad y_A = 2$$
$$x_3 = 6 \qquad y_B = 0$$
$$x_4 = 8 \qquad y_C = 0$$
$$x_5 = 10 \qquad y_D = 1$$
$$\qquad\qquad y_E = 0$$

objective function = $350.

This solution requires that we crash activity A 2 days ($200) and activity D 1 day ($150). Thus the total crashed project cost is $1700 + $350 = $2050. The crashed activity schedule for our CPM project is given in Table 14.8. Note that all activities are critical.

Resolving the linear programming model with alternate project completion dates [constraint (14.20)] will show the project manager the costs associated with crashing the project to meet alternate deadlines.

Due to the substantial formulation and computational effort associated with scheduling and controlling large projects, most applications of PERT and CPM involve the use of canned computer programs developed to perform the appropriate network analysis.

14.3 PERT/COST

As you have seen, PERT and CPM concentrate on the *time* aspect of a project and provide information which can be used to schedule and control individual activities so that the entire project is completed on time. While project time and the meeting of a scheduled completion date are primary considerations for almost every project, there are many situations in which the *cost* associated with the project is just as important as time. In this

TABLE 14.8 *Crashed Activity Schedule for the Maintenance Project*

Activity	Crashed Time	ES	LS	EF	LF	Slack
A	5	0	0	5	5	0
B	3	5	5	8	8	0
C	6	0	0	6	6	0
D	2	6	6	8	8	0
E	2	8	8	10	10	0

section, we show how the PERT/Cost project management technique can be used to help plan, schedule, and control project costs. The ultimate objective of a PERT/Cost system is to provide information which can be used to maintain project costs within a specified budget. Although the cost control technique we will describe can be applied to either a PERT or CPM network, it is generally referred to as *PERT/Cost*.

Planning and Scheduling Project Costs

The budgeting process for a project usually involves identifying all costs associated with the project and then developing a schedule or forecast of when the costs are expected to occur. Then, at various stages of project completion, the actual project costs incurred can be compared to the scheduled or budgeted costs. If actual costs are exceeding budgeted costs, corrective action can hopefully be taken to keep costs within the budget.

The first step in a PERT/Cost control system is to break down the entire project into components that are convenient in terms of measuring and controlling costs. While a PERT and/or CPM network may already show detailed activities for the project, we may find that these activities are too detailed for conveniently controlling project costs. In such cases related activities which are under the control of one department, subcontractor, or the like are often grouped together to form what are referred to as *work packages*. By identifying costs of each work package, a project manager can use a PERT/Cost system to help plan, schedule, and control project costs.

Since the projects we discuss in this chapter have a relatively small number of activities, we will find it convenient to define work packages as having only one activity. Thus, in our discussion of the PERT/Cost technique, we will be treating each activity as a separate work package. Realize, however, that in large and complex projects, we would almost always group related activities so that a cost control system could be developed for a more reasonable number of work packages.

In order to illustrate the PERT/Cost technique, let us consider the research and development project network shown in Figure 14.9. We are assuming that each activity is an acceptable work package and that a detailed cost analysis has been made on an activity basis. The activity cost estimates, along with the expected activity times, are shown in Table 14.9. In using the PERT/Cost technique, we will be assuming that activities (work packages) are defined such that costs occur at a constant rate over the duration of the activity. For example, activity B, which shows an estimated cost of $30,000 and an expected 3-month duration, is assumed to have a cost rate of $30,000/3 = $10,000 per month. The cost rates for all activities are provided in Table 14.9. Note that the total estimated or budgeted cost for the project is $87,000.

421

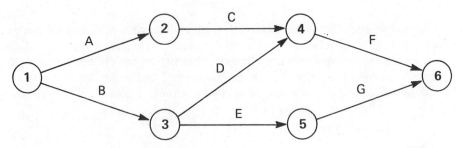

FIGURE 14.9   A Project Network

Using the expected activity times, we can compute the critical path for the project. A summary of the critical path calculations and the resulting activity schedule is shown in Table 14.10. Activities B, D, and F determine the critical path and provide an expected project duration of 8 months.

We are now ready to develop a budget for the project which will show when costs should occur during the 8-month project duration. First let us assume that all activities begin at their earliest possible starting date. Using the monthly activity cost rates shown in Table 14.9, we can prepare the month-by-month cost forecast as shown in Table 14.11. For example, using the earliest start date for activity A as 0, we expect activity A, which has a 2-month duration, to show a cost of $5000 in each of the first 2 months of the project. By similarly using the earliest starting date and monthly cost rate for each activity, we are able to complete Table 14.11 as shown. Note that by summing the costs in each column, we obtain the total cost anticipated for each month of the project. Finally, by accumulating the monthly costs, we can show the budgeted total cost schedule provided all activities are started at the *earliest* starting times. Table 14.12 shows the budgeted total cost schedule when all activities are started at the *latest* starting times.

If the project progresses on its PERT or CPM time schedule, each activity will be started somewhere between its earliest and latest starting times. This

TABLE 14.9   Activity Time and Cost Estimates

Activity	Expected Time (Months)	Budgeted or Estimated Cost	Budgeted Cost per Month
A	2	$10,000	$ 5,000
B	3	30,000	10,000
C	1	3,000	3,000
D	3	6,000	2,000
E	2	20,000	10,000
F	2	10,000	5,000
G	1	8,000	8,000

Total Project Budget = $87,000

TABLE 14.10 Activity Schedule

Activity	Earliest Start	Latest Start	Earliest Finish	Latest Finish	Slack	Critical Path
A	0	3	2	5	3	
B	0	0	3	3	0	Yes
C	2	5	3	6	3	
D	3	3	6	6	0	Yes
E	3	5	5	7	2	
F	6	6	8	8	0	Yes
G	5	7	6	8	2	

implies that the total project costs should occur at levels between the earliest start and latest start cost schedules. For example, using the data in Tables 14.11 and 14.12, we see that by month 3, total project costs should be between $30,000 (latest starting date schedule) and $43,000 (earliest starting date schedule). Thus, at month 3, a total project cost between $30,000 and $43,000 would be expected.

In Figure 14.10, we show the forecasted total project costs for both the earliest and latest starting time schedules. The shaded region between the two cost curves shows the possible budgets for the project. If the project manager is willing to commit activities to specific starting times, a specific project cost forecast or budget can be prepared. However, based on the above analysis, we know that such a budget will have to be in the feasible region shown in Figure 14.10.

TABLE 14.11 Budgeted Costs for an Earliest Starting
Date Schedule

Activity	Month 1	2	3	4	5	6	7	8
A	5	5						
B	10	10	10					
C			3					
D				2	2	2		
E				10	10			
F							5	5
G						8		
Monthly Cost	15	15	13	12	12	10	5	5
Total Project Cost	15	30	43	55.	67	77	82	87

(Costs are $ \times 10^3$)

423

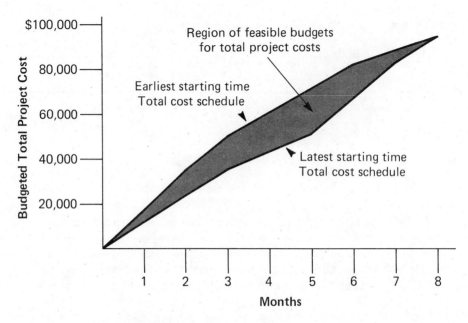

FIGURE 14.10 *Feasible Budgets for Total Project Costs*

TABLE 14.12 *Budgeted Costs for a Latest Starting Date Schedule*

Activity	1	2	3	Month 4	5	6	7	8
A				5	5			
B	10	10	10					
C						3		
D				2	2	2		
E						10	10	
F							5	5
G								8
Monthly Cost	10	10	10	7	7	15	15	13
Total Project Cost	10	20	30	37	44	59	74	87

(Costs are $ \times 10^3$)

Controlling Project Costs

The information that we have developed thus far is helpful in terms of planning and scheduling total project costs. However, if we are going to

424

have an effective cost control system, we will need to identify costs on a much more detailed basis. For example, information that the project's actual total cost is exceeding the budgeted total cost will be of little value unless we can identify the activity or group of activities that are causing the cost overruns.

The PERT/Cost system provides the desired cost control by budgeting and then recording actual costs on an activity (that is, work package) basis. Periodically throughout the project's duration, actual costs for all completed and in-process activities are compared to the appropriate budgeted costs. The project manager is then provided with up-to-date information on the cost status of each activity. If at any point in time actual costs exceed budgeted costs, we have a condition referred to as a cost overrun. On the other hand, if actual costs are less than the budgeted costs, we have a condition referred to as a cost underrun. By identifying the sources of cost overruns and underruns, the manager can take corrective action where necessary. The budgeted or estimated activity costs for the R&D project network of Figure 14.9 are shown again in Table 14.13.

Now at any point during the project's duration, the manager can use a PERT/Cost procedure to obtain an activity cost status report by collecting the following information for *each activity*.

1. Actual cost to date
2. Percent completion to date

While a PERT/Cost system will require a periodic—perhaps biweekly or monthly—collection of the above information, let us suppose we are at the end of the fourth month of the project and have the actual cost and percent completion data for each activity as shown in Table 14.14. This current status information shows that activities A and B have been completed, activities C, D, and E are in process, and activities F and G have not yet been started.

In order to prepare a cost status report, we will need to compute the value for all work completed to date. Let

V_i = value of work completed for activity i
p_i = percent completion for activity i
B_i = budget for activity i.

TABLE 14.13 *Activity Cost Estimates*

Activity	Budgeted Cost	Activity	Budgeted Cost
A	$10,000	E	$20,000
B	30,000	F	10,000
C	3,000	G	8,000
D	6,000		

425

TABLE 14.14 *Activity Cost and Percent Completion Data at the End of Month 4*

Activity	Actual Cost	% Completion
A	$12,000	100%
B	30,000	100%
C	1,000	50%
D	2,000	33%
E	10,000	25%
F	0	0
G	0	0

Total Actual Cost = $55,000

The following relationship is used to find the value of work completed for each activity.

$$V_i = \left(\frac{p_i}{100}\right) B_i. \tag{14.21}$$

For example, the values of work completed for activities A and C are as follows[4]:

$$V_A = (\tfrac{100}{100})(\$10,000) = \$10,000$$
$$V_C = (\tfrac{50}{100})(\$3000) = \$1500.$$

Cost overruns and cost underruns can now be found by comparing the actual cost of each activity with its appropriate budget value. Letting

AC_i = actual cost to date for activity i
D_i = difference in actual and budget value for activity i,

we have

$$D_i = AC_i - V_i. \tag{14.22}$$

A positive D_i indicates the activity has a cost *overrun,* while a negative D_i indicates a cost *underrun*. $D_i = 0$ indicates actual costs are in agreement with the budgeted costs.

For example,

$$D_A = AC_A - V_A = \$12,000 - \$10,000 = \$2000$$

shows that activity A, which has already been completed, has a $2000 cost overrun. However, activity C, with $D_C = \$1000 - \$1500 = -\$500$, is cur-

---

[4] Equation (14.21) and the succeeding calculations are based on the PERT/Cost assumption that activity costs occur at a constant rate over the duration of the activity. For details regarding this assumption see Wiest, J. D. and F. K. Levy, *A Management Guide to PERT/CPM*. Englewood Cliffs, N. J.: Prentice-Hall, 1969.

rently showing a cost underrun, or savings, of $500. A complete cost status report such as the one shown in Table 14.15 can now be prepared for the project manager.

This cost report shows the project manager that the costs to date are $6500 over the estimated or budgeted costs. On a percentage basis, we would say the project is experiencing a ($6500/$48,500) × 100 = 13.4% cost overrun, which for most projects is a serious situation. By checking each activity, we see that activities A and E are causing the cost overrun. Since activity A has been completed, its cost overrun cannot be corrected; however, activity E is in process and is only 25% complete. Thus, activity E should be reviewed immediately. Hopefully, corrective action can bring its actual costs closer to the budget. The manager may also want to consider cost reduction possibilities for activities C, D, F, and G in order to keep the total project cost within the budget.

While the PERT/Cost procedure described above can be an effective cost control system, it is not without possible drawbacks and implementation problems. First, the activity-by-activity cost recording system can require significant clerical effort, especially for firms with large and/or numerous projects. Thus the personnel and other costs associated with maintaining a PERT/Cost system may offset some of the advantages. Second, questions can arise as to how costs should be allocated to activities or work packages. Overhead, indirect, and even material costs can cause cost allocations and measurement problems. Third, and perhaps most critical, is the fact that PERT/Cost requires a system of cost recording and control that is significantly different from most cost accounting systems. Firms using departments or other organizational units as cost centers will need a substantially revised accounting system to handle the PERT/Cost activity-oriented

TABLE 14.15 Project Cost Status Report at Month 4

Activity	Actual Cost (AC)	Budgeted Value $\left(V = \dfrac{p}{100} B\right)$	Differences (D)
A	$12,000	$10,000	$2,000
B	30,000	30,000	0
C	1,000	1,500	−500
D	2,000	2,000	0
E	10,000	5,000	5,000
F	0	0	0
G	0	0	0
Totals	$55,000	$48,500	$6,500

Total Project Cost Overrun to Date

427

system. Problems of modifying accounting procedures and/or carrying dual accounting systems are not trivial matters.

14.4 SUMMARY

In this chapter we have introduced PERT, CPM, and PERT/Cost as network-based procedures designed to assist in the project planning, scheduling, and control process. PERT, which includes capabilities for handling variable or uncertain activity times, is better suited for new or unique projects such as those encountered in R&D activities. CPM provides the capability of reducing project completion times by crashing selected activities under increased but known costs. CPM uses a single-activity time estimate and is perhaps better suited for repeating projects where experience with activity times and resource requirements make it possible to obtain good estimates of their values. While PERT and CPM concentrate on the time aspect of the project, the PERT/Cost technique can be used to help plan, schedule, and control project costs. Because of the numerous computations associated with planning, updating, and revising PERT, CPM, and/or PERT/Cost networks, computer programs are frequently used to implement these project management techniques.

14.5 GLOSSARY

1. *Network*—A graphical description of a problem or situation consisting of numbered circles (nodes) interconnected by a series of lines (branches or arcs).
2. *Nodes*—The intersection or junction points of a network.
3. *Program evaluation and review technique (PERT)*—A network-based project management procedure.
4. *Activities*—Specific jobs or tasks that are components of a project. These are represented by arcs in a PERT network.
5. *Immediate predecessors*—The activities that must immediately precede another given activity.
6. *Branches*—The lines connecting the nodes which in general carry the flow through the network.
7. *Arcs*—Same as branches.
8. *Event*—An event occurs when *all* the activities leading into a node have been completed.
9. *Dummy activity*—A fictitious activity with zero activity time used to create a PERT-type network.
10. *Optimistic time*—A PERT activity time estimate based on the assumption that the activity will progress in an ideal manner.
11. *Most probable time*—A PERT activity time estimate for the most likely activity time.

12. *Pessimistic time*—A PERT activity time estimate based on the assumption that the most unfavorable conditions occur.
13. *Expected activity time*—The average activity time.
14. *Beta distribution*—A probability distribution used to describe PERT activity times.
15. *Path*—A sequence of branches (activities) connecting the starting and ending nodes of a network.
16. *Critical path*—The longest sequence of activities or path in a project management (PERT/CPM) network. The time it takes to traverse this path is the estimated project duration.
17. *Critical activities*—The activities on the critical path.
18. *Earliest start time*—The earliest time at which an activity may begin.
19. *Earliest finish time*—The earliest time at which an activity may be completed.
20. *Lastest start time*—The latest time at which an activity may begin without delaying the complete project.
21. *Latest finish time*—The latest time at which an activity may be completed without delaying the complete project.
22. *Forward pass*—A calculation procedure moving forward through the network which determines the early start and early finish times for each activity.
23. *Backward pass*—A calculation procedure moving backwards through the network which determines the latest start and latest finish times for each activity.
24. *Slack*—The length of time an activity can be delayed without affecting the project completion date.
25. *Critical path method (CPM)*—A network-based project management procedure which includes the capability of crashing a network.
26. *Crashing*—The process of reducing an activity time by adding resources and hence usually cost.
27. *PERT/Cost*—A technique designed to assist in the planning, scheduling, and controlling of project costs.
28. *Work package*—A natural grouping of interrelated project activities for purposes of cost control. A work package is a unit of cost control in a PERT/Cost system.

14.6 PROBLEMS

1. The USAVE Discount Store chain is designing a management training program for individuals at its corporate headquarters. The company would like to design the program so that the trainees can complete it as quickly as possible.

    There are important precedence relationships that must be maintained between tasks in the program. For example, a trainee is not allowed to

429

serve as an assistant to the store manager until he has obtained experience both in credit and sales. The activities below are the ones that must be completed by each trainee in the program.

Activity	Immediate Predecessor
A	—
B	—
C	A
D	A, B
E	A, B
F	C
G	D, F

Construct a PERT network for this problem. Do not attempt to perform any further analysis.

2. Given the following PERT network:

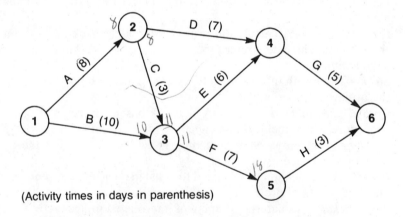

(Activity times in days in parenthesis)

   a. Identify the critical path.

   b. How long will it take to complete this project?

   c. Can activity E be delayed without delaying the entire project? If so, how many days?

   d. Can activity D be delayed without delaying the entire project? If so, how many days?

   e. What is the schedule for activity F (that is, start and completion times)?

3. Suppose the following estimates of activity times were provided for the PERT network shown in Problem 2.

Activity	Optimistic	Most Probable	Pessimistic
A	6	7	14
B	8	10	12
C	2	3	4
D	6	7	8
E	5	5.5	9
F	5	7	9
G	4	5	6
H	2.5	3	3.5

What is the probability the project will be completed within
a. 21 days?
b. 22 days?
c. 25 days?

4. Consider the project network given below:

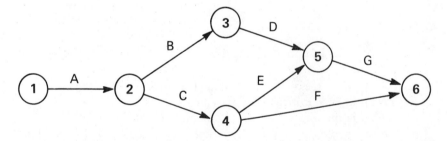

The appropriate activity managers have made estimates of the optimistic *(a)*, most probable *(m)*, and pessimistic *(b)* times (in days) for completion of the activities. These are given below.

Activity	Optimistic	Most Probable	Pessimistic
A	1	4	7
B	2	3	10
C	4	4	10
D	3	5	7
E	1	7	7
F	2	9	10
G	2	3	4

a. Find the critical path.
b. How much slack time, if any, is there in activity D?
c. Determine the expected project completion time and its variance.
d. Find the probability the project will be completed in 20 days or less.

5. Refer to the Porta-Vac project network shown in Figure 14.1. Suppose Daugherty's management revises the activity time estimates as follows:

Activity	Optimistic	Most Probable	Pessimistic
A	3	7	11
B	2	2.5	6
C	2	3	4
D	6	7	14
E	2	3	4
F	2.5	3	3.5
G	2.5	4	5.5
H	4.5	5.5	9.5
I	1	2	3
J	1	2	3

a. What are the expected times and variances for each activity?
b. What are the critical path activities?
c. What is the expected project completion date?
d. What is the new probability that the project will be completed before the 20-week deadline?
e. Show the new detailed activity schedule (see Table 14.4).

6. Doug Casey is in charge of planning and coordinating next spring's sales management training program for his company. Doug has listed the following activity information for this project:

Activity	Description	Immediate Predecessors	Times (weeks) Optimistic	Most Likely	Pessimistic
A	Plan topic	–	1.5	2	2.5
B	Obtain speakers	A	2	2.5	6
C	List meeting locations	–	1	2	3
D	Select location	C	1.5	2	2.5
E	Speaker travel plans	B, D	0.5	1	1.5
F	Final check with speakers	E	1	2	3
G	Prepare and mail brochure	B, D	3	3.5	7
H	Take reservations	G	3	4	5
I	Last-minute details	F, H	1.5	2	2.5

a. Show the PERT network for this project.
b. What are the critical path activities and the expected project completion time?
c. Prepare the activity schedule for this project.
d. If Doug wants a .99 probability of completing the project on time, how far ahead of the scheduled meeting date should he begin working on the project?

7. Construct the network for a project having the following activities:

Activity	Immediate Predecessor
A	–
B	–
C	A
D	A
E	C, B
F	C, B
G	D, E

The project is completed when both activities F and G are complete.

8. Assume that the project whose network was developed in Problem 7 will be scheduled and controlled by CPM. The activity times are as follows:

Activity	Time (months)
A	4
B	6
C	2
D	6
E	3
F	3
G	5

a. Find the critical path for the project network.
b. If the project has a $1\frac{1}{2}$ year completion deadline, should we consider crashing some activities? Explain.

9. For the CPM project in Problem 8 suppose that the following crash data are available:

Activity	Normal Time	Crash Time	Total Normal Cost ($\$\times10^3$)	Total Crash Cost ($\$\times10^3$)
A	4	2	50	70
B	6	3	40	55
C	2	1	20	24
D	6	4	100	130
E	3	2	50	60
F	3	3	25	25
G	5	3	60	75

a. Show a linear programming model that could be used to make the CPM crash decisions if the project had to be completed in T months.
b. If $T = 12$ months, what activities should be crashed, what is the crashing cost, and what are the critical activities?

434

10. Using the Daugherty Porta-Vac project shown in Figure 14.1, suppose expected activity costs are as follows:

Activity	Expected Cost $ \times 10^3$
A	90
B	16
C	3
D	100
E	6
F	2
G	60
H	20
I	4
J	2

Develop a total cost budget based on both an earliest start and latest start schedule. Show the graph of feasible budgets for the total project cost.

11. Using the Daugherty Porta-Vac project cost data given in Problem 10, prepare a PERT/Cost analysis for each of the following three points in time. For each case, show the percent overrun or underrun for the project to date and indicate any corrective action that should be undertaken. (Note: If an activity is not listed below, assume that it has not been started.)

a. At the end of 5th week:

Activity	Actual Cost ($ \times 10^3$)	% Completion
A	62	80%
B	6	50%

b. At the end of 10th week:

Activity	Actual Cost ($ \times 10^3$)	% Completion
A	85	100%
B	16	100%
C	1	33%
D	100	80%
E	4	100%
H	10	25%

c. At the end of 15th week:

Activity	Actual Cost	% Completion
A	85	
B	16	
C	3	
D	105	All 100%
E	4	Complete
F	3	
G	55	
H	25	
I	4	

12. The PERT network for the two-machine maintenance project discussed in Section 14.2 is shown below.

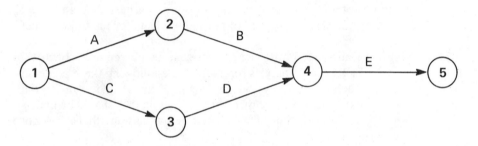

The recommended crashed schedule was shown in Table 14.8. Crashed times and budgeted costs for the project are as follows:

Activity	Expected Time (Days)	Cost
A	5	$ 700
B	3	200
C	6	500
D	2	350
E	2	300
		$2,050

a. Show the graph of feasible budgets for the project's total cost. Does this represent a usual or unusual feasible budget region? Explain.

b. Suppose at the start of day 8 we find the following activity status report.

Activity	Actual Cost	% Completion
A	$800	100%
B	100	67%
C	450	100%
D	250	50%
E	0	0

In terms of both time and cost, is the project on schedule? What action is recommended?

13. A firm is modifying its warehouse operation with the installation of an automated stock handling system. Specific activities include redesigning the warehouse layout, installing the new equipment, testing the new equipment, and so forth. The PERT project management network is shown below.

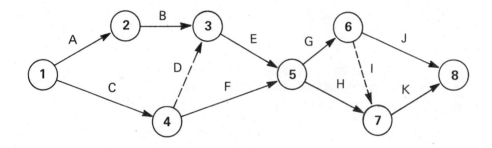

Note: D and I are dummy activities.

Pertinent time and cost data are as follows:

Activity	Expected Time (Weeks)	Variance	Budgeted Cost
A	3	.3	$ 6,000
B	2	.5	4,000
C	8	2.0	16,000
D	0	.0	0
E	6	1.0	18,000
F	4	.2	20,000
G	5	.4	15,000
H	1	.1	2,000
I	0	.0	0
J	5	1.0	5,000
K	6	.6	12,000

a. Develop a PERT activity schedule for the project.
   (1) What is the critical path?
   (2) What is the expected completion date?
   (3) What is the probability of meeting a desired 6-month (26 week) completion date?
b. Develop a PERT/Cost budget for total project costs over the project's duration. What should the range be for expenditures after 12 weeks of the project?

14. Referring to the network in Problem 13, suppose that after 12 weeks of operation the following data are available on all completed and in-process activities:

Activity	Actual Cost	% Completion
A	$ 5,000	100%
B	4,000	100%
C	18,000	100%
E	9,000	50%
F	18,000	75%

Is the project in control based on both time and cost considerations? What corrective action, if any, is desirable?

15

Inventory Mode

Expenses associated with financing and maintaining inventories are a substantial part of the cost of doing business for most companies. In large companies, especially those with many or expensive products, the costs associated with raw material, in-process, and finished goods inventories can run into millions of dollars. To gain an appreciation of how these costs arise and what managers can do to control them, let us consider the situation faced by the R & B Beverage Company. R & B Beverage is a distributor of beer, wine, and soft-drink products in central Ohio. From a main warehouse located in Columbus, R & B supplies nearly 1000 retail stores with beverage products.

R & B's beer inventory constitutes approximately 20% of the company's total inventory. The current beer inventory consists of approximately 240,000 cases. Since the average cost per case is roughly $3, R & B estimates the value of its beer inventory to be $720,000.

There are a number of costs associated with maintaining or carrying a given level of inventory. Taken together these costs are usually referred to as the *inventory holding costs*. First there is the cost of financing. If money is borrowed to maintain the inventory investments, an interest charge is incurred. If the firm's own money is used, there is an opportunity cost associated with not being able to use the money for other investments. In either case, a financing charge exists in the form of an interest cost for the capital tied up in inventory. This *cost of capital* is usually expressed as a percentage of the amount invested. Since R & B estimates its cost of capital at an annual rate of 9%, this portion of the inventory cost is 0.09 ($720,000) = $64,800 per year.

There are a number of other costs such as insurance, taxes, breakage, pilferage, and warehouse overhead which also depend for the most part on the value of the inventory. R & B estimates these other costs at an annual rate of approximately 6% of the value of its inventory. Thus total inventory holding cost for the R & B beer inventory is 15% of its value, which is 0.15 ($720,000) = $108,000 per year. When we consider that the beer constitutes only about 20% of R & B's total inventory, we can begin to see that inventory holding costs are a major expense for the R & B Beverage Company.

Inventory holding cost is a concern to every manager who is responsible for some form of inventory. Certainly, all managers are aware that inventories, which can be defined as any idle goods or materials that are waiting to be used, are necessary and important for the efficiency of business operations. Thus managers are faced with the dual problems of maintaining sufficient inventories to meet demand for goods and at the same time incurring the lowest possible inventory cost. Basically, managers attempt to solve these problems by making the best possible decisions with respect to

1. How much should be ordered when the inventory for a given item is replenished?
2. When should the inventory for a given item be replenished?

The purpose of this chapter is to introduce you to how quantitative models can assist in making the above decisions. While there are many basic similarities in all inventory systems, each system also has unique operating characteristics that prevent us from applying one or two general inventory decision models to all situations. In this chapter you will be introduced to the fundamental inventory decision models and some of the more common and most useful variations. In Sections 15.1 to 15.4, we consider inventory models where demand for the products is known in advance. These models are referred to as inventory models with *deterministic* demand. In Section 15.5, we discuss an inventory problem with an uncertain or *probabilistic* demand.

15.1 ECONOMIC ORDER QUANTITY (EOQ) MODEL

Undoubtedly the best known and most fundamental inventory decision model is the economic order quantity (EOQ) model. This model is potentially applicable when the entire quantity ordered arrives in the inventory at one point in time and when the demand for the item has a constant, or nearly constant, rate. The *constant demand rate* condition simply means that the same number of units are taken from inventory each period of time, such as 5 units every day, 25 units every week, 100 units every 4-week period, and so on. It is assumed that this constant demand rate is known in advance. Let us see how the EOQ model can be applied by the R & B Beverage Company.

R & B's warehouse manager has conducted a preliminary analysis of overall inventory costs and has decided to do a detailed study of one product for the purpose of establishing the *how-much*-to-order and *when*-to-order decision rules that will result in the lowest possible inventory cost for the product. The manager has selected R & B's number one selling beer, Bub, for his study.

In a meeting with the R & B purchaser in charge of Bub, the manager found that since Bub was the company's number one selling beer, the purchaser tended to order large quantities ahead of time and always maintain a sizable inventory so that the company would never experience a shortage. Actually no attention was being given to the costs associated with placing purchase orders or holding the inventory. Records showed that over the past year the purchaser had placed 13 orders of 8000 cases each (ordering about every 4 weeks) with a purchase price of $3.60 per case.

440

The historical demand data for Bub during the past 10 weeks are as follows.

Week	Demand (cases)
1	2000
2	2025
3	1950
4	2000
5	2100
6	2050
7	2000
8	1975
9	1900
10	2000
Total cases	20,000
Average cases per week	2000

Strictly speaking, the above weekly demand figures do not show a constant demand rate. However, given the relatively low variability exhibited by the weekly demands, inventory planning with a constant and known rate of demand of 2000 cases per week appears acceptable.

In practice you will find that the real inventory situation seldom, if ever, satisfies the assumptions of the model exactly. Thus in any particular application it is the job of the manager and the management scientist to determine if the model assumptions are close enough to reality for the model to be useful. In this situation, since demand varies from a low of 1900 cases to a high of 2100 cases, it appears that the assumption of constant demand is a reasonable approximation.

The *how-much*-to-order decision involves selecting an order quantity that draws a compromise between (1) keeping small inventories and ordering frequently and (2) keeping large inventories and ordering infrequently. The first alternative could result in undesirably high ordering costs, while the second alternative would probably result in undesirably high inventory holding costs. In order to find the optimal compromise between these conflicting objectives, let us develop a mathematical model that will show the total cost as the sum of the holding costs plus the ordering costs.

As mentioned in the previous section, *inventory holding* or *inventory carrying costs* are the costs that are dependent upon the size of the inventory; that is, as we encounter larger inventories, we also find larger inventory holding costs. As mentioned earlier, R & B estimated its annual inventory holding costs to be 15% of the value of its inventory, and the cost of one case of Bub beer was $3.60. Thus it costs (0.15) ($3.60) = $0.54 to store one case of Bub beer in inventory for 1 year. Note that defining the inventory holding cost as a percentage of value of the product is convenient because it is easily transferable to other products, even though product prices are different. For example, a case of Carle's Red Ribbon Beer ($3.20/case) has an annual inventory holding cost of 0.15($3.20) = $0.48 per case.

The next step is to determine the cost of placing an order. For R & B the largest portion of this cost involves the salaries of the purchasers. An analysis of the purchasing process showed that a purchaser spends approximately 30 minutes preparing and processing an order for Bub beer. This amount of time is required regardless of the number of cases ordered. With a wage rate and fringe benefit cost for purchasers of $15 per hour, the labor portion of the ordering cost is $7.50. Making allowances for paper, postage, telephone, and transportation costs at $1.50 per order, the manager estimated the cost of ordering to be $9 per order. That is, R & B is paying $9 per order regardless of the quantity requested in the order.

The inventory holding costs, the order costs, and the demand information are the three data items that must be prepared prior to the use of any EOQ model. Since these data have now been developed for our R & B example, let us see how they are used to develop a total cost model. We shall begin by defining the symbol Q to be the size of the order quantity. Thus the *how-much*-to-order decision involves trying to find that value of Q which will minimize the sum of ordering and holding costs.

The inventory level for Bub will have a maximum value of Q units when the order of size Q is received from the manufacturer. R & B will then supply its customers from inventory until the inventory is depleted, at which time another shipment of Q units will be received. With the assumption of a constant demand rate of 2000 units per week or, assuming R & B is open 5 days each week, 400 units per day, the sketch of the inventory level for Bub beer is shown in Figure 15.1.

Note that the sketch indicates that the average inventory level for the period in question is $\frac{1}{2}Q$. This should appear reasonable to you, since the maximum inventory level is Q, the minimum is 0, and the inventory level declines at a constant rate over the period.

Figure 15.1 shows the inventory pattern during one order cycle or period T. As time goes on, this pattern will repeat. The complete inventory pattern is shown in Figure 15.2. If the average inventory during each cycle is $\frac{1}{2}Q$, the average inventory level over any number of cycles is also $\frac{1}{2}Q$. Thus as long as the time period involved contains an integral number of order cycles, the average inventory for the period will be $\frac{1}{2}Q$.

The inventory holding cost can be calculated using the average inventory level. That is, we can calculate the inventory holding cost by multiplying the average inventory by the cost of carrying one unit in inventory for the stated period. The period of time selected for the model is up to you; it could be 1 week, 1 month, 1 year, or more. However, since the inventory carrying costs for many industries and businesses are often expressed as an *annual* percentage or rate, you will probably find most inventory models developed on an *annual cost* basis.

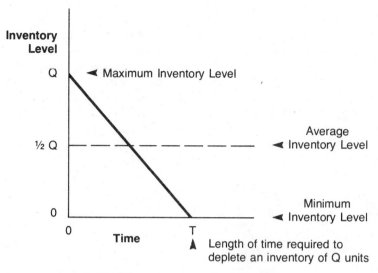

FIGURE 15.1 Sketch of the Inventory Level for Bub Beer

Letting

> I = annual inventory carrying charge (15% for R & B)
> C = unit cost of the inventory item ($3.60 for Bub beer)

the cost of storing one unit in inventory for the year, denoted by C_h, is given by $C_h = IC$, which for Bub is $(0.15)(\$3.60) = \$0.54$. Thus the general equation for annual inventory holding cost is as follows:

$$\begin{pmatrix} \text{annual inventory} \\ \text{holding cost} \end{pmatrix} = \begin{pmatrix} \text{average} \\ \text{inventory} \end{pmatrix}\begin{pmatrix} \text{annual holding} \\ \text{cost} \\ \text{per unit} \end{pmatrix}$$

$$= \tfrac{1}{2}QC_h. \tag{15.1}$$

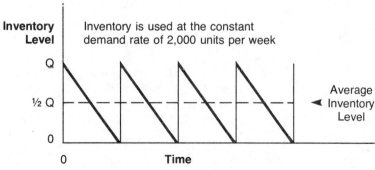

FIGURE 15.2 Inventory Pattern for the EOQ Inventory De-cision Model

443

To complete our total cost model, we must include the ordering cost. Our goal is to express this cost in terms of the order quantity Q. Since the inventory holding cost was expressed as an annual cost, we need to express ordering costs on an annual basis. The first question is, how many orders will be placed during the year? Letting D denote the annual demand for the product [for R & B, D = (52 weeks) (2000 per week) = 104,000], we know that by ordering Q units each time we order, we may have to place D/Q orders. For example, if Q = 52,000, we would only need to order twice a year to satisfy demand for Bub beer. If C_0 is the cost of placing one order ($9 for R & B), the general equation for the annual ordering cost is as follows:

$$\text{annual ordering cost} = \begin{pmatrix} \text{number of} \\ \text{orders} \\ \text{per year} \end{pmatrix} \begin{pmatrix} \text{cost} \\ \text{per} \\ \text{order} \end{pmatrix}$$

$$= \left(\frac{D}{Q}\right) C_0. \tag{15.2}$$

Thus the total cost can be expressed as follows:

$$\text{TC} = \tfrac{1}{2}QC_h + \frac{D}{Q}\, C_0. \tag{15.3}$$

Using the Bub beer data, the total cost model becomes

$$\text{TC} = \tfrac{1}{2}Q(\$0.54) + \frac{104{,}000}{Q}\,(\$9) = 0.27Q + \frac{936{,}000}{Q}. \tag{15.4}$$

The development of the above total cost model has gone a long way toward helping solve the inventory problem. We now are able to express the total annual cost as a function of one of the decisions, *how much* should be ordered. The development of a realistic total cost model is perhaps the most important part of applying quantitative techniques to inventory decision making. Equation (15.3) is the general total cost equation for inventory situations in which the assumptions of the economic order quantity model are valid.

The How-Much-to-Order Decision

The next step is to find the order quantity Q that does in fact minimize the total cost as stated in equation (15.4). Using a trial-and-error approach we can compute the total cost for several possible order quantities. As a starting point, let us use the current purchase policy for Bub which is Q = 8000. The total annual cost is

$$\text{TC} = 0.27(8000) + \frac{936{,}000}{8000} = \$2277.00.$$

TABLE 15.1 Inventory Holding and Ordering Costs for Various Order Quantities of Bub Beer

Order Quantity	Annual Inventory Holding Cost	Annual Ordering Cost	Annual Total Cost
5000	$1350.00	$187.20	$1537.20
4000	$1080.00	$234.00	$1314.00
3000	$ 810.00	$312.00	$1122.00
2000	$ 540.00	$468.00	$1008.00
1000	$ 270.00	$936.00	$1206.00

A trial with an order quantity of 5000 gives

$$TC = 0.27(5000) + \frac{936{,}000}{5000} = \$1537.20.$$

Several other trial order quantities are shown in Table 15.1. As can be seen, the lowest cost solution is around 2000 units. Graphs of the inventory holding, ordering, and total costs are shown in Figure 15.3.

The advantage and trial-and-error approach is that it is rather easy to do and provides the total cost for a number of possible order quantity decisions. Also, we can see that approximately 2000 units appears to be the minimum

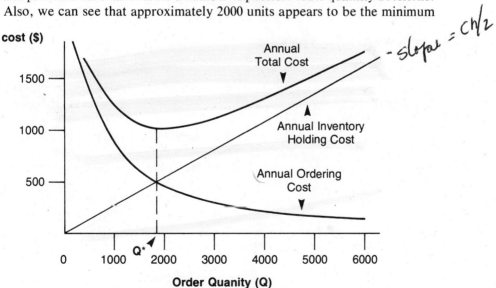

FIGURE 15.3 Graph of Annual Inventory Holding, Ordering, and Total Cost for Bub Beer

445

cost order quantity. The disadvantage of this approach, however, is that it does not provide the exact minimum cost order quantity.

Referring to Figure 15.3, you can see that the minimum total cost order quantity is an order size of Q^*. By using differential calculus it can be shown (see Appendix 15.1) that the value of Q^* which minimizes the total cost is given by the formula

$$Q^* = \sqrt{\frac{2DC_0}{C_h}} \, . \tag{15.5}$$

This formula is well known by management scientists and is referred to as the economic order quantity (EOQ) formula.

For Bub beer the minimum total cost order quantity is

$$Q^* = \sqrt{\frac{2(104,000)9}{0.54}} = \sqrt{3,466,667} \approx 1862.$$

Using an order quantity of 1862 in equation (15.4) shows that the minimum cost inventory policy for Bub beer results in a total cost of \$1005.42. Note that this inventory decision, that is $Q^* = 1862$, results in a \$2277.00 − \$1005.42 = \$1271.58, or 55.8% cost reduction from the current purchase policy of $Q = 8000$. Also you might note that this value of Q^* has balanced the inventory holding and ordering costs. Check for yourself to see that these costs, are equal.[1] Problem 2 at the end of the chapter asks you to show that this is a general property of the EOQ model.

The When-to-Buy Decision

Now that we know how much to order, we want to answer the second question of *when* to order. The when-to-order decision is most often expressed in terms of a *reorder point,* which is the inventory level at which an order should be placed.

The manufacturer of Bub beer guarantees a 2-day delivery on any order placed by R & B. Hence assuming a constant demand rate of 2000 cases per week or 400 cases per day, we expect (2 days) (400 cases/day) = 800 cases of Bub to be sold during the 2 days it takes a new order of Bub to reach the R & B warehouse. In inventory terminology, the 2-day delivery period is referred to as the *lead time* for a new order, and the 800 cases of demand anticipated during this period is referred to as the *lead time demand*. Thus R & B should order a new shipment of Bub beer from the manufacturer when the inventory

---

[1] Actually Q^* from equation (15.5) is 1861.9, but since we can not order fractional cases of beer, a Q^* of 1862 is shown. This value of Q^* may cause a few cents deviation between the two costs. Actually if Q^* is used at its exact value, the inventory holding and ordering costs will be exactly the same.

on hand reaches a reorder level of 800 cases. For inventory systems using the constant demand rate assumption, the reorder point is the same as the lead time demand.

The general expression for the reorder point is given as follows:

$$r = dm \qquad\qquad (15.6)$$

where

r = reorder point
d = demand per day
m = lead time for a new order in days.

The question of how frequently the order will be placed can also be answered now. This period between orders is referred to as the *cycle time*. Previously [see equation (15.2)] we defined D/Q as the number of orders that will be placed in a year. Thus $D/Q^* = 104,000/1862 = 56$ is the number of orders R & B will place for Bub each year. If we place 56 orders over 365 days, we will order approximately every $365/56 = 6.5$ days. Thus the cycle time is computed to be 6.5 days. The general expression for a cycle time of T days is given by

$$T = \frac{365}{D/Q^*} = \frac{365Q^*}{D} \cdot \qquad\qquad (15.7)$$

Sensitivity Analysis in the EOQ Model

Even though substantial time has been spent in arriving at the cost per order ($9) and inventory holding cost (15%) figures, we should realize that these figures are, at best, good estimates. Thus we may want to consider how much the order size recommendation would change if the estimated ordering and holding costs had been different. To determine this, we can calculate the recommended order quantity under several different cost conditions. These calculations are shown in Table 15.2. As you can see from the table, Q^* is

TABLE 15.2 Economic Order Quantities for Several Cost Possibilities

Possible Inventory Holding Cost (%)	Possible Cost per Order	Optimal Order Quantity (Q^*)	Projected Total Cost Using Q^*	Projected Total Cost Using $Q = 1862$
14	$ 8	1817	$ 916	$ 916
14	$10	2031	1024	1027
16	$ 8	1700	979	983
16	$10	1900	1094	1095

relatively stable, even with some variations in the cost estimates. Based on these results, it appears that the best order quantity for Bub is somewhere around 1700 to 2000 units and definitely not near the current order quantity of 8000 units. If operated properly, the total cost for the Bub inventory system should be close to $1000 per year. We also note that there is very little risk associated with implementing the calculated order quantity of $Q = 1862$. In the worst case (when the true optimal order quantity $Q^* = 1700$), it only results in a $4 increase in the total annual cost; that is, $983 - $979 = $4.

From the above analysis, we would say that this EOQ model is insensitive to small variations or errors in the cost estimates. This is a property of EOQ models in general, which indicates that if we have at least reasonable estimates of ordering and inventory holding costs, we should obtain a good approximation of the true minimum cost order quantity.

The Manager's Use of the EOQ Model

The inventory model and analysis had led to a recommended order quantity of 1862 units. Is this the final decision or should the manager's judgment enter into the establishment of the final inventory policy decisions? Although the model has provided us with a good order quantity recommendation, it may not have taken into account all aspects of the inventory situation. As a result, the decision maker should feel free to modify the final order quantity recommendation to meet the unique circumstances of his inventory situation. In this case the warehouse manager felt that it would be desirable to increase the order quantity from 1862 units to 2000 units in order to have an order quantity equal to 5 days' demand. By doing so, R & B can maintain a weekly order cycle.

The warehouse manager also realized that the EOQ model was based on the constant demand rate assumption of 2000 units per week. While this was close to the actual case, sometimes the demand might exceed this amount. If a reorder point of 800 units is used, we would be expecting an 800-unit demand during the lead time and the new order to arrive exactly when the inventory level reached zero. Such close timing would leave little room for error, and the scheduling of arrivals would be very critical if stockouts were to be avoided. To protect against shortages due to higher than expected demands or slightly delayed incoming orders, the warehouse manager recommended a 1200-unit reorder point. Thus, under normal conditions, R & B will order 2000 cases of Bub whenever the current inventory reaches 1200 units. During the expected 2-day lead time, 800 units should be demanded, and thus 400 units should be in inventory when an order arrives. The extra 400 units serves as a safety precaution against a higher than expected demand or a delayed incoming order. In general, the amount by which the reorder point exceeds the expected lead time demand is referred to as *safety stock.*

The decisions to adjust the order quantity and reorder point were purely management judgment decisions and were not necessarily made with a minimum cost objective in mind. However, they are examples of how judgment might interface with the inventory decision model to arrive at a sound inventory policy. The final decision of $Q = 2000$ with a 400-unit safety stock resulted in a total cost of $1224.[2] This was still a $2277 − $1224 = $1053, or 46%, savings over the current inventory policy.

How Has the EOQ Decision Model Helped

The EOQ model has objectively included inventory holding and ordering costs and, with the aid of some management judgment, has led to a cost-saving inventory decision. In addition, the general optimal order quantity model, equation (15.5), is potentially applicable to other R & B products. For example, Red Ribbon beer ($3.20/case), which has an ordering cost of $9, a constant demand rate of 1200 cases per week (62,400 cases/year), and a 2-day lead time period, has a recommended order quantity of

$$Q^* = \sqrt{\frac{2(62,400)(9.00)}{(0.15)(3.20)}} = 1530 \text{ cases}$$

a cycle time of $T = (1530/62,400)365 = 8.9$ days, and a reorder point of $r = (240)(2) = 480$ cases.

We will now investigate additional inventory decision models that are designed to make *how much* and *when* to order decisions for other types of inventory systems.

15.2 ECONOMIC PRODUCTION LOT SIZE MODEL

The following inventory decision model is similar to the first model in that we are attempting to determine *how much* we should order or produce and *when* the order should be placed. Again we will make the assumption of a constant demand rate. However, instead of the goods arriving at the warehouse in a shipment of size Q^* as assumed in the EOQ model, we will assume that units are supplied to inventory at a constant rate over several days or several weeks. The *constant supply rate* assumption implies that the same number of units are supplied to inventory each period of time (for example, 10 units every day, 50 units every week, and so on). This model is designed for

---

[2] A Q of 2000 units resulted in a total cost of $1008 (see Table 15.1). The additional safety stock inventory of 400 units increases the average inventory by 400 units since it is on hand all year long. Thus the inventory carrying charge is increased by $0.54(400) = 216. Therefore the total cost of the revised policy is $1224.

449

production situations in which once an order is placed, production begins and a constant number of units are added to inventory each day until the production run has been completed.

If we have a production system that produces 50 units per day and we decide to schedule 10 days of production each time we want additional units, we have a 50 (10) = 500-unit production run size. Alternative terminology may refer to the 500 units as the production lot size or lot quantity.

If, in general, we let Q indicate the production lot quantity, our approach to the inventory decisions will be similar to the EOQ model; that is, we will attempt to build an inventory holding and ordering cost model that expresses the total annual cost as a function of the production quantity. Then we will attempt to find the quantity that minimizes the total cost.

One other condition that should be mentioned at this time is that the model will only apply to production situations in which the production rate is greater than the demand rate. Stated more simply, the production system must be able to satisfy the demand. For example, if our constant demand rate is 2000 units per week, our production rate has to be at least 2000 units per week if we are going to satisfy our demand.

Since we have assumed that the production rate will exceed the demand rate, each day during a production run we will be manufacturing more units than we ship. Thus we will put the excess production in inventory, resulting in a gradual inventory buildup during the production period. When the production run is completed, the inventory will show a gradual decline until a new production run is started. The inventory pattern for this system is shown in Figure 15.4.

As in the EOQ model, we are now dealing with two costs, the inventory holding cost and the ordering cost. While the inventory holding cost is identical to our definition in the EOQ model, the interpretation of the ordering cost is slightly different. In fact, in a production situation the ordering cost may be more correctly referred to as production setup cost. This cost, which in-

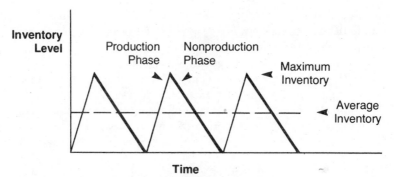

FIGURE 15.4 *Inventory Pattern for the Production Lot Size Inventory Model*

450

cludes man-hours, material, and lost production costs incurred while preparing the production system for operation, is a fixed cost which occurs for every production run, regardless of the production quantity.

Building the Total Cost Model

Let us begin building our model by attempting to write the inventory holding cost in terms of our production quantity Q. Again, our approach will be to develop an expression for average inventory, and then establish the holding costs associated with the average inventory level. We will use a 1-year time period and an annual cost for our model.

We saw in the EOQ model that the average inventory was simply one half the maximum inventory or $\frac{1}{2}Q$. Since Figure 15.4 shows a constant inventory buildup rate during the production run and a constant inventory depletion rate during the nonproduction period, the average inventory for the production lot size model will also be one half of the maximum inventory level. However, in this inventory system the production quantity Q does not go into inventory at one point in time, and thus the inventory level never reaches a level of Q units.

Let us see if we can compute the maximum inventory level. First we define the following symbols:

d = daily demand rate for the product
p = daily production rate for the product
t = number of days for a production run.

Since we are assuming p will be larger than d, the excess production each day is $p - d$, which is the daily rate of inventory buildup. If we run production for t days and place $p - d$ units in inventory each day, the inventory level at the end of the production run will be $(p - d)t$. From Figure 15.4 we can see that the inventory level at the end of the production run is also the maximum inventory level. Thus we can write

$$\text{maximum inventory} = (p - d)t. \tag{15.8}$$

If we know we are producing a production quantity of Q units at a daily production rate of p units, then $Q = pt$, and we can compute the length of the production run t to be

$$t = Q/p \text{ days.} \tag{15.9}$$

Thus

$$\text{maximum inventory} = (p - d)t = (p - d)(Q/p)$$
$$= (1 - d/p)Q. \tag{15.10}$$

The average inventory, which is one half of the maximum inventory, is given by

$$\text{average inventory} = \tfrac{1}{2}(1 - d/p)Q. \tag{15.11}$$

With an annual inventory holding cost of $C_h = IC$ per unit, the general equation for annual inventory holding cost is as follows:

$$\begin{pmatrix} \text{annual inventory} \\ \text{holding cost} \end{pmatrix} = \begin{pmatrix} \text{average} \\ \text{inventory} \end{pmatrix} \begin{pmatrix} \text{annual holding} \\ \text{cost} \\ \text{per unit} \end{pmatrix}$$

$$= \tfrac{1}{2}(1 - d/p)QC_h. \tag{15.12}$$

If D is the annual demand for the product and C_0 is the setup cost for a production run, then the total annual setup cost, which takes the place of the total annual ordering cost of the EOQ model, is as follows:

$$\text{annual setup cost} = \begin{pmatrix} \text{number of production} \\ \text{runs per year} \end{pmatrix} \begin{pmatrix} \text{setup cost} \\ \text{per run} \end{pmatrix}$$

$$= \left(\frac{D}{Q}\right) C_0. \tag{15.13}$$

Thus, the total annual cost (TC) model is

$$TC = \tfrac{1}{2}(1 - d/p)QC_h + \frac{D}{Q} C_0. \tag{15.14}$$

Suppose that a plant operates 250 days per year; 115 days are idle as a result of weekends and holidays. Then we could write daily demand d in terms of annual demand D as follows:

$$d = D/250.$$

If we let P denote the annual production for the product if it were produced every day, then

$$P = 250p \quad \text{or} \quad p = P/250.$$

Thus

$$d/p = \frac{D/250}{P/250} = D/P. \text{[3]}$$

Therefore we could write the total annual cost as follows:

$$TC = \tfrac{1}{2}(1 - D/P)QC_h + \frac{D}{Q} C_0. \tag{15.15}$$

---

[3] The ratio $d/p = D/P$ regardless of the number of days of operation; 250 days was used here merely as an illustration.

Equations (15.14) and (15.15) are equivalent. However, equation (15.15) may be used more frequently since an *annual* cost model tends to make the analyst think in terms of collecting *annual* demand *(D)* and *annual* production *(P)* data rather than daily rate data.

Finding the Economic Production Lot Size

Given the estimates of the inventory holding cost C_h, setup cost C_0, annual demand rate *D,* and annual production rate *P,* we can use a trial-and-error approach to compute the total annual cost for various lot sizes *Q.* However, we may also use the minimum cost formula for Q^* which has been developed using differential calculus (see Appendix 15.2). The equation is as follows:

$$Q^* = \sqrt{\frac{2DC_0'}{(1 - D/P)C_h}} \; . \tag{15.16}$$

An Example   Beauty Bar Soap is produced on a production line that has an annual capacity of 60,000 cases. The annual demand is estimated at 26,000 cases with the demand rate essentially constant throughout the year. The cleaning, preparation, and setup of the production line costs approximately $90. The manufacturing cost per case is $4.50, and an annual inventory holding cost is figured at a 16% rate. Thus $C_h = IC = (.16)(\$4.50) = 0.72$. What is your recommended production lot size?

Using equation (15.16) we have

$$Q^* = \sqrt{\frac{2(26,000)(90)}{\left(1 - \dfrac{26,000}{60,000}\right)(0.72)}} = \sqrt{\frac{4,680,000}{0.408}} = 3387$$

The total annual cost using equation (15.15) and $Q^* = 3387$ is estimated to be $1382.

Other relevant data include a 1-week lead time to schedule and set up a production run. Thus, a 1-week demand of $26,000/52 = 500$ cases is the reorder point. The cycle time between production runs, using equation (15.7) is estimated to be $T = [(365)(3387)]/26,000$, or about 47 days. Thus we should plan a production run of 3300 to 3400 units about every 47 days.

Certainly the manager will want to review the model recommendations. Adjusting the recommended $Q^* = 3387$ to a slightly more practical figure and/or adding safety stock may be desirable.

15.3   AN INVENTORY MODEL WITH PLANNED SHORTAGES

In many inventory situations a shortage or stockout—a demand that cannot be supplied from inventory or production—is undesirable and should be avoided if at all possible. However, there are other cases in which it may be desirable—from an economic point of view—to plan for and allow shortages. In practice these types of situations are most commonly found where the value per unit of the inventory is very high, and hence the inventory holding cost is high. An example of this type of situation is a new car dealer's inventory. It is not uncommon for a dealer not to have the specific car you want in stock. However, he is always willing to order it for you if you can wait.

The specific model developed in this section allows the type of shortage known as a *back order*. In a back-order situation an assumption is made that when a customer places an order and discovers that the supplier is out of stock, the customer does not withdraw the order. Rather, he waits until the next shipment arrives, and then the order is filled. Frequently the waiting period in back-ordering situations will be relatively short and, by promising the customer top priority and immediate delivery when the goods become available, companies can convince customers to wait for the order. In these cases the back-order assumption is valid. If for a particular product a firm finds that a shortage causes the customer to withdraw the order and a lost sale results, the back-order model would not be the appropriate inventory decision model.

Using the back-order assumption for shortages, we will now develop an extension to the EOQ model presented in Section 15.1. The EOQ model assumptions of the goods arriving in inventory all at one time and a constant demand rate for the product will be used. If we let S indicate the amount of the shortage or the number of back orders that have accumulated when a new shipment of size Q is received, then the inventory system for the back-order case has the following characteristics:

1. With S back orders existing when a new shipment of size Q arrives, the S back orders will be shipped to the appropriate customers immediately and the remaining $(Q - S)$ units will be placed in inventory.
2. $Q - S$ will be the maximum inventory level.
3. The inventory cycle of T days will be divided into two distinct phases; t_1 days when inventory is on hand and orders are filled as they occur and t_2 days when there is a stockout and all orders are placed on back order.

The inventory pattern for this model, where negative inventory represents the number of back orders, is shown in Figure 15.5.

With the inventory pattern now defined, we should be able to proceed with the basic step of all inventory models; namely, the development of a total cost expression. For the inventory model with back orders we will encounter the usual inventory holding costs and ordering costs. In addition, we will incur a back-ordering cost in terms of labor and special delivery costs di-

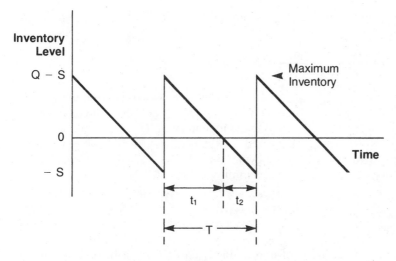

t_1 = length of inventory period

t_2 = length of stockout or backorder period

FIGURE 15.5 *Inventory Pattern for an Inventory Model with Back Orders*

rectly associated with the handling of the back orders. Another portion of the back-order cost can be expressed as a loss of goodwill because customers will have to wait for their orders. Since the *goodwill cost* depends upon how long the customer has to wait, it is customary to adopt the convention of expressing all back-order costs in terms of how much it costs to have a unit on back order for a stated period of time. This method of costing back orders on a time basis is similar to the method we have used to compute the inventory holding cost.

Using this method for approaching back-order costs, we can compute a total annual cost of back orders once the average back-order level and the back-order cost per unit per unit time is known. As you will recall, this is the same type of information that is needed to calculate inventory holding costs.

Admittedly, the back-order cost rate (especially the goodwill cost) is difficult to determine in practice. However, noting that EOQ models are rather insensitive to the cost estimates (see Table 15.2), we should feel confident that reasonable estimates of the back-order cost will lead to a good approximation of the overall minimum cost inventory decision.

Let us begin the development of our total cost model by showing how to calculate the inventory holding costs. First we use a small hypothetical example to suggest a procedure for computing the average inventory level. If we have an average inventory of two units for 3 days and no inventory on the fourth day, what is our average inventory level over the 4-day period? You should say

$$\frac{2 \text{ units}(3 \text{ days}) + 0 \text{ units}(1 \text{ day})}{4 \text{ days}} = \frac{6}{4} = 1.5 \text{ units.}$$

Referring to Figure 15.5, you can see that this is exactly what happens in the back-order model. With a maximum inventory of $Q - S$ units during the t_1 days we have inventory, an average inventory of $(Q - S)/2$ is on hand for the t_1 days. No inventory is carried for the t_2 days in which we experience back orders. Thus over the total cycle time of $T = t_1 + t_2$ days, we can compute the average inventory level as follows:

$$\begin{matrix} \text{average inventory} \\ \text{level} \end{matrix} = \frac{\left(\dfrac{Q-S}{2}\right) t_1 + 0t_2}{T} = \frac{\left(\dfrac{Q-S}{2}\right) t_1}{T}. \tag{15.17}$$

Can we find other ways of expressing t_1 and T? Since we know that the maximum inventory is $(Q - S)$ and d represents the constant daily demand, we have

$$t_1 = \frac{Q - S}{d} \text{ days.} \tag{15.18}$$

That is, the maximum inventory level of $Q - S$ units will be used up in $(Q - S)/d$ days. Since Q units are ordered and shipped each cycle, we know the length of a cycle must be

$$T = Q/d \text{ days.} \tag{15.19}$$

Using equations (15.18) and (15.19) with equation (15.17), we can write the following:

$$\begin{matrix} \text{average} \\ \text{inventory} \\ \text{level} \end{matrix} = \frac{\left(\dfrac{Q-S}{2}\right)\left(\dfrac{Q-S}{d}\right)}{Q/d} = \frac{(Q-S)^2}{2Q}. \tag{15.20}$$

Thus, the average inventory level is expressed in terms of two inventory decisions, how much we order (Q) and the maximum number of units back ordered we will allow (S).

The formula for the annual number of orders placed under this model is identical to that for the EOQ model. With D representing the annual demand we have

$$\text{annual number of orders} = D/Q. \tag{15.21}$$

The next step is to develop an expression for the average back-order level. Since there is a maximum of S back orders, we can use the same logic that we used to establish average inventory to find the average number of back orders. We have an average number of back orders during the period t_2 of $\frac{1}{2}$

456

the maximum number of back orders or $\frac{1}{2}S$. Since we do not have any back orders during the t_1 days we have inventory, we can calculate the average back-order level in a manner similar to equation (15.17). Using this approach we have

$$\text{average back-order level} = \frac{0t_1 + (S/2)t_2}{T} = \frac{(S/2)t_2}{T}. \tag{15.22}$$

Since we let the maximum number of units back ordered reach an amount S at a daily rate of d, the length of the back-order portion of the inventory cycle is

$$t_2 = S/d. \tag{15.23}$$

Using equations (15.23) and (15.19) in equation (15.22), we have

$$\text{average back-order level} = \frac{(S/2)(S/d)}{Q/d} = \frac{S^2}{2Q}. \tag{15.24}$$

Letting

C_b = cost to maintain one unit on back order for 1 year

our total annual cost expression (TC) for the inventory model with back orders becomes

$$TC = \frac{(Q-S)^2}{2Q} C_h + \frac{D}{Q} C_0 + \frac{S^2}{2Q} C_b. \tag{15.25}$$

Given the cost estimates and the annual demand D, we can begin to determine the minimum cost values for our inventory decisions, Q and S. With two decision components a trial-and-error approach, while valid, becomes cumbersome. Using calculus, management scientists have established the following minimum cost formulas for the order quantity Q^* and the planned back orders S^*:

$$Q^* = \sqrt{\frac{2DC_0}{C_h} \left(\frac{C_h + C_b}{C_b} \right)} \tag{15.26}$$

and

$$S^* = Q^* \left(\frac{C_h}{C_h + C_b} \right) \tag{15.27}$$

An Example Suppose the Higley Radio Components Company has a product for which the assumptions of the inventory model with back orders are valid. Information obtained by the company is as follows:

D = 2000 units per year
I = 20% per year
C = \$50 per unit
$C_h = IC$ = \$10 per unit per year
C_0 = \$25 per order.

457

The company is considering the possibility of allowing some back orders to occur for the product. A manager, using a 1-week back-order cost estimate of roughly \$0.50 to \$0.60 per unit, estimates the annual unit back-order cost at \$30 per unit per year. Using equations (15.26) and (15.27) we have

$$Q^* = \sqrt{\frac{2(2000)(25)}{10}\left(\frac{10+30}{30}\right)} = \sqrt{10,000\left(\frac{40}{30}\right)} = 115$$

and

$$S^* = 115\left(\frac{10}{10+30}\right) = 115\left(\frac{10}{40}\right) = 29.$$

If this solution is implemented, the system will operate with the following properties:

maximum inventory $= Q - S = 115 - 29 = 86$
cycle time $= T = (Q/D)(365) = 21$ days.

The total annual cost is

Inventory holding cost $= \dfrac{(86)^2}{2(115)}(10) = \$322$

Ordering cost $\quad\quad = \dfrac{2000}{115}(25) \quad = \$435$

Back-order cost $\quad\quad = \dfrac{(29)^2}{2(115)}(30) = \$110$

$\quad\quad\quad\quad\quad\quad\quad\quad\quad\quad\quad \overline{\quad\quad\$867}$

If the company had chosen to prohibit back orders and had adopted the regular EOQ model, the recommended inventory decision would have been

$$Q^* = \sqrt{\frac{2DC_0}{C_h}} = \sqrt{10,000} = 100.$$

This order quantity would have resulted in an inventory holding cost and ordering cost of \$500 each or a total annual cost of \$1000. Thus in this example, allowing back orders is projecting a $\$1000 - \$867 = \$133$ or 13.3% savings in cost from the no-stockout EOQ model. The above comparison and conclusion is based on the assumption that the back-order model (no lost sales) with an annual cost per back-ordered unit of \$30 is a valid model for the actual inventory situation. If the company has strong fears that stockouts might lead to lost sales, then the above savings might not be enough to warrant switching to an inventory policy that allowed for planned shortages.

Note that as the back-ordering cost C_b becomes large relative to the inventory holding cost C_h, the quantity $C_h/(C_h + C_b)$ in equation (15.27) will be relatively small and thus S^* will also be small. In this case the back-order model and the regular EOQ model provide very similar results. Also note that as the holding costs $(C_h = IC)$ become large, the number of back orders S becomes larger. This explains why many items which have a very high per unit cost C are handled on a back-order basis.

15.4 QUANTITY DISCOUNTS FOR THE EOQ MODEL

Quantity discounts occur in numerous businesses and industries where suppliers provide an incentive for large purchase quantities by offering lower unit costs when items are purchased in larger lots or quantities. In this section we show how the basic EOQ model can be used when quantity discounts are offered.

Assume that we have a product where the basic EOQ model is applicable, but instead of a fixed unit cost, our supplier quotes the following discount schedule.

Discount Category	Order Size	Discount	Unit Cost
1	0 to 999	0	$5.00
2	1000 to 2499	3%	$4.85
3	2500 and over	5%	$4.75

The 5% discount for the 2500-unit minimum order quantity looks tempting, but realizing that higher order quantities give us higher inventory carrying costs, we should prepare a thorough cost analysis before making a final ordering and inventory policy recommendation.

Suppose our data and cost analysis show an inventory holding cost rate of 20% per year, ordering costs of $49 per order, and an annual demand of 5000 units; what order quantity should we select? The following three-step procedure shows the calculations necessary to make this decision. In our preliminary calculations we will use Q_1 to indicate the order quantity for discount category 1, Q_2 for discount category 2, and Q_3 for discount category 3.

Step 1. Compute a Q^* using the EOQ formula for the unit cost associated with each discount category.

Recall the EOQ model $Q^* = \sqrt{2DC_0/C_h}$. In this case,

$$Q_1^* = \sqrt{\frac{2(5000)49}{1.00}} = 700$$

459

$$Q_2{}^* = \sqrt{\frac{2(5000)49}{0.97}} = 711$$

$$Q_3{}^* = \sqrt{\frac{2(5000)49}{0.95}} = 718.$$

Since the only differences in the models are slight differences in the inventory holding costs, the economic order quantities resulting from this step will be approximately the same. However, the calculated order quantities will usually not all be of the size necessary to qualify for the discount price assumed. In the above case, both $Q_2{}^*$ and $Q_3{}^*$ are insufficient order quantities to obtain their assumed unit costs of \$4.85 and \$4.75, respectively. For those order quantities for which the assumed price is incorrect, the following procedure must then be used.

Step 2. For those Q^*'s which are too small to qualify for the assumed discount price, adjust the order quantity upward to the nearest order quantity which will allow the product to be purchased at the assumed price.

In our example this causes us to set

$$Q_2{}^* = 1000$$

and

$$Q_3{}^* = 2500.$$

If a calculated Q^* for a given price is larger than the highest order quantity providing the particular discount price, this Q^* need not be considered any further since it cannot lead to an optimal solution. While this may not be obvious, it does turn out to be a property of the EOQ quantity discount model. Problem 16 at the end of the chapter asks you to show that this property is true.

In our previous inventory models we have ignored the annual purchase cost of the item because it was constant and never affected by the inventory order policy decision. However, in the quantity discount model total annual purchase cost will vary with the order quantity decision and the associated unit cost. Thus annual purchase cost (annual demand $D \times$ unit cost C) is included in the total cost model as shown below:

$$TC = \frac{Q}{2} C_h + \frac{D}{Q} C_0 + DC. \tag{15.28}$$

Using this total cost formula we can now determine the optimal order quantity for the EOQ discount model in Step 3 below.

Step 3. For each of the order quantities resulting from Step 1 and Step 2, compute the total annual cost using the unit price from the appropriate discount category and equation (15.28). The order quantity yielding the minimum total annual cost is the optimal order quantity.

460

TABLE 15.3   Total Annual Cost Calculations for the EOQ
             Quantity Discount Model

Category	Unit Cost	Order Quantity	Annual Inventory Cost	Annual Ordering Cost	Annual Purchase Cost	Total Annual Cost
1	$5.00	700	$ 350	$350	$25,000	$25,700
2	$4.85	1000	$ 485	$245	$24,250	$24,980
3	$4.75	2500	$1188	$ 98	$23,750	$25,036

The Step 3 calculations for our example problem are summarized in Table 15.3. As you can see, a decision to order 1000 units at the 3% discount rate yields the minimum cost solution. While the 2500-unit order quantity would result in a 5% discount, its excessive inventory holding cost makes it the second best solution.

15.5   AN ORDER QUANTITY—REORDER POINT MODEL WITH PROBABILISTIC DEMAND

Thus far in this chapter we have discussed inventory decision models where demand occurs at a constant rate. We now want to consider a variation of the EOQ model which provides "how-much-to-order" and "when-to-order" decision recommendations for situations in which the demand can only be described in probabilistic terms. Decision models used to analyze such inventory systems are referred to as *probabilistic demand* models. Just as with the EOQ model, we will be attempting to identify an inventory policy that minimizes the sum of ordering and inventory holding costs.

Since the level of mathematical sophistication required for an exact formulation of order quantity-reorder point inventory models with probabilistic demand is beyond the scope of this text, we will restrict our discussion of these inventory decision problems to a heuristic procedure that should enable you to obtain good, workable solutions without relying upon more advanced mathematical techniques. While this solution procedure can only be expected to provide approximations to the optimal inventory decisions, it has been found to yield very good decisions in many practical situations.

Let us consider the case of Dabco Industrial Lighting Distributors. Suppose Dabco purchases a special high-intensity light bulb for industrial lighting systems from a well-known light bulb manufacturer. Dabco would like a recommendation on how much it should order and when it should place an order so that a low-cost inventory operation can be realized. Pertinent facts are that ordering costs are $12 per order, one bulb costs $6, and Dabco uses a

20% annual holding cost rate for its inventory ($C_h = 0.20 \times 6 = \$1.20$). Dabco, which has over 1000 different customers, experiences a probabilistic demand in that the number of orders will vary considerably from day to day and week to week. While demand is not specifically known, historical sales data indicate that an annual demand of 8000 bulbs, while not exact, can be used as a good estimate of the anticipated annual volume.

The How-Much-to-Order Decision

Although we are in a probabilistic demand situation, we have a good estimate of the expected annual volume of 8000 units. As an approximation of the best order quantity we can apply the EOQ model with the expected annual volume substituted for the annual demand D. In Dabco's case,

$$Q^* = \sqrt{\frac{2DC_0}{C_h}} = \sqrt{\frac{2(8000)(12)}{(0.20)(6.00)}} = 400 \text{ units.}$$

When we studied the sensitivity of the EOQ models, we learned that the total cost of operating an inventory system was relatively insensitive to order quantities that were in the neighborhood of Q^* (see Table 15.2). Using this knowledge we expect 400 units per order to be a good approximation of the optimal order quantity. Even if annual demand were as low as 7000 units or as high as 9000 units, an order quantity of 400 units should be a relatively good low-cost order size. Thus given our best estimate of annual demand at 8000 units, we will use $Q^* = 400$.

We have established the 400-unit order quantity by ignoring the fact that demand is probabilistic. Using $Q^* = 400$, Dabco can anticipate placing approximately $D/Q^* = 8000/400 = 20$ orders per year with an average of approximately $365/20 = 18$ days between orders.

The When-to-Order Decision

We now want to establish a when-to-order decision rule or reorder point that will trigger the ordering process. Further pertinent data indicate that it usually takes one week for Dabco to receive a new supply of light bulbs from the manufacturer. With an average weekly demand of 8000/52 weeks = 154 units, you might first suggest a 154-unit reorder point. However, it now becomes extremely important to consider the probabilities of the various demands. If 154 is the average weekly demand, and if the demands are symmetrically distributed about 154, then weekly demand will be more than 154 units roughly 50% of the time.

When the demand during the 1-week lead time exceeds 154 units, Dabco will experience a shortage or stockout. Thus with a reorder point of 154

462

units, approximately 50% of the time (10 of the 20 orders a year) Dabco will be short of bulbs before the new supply arrives. This shortage rate would most likely be viewed as unacceptable. In order to determine a reorder point with a reasonably low likelihood or probability of a stockout it is necessary to establish a probability distribution for the lead time demand and analyze stockout probabilities.

Using historical data and some judgment, the *lead time demand distribution* for Dabco's light bulbs is assumed to be a normal distribution with a mean of 154 units and a standard deviation of 25 units. This is shown in Figure 15.6.

While the normal distribution of lead time demand is used in the Dabco problem, any demand probability distribution is acceptable. By collecting historical data on actual demands during the lead time period, an analyst should be able to determine if the normal distribution or some other probability distribution is the most realistic picture of the lead time demand distribution.

Given the lead time demand probability distribution, we can now determine how the reorder point *r* affects the probability of a stockout for the item. Since stockouts occur whenever the demand during the lead time exceeds the reorder point, we can find the probability of stockout by using the lead time demand distribution to compute the probability of demand exceeding *r*.

We could now approach the "when-to-order" problem by defining a cost per stockout and then attempting to include this cost in a total cost equation. Probably a more practical approach is to ask management to define an acceptable *service level,* where the service level refers to the average number of stockouts we are willing to allow per year. If demand for a product is probabilistic, a manager who says he will never tolerate a stockout is being somewhat unrealistic, because attempting to avoid stockouts completely will require high reorder points, high inventory levels, and an associated high inventory holding cost.

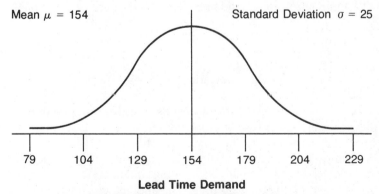

FIGURE 15.6   Distribution of Demand During the Lead Time for Dabco

463

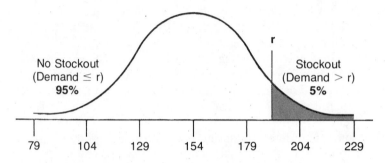

FIGURE 15.7 *Reorder Point r that Allows a 5% Chance of Stockout for Dabco Light Bulbs*

Suppose in this case that Dabco management is willing to tolerate an average of one stockout per year. This service level can be maintained if 1 out of the 20 planned orders, 5% of the orders, results in a stockout. This implies that for any one order there can be a 5% chance of a stockout. Thus the reorder point *r* can be found by using the lead time demand distribution to find the value of *r* for which there is only a 5% chance of having a lead time demand exceeding it. This situation is shown graphically in Figure 15.7.

From the normal distribution tables in Appendix B we see that an *r* value that is 1.645 standard deviations above the mean will allow stockouts 5% of the time. Therefore, for the assumed normal distribution for lead time demand with $\mu = 154$ and $\sigma = 25$, the reorder point *r* is determined by

$$r = 154 + 1.645(25) = 195.$$

If a normal distribution is used for lead time demand, the general equation for *r* is

$$r = \mu + z\sigma \tag{15.29}$$

where z is the number of standard deviations necessary to achieve the acceptable stockout probability.

Thus the recommended inventory decisions are to order 400 units whenever the inventory level reaches the reorder point of 195. Since the mean or expected demand during the lead time is 154 units, the $195 - 154 = 41$ units serve as a safety stock which absorbs higher than usual demand during the lead time. Roughly 95% of the time the 195 units will be able to satisfy demand during the lead time. The anticipated annual cost for this system is as follows:

464

ordering cost	$(D/Q)C_0 = (8000/400)12$	$= \$240.00$
holding cost—normal inventory	$(Q/2)C_h = (400/2)(1.20)$	$= \$240.00$
holding cost—safety stock	$(41)C_h = 41(1.20)$	$= \$\ \underline{49.20}$
		$\$529.20.$

If Dabco could have assumed that a known, constant demand rate of 8000 units per year existed for the light bulbs, a $Q^* = 400$, $r = 154$, and total annual cost of $\$240 + \$240 = \$480$ would have been expected. When demand is uncertain and can only be expressed in probabilistic terms, a larger total cost can be expected. The larger cost occurs in the form of larger inventory holding costs because more inventory must be maintained in order to prevent frequent stockouts. For Dabco this additional inventory or safety stock was 41 units, with an additional annual inventory holding cost of $\$49.20$.

15.6 SUMMARY

In this chapter you have seen some of the approaches that operations researchers take in attempting to develop inventory decision models that will assist managers in establishing low-cost operating policies for inventory systems. In Sections 15.1 to 15.4 we specifically studied cases where the demand for the product occurs at a rather stable or constant known rate. In analyzing these inventory systems, operations researchers attempt to develop total cost models which include ordering cost, inventory holding cost, and in some cases, back-ordering cost, and then use differential calculus to develop minimum cost formulas for the order quantity Q. A reorder point r can be established by considering the lead time demand for the item.

In Section 15.5, we introduced a decision model that took into consideration an uncertain or probabilistic demand. While the recommended order quantity was based on the EOQ model, the reorder point was adjusted upward in order to provide a safety stock and an acceptable service level.

In closing this chapter we reemphasize that inventory and inventory systems can be an extremely expensive phase of a firm's operation. It is of utmost economic importance for managers to be aware of the cost of inventory systems and to make the best possible operating policy decisions for the inventory system. Quantitative inventory decision models, as presented in this chapter, can help managers to develop good inventory policies.

15.7 GLOSSARY

1. *Inventory holding or inventory carrying cost*—All costs associated with maintaining an inventory investment: cost of the capital investment in

the inventory, insurance, taxes, warehouse overhead, and so on. This cost may be stated as a percentage of the inventory investment or a cost per unit.

2. *Cost of capital*—The cost a firm incurs, usually interest payments on borrowed funds or dividend payments on stocks, in order to obtain capital for investment. The cost of capital, which may be stated as an annual percentage rate, is part of the holding cost associated with maintaining inventory levels.

3. *Economic order quantity (EOQ)*—The order quantity which minimizes the total inventory costs in the most fundamental inventory decision model.

4. *Constant demand rate*—An assumption of many inventory decision models which states that the same number of units are taken from inventory in each period of time.

5. *Ordering cost*—The fixed cost (salaries, paper, transportation, and so on) associated with placing an order for an item.

6. *Reorder point*—The inventory level at which a new order should be placed.

7. *Lead time*—The time between the placing of an order and its receipt in the inventory system.

8. *Lead time demand*—The number of units demanded during the lead time period.

9. *Cycle time*—The length of time between the placing of two consecutive orders.

10. *Safety stock*—Inventory maintained in order to reduce the number of stockouts resulting from higher than expected demand during lead time.

11. *Constant supply rate*—The situation in which the inventory is built up at a constant rate over a period of time. This assumption applies to the production lot size model of this chapter.

12. *Back order*—The receipt of an order for a product when there are no units on hand in inventory. These back orders become shortages which are eventually satisfied when a new supply of the product becomes available.

13. *Quantity discounts*—Discounts or lower unit costs offered by the manufacturer when a customer purchases larger quantities of the product.

14. *Goodwill cost*—A cost associated with a back order, a lost sale, or any form of stockout or unsatisfied demand. This cost may be used to reflect the loss of future profits because a customer experienced an unsatisfied demand.

15. *Probabilistic demand*—Situations in which demand for the inventory item is not known exactly and probabilities must be used to describe the demand alternatives for the product.

16. *Lead time demand distribution*—In probabilistic inventory models, this is the distribution of demand that occurs during the lead time period.

17. *Service level*—The average number of stockouts allowed per year.

15.8 PROBLEMS

1. Suppose R & B Beverage Company has a soft-drink product that has a constant annual demand rate of 3600 cases. A case of the soft drink costs R & B $2.70. If ordering costs are $9 and inventory holding costs are charged at 15%, what is the economic order quantity and cycle time in days for this product?

2. A general property of the EOQ inventory model is that total inventory holding and total ordering costs are equal or balanced at the optimal solution. Use the data in Problem 1 to show that this result is observed for this problem. Use equations (15.1), (15.2), and (15.5) to show in general that total inventory holding costs and total ordering costs are equal whenever Q^* is used.

3. The XYZ Company purchases a component used in the manufacturing of automobile generators directly from the supplier. XYZ's generator production operation, which is operated at a constant rate, will require 1000 components per month throughout the year (12,000 units annually). If ordering costs are $25 per order, unit cost is $2.50 per component, and annual inventory holding costs are charged at 20%, answer the following inventory policy questions for XYZ.
   a. What is the EOQ for this component?
   b. What is the length of cycle time in months?
   c. What are the total annual inventory holding and ordering costs associated with your recommended EOQ?

4. Assuming 250 days of operation per year and a lead time of 5 days, what is the reorder point for the XYZ Company in Problem 3?

5. Suppose that XYZ's management in Problem 3 likes the operational efficiency of ordering in quantities of 1000 units and ordering once each month. How much more expensive would this policy be than your EOQ recommendation? Would you recommend in favor of the 1000-unit order quantity? Explain. What would the reorder point be if the 1000-unit quantity was acceptable?

6. Nation-Wide Bus Lines is quite proud of its 6-week bus driver training program that it conducts for all new Nation-Wide drivers. A 6-week training program costs Nation-Wide $15,000 for instructors, equipment, and so on, and is independent of the number of new drivers in the class as long as the class size remains less than or equal to 35. The Nation-Wide training program must provide the company with approximately five new fully trained drivers per month. After completing the training program, new drivers are paid $1000 per month, but do not work until a full-time driver position is open. Nation-Wide views the $1000 per month paid to each idle new driver as a holding cost necessary to maintain a supply of newly trained drivers available for immediate service. Viewing new drivers as inventory-type units, how large should the training classes be in order to minimize Nation-Wide's total annual

training and new driver idle-time costs? How many training classes should the company hold each year? What is the total annual cost of your recommendation?

7. All-Star Bat Manufacturing, Inc., supplies baseball bats to major and minor league baseball teams. After an initial order in January, demand over the 8-month baseball season is approximately constant at 1000 bats per month. Assuming that the bat production process can handle up to 4000 bats per month, the bat production setup costs are $150 per setup, the production cost is $10 per bat, and assuming that All-Star uses a 24% annual or 2% monthly inventory holding cost, what production lot size would you recommend to meet the demand during the baseball season? How often will the production process operate, and what is the length of a production run?

8. Assume a production line operates such that the production lot size model of Section 15.2 is applicable. Given $D = 6400$ units per year, $C_0 = \$100$, and $C_h = \$2$ per unit per year, compute the minimum cost production lot size for each of the following production rates:
   a. 8000 units per year.
   b. 10,000 units per year.
   c. 32,000 units per year.
   d. 100,000 units per year.

   Compute the EOQ recommended lot size using equation (15.5). What two observations can you make about the relationship between the EOQ model and the production lot size model?

9. Assume you are reviewing the production lot size decision associated with a production operation where $P = 8000$ units per year, $D = 2000$ units per year, $C_0 = \$300$, and $C_h = \$1.60$ per unit per year. Also assume current practice calls for production runs of 500 units every 3 months. Would you recommend changing the current production lot size? Why or why not? How much could be saved by converting to your production lot size recommendation?

10. Suppose the XYZ Company of Problem 3, with $D = 12,000$ units per year, $C_h = (2.50)(0.20) = \$0.50$, and $C_0 = \$25.00$, decided to operate with a back-order inventory policy. Back-order costs are estimated to be $5 per unit per year. Identify the following:
    a. Minimum cost order quantity.
    b. Maximum number of back orders.
    c. Maximum inventory level.
    d. Cycle time.
    e. Total annual cost.

11. Assuming 250 days of operation per year and a lead time of 5 days, what is the reorder point for the XYZ Company in Problem 10? Show the general formula for the reorder point for the EOQ model with back orders. In general, is the reorder point when back orders are allowed

468

greater than or less than the reorder point when back orders are not allowed? Explain.

12. A manager of an inventory system believes inventory models are important decision-making aids. While he frequently uses the EOQ policy, he has never considered a back-order model because he has always felt back orders were "bad" and should be avoided. However, with upper management's continued pressure for cost reduction, he has asked you to analyze the economics of a back-ordering policy for some products that he believes can possibly be back-ordered. For a specific product with $D = 800$ units per year, $C_0 = \$150$, $C_h = \$3.00$, and $C_b = \$20$, what is the economic difference between the EOQ and the planned back-order model? If the manager puts constraints that no more than 25% of the units can be back-ordered and that no customer will have to wait more than 3 weeks (21 days) for an order, should the back-order inventory policy be adopted?

13. If the lead time for new orders is 1 month for the inventory system discussed in Problem 12, find the reorder point for both the EOQ and the planned back-order models.

14. Assume the following quantity discount schedule is appropriate:

Order Size	Discount	Unit Cost
0 to 49	0%	$30.00
50 to 99	5%	$28.50
over 99	10%	$27.00

If annual demand is 120 units, ordering cost is $20 per order, and annual inventory carrying cost is 25%, what order quantity would you recommend?

15. Apply the EOQ model to the following quantity discount situation. What order quantity do you recommend?

Category	Order Size	Discount	Unit Cost
1	0 to 99	0	$10.00
2	over 99	3%	$ 9.70

$D = 500$ units per year, $C_0 = \$40$, and an annual inventory holding cost of 20% are given.

16. In the EOQ model with quantity discounts we stated that if the Q^* for a price category is larger than necessary to qualify for the category price, the category cannot be optimal. Use the two discount categories in

469

Problem 15 to show that this is true. That is, plot the total cost curves for the two categories and show that if the category 2 minimum cost Q is an acceptable solution, we do not have to consider category 1.

17. Floyd Distributors, Inc., provides a variety of auto parts to small local garages. Floyd purchases from the manufacturers according to the EOQ model and then ships from a regional warehouse direct to its customers. For a particular type of muffler, Floyd's EOQ analysis recommends orders with $Q^* = 25$ to satisfy an annual demand of 200 mufflers (average demand is approximately four units per week). Floyd has a 3-week lead time on all orders he places with his muffler supplier.

   a. What is the reorder point if Floyd assumes a constant demand of four units per week?

   b. Suppose Floyd's muffler demand shows some variability such that the lead time demand follows a normal distribution with $\mu = 12$ and $\sigma = 2.5$. If Floyd's management can tolerate one stockout per year, what is the revised reorder point?

   c. What is the safety stock for part b? If $C_h = \$5/\text{unit/year}$, what is the extra cost due to the uncertainty of demand?

18. For Floyd's Distributors in Problem 17, we were given $Q^* = 25$, $D = 200$, $C_h = \$5$, and a normal lead time demand distribution with $\mu = 12$ and $\sigma = 2.5$.

   a. What is Floyd's reorder point if the firm is willing to tolerate two stockouts during the year?

   b. What is Floyd's reorder point if the firm wants to restrict the probability of a stockout on any one cycle to 1%?

   c. What are the safety stock levels and the annual safety stock costs for the reorder points found in parts (a) and (b)?

19. A firm with an annual demand of approximately 1000 units has $C_0 = \$25.50$ and $C_h = 8$. The demand exhibits some variability such that the lead time demand follows a normal distribution with $\mu = 25$ and $\sigma = 5$.

   a. What is the recommended order quantity?

   b. What is the reorder point and safety stock if the firm desires a 2% probability of stockout on any given order cycle?

   c. If a manager sets the reorder point at 30, what is the probability of a stockout on any given order cycle? How many times would you expect to stockout during the year if this reorder point were used?

20. The B&S Novelty and Craft Shop in Bennington, Vermont, sells a variety of quality handmade items to tourists. B&S will sell approximately 300 hand-carved miniature replicas of a colonial soldier each year, but the demand pattern during the year is uncertain. The replicas sell for $20 each and B&S uses a 15% annual inventory holding cost rate. Ordering costs are $5 per order and demand during the lead time

follows a uniform distribution with the demand alternatives from 6 to 25 each having approximately the same probability of occurrence.

a. What is the recommended order quantity?

b. If B&S is willing to have a stockout roughly twice a year, what reorder point would you recommend? What is the probability B&S will have a stockout on any one order cycle?

c. What is the safety stock and annual safety stock costs for this product?

APPENDIX 15.1 DEVELOPMENT OF THE OPTIMAL ORDER QUANTITY Q* FORMULA FOR THE EOQ MODEL

Given equation (15.3) as the general total annual cost formula for the EOQ model,

$$\text{TC} = \tfrac{1}{2}QC_h + \frac{D}{Q}C_0 \qquad\qquad (15.3)$$

we can find the order quantity Q that minimizes the total cost by setting the derivative $d\text{TC}/dQ$ equal to zero and solving for Q^*.

$$\frac{d\text{TC}}{dQ} = \tfrac{1}{2}C_h - \frac{D}{Q^2}C_0 = 0$$

$$\tfrac{1}{2}C_h = \frac{D}{Q^2}C_0$$

$$C_h Q^2 = 2DC_0$$

$$Q^2 = \frac{2DC_0}{C_h}$$

Hence,

$$Q^* = \sqrt{\frac{2DC_0}{C_h}}. \qquad\qquad (15.5)$$

The second derivative is

$$\frac{d^2\text{TC}}{dQ^2} = \frac{2D}{Q^3}C_0.$$

Since the value of the second derivative is greater than zero for D, C_0, and Q greater than zero, Q^* from equation (15.5) is, in fact, the minimum cost solution.

471

APPENDIX 15.2   DEVELOPMENT OF THE OPTIMAL LOT SIZE Q* FOR THE PRODUCTION LOT SIZE MODEL

Given equation (15.15) as the total annual cost formula for the production lot size model,

$$TC = \tfrac{1}{2}(1 - D/P)QC_h + \frac{D}{Q} C_0 \qquad (15.15)$$

we can find the order quantity Q that minimizes the total cost by setting the derivative dTC/dQ equal to zero and solving for Q^*.

$$\frac{dTC}{dQ} = \tfrac{1}{2}(1 - D/P)C_h - \frac{D}{Q^2} C_0 = 0.$$

Solving for Q^* we have

$$\tfrac{1}{2}(1 - D/P)C_h = \frac{D}{Q^2} C_0$$

$$(1 - D/P)C_h Q^2 = 2DC_0$$

$$Q^2 = \frac{2DC_0}{(1 - D/P)C_h} \ .$$

Hence,

$$Q^* = \sqrt{\frac{2DC_0}{(1 - D/P)C_h}} \qquad (15.16)$$

The second derivative is

$$\frac{d^2TC}{dQ^2} = \frac{2DC_0}{Q^3} \ .$$

Since the value of the second derivative is greater than zero for D, C_0, and Q greater than zero, Q^* from equation (15.16) is a minimum cost solution.

16
Computer
Simulation

Computer simulation is a procedure that attempts to re-create a problem situation under study by developing a computer model of the process. Then, through a series of organized trial-and-error operations, the technique attempts to determine a good solution to the problem. Computer simulation ranks as one of the most often used quantitative solution techniques. The Turban study referred to in Chapter 1 indicated that computer simulation was used in approximately 25% of the projects involving operations research methodology. Some of the reasons why computer simulation is such a significant problem-solving tool are listed below.

1. Computer simulation can often be used to obtain good solutions to problems that are too complex and difficult to solve using existing analytical solution procedures such as linear programming, inventory models, and others.
2. The approach is relatively easy to explain and understand. As a result management confidence is increased, and consequently utilization of the technique is more easily obtained.
3. Computer manufacturers have developed extensive software packages which consist of specialized computer simulation programming languages, thus facilitating use by analysts.
4. In practice, the technique has been applied successfully to a wide range of decision-making problems.

In this chapter we introduce the concepts and procedures of computer simulation by studying how this technique can be used to solve a simple production quantity decision problem. The particular problem involves a daily production quantity decision when demand is uncertain. After describing how computer simulation can be used to solve this problem, we study and apply the computer simulation approach to a problem with two decision variables and two probabilistic components. Let us begin with the production quantity decision problem faced by the Stollar Bakery Shop.

16.1 THE STOLLAR BAKERY SHOP PROBLEM

Red Stollar, proprietor of the Stollar Bakery Shop, has the following problem. He would like to determine how many 10-inch white birthday cakes he

473

should produce each day in order to maximize his profits. Red's present method of determining the quantity to bake is based upon his best guess or estimate of the daily demand for the birthday cakes. For example, if Red estimates that the daily demand will be five cakes, then five cakes will be produced for the day's operation. Since it is more economical to process all the cakes in one batch, all five cakes would be produced early in the morning.

The production costs are $2 per cake. Thus, with a $4.50 selling price, the bakery realizes a $2.50 profit for each cake sold. However, if Red overestimates the daily demand, some cakes will be left over at the end of the day. The bakery's policy is to sell all leftover or surplus cakes to a local store that specializes in day-old bakery items. The bakery is currently receiving $1.50 per cake for the surplus cakes, thus incurring a loss of $0.50 per cake.

Unfortunately Red's daily decision of how many cakes to produce is difficult because the daily demand is uncertain. Red has experienced some days when there was no demand, and yet one day last week he experienced a demand for eight of the birthday cakes.

Red felt very uncomfortable with his daily production-quantity decision since it was based on his "guess" of the daily demand. More importantly, Red could not predict the profit associated with his final production quantity decision. Ideally, Red wanted a recommendation on the daily production quantity for birthday cakes that would maximize his profits over the long run. In attempting to determine a good production quantity, Red described a possible solution procedure by stating the following: "What I would really like to do is to try a variety of production sizes and see how each did. I guess I'm really thinking about some type of trial-and-error procedure. For example, I would like to try a production size of two cakes for a while, maybe for two or three weeks, and then observe the resulting sales and total profits; then try a production size of three cakes for the same length of time; then perhaps four cakes each day, and so on. Then all I would have to do is select the production quantity that resulted in a maximum profit."

Unfortunately, while Red's approach seems logical, this procedure would be very time-consuming because it would take Red 3 or 4 months to collect profit data on only five trial production-quantity alternatives. In addition, Red could experience several weeks of low profits or even losses if some of his trial production quantities were poor decisions. What Red needs is a way to carry out his trial-and-error procedure without actually performing the experiments in the bakery.

Actually, computer simulation can be used to experiment with production sizes in just this manner. In the computer simulation technique we will need to develop a mathematical model and a computer program that describe or re-create the bakery shop's operation for the sale of the white birthday cakes. In using the simulation model we will choose a trial production quantity, create or simulate a number of hypothetical daily demands, and compute the resulting total profit. Then, by choosing other production quantities, we can continue this trial-and-error procedure until we find what appears to be the profit-maximizing production quantity. While this trial-and-error procedure will not guarantee an optimal solution, the simulated "best" solution should be close to the optimal solution and thus a very good production quantity decision. In order to understand the simulation procedure, let us describe a simulation model of the Stollar Bakery Shop problem.

Model Development

We begin our development of the bakery simulation model by defining the following notation. Let

x = number of 10-inch birthday cakes produced
d = daily demand for 10-inch birthday cakes
z = daily profit associated with producing x 10-inch birthday cakes.

For example, if Red produces five cakes ($x = 5$) and the actual daily demand turns out to be seven ($d = 7$), Red would have two unfilled orders, and the daily profit would be

$$z = 5(\$2.50) = \$12.50.$$

daily profit   cakes sold   profit per cake

In the above illustration, Red underestimated the daily demand by two units. Note that although the bakery was unable to satisfy demand, there was no additional cost incurred as a result of the lost sales. However, a business that continually fails to meet demand can suffer significant losses due to customer dissatisfaction. This may result in customers reducing future purchases or taking their business elsewhere. In situations where there is a loss of goodwill associated with unsatisfied demand, a cost reflecting this loss would be subtracted in the calculation of z. While Red considered the possibility of a goodwill cost, he decided not to include it in the profit calculation at this time. Problem 4 at the end of the chapter asks you to show what happens to the production-quantity decision when a goodwill cost is considered.

If, on another day, the bakery produces five cakes to cover daily demand ($x = 5$) and the actual demand turns out to be only three ($d = 3$), then the profit resulting from overproducing by two units would be

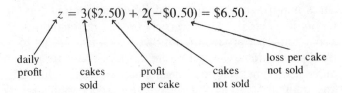

$$z = 3(\$2.50) + 2(-\$0.50) = \$6.50.$$

daily profit — cakes sold — profit per cake — cakes not sold — loss per cake not sold

Hence we see that the bakery's daily profit depends upon the daily demand; that is, in both illustrations Red has selected the same production quantity but the resulting daily profit has changed by $12.50 − $6.50 = $6.00. Let us consider one more case before attempting to write a general model for this problem.

Assume that Red decides to produce five cakes ($x = 5$) and that actual demand turns out to be five ($d = 5$). The profit resulting from meeting demand exactly would be

Thus we see that when the production quantity equals the actual daily demand, the daily profit is computed in exactly the same way as when the daily demand exceeds the production quantity. Hence when writing a mathematical model to describe how profits are related to the production quantity x and the daily demand d, we need only consider two separate cases: (1) the production quantity is less than or equal to the daily demand and (2) the production quantity is greater than the daily demand.

Case 1: Production Quantity Less than or Equal to Demand
If $x \leq d$,

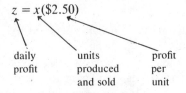

$$z = x(\$2.50)$$

daily profit — units produced and sold — profit per unit

or

$$z = 2.50x. \tag{16.1}$$

Case 2: Production Quantity Greater than Demand
If $x > d$,

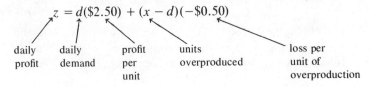

$$z = d(\$2.50) + (x - d)(-\$0.50)$$

daily profit — daily demand — profit per unit — units overproduced — loss per unit of overproduction

476

or

$$z = 3.00d - 0.50x. \tag{16.2}$$

The profit expressions of equations (16.1) and (16.2) are, of course, only applicable for the prices and costs associated with the bakery shop problem. To develop general formulas that are appropriate for similar problems, we must introduce some additional notation. Let

p = selling price of each unit
c = cost of each unit
s = day-old sales prices or salvage value for each unit that is not sold.

For the bakery shop problem, $p = \$4.50$, $c = \$2.00$, and $s = \$1.50$. We can now generalize our two cases.

Case 1: Production Quantity Less than or Equal to Demand
  If $x \leq d$,

$$z = (p - c)x. \tag{16.3}$$

Case 2: Production Quantity Greater than Demand
  If $x > d$,

$$z = d(p - c) + (x - d)(s - c)$$
$$= (p - s)d + (s - c)x. \tag{16.4}$$

16.2 SIMULATION OF THE STOLLAR BAKERY SHOP PROBLEM

A schematic representation of the model for the Stollar Bakery Shop problem is shown in Figure 16.1. The production size is the controllable input and the daily demand is the uncontrollable input. Since the daily demand is uncertain, we have a stochastic model of the bakery shop operation.

In Figure 16.1 we see that in order to simulate (re-create) the bakery shop's operation, we must first define the production quantity x and the daily demand d for each day of operation. With x and d defined, we can use the model to project the resulting daily profit. If we fix the production quantity x at a trial value and then input several daily demands, representing several hypothetical days of bakery shop operation, we can project the total profit that would result if the bakery produced x units each day during the hypothetical period of time. The total profit for the period would be an estimate of the total profit the bakery might realize if the trial production quantity was used over the same number of actual days of operation. Through this process we are simulating the bakery shop operation for a period of time under a trial production quantity. The flow chart of the simula-

477

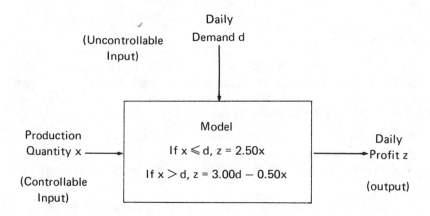

FIGURE 16.1 *Bakery Shop Model for the Sale of Birthday Cakes*

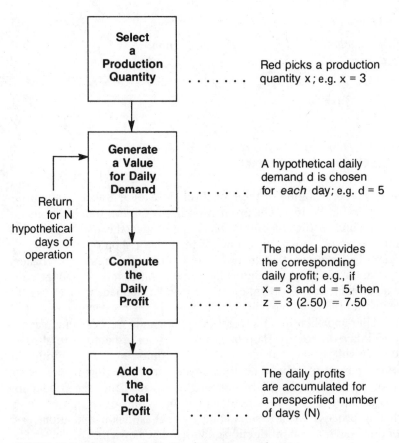

FIGURE 16.2 *Flowchart of the Simulation Process for N Days of the Stollar Bakery Shop Operation*

tion procedure of selecting a production quantity x, generating several hypothetical daily demands, and computing the resulting total profit is illustrated in Figure 16.2.

Generating Daily Demand

Note from the second block of Figure 16.2 that a major part of the simulation process consists of generating a hypothetical daily demand. Since we want the model to be a good representation of the real situation, it is important that the generated daily demand be a good representation of the actual daily demands that exist for the birthday cakes.

Assume that the bakery has available data showing the daily demand during the past month (20 days of operation). This history of daily demand is shown in Table 16.1.

We see that for the 20 days of operation a daily demand of 0 units occurred just one day, a daily demand of one unit occurred on two separate days, and so on. Red felt that this demand pattern was typical and would be representative of the levels of daily demand the bakery shop would receive in the future.

Based on Table 16.1 we can prepare a slightly different table that will help us generate hypothetical demands for the simulation model. The new table that we will develop contains the relative frequency distribution of daily

TABLE 16.1   Historical Daily Demand for the Birthday Cakes

Daily demand d	Frequency or Number of Days Observed
0	1
1	2
2	1
3	2
4	3
5	6
6	3
7	1
8	1
	20 days

demand, where the relative frequency of a particular value is defined as follows:

$$\text{relative frequency} = \frac{\text{frequency of observation}}{\text{total number of observations}}.$$

For example, a daily demand for five units ($d = 5$) occurred on 6 days during the 20 days of operation. Thus the relative frequency of a daily demand of $d = 5$ is given by

$$\text{relative frequency} = \frac{6}{20} = 0.30.$$

Table 16.2 presents the relative frequency distribution of the daily demand for the birthday cakes.

We see that 5% of the daily demands were for zero cakes, 10% were for one cake, 5% were for two cakes, and so on. If we believe that this relative frequency distribution is representative of the future pattern of daily demand, we can use it as the basis for generating hypothetical daily demand in our simulation model. This is a critical part of any simulation study and warrants serious consideration by both the analyst and the decision maker. If the demand distribution is not an accurate representation of the actual demand, the simulation results will be of little value. In general, decision models based on inaccurate or nonrepresentative inputs will not provide useful output information for the decision maker.

Assuming that Red accepts the above relative frequency distribution as an accurate portrayal of future daily demand, we must now devise a method of

TABLE 16.2 *Relative Frequency of Daily Demand for Birthday Cakes*

Daily Demand d	Relative Frequency
0	0.05
1	0.10
2	0.05
3	0.10
4	0.15
5	0.30
6	0.15
7	0.05
8	0.05
	1.00

480

generating or simulating daily demand of $d = 0, d = 1, d = 2, \ldots$. Our method should in the long run generate a demand of 0 units approximately 5% of the time, a demand of one unit approximately 10% of the time, and so on. Although we will eventually perform this process using a computer, let us initially describe a simple approach that you can employ with nothing more sophisticated than a pencil and a sheet of paper.

Take a sheet of paper and cut it into 20 equal-sized pieces. Following the historical daily demand frequency data of Table 16.1, write the number 0 on one piece of paper; this stands for a demand of zero units. On two of the remaining pieces write the number 1, which stands for a demand of one unit. Then, on one piece write the number 2; on two pieces write a 3; on three pieces write a 4; on six pieces write a 5; on three pieces write a 6; on one piece write a 7; and finally, on the last piece write an 8, which stands for a demand of eight units. Check the numbers you have written carefully, because this "deck" of 20 pieces of paper will be used to generate daily demands in our hand simulation of the process. Note that your deck was 5% 0's, 10% 1's, 5% 2's, and so on, and represents the historical relative frequency distribution of Table 16.2. Now shuffle your deck of 20 pieces of paper to thoroughly mix up the numbers. Since the slips are all the same size, if we select one slip of paper at random, we will have simulated drawing a specific daily demand from the distribution shown in Table 16.2.

Let us now see how we can use this "deck" in the simulation of the bakery shop operation. In Figure 16.2 we saw that the first step of the simulation procedure required the selection of a daily production quantity. For purposes of illustrating the simulation procedure, let us assume Red has selected three cakes as the production quantity ($x = 3$). The second block of Figure 16.2 indicates that the next step of the simulation process involves generating a hypothetical daily demand. Let us now use the deck of 20 slips of paper to generate a demand by selecting one slip of paper at random. Suppose the first slip drawn has a 5 written on it. We shall then use a demand of five cakes for the first simulated day of bakery shop operation. This level of demand, given Red's production quantity of three cakes, corresponds to an underproduction of two cakes. Since $x < d$, we can compute our first day's profit using the expression $2.50x = 2.50(3) = \$7.50$. Since this is our first day of simulation, the corresponding total profit is also $7.50. If we only wanted to simulate one day of operation we would stop at this point. However, to simulate additional days of operation, we return to the second block in Figure 16.2 and generate another hypothetical daily demand.

We generate a hypothetical demand for the second day of our simulation by returning the previously selected slip of paper to the deck, reshuffling all 20 pieces of paper, and then drawing another slip at random. On this second draw, suppose we obtain a demand of $d = 1$. Since $x > d$ on this second simulated day, the daily profit is computed using the expression $z = 3.00d - 0.50x$, which results in a daily profit of $3.00(1) - 0.50(3) = \$1.50$. Adding the

TABLE 16.3   Ten-Day Simulation Results for a Production
Quantity of x = 3.

Day	Generated Daily Demand d	Daily Profit	Total Profit ($)
1	5	7.50	7.50
2	1	1.50	9.00
3	6	7.50	16.50
4	3	7.50	24.00
5	4	7.50	31.50
6	4	7.50	39.00
7	8	7.50	46.50
8	0	−1.50	45.00
9	5	7.50	52.50
10	6	7.50	60.00

$1.50 profit for the second day to the $7.50 profit for the first day results in a total profit of $9 for 2 days of simulated operation. We continued this hand simulation process for 8 more days of operation and the results are summarized in Table 16.3. The total profit of $60 is the simulated or projected 10-day profit if the bakery uses a daily production quantity of 3.

If we perform similar 10-day simulations with other possible production quantity decisions, we will obtain projected 10-day profit information for other decision alternatives. The production quantity alternative resulting in the highest 10-day total profit is the simulation model recommendation of the best production-quantity decision. Using the same set of hypothetical daily demands $(5, 1, 6, 3, \ldots)$, we simulated 10 days of operation for production quantities from $x = 1$ to $x = 8$. A summary of the results from all 10-day simulations is presented in Table 16.4.

While the simulation results of Table 16.4 indicate that $x = 6$ is the best production quantity, the results are based upon only 10 days of simulated operation. A much longer simulation period is required to develop confidence in our best production quantity conclusion. Note that for our 10-day simulation we did not observe a daily demand of two units or seven units, and yet, according to Table 16.2, such demands occur 10% of the time. Running the model for a longer period of time will tend to make the simulated demands more closely follow the relative frequency distribution of Table 16.2.

Table 16.5 shows the results for 500 days of simulated bakery shop operation. As it turns out, the results from this longer simulation period also

482

TABLE 16.4   Ten-Day Simulation Results for Various
             Production Quantities

Production Size	Ten-Day Simulated Profit ($)
1	25
2	44
3	60
4	79
5	90
6	93
7	91
8	89

indicate that the best production size is 6. Because of the large number of calculations required by the 500 days of simulation, a computer program was used to perform these simulations. In Section 16.4 we will look more closely at the computer simulation process.

If Red is satisfied that the model and the frequency distribution of daily demand are appropriate for the bakery shop operation, the simulation model solution of $x = 6$ should be the recommended production quantity.

The simulation we have described for Stollar's Bakery Shop conveys the essence of what simulation is all about; that is, we build a model of the situation and then investigate how different decision alternatives affect the output. In the bakery shop problem we investigated how different production

TABLE 16.5   500-Day Simulation Results for Stollar's Bakery
             Shop

Production Size	Total Profit ($)	
1	1187	
2	2191	
3	3096	
4	3845	
5	4360	
6	4467 ◄———	Best simulation
7	4397	solution
8	4231	

quantities affect the bakery's profits. While a simulation model does not guarantee or mathematically prove that the recommended decision is optimal, it should provide information that will enable the decision maker to select a near-optimal or good decision.

16.3 THE ROLE OF RANDOM NUMBERS IN SIMULATION

In the previous section we described a method for simulating the daily demand for the birthday cakes by simply writing the various demands on pieces of paper and selecting a piece of paper, and therefore a specific demand, at random. By writing the more frequent demands on correspondingly more pieces of paper, we were able to provide simulated demands with a relative frequency distribution similar to the relative frequency distribution of the actual demand. While this method helped us demonstrate the simulation process and perhaps might be used for some small hand-simulation models, it would be inefficient and cumbersome for relatively large and complex simulation studies.

In this section we will show you how random numbers can be used to simulate the probabilistic inputs of a model. Specifically you will learn how random numbers can be used to provide the simulated demands for the Stollar Bakery Shop problem. Later you will see how the random number procedure offers a convenient method that can be used when a computer performs the simulation calculation.

Almost everyone who has been exposed to simple random sampling and basic statistics is familiar with tables of random digits or random numbers. Actually, there are complete handbooks[1] that contain nothing but table after table of random numbers. We have included one such table of random numbers in Appendix D. Thirty random numbers from the first line of this table are as follows:

> 63271   59986   71744   51102   15141   80714.

The specific digit appearing in a given position is simply a random selection of the digits 0, 1, 2, . . . , 9, with each digit having an equal chance of selection. Note that the grouping of the numbers in sets of five is simply for the convenience of making the table easier to read.

Now that we have random numbers available in Appendix D, let us see how we might use them to simulate daily demand for the Stollar Bakery Shop problem. Just as in the previous section where we had a specific demand associated with each piece of paper, we will now want a specific demand

---

[1] For example, *A Million Random Digits with 100,000 Normal Deviates*, RAND Corporation, 1955.

associated with each random number. Also, just as we had more pieces of paper for the more frequent demands, we will want more random numbers for the more frequent demands.

Suppose we select random numbers from our table in sets of two digits. This will provide us with 100 two-digit random numbers from 00 to 99 with each two-digit random number having a 1/100 or 0.01 chance of being selected. While we could select the two-digit random number from any part of our random number table, suppose we start by using the first row of random numbers from Appendix D. Our two-digit random numbers would be

63, 27, 15, 99, 86, 71, ...

Now let us see how we can define a daily demand corresponding to each of these two-digit random numbers. For example, let us consider the demand of zero units. Recall from the relative frequency distribution of Table 16.2 that we found that a daily demand of zero units occurred 5% of the time. Thus we will want 5% of our 100 possible two-digit random numbers to correspond to a demand of zero units. While any five numbers from 00 to 99 will do, for convenience, let us assign a demand of zero units to the first 5 two-digit random numbers: 00, 01, 02, 03, and 04. Thus any time one of these five random numbers are observed, we will create a simulated daily order of zero units. Since we expect one of the two-digit numbers from 00 to 04 to occur 5% of the time, the method will create a demand of zero units approximately 5% of the time.

Now suppose we consider the daily demand of one unit which historically has occurred 10% of the time (see Table 16.2). Letting 10% or 10 of our 100 two-digit random numbers such as 05, 06, 07, 08, 09, 10, 11, 12, 13, and 14 correspond to a simulated daily demand of one unit, will provide a demand of one unit approximately 10% of the time. Continuing to assign demands to sets of two-digit random numbers according to the relative frequency of the specific demands results in the random number and demand assignments shown in Table 16.6.

Note that associated with every demand level is an interval of random numbers. Furthermore, these intervals have been selected so that the probability of selecting a random number from any particular interval is the same as the probability of the associated demand. For example, the probability of selecting a random number from the interval 30 through 44 (that is, 0.15) is exactly the same as the probability that the demand will be 4. It is not important that we selected the random numbers 30 through 44 to correspond to a demand of four units, but it is important that we selected 15% or 15 of the 100 random numbers from 00 to 99. In fact, we could have selected any arbitrary set of 15 random numbers that had not already been assigned to other demand values. The choice of an interval of successive numbers is a matter of convenience and is the convention we will follow in the remainder of the chapter.

TABLE 16.6 *Random Number Intervals and the Associated Daily Demand for the Stollar Bakery Shop Problem*

Daily Demand	Relative Frequency	Interval of Random Numbers	Probability of Selecting a Random Number in Interval
0	0.05	00 to 04	0.05
1	0.10	05 to 14	0.10
2	0.05	15 to 19	0.05
3	0.10	20 to 29	0.10
4	0.15	30 to 44	0.15
5	0.30	45 to 74	0.30
6	0.15	75 to 89	0.15
7	0.05	90 to 94	0.05
8	0.05	95 to 99	0.05
	1.00		1.00

Using Table 16.6 and the two-digit random numbers in the first row of Appendix D (63, 27, 15, 99, 86, . . .), we can simulate the daily demand for the birthday cakes. The results are presented in Table 16.7. The first two-digit random number selected, 63, is in the interval from 45 through 74; thus we select a demand of 5. The second random number selected, 27, is in the interval from 20 through 29; thus we select a demand of 3, and so on. Hence we see how random numbers can be used to generate daily demands such that the simulated demands are from the same frequency distribution as the actual demands. Simulations that use a random number procedure to generate probabilistic inputs such as demand are referred to as *Monte Carlo simulations.*

For any simulation problem in which a relative frequency distribution of a variable can be developed, it is relatively easy to apply the above random-number-based procedure to simulate values of the variable. First develop a table similar to Table 16.6 by associating an interval of random numbers with each possible value of the variable and making sure that the probability of selecting a random number from each interval is the same as the relative frequency of the associated value of the variable. Then as each random number is selected, you can simply check the corresponding interval and find the associated value of the variable.

TABLE 16.7 Results of Simulating 10 Daily Demands for Stollar's Bakery Shop Using the Random Number Table

Random Number	Simulated Daily Demand
63	5
27	3
15	2
99	8
86	6
71	5
74	5
45	5
11	1
02	0

16.4 THE ROLE OF THE COMPUTER IN SIMULATION

We stated in Section 16.2 that a computer simulation was used to generate the 500-day simulation results shown in Table 16.5. Obviously, for long and/or complex simulations that require numerous calculations, a high-speed computer simulation process is desirable and perhaps necessary. Let us first see how a computer can be programmed to use the random number procedure presented in the previous section. Then we will discuss the computer simulation procedure for the Stollar Bakery Shop problem.

If a computer procedure is going to be used to perform the simulation calculations, we will need a way to generate random numbers and values for the probabilistic components of the model. While the computer could be programmed to store random number tables and then follow the procedure outlined in the previous section, the computer storage space required for the random number tables would be substantial, and, in general, this method would be an inefficient use of the computer. For this reason, computer simulations make use of mathematical formulas that generate numbers which, for all practical purposes, have all the properties of the numbers selected from random number tables. Since the computer-generated random numbers are based on mathematical formulas, they do not represent "pure" random numbers. As a result, these numbers are *pseudo-random numbers*. In computer simulations pseudo-random numbers are used in exactly the same way as the random numbers selected from random number tables.

Most of the mathematical formulas for generating pseudo-random numbers are designed to produce a number from 0 up to but not including 1 (that is, 0 to 0.999 ···). In order to simulate a particular demand, we would associate an interval of pseudo-random numbers with the specific demand so that the probability of generating a pseudo-random number in that interval would be exactly the same as the probability of that level of demand. Table 16.8 shows how this would be done for the Stollar Bakery Shop daily demand. Note, for example, that any pseudo-random number greater than or equal to 0.05 but less than 0.15 would correspond to a demand of 1. Any pseudo-random number greater than or equal to 0.45 but less than 0.75 would correspond to a demand of 5, and so on.

In the Stollar Bakery Shop problem we initially carried out a hand-simulation process for a 10-day period. As we mentioned earlier, it would be very risky to make a decision based on the results of such a short period of simulation. When we think of performing the simulation calculations for a

TABLE 16.8 Pseudo-Random Number Intervals and the Associated Daily Demand for the Stollar Bakery Shop Problem

Daily Demand	Relative Frequency	Interval of Pseudo-Random Numbers	Probability of Selecting a Pseudo-Random Number in Interval
0	0.05	0.00 to 0.04999 ...	0.05
1	0.10	0.05 to 0.14999 ...	0.10
2	0.05	0.15 to 0.19999 ...	0.05
3	0.10	0.20 to 0.29999 ...	0.10
4	0.15	0.30 to 0.44999 ...	0.15
5	0.30	0.45 to 0.74999 ...	0.30
6	0.15	0.75 to 0.89999 ...	0.15
7	0.05	0.90 to 0.94999 ...	0.05
8	0.05	0.95 to 0.99999 ...	0.05
	1.00		1.00

simulated period as long as 500 days, the problems of carrying out the simulation for even a case as small as the bakery shop problem are significant. For example, let us consider what is involved in simulating the process for 500 days of the bakery operation. The mathematical model does not change, but the "dog work" we have to go through to evaluate the results certainly expands. We would have to create a table similar to Table 16.4 to evaluate each order size for 500 days of operation. For each day we would have to generate a value for demand, compute the daily profit, and add the daily profit to the total profit. For an efficient worker, this might take 1 minute for each day of simulation. Thus for a 500-day simulation, it might easily take an analyst 500 minutes or over 8 hours to perform a simulation for one production size. If the analyst wanted to consider just five different production sizes, performing the simulation in this fashion could easily consume as much as 40 hours of calculation time.

It should be obvious that in order for simulation to be an effective problem-solving tool, some means for automating the simulation calculations is necessary. By using a computer to carry out the set of well-defined steps and calculations that make up the simulation process, we are able to perform large simulations in reasonable amounts of time. While the simulation approach to problem solving has been known for many years, it was not until the advent of electronic computers that simulation became a practical problem-solving tool. The frequent usage of the computer in performing simulation calculations is the reason why the adjective "computer" often precedes simulation. In addition, it is common terminology to refer to the computer program that performs the simulation calculations as the *simulator*.

The use of simulation has grown rapidly in recent years, and users, as well as computer manufacturers, have recognized that most computer simulations have many common features: values of variables have to be generated from probability distributions, tables must be developed to keep track of the simulation results, and so on. Thus special computer programming languages have been developed to enable analysts to more easily describe simulation models in computer form. Two of the more common languages in use today are GPSS (general purpose simulation system) and SIMSCRIPT. Since it is not our purpose to describe computer languages in detail, we suggest that if you are interested in learning more about these languages you consult any of the number of excellent texts available or consult the manuals published by a number of computer companies that support these simulation languages. In addition, many analysts make use of general-purpose programming languages such as FORTRAN and PL/I to develop computer simulations.

Now that we have a basic understanding of the simulation process and the role of the computer in this process, let us see how simulation can be applied to problem situations where more than one probabilistic component is present.

16.5 AN INVENTORY SIMULATION WITH TWO DECISION VARIABLES AND TWO PROBABILISTIC COMPONENTS

The Stollar Bakery Shop problem which we have used in the previous sections is not a particularly difficult simulation problem. It has only one probabilistic component, daily demand, and only one decision variable, the production quantity. Using techniques from decision theory (Chapter 4), an expected value analysis could have been used to solve this problem analytically. While computer simulation may be used as an alternative solution procedure for problems that can also be solved analytically, the real value of computer simulation occurs when it is used to analyze and solve problems that either cannot be solved, or are extremely difficult to solve, analytically. In this section we will present an inventory problem with two decision variables and two probabilistic components. While some analysts might attempt to solve this problem by a mathematical analysis and not computer simulation, the problem is rather complex, and thus we believe that many analysts would employ a computer simulation model to develop a solution or decision recommendation.

Art's Auto Supplies, Inc., is a specialty auto supplies store that carries over 1000 items in inventory. While Art has used inventory models to determine how-much-to-order and when-to-order decisions for most of his products, he has become especially concerned about the inventory problem he has been experiencing with a deluxe tool cabinet product. Demand for the cabinets has been relatively low but subject to some variability. While on approximately one half of the days the store is open for business no one orders a cabinet, about one day per month three or four orders may occur for the cabinets. If variable demand were the only source of uncertainty, Art believes his order quantity and reorder point decisions could be based on an inventory model, perhaps similar to the inventory model discussed in Section 15.5. However, the tool cabinet inventory problem is further complicated by the fact that the lead time—the time between order placement and order arrival—also varies. Historically the length of the lead time has been anywhere between 1 and 5 days. The long lead times have caused Art to run out of inventory on several occasions. Orders received during the out-of-stock period have caused lost sales. Thus given this situation, Art would like to establish order quantity and reorder point decisions that provide a minimum total cost which includes an ordering, inventory holding, and stockout or shortage cost.

The Art's Auto Supplies problem is more complex than the Stollar Bakery Shop problem because it involves two decision variables and two probabilistic components. In addition, the auto supplies problem allows inventory to be carried from day to day, while the daily bakery shop problem did not. Let us see how a computer simulation model can be used to solve the Art's Auto Supplies, Inc., problem.

First we must develop the necessary probability distributions to generate demands and lead times. If Art had a complete set of records showing the demand for the cabinets over some recent period of time, we could develop a distribution for demand in the same manner as we did for the bakery shop problem. However, if no records are available, we would have to use subjective judgment, experience, and/or intuition to arrive at an estimate of the probability distribution for demand. The same approach for developing a probability distribution is applicable for lead times; that is, either historical data or subjective criteria must be used. Once these probability distributions have been developed, we can establish a computer simulation procedure for generating demands and lead times.

After an analysis of delivery charges and other costs associated with each order, Art was able to estimate his order costs at $20 per order. An analysis of interest, insurance, and other inventory carrying costs led Art to estimate the holding cost at $0.10 per unit per day. Finally, Art estimated his shortage cost at $50 per unit. The total cost of the system is given by the sum of the ordering cost, the holding cost, and the shortage cost. Art's objective is to find the order quantity and reorder point combination that will result in the lowest possible total cost.

A first step in the simulation approach to Art's problem is to develop a model that can be used to simulate the total costs corresponding to a specific order size and reorder point. Then, using this model, the two decision variables can be varied systematically in order to determine what appears to be the lowest cost combination. Let us see what is involved in developing such a model to carry out a 1-day simulation of the inventory process.

Assume that a specific reorder point and order quantity have already been selected. We must begin each day of the simulation by checking whether any inventory that had been ordered has just arrived. If so, the current inventory on hand must be increased by the quantity of goods received. Note that this assumes that orders are received and inventory on hand is updated at the start of each day. If this assumption is not appropriate, a different model, perhaps calling for goods to be received at the end of the day, would have to be developed.

Next our simulator must generate a value for the daily demand from the appropriate probability distribution. If there is sufficient inventory on hand to meet the daily demand, the inventory on hand will be decreased by the amount of the daily demand. If, however, inventory on hand is not sufficient to satisfy all the demand, we will satisfy as much of the demand as possible. The inventory will then be zero, and a shortage cost will be computed for all unsatisfied demand. In using this procedure we are assuming that if a customer orders more cabinets than Art has in inventory, the customer will take

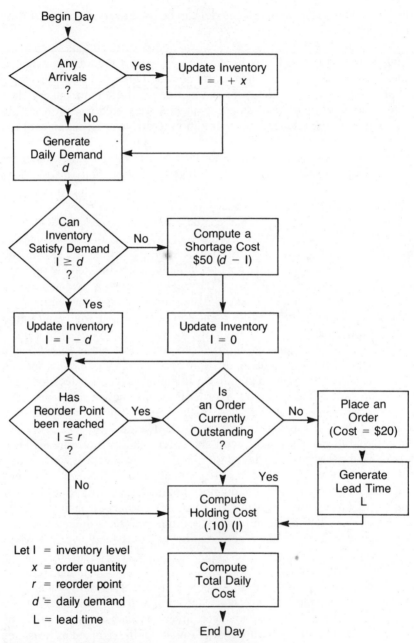

FIGURE 16.3 Flowchart of the Simulation of One Day of Operation for the Art's Auto Supplies Inventory System

what is available and shop elsewhere for the remainder of the order. With another auto supplies store only two blocks away, Art is sure unsatisfied demands will be lost sales and a $50 goodwill cost for each shortage is appropriate.

After the daily order has been processed by the simulator, the next step is to determine if the daily ending inventory has reached the reorder point and a new order should be placed. However, prior to placing a new order, we must check to see if a recent order is outstanding and should be arriving shortly. If so, we do not place an order.[2] Otherwise, an order is placed and the company incurs an ordering cost. If a new order is placed, a lead time must be randomly generated to reflect the time between the placement and the receipt of the goods.

Finally, an inventory holding cost, which is $0.10 for each unit in the daily ending inventory, is computed. The sum of the shortage costs, ordering costs, and inventory holding costs becomes the total daily cost for the simulation. Performing the above sequence of operations would complete 1 day of simulation. Figure 16.3 depicts this daily simulation process for the deluxe tool cabinet inventory operation.

The daily simulation process should be repeated for as many days as necessary to obtain meaningful results. The output from the simulation will show the total cost involved in using one particular order quantity and reorder point combination. By simulating the inventory operation with different order quantity-reorder point combinations, we can compare total operating costs and select the apparent "best" order quantity and reorder point decisions for the deluxe tool cabinets.

16.6 SIMULATION RESULTS FOR THE ART'S AUTO SUPPLIES PROBLEM

Suppose Art has a complete set of records showing the demand for the deluxe tool cabinets for the past year of operation (300 days). Furthermore, suppose he has records showing the number of days between placement and receipt of each order over the same period of time. Table 16.9 shows the frequency and relative frequency distributions for demand, and Table 16.10 shows the frequency and relative frequency distributions for lead time.

In order to carry out the simulation steps depicted in Figure 16.3, we must develop the procedure for generating values from the demand and lead time distributions. As before, we shall associate with each value of the random variable an interval of pseudo-random numbers such that the probability of generating a pseudo-random number in that interval is the same as the rela-

---

[2] We are assuming that it will never be necessary to have two orders outstanding simultaneously.

TABLE 16.9 Frequency and Relative Frequency Distributions for Demand in Art's Auto Supplies Problem

Demand (units)	Frequency (days)	Relative Frequency
0	150	0.50
1	75	0.25
2	45	0.15
3	15	0.05
4	15	0.05
	300	1.00

tive frequency of the associated demand and lead time. The relative frequency distributions are summarized in Tables 16.11 and 16.12.

To appreciate how the simulation method works for this problem, we will follow a 10-day simulation of the process. Let us assume that Art wants to determine the effect of using an order quantity of five units with a reorder point of three units. For purposes of starting the simulation, let us assume that we have a beginning inventory of five units at the start of day 1 of our 10-day simulation.

Referring to the flowchart in Figure 16.3, the first step is to check to see if any shipments have arrived. Since this is the first day of the simulation, we assume no arrivals and generate the daily demand for day 1. Let us assume we use a computer to generate pseudo-random numbers between 0 and 0.999 and that the first number generated is 0.093. From Table 16.11 we see that this pseudo-random number corresponds to a demand of zero units.

TABLE 16.10 Frequency and Relative Frequency Distributions for Lead Time in Art's Auto Supplies Problem

Lead Time (days)	Frequency (days)	Relative Frequency
1	6	0.20
2	3	0.10
3	12	0.40
4	6	0.20
5	3	0.10
	30	1.00

494

TABLE 16.11 *Pseudo-Random Numbers and Associated Daily Demands for Art's Auto Supplies Problem*

Daily Demand	Relative Frequency	Interval of Pseudo-Random Numbers	Probability of Selecting a Pseudo-Random Number in Interval
0	0.50	0.00 to 0.49999 . . .	0.50
1	0.25	0.50 to 0.74999 . . .	0.25
2	0.15	0.75 to 0.89999 . . .	0.15
3	0.05	0.90 to 0.94999 . . .	0.05
4	0.05	0.95 to 0.99999 . . .	0.05
	1.00		1.00

Thus we have no shortage costs to compute, and since inventory on hand (five units) is greater than the reorder point (three units), we do not place an order. The holding costs for day 1 are computed by ($0.10)5, or $0.50. With no shortages and no ordering, the total cost for day 1 is just the holding cost of $0.50. Continuing our simulation in this manner, we observe the computer-generated results in Table 16.13 for the 10 days of simulated operation.

At the start of day 4 the beginning inventory was four units. The random number selected to generate daily demand was 0.528; thus a daily demand of

TABLE 16.12 *Pseudo-Random Numbers and Associated Lead Times for Art's Auto Supplies Problem*

Lead Time (days)	Relative Frequency	Interval of Pseudo-Random Numbers	Probability of Selecting a Pseudo-Random Number in Interval
1	0.20	0.00 to 0.19999 . . .	0.20
2	0.10	0.20 to 0.29999 . . .	0.10
3	0.40	0.30 to 0.69999 . . .	0.40
4	0.20	0.70 to 0.89999 . . .	0.20
5	0.10	0.90 to 0.99999 . . .	0.10
	1.00		1.00

TABLE 16.13 Computer Simulation Results for 10 Days of Operation of Art's Auto Supplies with an Order Quantity of 5 and Reorder Point of 3.

Day	Beg Inv	Units Rcvd	Rndm Numb	Units Demd	End Inv	Rndm Numb	Lead Time	Holding Cost	Order Cost	Short Cost	Total Cost
1	5	0	0.093	0	5			0.50	0.00	0.00	0.50
2	5	0	0.681	1	4			0.40	0.00	0.00	0.40
3	4	0	0.292	0	4			0.40	0.00	0.00	0.40
4	4	0	0.528	1	3	0.620	3	0.30	20.00	0.00	20.30
5	3	0	0.866	2	1			0.10	0.00	0.00	0.10
6	1	0	0.975	4	0			0.00	0.00	150.00	150.00
7	0	5	0.622	1	4			0.40	0.00	0.00	0.40
8	4	0	0.819	2	2	0.939	5	0.20	20.00	0.00	20.20
9	2	0	0.373	0	2			0.20	0.00	0.00	0.20
10	2	0	0.353	0	2			0.20	0.00	0.00	0.20
						Average cost for 10 Simulated days		0.27	4.00	15.00	19.27

one unit was generated. As a result, the ending inventory dropped to three units and an order for five units was placed. Generating another random number, in this case 0.620, indicates (see Table 16.12) a lead time of 3 days, which means that the new order will be available on day 7. The day 4 costs are ($0.10)3 = $0.30 for the inventory holding cost and $20 for the ordering cost. Since there was no shortage cost, the total cost for the day was $20.30. The figures at the bottom of Table 16.13 provide the average holding cost, average ordering cost, average shortage cost, and average total cost for the 10-day simulation. Prior to drawing any firm conclusions based on these limited simulation results, we should run the simulation for many more days. Also we will want to test many other order quantity-reorder point combinations.

A computer programmer could develop a computer simulation program or simulator that would enable Art to explore a variety of order quantities and reorder points for a larger number of simulated days. In Table 16.14 we present output from a simulator that was developed to solve inventory problems such as the auto supplies problem. In this simulator the decision maker has the option of selecting a variety of order quantities and reorder points. For purposes of illustration, the computer simulation output is shown for simulations with order quantities of from 5 units to 50 units in increments of five and the reorder points of from 1 to 10 in increments of one. A total of 1000 days are represented in the simulation of each order quantity-reorder point combination.

TABLE 16.14   Simulated Average Daily Cost for 1000 Days
             of Art's Auto Supplies Inventory Problem

Reorder Level	Order Quantity									
	5	10	15	20	25	30	35	40	45	50
1	14.35	8.30	6.58	5.20	5.35	4.16	3.30	4.42	3.98	5.22
2	11.51	5.93	5.46	3.92	3.91	3.44	2.96	3.69	3.62	3.71
3	9.34	5.64	3.37	3.01	3.03	2.84	3.96	3.29	2.90	3.07
4	6.90	4.12	3.47	2.78	3.14	2.79	3.29	3.25	3.37	3.42
5	5.41	3.31	2.85	2.42	2.61	3.24	3.25	2.93	3.18	3.22
6	4.72	2.75	2.69	2.60	(2.39)	2.74	2.93	3.06	3.13	3.34
7	4.72	2.85	2.52	2.60	2.76	2.71	3.06	2.99	3.02	3.28
8	5.50	2.89	2.66	2.50	2.62	2.75	2.99	3.05	3.33	3.56
9	4.36	3.11	2.62	2.62	2.66	2.77	3.05	3.18	3.34	3.49
10	4.68	3.05	2.75	2.72	2.80	2.85	3.18	3.28	3.31	3.72

We see that the results of this computer simulation indicate that the lowest cost solution occurs at an order quantity of 25 units and a reorder point of 6 units; in this case the resulting average total cost is $2.39 per day. After studying these results, Art might wish to explore other order quantities near the apparent "best" order quantity of 25. In Table 16.15 the results of varying the order quantity from 21 to 30 in increments of one and reorder points from 4 to 8 are shown. The smallest simulated average total cost of $2.33 now occurs when the order quantity is 22 units and the reorder point is 6 units. Note, however, that in this second set of simulations the previously best order quantity of 25 units and a reorder point of 6 units now has a total

TABLE 16.15   Simulated Average Daily Cost for 1000 Days
             of Art's Auto Supplies Inventory Problem

Reorder Level	Order Quantity									
	21	22	23	24	25	26	27	28	29	30
4	2.94	3.02	3.13	2.74	2.89	2.56	2.74	3.07	2.67	3.24
5	2.59	2.58	2.84	2.70	2.66	2.59	2.88	2.57	2.48	2.75
6	2.55	(2.33)	2.87	2.35	2.75	2.45	2.81	2.79	2.61	2.60
7	2.52	2.45	2.47	2.51	2.57	2.62	2.61	2.63	2.62	2.67
8	2.50	2.69	2.48	2.49	2.63	2.57	2.63	2.69	2.69	2.71

cost of $2.75 per day. Since different random numbers were used in the two simulations, different total costs are to be expected. The selection of the "best" order quantity and reorder point is now up to the analyst. What decisions would you make? While you might want to run more or longer simulations, the simulation data of Tables 16.14 and 16.15 indicate that good solutions apparently exist with order quantities around 20 to 25 units and reorder points around 6 or 7 units. Thus while simulation has not guaranteed an optimal solution, it has enabled us to identify apparent low-cost or "near-optimal" decisions for the inventory problem. The final decision for an order quantity and reorder point will be based on Art's preference for the "near-optimal" solution that he would like to adopt.

16.7 ADVANTAGES AND DISADVANTAGES OF COMPUTER SIMULATION

Earlier we mentioned that analytical procedures were available for solving the Stollar Bakery Shop problem, but that for Art's Auto Supplies inventory problem analytical procedures were generally not available. If it had turned out that the distribution for demand and lead time for the tool cabinets had followed a standard distribution, such as the Poisson distribution, a mathematical or analytical solution, while rather complex, could have been used. However, when mathematically convenient distributions are not applicable to the problem situation, an analytical analysis may be impossible. Thus a simulation model becomes the best approach available to the operations research analyst. Thus the biggest advantage of simulation is that it is a useful solution procedure for problems that are too complex to be solved by other modeling techniques, such as those discussed in this book. In general, as the number of random components in the problem become larger, the more likely simulation will be the best (or only) operations research solution technique applicable.

Another advantage of the simulation approach is that the simulation model and simulator provide a convenient experimental laboratory. Once the computer program has been developed, it is usually relatively easy to experiment with the model. For example, if we wanted to know the effect of an increase in shortage cost on the recommended solution to our inventory problem, we could have simply changed the shortage cost input value and rerun the simulation. The effect of experimental changes in other inputs, such as the probability distributions of demand and lead time, could also be investigated.

Simulation is not without its disadvantages. One obvious disadvantage is that someone must develop the computer programs. For large simulation projects this is usually a substantial undertaking. Hence one should certainly not attempt to develop a simulation model unless the potential gains promise

498

to outweigh the costs of model development. This disadvantage has been reduced in recent years with the development of computer simulation languages such as GPSS and SIMSCRIPT. The use of these languages often leads to considerable savings in time and money as the computer program or simulator is developed.

Another disadvantage of simulation is that it may not lead to the optimal solution to the problem. Remember, simulation is a trial-and-error approach. One usually selects those values of the decision variables to test in the model that have a good chance of being near the optimal solution. But since it is usually too costly to try all values of the decision variables, and since different simulations may provide different results, there is no guarantee that the best simulation solution found is the overall optimal solution. However, the danger of obtaining bad solutions is slight if good judgment is exercised in developing and running the simulation model. The decision maker usually has a good idea of reasonable values to try for the decision variables, and it is usually possible to run the simulation long enough to identify the apparent best decisions.

16.8 SUMMARY

In this chapter we have seen how two different problem situations could be analyzed and solved using the computer simulation technique. Based on these two simulation models, we can make the following general observations about the simulation approach to decision making.

1. Simulation is perhaps most appropriate when the problem is too complex or difficult to solve by another quantitative technique.
2. Simulation is trial-and-error approach to problem solving.
3. A mathematical model must be developed to represent the various relationships existing in the problem situation.
4. A process such as a random number generator must be employed to generate values of the probabilistic components in the model.
5. A bookkeeping procedure must be developed to keep track of what is happening in the simulation process (see Table 16.13).
6. Because of the numerous calculations required in most simulations, a computer program or simulator is required.
7. The simulation process must be conducted for many days or periods in order to establish the long-run evaluations of the decision alternatives.
8. Simulation does not guarantee an optimal solution; however, it should be very helpful in identifying good, or near-optimal, solutions.

In both problem situations studied in this chapter, the random components resulted from discrete probability distributions; that is, the random variables involved could only take on a finite number of values. In many computer simulation experiments it is common to experience factors that follow continuous distributions such as the normal distribution. The basic simulation approach we have developed in this chapter is still appropriate for these situations. The only difference concerns the method of generating random values from the appropriate continuous probability distributions.

16.9 GLOSSARY

1. *Simulation*—A procedure that involves developing a model to re-create the process or system under study. Most often this technique employs a computer model (computer program) to re-create the process and then, by trial-and-error experiments, identifies near-optimal solutions.
2. *Monte Carlo simulation*—Simulations that use a random number procedure to create values for the probabilistic components of a simulation model.
3. *Pseudo-random numbers*—Computer-generated numbers developed from mathematical expressions which have the properties of random numbers.
4. *Simulator*—The computer program written to perform the simulation calculations.
5. *GPSS and SIMSCRIPT*—Two common computer programming languages used for simulation studies.

16.10 PROBLEMS

The problems in this section are specifically designed to enable you to perform simulations with hand calculations. To keep the hand calculations reasonable, we will only ask you to consider a few decision alternatives and relatively short periods of simulation. While this should give you a good understanding of the simulation process, the simulation results will not be sufficient to make final conclusions or decisions about the problem situation. If you have access to a computer, we suggest that you develop a computer simulation model for some of the problems. Then, by using the model to test several decision alternatives over a much longer simulated period of time, you will be able to obtain the desired decision-making information.

Also note that most problems in this section are relatively simple, and hence analytical solution techniques, as well as simulation, may be used to provide recommended decisions. While our purpose is to emphasize the simulation procedure, you may want to consider an analytical solution procedure for the problems. A comparison of the analytical solution and your simulated solution will give you a better understanding of the simulation process.

1. Queen-Quik Markets has experienced the following historical weekly sales for Bash beer.

Sales (cases)	Frequency (weeks)
10	2
11	4
12	7
13	3
14	2
15	2
	20

   a. Develop a relative frequency distribution for the above data.
   b. Use random numbers to simulate weekly sales for a 15-week period.

2. Given below is 50 weeks of historical sales data for Chevrolets sold by a new car dealer in Newton, Ohio.

Number of Sales	Number of Weeks		
0	2	.04	.00 - .03
1	5	.10	.04 - .03
2	8	.16	.14 - .29
3	22	.44	.29 .73
4	10	.20	.73 - .93
5	3	.6	.93 .
	50		

   a. Develop the relative frequency distribution for these data.
   b. Use a random number procedure to simulate weekly automobile sales for a 12-week period.

3. For the Stollar Bakery Shop problem presented in Section 16.1, use a new set of random numbers to develop your own simulation results for

production quantities of five, six, and seven. How do your simulation results compare to the results shown in Table 16.4? What is the reason for any differences?

4. Assume that in the Stollar Bakery Shop problem we wished to consider a goodwill cost of $2 for each unsatisfied daily order.

   a. Show the profit model for this problem when the goodwill cost is included.

   b. Use the 10 days of simulated daily orders in Table 16.3 to simulate 10 days of operation when this cost is considered. Use trial production quantities of six, seven, and eight.

   c. What is the "best" production quantity for the 10-day simulation? In general, what do you expect to happen to the production-quantity decision when goodwill costs are included? Explain.

5. Jim Nelson has two alternative ways to get to work each day: (1) he can take the city bus to his general work area and walk to his office; (2) he can drive his car to his general work area, locate a parking spot in his company's parking lot, and then walk from the parking lot to his office. The time distributions are as follows.

Taking the bus to the work area and walking:

Time (minutes)	Relative Frequency
25	0.50
30	0.25
35	0.15
40	0.10

Driving the car from home to the parking lot:

Time (minutes)	Relative Frequency
20	0.40
25	0.40
30	0.10
35	0.10

Locating a parking spot after reaching the parking area and walking to the office:

502

Time (minutes)	Relative Frequency
2	0.15
4	0.75
6	0.10

a. Show the random number intervals that could be used to simulate times for each of the three distributions.

b. Simulate 10 days of trips using the two alternatives and recommend a policy for Jim to follow.

6. Charlestown Electric Company is building a new generator for its Mt. Washington plant. Even with good maintenance procedures, the generator will have periodic failures or breakdowns. Historical figures for similar generators indicate that the relative frequency of failures during a year is as follows.

Number of Failures	Relative Frequency
0	0.80
1	0.15
2	0.04
3	0.01

Assuming that the useful lifetime of the generator is 25 years, use simulation to estimate the number of breakdowns that will occur in the 25 years of operation. Is it common to have 5 or more consecutive years of operation without a failure?

7. Smooth-on Paints, Inc., (SOP) is a small firm that produces only one type of paint. SOP maintains an inventory of the paint which is used to supply the weekly orders for Swellons and Mac's paint supplies stores. The problem is to determine how many cases of paint SOP should have in inventory at the beginning of each week. SOP would like to select the lowest possible beginning-of-the-week inventory level that would have a 95% probability of satisfying the combined weekly orders from both retailers. The demand distributions for the retailers are as follows.

Weekly Demand (gallons)	Relative Frequency
Swellons	
100	0.20
150	0.25
200	0.40
250	0.10
300	0.05
Mac's	
300	0.10
400	0.50
500	0.20
600	0.20

Simulate 20 weeks of operation for beginning inventory sizes of 700 and 800 gallons. Based on your limited simulation results, how many cases should SOP maintain in inventory? Discuss what you would want to do in a full-scale computer simulation of this problem.

8. Phil Williams is currently completing the design for a drive-in movie theater to be located in Big Flats, New York. Phil has purchased the land and is now in the planning stages of determining the number of automobiles to accommodate. Each automobile location requires installing a speaker system at a total cost of $250 per location. Based upon his experience with the five other drive-ins he has been operating for the past 8 years, Phil estimates that the nightly attendance will range from 100 to 500 automobiles with the relative frequencies shown below.

Approximate Number of Automobiles	Relative Frequency
100	0.10
200	0.25
300	0.40
400	0.15
500	0.10

504

a. Simulate 20 days of attendance for capacities of 300, 400, and 500.

b. In the 20 days of simulated operation, how many daily demands of 300 would you have expected? Did you observe this many in your simulation? Should you have? Explain.

c. After considering personnel and other operating costs, the average profit is $1 per car. Using your 20 days of simulated data, what is the average nightly profit for the capacities of 300, 400, and 500? How many days of operation will it take Phil to recover the speaker installation cost if all profits are allocated to this cost?

9. A door-to-door magazine salesman has the following historical sales record. If the salesman talks to the lady of the house, he has a 15% chance of making a sale. Furthermore, if he does convince her to purchase some magazines, the relative frequency distribution for the number of subscriptions ordered is as follows.

Number of Subscriptions	Relative Frequency
1	0.60
2	0.30
3	0.10

On the other hand, if the man of the house answers the door, the salesman's chances of making a sale are 25%. In addition the relative frequency distribution for the number of subscriptions ordered is as follows.

Number of Subscriptions	Relative Frequency
1	0.10
2	0.40
3	0.30
4	0.20

The salesman has found that no one answers the door at about 30% of the houses he contacts. However, of the people who do answer the door, 80% are women and 20% are men. The salesman's profit is $2 for each subscription sold.

505

a. Prepare a simulation model flowchart (see Figure 16.3) for this problem. The output of the model should be the total profit the salesman makes from calling upon N houses.

b. Simulate this problem and show the house-by-house results for 25 calls. What is the total profit projected for the 25 calls?

c. Based upon your results from part (b), how many subscriptions should the salesman expect to sell if he calls on 100 houses per day? What is the salesman's expected daily profit?

10. For the Art's Auto Supplies problem in Section 16.5, develop a 10-day simulation when the following demand distribution is assumed.

Demand	Relative Frequency
0	0.25
1	0.50
2	0.15
3	0.05
4	0.05

Using an order quantity of five and a reorder point of three, show your results in the format of Table 16.13.

11. Bill Bristol, owner and proprietor of Bristol Bikes, would like to develop an order quantity and reorder point policy that would minimize the total costs associated with the company's inventory of exercise bikes. The relative frequency distribution for retail demand on a weekly basis is shown below.

Demand	Relative Frequency
0	0.20
1	0.50
2	0.10
3	0.10
4	0.05
5	0.05

The relative frequency distribution for lead time is as follows.

Lead Time (weeks)	Relative Frequency
1	0.10
2	0.25
3	0.60
4	0.05

The inventory holding costs are $1 per unit per week, the ordering cost is $20 per order, the shortage cost is $25 per unit, and the beginning inventory is seven units. Using an order quantity of 12 and a reorder point of 5, simulate 10 weeks of operation of this inventory system.

12. A medical consulting firm has been asked to determine the facilities required in the x-ray laboratory of a new hospital. In particular, the firm should provide recommendations on the number of x-ray units for the laboratory. How could computer simulation assist in reaching a good decision? What factors would you consider in a simulation model of this problem?

13. Consider a medium-sized community that currently has only one fire station. You have been hired by the city manager to assist in the determination of the best location for a second fire station. What would be your objective for this problem? Explain how computer simulation might be used to evaluate alternative locations and help identify the best location.

14. A bus company is considering adding a new 10-stop route to its operation. The bus will be scheduled to complete the route once each hour. If the company has determined the approximate demand distribution for each location, discuss how simulation might be used to project the hourly profit associated with the new route. If the company can assign a regular bus or a more economical minibus to this route, discuss how simulation might help make this decision. Note that with the minibus the company's management is concerned about being unable to pick up customers if the bus is already carrying its maximum number of riders.

17
Waiting Line Models

Everyone has experienced waiting line situations such as a line of customers at a supermarket checkout counter, a line of customers at a teller window of a bank, or a line of cars at a traffic light. In these and many other situations, *waiting* time is an undesirable occurrence for all parties concerned. For example, the customer in the supermarket checkout line can become very annoyed with excessive waiting times. In addition, the excessive waiting times, while indicative of many customers, are equally undesirable for the manager of the supermarket. The manager realizes that long waiting lines mean that customers are not being promptly serviced. More importantly, he realizes that these long waiting times may cause potential repeat customers to seek better service elsewhere, thus proving costly in terms of lost future sales.

If the manager in our supermarket example is concerned about the existence of long waiting lines, one obvious answer would be to add more checkout counters. This added service capability should provide better service and correspondingly shorter customer waiting lines. However, adding additional supermarket checkout counters will lead to greater costs in terms of additional personnel, equipment, and space requirements. Thus the supermarket waiting line problem will require the manager to balance the benefits of better service with the added costs involved.

Quantitative models have been developed to help managers understand and make better decisions concerning the operation of waiting lines. In operations research terminology, *queuing theory* involves the study of waiting lines, where the waiting line is referred to as the *queue*. Thus in our supermarket example, the customers in the waiting line could have been referred to as the customers in the queue.

For a given waiting line problem, queuing models may be used to identify the system's *operating characteristics* such as

1. The percent of time or probability that the service facilities (checkout counters) are idle
2. The probability of a specific number of units (customers) in the system[1]
3. The average number of units in the system
4. The average time each unit spends in the system (waiting time plus service time)

[1] The system includes the waiting line and the service facilities.

5. The average number of units in the waiting line or queue
6. The average time each unit spends in the waiting line
7. The percent of time or probability that an arriving unit will have to wait.

With the above information together with service cost estimates, customer waiting line limitations, and customer waiting time costs, the manager will be better equipped to make decisions that balance desirable service levels with service costs for the waiting line.

In this chapter we discuss how analytical and simulation models of waiting lines can assist in developing good decisions for waiting line problems. As an illustration of an application of a waiting line model, let us consider the problem Schips, Inc., is presently having with the truck dock at the company's Western Hills store.

17.1 THE SCHIPS, INC., TRUCK DOCK PROBLEM

Schips, Inc., is a large department store chain which has six branch stores located throughout the city. The company's Western Hills store, which was built some years ago, has recently been experiencing some problems in its receiving and shipping department because of the substantial growth in the branch's sales volume. Unfortunately, the loading dock was designed to handle only one truck at a time, and with the branch's increased business, the increase in receiving and shipping operations has led to a bottleneck problem in the loading dock area. At times the branch manager has observed as many as five Schips trucks waiting to be loaded or unloaded. However, at other times the manager has noticed that the two-man dock crew was idle because no trucks were at the store. Nevertheless, the recent trend has been toward less idle time and greater truck waiting times. The manager is considering increasing the dock crew size in order to decrease loading and unloading times and thereby reduce the waiting time problem.

What should the dock crew size be? Obviously, the manager needs more information before making this decision. While an increased crew size can be expected to help reduce the existing bottleneck, it will also result in a increase in personnel costs. The manager will want to know how much waiting time can be saved before making a final crew size decision. Let us see how a waiting line model of the loading dock operation can be used to help make the crew size decision.

17.2 THE SINGLE-CHANNEL WAITING LINE

The Schips receiving and shipping operation is an example of a *single-channel* or *single-server* waiting line. By this we mean that every truck entering the system must pass through *one* server—the one loading dock—before completing the unloading or loading process. The trucks form a single waiting line and wait for the single server. A diagram of our single-channel waiting line is shown in Figure 17.1.

In order to develop a waiting line model for the truck dock operation, we will need to identify some important characteristics of the system: (1) the arrival distribution for the trucks; (2) the service time distribution for the truck loading and unloading operation; and (3) the waiting line or queue discipline for the trucks. This information will be necessary to determine which of many waiting line models is most representative of the Schips truck dock waiting line.

17.3 ARRIVAL DISTRIBUTION

Defining the arrival distribution for a waiting line involves determining how many units arrive at the service mechanism in a given period of time. For example, in the Schips waiting line problem we will be interested in determining the number of trucks that arrive at the loading dock in a one-hour period. Since the number of trucks arriving each hour is not necessarily constant, we will need to define a probability distribution that describes the hourly truck arrivals.

For many waiting lines, the number of arrivals in a given period of time appears to have a *random pattern;* that is, while we may have a good estimate of the total number of arrivals expected each day, arrivals are independent of preceding arrivals and we cannot predict exactly when the arrivals will occur. In such cases, operations researchers have found that the *Poisson* probability distribution best describes this random arrival pattern.

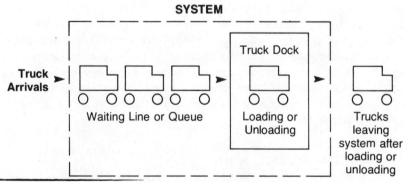

FIGURE 17.1 *Diagram of Schips Single-Channel Truck Dock Waiting Line*

The Poisson probability distribution is defined as follows:

$$P(x) = \frac{\lambda^x e^{-\lambda}}{x!} \qquad \text{for } x = 0, 1, 2, \cdots \qquad\qquad (17.1)$$

where, in waiting line applications,

x = number of arrivals in a specific period of time

λ = average or expected number of arrivals for the specific period of time

e = 2.71828.

In the Schips loading dock problem, busy periods would often have as many as seven or eight trucks arriving at the loading dock in a 1-hour period. However, during slow times it was not uncommon to have no arrivals during a 1-hour period. Since truck arrivals were not scheduled and occurred in an unpredictable fashion, a random arrival pattern appeared to exist for the trucks. Thus the Poisson distribution should provide an accurate description of the arrival pattern. Since Schips handles an average of 24 trucks per 8-hour day, or 3 trucks per hour ($\lambda = 3$), we can use the following Poisson distribution to compute the probability of x truck arrivals at the loading dock in an hour.[2]

$$P(x) = \frac{3^x e^{-3}}{x!}.$$

The probabilities for zero, one, and two trucks arriving in an hour are as follows.

$$P(x = 0) = \frac{3^0 e^{-3}}{0!} = e^{-3} = 0.0498$$

$$P(x = 1) = \frac{3^1 e^{-3}}{1!} = 3e^{-3} = 0.1494$$

$$P(x = 2) = \frac{3^2 e^{-3}}{2!} = \frac{9e^{-3}}{2} = 0.2241$$

Using the Poisson probability distribution we would expect no arrivals in an hour 4.98% of the time, exactly one arrival in an hour 14.94% of the time, exactly two arrivals in an hour 22.41% of the time, and so on. Continuing these probability calculations will show that the probability of nine or more truck arrivals in 1 hour is only 0.0038. Figure 17.2 shows the arrival distribution for Schips trucks based on the Poisson distribution assumption.

In the analysis that follows, we will use the Poisson distribution to describe the truck arrivals for Schips. You will see that the assumption of a Poisson arrival distribution will help simplify our analysis of the waiting line

---

[2] Values of $e^{-\lambda}$ are provided in Appendix E.

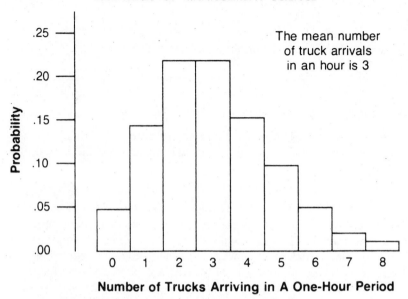

FIGURE 17.2 *Poisson Distribution of Truck Arrivals for Schips*

problem. In practice you would want to record the actual number of arrivals per time period for several days or weeks and compare the frequency distribution of the observed number of arrivals to the Poisson distribution to see if the Poisson distribution is a good approximation of the arrival distribution for the waiting line.

17.4 SERVICE TIME DISTRIBUTION

A service time distribution is needed to describe how long it takes to load or unload (that is, service) a truck once the dock crew begins the loading or unloading operation. Since the trucks carry different quantities of different items, the loading and unloading service times will vary. If the service times for the trucks occur in a random fashion, operations researchers have found that the *exponential* probability distribution best describes the service time distribution. Another particularly important reason for considering the exponential distribution is that if exponential service times and Poisson arrivals exist for a waiting line, the mathematical analysis required for determining the operating characteristics of the waiting line are relatively easy to develop and use.

The exponential probability distribution is defined as follows:

$$f(t) = \mu e^{-\mu t} \qquad \text{for } t \geq 0. \tag{17.2}$$

In waiting line applications.

> t = service time
> μ = expected number of units the service facility can handle in a specific period of time
> e = 2.71828.

The mean or average service time $\bar{t}$ is given by $1/\mu$.

If an exponential service time distribution is used, the probability that the service is completed within a specific period of time T is given by

$$P(t \leq T) = 1 - e^{-\mu T}. \tag{17.3}$$

The Schips trucks are loaded or unloaded by the two-man crew in an average of $\bar{t} = 0.25$ hours per truck. Therefore, since $\bar{t} = 1/\mu$, we find that $\mu = 4$, and hence the following exponential distribution for service times:

$$f(t) = 4e^{-4t}.$$

Using equation (17.3), we can compute the probability a truck is loaded and/or unloaded (serviced) within a specified time T. For example,

> $P(t \leq 0.1 \text{ hour}) = 1 - e^{-4(0.1)} = 1 - e^{-0.4} = 0.3297$
> $P(t \leq 0.3 \text{ hour}) = 1 - e^{-4(0.3)} = 1 - e^{-1.2} = 0.6988$
> $P(t \leq 0.5 \text{ hour}) = 1 - e^{-4(0.5)} = 1 - e^{-2} = 0.8647.$

Thus using the exponential distribution we would expect 32.97% of the trucks to be serviced in 6 minutes or less ($T = 0.1$), 69.88% in 18 minutes or less ($T = 0.3$), and 86.47% in 30 minutes or less ($T = 0.5$). Figure 17.3 shows graphically the probability that T hours or less will be required to service a Schips truck.

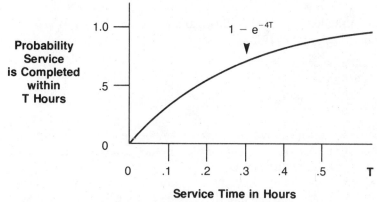

FIGURE 17.3 *Probability a Schips Truck Will Be Serviced within T Hours*

513

In the analysis of a specific waiting line the quantitative analyst will want to collect data on actual service times to see if the exponential distribution assumption is appropriate. If you find that other service time patterns such as a normal service time distribution or a constant service time exist, the exponential distribution should not be used. For the Schips problem we will assume that it has already been determined that the exponential distribution is the most appropriate representation of the service times.

17.5 QUEUE DISCIPLINE

In describing a waiting line, we will want to define the manner in which the waiting units are ordered for service. For the Schips, Inc., problem, and in general for most customer-oriented waiting lines, the waiting units are ordered on a first-come, first-served basis, which is referred to as a first-in-first-out (FIFO) queue discipline. When people wait in line for an elevator, it is usually the last one in line that is the first one serviced (that is, to leave the elevator). This is an example of last-in-first-out (LIFO) queue discipline. Other types of queue disciplines assign priorities to the waiting units and service the unit with the highest priority first. We will restrict our attention to waiting lines with a FIFO queue discipline. In situations where the FIFO queue discipline is not used, waiting line models other than those discussed in this chapter must be used.

17.6 THE SINGLE-CHANNEL WAITING LINE MODEL WITH POISSON ARRIVALS AND EXPONENTIAL SERVICE TIMES

The waiting line model presented in this section can be applied to waiting lines where the following conditions exist:

1. Single-channel waiting line
2. Poisson distribution of arrivals
3. Exponential distribution of service times
4. First-in-first-out (FIFO) queue discipline.

Since we assumed that the above conditions were applicable for the Schips problem, we will show how this waiting line model can be used to help determine the best loading dock crew size.

The quantitative methodology used in the development of most waiting line models is rather complex and outside the scope of this text. However, we show the quantitative expressions that have been developed for analyzing single-channel waiting lines and then show you how these expressions can be applied to the Schips waiting line problem.

Let us begin by reviewing some of our notation:

λ = expected number of arrivals per time period (mean arrival rate)
$\bar{t}$ = mean service time
$\mu = 1/\bar{t}$ = expected number of services possible per time period (mean service rate).

For the Schips problem we have $\lambda = 3$, $\bar{t} = 0.25$, and $\mu = 1/0.25 = 4$.

Using the assumptions of Poisson arrivals and exponential service times, operations researchers have developed the following expressions which define the operating characteristics of a single-channel waiting line.[3]

1. The probability that the service facility is idle (that is, the probability of 0 units in the system):

$$P_0 = \left(1 - \frac{\lambda}{\mu} \right). \tag{17.4}$$

2. The probability of n units in the system:

$$P_n = \left(\frac{\lambda}{\mu} \right)^n P_0 = \left(\frac{\lambda}{\mu} \right)^n \left(1 - \frac{\lambda}{\mu} \right). \tag{17.5}$$

3. The average number of units in the system:

$$L = \frac{\lambda}{\mu - \lambda}. \tag{17.6}$$

4. The average time a unit spends in the system (waiting time + service time):

$$W = \frac{1}{\mu - \lambda} = \frac{L}{\lambda}. \tag{17.7}$$

5. The average number of units in the queue waiting for service:

$$L_q = \frac{\lambda^2}{\mu(\mu - \lambda)}. \tag{17.8}$$

6. The average time a unit spends in the queue waiting for service:

$$W_q = \frac{\lambda}{\mu(\mu - \lambda)} = \frac{L_q}{\lambda}. \tag{17.9}$$

7. The probability that an arriving unit has to wait for service:

$$P_w = \frac{\lambda}{\mu}. \tag{17.10}$$

---

[3] These equations apply to the *steady-state* operation of a waiting line, which occurs after an initial or transient period at the start of the waiting line operation.

The ratio of the mean arrival rate λ to the mean service rate μ, given by λ/μ, is an important component in the above formulas. From equation (17.10) we see that the value of λ/μ is simply the probability the server is busy or in use. Thus λ/μ is often referred to as the *utilization factor* for the waiting line.

Since we know the probability that the server is busy, λ/μ, cannot be greater than one, we see that we cannot consider a utilization factor of $\lambda/\mu > 1$ in equations (17.4) to (17.10). In addition, if we attempt to use $\lambda/\mu = 1$, or $\lambda = \mu$, we see from equations (17.6) and (17.7) that the number of units in the system L and the average time a unit spends in the system W both become infinitely large. This tells us that if we attempt to operate a single-channel waiting line system with Poisson arrivals and exponential service times at a utilization factor of $\lambda/\mu = 1$, both the waiting line and waiting time will grow without limit.

Based on the above discussion it should be clear that the formulas for determining the operating characteristics of a single-channel waiting line presented in equations (17.4) to (17.10) are only applicable when $\lambda/\mu < 1$. This condition occurs when the mean service rate μ is greater than the mean arrival rate λ, and hence the service rate is sufficient to process or service all arrivals.

Returning to the Schips loading dock problem, we see that with $\lambda = 3$ trucks per hour, $\mu = 4$ trucks per hour, and $\lambda/\mu = \frac{3}{4}$, we can use equations (17.4) to (17.10) to determine the operating characteristics of the loading dock operation:

$$\text{crew utilization } \frac{\lambda}{\mu} = \frac{3}{4} = 0.75$$

$$P_0 = \left(1 - \frac{\lambda}{\mu}\right) = \left(1 - \frac{3}{4}\right) = 0.25 \quad \text{(probability of being idle)}$$

$$L = \frac{\lambda}{\mu - \lambda} = \frac{3}{4 - 3} = 3 \text{ trucks} \quad \text{(average number of units in system)}$$

$$W = \frac{L}{\lambda} = \frac{3}{3} = 1 \text{ hour per truck} \quad \text{(average time in system)}$$

$$L_q = \frac{\lambda^2}{\mu(\mu - \lambda)} = \frac{(3)^2}{4(4 - 3)} = 2.25 \text{ trucks} \quad \left(\begin{array}{l}\text{average number waiting} \\ \text{for service}\end{array}\right)$$

$$W_q = \frac{L_q}{\lambda} = \frac{2.25}{3} = 0.75 \text{ hour per truck} \quad \left(\begin{array}{l}\text{average time a unit} \\ \text{waits for service}\end{array}\right)$$

$$P_w = \frac{\lambda}{\mu} = \frac{3}{4} = 0.75 \quad \text{(probability of a unit having to wait).}$$

By looking at the above data for the waiting line, we can learn several important things about the loading dock operation. In particular, the fact that trucks wait an average of 0.75 hour or 45 minutes before being loaded or unloaded appears excessive and undesirable. In addition, the facts that the average waiting line is 2.25 trucks and that 75% of the arriving trucks have to wait for service are indicators that something should be done to improve the efficiency of the loading dock operation.

The branch manager believes that increasing the size of the dock crew will help improve the situation by speeding up the service times. He is willing to assume that an increase in the crew will result in a proportional decrease in the **mean** service time. Since the current two-man crew has a mean service time of $\bar{t} = 0.25$ hour, the trucks appear to require an average of 2(0.25) or 0.5 man-hours per truck. A general expression for the mean service time for the Schips trucks is given by $\bar{t} = (0.5/\text{crew size})$ hours per truck.

Using the above equation for $\bar{t}$ and computing a corresponding mean service rate $\mu = 1/\bar{t}$, we will be able to use equations (17.4) to (17.10) to predict the effect on our loading dock operation of crew sizes of three, four, and five. These data are summarized in Table 17.1.

In general we can see that a larger dock crew does improve service. The average waiting time per truck, the average number of trucks waiting, and the probability of an arriving truck having to wait all improve with a larger dock crew. As you might expect, however, the idle time of the crew increases as the crew size gets larger. What is your recommendation for crew size?

While the reduction in truck waiting time will result in a cost savings due to reducing the idleness of the trucks, the larger crew size represents an

TABLE 17.1   Waiting Line System Characteristics for the Schips Truck Dock Problem

	Crew Size			
	2	3	4	5
Mean service time $\bar{t}$, hours	0.25	0.167	0.125	0.1
Mean service rate μ, per hour	4	6	8	10
Crew utilization factor	0.75	0.5	0.375	0.3
Probability the crew is idle P_0	0.25	0.5	0.625	0.7
Average number of trucks in system L	3	1	0.6	0.429
Average time a truck spends in system W, hours	1	0.33	0.2	0.143
Average number of trucks in queue L_q	2.25	0.5	0.225	0.129
Average time a truck spends in queue W_q, hours	0.75	0.167	0.075	0.043
Probability that an arriving unit has to wait for service P_w	0.75	0.5	0.375	0.3

increased cost. Before reaching a final decision on crew size, we need to estimate the economic impact of the various crew size alternatives.

17.7 ECONOMIC ANALYSIS OF WAITING LINES

Waiting line models, such as the single server in the previous section, are valuable in that they describe or predict how the waiting line will function under a variety of operating alternatives. They are extremely helpful in identifying potential waiting times, queue sizes, idle times, and so on. However, these models do not directly recommend or identify minimum cost or optimal decisions.

As we stated earlier in this chapter, the solution to a waiting line problem may require the manager to balance or trade off the cost reductions resulting from better service with the increased cost of achieving the better service. In defining the costs of the Schips loading dock problem, we will want to consider the waiting time cost for the trucks, both in the queue and while being serviced at the dock, and the personnel costs for the loading dock crew. We can develop mathematical expressions for these costs as follows. Let

c_1 = truck cost per hour
c_2 = crew cost per hour for *one* crew member
d = dock crew size.

Then

total hourly cost for trucks
   waiting in the queue and
    being serviced $= Lc_1$
hourly cost for the dock crew $= dc_2$
total cost per hour $= Lc_1 + dc_2.$ (17.11)

By evaluating the above total cost model for several possible crew sizes, we will be able to obtain the cost information necessary to make a minimum operating cost decision. For example, suppose that the Schips trucks are operated at a cost of $15 per hour and that each dock crew member is paid $7 an hour. Table 17.2 summarizes the costs for the Schips loading dock operation.

What decision would you make if you were the Schips branch manager? Now that you have cost data in Table 17.2, you should increase your loading dock crew size to three, which, according to the waiting line analysis, will reduce cost by $59 − $36 = $23 per hour. This is a 39% cost reduction over the cost of the current loading dock operation.

In addition, the waiting line model tells us (Table 17.1) that we can

TABLE 17.2   Total Hourly Cost Summary for the Schips
            Truck Dock Problem

Crew Size	Truck Waiting and Service Time Cost per Hour Lc_1	Crew Cost per Hour dc_2	Total Cost per Hour
2	(3.00)(15)=45.00	2(7)=14.00	$59.00
3	(1.00)(15)=15.00	3(7)=21.00	$36.00
4	(0.60)(15)= 9.00	4(7)=28.00	$37.00
5	(0.429)(15)= 6.44	5(7)=35.00	$41.44

expect the trucks to wait on the average 0.167 hours, approximately 10 minutes. Approximately 50% of the trucks will experience some waiting time, and the crew will be loading or unloading approximately 50% of the time. With this crew utilization information, the manager knows his crew will be free about 4 hours per day and can possibly be assigned to other tasks in the loading dock or warehouse area.

Note that by increasing the crew size to four, the branch could further reduce truck waiting time and provide an even better loading and unloading service. Table 17.1 shows that the average waiting time for trucks with a four-man crew is reduced to 0.075 hours or 4.5 minutes per truck. However, the cost model shows that the cost of going to a four-man crew slightly exceeds the economic benefits associated with faster service, and thus the three-man crew is the minimum cost recommendation.

The Schips loading dock problem is an example of how quantitative models of waiting lines (queueing models) can help in the decision-making process. While equations (17.4) to (17.10) are the general equations for the single-channel waiting line with Poisson arrivals and exponential service times, cost equation (17.11) was specifically developed for the Schips problem. Thus for similar waiting line problems, while you may use equations (17.4) to (17.10) to compute the operating characteristics of the system, you may need to develop a modified cost model to describe the costs associated with your specific problem.

17.8   THE MULTIPLE-CHANNEL WAITING LINE MODEL WITH POISSON ARRIVALS AND EXPONENTIAL SERVICE TIMES

A logical extension of the single-channel waiting line is the *multiple-channel* waiting line. By multiple-channel waiting lines we mean that two or more

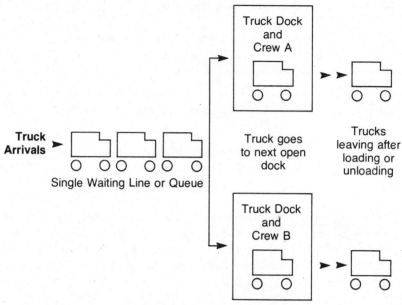

*FIGURE 17.4 Flow Diagram of Schips Two-Channel Waiting
Line System*

servers (channels) are available and that the customers arriving for service form a single waiting line and wait for any one of the servers to become available.

For the Schips loading dock problem we would use a multiple-channel waiting line model if the loading dock area had two or more loading docks. The flow diagram for a two-channel loading dock operation is shown in Figure 17.4.

If we make the assumptions that the multiple servers are identical in terms of providing exponential service times with the same mean service time or service rate, that the arrival distribution can be described by the Poisson distribution, and that a first-in-first-out queue discipline is appropriate, we have the basic multiple-channel waiting line with Poisson arrivals and exponential service times. Operations researchers have developed the following formulas for determining the operating characteristics of this type of multiple-channel waiting line. Let

k = number of channels (that is, the number of servers)
λ = mean arrival rate for the system
μ = mean service rate for *each* channel (servers are assumed to be identical).

1. The probability that all k service channels are idle (that is, the probability of zero units in the system):

$$P_0 = \frac{1}{\left[\displaystyle\sum_{n=0}^{n=k-1} \frac{1}{n!}\left(\frac{\lambda}{\mu}\right)^n\right] + \frac{1}{k!}\left(\frac{\lambda}{\mu}\right)^k \frac{k\mu}{k\mu - \lambda}} \qquad \text{for } k\mu > \lambda. \qquad (17.12)$$

2. The probability of n units in the system:

$$P_n = \frac{1}{k!k^{n-k}}\left(\frac{\lambda}{\mu}\right)^n P_0 \qquad \text{for } n > k \qquad (17.13)$$

$$P_n = \frac{1}{n!}\left(\frac{\lambda}{\mu}\right)^n P_0 \qquad \text{for } n \leq k. \qquad (17.14)$$

3. The average number of units in the system:

$$L = \frac{\lambda\mu(\lambda/\mu)^k}{(k-1)!\,(k\mu - \lambda)^2} P_0 + \frac{\lambda}{\mu}. \qquad (17.15)$$

4. The average time a unit spends in the system (waiting time + service time):

$$W = \frac{\mu(\lambda/\mu)^k}{(k-1)!\,(k\mu - \lambda)^2} P_0 + \frac{1}{\mu} = \frac{L}{\lambda}. \qquad (17.16)$$

5. The average number of units in the queue waiting for service:

$$L_q = L - \frac{\lambda}{\mu}. \qquad (17.17)$$

6. The average time a unit spends in the queue waiting for service:

$$W_q = W - \frac{1}{\mu} = \frac{L_q}{\lambda}. \qquad (17.18)$$

7. The probability that an arriving unit has to wait for service:

$$P_w = \frac{1}{k!}\left(\frac{\lambda}{\mu}\right)^k \frac{k\mu}{k\mu - \lambda} P_0. \qquad (17.19)$$

While the equations describing the operating characteristics of a multiple-channel waiting line with Poisson arrivals and exponential service times are somewhat more complex than the single-channel equations, they provide the same information and are used exactly like we used the results from the single-channel model. In fact, the single-channel model is a special case of the general multiple-channel model where $k = 1$; that is, if we use $k = 1$ in equations (17.12) to (17.19), we will generate the corresponding single-channel results of equations (17.4) to (17.10).

For an application of the multiple-channel waiting line model, suppose we return to the Schips loading dock problem. The analysis of the single-channel model led to the decision to use a three-man crew with an estimated operating cost of $36 per hour. Suppose the manager would like to consider the desirability of expanding the loading dock area to provide space to load and/or unload two trucks simultaneously. If this were done, the manager would assign a two-man crew to each of the two docks and operate with a two-channel waiting line. How does this alternative compare to the single-channel, three-man crew alternative?

We can answer this question by applying equations (17.12) to (17.19) specifically for the two-channel ($k = 2$) waiting line. Using $\lambda = 3$ trucks per hour and $\mu = 4$ trucks per hour for each two-man crew, we have the following operating condition:

$$P_0 = \frac{1}{\left[\sum_{n=0}^{1} \frac{1}{n!}\left(\frac{3}{4}\right)^n\right] + \frac{1}{2!}\left(\frac{3}{4}\right)^2 \frac{2(4)}{2(4) - 3}}$$

$$= \frac{1}{1 + \frac{3}{4} + \frac{1}{2}\left(\frac{3}{4}\right)^2\left(\frac{8}{8 - 3}\right)} = 0.4545$$

$$L = \frac{3(4)(3/4)^2}{(1)! \, (8 - 3)^2}(0.4545) + \frac{3}{4} = 0.873 \text{ trucks}$$

$$W = \frac{0.873}{3} = 0.291 \text{ hours}$$

$$L_q = 0.873 - 3/4 = 0.123 \text{ trucks}$$

$$W_q = \frac{0.123}{3} = 0.041 \text{ hours}$$

$$P_w = \frac{1}{2!}\left(\frac{3}{4}\right)^2 \frac{2(4)}{(2(4) - 3)}(0.4545) = 0.2045.$$

In order to evaluate this system on an economic basis, we would use a $15 per hour truck cost, a $7 per hour crew member cost, a total crew size of four, and the total cost model of equation (17.11). This provides the following total hourly cost for Schips' two-channel loading dock:

$$\begin{aligned} TC &= Lc_1 + dc_2 \\ &= 0.873(15) + 4(7) \\ &= 13.10 + 28.00 = \$41.10 \text{ per hour.} \end{aligned}$$

Thus we see that the three-man single-channel loading dock operation remains the most economical system. It is interesting to note that the four-man crew for the single-channel system ($37/hour) is more economical than the 2 two-man crews for the multiple-channel system ($41.10/hour). In Table 17.1 we saw that the average waiting time in the queue with the four-man crew single-channel system W_q was 0.075 hour or 4.5 minutes per truck. The corresponding waiting time for the two-channel system was 0.041 hours or 2.5 minutes per truck. Thus the waiting time in the queue was slightly reduced by the two-channel operation. In addition, the two-channel system has reduced the percent of trucks having to wait to 20.45%. However, with the single-channel four-man crew the trucks are loaded or unloaded in an average of 0.125 hour or 7.5 minutes per truck, while the multiple-channel two-man crews each require 0.25 hour or 15 minutes per truck. Thus while the two-channel system decreases waiting time in the queue, its slower mean service time per truck makes it less economical than the four-man crew single-channel system.

17.9 OTHER WAITING LINE MODELS

In this chapter you have been exposed to single-channel and multiple-channel waiting lines with Poisson arrivals and exponential service times. However, many variations of these specific systems may exist in actual waiting line situations. Operations researchers have analyzed a wide variety of possible waiting lines and developed general expressions for average customer waiting time, average number of customers in the system, percent of the time servers are idle, and other operating characteristics of the system. Specifically, models are available covering some of the following types of waiting line situations:

1. Arrivals other than Poisson
2. Service times other than exponential
3. Arrivals in bulk quantities rather than one at a time
4. Limited or finite waiting lines called truncated queues
5. Mean arrival and service rates that vary with the number of the units waiting for service
6. Queue disciplines other than first-in-first-out
7. Sequential waiting lines where units pass through a fixed sequence or series of servers.

With these and other analytical models of waiting lines, a decision maker with a specific waiting line problem should attempt to identify a general waiting line model that closely approximates his specific problem; that is, he should attempt to identify a waiting line model with an arrival distribution, service time distribution, queue discipline, and so on, that closely approximates the actual situation. Even with the numerous waiting line models in existence, many practical waiting line problems are so complex that operations researchers have been unable to develop the analytical expressions necessary to determine the operating characteristics. Thus if the decision maker is unable to find an analytical model applicable to the specific waiting line, a computer simulation model of the problem may be used to develop the necessary operating characteristics data.

17.10 SIMULATION OF WAITING LINES

Computer simulation models offer an attractive alternative to the use of mathematical models when studying the behavior and operating characteristics of waiting lines. The attractiveness of computer simulation models rests primarily with their versatility. Although we pointed out that mathematical models have been developed for waiting line situations that differ from the Poisson-exponential systems described in this chapter, the complexity and diversity of waiting lines often prohibits an analyst from finding an existing model that fits the specific situation being studied. Even when models that appear to be good approximations of the problem can be identified, the mathematics of the models are often so complex that many practitioners are unable to determine whether the models are applicable or not. Thus a computer simulation model of a waiting line problem offers another approach to studying waiting line situations.

Let us consider a deviation from the assumptions which enabled us to utilize existing mathematical models for the Schips truck dock waiting line. One key assumption was that the service times in the Schips problem were essentially random *and* independent of all other conditions. This enabled us to use the same exponential distribution and mean service rate for all trucks. Let us suppose that the Schips truck dock crew does not work independently of the number of trucks waiting to be serviced. That is, suppose that management has observed that as the length of the waiting line increases, the rate at which the dock crew loads and unloads also increases. Thus our previous assumption that service times are always exponentially distributed with a mean service time of 0.25 hour per truck would not reflect the actual situation. Hence while the decision maker might still elect to use the Poisson-exponential model as a rough approximation, he may want to develop a computer simulation model that attempts to account for the varying work rates of the crew.

Also recall that the waiting line models in this chapter employ a first-in-first-out queue discipline. Suppose the branch manager wanted to evaluate the policy of having the dock crews load customer delivery trucks before unloading incoming shipments from the central warehouse. How would the waiting times and operating costs be affected by this policy? We cannot answer this question with a waiting line model that assumes a first-in-first-out queue discipline. However, a computer simulation model could be used to test this new priority policy.

Finally, suppose that we collected actual arrival and service time data for the Schips trucks for a 2-week period and found that arrivals did not follow a Poisson distribution and the service times did not follow an exponential distribution. We might try to identify the general distributions that these data follow and attempt to identify an existing waiting line model based on these distributions. However, if an existing model cannot be found or if the arrivals and/or service times do not follow any recognizable probability distribution, we could input the observed relative frequency data for the arrival and service times into a simulation model and use computer simulation to generate the operating characteristics of the loading dock.

Although we have only mentioned a few specific changes in the characteristics of the Schips waiting line problem, it should be apparent that many other possibilities could be considered. Again, this is where computer simulation starts to become especially attractive as a solution procedure. Instead of using an existing waiting line model that is perhaps a poor approximation of the waiting line being studied, we develop a computer simulation model that more closely reflects the true characteristics of the waiting line.

17.11 SUMMARY

Waiting line problems occur in a variety of practical situations in which customers or other units may wait for a service. Queueing models have been developed which provide information regarding waiting times, idle time, number of people waiting, and other operating characteristics of a waiting line. This information along with cost data may be used to balance the benefits of improved service with the cost necessary to improve the service.

In this chapter we have presented models for single-channel and multiple-channel waiting lines with Poisson arrivals and exponential service times. In addition, we pointed out that models exist which consider a variety of other waiting line situations. However, a computer simulation model of the waiting line is recommended if the assumptions of existing waiting line models do not closely approximate the specific problem under study.

17.12 GLOSSARY

1. *Queueing theory*—The operations research term for the study of waiting lines.
2. *Queue*—A waiting line.
3. *Single-channel*—A waiting line with only one server.
4. *Multiple-channel*—A waiting line with two or more parallel identical servers.
5. *Mean arrival rate*—The expected number of customers or units arriving or entering the system in a given period of time.
6. *Poisson distribution*—A probability distribution used to describe the random arrival pattern for some waiting lines.
7. *Mean service rate*—The expected number of customers or units that can be serviced by one server in a given period of time.
8. *Exponential distribution*—A probability distribution used to describe the pattern of service times for some waiting lines.

9. *Queue discipline*—The way in which customers in the waiting line are ordered for service.
10. *Steady state*—The normal operation of the waiting line after an initial transient or startup period of time.
11. *Utilization factor*—The ratio of the mean arrival rate to the mean service rate λ/μ. It indicates the proportion of the time the service facilities are in use.
12. *Operating characteristics*—The performance characteristics of a waiting line such as average number of customers in the system, average queue size, average waiting time, and so on.

17.13 PROBLEMS

The following waiting line problems are all based upon the assumptions of Poisson arrivals and exponential service times.

1. The demand for a computer facility occurs at a mean rate of five programs per hour ($\lambda = 5$).
   a. What is the probability no one will request a computer run in a given 1-hour period?
   b. What is the probability of exactly one request? Exactly two requests?
   c. What is the probability the computer facility will have three or more requests in an hour?
2. Computer programs require on the average of 10 minutes of computer time.
   a. What is the mean service rate in programs per hour?
   b. What percent of the programs will be completed in 5 minutes or less ($T = 1/12$ hour)?
   c. What percent in 10 minutes or less?
   d. What percent of the computer programs will require *more than* 30 minutes to complete?
3. If a computer system has a mean arrival rate of five new programs per hour and a mean service rate of six programs per hour, consider the following questions.
   a. What is the utilization factor for the computer system?
   b. What is the probability that the system is idle?
   c. What is the average turnaround time (waiting time plus service time) for a program?
   d. What is the average number of programs that will be waiting in the queue?

4. Ships using a single-channel loading dock in New York Harbor have a mean arrival rate of two per day. The loading and unloading rate is three per day.
   a. What is the probability the dock will be idle?
   b. What is the probability of one ship in the system?
   c. What is the probability that at least one ship will be waiting (that is, the probability of at least two ships in the system)?
   d. What is the probability a new arrival will have to wait?
5. New orders, which are filled from inventory, are processed by a single shipping clerk. The orders have a mean arrival rate of 15 per week and a mean service rate of 20 per week. Assume a week consists of 5 work days.
   a. What is the average time in days an order spends in the system?
   b. What is the average time in days an order spends in the queue waiting for the clerk to begin service?
   c. Verify that the answer to part a is equal to the answer to part b plus $1/\mu$. Does this make sense? Explain.
6. For the Schips single-channel waiting line, assume the mean arrival rate is four trucks per hour and the mean service rate for the two-man crew is five trucks per hour.
   a. What is the probability the dock crew will be idle?
   b. What is the average number of trucks in the system?
   c. What is the average time a truck spends in the system?
   d. What is the average number of trucks in the queue?
   e. What is the average time a truck spends in the queue waiting for service?
   f. What is the probability an arriving truck will have to wait?
   g. What is the probability that at least one unit will be waiting?
   h. Does this waiting line provide more or less service than the original Schips two-man crew operation (see Table 17.1)?
7. Using the $15 per hour truck cost and the $7 per hour crew member cost, what crew size would you recommend for the single-channel Schips loading dock with $\lambda = 4$ and $\mu = 5$? Assume that the average service time $\bar{t}$ is given by $\bar{t} = 0.4/(\text{crew size})$. What are the operating characteristics of the truck waiting line if Schips adopts your crew size recommendation?
8. Perform a two-channel analysis of the Schips loading dock with $\lambda = 4$, $\mu = 5$, and $\bar{t} = 0.4/(\text{crew size})$ per channel. What is the hourly cost of the 2 two-man crews operation? Comparing these results to the four-man crew single-channel system in Problem 7, what is your recommendation?
9. Consider a two-channel waiting line with a mean arrival rate of 50 per hour and a mean service rate of 75 per hour for each channel.

    a.   What is the probability of an empty system?

    b.   What is the probability that an arrival will have to wait?

    c.   Would the answers to parts (a) and (b) change if the mean arrival rate were two per hour and the mean service rate were three per hour? Why?

10.   For a two-channel waiting line with a mean arrival rate of 15 per hour and a mean service rate of 10 per hour per channel, determine the probability that an arrival has to wait. What is the probability of waiting if the system is expanded to three channels?

11.   Pete's market is a small local grocery store with only one checkout counter. Assuming that shoppers arrive at the checkout lane at an average rate of 15 customers per hour and that the average order takes 3 minutes to ring up and bag, what information would you develop for Pete to aid him in analyzing his current operation? If Pete does not want the average waiting time in the queue to exceed 5 minutes, what would you tell Pete about his current system?

12.   In Problem 11 we analyzed the checkout waiting line for Pete's market. After reviewing our analysis, Pete felt it would be desirable to hire a full-time person to assist in the checkout operation. Pete believed that if the new employee assisted the checkout cashier, service time could be reduced to 2 minutes. However, Pete was also considering installing a second checkout lane which could be operated by the new person. This second alternative would provide a two-channel system with the average service time of 3 minutes for each server. Should Pete use the new employee to assist on the current checkout counter or operate a second counter? Justify your recommendation.

13.   Keuka Park Savings and Loan currently has one drive-in teller window. The arrival of cars occurs at a mean rate of 10 cars per hour. The mean service rate is 12 cars per hour.

    a.   What is the probability the service facility will be idle?

    b.   If you were to drive up to the facility, what is the expected number of cars you would see waiting and being serviced.

    c.   What is the probability that at least one car will be waiting to be serviced?

    d.   What is the average time in the queue waiting for service?

    e.   As a potential customer of the system would you be satisfied with the above waiting line characteristics? How do you think management could go about assessing the feelings of its customers with respect to the operation of the current system?

14.   In order to improve the service to the customer, Keuka Park Savings and Loan wants to investigate the effect of a second drive-in teller window. Assume a mean arrival rate of 10 cars per hour and a mean service rate of 12 cars per hour for each drive-in window. What effect

would the addition of a new teller window have upon the system? Does this system appear acceptable?

15. Fore and Aft Marina is a newly planned marina that is to be located on the Ohio river near Madison, Indiana. Assuming that Fore and Aft decides to build one docking facility, and a mean arrival rate of 5 boats per hour and a mean service rate of 10 boats per hour are expected, consider the following questions.

    a. What is the probability that the boat dock will be idle?

    b. What is the average time a boat will spend waiting for service? What is the average time a boat will spend at the dock?

    c. What is the average number of boats that will be waiting in the queue for service?

    d. If you were the management of Fore and Aft Marina and believed that the above arrival and service rates were accurate, would you be satisfied with the service level your system would be providing?

16. Management of the Fore and Aft Marina project in Problem 15 wants to investigate the possibility of adding a second dock. Assume a mean arrival rate of 5 boats per hour and a mean service rate of 10 boats per hour for each channel.

    a. What is the probability that a boat that stops for fuel will have to wait?

    b. What is the average waiting time a boat will spend in the queue?

    c. What is the probability the system is idle?

    d. Would you consider this good service? Is it too good?

17. Big Al's Quickie Car Wash is a chain of 50-cent car wash stations. Each of Al's stations has two wash areas with a mean service time of 4 minutes per car. Cars arrive at a station at the rate of 10 cars per hour on the average, join the waiting line, and select the next open wash area when it becomes available.

    a. What is the probability a station will be empty?

    b. What is the probability that a customer who arrives at a station will have to wait?

    c. As a customer of Big Al's Quickie Car Wash, do you think the service of the system favors the customer? If you were Al, what would your attitude be relative to this service level?

18. In Section 17.8 we determined the operating characteristics and prepared an economic analysis of the Schips problem for the case of two loading docks. One of the assumptions that was implicit in our analysis was that the crews would not work together.

Suppose, however, that when one of the dock crews was idle and the other was busy, the idle crew would help the busy crew with its loading and unloading. Thus none of the dock workers would be idle unless there were no trucks in the system.

The formulas presented in Section 17.8 are not applicable to this new situation and hence should not be applied. This is a case in which a simulation model would be useful.

a. Discuss in a step-by-step fashion how you would develop a simulation model to determine the operating characteristics of this waiting line system.

b. What type of output would you like to have as a result of the simulation?

18
Markov Processes

Markov process models are useful in studying the evolution of certain systems over repeated trials. These repeated trials are often successive time periods where the state or outcome of the system in any particular time period cannot be determined with certainty. Rather, a set of transition probabilities is used to describe the manner in which the system makes transitions from one period to the next. Hence we talk about the probability of the system being in a particular state at a given time period.

Markov processes have been used to describe the probability that a machine which is functioning in one period will continue to function or will break down in the next period. They have also been used to describe the probability that a consumer purchasing brand A in one period will purchase brand B in the next period. In this chapter we study a marketing application of Markov process models that involves an analysis of the store switching behavior of supermarket customers. As a second illustration of Markov process models, we consider an accounting application that is concerned with the transitioning of accounts receivable dollars to different aging categories.

Since an in-depth treatment of Markov processes is beyond the scope of this text, our analysis in both illustrations is restricted to Markov processes in which there are a finite number of states, the transition probabilities remain constant over time, and the probability of being in a particular state at any one time period depends only upon the state of the process in the immediately preceding period. Such Markov processes are often referred to as Markov chains with stationary transition probabilities.

18.1 MARKET SHARE ANALYSIS

Suppose that we are interested in analyzing the market share and customer loyalty for Murphy's Food Liner and Ashley's Super Market, the only two grocery stores in a small town. We focus our attention on the sequence of shopping trips of one customer. We assume that the customer makes one shopping trip each week and that he will select either Murphy's Food Liner or Ashley's Super Market, but not both, on each weekly trip.

Using the terminology of Markov processes, we refer to the weekly time periods or shopping trips as the *trials of the process*. Thus at each trial the customer will shop at either Murphy's Food Liner or Ashley's Super Market. The particular store selected in a given week is referred to as the *state of the system* in that time period. Since the customer has two shopping alternatives at each trial, we say the system has two possible states. Since the number of states is finite, we can list and identify each state in detail. The two possible states are

State 1:   The customer shops at Murphy's Food Liner

State 2:   The customer shops at Ashley's Super Market.

If we say the system is in state 1 at trial 3, we are simply saying that the customer shops at Murphy's during the third weekly shopping period.

As we continue the shopping trip process into the future, we cannot say for certain where the customer will shop during a given week or trial. In fact, we realize that during any given week, the customer may be a Murphy's customer or an Ashley's customer. However using a Markov process model we will be able to compute the probability the customer shops at each store during any time period. For example, we may find there is a 0.6 probability that the customer will shop at Ashley's during a particular week and a 0.4 probability that he will shop at Murphy's.

In order to determine the probabilities of the various states occurring at successive trials of the Markov process, we need information on the probability that a customer remains with the same store or switches to the competing store as the process continues from trial to trial or week to week.

Suppose as part of a market research study we collect data from 100 shoppers over a 10-week period. Suppose further that these data show each customer's weekly shopping-trip pattern in terms of the sequence of visits to Murphy's and Ashley's. In order to develop a Markov process model for the sequence of weekly shopping trips, we need to express the probability of selecting each store (state) in a given time period solely in terms of the store (state) that was selected during the previous time period. In reviewing the data, suppose we find that out of all customers who shopped at Murphy's in a given week, 90% shopped at Murphy's the following week while 10% switched to Ashley's. Suppose that similar data for the customers who shopped at Ashley's in a given week show that 80% shopped at Ashley's the following week while 20% switched to Murphy's. Probabilities based on these data are shown in Table 18.1. Since these are the probabilities that a customer moves or makes a transition from a state in a given period to a state in the following period, these probabilities are given the special name of *transition probabilities*.

An important property of the table of transition probabilities is that the sum of the entries in each row is 1; this indicates that each row of the table provides a probability distribution. For example, a customer who shops at Murphy's one week must either shop at Murphy's or Ashley's the next week. The entries in row 1 give the probabilities associated with each of these events.

The 0.9 and 0.8 probabilities in Table 18.1 can be interpreted as measures

TABLE 18.1 Transition Probabilities for Murphy's and Ashley's Supermarkets

		Next Weekly Shopping Period	
		Murphy's Food Liner	Ashley's Super Market
Current Weekly Shopping Period	Murphy's Food Liner	0.9	0.1
	Ashley's Super Market	0.2	0.8

of store loyalty in that they indicate the probability of a repeat visit to the same store. Similarly, the 0.1 and 0.2 probabilities are measures of the store switching characteristics of customers.

It is important to realize that in developing a Markov process model for our problem, we are assuming that the transition probabilities will be the same for any customer and that the transition probabilities will not change over time; that is, at any point in time, the transition probabilities can be used to assess the probability a customer will shop at Murphy's or Ashley's in the next period, given we know where the customer is shopping during the current time period.

Note that the table of transition probabilities, Table 18.1, has one row and one column for each state of the system. We will use the symbol p_{ij} to represent the individual transition probabilities and the symbol P to represent the matrix (table) of transition probabilities; that is,

p_{ij} = probability of making a transition from state i in a given time period to state j in the next time period.

For our supermarket problem we have

$$P = \begin{bmatrix} p_{11} & p_{12} \\ p_{21} & p_{22} \end{bmatrix} = \begin{bmatrix} 0.9 & 0.1 \\ 0.2 & 0.8 \end{bmatrix}$$

Using the matrix of transition probabilities, we can now determine the probability that a customer will be a Murphy's or an Ashley's customer at some time period in the future. Let us begin by assuming that we have a customer whose last weekly shopping trip was to Murphy's. What is the probability that this customer will shop at Murphy's on the next weekly shopping trip, time period 1? In other words, what is the probability that the system will be in state 1 after the first transition? The matrix of transition probabilities indicates that this probability is $p_{11} = 0.9$.

Now let us consider the state of the system in period 2. A useful way of depicting what can happen on the second weekly shopping trip is to draw a tree diagram of the possible outcomes (see Figure 18.1). Using this tree diagram, we see that the probability that the customer shops at Murphy's during both the first and second weeks is $(0.9)(0.9) = 0.81$. Also, note that the probability of the customer switching to Ashley's on the first trip and then switching back to Murphy's on the second trip is $(0.1)(0.2) = 0.02$. Since these are the only two ways that the customer can be in state 1

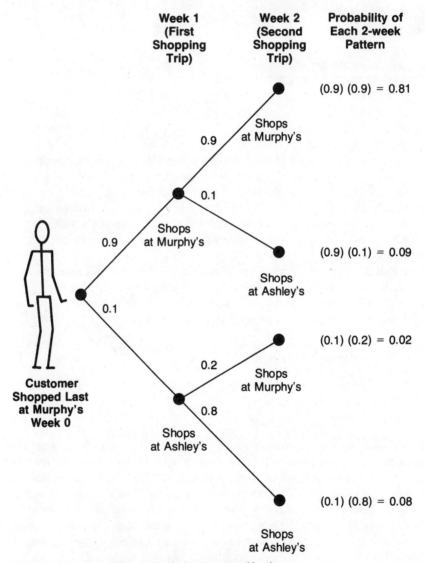

FIGURE 18.1 *Tree Diagram Depicting Two Weekly Shopping Trips of a Customer Who Shopped Last at Murphy's*

(shopping at Murphy's) during the second period, the probability of the system being in state 1 during the second period is $0.81 + 0.02 = 0.83$. Similarly, the probability of the system being in state 2 during the second period of the process is $0.09 + 0.08 = 0.17$.

As desirable as the tree diagram approach may be from an intuitive point of view, this approach becomes very cumbersome when we want to extend the analysis three, four, or more periods into the future. Fortunately, there is an easier way to calculate the probabilities of the system being in state 1 or state 2 for any subsequent period. First, we introduce notation that will allow us to represent the probability of the system being in state 1 or state 2 for any given period of time. Let

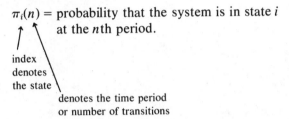

$$\pi_i(n) = \text{probability that the system is in state } i \text{ at the } n\text{th period.}$$

index denotes the state

denotes the time period or number of transitions

For example, $\pi_1(1)$ would represent the probability of the system being in state 1 in period 1 (that is, after 1 transition), while $\pi_2(1)$ denotes the probability of the system being in state 2 after one transition. Since $\pi_i(n)$ is the probability that the system is in state i at period n, this probability is referred to as a *state probability*.

$\pi_1(0)$ and $\pi_2(0)$ will denote the probability of the system being in state 1 or state 2 at some initial or starting time period. Period or week 0 represents the most recent time period when we are beginning the analysis of a Markov process. If we set $\pi_1(0) = 1$ and $\pi_2(0) = 0$, we are saying that as an initial condition the customer shopped last week at Murphy's; whereas if we set $\pi_1(0) = 0$ and $\pi_2(0) = 1$, we would be starting the system with a customer who shopped last week at Ashley's. In our tree diagram of Figure 18.1 we considered the situation where the customer shopped last at Murphy's. Thus

$$[\pi_1(0)\ \pi_2(0)] = [1\ \ 0]$$

is a vector that represents the initial state probabilities of our system. In general, we use the notation

$$\Pi(n) = [\pi_1(n)\ \pi_2(n)]$$

to denote the vector of state probabilities for the system at period n. In our shopping example, $\Pi(1)$ is a vector representing the state probabilities for the first week, $\Pi(2)$ is a vector representing the state probabilities for the second week, and so on.

Using this notation, we can find the state probabilities for period $n + 1$ by simply multiplying the known state probabilities for period n by the transi-

535

tion probability matrix. Using the vector of state probabilities and the matrix of transition probabilities, this multiplication[1] can be expressed as follows:

$$\Pi(\text{next period}) = \Pi(\text{current period})P$$

or

$$\Pi(n + 1) = \Pi(n)P. \tag{18.1}$$

Beginning with the system in state 1 at period 0, we have $\Pi(0) = [1,0]$. We can compute the state probabilities for period 1 as follows:

$$\Pi(1) = \Pi(0)P$$

or

$$[\pi_1(1) \quad \pi_2(1)] = [\pi_1(0) \quad \pi_2(0)]\begin{bmatrix} p_{11} & p_{12} \\ p_{21} & p_{22} \end{bmatrix}$$

$$= [1 \quad 0]\begin{bmatrix} 0.9 & 0.1 \\ 0.2 & 0.8 \end{bmatrix}$$

$$= [0.9 \quad 0.1].$$

The state probabilities $\pi_1(1) = 0.9$ and $\pi_2(1) = 0.1$ are the probabilities that a customer shops at Murphy's or Ashley's during week 1, given that he shopped at Murphy's during week 0.

Using equation (18.1), we can compute the state probabilities for the second week as follows:

$$\Pi(2) = \Pi(1)P$$

or

$$[\pi_1(2) \quad \pi_2(2)] = [\pi_1(1) \quad \pi_2(1)]\begin{bmatrix} p_{11} & p_{12} \\ p_{21} & p_{22} \end{bmatrix}$$

$$= [0.9 \quad 0.1]\begin{bmatrix} 0.9 & 0.1 \\ 0.2 & 0.8 \end{bmatrix}$$

$$= [0.83 \quad 0.17].$$

We see that the probability of shopping Murphy's during the second week is 0.83, while the probability of shopping Ashley's during this time period is 0.17. These same results were previously obtained using the tree diagram of Figure 18.1. By continuing to apply equation (18.1), we can easily compute the state probabilities for any future time period; that is,

[1] Appendix F provides the step-by-step procedure for vector and matrix multiplication.

$$\Pi(3) \quad = \Pi(2)P$$
$$\Pi(4) \quad = \Pi(3)P$$
$$\cdot \qquad \cdot$$
$$\cdot \qquad \cdot$$
$$\cdot \qquad \cdot$$
$$\Pi(n + 1) = \Pi(n)P.$$

Table 18.2 shows the result of carrying out these calculations for a number of periods in the future.

The vectors $\Pi(1)$, $\Pi(2)$, $\Pi(3)$, . . . contain the probabilities that a customer who started out as a Murphy customer will be in state 1 or state 2 in the first period, the second period, the third period, and so on. In Table 18.2 we see that after a large number of periods these probabilities do not change much from one period to the next. In fact, the probability of the system being in state 1 or state 2 is approaching $\frac{2}{3}$ and $\frac{1}{3}$ after a large number of shopping periods.

If we had started with 1000 Murphy customers, that is, 1000 consumers who last shopped at Murphy's, our analysis indicates that during the fifth subsequent weekly shopping period 723 would be customers of Murphy's and 277 would be customers of Ashley's. Moreover, after a large number of shopping periods, approximately 667 would be customers of Murphy's and 333 customers of Ashley's.

Now let us repeat our analysis, but this time we will begin the process with a customer who shopped last at Ashley's. Thus,

$$\Pi(0) = [\pi_1(0) \ \pi_2(0)] = [0 \ 1].$$

Using equation (18.1) the probability of the system being in state 1 or state 2 in period 1 is given by

$$\Pi(1) = \Pi(0)P$$

or

$$[\pi_1(1) \quad \pi_2(1)] = [\pi_1(0) \quad \pi_2(0)]\begin{bmatrix} p_{11} & p_{12} \\ p_{12} & p_{22} \end{bmatrix}$$
$$= [0 \quad 1]\begin{bmatrix} 0.9 & 0.1 \\ 0.2 & 0.8 \end{bmatrix}$$
$$= [0.2 \quad 0.8].$$

Proceeding as before we can calculate subsequent state probabilities. Doing so, we obtain the results shown in Table 18.3.

On the fifth shopping period the probability that the customer will be shopping at Murphy's is 0.555 and the probability that he will be shopping at Ashley's is 0.445. After a large number of shopping periods the probability of the system being in state 1 approaches $\frac{2}{3}$ and the probability of it being in

TABLE 18.2 *Probabilities of States for Future Periods Beginning Initially with a Murphy's Customer,* $\Pi(0) = (1\ 0)$

State Probability	Period (n)											
	0	1	2	3	4	5	6	7	8	9	10	Large n
$\pi_1(n)$	1	0.9	0.83	0.781	0.747	0.723	0.706	0.694	0.686	0.680	0.676	$\rightarrow \frac{2}{3}$
$\pi_2(n)$	0	0.1	0.17	0.219	0.253	0.277	0.294	0.306	0.314	0.320	0.324	$\rightarrow \frac{1}{3}$

TABLE 18.3 *Probabilities of States for Future Periods Beginning Initially with an Ashley's Customer,* $\Pi(0) = [0\ 1]$

State Probability	Period (n)											
	0	1	2	3	4	5	6	7	8	9	10	Large n
$\pi_1(n)$	0	0.2	0.34	0.438	0.507	0.555	0.589	0.612	0.628	0.640	0.648	$\rightarrow \frac{2}{3}$
$\pi_2(n)$	1	0.8	0.66	0.562	0.493	0.445	0.411	0.388	0.372	0.360	0.352	$\rightarrow \frac{1}{3}$

state 2 approaches $\frac{1}{3}$. These are the same as the probabilities obtained after a large number of transitions when the system started in state 1. Thus we see that the probability of the system being in a particular state after a large number of periods is independent of the beginning state of the system. The probabilities that we approach after a large number of transitions are referred to as *steady-state probabilities*. We shall denote the steady-state probability for state 1 with the symbol π_1 and the steady-state probability for state 2 with the symbol π_2. We simply omit the period designation from $\pi_i(n)$ since it is no longer necessary.

Thus if we have 1000 customers in the system, the Markov process model tells us that in the long run, with steady-state probabilities $\pi_1 = \frac{2}{3}$ and $\pi_2 = \frac{1}{3}$, approximately two thirds or 667 customers would be Murphy's, while approximately one third or 333 customers would be Ashley's. These steady-state probabilities can be interpreted as the market shares for the two stores.

The analysis of Tables 18.2 and 18.3 indicates that as n gets larger, the difference between the state probabilities for the nth shopping period and the $(n + 1)$th period becomes very small. This leads us to the conclusion that as n gets extremely large, the state probabilities at the $(n + 1)$th period are essentially equal to those at the nth period. This observation provides the basis for a simple method for computing the steady-state probabilities without having to actually carry out a large number of calculations.

In general we know from equation (18.1) that

$$[\pi_1(n + 1) \quad \pi_2(n + 1)] = [\pi_1(n) \quad \pi_2(n)] \begin{bmatrix} p_{11} & p_{12} \\ p_{21} & p_{22} \end{bmatrix}$$

Since for sufficiently large n the difference between $\Pi(n + 1)$ and $\Pi(n)$ is negligible, we see that in the steady state $\pi_1(n + 1) = \pi_1(n) = \pi_1$ and $\pi_2(n + 1) = \pi_2(n) = \pi_2$. Thus we have

$$[\pi_1 \quad \pi_2] = [\pi_1 \quad \pi_2] \begin{bmatrix} p_{11} & p_{12} \\ p_{21} & p_{22} \end{bmatrix}$$

$$= [\pi_1 \quad \pi_2] \begin{bmatrix} 0.9 & 0.1 \\ 0.2 & 0.8 \end{bmatrix}$$

After carrying out the above multiplications we obtain

$$\pi_1 = 0.9\pi_1 + 0.2\pi_2 \tag{18.2}$$

and

$$\pi_2 = 0.1\pi_1 + 0.8\pi_2. \tag{18.3}$$

However, we also know that

$$\pi_1 + \pi_2 = 1 \tag{18.4}$$

since the sum of the probabilities must equal 1.

Using equation (18.4) to solve for π_2 and substituting the result in equation (18.2), we obtain

$$\pi_1 = 0.9\pi_1 + 0.2(1 - \pi_1)$$
$$\pi_1 = 0.9\pi_1 + 0.2 - 0.2\pi_1$$
$$\pi_1 - 0.7\pi_1 = 0.2$$
$$0.3\pi_1 = 0.2$$
$$\pi_1 = \tfrac{2}{3}.$$

Then using equation (18.4), we can conclude that $\pi_2 = \tfrac{1}{3}$.

Thus we see that solving the simultaneous equations given by equations (18.2) and (18.4) allows us to solve for the steady-state probabilities directly. You can check for yourself that we could have obtained the same result using equations (18.3) and (18.4).[2] In our example, these steady-state probabilities represent the share of the market each store would receive in the long run regardless of its initial market share.

This market share information is often quite valuable in decision-making situations. For example, suppose Ashley's Super Market is contemplating an advertising campaign to attract more of Murphy's customers to its store. Let us suppose further that Ashley's believes this promotional strategy will increase the probability of a Murphy's customer switching to Ashley's from 0.10 to 0.15. The new transition probabilities which would result are given in Table 18.4.

Given the new transition probabilities, we can solve for the new steady-state probabilities or market shares as we did before using equations (18.2) and (18.4). Thus we obtain

$$\pi_1 = 0.85\pi_1 + 0.20\pi_2$$

TABLE 18.4   *New Transition Probabilities for Murphy's and Ashley's Supermarkets*

		Next Weekly Shopping Period	
		Murphy's Food Liner	Ashley's Super Market
Current Weekly Shopping Period	Murphy's Food Liner	0.85	0.15
	Ashley's Super Market	0.20	0.80

[2] Even though equations (18.2) and (18.3) provide us with two equations and two unknowns, we must include equation (18.4) when solving for π_1 and π_2 to ensure that the sum of steady-state probabilities will equal 1.

and substituting $\pi_2 = 1 - \pi_1$ from equation (18.4), we get

$$\pi_1 = 0.85\pi_1 + 0.20(1 - \pi_1)$$
$$\pi_1 = 0.85\pi_1 + 0.20 - 0.20\pi_1$$
$$\pi_1 - 0.65\pi_1 = 0.20$$
$$0.35\pi_1 = 0.20$$
$$\pi_1 = 0.57$$

and

$$\pi_2 = 1 - 0.57 = 0.43.$$

Thus we see that the proposed promotional strategy will lead to approximately a 10% increase in Ashley's market share. Suppose that the total market consists of 6000 customers per week. The new promotional strategy will approximately increase the number of customers doing their weekly shopping at Ashley's from 2000 to 2580. If the average weekly profit per customer is $1, the proposed promotional strategy can be expected to increase Ashley's profits by $580 per week. Clearly, then, if the cost of the promotional campaign is less than $580 per week, Ashley should seriously consider such a strategy.

This is but one illustration of how a Markov analysis of a firm's market share can be useful in a decision-making situation. Suppose that instead of trying to attract customers away from Murphy's Food Liner, Ashley's directed a promotional effort at increasing the loyalty of its own customers. In this case p_{22} would increase and p_{21} would decrease. Once we knew the amount of the change, we could calculate new steady-state probabilities and compute the impact on profits. Let us now see how Markov process models can be useful in accounting.

18.2 ACCOUNTS RECEIVABLE ANALYSIS

Another area in which Markov processes have produced useful results involves the estimation of the allowance for doubtful accounts. This allowance is an estimate of the amount of accounts receivable that will ultimately prove to be uncollectible (that is, bad debts).

Let us begin our analysis by considering the accounts receivable for Heidman's Department Store. Heidman's has two aging categories for its accounts receivable: (1) accounts that are classified as 0-30 days old and (2) accounts that are classified as 31-90 days old. If any portion of an account balance becomes over 90 days old that portion is written off as a bad debt. Heidman's follows the procedure of aging the total balance in any customer's account according to the oldest unpaid bill. For example, suppose one customer's account balance on September 30 is as follows.

Data of Purchase	Amount Charged
August 15	$25
September 18	10
September 28	50
Total	$85

An aging of accounts receivable on September 30 would assign the total balance of $85 to the 31–90 day old category because the oldest unpaid bill of August 15 is 46 days old. Let us assume that one week later, October 7, the customer pays the August 15 bill of $25. The remaining total balance of $60 would now be placed in the 0–30 day aging category since the oldest unpaid amount, corresponding to the September 18 purchase, is less than 31 days old. This method of aging accounts receivable is called the "total balance" method since the total account balance is placed in the age category corresponding to the oldest unpaid amount.

Note that under the total balances method of aging accounts receivable, dollars appearing in a 31–90 day age category at one point in time may appear in a 0–30 day age category at a later point in time. In the above example this was true for $60 of September billings which shifted from a 31–90 day to a 0–30 day aging category after the August bill had been paid.

Let us assume that on December 31 Heidman's shows a total of $3000 in its accounts receivable and that the firm's management would like an estimate of how much of the $3000 will eventually be collected and how much will eventually result in bad debts. The estimated amount of bad debts will appear as an allowance for doubtful accounts in the year-ending financial statements.

Let us see how we can view the accounts receivable operation as a Markov process. First, concentrate on what happens to *one* dollar currently in accounts receivable. As the firm continues to operate into the future, we can consider each week as a trial of a Markov process with a dollar existing in one of the following states of the system.

State 1: Paid category

State 2: Bad debt category

State 3: 0–30 day age category

State 4: 31–90 day age category

Thus we can track the week-by-week status of one dollar by using a Markov analysis to identify the state of the system at a particular week or time period in the future.

542

Using a Markov process model with the above states, we define our transition probabilities as follows:

p_{ij} = probability of a dollar in state i in one week moving to state j in the next week.

Based on historical transitions of accounts receivable dollars, the following transition matrix P has been developed for Heidman's Department Store:

$$P = \begin{bmatrix} p_{11} & p_{12} & p_{13} & p_{14} \\ p_{21} & p_{22} & p_{23} & p_{24} \\ p_{31} & p_{32} & p_{33} & p_{34} \\ p_{41} & p_{42} & p_{43} & p_{44} \end{bmatrix} = \begin{bmatrix} 1 & 0 & 0 & 0 \\ 0 & 1 & 0 & 0 \\ 0.4 & 0 & 0.3 & 0.3 \\ 0.4 & 0.2 & 0.3 & 0.1 \end{bmatrix}.$$

From the transition matrix we see that the probability of a dollar in the 0–30 day age category (state 3) moving to the paid category (state 1) in the next period is 0.4. Also we see that there is a 0.3 probability that this dollar will remain in the 0–30 day category (state 3) 1 week later, while there is a 0.3 probability that it will be in the 31–90 day category (state 4) 1 week later. Note that a dollar in a 0–30 day account cannot transition to a bad debt (state 2) in 1 week.

An important property of the Markov process model for Heidman's accounts receivable is the presence of *absorbing states*. Note that once a dollar makes a transition to state 1, the paid state, the probability of making a transition to any other state is zero. Similarly, once a dollar is in state 2, the bad debt state, the probability of a transition to any other state is zero. Thus once a dollar reaches state 1 or state 2, the system will remain in this state indefinitely. This leads us to conclude that all accounts receivable dollars will eventually be absorbed into either the paid or bad debt state, hence, the name absorbing state.

When a Markov process has absorbing states present, we do not compute steady-state probabilities in the context of the previous section because the process will eventually end up in one of the absorbing states. However, we may be interested in knowing the probability that the dollar will end up in each of the absorbing states. To determine these probabilities, we need to develop the notion of a fundamental matrix.

The Fundamental Matrix and Associated Calculations

In the following discussion we present the appropriate formulas for determining the probability that a dollar starting in state 3 or 4 will end up in each of the absorbing states. The underlying concept in the analysis involves the notion of a *fundamental matrix*. We begin the development of this concept by partitioning the matrix of transition probabilities into four parts; that is, we let

$$P = \begin{bmatrix} 1 & 0 & 0 & 0 \\ 0 & 1 & 0 & 0 \\ 0.4 & 0 & 0.3 & 0.3 \\ 0.4 & 0.2 & 0.3 & 0.1 \end{bmatrix} = \begin{bmatrix} I & O \\ R & Q \end{bmatrix}$$

where

$$I = \begin{bmatrix} 1 & 0 \\ 0 & 1 \end{bmatrix} \qquad O = \begin{bmatrix} 0 & 0 \\ 0 & 0 \end{bmatrix}$$

$$R = \begin{bmatrix} 0.4 & 0 \\ 0.4 & 0.2 \end{bmatrix} \qquad Q = \begin{bmatrix} 0.3 & 0.3 \\ 0.3 & 0.1 \end{bmatrix}$$

A matrix N, called a *fundamental matrix,* can be calculated using the following formula:

$$N = (I - Q)^{-1}. \tag{18.5}$$

The superscript -1 is used to indicate the inverse of the matrix $(I - Q)$. In Appendix F we present formulas for finding the inverse of any matrix with two rows and two columns. In our current problem,

$$I - Q = \begin{bmatrix} 1 & 0 \\ 0 & 1 \end{bmatrix} - \begin{bmatrix} 0.3 & 0.3 \\ 0.3 & 0.1 \end{bmatrix}$$

$$= \begin{bmatrix} 0.7 & -0.3 \\ -0.3 & 0.9 \end{bmatrix}$$

and (see Appendix F)

$$N = (I - Q)^{-1} = \begin{bmatrix} 1.67 & 0.56 \\ 0.56 & 1.30 \end{bmatrix}.$$

If we multiply the fundamental matrix N times the R portion of the P matrix, we obtain the probabilities that accounts receivable dollars initially in states 3 or 4 will eventually reach each of the absorbing states. The multiplication of N times R for the Heidman's Department Store problem is shown below. (See Appendix F for the steps of this matrix multiplication.)

$$NR = \begin{bmatrix} 1.67 & 0.56 \\ 0.56 & 1.30 \end{bmatrix} \begin{bmatrix} 0.4 & 0 \\ 0.4 & 0.2 \end{bmatrix} = \begin{bmatrix} 0.89 & 0.11 \\ 0.74 & 0.26 \end{bmatrix}.$$

The first row of the product NR is the probability that a dollar in the 0–30 age category will end up in each of the absorbing states. Thus we see that there is a 0.89 probability a dollar in the 0–30 day old category will eventually be paid and a 0.11 probability that it will become a bad debt. Similarly, the second row tells us the probabilities associated with a dollar in the 31–90 day category; that is, a dollar in the 31–90 day category has a 0.74 probability of eventually being paid and a 0.26 probability of proving to be uncollectible. Using this information we can predict the amount of money that will be paid and the amount that will be lost as bad debts.

Establishing the Allowance for Doubtful Accounts

Let B represent a two-element vector which contains the current accounts receivable balances in the 0–30 day and the 31–90 day age categories; that is,

$$B = [b_1 \quad b_2]$$

total dollars in the 0–30 day category   total dollars in the 31–90 day category

Suppose that the December 31 balance of accounts receivable for Heidman's shows $1000 in the 0–30 day category (state 3) and $2000 in the 31-90 day category (state 4).

$$B = [1000 \quad 2000]$$

We can multiply B times NR to determine how much of the $3000 will be collected and how much will be lost. In our example,

$$BNR = [1000 \quad 2000]\begin{bmatrix} 0.89 & 0.11 \\ 0.74 & 0.26 \end{bmatrix}$$

$$= [2370 \quad 630].$$

Thus we see that $2370 of the accounts receivable balances will be collected and $630 will eventually have to be written off as a bad debt expense. Based on this analysis, the accounting department of the company would set up an allowance for doubtful accounts of $630.

The matrix multiplication of BNR is simply a convenient way of computing the eventual collections and bad debts of the accounts receivable. Recall that the NR matrix provided a 0.89 probability of collecting dollars in the 0–30 day category and a 0.74 probability of collecting dollars in the 31–90 day category. Thus as was shown by the BNR calculation, we expect to collect a total of $0.89(1000) + 0.74(2000) = 890 + 1480 = \$2370$.

Suppose that on the basis of the previous analysis Heidman's would like to investigate the possibility of reducing the amount of bad debts. Recall that our analysis indicated that a 0.11 probability or 11% of the dollars in the 0–30 day age category and 26% of the amount in the 31–90 day age category will prove to be uncollectible. Let us assume that Heidman's is considering instituting a new credit policy involving a discount for prompt payment.

Management believes that the policy under consideration will increase the probability of a transition from the 0–30 day age category to the paid category and decrease the probability of a transition from the 0–30 day to the 31–90 day age category. Let us assume that a careful study of the effects of this new policy leads management to conclude that the following transition matrix would be applicable:

$$P = \begin{bmatrix} 1 & 0 & \vdots & 0 & 0 \\ 0 & 1 & \vdots & 0 & 0 \\ \hdashline 0.6 & 0 & \vdots & 0.3 & 0.1 \\ 0.4 & 0.2 & \vdots & 0.3 & 0.1 \end{bmatrix}$$

We see that the probability of a dollar in the 0–30 day age category making a transition to the paid category in the next period has increased to 0.6 and that the probability of a dollar in the 0–30 day age category making a transition to the 31–90 day category has decreased to 0.1. To determine the effect of these changes on bad debt expense we must calculate N, NR, and BNR. We begin by using equation (18.5) to calculate the fundamental matrix N.

$$N = (I - Q)^{-1} = \left\{ \begin{bmatrix} 1 & 0 \\ 0 & 1 \end{bmatrix} - \begin{bmatrix} 0.3 & 0.1 \\ 0.3 & 0.1 \end{bmatrix} \right\}^{-1}$$

$$= \begin{bmatrix} 0.7 & -0.1 \\ -0.3 & 0.9 \end{bmatrix}^{-1}$$

$$= \begin{bmatrix} 1.5 & 0.17 \\ 0.5 & 1.17 \end{bmatrix}$$

By multiplying N times R we obtain the new probabilities that the dollars in each age category will end up in the two absorbing states:

$$NR = \begin{bmatrix} 1.5 & 0.17 \\ 0.5 & 1.17 \end{bmatrix} \begin{bmatrix} 0.6 & 0 \\ 0.4 & 0.2 \end{bmatrix}$$

$$= \begin{bmatrix} 0.97 & 0.03 \\ 0.77 & 0.23 \end{bmatrix}$$

We see that with the new credit policy we would only expect 3% of the funds in the 0–30 day age category and 23% of the funds in the 31–90 day age category to prove to be uncollectible. If, as before, we assume that there is a current balance of $1000 in the 0–30 day age category and $2000 in the 31–90 day age category, we can calculate the total amount of accounts receivable that will end up in the two absorbing states by multiplying B times NR. We obtain

$$BNR = \begin{bmatrix} 1000 & 2000 \end{bmatrix} \begin{bmatrix} 0.97 & 0.03 \\ 0.77 & 0.23 \end{bmatrix}$$

$$= \begin{bmatrix} 2510 & 490 \end{bmatrix}.$$

Under the previous credit policy we found the bad debt expense to be $630. Thus a savings of $630 - 490 = $140 could be expected as a result of the new credit policy. Given our total accounts receivable balance of $3000, this is a 4.7% reduction in bad debt expense. After considering the costs involved, management can evaluate the economics of adopting the new credit policy. If the cost, including discounts, is less than 4.7% of the accounts receivable balance, we would expect the new policy to lead to increased profits for Heidman's Department Store.

18.3 SUMMARY

In this chapter we have presented Markov process models as well as examples of their application. We saw that a Markov analysis could provide helpful decision-making information about a process or situation which involved a sequence of repeated trials with a number of possible outcomes or states on each trial. A primary objective of our analysis was obtaining information about the probability of each state occurring a certain number of transitions or time periods in the future.

A market share analysis showed the computational procedure for determining the steady-state probabilities which could be interpreted as market shares for two competing supermarkets. In an accounts receivable application of Markov processes we introduced the notion of absorbing states. The two absorbing states were bad debt and paid categories, and we showed how to determine the percentage of accounts receivable balances that would be absorbed in each of these states.

18.4 GLOSSARY

1. *Trials of the process*—The events that trigger transitions of the system from one state to another. In many applications successive time periods represent the trials of the process.
2. *State of the system*—The condition of the system at any particular trial or time period.
3. *Transition probability*—Given the system is in state i during one period, the transition probability p_{ij} is the probability that the system will be in state j during the next period.
4. *State probability*—The probability the system will be in any particular state. ($\pi_i(n)$ is the probability that the system will be in state i during period n.)
5. *Steady-state probability*—The probability that the system will be in any particular state after a large number of transitions. Once steady-state has been reached, the state probabilities do not change from period to period.
6. *Absorbing state*—A state is said to be absorbing if the probability of making a transition out of that state is zero. Thus once the system has made a transition into an absorbing state, it will remain there forever.
7. *Fundamental matrix*—A matrix necessary for the computation of probabilities associated with absorbing states of a Markov process.

547

18.5 PROBLEMS

1. In the market share analysis of Section 18.1 suppose that we are considering the Markov process associated with the shopping trips of one customer but we do not know where the customer shopped during the last week. Thus we might make the assumption that there is a 0.5 probability that the customer shopped at Murphy's and a 0.5 probability that the customer shopped at Ashley's at time period 0; that is, $\pi_1(0) = 0.5$ and $\pi_2(0) = 0.5$. Given these initial state probabilities, develop a table similar to Table 18.2 showing the probability of each state in future periods. What do you observe about the long-run probabilities of each state?

2. Management of the New Fangled Softdrink Company believes that the probability of a customer purchasing Red-Rot Pop and the company's major competition, Super Cola, is based on the customer's most recent purchase. Suppose the following transition matrix is appropriate.

		To	
		Red-Rot Pop	Super Cola
From	Red-Rot Pop	0.9	0.1
	Super Cola	0.1	0.9

a. Show the two-period tree diagram for one customer who last purchased Red-Rot Pop. What is the probability that this customer purchases Red-Rot Pop on the second purchase?

b. What is the long-run market share for each of these two products?

c. A major advertising campaign is being planned to increase the probability of attracting Super Cola customers. Management believes that the new campaign will result in the probability of a customer switching from Super Cola to Red-Rot Pop to increase to 0.15. What is the projected effect of the advertising campaign on the market shares?

3. The computer center at Rockbottom University has been experiencing substantial periods of computer down time. Let us assume that the trials of an associated Markov process are defined to be 1-hour periods and that the probability of the system being in a running state or a down state is based upon the state of the system in the previous period. Historical data show the following transition probabilities.

		To	
		Running	Down
From	Running	0.90	0.10
	Down	0.30	0.70

a. If the system is initially running, what is the probability of the system being down in the next hour of operation?

b. What are the steady-state probabilities of the system being in the running state and in the down state?

4. In Problem 3 one cause of the down-time problem was traced to a specific piece of computer hardware. Management believes that switching to a different hardware component will result in the following transition probability matrix.

		To	
		Running	Down
From	Running	0.95	0.05
	Down	0.60	0.40

a. What are the steady-state probabilities of the system being in the running and down states?

b. If the cost of the system being down for any period is estimated to be $500 (including lost profits for time down and maintenance), what is the breakeven cost for the new hardware component on a time-period basis?

5. A major traffic problem in the greater Cincinnati area involves traffic attempting to cross the Ohio River from Cincinnati to Kentucky using Interstate I-75. Let us assume that the probability of no traffic delay in one period, given no traffic delay in the preceding period, is 0.85 and that the probability of finding a traffic delay in one period, given a delay in the preceding period, is 0.75. Traffic will be classified as having either a delay or no-delay state and a time period will be considered to be 30 minutes.

a. Assuming you are a motorist entering the traffic system and receive a radio report of a traffic delay, what is the probability that for the next 60 minutes (two time periods) the system will be in the delay state? Note that this is the probability of being in the delay state for two consecutive periods. A tree diagram should be helpful.

b. What is the probability that in the long run the traffic will not be in the delayed state?

c. An important assumption of the Markov process models presented in this chapter has been the constant or stationary transition probabilities as the system operates in the future. Do you believe this assumption is appropriate in the above traffic problem? Explain.

6. The purchase patterns of two brands of toothpaste can be expressed as a Markov process with the following transition probabilities.

		To	
		Special B	MDA
From	Special B	0.90	0.10
	MDA	0.05	0.95

a. Which brand appears to have the most loyal customers? Explain.

b. What are the projected market shares for the two brands?

7. Suppose that in Problem 6 a new toothpaste brand enters the market such that the following transition probabilities exit.

		To		
		Special B	MDA	T-White
	Special B	0.80	0.10	0.10
From	MDA	0.05	0.75	0.20
	T-White	0.40	0.30	0.30

What are the new long-run market shares? Which brand will suffer most from the introduction of the new brand of toothpaste? Note that solving for the steady-state probabilities for this problem requires the solution of three equations and three unknowns.

8. Given the following transition matrix with states 1 and 2 as absorbing states, what is the probability that units in state 3 and state 4 end up in each of the absorbing states?

$$P = \begin{bmatrix} 1 & 0 & 0 & 0 \\ 0 & 1 & 0 & 0 \\ 0.2 & 0.1 & 0.4 & 0.3 \\ 0.2 & 0.2 & 0.1 & 0.5 \end{bmatrix}$$

9. In the Heidman's Department Store problem of Section 18.2, suppose the following transition matrix is appropriate.

$$P = \begin{bmatrix} 1 & 0 & 0 & 0 \\ 0 & 1 & 0 & 0 \\ 0.5 & 0 & 0.25 & 0.25 \\ 0.5 & 0.2 & 0.05 & 0.25 \end{bmatrix}$$

If Heidman's has $4000 in the 0–30 day age category and $5000 in the 31–90 day age category, what is your estimate of the amount of bad debts the company will experience?

10. The KLM Christmas Tree Farm owns a plot of land with 5000 ever-green trees. Each year KLM allows retailers of Christmas trees to select and cut trees for sale to individual customers. KLM protects small trees (usually less than 4 feet tall) so that they will grow and be available for sale in future years. Currently 1500 trees are classified as protected trees while the remaining 3500 are available for cutting. However, even though a tree is available for cutting in a given year, it may not be selected for cutting until future years. While most trees not cut in a given year live until the next year, some trees die during the year and are lost.

In viewing the KLM Christmas trees operation as a Markov process with yearly time periods, we define the following four states:

State 1: Cut and sold

State 2: Lost to disease

State 3: Too small for cutting

State 4: Available for cutting but not cut and sold.

The following transition matrix is appropriate:

$$P = \begin{bmatrix} 1 & 0 & 0 & 0 \\ 0 & 1 & 0 & 0 \\ 0.1 & 0.2 & 0.5 & 0.2 \\ 0.4 & 0.1 & 0 & 0.5 \end{bmatrix}$$

How many of the Farm's 5000 trees will be sold eventually and how many will be lost?

19

Quantitative Decision Making and Management Information Systems

In order to be effective, managers need accurate and timely information which can be used as a basis for decision making. Just as a production manager needs the latest and best possible product forecast information in order to prepare his production schedule, a stockbroker needs good up-to-date information on stock market behavior in order to make effective portfolio management decisions. We will refer to the specific information the manager uses in the decision-making process as *management information*. Since the desired management information often comes from a variety of sources and since the total information needs of the manager may be large, many organizations have designed and implemented formal systems for collecting, analyzing, and reporting information to the managers. Such systems are referred to as *management information systems*.

A complete introduction to management information systems would range from a broad, philosophical discussion of the management function to the information system details of data file organization, data base management, and data retrieval codes. It is not our intent to provide such an extensive treatment. Our purpose in this chapter is twofold: to provide a brief introduction and description of the types of management information systems and, more importantly, to identify the interaction between management information systems and the quantitative decision-making aids you have been studying in this text.

19.1 MANAGEMENT INFORMATION SYSTEMS (MIS)

Simply stated, a management information system is any procedure or system designed to collect, organize, and process data to provide the information management needs to make decisions.

552

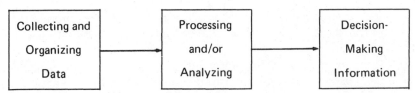

FIGURE 19.1   The Management Information System Process

The essential role of a management information system is to transform data describing the operation of the business into information that is useful for decision making. For example, data on historical sales volumes may not be helpful to the production manager until it has been processed by a fore-casting procedure in order to provide the projected sales information needed in the scheduling decision process. The overall management information system process of transforming data into information is shown in Figure 19.1.

It is essential that the data be captured and transformed into the desired management information so that the information will be readily available to the decision maker when it is needed. Although there have been and still do exist information systems that operate without the use of a computer, the time demands for information, coupled with the sheer volume of data and information needed, have tended to make the computer an essential part of most information systems. Because of the increasingly important role computers play in management information systems, our discussion assumes that a computer is used as an integral part of the information system.

Virtually all organizations have some form of a management information system. According to Terrance Hanold, president of the Pillsbury Company, "Theoreticians may debate the topic fruitlessly, but a management information system has become an absolute necessity for successful operation of a large and complex business enterprise."[1] The more successful organizations more often than not have excellent systems, while those organizations that have not fared as well can often attribute at least a portion of their lack of success to improper planning and use of their management information system.

19.2   A CLASSIFICATION OF MANAGEMENT INFORMATION SYSTEMS

The starting point for any management information system is an organized collection of data that is generally referred to as the *data base*. Because of the large volume of data available in many organizations, the data base is fre-

[1] Hanold, T., "An Executive View of MIS," *Datamation*, Nov. 1972.

quently stored in a computerized system. The purpose of the information system is to transform the raw data contained in the data base into useful output information.

There are many different computer hardware and/or software systems currently being used to make the transformation from raw data to information. As a result, management information systems are often classified as being one type or another, based upon hardware and/or software differences.[2] However, a much more important criterion for classifying management information systems is the *type of output information* the system provides. Using a type-of-output criterion for classification, we can identify three types of management information systems:

1. Report-generator MIS
2. "What-if" MIS
3. Management information-decision system (MIDS).

Report-Generator MIS

The report-generator MIS is the simplest type of management information system in that it simply transforms the raw data contained in the data base into summary reports. Essentially the reports (information) produced by these systems attempt to capture and convey the results of business activities that have happened in the past or currently exist. Examples of the kinds of reports created by report-generator MIS are as follows:

1. Profit and loss statements
2. Balance sheets
3. Production efficiency reports
4. Personnel absenteeism reports
5. Current inventory status
6. Current accounts receivable status.

In its basic form, the report-generator MIS consists of several computer programs each of which has been specially designed to access the data base and create a specific report. To use this management information system, the manager merely requests the desired report-generating program. The more advanced systems often permit the user to select specific information and then custom design the output form of the reports generated. In order to obtain this user flexibility and a fast-response capability, these versions of the report-generator MIS are often operated in a time-sharing computer environment. Thus the report-generator MIS has the fundamental objective of

---

[2] Definitions of the computer terminology mentioned in this chapter are provided in the Glossary (see Section 19.6).

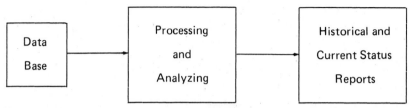

FIGURE 19.2 The Report-Generator MIS Concept

transforming the data base into historical or current status reports on business activities. The report-generator MIS concept is depicted in Figure 19.2.

The value of the report-generator MIS is that the manager will (hopefully) be able to utilize the information generated by these reports to make better decisions. In this sense, one of the most important uses of the information occurs when the decision maker attempts to predict future consequences or outcomes of various decision alternatives. Since the report-generator MIS does not provide the necessary prediction information directly, the "what-if" concept has been developed.

"What-If" MIS

The "what-if" MIS takes management what-if questions or inputs and operates upon the data base to create information in the form of summary reports. The essential difference between the "what-if" MIS and the report-generator MIS is that the "what-if" system creates reports that attempt to identify the *potential consequences* of future conditions or decisions. This type of management information system provides the user with answers to what-if questions such as:

What if product prices are changed? (What will be the effect on cash flow and/or profits?)

What if a proposed new item of equipment is purchased or leased? (What will be the effect on profits and cash flow?)

What if a wage increase is granted? (What will be the effect on production rate and the use of overtime?)

In general, then, the questions usually asked of the "what-if" MIS will be of the following forms:

1.   What would be the effect if this condition were to occur?
2.   What would be the effect if this decision were made?

The output from this type of management information system includes the corresponding projected version of each of the report-generator's reports (such as projected profit and loss, projected inventory reports, and so on). The "what-if" MIS concept is depicted in Figure 19.3.

555

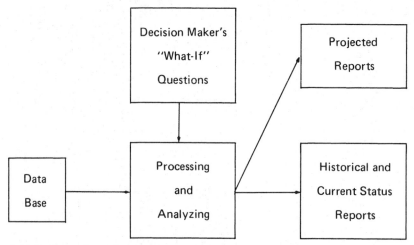

FIGURE 19.3   The "What-If" MIS Concept

The MIS processing and analyzing procedures have to be more than just data organizers and summarizers. If the "what-if" MIS is to do the job of projecting various user reports, it will have to contain data analysis procedures. For example, it should have statistical routines that perform correlation and regressional analyses as well as forecasting routines that could be used to project the future levels of sales, inventory, and so on. In addition, the system should contain the mathematical expressions for computing cash flows, profit, etc. The critical part of this type of management information system is the mathematical models that project output based on the what-if question inputs of the decision maker. The data analysis procedures plus the mathematical models give the "what-if" system the ability to move from the report-generator level to the projected-report level.

As an illustration of this type of system, suppose the basic economic order quantity model of Chapter 15 was applicable for a given product. The total cost model (see Section 15.1) is

$$TC = \frac{Q}{2}\, C_h + \frac{D}{Q}\, C_0$$

and the time in days between orders is given by

$$T = \frac{365Q}{D}$$

A "what-if" MIS might have these models available as an analysis option. The decision maker could use the "what-if" MIS to evaluate how changes in the order quantity Q would affect the total cost and the time between orders; that is, given the trial or test input of Q, the MIS would select C_h, C_0, and D

for this product from the data base and then provide total cost TC and order period T information to the decision maker.

In addition, the decision maker might want to learn about other "what-if" questions such as changes in C_0, C_h, and/or D. By inputting trial changes in these values, the decision maker could obtain revised total cost and order period information.

Whether the "what-if" MIS is directed at a basic inventory problem or a complex ordering-production-shipping system, it utilizes a data base and one or more mathematical models to generate information about the consequences of future decisions or changes in the situation under study. The "what-if" MIS allows the decision maker to test prospective decisions or changes before making a final decision.

In its most advanced form, the "what-if" MIS has the ability to provide the decision maker with the projected consequences of various decisions on a real-time basis. Thus we are talking about man-system interaction via time-shared computers. The decision maker inputs what-if questions such as decision alternatives and obtains the projected results. He can then modify his what-if questions and continue interactive communication with the system until he has the desired information. This interactive capability of the "what-if" MIS is shown in Figure 19.4.

There is no question that the "what-if" MIS has many decision-making advantages over the report-generator MIS, and that when correctly used, it can provide valuable input to the decision-making process.

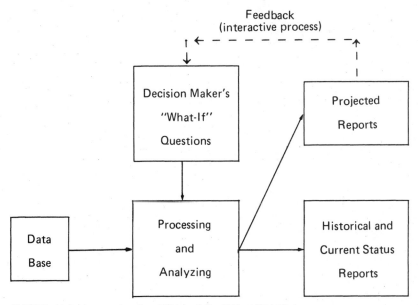

FIGURE 19.4 Interactive Capabilities of the "What-if" MIS

Management Information–Decision Systems (MIDS)

The management information–decision system is a new and more sophisticated class of management information system that ultimately transforms the "what-if" MIS information into recommended decisions. Basically we are referring to a generalized management information system component that would incorporate decision-making capabilities into the framework of the "what-if" MIS. Thus, using the MIDS approach, the decision maker would receive the potential consequence information as simulated by the "what-if" MIS. Further, he would receive information in terms of recommended course of action. The basic configuration of a MIDS is shown in Figure 19.5.

The decision-making component of a MIDS may take a variety of forms. Basically it is a mathematical model that uses the "what-if" information to recommend decision alternatives. For example, let us return to the economic order quantity problem. We know (see Section 15.1) that the minimum total cost order quantity is given by

$$Q^* = \sqrt{\frac{2DC_0}{C_h}} .$$

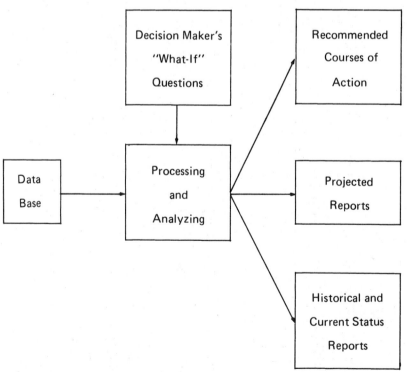

FIGURE 19.5 The MIDS Concept

Thus if a decision maker wanted to consider an up-date or revision in the demand *D,* he could input the what-if change to the MIDS and obtain information on total cost, order period, and, with the above model as part of the MIDS, the revised minimum cost order quantity.

Actually a MIDS is the "what-if" MIS with a decision model component that provides the decision recommendation. In a more extensive MIDS for production scheduling, the data base would contain machine production rate, product routing, manpower requirements, and so on. What-if questions concerning maintenance shutdown of machines, purchases of new machines, revised product forecasts, and so on, could be considered. A MIDS decision model component based on a linear programming representation of the production system could provide the manager with information such as inventory levels, machine utilization, and, most important, a recommendation for a minimum cost production schedule.

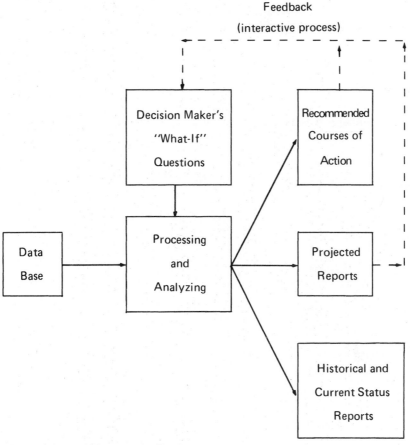

FIGURE 19.6   MIDS Interactive Process

In order to utilize the MIDS to its fullest potential there must be on-line interactive capabilities such as those available in time-sharing systems. This interactive capability of the MIDS system is depicted in Figure 19.6. While the changes in the projected reports will be of interest to the decision maker, the critical question MIDS will attempt to answer is how should these changes affect the decisions.

Even with the MIDS concept, decision making will ultimately rest with management evaluation and judgment. The purpose of the MIDS output is not to impose a decision on the manager or claim an absolute optimal decision for the problem. The results are only meant to provide a recommendation to the manager. The decision maker should consider and evaluate the MIDS recommendation, incorporate his management skills, and then make the final decision.

Hopefully, you have recognized the role quantitative analysis or operations research can play in the development of management information systems. Not only can mathematical models aid in the process of transforming raw data describing the operation of a business into useful management information, but coupled with information systems such as the MIDS, quantitative analysis procedures can also provide managers with recommended decisions.

19.3 THE INTERACTION OF MIS AND THE QUANTITATIVE MODELS OF MANAGEMENT SCIENCE

In the preceding section we discussed three classifications of management information systems. While the report-generator MIS may be as simple as selecting and organizing elements of the data base into a meaningful management report, the "what-if" MIS and MIDS both require a mathematical model component to generate the desired information. In addition, the decision-recommending capabilities of the MIDS require a model solution procedure such as linear programming, PERT, an inventory model, a waiting line model, and so on. Thus we see that the quantitative models of operations research and management science play an important role in achieving the maximum potential and utilization of management information systems.

Just as we believe that the use of quantitative models is essential to obtain the maximum benefit from management information systems, management information systems and especially good data bases are essential to obtaining the maximum benefit from quantitative aids for decision making.

In Chapter 1 we discussed a five-step approach to the quantitative analysis of a managerial decision: (1) problem definition, (2) model development, (3) data preparation, (4) model solution, and (5) report generation. The data-preparation step involved the collection of the data used as input to the model

560

and the preparation of the data in the form necessary for the solution procedure. A key component of the management information system is the data base. When a data base currently exists as part of a management information system, the data-preparation step can be greatly simplified and, as a result, the use of a mathematical model can often be cost justified by virtue of the fact that data needed by the model are readily available.

To make use of most of the quantitative models we have discussed in this text, we need data describing the situation under study. In applying an inventory model, such as the economic order quantity model, we would hope to use the data base of a management information system to find the holding cost C_h, order cost C_0, and annual demand D for each product we might want to analyze via this model. Thus, while MIS and quantitative approaches to decision making are often treated as separate topics, they have important interactions that make each dependent upon the other in terms of maximizing the contribution to the decision-making process. Since both management information systems and mathematical models strive to provide decision-assisting information, it makes sense that the greatest contribution to decision making can be made by integrating the quantitative analysis and management information systems.

19.4 THE ROLE OF MANAGEMENT SCIENCE IN DEVELOPING MANAGEMENT INFORMATION SYSTEMS

Let us assume that you are working for a company that wanted to develop an integrated marketing management information system. Management has broadly stated that the system developed must integrate the company's existing sales analysis function, inventory control system, and production control information system. In addition, management would like to see an on-line order-entry system developed; that is, an order-entry system in which the salesmen could contact the inventory system through computer terminals in order to check the status of current inventory levels, record a sales transaction whenever it occurs, and so on. The total system would be integrated because it would tie together three major corporate functions that are currently being handled by separate and distinct processing components.

How should the company plan, design, and implement this new system? It is not necessary to be an information systems expert to recognize that a project of this scope is a major undertaking for the company. How can management science assist in assuring that the corporation's resources are best utilized in developing this new system? In Chapter 14 we discussed two related techniques developed to assist management in planning for and controlling large scale projects, PERT and CPM. These tools can be used to

561

help plan the development of the new marketing management information system.

Can you think of other ways in which any of the techniques we have covered in this text could be used to develop this new system? What if the system design team came up with four or five alternative designs for the new system and was trying to determine the best system to recommend for implementation. For example, one design might call for inventory levels to be updated whenever a salesman called in an order; an alternative system design might call for collecting all the sales orders that come in during the day and then updating the inventory status each evening. Suppose the computer system configurations required for both approaches differ in size and cost, and the design team is trying to determine which system to recommend. What should be done?

In Chapter 16, Computer Simulation, we discussed a technique for analyzing complex problem situations. In the above problem, one alternative available to the design team would be to develop computer simulation models of the different designs being considered. By varying the factors affecting the proposed system, such as the number of sales transactions made each day, the computer system capabilities, and so on, the design team could effectively compare the various proposed designs and thus make a better recommendation to management.

In assisting with the development of management information systems, the management scientist or operations research analyst will most likely be part of a team that consists of marketing specialists, computer systems people, information systems analysts, and others. The management scientist's role will not be that of an expert in the development of information systems per se. Nonetheless, a minimal amount of knowledge of management information systems, the functional business areas, and computer systems will be necessary. However, his most important contribution will come from his understanding of various techniques such as PERT, CPM, simulation, and so on, and, more importantly, how they can be applied in the information system development process.

19.5 SUMMARY

In this chapter we have presented an overview of the management information system concept, with the goal of illustrating how management information systems relate to the central theme of the book: quantitative models for decision making. We have discussed how models currently are and will become even more significant components of information systems that attempt to provide decision makers with something more than just information. In addition, we have discussed the data-supply role information systems play in the data-preparation step of applying quantitative analysis. The combination of quantitative models and management information systems can make significant contributions to the managerial decision-making process.

19.6 GLOSSARY

1. *Management information system (MIS)*—A system intended to provide the information management needs to make decisions.
2. *Data base*—An organized collection of data.
3. *Report-generator MIS*—Creates historical or current status reports on business activities.
4. *"What-if" MIS*—Creates reports of the projected consequences of possible decisions or what-if questions.
5. *Management information-decision system (MIDS)*—Transforms "what-if" MIS information into recommended decisions.
6. *Hardware*—The physical equipment used in the processing of data, such as the computer and the peripheral equipment such as card readers, tape drives, disk drives, and so on.
7. *Software*—The computer programs, procedures, and documentation used in the processing of data.
8. *On-line*—A component of a computer system is said to be on line if it is under the direct control of the computer. When the user has the ability to directly interact with the computer, we say the user is on line.
9. *Time-sharing*—The utilization of the computer by a number of different users. The term usually implies that the user communicates with the computer through a remote terminal.
10. *Remote terminal*—A device that allows the user to enter data and the computer to output data to a location that is remote from the computer.
11. *Real-time system*—A computer system is said to operate in a real-time mode if the results of the processing are immediately available to the user.

APPENDICES

APPENDIX A. BINOMIAL PROBABILITIES

Example: Suppose $n = 3$, $x = 2$, $P = .30$.

$P(x) = .1890$.

n	x	.05	.10	.15	.20	.25	.30	.35	.40	.45	.50
1	0	.9500	.9000	.8500	.8000	.7500	.7000	.6500	.6000	.5500	.5000
	1	.0500	.1000	.1500	.2000	.2500	.3000	.3500	.4000	.4500	.5000
2	0	.9025	.8100	.7225	.6400	.5625	.4900	.4225	.3600	.3025	.2500
	1	.0950	.1800	.2550	.3200	.3750	.4200	.4550	.4800	.4950	.5000
	2	.0025	.0100	.0225	.0400	.0625	.0900	.1225	.1600	.2025	.2500
3	0	.8574	.7290	.6141	.5120	.4219	.3430	.2746	.2160	.1664	.1250
	1	.1354	.2430	.3251	.3840	.4219	.4410	.4436	.4320	.4084	.3750
	2	.0071	.0270	.0574	.0960	.1406	.1890	.2389	.2880	.3341	.3750
	3	.0001	.0010	.0034	.0080	.0156	.0270	.0429	.0640	.0911	.1250
4	0	.8145	.6561	.5220	.4096	.3164	.2401	.1785	.1296	.0915	.0625
	1	.1715	.2916	.3685	.4096	.4219	.4116	.3845	.3456	.2995	.2500
	2	.0135	.0486	.0975	.1536	.2109	.2646	.3105	.3456	.3675	.3750
	3	.0005	.0036	.0115	.0256	.0469	.0756	.1115	.1536	.2005	.2500
	4	.0000	.0001	.0005	.0016	.0039	.0081	.0150	.0256	.0410	.0625
5	0	.7738	.5905	.4437	.3277	.2373	.1681	.1160	.0778	.0503	.0312
	1	.2036	.3280	.3915	.4096	.3955	.3602	.3124	.2592	.2059	.1562
	2	.0214	.0729	.1382	.2048	.2637	.3087	.3364	.3456	.3369	.3125
	3	.0011	.0081	.0244	.0512	.0879	.1323	.1811	.2304	.2757	.3125
	4	.0000	.0004	.0022	.0064	.0146	.0284	.0488	.0768	.1128	.1562
	5	.0000	.0000	.0001	.0003	.0010	.0024	.0053	.0102	.0185	.0312
6	0	.7351	.5314	.3771	.2621	.1780	.1176	.0754	.0467	.0277	.0156
	1	.2321	.3543	.3993	.3932	.3560	.3025	.2437	.1866	.1359	.0938
	2	.0305	.0984	.1762	.2458	.2966	.3241	.3280	.3110	.2780	.2344
	3	.0021	.0146	.0415	.0819	.1318	.1852	.2355	.2765	.3032	.3125
	4	.0001	.0012	.0055	.0154	.0330	.0595	.0951	.1382	.1861	.2344
	5	.0000	.0001	.0004	.0015	.0044	.0102	.0205	.0369	.0609	.0938
	6	.0000	.0000	.0000	.0001	.0002	.0007	.0018	.0041	.0083	.0156
7	0	.6983	.4783	.3206	.2097	.1335	.0824	.0490	.0280	.0152	.0078
	1	.2573	.3720	.3960	.3670	.3115	.2471	.1848	.1306	.0872	.0547
	2	.0406	.1240	.2097	.2753	.3115	.3177	.2985	.2613	.2140	.1641
	3	.0036	.0230	.0617	.1147	.1730	.2269	.2903	.2918	.2388	.2734
	4	.0002	.0026	.0109	.0287	.0577	.0972	.1442	.1935	.2388	.2734
	5	.0000	.0002	.0012	.0043	.0115	.0250	.0466	.0774	.1172	.1641
	6	.0000	.0000	.0001	.0004	.0013	.0036	.0084	.0172	.0320	.0547
	7	.0000	.0000	.0000	.0000	.0001	.0002	.0006	.0016	.0037	.0078
8	0	.6634	.4305	.2725	.1678	.1001	.0576	.0319	.0168	.0084	.0039
	1	.2793	.3826	.3847	.3355	.2670	.1977	.1373	.0896	.0548	.0312
	2	.0515	.1488	.2376	.2936	.3115	.2965	.2587	.2090	.1569	.1094
	3	.0054	.0331	.0839	.1468	.2076	.2541	.2786	.2787	.2568	.2188
	4	.0004	.0046	.0185	.0459	.0865	.1361	.1875	.2322	.2627	.2734
	5	.0000	.0004	.0026	.0092	.0231	.0467	.0808	.1239	.1719	.2188
	6	.0000	.0000	.0002	.0011	.0038	.0100	.0217	.0413	.0703	.1094
	7	.0000	.0000	.0000	.0001	.0004	.0012	.0033	.0079	.0164	.0312
	8	.0000	.0000	.0000	.0000	.0000	.0001	.0002	.0007	.0017	.0039

						$P(x)$					
n	x	.05	.10	.15	.20	.25	.30	.35	.40	.45	.50
9	0	.6302	.3874	.2316	.1342	.0751	.0404	.0207	.0101	.0046	.0020
	1	.2985	.3874	.3679	.3020	.2253	.1556	.1004	.0605	.0339	.0176
	2	.0629	.1722	.2597	.3020	.3003	.2668	.2162	.1612	.1110	.0703
	3	.0077	.0446	.1069	.1762	.2336	.2668	.2716	.2508	.2119	.1641
	4	.0006	.0074	.0283	.0661	.1168	.1715	.2194	.2508	.2600	.2461
	5	.0000	.0008	.0050	.0165	.0389	.0735	.1181	.1672	.2128	.2461
	6	.0000	.0001	.0006	.0028	.0087	.0210	.0424	.0743	.1160	.1641
	7	.0000	.0000	.0000	.0003	.0012	.0039	.0098	.0212	.0407	.0703
	8	.0000	.0000	.0000	.0000	.0001	.0004	.0013	.0035	.0083	.0176
	9	.0000	.0000	.0000	.0000	.0000	.0000	.0001	.0003	.0008	.0020
10	0	.5987	.3487	.1969	.1074	.0563	.0282	.0135	.0060	.0025	.0010
	1	.3151	.3874	.3474	.2684	.1877	.1211	.0725	.0403	.0207	.0098
	2	.0746	.1937	.2759	.3020	.2816	.2335	.1757	.1209	.0763	.0439
	3	.0105	.0574	.1298	.2013	.2503	.2668	.2522	.2150	.1665	.1172
	4	.0010	.0112	.0401	.0881	.1460	.2001	.2377	.2508	.2384	.2051
	5	.0001	.0015	.0085	.0264	.0584	.1029	.1536	.2007	.2340	.2461
	6	.0000	.0001	.0012	.0055	.0162	.0368	.0689	.1115	.1596	.2051
	7	.0000	.0000	.0001	.0008	.0031	.0090	.0212	.0425	.0746	.1172
	8	.0000	.0000	.0000	.0001	.0004	.0014	.0043	.0106	.0229	.0439
	9	.0000	.0000	.0000	.0000	.0000	.0001	.0005	.0016	.0042	.0098
	10	.0000	.0000	.0000	.0000	.0000	.0000	.0000	.0001	.0003	.0010
11	0	.5688	.3138	.1673	.0859	.0422	.0198	.0088	.0036	.0014	.0005
	1	.3293	.3835	.3248	.2362	.1549	.0932	.0518	.0266	.0125	.0054
	2	.0867	.2131	.2866	.2953	.2581	.1998	.1395	.0887	.0513	.0269
	3	.0137	.0710	.1517	.2215	.2581	.2568	.2254	.1774	.1259	.0806
	4	.0014	.0158	.0536	.1107	.1721	.2201	.2428	.2365	.2060	.1611
	5	.0001	.0025	.0132	.0388	.0803	.1321	.1830	.2207	.2360	.2256
	6	.0000	.0003	.0023	.0097	.0268	.0566	.0985	.1471	.1931	.2256
	7	.0000	.0000	.0003	.0017	.0064	.0173	.0379	.0701	.1128	.1611
	8	.0000	.0000	.0000	.0002	.0011	.0037	.0102	.0234	.0462	.0806
	9	.0000	.0000	.0000	.0000	.0001	.0005	.0018	.0052	.0126	.0269
	10	.0000	.0000	.0000	.0000	.0000	.0000	.0002	.0007	.0021	.0054
	11	.0000	.0000	.0000	.0000	.0000	.0000	.0000	.0000	.0002	.0005
12	0	.5404	.2824	.1422	.0687	.0317	.0138	.0057	.0022	.0008	.0002
	1	.3413	.3766	.3012	.2062	.1267	.0712	.0368	.0174	.0075	.0029
	2	.0988	.2301	.2924	.2835	.2323	.1678	.1088	.0639	.0339	.0161
	3	.0173	.0852	.1720	.2362	.2581	.2397	.1954	.1419	.0923	.0537
	4	.0021	.0213	.0683	.1329	.1936	.2311	.2367	.2128	.1700	.1208
	5	.0002	.0038	.0193	.0532	.1032	.1585	.2039	.2270	.2225	.1934
	6	.0000	.0005	.0040	.0155	.0401	.0792	.1281	.1766	.2124	.2256
	7	.0000	.0000	.0006	.0033	.0115	.0291	.0591	.1009	.1489	.1934
	8	.0000	.0000	.0001	.0005	.0024	.0078	.0199	.0420	.0762	.1208
	9	.0000	.0000	.0000	.0001	.0004	.0015	.0048	.0125	.0277	.0537
	10	.0000	.0000	.0000	.0000	.0000	.0002	.0008	.0025	.0068	.0161
	11	.0000	.0000	.0000	.0000	.0000	.0000	.0001	.0003	.0010	.0029
	12	.0000	.0000	.0000	.0000	.0000	.0000	.0000	.0000	.0001	.0002
13	0	.5133	.2542	.1209	.0550	.0238	.0097	.0037	.0013	.0004	.0001
	1	.3512	.3672	.2774	.1787	.1029	.0259	.0259	.0113	.0045	.0016
	2	.1109	.2448	.2937	.2680	.2059	.1388	.0836	.0453	.0220	.0095
	3	.0214	.0997	.1900	.2457	.2517	.2181	.1651	.1107	.0660	.0349
	4	.0028	.0277	.0838	.1535	.2097	.2337	.2222	.1845	.1350	.0873
	5	.0003	.0055	.0266	.0691	.1258	.1803	.2154	.2214	.1989	.1571
	6	.0000	.0008	.0063	.0230	.0559	.1030	.1546	.1968	.2169	.2095
	7	.0000	.0001	.0011	.0058	.0186	.0442	.0833	.1312	.1775	.2095
	8	.0000	.0000	.0001	.0011	.0047	.0142	.0336	.0656	.1089	.1571
	9	.0000	.0000	.0000	.0001	.0009	.0034	.0101	.0243	.0495	.0873
	10	.0000	.0000	.0000	.0000	.0001	.0006	.0022	.0065	.0162	.0349
	11	.0000	.0000	.0000	.0000	.0000	.0001	.0003	.0012	.0036	.0095
	12	.0000	.0000	.0000	.0000	.0000	.0000	.0000	.0001	.0005	.0016
	13	.0000	.0000	.0000	.0000	.0000	.0000	.0000	.0000	.0000	.0001

n	x	.05	.10	.15	.20	.25	.30	.35	.40	.45	.50
							P(x)				
14	0	.4877	.2288	.1028	.0440	.0178	.0068	.0024	.0008	.0002	.0001
	1	.3593	.3559	.2539	.1539	.0832	.0407	.0181	.0073	.0027	.0009
	2	.1229	.2570	.2912	.2501	.1802	.1134	.0634	.0317	.0141	.0056
	3	.0259	.1142	.2056	.2501	.2402	.1943	.1366	.0845	.0462	.0222
	4	.0037	.0349	.0998	.1720	.2202	.2290	.2022	.1549	.1040	.0611
	5	.0004	.0078	.0352	.0860	.1468	.1963	.2178	.2066	.1701	.1222
	6	.0000	.0013	.0093	.0322	.0734	.1262	.1759	.2066	.2088	.1833
	7	.0000	.0002	.0019	.0092	.0280	.0618	.1082	.1574	.1952	.2095
	8	.0000	.0000	.0003	.0020	.0082	.0232	.0510	.0918	.1398	.1833
	9	.0000	.0000	.0000	.0003	.0018	.0066	.0183	.0408	.0762	.1222
	10	.0000	.0000	.0000	.0000	.0003	.0014	.0049	.0136	.0312	.0611
	11	.0000	.0000	.0000	.0000	.0000	.0002	.0010	.0033	.0093	.0222
	12	.0000	.0000	.0000	.0000	.0000	.0000	.0001	.0005	.0019	.0056
	13	.0000	.0000	.0000	.0000	.0000	.0000	.0000	.0001	.0002	.0009
	14	.0000	.0000	.0000	.0000	.0000	.0000	.0000	.0000	.0000	.0001
15	0	.4633	.2059	.0874	.0352	.0134	.0047	.0016	.0005	.0001	.0000
	1	.3658	.3432	.2312	.1319	.0668	.0305	.0126	.0047	.0016	.0005
	2	.1348	.2669	.2856	.2309	.1559	.0916	.0476	.0219	.0090	.0032
	3	.0307	.1285	.2184	.2501	.2252	.1700	.1110	.0634	.0318	.0139
	4	.0049	.0428	.1156	.1876	.2252	.2186	.1792	.1268	.0780	.0417
	5	.0006	.0105	.0449	.1032	.1651	.2061	.2123	.1859	.1404	.0916
	6	.0000	.0019	.0132	.0430	.0917	.1472	.1906	.2066	.1914	.1527
	7	.0000	.0003	.0030	.0138	.0393	.0811	.1319	.1771	.2013	.1964
	8	.0000	.0000	.0005	.0035	.0131	.0348	.0710	.1181	.1647	.1964
	9	.0000	.0000	.0001	.0007	.0034	.0116	.0298	.0612	.1048	.1527
	10	.0000	.0000	.0000	.0001	.0007	.0030	.0096	.0245	.0515	.0916
	11	.0000	.0000	.0000	.0000	.0001	.0006	.0024	.0074	.0191	.0417
	12	.0000	.0000	.0000	.0000	.0000	.0001	.0004	.0016	.0052	.0139
	13	.0000	.0000	.0000	.0000	.0000	.0000	.0001	.0003	.0010	.0032
	14	.0000	.0000	.0000	.0000	.0000	.0000	.0000	.0000	.0001	.0005
	15	.0000	.0000	.0000	.0000	.0000	.0000	.0000	.0000	.0000	.0000
16	0	.4401	.1853	.0743	.0281	.0100	.0033	.0010	.0003	.0001	.0000
	1	.3706	.3294	.2097	.1126	.0535	.0228	.0087	.0030	.0009	.0002
	2	.1463	.2745	.2775	.2111	.1336	.0732	.0353	.0150	.0056	.0018
	3	.0359	.1423	.2285	.2463	.2079	.1465	.0888	.0468	.0215	.0085
	4	.0061	.0514	.1311	.2001	.2252	.2040	.1553	.1014	.0572	.0278
	5	.0008	.0137	.0555	.1201	.1802	.2099	.2008	.1623	.1123	.0667
	6	.0001	.0028	.0180	.0550	.1101	.1649	.1982	.1983	.1684	.1222
	7	.0000	.0004	.0045	.0197	.0524	.1010	.1524	.1889	.1969	.1746
	8	.0000	.0001	.0009	.0055	.0197	.0487	.0923	.1417	.1812	.1964
	9	.0000	.0000	.0001	.0012	.0058	.0185	.0442	.0840	.1318	.1746
	10	.0000	.0000	.0000	.0002	.0014	.0056	.0167	.0392	.0755	.1222
	11	.0000	.0000	.0000	.0000	.0002	.0013	.0049	.0142	.0337	.0667
	12	.0000	.0000	.0000	.0000	.0000	.0002	.0011	.0040	.0115	.0278
	13	.0000	.0000	.0000	.0000	.0000	.0000	.0002	.0008	.0029	.0085
	14	.0000	.0000	.0000	.0000	.0000	.0000	.0000	.0001	.0005	.0018
	15	.0000	.0000	.0000	.0000	.0000	.0000	.0000	.0000	.0001	.0002
	16	.0000	.0000	.0000	.0000	.0000	.0000	.0000	.0000	.0000	.0000
17	0	.4181	.1668	.0631	.0225	.0075	.0023	.0007	.0002	.0000	.0000
	1	.3741	.3150	.1893	.0957	.0426	.0169	.0060	.0019	.0005	.0001
	2	.1575	.2800	.2673	.1914	.1136	.0581	.0260	.0102	.0035	.0010
	3	.0415	.1556	.2359	.2393	.1893	.1245	.0701	.0341	.0144	.0052
	4	.0076	.0605	.1457	.2093	.2209	.1868	.1320	.0796	.0411	.0182
	5	.0010	.0175	.0668	.1361	.1914	.2081	.1849	.1379	.0875	.0472
	6	.0001	.0039	.0236	.0680	.1276	.1784	.1991	.1839	.1432	.0944
	7	.0000	.0007	.0065	.0267	.0668	.1201	.1685	.1927	.1841	.1484
	8	.0000	.0001	.0014	.0084	.0279	.0644	.1134	.1606	.1883	.1855
	9	.0000	.0000	.0003	.0021	.0093	.0276	.0611	.1070	.1540	.1855
	10	.0000	.0000	.0000	.0004	.0025	.0095	.0263	.0571	.1008	.1484
	11	.0000	.0000	.0000	.0001	.0005	.0026	.0090	.0242	.0525	.0944
	12	.0000	.0000	.0000	.0000	.0001	.0006	.0024	.0081	.0215	.0472
	13	.0000	.0000	.0000	.0000	.0000	.0001	.0005	.0021	.0068	.0182
	14	.0000	.0000	.0000	.0000	.0000	.0000	.0001	.0004	.0016	.0052

n	x	.05	.10	.15	.20	.25	.30	.35	.40	.45	.50
							$P(x)$				
17	15	.0000	.0000	.0000	.0000	.0000	.0000	.0000	.0001	.0003	.0010
	16	.0000	.0000	.0000	.0000	.0000	.0000	.0000	.0000	.0000	.0001
	17	.0000	.0000	.0000	.0000	.0000	.0000	.0000	.0000	.0000	.0000
18	0	.3972	.1501	.0536	.0180	.0056	.0016	.0004	.0001	.0000	.0000
	1	.3763	.3002	.1704	.0811	.0338	.0126	.0042	.0012	.0003	.0001
	2	.1683	.2835	.2556	.1723	.0958	.0458	.0190	.0069	.0022	.0006
	3	.0473	.1680	.2406	.2297	.1704	.1046	.0547	.0246	.0095	.0031
	4	.0093	.0700	.1592	.2153	.2130	.1681	.1104	.0614	.0291	.0117
	5	.0014	.0218	.0787	.1507	.1988	.2017	.1664	.1146	.0666	.0327
	6	.0002	.0052	.0301	.0816	.1436	.1873	.1941	.1655	.1181	.0708
	7	.0000	.0010	.0091	.0350	.0820	.1376	.1792	.1892	.1657	.1214
	8	.0000	.0002	.0022	.0120	.0376	.0811	.1327	.1734	.1864	.1669
	9	.0000	.0000	.0004	.0033	.0139	.0386	.0794	.1284	.1694	.1855
	10	.0000	.0000	.0001	.0008	.0042	.0149	.0385	.0771	.1248	.1669
	11	.0000	.0000	.0000	.0001	.0010	.0046	.0151	.0374	.0742	.1214
	12	.0000	.0000	.0000	.0000	.0002	.0012	.0047	.0145	.0354	.0708
	13	.0000	.0000	.0000	.0000	.0000	.0002	.0012	.0045	.0134	.0327
	14	.0000	.0000	.0000	.0000	.0000	.0000	.0002	.0011	.0039	.0117
	15	.0000	.0000	.0000	.0000	.0000	.0000	.0000	.0002	.0009	.0031
	16	.0000	.0000	.0000	.0000	.0000	.0000	.0000	.0000	.0001	.0006
	17	.0000	.0000	.0000	.0000	.0000	.0000	.0000	.0000	.0000	.0001
	18	.0000	.0000	.0000	.0000	.0000	.0000	.0000	.0000	.0000	.0000
19	0	.3774	.1351	.0456	.0144	.0042	.0011	.0003	.0001	.0000	.0000
	1	.3774	.2852	.1529	.0685	.0268	.0093	.0029	.0008	.0002	.0000
	2	.1787	.2852	.2428	.1540	.0803	.0358	.0138	.0046	.0013	.0003
	3	.0533	.1796	.2428	.2182	.1517	.0869	.0422	.0175	.0062	.0018
	4	.0112	.0798	.1714	.2182	.2023	.1491	.0909	.0467	.0203	.0074
	5	.0018	.0266	.0907	.1636	.2023	.1916	.1468	.0933	.0497	.0222
	6	.0002	.0069	.0374	.0955	.1574	.1916	.1844	.1451	.0949	.0518
	7	.0000	.0014	.0122	.0443	.0974	.1525	.1844	.1797	.1443	.0961
	8	.0000	.0002	.0032	.0166	.0487	.0981	.1489	.1797	.1771	.1442
	9	.0000	.0000	.0007	.0051	.0198	.0514	.0980	.1464	.1771	.1762
	10	.0000	.0000	.0001	.0013	.0066	.0220	.0528	.0976	.1449	.1762
	11	.0000	.0000	.0000	.0003	.0018	.0077	.0233	.0532	.0970	.1442
	12	.0000	.0000	.0000	.0000	.0004	.0022	.0083	.0237	.0529	.0961
	13	.0000	.0000	.0000	.0000	.0001	.0005	.0024	.0085	.0233	.0518
	14	.0000	.0000	.0000	.0000	.0000	.0001	.0006	.0024	.0082	.0222
	15	.0000	.0000	.0000	.0000	.0000	.0000	.0001	.0005	.0022	.0074
	16	.0000	.0000	.0000	.0000	.0000	.0000	.0000	.0001	.0005	.0018
	17	.0000	.0000	.0000	.0000	.0000	.0000	.0000	.0000	.0001	.0003
	18	.0000	.0000	.0000	.0000	.0000	.0000	.0000	.0000	.0000	.0000
	19	.0000	.0000	.0000	.0000	.0000	.0000	.0000	.0000	.0000	.0000
20	0	.3585	.1216	.0388	.0115	.0032	.0008	.0002	.0000	.0000	.0000
	1	.3774	.2702	.1368	.0576	.0211	.0068	.0020	.0005	.0001	.0000
	2	.1887	.2852	.2293	.1369	.0669	.0278	.0100	.0031	.0008	.0002
	3	.0596	.1901	.2428	.2054	.1339	.0716	.0323	.0123	.0040	.0011
	4	.0133	.0898	.1821	.2182	.1897	.1304	.0738	.0350	.0139	.0046
	5	.0022	.0319	.1028	.1746	.2023	.1789	.1272	.0746	.0365	.0148
	6	.0003	.0089	.0454	.1091	.1686	.1916	.1712	.1244	.0746	.0370
	7	.0000	.0020	.0160	.0545	.1124	.1643	.1844	.1659	.1221	.0739
	8	.0000	.0004	.0046	.0222	.0609	.1144	.1614	.1797	.1623	.1201
	9	.0000	.0001	.0011	.0074	.0271	.0654	.1158	.1597	.1771	.1602
	10	.0000	.0000	.0002	.0020	.0099	.0308	.0686	.1171	.1593	.1762
	11	.0000	.0000	.0000	.0005	.0030	.0120	.0336	.0710	.1185	.1602
	12	.0000	.0000	.0000	.0001	.0008	.0039	.0136	.0355	.0727	.1201
	13	.0000	.0000	.0000	.0000	.0002	.0010	.0045	.0146	.0366	.0739
	14	.0000	.0000	.0000	.0000	.0000	.0002	.0012	.0049	.0150	.0370
	15	.0000	.0000	.0000	.0000	.0000	.0000	.0003	.0013	.0049	.0148
	16	.0000	.0000	.0000	.0000	.0000	.0000	.0000	.0003	.0013	.0046
	17	.0000	.0000	.0000	.0000	.0000	.0000	.0000	.0000	.0002	.0011
	18	.0000	.0000	.0000	.0000	.0000	.0000	.0000	.0000	.0000	.0002
	19	.0000	.0000	.0000	.0000	.0000	.0000	.0000	.0000	.0000	.0000
	20	.0000	.0000	.0000	.0000	.0000	.0000	.0000	.0000	.0000	.0000

Source: From *Handbook of Probability and Statistics with Tables* by Burlington & May. Copyright © 1970 by McGraw-Hill, Inc. Used with permission of McGraw-Hill Book Company.

APPENDIX B. **AREAS FOR THE STANDARD
NORMAL DISTRIBUTION**

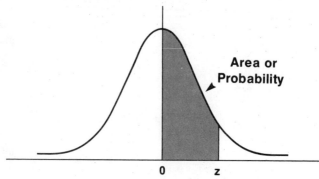

Entries in the table give the area under the curve between the mean and z standard deviations above the mean. For example, for $z=1.25$ the area under the curve between the mean and z is 0.3944.

z	0.00	0.01	0.02	0.03	0.04	0.05	0.06	0.07	0.08	0.09
0.0	0.0000	0.0040	0.0080	0.0120	0.0160	0.0199	0.0239	0.0279	0.0319	0.0359
0.1	0.0398	0.0438	0.0478	0.0517	0.0557	0.0596	0.0636	0.0675	0.0714	0.0753
0.2	0.0793	0.0832	0.0871	0.0910	0.0948	0.0987	0.1026	0.1064	0.1103	0.1141
0.3	0.1179	0.1217	0.1255	0.1293	0.1331	0.1368	0.1406	0.1443	0.1480	0.1517
0.4	0.1554	0.1591	0.1628	0.1664	0.1700	0.1736	0.1772	0.1808	0.1844	0.1879
0.5	0.1915	0.1950	0.1985	0.2019	0.2054	0.2088	0.2123	0.2157	0.2190	0.2224
0.6	0.2257	0.2291	0.2324	0.2357	0.2389	0.2422	0.2454	0.2486	0.2518	0.2549
0.7	0.2580	0.2612	0.2642	0.2673	0.2704	0.2734	0.2764	0.2794	0.2823	0.2852
0.8	0.2881	0.2910	0.2939	0.2967	0.2995	0.3023	0.3051	0.3078	0.3106	0.3133
0.9	0.3159	0.3186	0.3212	0.3238	0.3264	0.3289	0.3315	0.3340	0.3365	0.3389
1.0	0.3413	0.3438	0.3461	0.3485	0.3508	0.3531	0.3554	0.3577	0.3599	0.3621
1.1	0.3643	0.3665	0.3686	0.3708	0.3729	0.3749	0.3770	0.3790	0.3810	0.3830
1.2	0.3849	0.3869	0.3888	0.3907	0.3925	0.3944	0.3962	0.3980	0.3997	0.4015
1.3	0.4032	0.4049	0.4066	0.4082	0.4099	0.4115	0.4131	0.4147	0.4162	0.4177
1.4	0.4192	0.4207	0.4222	0.4236	0.4251	0.4265	0.4279	0.4292	0.4306	0.4319
1.5	0.4332	0.4345	0.4357	0.4370	0.4382	0.4394	0.4406	0.4418	0.4429	0.4441
1.6	0.4452	0.4463	0.4474	0.4484	0.4495	0.4505	0.4515	0.4525	0.4535	0.4545
1.7	0.4554	0.4564	0.4573	0.4582	0.4591	0.4599	0.4608	0.4616	0.4625	0.4633
1.8	0.4641	0.4649	0.4656	0.4664	0.4671	0.4678	0.4686	0.4693	0.4699	0.4706
1.9	0.4713	0.4719	0.4726	0.4732	0.4738	0.4744	0.4750	0.4756	0.4761	0.4767
2.0	0.4772	0.4778	0.4783	0.4788	0.4793	0.4798	0.4803	0.4808	0.4812	0.4817
2.1	0.4821	0.4826	0.4830	0.4834	0.4838	0.4842	0.4846	0.4850	0.4854	0.4857
2.2	0.4861	0.4864	0.4868	0.4871	0.4875	0.4878	0.4881	0.4884	0.4887	0.4890
2.3	0.4893	0.4896	0.4898	0.4901	0.4904	0.4906	0.4909	0.4911	0.4913	0.4916
2.4	0.4918	0.4920	0.4922	0.4925	0.4927	0.4929	0.4931	0.4932	0.4934	0.4936
2.5	0.4938	0.4940	0.4941	0.4943	0.4945	0.4946	0.4948	0.4949	0.4951	0.4952
2.6	0.4953	0.4955	0.4956	0.4957	0.4959	0.4960	0.4961	0.4962	0.4963	0.4964
2.7	0.4965	0.4966	0.4967	0.4968	0.4969	0.4970	0.4971	0.4972	0.4973	0.4974
2.8	0.4974	0.4975	0.4976	0.4977	0.4977	0.4978	0.4979	0.4979	0.4980	0.4981
2.9	0.4981	0.4982	0.4982	0.4983	0.4984	0.4984	0.4985	0.4985	0.4986	0.4986
3.0	0.4986	0.4987	0.4987	0.4988	0.4988	0.4989	0.4989	0.4989	0.4990	0.4990

APPENDIX C.   VALUES OF THE UNIT NORMAL LOSS INTEGRAL

$$L_N(Z_b) \text{ where } Z_b = \left| \frac{x_b - \mu}{\sigma} \right|$$

Example.   Suppose $x_b = 20,000$, $\mu = 21,000$, $\sigma = 3.125$.

$$Z_b = \left| \frac{x_b - \mu}{\sigma} \right| = \left| \frac{20,000 - 21,000}{3125} \right| = .32.$$

Therefore, $L_N(z_b) = L_N(.32) = .2592$

Z_b	.00	.01	.02	.03	.04	.05	.06	.07	.08	.09
.0	.3989	.3940	.3890	.3841	.3793	.3744	.3697	.3649	.3602	.3556
.1	.3509	.3464	.3418	.3373	.3328	.3284	.3240	.3197	.3154	.3111
.2	.3069	.3027	.2986	.2944	.2904	.2863	.2824	.2784	.2745	.2706
.3	.2668	.2630	.2592	.2555	.2518	.2481	.2445	.2409	.2374	.2339
.4	.2304	.2270	.2236	.2203	.2169	.2137	.2104	.2072	.2040	.2009
.5	.1978	.1947	.1917	.1887	.1857	.1828	.1799	.1771	.1742	.1714
.6	.1687	.1659	.1633	.1606	.1580	.1554	.1528	.1503	.1478	.1453
.7	.1429	.1405	.1381	.1358	.1334	.1312	.1289	.1267	.1245	.1223
.8	.1202	.1181	.1160	.1140	.1120	.1100	.1080	.1061	.1042	.1023
.9	.1004	.09860	.09680	.09503	.09328	.09156	.08986	.08819	.08654	.08491
1.0	.08332	.08174	.08019	.07866	.07716	.07568	.07422	.07279	.07138	.06999
1.1	.06862	.06727	.06595	.06465	.06336	.06210	.06086	.05964	.05844	.05726
1.2	.05610	.05496	.05384	.05274	.05165	.05059	.04954	.04851	.04750	.04650
1.3	.04553	.04457	.04363	.04270	.04179	.04090	.04002	.03916	.03831	.03748
1.4	.03667	.03587	.03508	.03431	.03356	.03281	.03208	.03137	.03067	.02998
1.5	.02931	.02865	.02800	.02736	.02674	.02612	.02552	.02494	.02436	.02380
1.6	.02324	.02270	.02217	.02165	.02114	.02064	.02015	.01967	.01920	.01874
1.7	.01829	.01785	.01742	.01699	.01658	.01617	.01578	.01539	.01501	.01464
1.8	.01428	.01392	.01357	.01323	.01290	.01257	.01226	.01195	.01164	.01134
1.9	.01105	.01077	.01049	.01022	$.0^2 9957$	$.0^2 9698$	$.0^2 9445$	$.0^2 9198$	$.0^2 8957$	$.0^2 8721$

Z_b	.00	.01	.02	.03	.04	.05	.06	.07	.08	.09
2.0	$.0^{2}8491$	$.0^{2}8266$	$.0^{2}8046$	$.0^{2}7832$	$.0^{2}7623$	$.0^{2}7418$	$.0^{2}7219$	$.0^{2}7024$	$.0^{2}6835$	$.0^{2}6649$
2.1	$.0^{2}6468$	$.0^{2}6292$	$.0^{2}6120$	$.0^{2}5952$	$.0^{2}5788$	$.0^{2}5628$	$.0^{2}5472$	$.0^{2}5320$	$.0^{2}5172$	$.0^{2}5028$
2.2	$.0^{2}4887$	$.0^{2}4750$	$.0^{2}4616$	$.0^{2}4486$	$.0^{2}4358$	$.0^{2}4235$	$.0^{2}4114$	$.0^{2}3996$	$.0^{2}3882$	$.0^{2}3770$
2.3	$.0^{2}3662$	$.0^{2}3556$	$.0^{2}3453$	$.0^{2}3352$	$.0^{2}3255$	$.0^{2}3159$	$.0^{2}3067$	$.0^{2}2977$	$.0^{2}2889$	$.0^{2}2804$
2.4	$.0^{2}2720$	$.0^{2}2640$	$.0^{2}2561$	$.0^{2}2484$	$.0^{2}2410$	$.0^{2}2337$	$.0^{2}2267$	$.0^{2}2199$	$.0^{2}2132$	$.0^{2}2067$
2.5	$.0^{2}2004$	$.0^{2}1943$	$.0^{2}1883$	$.0^{2}1826$	$.0^{2}1769$	$.0^{2}1715$	$.0^{2}1662$	$.0^{2}1610$	$.0^{2}1560$	$.0^{2}1511$
2.6	$.0^{2}1464$	$.0^{2}1418$	$.0^{2}1373$	$.0^{2}1330$	$.0^{2}1288$	$.0^{2}1247$	$.0^{2}1207$	$.0^{2}1169$	$.0^{2}1132$	$.0^{2}1095$
2.7	$.0^{2}1060$	$.0^{2}1026$	$.0^{3}9928$	$.0^{3}9607$	$.0^{3}9295$	$.0^{3}8992$	$.0^{3}8699$	$.0^{3}8414$	$.0^{3}8138$	$.0^{3}7870$
2.8	$.0^{3}7611$	$.0^{3}7359$	$.0^{3}7115$	$.0^{3}6879$	$.0^{3}6650$	$.0^{3}6428$	$.0^{3}6213$	$.0^{3}6004$	$.0^{3}5802$	$.0^{3}5606$
2.9	$.0^{3}5417$	$.0^{3}5233$	$.0^{3}5055$	$.0^{3}4883$	$.0^{3}4716$	$.0^{3}4555$	$.0^{3}4398$	$.0^{3}4247$	$.0^{3}4101$	$.0^{3}3959$
3.0	$.0^{3}3822$	$.0^{3}3689$	$.0^{3}3560$	$.0^{3}3436$	$.0^{3}3316$	$.0^{3}3199$	$.0^{3}3087$	$.0^{3}2978$	$.0^{3}2873$	$.0^{3}2771$
3.1	$.0^{3}2673$	$.0^{3}2577$	$.0^{3}2485$	$.0^{3}2396$	$.0^{3}2311$	$.0^{3}2227$	$.0^{3}2147$	$.0^{3}2070$	$.0^{3}1995$	$.0^{3}1922$
3.2	$.0^{3}1852$	$.0^{3}1785$	$.0^{3}1720$	$.0^{3}1657$	$.0^{3}1596$	$.0^{3}1537$	$.0^{3}1480$	$.0^{3}1426$	$.0^{3}1373$	$.0^{3}1322$
3.3	$.0^{3}1273$	$.0^{3}1225$	$.0^{3}1179$	$.0^{3}1135$	$.0^{3}1093$	$.0^{3}1051$	$.0^{3}1012$	$.0^{4}9734$	$.0^{4}9365$	$.0^{4}9009$
3.4	$.0^{4}8666$	$.0^{4}8335$	$.0^{4}8016$	$.0^{4}7709$	$.0^{4}7413$	$.0^{4}7127$	$.0^{4}6852$	$.0^{4}6587$	$.0^{4}6331$	$.0^{4}6085$
3.5	$.0^{4}5848$	$.0^{4}5620$	$.0^{4}5400$	$.0^{4}5188$	$.0^{4}4984$	$.0^{4}4788$	$.0^{4}4599$	$.0^{4}4417$	$.0^{4}4242$	$.0^{4}4073$
3.6	$.0^{4}3911$	$.0^{4}3755$	$.0^{4}3605$	$.0^{4}3460$	$.0^{4}3321$	$.0^{4}3188$	$.0^{4}3059$	$.0^{4}2935$	$.0^{4}2816$	$.0^{4}2702$
3.7	$.0^{4}2592$	$.0^{4}2486$	$.0^{4}2385$	$.0^{4}2287$	$.0^{4}2193$	$.0^{4}2103$	$.0^{4}2016$	$.0^{4}1933$	$.0^{4}1853$	$.0^{4}1776$
3.8	$.0^{4}1702$	$.0^{4}1632$	$.0^{4}1563$	$.0^{4}1498$	$.0^{4}1435$	$.0^{4}1375$	$.0^{4}1317$	$.0^{4}1262$	$.0^{4}1208$	$.0^{4}1157$
3.9	$.0^{4}1108$	$.0^{4}1061$	$.0^{4}1016$	$.0^{5}9723$	$.0^{5}9307$	$.0^{5}8908$	$.0^{5}8525$	$.0^{5}8158$	$.0^{5}7806$	$.0^{5}7469$
4.0	$.0^{5}7145$	$.0^{5}6835$	$.0^{5}6538$	$.0^{5}6253$	$.0^{5}5980$	$.0^{5}5718$	$.0^{5}5468$	$.0^{5}5227$	$.0^{5}4997$	$.0^{5}4777$
4.1	$.0^{5}4566$	$.0^{5}4364$	$.0^{5}4170$	$.0^{5}3985$	$.0^{5}3807$	$.0^{5}3637$	$.0^{5}3475$	$.0^{5}3319$	$.0^{5}3170$	$.0^{5}3027$
4.2	$.0^{5}2891$	$.0^{5}2760$	$.0^{5}2635$	$.0^{5}2516$	$.0^{5}2402$	$.0^{5}2292$	$.0^{5}2188$	$.0^{5}2088$	$.0^{5}1992$	$.0^{5}1901$
4.3	$.0^{5}1814$	$.0^{5}1730$	$.0^{5}1650$	$.0^{5}1574$	$.0^{5}1501$	$.0^{5}1431$	$.0^{5}1365$	$.0^{5}1301$	$.0^{5}1241$	$.0^{5}1183$
4.4	$.0^{5}1127$	$.0^{5}1074$	$.0^{5}1024$	$.0^{6}9756$	$.0^{6}9296$	$.0^{6}8857$	$.0^{6}8437$	$.0^{6}8037$	$.0^{6}7655$	$.0^{6}7290$
4.5	$.0^{6}6942$	$.0^{6}6610$	$.0^{6}6294$	$.0^{6}5992$	$.0^{6}5704$	$.0^{6}5429$	$.0^{6}5167$	$.0^{6}4917$	$.0^{6}4679$	$.0^{6}4452$
4.6	$.0^{6}4236$	$.0^{6}4029$	$.0^{6}3833$	$.0^{6}3645$	$.0^{6}3467$	$.0^{6}3297$	$.0^{6}3135$	$.0^{6}2981$	$.0^{6}2834$	$.0^{6}2694$
4.7	$.0^{6}2560$	$.0^{6}2433$	$.0^{6}2313$	$.0^{6}2197$	$.0^{6}2088$	$.0^{6}1984$	$.0^{6}1884$	$.0^{6}1790$	$.0^{6}1700$	$.0^{6}1615$
4.8	$.0^{6}1533$	$.0^{6}1456$	$.0^{6}1382$	$.0^{6}1312$	$.0^{6}1246$	$.0^{6}1182$	$.0^{6}1122$	$.0^{6}1065$	$.0^{6}1011$	$.0^{7}9588$
4.9	$.0^{7}9096$	$.0^{7}8629$	$.0^{7}8185$	$.0^{7}7763$	$.0^{7}7362$	$.0^{7}6982$	$.0^{7}6620$	$.0^{7}6276$	$.0^{7}5950$	$.0^{7}5640$

APPENDIX D. RANDOM DIGITS

63271	59986	71744	51102	15141	80714	58683	93108	13554	79945
88547	09896	95436	79115	08303	01041	20030	63754	08459	28364
55957	57243	83865	09911	19761	66535	40102	26646	60147	15702
46276	87453	44790	67122	45573	84358	21625	16999	13385	22782
55363	07449	34835	15290	76616	67191	12777	21861	68689	03263
69393	92785	49902	58447	42048	30378	87618	26933	40640	16281
13186	29431	88190	04588	38733	81290	89541	70290	40113	08243
17726	28652	56836	78351	47327	18518	92222	55201	27340	10493
36520	64465	05550	30157	82242	29520	69753	72602	23756	54935
81628	36100	39254	56835	37636	02421	98063	89641	64953	99337
84649	48968	75215	75498	49539	74240	03466	49292	36401	45525
63291	11618	12613	75055	43915	26488	41116	64531	56827	30825
70502	53225	03655	05915	37140	57051	48393	91322	25653	06543
06426	24771	59935	49801	11082	66762	94477	02494	88215	27191
20711	55609	29430	70165	45406	78484	31639	52009	18873	96927
41990	70538	77191	25860	55204	73417	83920	69468	74972	38712
72452	36618	76298	26678	89334	33938	95567	29380	75906	91807
37042	40318	57099	10528	09925	89773	41335	96244	29002	46453
53766	52875	15987	46962	67342	77592	57651	95508	80033	69828
90585	58955	53122	16025	84299	53310	67380	84249	25348	04332
32001	96293	37203	64516	51530	37069	40261	61374	05815	06714
62606	64324	46354	72157	67248	20135	49804	09226	64419	29457
10078	28073	85389	50324	14500	15562	64165	06125	71353	77669
91561	46145	24177	15294	10061	98124	75732	00815	83452	97355
13091	98112	53959	79607	52244	63303	10413	63839	74762	50289
73864	83014	72457	22682	03033	61714	88173	90835	00634	85169
66668	25467	48894	51043	02365	91726	09365	63167	95264	45643
84745	41042	29493	01836	09044	51926	43630	63470	76508	14194
48068	26805	94595	47907	13357	38412	33318	26098	82782	42851
54310	96175	97594	88616	42035	38093	36745	56702	40644	83514
14877	33095	10924	58013	61439	21882	42059	24177	58739	60170
78295	23179	02771	43464	59061	71411	05697	67194	30495	21157
67524	02865	39593	54278	04237	92441	26602	63835	38032	94770
58268	57219	68124	73455	83236	08710	04284	55005	84171	42596
97158	28672	50685	01181	24262	19427	52106	34308	73685	74246
04230	16831	69085	30802	65559	09205	71829	06489	85650	38707
94879	56606	30401	02602	57658	70091	54986	41394	60437	03195
71446	15232	66715	26385	91518	70566	02888	79941	39684	54315
32886	05644	79316	09819	00813	88407	17461	73925	53037	91904
62048	33711	25290	21526	02223	75947	66466	06232	10913	75336
84534	42351	21628	53669	81352	95152	08107	98814	72743	12849
84707	15885	84710	35866	06446	86311	32648	88141	73902	69981
19409	40868	64220	80861	13860	68493	52908	26374	63297	45052
57978	48015	25973	66777	45924	56144	24742	96702	88200	66162
57295	98298	11199	96510	75228	41600	47192	43267	35973	23152
94044	83785	93388	07833	38216	31413	70555	03023	54147	06647
30014	25879	71763	96679	90603	99396	74557	74224	18211	91637
07265	69563	64268	88802	72264	66540	01782	08396	19251	83613
84404	88642	30263	80310	11522	57810	27627	78376	36240	48952
21778	02085	27762	46097	43324	34354	09369	14966	10158	76089

Used by permission from *A Million Random Digits with 100,000 Normal Deviates*, The Rand Corporation, 1955.

APPENDIX E.   VALUES OF $e^{-\lambda}$

λ	$e^{-\lambda}$	λ	$e^{-\lambda}$
0.0	1.0000	3.1	0.0450
0.1	0.9048	3.2	0.0408
0.2	0.8187	3.3	0.0369
0.3	0.7408	3.4	0.0334
0.4	0.6703	3.5	0.0302
0.5	0.6065	3.6	0.0273
0.6	0.5488	3.7	0.0247
0.7	0.4966	3.8	0.0224
0.8	0.4493	3.9	0.0202
0.9	0.4066	4.0	0.0183
1.0	0.3679	4.1	0.0166
1.1	0.3329	4.2	0.0150
1.2	0.3012	4.3	0.0136
1.3	0.2725	4.4	0.0123
1.4	0.2466	4.5	0.0111
1.5	0.2231	4.6	0.0101
1.6	0.2019	4.7	0.0091
1.7	0.1827	4.8	0.0082
1.8	0.1653	4.9	0.0074
1.9	0.1496	5.0	0.0067
2.0	0.1353	5.1	0.0061
2.1	0.1225	5.2	0.0055
2.2	0.1108	5.3	0.0050
2.3	0.1003	5.4	0.0045
2.4	0.0907	5.5	0.0041
2.5	0.0821	5.6	0.0037
2.6	0.0743	5.7	0.0033
2.7	0.0672	5.8	0.0030
2.8	0.0608	5.9	0.0027
2.9	0.0550	6.0	0.0025
3.0	0.0498		

APPENDIX F.   MATRIX NOTATION AND OPERATIONS

Matrix Notation

We define a matrix to be a rectangular arrangement of numbers. For example, the following arrangement of numbers is a matrix named D:

$$D = \begin{bmatrix} 1 & 3 & 2 \\ 0 & 4 & 5 \end{bmatrix}$$

The matrix D is said to consist of six elements, where each element of D is a number. In order to identify a particular element of a matrix, we have to specify its precise location. To do this, we introduce the notion of rows and columns.

All elements across some horizontal line in a matrix are said to be in a row of the matrix. For example, elements 1, 3, and 2 in matrix D are in the first row of D, and elements 0, 4, and 5 are in the second row of D. Thus we see that D is a matrix that has two rows. By convention, we always refer to the top row as row 1, the second row from the top as row 2, and so on.

All elements along some vertical line are said to belong to a column of the matrix. Elements 1 and 0 in matrix D are elements in the first column of D, elements 3 and 4 are elements of the second column, and elements 2 and 5 are elements of the third column. Thus we see that matrix D has three columns. By convention, we always refer to the leftmost column as column 1, the next column to the right of column 1 as column 2 and so on.

Thus an easy way of identifying a particular element in a matrix is to specify its row and column position. For example, the element in row 1 and column 2 of matrix D is the number 3. This is written as

$$d_{12} = 3.$$

In general we use the following notation to refer to specific elements of matrices:

d_{ij} = element located in the ith row and jth column of D.

We always use capital letters for the names of matrices and lowercase versions of the same letter with two subscripts to denote the elements.

The *size* of a matrix is defined to be the number of rows and columns in the matrix and is written as "the number of rows X the number of columns." Thus the size of matrix D above is 2X3.

Frequently we will encounter matrices that have only one row or one column. For example,

$$G = \begin{bmatrix} 6 \\ 4 \\ 2 \\ 3 \end{bmatrix}$$

is a matrix that has only one column. Whenever we have a matrix that has only one column like G, we call the matrix a column vector. In a similar manner, any matrix that has only one row is called a row vector. Using our previous notation for elements of a matrix, we could refer to specific elements in G by writing g_{ij}. However, since G has only one column, the column position is unimportant, and we only need specify the row the element of interest is in. That is, instead of referring to elements in a vector using g_{ij}, we only specify one subscript which denotes the position of the element in the vector. For example,

$$g_1 = 6$$

$$g_2 = 4$$

$$g_3 = 2$$

$$g_4 = 3.$$

Matrix Operations

Matrix Transpose

Given any matrix, we can form the transpose of the matrix by making the rows in the original matrix the columns in the transpose matrix, and by making the columns in the original matrix the rows in the transpose matrix. For example, if we take the transpose of the matrix

$$D = \begin{bmatrix} 1 & 3 & 2 \\ 0 & 4 & 5 \end{bmatrix}$$

we get

$$D^t = \begin{bmatrix} 1 & 0 \\ 3 & 4 \\ 2 & 5 \end{bmatrix}$$

Here you will note that we use the superscript t to denote the transpose of a matrix.

574

Matrix Multiplication

We will demonstrate how to perform two types of matrix multiplication: (1) how to multiply two vectors, and (2) how to multiply a matrix times a matrix.

The product of a row vector of size $1 \times n$ times a column vector of size $n \times 1$ is the number obtained by multiplying the first element in the row vector times the first element in the column vector, the second element in the row vector times the second element in the column vector, and continuing on through the last element in the row vector times the last element in the column vector, and then summing the products. Suppose, for example, that we wanted to multiply the row vector H times the column vector G where

$$H = [2 \quad 1 \quad 5 \quad 0] \quad \text{and} \quad G = \begin{bmatrix} 6 \\ 4 \\ 2 \\ 3 \end{bmatrix}.$$

The product HG is given by

$$HG = 2(6) + 1(4) + 5(2) + 0(3) = 26.$$

The product of a matrix of size $p \times n$ and a matrix of size $n \times m$ is a new matrix of size $p \times m$. The element in the i-th row and j-th column of the new matrix is given by the vector product of the ith row of the $p \times n$ matrix times the j-th column of the $n \times m$ matrix. Suppose, for example, that we want to multiply D times A, where

$$D = \begin{bmatrix} 1 & 3 & 2 \\ 0 & 4 & 5 \end{bmatrix} \quad \text{and} \quad A = \begin{bmatrix} 1 & 3 & 5 \\ 2 & 0 & 4 \\ 1 & 5 & 2 \end{bmatrix}.$$

Let us denote by $C = DA$ the product of D times A. The element in row 1 and column 1 of C is given by the vector product of the first row of D times the first column of A. Thus we get

$$c_{11} = [1 \quad 3 \quad 2] \begin{bmatrix} 1 \\ 2 \\ 1 \end{bmatrix} = 1(1) + 3(2) + 2(1) = 9.$$

The element in row 2 and column 1 of C is given by the vector product of the second row of D times the first column of A. Thus we get

$$c_{21} = [0 \quad 4 \quad 5] \begin{bmatrix} 1 \\ 2 \\ 1 \end{bmatrix} = 0(1) + 4(2) + 5(1) = 13.$$

Calculating the remaining elements of C in a similar fashion we obtain

$$C = \begin{bmatrix} 9 & 13 & 21 \\ 13 & 25 & 26 \end{bmatrix}$$

Clearly the product of a matrix and a vector is just a special case of multiplying a matrix times a matrix. For example, the product of a matrix of size $m \times n$ and a vector of size $n \times 1$ is a new vector of size $m \times 1$. The element in the ith position of the new vector is given by the vector product of the ith row of the $m \times n$ matrix times the $m \times 1$ column vector. Suppose for example, that we want to multiply D times k, where

$$D = \begin{bmatrix} 1 & 3 & 2 \\ 0 & 4 & 5 \end{bmatrix} \quad \text{and} \quad k = \begin{bmatrix} 1 \\ 4 \\ 2 \end{bmatrix}.$$

The first element of Dk is given by the vector product of the first row of D times k. Thus we get

$$[1 \quad 3 \quad 2] \begin{bmatrix} 1 \\ 4 \\ 2 \end{bmatrix} = 1(1) + 3(4) + 2(2) = 17.$$

The second element of Dk is given by the vector product of the second row of D and k. Thus we get

$$[0 \quad 4 \quad 5] \begin{bmatrix} 1 \\ 4 \\ 2 \end{bmatrix} = 0(1) + 4(4) + 5(2) = 26.$$

Hence we see that the product of the matrix D times the vector k is given by

$$Dk = \begin{bmatrix} 1 & 3 & 2 \\ 0 & 4 & 5 \end{bmatrix} \begin{bmatrix} 1 \\ 4 \\ 2 \end{bmatrix} = \begin{bmatrix} 17 \\ 26 \end{bmatrix}.$$

Can any two matrices be multiplied? The answer is obviously no! For us to multiply two matrices, the number of the columns in the first matrix must equal the number of rows in the second. If this property is satisfied, the matrices are said to conform for multiplication. Thus in our example D and k could be multiplied because D had three columns and k had three rows.

Matrix Inverse

The inverse, of any square matrix A denoted by A^{-1}, consisting of two rows and two columns is computed as follows:

$$A = \begin{bmatrix} a_{11} & a_{12} \\ a_{21} & a_{22} \end{bmatrix}$$

$$A^{-1} = \begin{bmatrix} a_{22}/d & -a_{12}/d \\ -a_{21}/d & a_{11}/d \end{bmatrix}$$

where $d = a_{11}a_{22} - a_{21}a_{12}$ is the determinant of the 2×2 matrix A. For example, if

$$A = \begin{bmatrix} 0.7 & -0.3 \\ -0.3 & 0.9 \end{bmatrix}$$

then $d = (0.7)(0.9) - (-0.3)(-0.3) = 0.54$

and

$$A^{-1} = \begin{bmatrix} 0.9/0.54 & 0.3/0.54 \\ 0.3/0.54 & 0.7/0.54 \end{bmatrix} = \begin{bmatrix} 1.67 & 0.56 \\ 0.56 & 1.30 \end{bmatrix}$$

REFERENCES
AND
BIBLIOGRAPHY

THE ROLE AND NATURE OF MANAGEMENT SCIENCE (CHAPTER 1)

Churchman, C. W., R. L. Ackoff, and E. L. Arnoff, *Introduction to Operations Research,* New York: John Wiley & Sons, Inc., 1957.

Grayson, C. J., Jr., "Management Science and Business Practice," *Harvard Business Review* 51 (1973): 41–48.

Hillier, F., and G. J. Lieberman, *Introduction to Operations Research,* 2nd ed. San Francisco: Holden-Day, 1974.

Radnor, M., and R. D. Neal, "The Progress of Management Science Activities in Large U.S. Industrial Corporations," *Operations Research* 21 (1973) 427–450.

Turban, E., "A Sample Survey of Operations Research Activities at the Corporate Level," *Operations Research,* vol. 20, pp. 708–721, 1972.

Wagner, H., *Principles of Operations Research with Applications to Managerial Decisions,* Englewood Cliffs, N. J.: Prentice-Hall, 1969.

PROBABILITY, DECISION THEORY, AND UTILITY (CHAPTERS 2–7)

Chernoff, H., and L. E. Moses, *Elementary Decision Theory,* New York: John Wiley & Sons, 1959.

Feller, W., *An Introduction to Probability Theory and Its Applications,* 3rd ed. New York: John Wiley & Sons, Inc., 1968.

Freund, John E., *Mathematical Statistics,* 2nd ed., Englewood Cliffs, N. J.: Prentice-Hall, Inc., 1971.

Freund, J., and F. Williams, *Modern Business Statistics,* 2nd ed., Englewood Cliffs, N. J.: Prentice-Hall, Inc., 1969.

Hamburg, M., *Statistical Analysis for Decision Making,* 2nd ed., New York: Harcourt Brace Jovanovich, 1977.

579

Luce, R. D., and H. Raiffa, *Games and Decisions,* New York: John Wiley & Sons, 1957.

Raiffa, H., *Decision Analysis,* Reading, Mass.: Addison-Wesley, 1968.

Schlaifer, R., *Analysis of Decisions under Uncertainty,* New York: McGraw-Hill Book Co., 1969.

Schlaifer, R., *Introduction to Statistics for Business Decisions,* New York: McGraw-Hill Book Co., 1961.

Winkler, R. L., *An Introduction to Bayesian Inference and Decision,* New York: Holt, Rinehart, and Winston, 1972.

Winkler, R. L., and W. L. Hays, *Statistics: Probability, Inference and Decision,* 2nd ed. New York: Holt, Rinehart and Winston, Inc., 1975.

LINEAR PROGRAMMING, TRANSPORTATION, AND ASSIGNMENT (CHAPTERS 8–13)

Anderson, D. R., D. J. Sweeney, and T. A. Williams, *Linear Programming for Decision Making,* St. Paul, Mn.: West Publishing Co., 1974.

Bazarra, M. S., and J. J. Jarvis, *Linear Programming and Network Flows,* New York: John Wiley & Sons, Inc., 1977.

Daellenbach, Hans G., and J. Bell, *User's Guide to Linear Programming,* Englewood Cliffs, N. J.: Prentice-Hall, Inc., 1970.

Dantzig, G. B., *Linear Programming and Extensions,* Princeton, N. J.: Princeton University Press, 1963.

Gass, S., *Linear Programming,* 4th ed., New York: McGraw-Hill Book Co., 1975.

Gass, Saul J., *An Illustrated Guide to Linear Programming,* New York, McGraw-Hill Book Co., 1970.

Hadley, G., *Linear Programming,* Reading, Mass.: Addison-Wesley, 1962.

Hiller, F., and G. J. Lieberman, *Introduction to Operations Research,* 2nd ed., San Francisco: Holden-Day, 1974.

Hughes, A. J., and Grawoig, D. E., *Linear Programming: An Emphasis on Decision Making,* Reading, Mass.: Addison-Wesley, 1973.

Levin, R. I., and R. P. Lamone, *Linear Programming for Management Decisions,* Homewood, Ill.: Richard D. Irwin, 1969.

Wagner, H., *Principles of Operations Research with Applications to Managerial Decisions,* Englewood Cliffs, N. J.: Prentice-Hall, 1969.

PERT AND CPM (CHAPTER 14)

Evarts, H. F., *Introduction to PERT,* Boston: Allyn and Bacon, Inc., 1964.

Moder, J. J., and C. R. Phillips, *Project Management with CPM and PERT,* 2nd ed., New York: Van Nostrand, 1970.

Wagner, H., *Principles of Operations Research with Applications to Managerial Decisions,* Englewood Cliffs, N. J.: Prentice-Hall, 1969.

Wiest, J., and F. Levy, *Management Guide to PERT-CPM,* Englewood Cliffs, N. J., Prentice-Hall, 1969.

INVENTORY MODELS (CHAPTER 15)

Greene, J. H., *Production and Inventory Control Handbook,* New York: McGraw-Hill Book Co., 1970.

Hadley, G., and T. M. Whitin, *Analysis of Inventory Systems,* Englewood Cliffs, N. J.: Prentice-Hall, 1963.

Hillier, F., and G. J. Lieberman, *Introduction to Operations Research,* 2nd ed., San Francisco: Holden-Day, 1974.

Naddor, E., *Inventory Systems,* New York: John Wiley & Sons, 1966.

Starr, M., and D. Miller, *Inventory Control: Theory and Practice,* Englewood Cliffs, N. J.: Prentice-Hall, 1962.

Stockton, R. S., *Basic Inventory Systems: Concepts and Analysis,* Boston: Allyn and Bacon, 1965.

Wagner, H., *Principles of Operations Research with Applications to Managerial Decisions,* Englewood Cliffs, N. J.: Prentice-Hall, 1969.

SIMULATION (CHAPTER 16)

Emshoff, J. R., and R. L. Sisson, *Design and Use of Computer Simulation Models,* New York: MacMillan, 1970.

Maisel, H., and G. Gnugnoli, *Simulation of Discrete Stochastic Systems,* Chicago: SRA Inc., 1972.

Naylor, T. H., *Computer Simulation Experiments with Models of Economic Systems,* New York: John Wiley & Sons, 1971.

Naylor, T. H., J. L. Balintfy, D. S. Burdick, and K. Chu, *Computer Simulation Techniques,* New York: John Wiley & Sons, 1968.

Schmidt, J. W., and R. E. Taylor, *Simulation and Analysis of Industrial Systems,* Homewood, Ill.: Richard D. Irwin, Inc., 1970.

Trueman, R. E., *An Introduction to Quantitative Methods for Decision Making,* 2nd ed., New York: Holt, Rinehart, and Winston, 1977.

WAITING LINES (CHAPTER 17)

Bhat, U. N., *Elements of Applied Stochastic Processes,* New York: John Wiley & Sons, Inc., 1972.

Cooper, R. B., *Introduction to Queueing Theory,* New York: MacMillan, 1972.

Cox, D. R., and W. L. Smith, *Queues,* New York: John Wiley & Sons, Inc., 1965.

Gross, D., and C. M. Harris, *Fundamentals of Queueing Theory,* New York: John Wiley & Sons, 1974.

Hillier, F. and G. J. Lieberman, *Introduction to Operations Research,* 2nd ed., San Francisco: Holden-Day, 1974.

Newell, G. F., *Applications of Queueing Theory,* London: Chapman and Hall, Ltd., 1971.

MARKOV PROCESSES (CHAPTER 18)

Derman, C., *Finite State Markovian Decision Processes,* New York: Academic Press, 1970.

Howard, R. A., *Dynamic Programming and Markov Processes,* Cambridge, Mass.: M. I. T. Press, 1960.

Kemeny, J. G., and J. L. Snell, *Finite Markov Chains,* Englewood Cliffs, N. J.: Prentice-Hall, Inc., 1960.

Ross, S. M., *Applied Probability Models with Optimization Applications,* San Francisco: Holden-Day, Inc.. 1970.

MANAGEMENT INFORMATION SYSTEMS
(CHAPTER 19)

Burch, J. G., Jr., and F. R. Strater, Jr., *Information Systems: Theory and Practice,* Hamilton Publishing Co., 1974.

Davis, G. B., *Management Information Systems: Conceptual Foundations, Structure, and Development,* New York: McGraw-Hill, 1974.

Mockler, R. J., *Information Systems for Management,* Columbus, Oh.: Charles E. Merrill Co., 1974.

Ross, J. E., *Modern Management and Information Systems,* Reston, Va.: Reston Publishing Co., 1976.

Voich, D. J., H. J. Mottice, and W. A. Shrode, *Information Systems for Operations and Management,* Cincinnati: South-Western Publishing Co., 1975.

A GLOSSARY
OF KEY TERMS I
MANAGEMENT
SCIENCE

Absorbing state In Markov processes, a state from which there is a zero probability of making a transition out of the state. Thus once the system has made a transition into an absorbing state, it will remain there forever.

Activities In PERT and CPM, the specific jobs or tasks that are the components of a particular project.

Addition law A probability law used to compute the probability of a union, $P(A \cup B) = P(A) + P(B) - P(A \cap B)$.

Algorithm A step–by–step procedure that can be used to find the optimal solution for a particular type of problem.

Alternate optima Refers to the situation where a problem has two or more optimal solutions.

Artificial variable A variable that has no physical meaning in terms of the linear programming problem, but is necessary in order to create a starting solution for the Simplex method.

Assignment problem A special type of problem involving for example the assignment of jobs to machines, workers to tasks, etc. such that one job or worker is assigned to one and only one machine or task. The objective is usually expressed in terms of finding the assignment that minimizes costs, minimizes time, maximizes profits, etc.

Backorder The receipt of a demand for a product when there are no units on hand in inventory. These backorders become shortages which are eventually satisfied when a new supply of the product becomes available.

Bayes' Theorem The probability law or relationship which shows how prior probabilities and new information can be combined to compute posterior probabilities.

Binomial distribution The probability distribution for a discrete random variable denoting the number of successes in independent trails. The probability of a success is constant from trial to trial.

Breakeven point A volume level where total revenue exactly balances or equals total cost. Volumes above the breakeven point result in profits, while volumes below the breakeven point result in losses.

Classical method   A method of assigning probabilities based upon the assumption that the outcomes for the experiment are equally likely.

Complement of event A   The event containing all sample points that are not in A.

Conditional probability   The probability of a particular event based on the given condition that another event has occurred.

Constant demand rate   An assumption of many inventory decision models which states that the same number of units will be taken from inventory in each period of time.

Constraints   Restrictions or limitations imposed on a particular problem situation.

Continuous random variable   A random variable that can take on an infinite number of values in an interval or range of values.

Crashing   In CPM, the process of reducing an activity time by adding resources and hence usually cost.

Critical activities   The activities on the critical path.

Critical path   In PERT and CPM, the longest sequence of activities or longest path in the network. The time required to traverse the critical path is the estimated project duration.

Critical path method (CPM)   A network–based procedure used to assist in the planning, scheduling, and controlling of the various activities associated with a particular program or project.

Data base   An organized collection of data. Often referred to in the context of a management information system.

Decision theory   Quantitative decision analysis procedures which can be used to determine optimal decision strategies when a decision maker is faced with several decision alternatives and an uncertain pattern of future events.

Decision tree   A graphical representation of a decision–making situation.

Degeneracy   In linear programming, the condition that occurs whenever a linear program with m constraints has less than m variables taking on values greater than zero.

Deterministic model   A model where all uncontrollable inputs or components are known and do not vary.

Discrete random variable   A random variable that can only take on a countable or finite number of values.

586

Economic order quantity (EOQ)   The order quantity which minimizes the total cost in the most fundamental inventory decision model.

Event   In probability, a collection of sample points which is of interest to the decision maker. In PERT, a point in time occurring when all activities leading into a particular node have been completed.

Expected opportunity loss   The expected value decision theory criterion applied to opportunity loss or regret values.

Expected utility   In decision theory, a decision criterion which weights the utility values for each decision alternative by their probability of occurrence. The recommended decision is the one with the best expected utility.

Expected value   In probability, the mean value of the random variable. For a discrete random variable it is computed by a weighted sum of all values of the random variable, where the probability associated with each value is used as its weight. In decision theory, expected value is a decision criterion which weights the payoffs for each decision alternative by their probability of occurrence. The recommended decision is the one with the best expected value.

Expected value of perfect information (EVPI)   The expected value of the information which would tell the decision maker exactly which state of nature was going to occur (that is, perfect information). EVPI is equal to the expected opportunity loss associated with the best decision alternative.

Expected value of sample information (EVSI)   The difference between the expected value of an optimal strategy based on new information and the expected value of the "best" decision prior to the new information. It is a measure of the value of the new or sample information.

Experiment   In probability, any process which generates observable well–defined outcomes.

Extreme point   In linear programming, extreme points refer to feasible solutions occurring at the vertices or "corners" of the feasible region. The optimal solution to a linear programming problem will always occur at an extreme point.

Feasible region   The set of satisfying all the problem constraints.

Feasible solution   A solution or decision that satisfies all the constraints of a particular problem.

Fixed costs   Costs that are not related to volume.

Goodwill cost   A cost associate with a backorder, a lost sale, or any form of stockout or unsatisfied demand. This cost may be used to reflect the loss of

587

future profits due to the fact that a customer experienced an unsatisfied demand and may buy elsewhere in the future.

Graphical method A graphical solution technique for linear programming problems.

Hungarian method A solution procedure for the assignment problem.

Incremental or marginal analysis The solution technique whereby the analyst considers the marginal profit or cost associated with incrementing the order quantity by 1 unit.

Independent events In probability, events that have no influence on each other. That is for two independent events A and B, $P(A \mid B) = P(A)$ and $P(B \mid A) = P(B)$.

Infeasible solution A solution or decision that violates one or more constraints of a particular problem.

Intersection of events (A ∩ B) The event containing all sample points that are in both A and B.

Inventory holding or inventory carrying cost All costs associated with maintaining an inventory, including the cost of the capital invested in the inventory, insurance, taxes, warehouse overhead, and so on. This cost is often stated as a percentage of the cost of the units stored in inventory.

Lead time In inventory systems, the time between the placing of an order and its receipt in the inventory system.

Lead time demand The number of units demanded and removed from inventory during the lead time period.

Lead time demand distribution In probabilistic inventory models, this is the probability distribution that describes the possible number of units demanded during the lead time period.

Linear equations or functions Mathematical expressions in which the variables appear in separate terms and are raised to the first power. For example, $10x_1 + 9x_2$ is linear in terms of the variables x_1 and x_2.

Linear loss function An equation relating loss and volume such that loss is a linear function of volume.

Linear profit function An equation relating profit and volume such that profit is a linear function of volume.

Linear program A mathematical model with a linear objective function and a set of linear constraints.

588

Lottery A hypothetical decision alternative used in constructing utility functions with a probability p of obtaining the best possible payoff and a probability of $(1-p)$ of obtaining the worst possible payoff in a payoff table.

Management information system (MIS) A system designed to provide the information that management needs to make a decision.

Mathematical model A model which represents a real situation through the use of mathematical symbols and expressions.

Maximax A maximization decision criterion which recommends the decision alternative providing the maximum of the maximum payoffs.

Maximin A maximization decision criterion which recommends the decision alternative providing the maximum of the minimum payoffs.

Minimax A minimization decision criterion which identifies the decision alternative providing the minimum of the maximum payoffs as the best alternative.

Minimax regret A decision theory criterion which identifies the decision alternative providing the minimum of the maximum regrets as the best alternative.

Minimin A minimization decision criterion which identifies the decision alternative providing the minimum of the minimum payoffs as the best alternative.

Model A representation of a real object or situation. Analysis and study of the model often provides a better understanding of the object or situation, including information that can be used in a decision–making role.

Modified distribution method (MODI) A procedure used to find the optimal solution for a transportation problem.

Monte Carlo simulation Simulation that uses a random number procedure to create values for the probabilistic components or inputs to a simulation model.

Most probable time A PERT activity time estimate for the most likely activity time.

Multiple–channel queue A waiting line with two or more parallel, identical servers.

Multiplication law A probability law used to compute the probability of an intersection, $P(A \cap B) = P(A)P(B/A)$.

Mutually exclusive events Events that have no sample points in common. That is, any one particular outcome from the experiment will result in at most one of the mutually exclusive events.

Network A graphical description of a problem or situation consisting of circles (nodes) interconnected by a series of lines (branches or arcs).

Nonnegativity constraints In linear programming, a set of constraints that requires all variables to be nonnegative.

Normal distribution A continuous probability distribution that is bell-shaped.

Northwest corner rule A procedure used to find an initial feasible solution for a transportation problem.

Objective function A mathematical expression used to identify a goal or objective of a particular problem situation.

Opportunity loss or regret The amount of loss (lower profit or higher cost) due to not making the best decision. That is, the difference between the payoff realized and the payoff that would have occurred had the best decision been made.

Optimal solution A feasible solution that maximizes (or minimizes) the value of the objective function.

Optimistic time A PERT activity time estimate based on the assumption that the activity will progress in an ideal manner.

Ordering cost The fixed cost (salaries, paper, transportation, and so on) associated with placing an order for an item.

Path In networks, a sequence of branches connecting the origin and destination of a network.

Payoff The value associated with a particular outcome usually measured in terms such as profit, cost, etc. In decision theory, each combination of a decision alternative and a state of nature has a specific payoff.

Payoff table A tabular representation of the payoffs associated with a decision theory problem.

Pessimistic time A PERT activity time estimate based on the assumption that the most unfavorable conditions will occur.

Posterior (revised) probability Probability values for events or states of nature that have been revised on the basis of new information.

Prior probability Initial probability values for events or states of nature.

Probability A numerical measure of the likelihood that an event will occur.

Program evaluation and review technique (PERT) A network–based procedure used to assist in the planning, scheduling, and controlling of the various activities associated with a particular program or project.

590

Pseudo–random numbers   Numbers, often computer generated, which are developed from mathematical expressions and which have the properties of random numbers. Pseudo–random numbers are frequently used in simulation models.

Quantity discounts   Discounts or lower unit costs offered by a manufacturer whenever a customer purchases larger quantities of the product.

Queue   A waiting line.

Queue discipline   The way in which customers or units in a waiting line are ordered for service.

Queueing theory   Quantitative study of waiting line systems.

Random variable   A numerical description of the possible experimental outcomes.

Redundant constraint   A constraint which does not affect the feasible region. Redundant constraints may be removed from the problem without affecting the solution.

Relative frequency method   A method of assigning probabilities based upon experimentation or historical data.

Reorder point   The inventory level at which a new order should be placed.

Safety stock   Inventory maintained in order to reduce the number of stockouts due to the variability in demand.

Sample points   In probability, the individual outcomes of an experiment.

Sample space   In probability, the collection of all possible sample points.

Sensitivity analysis   The study of how the optimal solution and the value of the objective function are affected by changes in the various inputs or components of the model.

Service level   In inventory systems, the average number of stockouts allowed over a specified period of time.

Shadow price   The value of one additional unit of the resource associated with a linear programming constraint. The shadow prices for all resources can be found in the final tableau of the Simplex method calculations.

Simplex method   An algebraic procedure for solving linear programming problems.

Simplex tableau   A table used to keep track of the calculations made when the Simplex solution method is employed.

Simulation A procedure that involves developing a model to recreate the process or system under study. Most often this technique employs a computer model (computer program) to recreate the process and then identify near–optimal solutions or decisions.

Simulator The computer program written to perform the simulation calculations.

Simultaneous linear equations A system of linear equations. "Simultaneous" refers to the fact that we will be attempting to identify values for the variables that will satisfy all of the equations.

Single–channel queue A waiting line with only one server.

Single–period inventory models Inventory models in which it is assumed that only one order is placed for the product and at the end of the period the item has either sold out or the surplus of unsold items will be sold for a salvage value.

Slack In PERT and CPM, the length of time an activity can be delayed without affecting the project completion date.

Slack variable In linear programming, a variable added to the left–hand side of a less–than–or–equal–to constraint in order to convert the constraint into an equality. The value of this variable can usually be interpreted as the amount of unused resource.

Standard deviation The positive square root of the variance.

Standard normal distribution A normal distribution with a mean of 0 and a standard deviation of 1.

State probability In Markov processes, the probability the system is in a particular state or condition.

States of nature The uncontrollable events that ultimately affect the payoff or value associated with a decision.

Steady state The normal operation of a system after an initial transient or startup period.

Stepping–stone method A procedure used to find the optimal solution for a transportation problem.

Stochastic model A model where at least one of the data inputs or components is uncertain and subject to variation. Since concepts from probability are often used to describe the uncertainty or variability, these models may also be referred to as probabilistic models.

Subjective method A method of assigning probabilities based upon judgment.

Surplus variable   In linear programming, a variable subtracted from the left–hand side of a greater–than–or–equal–to constraint in order to convert the constraint into an equality. The value of this variable can usually be interpreted as the amount over and above the required minimum level.

Transition probability   In Markov processes, the probability p_{ij} that a system which is in state or condition i during one period will be in state or condition j during the next period.

Transportation problem   A special type of problem usually involving the determination of how many units should be shipped from each of several supply locations to each of several demand locations such that all demands are satisfied and transportation costs are minimized.

Unbounded   A problem is described as unbounded whenever the value of the objective function can be made infinitely large (or small in minimization problems) without violating any of the constraints.

Union of events (A ∪ B)   The event containing all sample points that are in A or B or both.

Utility   A measure of the total worth of an outcome reflecting a decision maker's attitude toward considerations such as profit, loss, and intangibles like risk.

Utility function for money   A function or curve that depicts the relationship between monetary values and utility values.

Utilization factor   In waiting line systems, the ratio of the mean arrival rate to the mean service rate. It indicates the proportion of the time the service facilities are in use.

Variable costs   Costs that depend directly on volume with higher volumes providing proportionally higher costs.

Variance   A measure of the dispersion in the values of the random variable.

Vogel's approximation method   A procedure used to find an initial feasible solution for a transportation problem.

INDEX